Broad
are the
Branches

AN AMERICAN SAGA

⊰ *Part III* ⊱

REBELLION

BROOKIE CONDIE SWALLOW

Broad are the Branches: An American Saga – Volume II

BookWise Publishing
3138 Matterhorn Drive
West Jordan, UT 84084

www.bookwise.com

Front cover painting: *Oregon Coast* by artist LILLIE CONDIE CLAY

Back cover paintings:
Heber, Utah, landscape, by BENJAMIN DUKE;
American Eagle, by MARY ANN HESS; and *Christ in the Garden,* by BROOKIE CONDIE SWALLOW

Back cover photographs:
Cape Cod Sunset, by TROY RUSHTON; *Boston, August 2001,* by BROOKIE CONDIE SWALLOW

Cover and book design by Eden Graphics, LLC

Library of Congress Cataloging-in-Publication Data
Swallow, Brookie Condie
Part III: REBELLION; Part IV: UNITED STATES ? /Brookie Condie Swallow
LCN 2012918399
ISBN 978-1-60645-106-9

10 9 8 7 6 5 4 3 2 1

First Printing

1600

1700

General / European Chronology

11. Gustavus Adolphus the Great.
Grotius.
Galileo.
18. The Thirty Years' War begins.
Kepler.
21-12. Richelieu.
48. Peace of Westphalia.
43. Louis XIV.

Shakespeare.
Milton.
Bacon.
49. Cromwell.
Locke.
60. The Restoration.
64. Charles II.

3. James VI. }
James I. }
9. Charles I.
25. Charles I.
42. The Revolution.

89. Peter the Great.
97. Charles XII.
War of the Spanish Succession.
Leibnitz.
13. Peace of Utrecht.
15. Louis XV.
Newton.
William and Mary, and after the death of Mary, 94. William III.
85. James II.
2. Anne.
14. George I.
27. George II.

40. Frederick the Great.
62. Catharine II.
War of the Austrian Succession terminated by 48. Peace of Aix-la-Chapelle.
74. Louis XVI.
Voltaire.
Dr. Johnson.
65. The Rockingham ministry.
Chatham.
55. War between France and England.
65. The Stamp Act.
60. George III.

89. French Revolution.
93. Reign of Terror.
Burke. Pitt. Fox.

85. Revocation of Edict of Nantes.
87. Habeas corpus.
88. Second Revolution.

38. Royal government established.
Dr. Benjamin Franklin.
41. New Hampshire finally separated from Massachusetts.
61. Writs of Assistance.
67. The tea tax.
73. The Boston "Tea Party."
75. Lexington.
74. Boston Port Bill.
68. General Gage arrives in Boston.
70. Tumult in Boston.
75. Bunker Hill.
44. Negro plot.
58. Fall of Lewisburg.
65. Declaration of Rights.
54. French and Indian War.
65. First Colonial Congress assembles at [New York.

7. VIRGINIA colonized by the London Company at Jamestown.

John Smith, governor.
19. Introduction of Slavery.
24. Dissolution of the London Company.
9. Second Charter granted.
12. The Third Charter.
19. House of Burgesses established.
42. Berkeley's administration.
44. Indian massacre.
51. First Navigation Act.
76. Bacon's Rebellion.
77. Virginia becomes a proprietary government.
84. Royal government re-established.
82. Birth of Washington.
65. The Virginia Resolutions.

50. NORTH CAROLINA settled by the English.

63. Grant made to Lord Clarendon.
65. Sir John Yeamans, governor.
77. Culpepper's rebellion.
83. Seth Sothel, governor.
9. Arrival of the German immigrants.
11. The Coree War.
29. Final separation of the Carolinas.

34. MARYLAND settled by the Catholics under Lord Baltimore.

39. Representative government established.
75. Charles Calvert.
85. Sir John Archdale, governor.
91. Maryland becomes a royal government.

14. NEW YORK settled by the Dutch.

25. Minuits, governor.
38. Wilmington settled by the Swedes.
38. Governor Kief.
47. Stuyvesant.
56. New York City founded.
64. Taken by the English.
Berkeley and Carteret.
70. Lovelace.
74. Edmund Andros.
83. Lionel Copley.
91. Sloughter, governor.
92. Fletcher.
98. Bellamont.
1. Cornbury.
32. Cosby, governor.

23. NEW JERSEY settled by the Dutch.

separated from New York.
Union of East and West Jersey.
81. First General Assembly.

29. NEW HAMPSHIRE settled.

30. Boston founded.
79. New Hampshire as a distinct colony.

30. MAINE settled.

20. MASSACHUSETTS settled by the Puritans at Plymouth.

30. Winthrop, governor.
36. Harvard College founded.
39. First printing-press set up at Cambridge.
76. King Philip's defeat and death.
84. Massachusetts loses her charter.
90. First issue of paper money.
90. King William's War.
92. Witch craft excitement.
2. Queen Anne's War.
4. First Newspaper.
10. First post-office.
20. Introduction of tea.
98. United with Massachusetts.
44. King George's War.
45. Louisburg taken.
59. Quebec taken.

36. RHODE ISLAND settled by Roger Williams.

39. Newport founded.
87. Rhode Island joined to New York.
89. Administration of Governor Bull.

30. CONNECTICUT granted to the earl of Warwick.

33. Hartford founded.
35. Saybrook founded.
37. Pequod War.
62. New charter granted.
89. The hiding of the charter.
1. Yale College founded.

82. DELAWARE separated from New York.

70. SOUTH CAROLINA settled by the English.

Locke's Constitution adopted.
86. Arrival of the Huguenots.
2. Expedition against St. Augustine.
29. Royal government established.

82. PENNSYLVANIA settled by the Quakers under Penn.

88. Founding of Philadelphia.
92. Penn loses his commission.
1. Penn returns to England.
18. Death of Penn.

33. GEORGIA settled by the English under Oglethorpe.

36. The Moravians in Georgia.
52. Royal government established.
55. Braddock's defeat.
74. Second Congress assembles at Philadelphia.
76. Independence.

CHRONOLOGICAL CHART NO. VII.

SHOWING

THE PROGRESS OF COLONIAL SETTLEMENTS IN AMERICA.

From 1607 to 1776 A. D.

Prepared by JOHN CLARK RIDPATH, LL. D.

CONTENTS

~ Introduction ~

Broad are the Branches—an American Saga

Part III: Rebellion

And a short review of
Part I: Driven and Part II: Standing Firm

In 1829, my third-great-grandparents ANDERSON IVIE, his wife SARAH (SALLY) ALLRED IVIE, and their families crossed the Mississippi Rivier from Tennessee to establish new homes in the new pioneer state of Missouri. Their older children, who accompanied them, were married with children of their own. The Missouri Compromise, which admitted Missouri into the Union as a slave state in February 1821 declared also that all territory west of Missouri and north of latitude 36° 30' should forever be free from slavery—they brought a few slaves with them. Their land was in Ralls County, where the two branches of the Salt River joined together. Ralls County would very soon be split, and this land would be in Monroe County.

ANDERSON IVIE was born in the tidewater area of southern Virginia in 1774, just before the Revolutionary War. His relations along the James River were very numerous, because his ancestors had been part of the gentlemen of the London Company and had settled in this new American country as early as 1613. He had a distant uncle, JOHN ARGENT who was with Captain John Smith in his early explorations around Jamestown. JOHN's neice ANN ARGENT married THOMAS IVIE (or IVY—IVEY) in Middlesex County, England, and the young adventurous couple came to Virginia in 1636, settling in Lower Norfolk where the United States Naval Yards are now located. They became parents of four sons and a daughter. Both parents died of a fever. Their orphaned children were sent back to England until they were old enough to claim their inheritance. The four sons returned in the 1660s.

ANDERSON IVIE's third-great-grandfather was GEORGE IVIE, the second orphaned son. He married ELIZABETH LANGLEY, daughter of WILLIAM LANGLEY of the London Company and the granddaughter of ELIZABETH MASON (THELABALL), whose husband was a wealthy French Huguenot who had escaped from France during their persecutions after the *Edict of Nantes* was repealed by King Louis XIV. Some LANGLEYs and MASONs were early members of the House of Burgesses at Williamsburg representing Lower Norfolk in those colonial days before the American Revolution. The original THOMAS IVIE had many Church of England (Episcopal) assignments, which was the official church in Virginia. He was an undersheriff and, in bad weather, their court was held in his home.

SARAH ALLRED's paternal grandparents had been English pioneers that came down the Great Wagon Road from Pennsylvania into the very large Orange County, North Carolina, of the 1750s—which, when divided, became Randolph County. Her mother, ELIZABETH THRASHER, was descended from the very early 1620's gentlemen of the tidewater country of the London Company. Their original land was located on the north side of the James River near Elizabeth City—across Hampton Roads from the Norfolk peninsula. Many of them moved westward, as it became safer, into the low lands east of the Blue Ridge Mountains—the area of Pittsylvania County, Virginia, and across the border into North Carolina—now Rockingham County. The ALLREDs of North Carolina were greatly involved in the War of the Regulators, which rebellion against the British government would occur in North Carolina in the latter part of the 1760s.

When the Revolutionary War ended, the British general Cornwallis and his troops had created great destruction of property in the Chesapeake/James River area of Virginia and throughout the back country of North Carolina. ANDERSON IVIE, as a young man left his home and family in Virginia and traveled west with his uncle NATHAN LOT IVIE and his family into Surry County, North Carolina, to seek their fortunes. They had problems with the double deeding of land and went south to Pendleton, South Carolina, with many of my other relations from this area. ANDERSON IVIE was in his twenties when he married SARAH ALLRED, while they were living in South Carolina.

When the Franklin County, Georgia, land lottery occurred (that gave this new former Cherokee Indian lands in Georgia to the fortunate winners of the lottery) in the very early 1800s, we can find these relations' names among the many that tried to obtain this property. ANDERSON and SALLY ALLRED IVIE were not successful winners, for his name appeared in the lottery every year. His uncle LOT IVIE was awarded some land in Jasper County (a short distance south from Atlanta). LOT moved there with several of his children and their families.

ANDERSON and SALLY IVIE are listed as charter members of the Baptist Church of Franklin County, where he was assigned as their clerk. He had beautiful handwriting. My second-great-grandfather JAMES RUSSELL IVIE was born in Franklin County, Georgia, in 1802. Unsuccessful in obtaining their land in Georgia, the family moved on to Bedford County, Tennessee, where many of their ALLRED and other relations would join them on Duck Creek. Second-great-grandfather JAMES RUSSELL IVIE married ELIZA McKEE FAUSETT, and they owned property in Tennessee. Her grandfather, ALEXANDER McKEE had been given land in Tennessee for his services as a private in the Revolutionary War. ELIZA's grandmother McKEE is believed to be MARY BEAN, and just after their daughter MARY married RICHARD FAUSETT, the two families left Orange County, North Carolina, and went through the Cumberland pass into, at first, Sumner County, Tennessee.

Still unhappy with their situation after the War of 1812 and its aftermath, the IVIEs moved on to Missouri in 1829. ANDERSON IVIE and his wife SARAH would die there in 1852 and 1862. JAMES and ELIZA joined the early *Mormon* Church in Missouri, and when my great-grandfather was born in 1833, they named him JOHN LEHI IVIE. Lehi was the name of the *Book of Mormon* prophet that left Jerusalem before its destruction in 600 B. C. and came to this American Continent—the ancient father of the American Indians. He was of the tribe of Manasseh—one of the sons of Joseph, who was sold into Egypt. ELIZA McKEE FAUSETT's ancestors were perhaps descendents of the early

THOMAS McKEE, a young British Indian agent of Pennsylvania who was told by the king to marry an Indian maiden to help keep friendly relations between the two nations. His wife was Shawnee.

ELIZA's grandfather WILLIAM FAUSETT had come from Northern Ireland in the 1760s. He carried a letter with him from a protestant church pastor stating that he had been a good member of his church while his family had been in Ireland, but had come to them as an exiled Huguenot from France.

ANDERSON and SARAH ALLRED IVIE sold part of their Missouri land to some developers that divided it into lots which were advertised for sale. Their son WILLIAM SHELTON IVIE is listed on the tax roles of this small town that was named Florida. Great-grandfather JOHN LEHI IVIE was born there in 1833. The Clemens family from Virginia bought one of the lots. Their son Samuel was born in Florida, Monroe, Missouri, in 1835. They would move to Hannibal in 1840, but Samuel Clemens would return to his uncle's farm during the summers until he was old enough to be hired in his brother's print shop in Hannibal. Today his old haunts are labeled with the well-known names of Tom Sawyer and Huckleberry Finn. Their old home in Florida is preserved. Probably the largest and maybe the newest building in the tiny town is the museum honoring "Mark Twain's Birthplace." There is a much smaller monument in the Florida Cemetery honoring my third-great-grandfather ANDERSON IVIE.

The true story of JAMES RUSSELL IVIE and his family and relations is told in Volume I of my history books, which includes Part 1: DRIVEN and Part II: STANDING FIRM. In 1852, my great-grandfather JOHN LEHI IVIE married great-grandmother MARY CATHERINE BARTON in Salt Lake City, Territory of Utah. They were very young. It was a decade before the Civil War began, but it was a very troubled time for the IVIE and ALLRED families. Volume I continues their story as members of The Church of Jesus Christ of Latter-day Saints, commonly called the *Mormons* for their belief (in addition to the *Holy Bible*) in the *Book of Mormon, another Testament of Jesus Christ.* The church is also called the L. D. S. Church—short for Latter-day Saints. Great-grandfather Colonel JOHN LEHI IVIE participated in eight Utah Indian battles. He led three of them—yet he really loved the Indians.

Great-grandmother MARY CATHERINE BARTON's third-great-grandfather was Captain ELISHA BARTON of the Revolutionary War

Pennsylvanian Continentals. His family lived in Hunterdon County, New Jersey—by the Delaware River, near Washington's Crossing, with close relations in Pennsylvania's Bucks County. MARY CATHERINE had some prominent early American relations from all the original northern colonies. Much more will be said about them in this Volume II—Part III: REBELLION. She is a first-cousin several times removed to Quaker STEPHEN HOPKINS of Rhode Island, who signed the Declaration of Independence, and to ELIZABETH SCHUYLER (Hamilton), wife of ALEXANDER HAMILTON—and the daughter of major general PHILIP SCHYULER of the Northern Theater of the Revolutionary War. MARY CATHERINE BARTON has at least three famous sixth-cousins—ABRAHAM LINCOLN, CLARA BARTON, and the financer J. P. MORGAN—all of whom were descendents of seventeenth century American colonists. There are Quakers, Reformed Dutch, Puritans, Royalists, Catholics, French Huguenots, Presbyterians, Anabaptists, and Pilgrims. Their 1620 to 1740 early history is told in the last Chapters of Part II: STANDING FIRM. Part III: REBELLION begins in 1744 with a journey through these northern colonies.

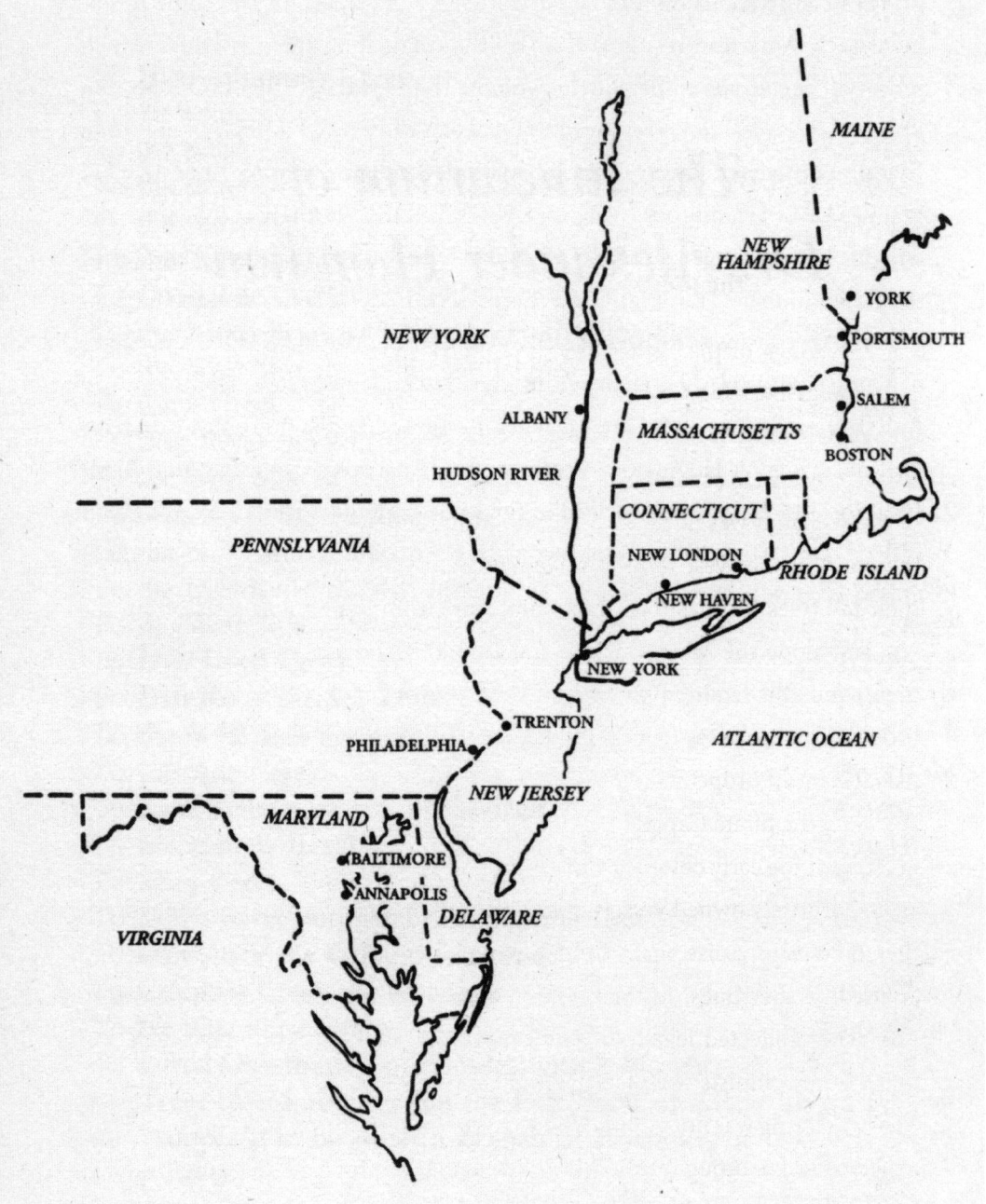

◦ 59 ◦

NORTH BY HORSEBACK IN THE SUMMER OF 1744

The Journey from Maryland to Philadelphia

The Kings of the British Isles and Europe saw the American continents much like a big apple pie—to be divided and eaten—that they might become fatter in their own power and wealth. The colonies were in a sense their slaves or pawns to accomplish this. Gold and mineral wealth had been their first desire. When it was not found in great supply, tobacco and sugar cane became the crops of the West Indies. In New England and Canada, the Kings wanted their tall trees for masts on their ships, furs from their animals, fish from the sea, and along the Massachusetts and Rhode Island coastal area, they wanted their rum. This required sugar cane, so those who could afford merchant ships brought the molasses from the West Indies, made rum and sold it across the Atlantic into Europe and Africa. Rhode Island's seaport was strategicslly situated, and the pirate Captain Kidd defied European authority, adding to the difficulties of the early colonists during the 17th century. There were privateers—armed privately owned vessels that were commissioned by the governments of the colonies to cruise against the commerce or war vessels of the enemy—as defined by the Kings. In the mid-1740s the enemy was France. Great wealth was being collected legally by some of these more enterprising seamen, but mostly the colonists were kept humble and reliant on their mother countries. Manufacturing was not allowed in the colonies, and cloth and many other desirable items were brought from Europe to maintain a trade dependency.

Black slavery was introduced into the Virginia London Company in the mid-1660s. It was slow in the beginning. The gentlemen of Virginia brought their English servants with them from England, and gained land by paying for their transportation, increasing the white population. The speed of the "slave trade" would increase rapidly when cotton became king on the larger plantations.

Dr. Hamilton, a popular physician of Annapolis, Maryland, and son of the Rev. William Hamilton of the University of Edinburgh, Scotland, suffered from consumption [tuberculosis.] The 31-year-old Hamilton stated in a letter, November 1743 that,

> "I shall only say I am not well in health, and for that reason chiefly continue still a Batchellor. I have more fatigue and trouble than I care for. I find it a very hard matter to live well and grow rich."

So on 30 May 1744, he left Annapolis, Maryland, with his black servant Dromo on a northern tour, where he hoped to find superior weather and alleviate his symptoms. He kept a journal. Because each colony had their own currency, the doctor carried letters of introduction to prominent gentlemen along the route, which served as both financial and social passports. The spelling is given as he wrote it. Ancestors and their relations are shown in capitals.

Philadelphia—Quakers—
PRESTON, WILKINSON, LACEY, PARLETT

His route on horseback took him north to Baltimore, across the Susquehanna River by ferry, to Newtown, Pennsylvania—upon the Chester River, to Chester and Darby, crossing on the Skuylkill ferry into Philadelphia:

> "On Friday, June 8 . . . I dined att a taveren with a very special mixed company of different nations and religions. There were Scots, English, Dutch, Germans and Irish; there were Roman Catholicks, Church men, Presbyterians, Quakers, Newlightmen, Methodists, Seventh day men, Moravians, Anabaptists, and one Jew. The whole company consisted of 25 planted around an oblong table in a great hall well stoked with flys. The company divided into committees in conversation; the prevailing topick was politicks and conjectures of a French war. A knott of Quakers there talked only about selling of flower and the price it bore. They touched a little upon religion, and high words arose among some of the sectaries, but their blood was not hot enough to quarrell, or, to speak in the canting phraze, their zeal wanted fervency . . . I went to see some ships that lay in the river. Among the rest were three vessels a fitting out for privateers—-a ship, a sloop, and a schooner. The ship was a large vessel, very high and full

rigged; one Capt. MACKEY intended to command her upon the cruise."

[Note: Nineteen-year-old, fourth-great-grandmother MARY PRESTON married Quaker fourth-great-grandfather SAMUEL LIPPINCOTT of Shrewsbury, New Jersey, on 7 Apr 1743, in Bucks County, Pennsylvania. She was born in Philadelphia in 1724. Her Quaker grandfather WILLIAM PRESTON had come from Newcastle-upon-the-Tyne, England. WILLIAM had many children and grandchildren who remained in Philadelphia. He had died 19 Jul 1717.]

"Saturday, June 9th. This morning there fell a light rain which proved very refreshing . . . The heat in this city is excessive, the sun's rays being reflected with such power from the brick houses and from the street pavement which is brick. The people commonly use awnings of painted cloth . . . over their shop doors and windows and, att sun set, throw buckets full of water upon the pavement which gives a sensible cool. They are stocked with plenty of excellent water . . . there being a pump att almost every 50 paces distance. There are a great number of balconies to their houses where sometimes the men sit in a cool habit and smoke.

"The market in this city is perhaps the largest in North-America. It is kept twice a week upon Wednesdays and Saturdays. The street where it stands, called Market Street, is large and spacious, composed of the best houses in the city. They have but one publick clock here which strikes the hour but has neither index nor dial plate. It is strange they should want such an ornament and conveniency in so large a place, but the chief part of the community consisting of Quakers, they would seem to shun ornament in their publick edifices as well as in their aparrell or dress. The Quakers here have two large meetings, the Church of England one great church in Second Street, and another built for Whitfield in which one Tennent, a fanatick, now preaches, the Romans one chapell, the Anabaptists one or two meetings, and the Presbyterians two.

"The Quakers are the richest and the people of greatest interest in this government; of them their House of Assembly is chiefly composed. They have the character of an obstinate, stiff necked generation and a perpetuall plague to their governors. The present governour, Mr. Thomas, has fallen upon a way to manage them better than any of his predecessors did and, att the same time, keep pritty much in their good graces and share some of their favours. However, the standing or falling of the Quakers in the House of Assembly depends upon their making sure the interest of the Palatines [chief ministers] in this province, who of late have turned so numerous that they can sway the votes which way they please."

[Note: One of their leaders was sixth-great-grandfather JOHN WILKINSON (Sr.), who died in 1751. He and his family were Quakers whose roots were in Rhode Island and England. He had large land holdings on both sides of the Neshaminy River and resided near Wrightstown in Bucks County—a gentleman of wealth and influence. He was the justice of the peace for many years, of the Court of Common Pleas, Orphan's Court, and Court of Quarter Sessions of the Peace, for the county of Bucks, which borders Philadelphia County on the north.]

Dr. Hamilton's journal continues:

"Here is no publick magazine of arms nor any method of defence, either for city or province, in case of the invasion of an enemy . . . This is owing to the obstinacy of the Quakers in maintaining their principle of non-resistance. . . . I never was in a place so populous where the gout for publick gay diversions prevailed so little. There is no such things as assemblys of the gentry among them, either for dancing or musick; these they have had an utter aversion to ever since Whitefield preached among them. Their chief employ, indeed, is traffick and mercantile business which turns their thoughts from these levitys. Some of the Virginia gentlemen that came here with the Commissioners of the Indian Treaty were desirous of having a ball but could find none of the feemale sex in a humour for it. Strange influence of religious enthusiasm upon human nature to excite an aversion at these innocent amusements, for the most part so agreeable and entertaining to the young and gay, and indeed, in the opinion of moderate people, so conducive to the improvement of politeness, good manners, and humanity. . . . In the evening I drank tea . . . . Att 7 a'clock I went to the Governour's Club where were a good many strangers, among the rest Captain MACKY, commander of the privateer ship. The conversation run chiefly upon trade and the late expedition att Cartagene. Severall toasts were drank, among which were some celebrated ones of the female sex.

"Tuesday, June 12. This seemed to me an idle kind of a day, and the heat began to return. I prepared my baggage, intending tomorrow to proceed on my journey towards New York, which city I proposed to be my next resting place . . . . I drank tea with Mrs. Cume att 5 a'clock. There was with her a masculin faced lady, very much pitted with the small pox. I soon found she was a Presbyterian. And a strait laced one too . . . . [She] was pritty well versed in the church history of Maryland. 'I am surprised,' said she, 'how your government can suffer such a rascally clergy. Maryland has become a receptical and, as it were, a common shore for all the filth and scum of that order. I am informed that taylors, coblers, blacksmiths, and such fellows, when they cannot live like gentlemen by their trade in that place, go home to take orders of some latitudinarian bishop and return learned preachers, setting up for teachers of the people, that have more need of schooling themselves.' I heard this long harangue with patience and attempted to speak in defence of our clergy, but this lady's instructions bore such credit with her that she would not be contradicted . . . . There is a polite conversation here among the better sort, among whom there is no scarcity of men of learning and good sense. The ladies, for the most part, keep att home and seldom appear in the streets, never in publick assemblies except att the churches or meetings . . . . but to be sure the Philadelphian dames are as handsome as their neighbors.

"The staple of this province is bread, flower, and pork. They make no tobacco but a little for their own use. The country is generally plain and levell, fruitfull in grain and fruits, pretty well watered, and abounding in woods backward. It is upon the growing hand, more than any of the provinces of America. The Germans and High Dutch are of late become very numerous here.

"Wednesday, June 13. Early in the morning I set out from Philadelphia, being willing to depart that city where, upon account of the excessive heat, it was a pain to live and breath . . . . I remarked . . . stone bridges, the first that I had seen in America. The country people whom I met asked in generall whether war had been proclaimed against France."

[Note: He crossed the Delaware River into New Jersey on a ferry near Trenton. Further up the Delaware River near the spot where George Washington would later cross the Delaware on his surprise visit to Trenton, were the ironworks of LACEY township. These ironworks were built by brothers JOHN and THOMAS LACEY and their brother-in-law JOHN HESTON. The settlement was known as Wycombe, patented to WILLIAM LACEY, father of the LACEY boys. The patent was executed by commissioners acting for William Penn in 1718, and superseded an earlier grant to WILLIAM PARLET, father-in-law of WILLIAM LACEY, who came from the Isle of Wight to Philadelphia with William Penn. WILLIAM LACEY divided the land into two parts and gave 192 acres to his son, JOHN, whose granddaughter MARY LACEY married the older son, JOHN (Jr.), of JOHN WILKINSON (Sr.), and 100 acres to THOMAS, his second son, whose daughter, fourth-great-grandmother BARBARA LACEY, became the wife of his second son, JOSEPH WILKINSON, who inherited the WILKINSON lands in Hunterdon County, New Jersey—across the Delaware River.

William Penn's first 100 came to New Castle (Delaware) on 27 Oct 1682. William Penn then returned to England until 9 Sep 1699, when he brought his family to Philadelphia; but he had to again return to England. On 4 Oct 1712, William Penn had a paralytic stroke, which deprived him of his memory and locomotion. He died 30 July 1718.]

Passing through New Jersey—Trenton to Perth Amboy—MORGAN

Our traveler continued on to Trenton, New Jersey.

"I put up att one Eliah Bond's att the 'Sign of the Wheat Sheaf.' Two gentlemen of the town came there and invited me into their company. One was named Cadwaller, a doctor in the place and, as I understood, a fallen off Quaker . . . . Cadwaller gave me the character of the constitution and [New Jersey] government. The House of Assembly here, he told me, was chiefly composed of mechanicks and ignorant wretches, obstinate to the last degree; that there were a number of proprietors in the government, and a multitude of Quakers. He enlarged a little in the praise of Governour Morris, who is now a very old man. From politicks the discourse turned to religion and then to physick [medicine].

"Thursday, June 14. A little after 5 in the morning I departed Trenton and rid twelve miles of a very pleasant road well stored with houses of entertainment. The country round about displays a variety of agreeable prospects and rurall scenes. I observed many large fields of wheat, barley, and hemp, which is a great staple and commodity now in this province, but very little maiz or Indian corn; only two or three small fields I observed in riding about 40 miles. They plant it here much thicker than in Maryland . . . . . All round you in this part of the country you observe a great many pleasant fertile meadows and pastures which diffuse, att this season of the year in the cool of the morning, a sweet and refreshing smell. The houses upon the road are many of them built with rough stone.

"I passed thro' Princetown, a small village at eight in the morning and was saluted . . . . by an Indian traveler . . . . Att half an hour after eight in the morning I put up att one Leonards's att the 'Sign of the Black Lyon' in Kingstown, another small village upon the road. I breakfasted there upon a dish of tea and was served by a pritty smiling girl, the landlord's daughter. After breakfast, as I sat in the porch, there arrived a waggon with some company. There were in it two Irishman, a Scotsman, and a Jew. The Jew's name was Abraham Du-bois, a French man by birth. He spoke such bad English that I could scarce understand him. He told me he had been att Conestogo to visit some relations he had there; that he left that place upon Monday last, and att that time there had arived there 40 canoes of Indians of the tribes of the Mohooks and 5 Nations going to treat [make a treaty] with Governours and Commissioners of the American provinces.

"The Jew and the company that were with him begun a dispute about sacred history. He insisted much upon the books of Moses and the authority of the Old Testament. He asked the Scotsman in particular if he believed the Old Testament. He replied that now a days there were few Old Testament people, all having become 'New Light men, for,' says he, 'among the Christians, one wife is sufficient for one man, but your Old Testament . . . . allowed a plurality of wives and as many concubines as they could afford to maintain.' The Jew made no answer to this nonsensicall reply but began very wisely to settle what day of the week it was and what time of that day that God began the creation of the world . . . . after a deal of such stuff about the Jewish Sabbath and such like subjects, the waggon and company departed. They travell here in light, convenient waggons made somewhat chaise fashion, being high behind and low before, many of them running upon 4 wheels so that the horses bear no weight but only draw, and by this means they can travel att a great rate, perhaps 40 or 50 miles a day.

"Betwixt twelve a'clock and three in the afternoon there came up three smart thunder gusts with which fell a deal of rain, but it did not much cool the air. In the middle of the first rain a solemn old fellow lighted att the door. He was in a homely rustick dress, and I understood his name was MORGAN. 'Look ye here,' says the landlord to me, 'here comes a famous philosopher.' 'Your servant, Mr. MORGAN, How d'ye?' The old fellow had not settled himself long upon his seat before he entered upon a learned discourse concerning astrology and the influences of the stars, in which he seemed to put a great deal more confidence than I thought requisite. From that he made a transition to the causes of the tides, the shape and dimensions of the earth, the laws of gravitation, and 50 other physicall subjects in which he seemed to me not to talk so much out of the way as he did upon the subject of judiciall astrology. Att every period of this old philosopher's discourse, the landlord's address to him was, 'Pray, Mr. MORGAN, you that are a philosopher know such and such reasons for such and such things, please inform the gentleman of your opinion.' Then he fell upon physick and told us that he was a riding for his health. I found him very deficient in his knowledge that way, tho a great pretender. All that passed while the old fellow drank half a pint of wine, which done, the old don took to his horse and rid off in a very slow solemn pace, seemingly well satisfied with his own learning and knowledge. When he was gone, I enquired of the landlord more particularly concerning him, who told me that he was the most conspicuous and notorious philosopher in all these American parts; that he understood mademadigs [mathematics] to a hair's breadth and had almost discovered whereabouts the longitude lay and had writ home to the States of Holland and some other great folks about it a great while agoe but had as yet received no answer."

[Note: Dr. Hamilton discovered later in his journey that Mr. MORGAN was then a curate to his Hudson River traveling companion, Mr. Milne, "a minister at *Shrewsbery* in the Jersies." The plural "Jersies" refers to East Jersey (Calvinistic) and West Jersey, which was dominated by the Quakers. New Jersey was originally settled by the Swedes; then it was claimed by the Dutch. Of course, the Delaware Indian tribe was an earlier settler. When the English conquered the Dutch in 1664, Englishmen were permitted to settle New Jersey. The LIPPINCOTT ancestors were chartered large land holders in Shrewsbery, in 1669. [*Part II: STANDING FIRM*]

Fifth-great-grandmother DOROTHY MORGAN, born about 1704, married a Dutchman HENRY

VAN KIRK of Freehold, New Jersey (about 10 miles west of Shrewsbury). They moved to Hopewell, New Jersey (a little northwest of Princeton) where they raised their family. Perhaps, Mr. MORGAN was her father [and my sixth-great-grandfather] traveling from Shrewsbury across New Jersey to visit his daughter's family at Hopewell in 1744. The three MORGAN brothers came from Wales to America in 1636 and settled in Connecticut. Ancestor JAMES MORGAN and many of his descendants lived in the Preston, New London, and New Haven, Connecticut area. They had large families and some spread westward into New York and beyond. Second brother JOHN was a minister. Several other relatives in the MORGAN family were ministers in the Church. The third brother MILES MORGAN settled in Hartford and is the ancestor of J. P. MORGAN.]

Dr. Hamilton then proceeded to Brunswick,

"a neat small city in East Jersey upon the Raretin River about 60 miles northeast of Philadelphia."

Dr. Hamilton forded the Raretin River on Friday June 15th before 6 in the morning

"the tide being low and the skeow aground."

On way to Perth Amboy

"I was overtaken by two men, a young man and an old, grave, sedate fellow. The young man gave me the salute which I returned and told him that if he was going to Amboy, I should be glad of company . . . . First of all (as is natural) we enquired concerning news. I gave him an account of such scraps of news as I had picked up att Philadelphia, and he gave me an account of a capture that had well nigh been made of an English sloop by a Frenchman that had the impudence to pursue her into the hook at the entrance of York Bay, but the English vessel getting into Amboy harbour, the Frenchman betook himself to sea again. 'But had this French rogue known Amboy as well as I,' added my newsmonger, 'he would have taken her there at anchor.' After discussing news, we discoursed concerning horses, by which I discovered that my chap was a jockey by trade. This topic lasted till we came to Perth Amboy, and the old don spoke not one word all the way but coughd and chawd tobacco.

"At nine in the morning we stoped att the 'Sign of the King's Arms' in Amboy where I breakfasted. As I sat in the porch I observed an antick figure pass by having an old plaid banyan, a pair of thick worsted stockings, ungartered, a greasy worsted nightcap, and no hat. 'You see that originall,' said the landlord. 'He is an old batchellor, and it is his humour to walk the street always in that dress. Tho he makes but a pitifull appearance, yet is he proprietor of most of the houses in town. He is very rich, yet for all that, has no servant but milks his own cow, dresses his own vittles, and feeds his own poultry himself.'

"Amboy is a small town (older than the city of New York) being a chartered city, much less than our Annapolis, and here frequently the Supream Court and Assembly sit. It has in it one Presbyterian meeting and a pritty large market house, lately built. It is the principall town in New Jersey and appears to be laid out in the shape of a St. George's cross, one main street cutting the other att right angles. Tis a sea port, having a good harbour but small trade. They have here the best oysters I have eat in America. It lyes close upon the water, and the best houses in town are ranged along the water side. In the Jerseys the people are chiefly Presbyterians and Quakers, and there are so many proprietors that share the lands in New Jersey, and so many doubtfull titles and rights that it creates an inexhaustible and profitable pool for the lawers."

Kings County, Long Island—COOL, VAN KIRK

From here he took a ferry to Staten Island and proceeded "on the pritty stony, sandy, and uneven road" to the Narrow's ferry.

"I came to the Narrows att two a'clock and dined att one Corson's that keeps the ferry. The landlady spoke both Dutch and English. I dined upon what I never had eat in my life before—a dish of fryed clams, of which shell fish there is abundance in these parts. As I sat down to dinner I observed a manner of saying grace quite new to me. My landlady and her two daughters put on solemn, devout faces, hanging down their heads and holding up their hands for half a minute. I, who had gracelessly fallen too without remembering that duty according to a wicked custom I had contracted, sat staring att them with my mouth choak full, but after a short meditation was over, we began to lay about us and stuff down the fryed clams with ryebread and butter. They took such a deal of chawing that we were long att dinner, and the dish began to cool before we had eat enough. The landlady called for the bedpan. I could not guess what she intended to do with it unless it was to warm her bed to go to sleep after dinner, but I found that it was used by way of a chaffing dish to warm our dish of clams. I stared att the novelty for some time, and reaching over for a mug of beer that stood on the opposite side of the table, my bag sleeve catched hold of the handle of the bed pan and unfortunately overset the clams, at which the landlady was a little ruffled and muttered a scrape of Dutch of which I understood not a word except mynheer, but I suppose she swore, for she uttered her speech with an emphasis. After dinner I went on board the ferry boat and, with a pritty good breeze, crossed the Narrows in half an hour to Long Island.

Att the entry of this bay is a little craggy island about one or two miles long called Coney Island. Before I came to New York Ferry, I rid a bye way where, in seven miles riding, I had 24 gates to open . . . . The road here for severall miles is planted thick upon each side with rows of cherry trees, like hedges, and the lots of land are mostly inclosed with stone fences."

[Note: He proceeded to Flatlands Bay. A distant cousin GERRET STOOTHOFF would drown in this bay two years later on 1 Aug 1746. GERRET was the great-grandson of ALTJE COOL, who first married Gerret Wolfertsz Van Couwenhoven and, after his death, married Elbert Elbertsz Stoothoff, and had children by both husbands. ALTJE was the daughter of ninth-great-grandfather, CORNELIS LAMBERTSZEN COOL, a very early settler in Flatlands, Kings County, Long Island. Today, it is 8 miles on Flatbush Avenue from the coastal Parkway Highway through Flatlands to the Brooklyn and Manhattan Bridges. The Flatbush Dutch Reformed Church, where many relatives were baptized and married, was midway on this road.

The VAN KIRKS settled first in Kings County. When New Jersey land was available for sale about 1698 to 1700, a large migration of the younger sons of the Dutch and New Englanders into New Jersey occurred. In the VAN KIRK family, the oldest son inherited his father's estate in Flatlands, while the younger sons went west: AERT into Delaware and then to Monmouth County, New Jersey; JAN, the first of the children to be born in America, moved directly to Monmouth County, New Jersey, and the youngest son, BARENT went to Bucks County, Pennsylvania. Fourth-great-grandfather HENRY VAN KIRK who married DOROTHY MORGAN was either the son of JAN or the grandson of AERT—genealogists seem to differ.]

Up the Hudson River to Albany and back—the Dutch—
COOL, RENSSELAER

Dr. Hamilton entered New York City on the ferry. On Wednesday, 20 June, he met a Mr. Milne,

"a minister at *Shrewsbery* in the Jerseys, who had formerly been for some years minister att *Albany*. I made an agreement to go to Albany with him the first opportunity that offered.

"Thursday, June 21 . . . After getting my baggage and some provisions ready, I went on board the Albany sloop where I found Mr. Milne and his wife, an old jolly, fat Dutchwoman, mother to the Patroon [JEREMIAH RENSSELAER] att Albany, a gentleman there of Dutch extract, the chief landed man in the place."

[Note: JEREMIAH RENSSELAER, 5th Patroon, was the son of KILIAEN VAN RENSSELAER, 4th Patroon, and MARITJE VAN CORTLAND, evidently the jolly, fat Dutchwoman referred to. KILIAEN and MARITJE were married 15 Oct 1701. The Cortland's had vast estates on the Hudson River between Albany and New York and as a family were greatly involved in New York politics and society. She married Mr. Milne after the death of her first husband. KILIAEN was a great-grandson of our common ancestor HENRI VAN RENSSELAER— a wealthy contemporary in Holland of the English Queen Elizabeth.]

"Having a contrary wind and an ebb tide, we dropt anchor about half a mile below New York and went ashore upon Nutting Island [Governor's Island that had belonged to Governor Van Twiller], which is about half a mile in dimension every way, containing about 60 or 70 square acres. We there took in a cask of spring water. One half of this island was made into hay, and upon the other half stood a crop of good barley, much dammaged by a worm which they have here which, so soon as their barley begins to ripen, cuts off the heads of it. There lived an old Scots-Irishman upon the island with his family in a ruinous house, a tennant of the Governour's to whom the island belongs durante officio. This old man treated us with a mug of ship beer and entertained us with a history of some of the adventures of the late Governour Cosby upon the island. It is called Nutting Island from its bearing nuts in plenty, but what kind of nuts they are I know not, for I saw none there . . . . The banks of the island are stonny and steep in some places. It is a good place to erect a battery upon to prevent an enimy's approach to the town, but there is no such thing, and I believe that an enimy might land on the back of this island out of reach of the town battery and plant cannon against the city or even throw boombs from behind the island upon it. We had on board this night 6 passengers, among whom were three women. They all could talk Dutch but myself and Dromo [his servant], and all but Mr. Milne seemed to preferr it to English. Att eight a'clock att night, the tide serving us, we weighed anchor and turned it up to near the mouth of North River [Hudson] and dropt anchor again att 10 just opposite to the great church in New York."

[Note: The colored stained glass windows in this Dutch Reformed New York Church and those in the Albany Dutch Reformed Church, representing the coats of arms of the members, were among the masterpieces of the painter and glazier EVERT DUYCKINCK and his son GERRIT. EVERT's daughter, ANNETJE, married PIETER CORNELISSON COOL, a grandson of ninth-great-grandfather CORNELIS LAMBERTSON COOL.]

"Friday June 22d. While we waited the tide in the morning, Mr. Milne and I went ashore . . . where we breakfasted and went from thence to see the new Dutch church, a pritty large but heavy stone building, as most of the Dutch edifices are, quite destitute of taste or elegance. The pulpit of this church is prittily wrought, being of black walnut. There is a brass supporter for the great Bible that turns upon a swivell, and the pews are in a very regular order. The church within is kept very clean, and when one speaks or hollows, there is a fine eccho. We went up into the steeple where there is one pritty large and handsom bell, cast att Amsterdam, and a publick clock. From this steeple we could have a full view of the city of New York.

"Early this morning two passengers came on board of the sloop, a man and a woman, both Dutch. The man was named Marcus Van Bummill. He came on board drunk and gave us a surfet of bad English. If any body laughed when he spoke, he was angry, being jealous that they thought him a fool. He had a good deal of the bully and braggadocio in him, but when thwarted or threatened, he seemed faint hearted and cowardly. Understanding that I was a valitudinarian, he began to advise me how to manage my constitution. 'You drink and whore too much,' said he, 'and that makes you thin and sickly. Could you abstain as I have done and drink nothing but water for 6 weeks, and have to do with no women but your own lawfull wife, your belly and cheeks would be like mine, look ye, plump and smooth and round.' With that he clapt his hands upon his belly and blowd up his cheeks like a trumpeter. He brought on board with him a runlett of rum, and, taking it into his head that somebody had robed him of a part of it, he went down into the hold and fell a swearing bitterly . . . . He was for having us all before a magistrate about it, but att last Knockson, the master of the sloop, swore him into good humour again and perswaded him that his rum was all safe. He quoted a deal of scripture, but his favorite topics when upon that subject was about King David, and King Solomon, and the shape and size of the Tower of Babel . . . . After a deal of talk and rattle, he went down and slept for four hours . . . . There was a Dutch woman on board, remarkably ugly, upon whom this Van Bummill cast a loving eye and wanted much to be att close conference with her.

"Att twelve a'clock we passed a little town, starboard, called Greenwitch, consisting of eight or ten neat houses, and two or three miles above that on the same shoar, a pritty box of a house with an avenue fronting the river, belonging to Oliver Dulancie. On the left hand some miles above York, the land is pritty high and rockey, the west bank of the river for severll miles being a steep precipice above 100 foot high.

"Mr. M. read a treatis upon microscopes and wanted me to sit and hear him, which I did, tho' with little relish, the piece being trite and vulgar, and tiresome to one who had seen Leewenhoek [the discoverer of the microscope] and some of the best hands upon that subject . . . . I found him an intire stranger to the mathematicks, so as that he knew not the difference betwixt a cone and a pyramid, a cylinder and a prism . . . . In some parts of learning, such as the languages, he seemed pritty well versed. He could talk Latine and French very well and read the Greek authors, and I was told that he spoke the Dutch to perfection . . . . I was informed by him that MORGAN, the philosopher and mathematician whom I had seen att Kingstown, was his curate.

"We had several learned discourses in the evening from Van Bummill concerning doctors. 'You are a doctor,' says he to me; 'what signifys your knowledge? You pretend to know inward distempers and to cure them, but to no purpose; your art is vain. Find me out a doctor among the best of you that can mend a man's body half so well as a joiner can help a crazy table or stool. I myself have spent more money on doctors than I would give for the whole tribe of them if I had it in my pocket again . . . . We had a fresh westerly wind att night, which died away att 10 a'clock, and we dropt anchor about 40 miles above York.

"Saturday, June 23. We weighed anchor about 4 in the morning, having the wind northeast and contrary, and the tide beginning to fall, we dropt anchor again att 7 . . . . We went ashore to fill water near a small log cottage on the west side of the river inhabited by one Stanespring and his family. The man was about 37 years of age, and the woman 30. They had seven children . . . . The children seemed quite wild and rustick. They stared like sheep upon Milne and I when we entered the house, being amazed at my laced hat and sword . . . . This cottage was very clean and neat but poorly furnished. Yet Mr. M observed severall superfluous things which showed an inclination to finery in these poor people, such as a looking glass with a painted frame, half a dozen pewter spoons and as many plates, old and wore out but bright and clean, a set of stone tea dishes, and a tea pot. These Mr. M said, were superfluous and too splendid for such a cottage, and therefor they ought to be sold to buy wool to make yarn; that a little water in a wooden pail might serve for a looking glass, and wooden plates and spoons would be as good for use . . . . As for the tea equipage it was quite unnecessary, but the man's musket, he observed, was as usefull a piece of furniture as any in the cottage. We had a pail of milk here which we brought on board, and the wind coming southerly att eleven a'clock, we weighed anchor and entered the Highlands which presented a wild, romantick scene of rocks and mountains covered with small craggy wood, mostly oak. . . . . At 6 a'clock we passed Dancing Hall larboard, a little square and level promontory which runs about 50 paces into the river, overgrown with bushes where, they report, about 60 or 70 years agoe, some young people from Albany, making merry and dancing, were killed by some Indians who lay in ambush in the woods . . . . We anchored att eight o'clock att the entry of that part of the river called Long Reach, the weather being very thick and rainy, and close by us on the starboard side stood a small village called Poughcapsy.

"Sunday, June 24th. At four in the morning Mr. M and I went ashore to the taveren, and there we met with a justice of the peace and a New Light taylor . . . . The taylor's phizz [face] was screwed up to a santified pitch, and he seemed to be either under great sorrow for his sins or else a hatching some mischief in his heart, for I have heard that your hipocriticall rogues always put on their most solemn countenance or vizzard when they are contriving how to perpetrate their villanies. We soon discovered that this taylor was a Moravian. The Moravians are a wild, fanatick sect with which both this place and the Jerseys are pestered. They live in common, men and women mixed in a great house or barn where they sometimes eat and drink, sometimes sleep, and sometimes preach and howl, but are quite idle and will employ themselves in no usefull work. They think all things should be in common and say that religion is intirely corrupted by being too much blended with the laws of the country. They call their religion the true religion . . . . and they commonly term themselves the followers of the Lamb, which I believe is true in so far as some of them may be wolves in sheep's clothing.

"We weighed anchor att 7 a'clock with the wind south west and fresh and half an hour after passed by Sopus [Esopus—across from Hyde Park—the home of Franklin D. Roosevelt—with the Vanderbilt Mansion slightly south of it.] . . . [Esopus is] a pleasant village situated upon the west side of the river, famous for beer and ale . . . . Att Sopus we passed by the Governour's fleet consisting of three painted sloops. That therein Clinton was had the union flag a stern. He had been att Albany treating with the Indians. We now had a sight of the range of mountains called the Catskill, or Blue Mountains . . . . Here the river is about 2 miles broad, and the land low, green and pleasant. Large open fields and thickets of woods, alternatly mixed, entertains the eye with variety of landskips . . . . Att one a'clock we scudded by Livingston Mannor."

[Note: PHILIP LIVINGSTON and ROBERT R. LIVINGSTON were New York's representatives to the Continental Congress and PHILIP was a signer of the Declaration of Independence. This mannor is part of present day "Clermont State Park" on the border of Dutchess and Columbia Counties. It is about 7 miles north of Red Hook, near the Rombout area to the east, where possible ancestor THOMAS POYER later wrote his will and died a few years later.]

"Monday, June 25th . . . Att seven o'clock, the wind being southerly, we hoised anchor, and sailing up the river we passed a large stone, larboard, called Prec Stone, or Preaching Stone, from its resemblance to a pulpit. We had not made much way before the wind changed to north west so we resolved to go to Albany in the sloop's canoe and went ashore to borrow another to carry our baggage. We found the poor people there in great terror of the Indians; they being apprehensive that they would begin their old trade of scalping. We set off in the canoes att nine a clock and saw Albany att a distance. We landed upon a island belonging to Mr. Milne, upon which there was fine grass of different sorts and very good crops of wheat and pease, of which they bring up great quantitys here for the use of the ships—the bug not getting into their pease there as with us . . . . We met severall Dutchmen on the island who had rented morgans of land upon it; they call half an acre of land there a morgan.

"These people . . . told us of a French man and his wife that had been att Albany the day before we arrived. They had come from Canada, and it was they we saw on board the sloop that passed us last night. The Frenchman was a fugitive, according to his own account, and said he had been a priest and was expelled his convent for having an intrigue with that lady who was now his wife. The lady had been prosecuted att law and had lost the greatest part of her estate which went among these cormorants, the lawers. The Governour of Canada, Mons'r Bon Harnois, being her enimy, she could not expect justice, and therefor fled with this priest to the English settlements in order to prevent her being intirely beggar'd, taking the residue of her estate along with her. This Bonharnois is now a very old man and, they say, behaves himself tyrranically in this government. He was a courtier in Lewis XIVth's time and then went by the name of Mons'r Bon Vit, which being an ugly name in the French language, the King changed his name to Bonharnois. This day there came some Canada Indians in two canoes to Albany to pursue this priest and his lady. 15,000 livres were laid upon each of their heads by the Governour. They said they had orders to bring back the priest dead or alive, if dead to scalp him and take the consecrated flesh from his thumb and forefinger. The lady they were to bring back alive, but they came too late to catch their game.

"Tuesday, June 26th. Early this morning I went with Mr. M to Albany, being a pleasant walk of two miles from the island. We went a small mile out of town to the house of JEREMIAH RANSLAER, who is dignified here with the title of Patroon. He is the principal landed man in these parts, having a large mannor, 48 miles long and 24 broad, bestowed upon his great grandfather by K. Charles the Second after his restoration. The old man [KILIAEN VAN RENSSELAER, born in 1580 was a son of my ancestor HENRI VAN RENSSELAER] it seems, had prophesied his recovering of his kingdoms ten years before it happened. The King had been his lodger when he was in Holland, and thereby he had an opportunity to ingratiate himself and procure the royall favour. This mannor is divided into two equall haves by Hudson's River, and the city of Albany stands in the middle of it. This city pays him a good yearly rent for the liberty of cutting their fire wood. The Patroon is a young man of good mein and presence. He is a batchellor, nor can his friends perswade him to marry. By paying too much hommage to Bacchus, he has acquired a hypochondriac habit. He has a great number of tennants upon his mannor, and he told me himself that he could muster 600 men fit to bear arms. Mr. Milne and I dined att his house and were handsomly entertained with good viands and wine. After dinner he showed us his garden and parks, and Milne got into one of his long harangues of farming and improvement of ground."

[Note: Albany (Fort Orange) saw the overthrow of Dutch rule on 24 Sep 1664. It was restored again to the Dutch on 5 Aug 1673. Charles I of Great Britain was executed by Cromwell and his people in London on 30 Jan 1649. Charles II fled to Holland as a refugee. On 29 May 1660 Charles II returned to London as their King amid cheers and acclamations. The Netherlands had the world's greatest navy after the sinking of the Spanish Armada—having helped the English with its destruction (1588). Henry Hudson, an Englishman, was given the *Half Moon* by the Dutch, and his claims in the new world were for the Dutch. In 1666, there was a war for naval supremacy between the two countries. When the British claimed New Netherlands, evidently RENSSELAER's large land holdings were also seized, but were later restored. Charles II died in London 6 Feb 1685. Neither RENSSELAER nor Charles II ever set foot in this new country. PART II: STANDING FIRM tells of the early days and relationships.]

ENGLISH KING CHARLES II

"At 4 a'clock Milne and I returned to town where Milne, having a generall acquaintance, for he had practised physick ten years in the city and was likewise the Church of England minister there, he introduced me into about 20 or 30 houses where I went thro' the farce of kissing most of the women, a manner of salutation which is expected (as Mr. M told me) from strangers coming there. I told him it was very well, if he led the way I should follow, which he did with clericall gravity. This might almost pass for pennance, for the generality of the women here, both old and young, are remarkably ugly.

"Att night we went to the island, where we supped. While we were att supper we smelt something very strong like burnt oatmeal which they told me was an animall called schunk, the urine of which could be smelt att a great distance, something of the nature of the polecat.

"Wednesday, June 27. I went this morning with the Patroon's brother, STEPHEN RENSLAER, to see the Cochoos, a great fall of water 12 miles above Albany. The water falls over a rock almost perpendicular, 80 foot high and 900 foot broad, and the noise of it is easily heard att 4 miles distance; but in the spring of the year when the ice breaks, it is heard like great guns all the way att Albany. There is a fine mist scattered about where it falls for above half a mile below it, upon which when the sun shines opposite, appears a pritty rainbow. Near the fall the noise is so great that you cannot discern a man's voice unless he hollows pritty loud. Below the fall the river is very narrow and very deep, running in a rockey channell about 200 foot wide, att each side of which channell there is a bank of sollid rock about 3 or 400 foot wide, as smooth and levell as a table.

"In this journey we met a Mohook Indian and his family going hunting. His name was Solomon. He had a squaw with him over whom he seemed to have an absolute authority. We travelled for two miles thro impenetrable woods, this Indian being our guide, and when we came to the banks of the river near the falls, we were obliged to leave our horses and descend frightfull precipices. One might walk across the river on top of the rock whence the water falls was it not for fear of being carried down by the force of the water, and Solomon told us that the Indians sometimes run across it when the water is low.

"We rid att a pritty hard rate 15 or 16 miles farther to the Mohooks town standing upon the same river. In it there are severall wooden and brick houses, built after the Dutch fashion, and some Indian wigwams or huts, with a church where one Barclay preaches to a congregation of Indians in their own language, for the bulk of the Mohooks up this way are Christians.

"Returning from here we dined att Coll. SKUYLER's about 4 a'clock in the afternoon, who is naturalized among the Indians, can speak severall of their languages, and has lived for years among them. We spent part of the evening att the Patroon's, and going to town att night I went to the taveren with Mr. LIVINGSTON, a man of estate and interest there.

[Note: This was John Schuyler who had a large estate in Albany, the father of General PHILIP J. SCHUYLER of the Revolutionary War. PHILIP SCHUYLER, born 20 Nov 1733 at Albany, married CATHERINE VAN RENNSELAER 17 Sep 1755. They had 11 children and their daughter ELIZABETH married ALEXANDER HAMILTON, the future U.S. Treasurer.]

"Thursday, June 28. Early this morning I took horse and went in company with one Collins, a surveyor here, to a village call[ed] Schenectady about 16 miles from Albany and pleasantly situated upon the Mohook's River."

[Note: It was originally settled by my distant great uncle ARENDT VAN CULER, whom the Indians and French called COLEAR, of Fort Orange (Albany.) He was the nephew and representative of KILIAEN

VAN RENSSELAER, 1580-1646, the first patroon, and was greatly loved by the Indians.]

"It is a trading village, the people carrying on a traffic with the Indians—their chief commodity is wampum, knives, needles, and other such pedlary ware. The village is pritty near as large as Albany and consists chiefly of brick houses, built upon a pleasant plain, inclosed all round att about a mile's distance with thick pine woods. These woods form a copse above your head almost all the way betwixt Albany and Schenectady, and you ride over a plain, levell, sandy road till, coming out of the covert of the woods, all att once the village strikes surprizingly your eye, which I can compare to nothing but the curtain rising in a play and displaying a beautiful scene.

"We returned to Milne's Island, from whence between twelve and one a'clock I went to Albany in a canoe . . . . I went to see the school in this city in which are about 200 schollars, boys and girls. I dined at the Patroon's; after dinner Mr. Shakesburrough, surgeon to the fort, came in, who by his conversation, seemed to have as little of the quack in him as any half hewn doctor ever I had met with. The doctors in Albany are mostly Dutch, all empyricks, having no knowledge or learning but what they have acquired by bare experience. They study chiefly the virtues of herbs, and the woods there furnish their shops with all the pharmacy they use. A great many of them take the care of a family for the value of a Dutch dollar a year, which makes the practise of physick a mean thing and unworthy of the application of a gentleman. This afternoon I went a visiting Milne and had the other kissing bout to go thro'. We went at night to visit STEPHEN RENSLAER's where we supped."

[Note: STEPHEN VAN RENSSELAER would become the 6th Patroon, as JEREMIAH never married. STEPHEN and his wife Elizabeth Groesbeck had a son STEPHEN who would become the 7th Patroon. STEPHEN, the 6th Patroon, also had a daughter ELIZABETH who married General ABRAHAM TEN BROECK at Albany, 1 Nov 1763. ABRAHAM was the son of Mayor DIRCK TEN BROECK and MARGARITA CUYLER. ABRAHAM was twice Mayor of Albany from 9 Apr 1779 to 26 Jun 1783 and again from 15 Oct 1796 to 31 Dec 1798. He died on 19 Jan 1810. STEPHEN RENNSELAER, the 7th Patroon, married CATHERINE LIVINGSTON, a daughter of PHILIP LIVINGSTON who was the signer of the Declaration of Independence for New York state. PHILIP was married to CHRISTINA TEN BROECK.]

"Friday, June 29th. After breakfast I walked out with Mr. Milne and visited some more old women, where I had occasion to prescribe and enter into a dispute with a Dutch doctor . . . . About this time one KUYLER [questionably believed to be a nephew of ancestor, ROBERT COLES], mayor of the city, was suspected of trading with the Canada Indians and selling powder to them. The people of the town talked pritty openly of it, and the thing coming to Governour Clinton's ears, he made him give security for his appearance att the Generall Court to have the affair tried and canvassed.

"I went before dinner with Milne and saw the inside of the Town House. The great hall where the court sits is about 40 foot long and thirty broad. This is a clumsy, heavy building both without and within. We went next and viewd the workmen putting up new palisading or stockadoes to fortify the town, and att ten a'clock we walked to the island and returned to town again att 12. Mr. Milne and I dined upon cold gammon att one Stevenson's, a Scots gentleman of some credit there. We drank tea att STEPH. RANSLAER's and supped at Widow SKUYLER's where the conversation turned upon the Moravian enthusiasts and their doctrines.

"Saturday, June 30 . . . We supped by invitation att the taveren with some of the chief men in the city, [Albany], it being muster day and a treat given by the officers of the fort to the muster masters. There was Messrs. KUYLLER the Mayor, TANSBROOK the Recorder [Mayor JOHN CUYLER of Albany was married to ELSIA TEN BROEK], Holland the Sherriff, Surveyor Collins, Captain Blood, Captain Haylin of the fort, and several others. The conversation was rude and clamorous, but the viands and wine were good. We had news of the French having taken another small fort besides Cansoe. I walked with Milne to the island at 10 at night.

"Sunday, July 1. At six a'clock this morning a sharp thunder gust came up with a heavy rain . . . . At 10 a'clock we went to the English Church where was the meanest congregation ever I beheld, there not being above 15 or 20 in church besides the souldiers of the fort who sat in a gallery. Milne preached and gave us an indifferent good discourse against worldly riches, the text being 'It is easier for a camel to pass thro' the eye of a needle than for a rich man to enter the kingdom of heaven.' This discourse, he told me, was calculated for the naturall vice of that people, which was avarice, and particularly for Mr. LIVINGSTON, a rich but very covetous man in town who valued himself much for his riches. But unfortunately LIVINGSTON did not come to church to hear his reproof.

"Att 12 a'clock another thunder gust came up. We dined at ST. RENSLAER'S and made severall visits in the afternoon. Among the rest we went to see Captain Blood at the fort. He is nephew to the famous Blood that stole the crown. This man is a downright old souldier, having in his manner an agreeable mixture of roughness and civility . . . . We supped att ST. RENSLAER's.

"Monday, July 2d, I now began to be quite tired of this place where was no variety or choise, either of company or conversation, and one's ears perpetually invaded and molested with volleys of rough sounding Dutch, which is the language most in use here. I therefor spoke to one Wendall, master of a sloop which was to sail this evening for York . . . . Att half an hour after two a'clock I saw Wendall's sloop falling down the river with the tide, and they having given me the signall of a gun which was agreed upon, they sent their canoe for me. Att three o'clock I took my leave of Milne and his wife, thanking them for all their civilitys and the hospitality . . . . I followed the sloop for near two miles in the canoe before I overtook her and went on board half an hour after three. We had scarce been half an hour under sail after I came on board when we run aground upon some shoals about a mile above the Oversleigh and dropt anchor till after 6. The tide rising we were afloat again and went down with the wind N. by East. Rainy.

"The city of Albany lyes on the west side of Hudson's River upon a rising hill about 30 or 40 miles below where the river comes out of the lake and 160 miles above New York. The hill whereon it stands faces south east. The city consists of three pritty compact streets, two of which run paralell to the river and are pritty broad, and the third cuts the other two att right angles, running up towards the fort, which is a square stone building about 200 foot square with a bastion att each corner, each bastion mounting eight or ten great guns, most of them 32 pounders. In the fort are two large, brick houses facing each other where there is lodging for the souldiers. There are three market houses in this city and three publick edifices, upon two of which are cupolos or spires, vizt., upon the Town House and the Dutch church. The English church is a great, heavy stone building without any steeple, standing just below the fort. The greatest length of the streets is half a mile. In the fort is kept a garrison of 300 men under the King's pay, who now and then send reinforcements to Oswego, a frontier garrison and trading town . . . . This city [Albany] is inclosed by a rampart or wall of wooden palisadoes about 10 foot high and a foot thick, being the trunks of pine trees rammed into the ground, pinned close together, and ending each in a point att top. Here they call them stockadoes. Att each 200 foot distance round this wall is a block house, and from the north gate of the city runs a thick stone wall down into the river, 200 foot long, att each end of which is a block house. In these block houses about 50 of the city militia keep guard every night, and the words all's well walks constantly round all night long from centry to centry and around the fort. There are 5 or 6 gates to this city, the chief of which are the north and south gates. In the city are about 4,000 inhabitants, mostly Dutch or of Dutch extract.

"The Dutch here keep their houses very neat and clean, both without and within. Their chamber floors are generally laid with rough plank which, in time, by constant rubbing and scrubbing becomes as smooth as if it had been plained. Their chambers and rooms are large and handsom. They have their beds generally in alcoves so that you may go thro all the rooms of a great house and see never a bed. They affect pictures much, particularly scripture history, with which they adorn their rooms. They set out their cabinets and bouffetts much with china. Their kitchens are likewise very clean, and there they hang earthen or delft plates and dishes all round the walls in manner of pictures, having a hole drilled thro the edge of the plate or dish and a loop of ribbon put into it to hang it by. But notwithstanding all this nicety and cleanliness in their houses, they are in their persons slovenly and dirty. They live here very frugally and plain, for the chief merit among them seems to be riches, which they spare no pains or trouble to acquire, but are a civil and hospitable people in their way but, att best, rustick and unpolished. I imagined when I first came there that there were some very rich people in the place. They talked of 30, 40, 50 and 100 thousand pounds as of nothing, but I soon found that their riches consisted more in large tracts of land than in cash. They trade pritty much with the Indians and have their manufactorys for wampum, a good Indian commodity. It is of two sorts—the black, which is the most valuable, and the white wampum. The first kind is a bead made out of the bluish black part of a clam shell. It is valued att 6 shillings York money per 100 beads. The white is made of a conch shell from the W. Indies and is not so valuable. They grind the beads to a shape upon a stone, and then with a well tempered needle dipt in wax and tallow, they drill a hole thro' each bead. This trade is apparently triffling but would soon make an estate to a man that could have a monopoly of it, for being in perpetuall demand among the Indians from their custome of burying quantitys of it with their dead, they are very fond of it, and they will give skins or money or any thing for it, having (tho they first taught the art of making it to the Europeans) lost the art of making it themselves.

"They live in their houses in Albany as if it were in prisons, all their doors and windows being perpetually shut. But the reason of this may be the little desire they have for conversation and society, their whole thoughts being turned upon profit and gain which necessarily makes them live retired and frugall. Att least this is the common character of the Dutch every where. But indeed the excessive cold winters here obliges them in that season to keep all snug and close, and they have not summer sufficient to revive heat in their veins so as to make them uneasy or put it in their heads to air themselves. They are a healthy long lived people, many in this city being in age near or above 100 years, and 80 is a common age. They are subject to rotten teeth and scorbutick gumms which, I suppose, is caused by the cold air and their constant diet of salt provisions in the winter, for in that season they are obliged to lay in as for a sea voyage, there being no stirring out of doors then for fear of never stirring again. As to religion they have little of it among them and of enthusiasm not a grain. The bulk of them, if any thing, are of the Lutheran church. Their women in general, both old and young, are the hardest favoured ever I beheld. Their old women wear a comicall head dress, large pendants, short petticoats, and they stare upon one like witches. They generally eat to their morning's tea raw hung beef sliced down in thin chips in the manner of parmezan cheese. Their winter here is excessive cold so as to freeze their cattle stiff in one night in the stables.

"To this city belongs about 24 sloops about 50 tons burden that go and come to York. They chiefly carry plank and rafters. The country about is very productive of hay and good grain, the woods not much cleared."

[Note: Lumber was a cash crop very much in demand in Europe and the American coastal colonies to build ships as well as homes. The tall pines for the masts of ships were difficult to find in Europe.]

"The neighbouring Indians are the Mohooks to the north west, the Canada Indians to the northward, and to the southward a small scattered nation of the Mohackanders.

"The young men here call their sweethearts luffees, and a young fellow of 18 is reckoned a simpleton if he has not a luffee; but their women are so homely that a man must never have seen any other luffees else they will never entrap him."

JESUIT MISSIONARIES AMONG THE INDIANS,

DRAWN BY WM. L. SHEPARD.

[Note: This ink drawing is shown in the early histories of Northumberland County, Pennsylvania, explaining that the Jesuits came early into this territory where my great-grandmother MARY CATHERINE BARTON was born in 1837. The Catholic French tried very hard to establish their colonies and religion in the Ohio, Pennsylvania, and west along the Mississippi River. It began when La Salle sailed down the Mississippi in 1681 to the Gulf of Mexico. The animosity between the English and French would increase steadily until the actual conflict would begin in 1749.]

60

ACROSS LONG ISLAND TO NEW LONDON, RHODE ISLAND, AND ON TO BOSTON IN 1744

Our traveler Dr. Hamilton sailed back to New York on the Hudson River. He commented:

"I was never so destitute of conversation in my life as in this voyage. I heard nothing but Dutch spoke all the way . . . . I went to my lodging att Mrs. Hog's where I first heard the melancholly news of the loss of the Philadelphia privateer. I dined att Todd's where there was a mixed company, among the rest . . . . the city recorder, Oliver Dulancie . . . . In this company there was one of these despicable fellows whom we may call c(our)t spys, a man, as I understood, pritty intimate with G(overno)r C(linto)n, who might perhaps share some favour for his dexterity in intelligence. This fellow, I found, made it his business to foist himself into all mixed companies to hear what was said and to enquire into the business and character of strangers. After dinner I happened to be in a room near the porch fronting the street and overheard this worthy intelligencer a pumping of Todd, the landlord . . . . Todd . . . informed him who I was, upon his asking the question. 'You mean the pock-fretten man,' said he, 'with the dark coloured silk coat. He is a countryman of mine . . . one Hamilton from Maryland. They say he is a doctor and is travelling for his health.' Hearing this stuff, 'this is afternoon's news,' thinks I, 'for the G(overno)r,' and just as the inquisitor was desiring Todd to speak lower, he was not deaf, I bolted out upon them and put an end to the enquiry, and the inquisitor went about his business.

"I went to the inn to see my horses, and finding them in good plight, Mr. Waghorn desired me to walk into a room where were some Boston gentlemen that would be company for me in my joruney there. I agreed to set out with them for Boston upon Monday morning . . . .

"Monday, July 9th. I waited upon Mr. Bayard this morning and had letters of credit drawn upon Mr. Lechmere at Boston . . . . We heard news this day of an English vessel loaden with ammunition and bound for New England being taken on the coast . . . . The people of New York att the first appearance of a stranger are seemingly civil and courteous, but this civility and complaisance soon relaxes if he be not either highly recommended or a good toaper. To drink stoutly with the Hungarian Club, who are all bumper men, is the readiest way for a stranger to recommend himself, and a sett among them are very fond of making a stranger drunk. To talk bawdy and to have a knack att punning passes . . . . Govr. C(linto)n himself is a jolly toaper and gives good example and, for that one quality, is esteemed among these dons.

"The staple of New York is bread flower and skins. It is a very rich place, but it is not so cheap living here as att Philadelphia. They have very bad water in the city, most of it being hard and brackish. Ever since the negroe conspiracy, certain people have been appointed to sell water in the streets, which they carry on a sledge in great casks and bring it from the best springs about the city, for it was when the negroes went for tea water that they held their caballs and consultations, and therefor they have a law now that no negroe shall be seen upon the streets without a lanthorn after dark.

"In this city are a mayor, recorder, aldermen, and common council. The goverment is under English law, but the chief places are possessed by Dutchmen, they composing the best part of the House of Assembly. The Dutch were the first settlers of this province, which is very large and extensive, the States of Holland having purchased the country of one Hudson who pretended first to have discovered it, but they att last exchanged it with the English for Saranam, and ever since there have been a great number of Dutch here, tho now their language and customs begin pritty much to wear out and would very soon die were it not for a parcell of Dutch domines here who, in the education of their children, endeavour to preserve the Dutch customs as much as possible. There is as much jarring here betwixt the powers of the legislature as in any of the other American provinces.

"There are a great many handsome women in this city. They appear much more in publick than att Philadelphia. It is customary here to ride thro the street in light chairs. When the ladys walk the streets in the day time, they commonly use umbrellas, prittily adorned with feathers and painted. There are two coffee-houses in this city, and the northeren and southeren posts go and come here once a week. I was tired of nothing here but their excessive drinking, for in this place you may have the best company and conversation as well as att Philadelphia."

Eastern Long Island, crossing the Sound to Connecticut—BARTON

"Tuesday, July 10th. Early in the morning we got up, and after preparing all my baggage, Messrs. Parker, Laughton, and I mounted horse and crossed the ferry att seven a'clock over to Long Island. After a tedious passage and being detained sometime att Baker's, we arrived a quarter after 10 at Jamaica, a small town upon Long Island just bordering upon Hampstead Plain. It [Jamaica] is about half a mile long, the houses sparse. There are in it one Presbyterian meeting, one English, and one Dutch church. The Dutch church is built in the shape of an octagon, being a wooden structure. We stopt there att the Sign of the Sun and paid dear for our breakfast, which was bread and mouldy cheese, stale beer and sower cyder."

[Note: Jamaica is close to the center of Queens County, currently near the main route to John F. Kennedy International Airport, which is directly south of it. JOSEPH BARTON (1670?), youngest son of our emigrant ancestor ROGER BARTON, had settled at Jamaica, Long Island, when he married his second wife Rachel about 1713. About 1721 he removed to Scarsdale Manor, Westchester, New York. Ten years later he moved to Greenwich, Fairfield County, Connecticut. One year previous to Dr. Hamilton's journey, in 1743, he settled at Filkintown in Crum Elbow precinct, Dutchess County, New York, where he died in 1762. At least two of his sons, LEWIS and CALEB accompanied him there. JOSEPH's descendants became prominent people in this county. It is believed by some genealogists that JOSEPH's sons, WILLIAM and JOSEPH BARTON, are the early settlers of that name in Philadelphia County, Pennsylvania, of whom more will be said later.]

"We set out again and arrived att Hampstead, a very scattered town standing upon the great plain to which it gives name . . . going across this great plain, we could see almost as good a horizon around us as when one is at sea, and in some places of the plain, the latitude might be taken by observation att noon day. It is about 16 miles long. The ground is hard and gravelly, the road very smooth but indistinct and intersected by severall other roads which makes it difficult for a stranger to find the way. There is nothing but long grass grows upon this plain, only in some particular spots small oak brush, not above a foot high. Near Hampstead there are severall pritty winding brooks that run thro' this plain. We lost our way here and blundered about a great while. Att last we spyed a woman and two men at some distance. We rid up towards them to enquire, but they were to wild to be spoke with, running over the plain as fast as wild bucks upon the mountains. Just after we came out of the plain and sunk into the woods, we found a boy lurking behind a bush. We wanted to enquire the way of him, but as soon as we spoke the game was started and away he run.

"We arrived att Huntington att eight a'clock att night, where we put up at one Flat's att the Sign of the Half Moon and Heart. We no sooner sat down when there came in a band of the town politicians in short jackets and trowsers, being probably curious to know who them strangers were who had newly arrived in town. Among the rest was a fellow with a worsted cap and great black fists. They stiled him doctor. Flat told me he had been a shoemaker in town and was a notable fellow att his trade, but happening two years agoe to cure an old woman of a pestilent mortal disease, he thereby acquired the character of a physition, was applied to from all quarters, and finding the practise of physick a more profitable business than cobling, he laid aside his awls and leather, got himself some gallipots, and instead of cobling of soals, fell to cobling of human bodies."

On July 11, they left Huntington in the morning, and after riding some thro' "some very barren, unequal, and stonny land" they forded the Smithtown River and viewed

"about 24 miles farther to the northward, the coast of New England or the province of Connecticut. We arrived at a scattered town called Brookhaven, or by the Indians, Setoquet, about two a'clock afternoon and dined att one Buchannan's there. Brookhaven is a small scattered village standing upon barren, rocky land near the sea. In this town is a small windmill for sawing of plank, and a wooden church with a small steeple. Att about 50 miles' distance from this town eastward is a settlement of Indians upon a sandy point which makes the south fork of the island and runs out a long narrow promontory into the sea almost as far as Block Island."

[Note: Brookhaven was settled in 1655 and joined the Connecticut Colony in 1661. In 1664 the name "ROG. BARONES" appears as a recorder on several copies of documents in these Brookhaven records from the Court of Connecticut. So immigrant ancestor ROGER BARTON was probably the earliest town-clerk of Brookhaven. As a freeman of the Connecticut Colony, he secured land at Rye Neck, also called Barton's Neck, about 1670. He sold some land in 1678. ROGER BARTON built a house in Westchester town in November 1684. On 6 Aug 1688, the Sheriff was ordered to put BARTON in Possession because a dispute developed between the members of the English and Dutch Churches in that area. He left Westchester and probably died later that year. (Barton & Hummell Family Histories p. 89)]

"While we were at Buchanan's, an old fellow named Smith called att the house. He said he was a travelling to York to get a license or commission from the Governour to go a privateering and swore he would not be under any commander but would be chief man himself. He showed us severall antick tricks such as jumping half a foot high upon his bum without touching the floor with any other part of his body. Then he turned and did the same upon his belly. Then he stood upright upon his head. He told us he was 75 years of age and swore d___n his old shoes if any man in America could do the like.

"We took horse again att half an hour after 5 o'clock, and scarce got a mile from Brookhaven when we lost our way but were directed right again by a man whom we met. After riding 10 miles thro' woods and marshes in which we were pestered with muscettoes, we arrived at eight o'clock att night att one Brewster's where we put up for all night, and in this house we could get nothing either to eat or drink and so were obliged to go to bed fasting or supperless. I was conducted up stairs to a large chamber. The people in this house seemed to be quite savage and rude.

"Thursday, July 12. When I waked this morning I found two beds in the room besides that in which I lay, in one of which lay two great hulking fellows with long black beards, having their own hair and not so much as half a nightcap betwixt them both. I took them for weavers, not only from their greasy appearance, but because I observed a weaver's loom at each side of the room. In the other bed was a raw boned boy who, with the two lubbers, huddled on his cloths and went reeling down stairs making as much noise as three horses.

"We set out from this desolate place at 6 a'clock and rid 16 miles thro very barren and waste land . . . . In all this way we met not one living soul nor saw any house, but one in ruins. Some of the inhabitants here call this place the Desart of Arabia. It is very much infested with muscettoes. We breakfasted att one *Fanning's*. [Perhaps a relative of the North Carolina *Fanning* mentioned later—a graduate lawyer from Yale.] Near his house stands the county court house, a decayed wooden building, and close by his door runs a small rivulett into an arm of the sea about 20 miles distance, which makes that division of the eastern end of Long Island called the Fork.

"This day was rainy, but we took horse and rid . . . to the town of Southhold, near which the road is levell, firm and pleasant, and in the neighbourhood are a great many windmills. The houses are pritty thick along the road here. We put up att one Mrs. More's in Southhold. In her house appeared nothing but industry. She and her grandaughters were busied in carding and spinning of wool . . . . After dinner we sent to enquire for a boat to cross the Sound . . . .

"Friday, July 13. We took horse after 6 in the morning and rid 5 or 6 miles close by the Sound till we came to one Brown's who was to give us passage in his boat. Then we proceeded 7 miles farther and stopped att one King's to wait the tide, when Brown's boat was to fall down the river to take us in . . . . At two a'clock we observed the boat falling down the river, and having provided our selves with a store of bread and cheese and some rum and sugar in case of being detained upon the water, that part of the Sound

35

which we had to cross being 18 miles broad, we put our horses on board 10 minutes before three and set sail with a fair wind from the Oyster Pond. Att three a'clock we passed the Gutt, a rapid current betwixt the main of Long Island and Shelter Island caused by the tides. Att a quarter after three we cleared Shelter Island, larboard, upon our weather bow. Gardiner's Island bore east by north, starboard, about three leagues' distance. This island is in the possession of one man and takes its name from him. It had been a prey to the French privateers in Queen Anne's war, who used to land upon it and plunder the family and tennants of their stock and provisions, the island lying very bleak upon the ocean just att the eastermost entry of the Sound betwixt Long Island and the main of Connecticut. [This area was a favorite place for the pirate Captain Kidd.].

Connecticut Government, New London—MORGAN

"We arrived in the harbour att New London att half an hour after 6 and put up att Duchand's att the Sign of the Anchor."

[Note: Eighth-great-grandfather JAMES MORGAN (born ca. 1607 in Wales) had been a large landed proprietor here in a district east of the River Thames from about 1650 till his death. His wife was MARGERY HILL, who was born in Great Barnstead, Essex, England—a few miles from where the SWALLOW ancestry came from 260 years later. On his death, his estate was divided among his four surviving children. His two older sons, JAMES and JOHN, were Captains and his third son, JOSEPH, was a Lieutenant. Captain JOHN MORGAN, moved nine miles to Preston City, New London, Connecticut, where he died in 1712. He had two wives. The first had seven children before she died. His second wife was ELIZABETH EATON, who is said to have added eight additional children. She is believed to be the daughter of the first Connecticut governor of New Haven, THEOPHILUS EATON, and his second wife the heiress, ANNE (LLOYD) MORTON, whose first husband was THOMAS YALE of London—probably the grandparents of ELIHUE YALE, who originally financed Yale University at New Haven. Many of their fifteen children remained in Connecticut.

Third son, Lieutenant JOSEPH MORGAN, married DOROTHY PARKE, 26 Apr 1670. Both were born in New London, Connecticut. They were the parents of a son, JOSEPH, and ten daughters, which were born in Preston. Although some genealogies show Captain JOHN as our ancestor, it seems Lieutenant JOSEPH, with his wife named DOROTHY, may be the actual great-grandparents of our DOROTHY MORGAN, who married HENRY VAN KIRK in Freedom, New Jersey.]

"The town of New London is irregularly built along the water side, in length about a mile. There is in it one Presbyterian meeting and one church. 'Tis just such another desolate expensive town as Annapolis in Maryland, the houses being mostly wood. The inhabitants were allarmed this night att a sloop that appeared to be rowing up into the harbour, they having heard a little before a firing of guns out in the Sound and seen one vessell, as they thought, give chase to another. There was a strange clamour and crowd in the street, chiefly of women. The country station sloop lay in the harbour, who, when she was within shot, sent a salute, first one gun, sharp shot, but the advancing sloop did not strike; then she bestowed upon her another, resolving next to proceed to a volley; but att the second shot, which whistled thro' her rigging, she struck and made answer that it was one Captain Trueman from Antequa. Then the people's fears were over, for they imagined it was old Morpang, the French rover, who in former times used to plunder these parts when he wanted provision."

Newport, Rhode Island—BARTON, WILBOR, TALLMAN

Traveling east through Kingston, Rhode Island, Dr. Hamilton crossed into Newport, Rhode Island, on Monday, July 16. He describes it as

"a pleasant, open spot of land, being an intire garden of farms, 12 or 13 miles long and 4 or 5 miles broad at its broadest part. The town Newport is about a mile long, lying pritty near north and south. It stands upon a very levell spot of ground and consists of one street, narrow but so streight that standing att one end of it you may see to the other. It is just close upon the water. There are severall lanes going from this street on both sides. Those to the landward are some of them pritty long and broad. There is one large market house near the south end of the main street. The Town House stands a little above this market house away from the water and is a handsom brick edifice, lately built, having a cupola at top. There is, besides, in this town two Presbyterian meetings, one large Quaker meeting, one Anabaptist, and one Church of England. The church has a very fine organ in it, and there is a publick clock upon the steeple as also upon the front of the town House. The fort is a square building of brick and stone, standing upon a small island which makes the harbour. This place is famous for privateering, and they had about this time brought in severall prizes, among which was a large Spanish snow near 200 ton burden which I saw in the harbour with her bowsplitt shot off. This town is as remarkable for pritty women as Albany is for ugly ones, many of whom one may see sitting in the shops in passing along the street."

[Note: On the north end of this island is Portsmouth, where RUFUS BARTON, brother of ancestor ROGER BARTON, settled when the Dutch drove him from New Amsterdam about 100 years before this time. His daughter ELIZABETH married THOMAS GREENE, and this couple named their youngest son NATHANIEL. They are close relations to George Washington's highly competent Continental Army General NATHANIEL GREENE of Rhode Island. About 6 miles west of Newport, across the Sakonnot River is Little Crompton, Rhode Island. This was the childhood home of sixth-great-grandmother HANNAH WILBOR, the mother of SAMUEL LIPPINCOTT, who married MARY PRESTON of Philadelphia. HANNAH's great-grandfather was JOHN WILBORE of Felstead, Essex, Engand, which is five miles from Stebbing, the home of my husband's SWALLOW and CROW ancestors, who came to Utah in the early 1870s. The WILBORs came to Rhode Island in the 1640s, and many of HANNAH's nieces and nephews were still there in 1744. HANNAH's mother was SARAH TALLMAN, whose grandfather came to Portsmouth, Rhode Island, from Hamburg, Germany.]

On to Boston and New Hampshire—
LIPPINCOTT, BARBER, BARTON, MORGAN

"Tuesday, July 17th . . . As we entered the Province of the Massachusets Bay, upon the left hand we saw a hill called Mount Hope, formerly the strong hold or refuge of an Indian king named Philip who held the place a long time against the first settlers and used to be very troublesome by making excursions. We passed thro' Bristol, a small trading town laid out in the same manner as Philadelphia, about three a'clock . . . We crossed another little ferry att 5 a'clock and baited att one Hunt's, then riding 10 miles farther we parted with Mr. Lee and lay that night att one Slake's, att the Sign of the White Horse."

[Note: The city of Bristol is in Rhode Island and the surrounding area borders Bristol County, Massachusetts, which was one of the areas settled by the early New England THRASHERs. I have tried, as yet unsuccessfully, to tie them to our southern THRASHER ancestry. Although most of them were strongly supportive of the colonial fight for independence, a BENJAMIN THRASHER, of Taunton, Bristol, Massachusetts, was one of the loyalist leaders. Evidently, he and John Adams opposed each other in several debates. As troubles increased, BENJAMIN moved back to England.]

"Wednesday, July 18 . . . While we were att dinner (at Robins's) . . . We had news . . . of the French having, along with the Cape Sable and St. John Indians, made an attack upon Annapolis Royall, [Nova Scotia] and that they had killed all their cattle and severall men there and burnt down all the houses in the town; so that the inhabitants, in the outmost distress, were obliged to betake themselves to the fort where they were scanty of provisions and ready to surrender when Captain Ting, master of the Boston gally, came seasonably to their assistance with a reinforcement of men and a fresh supply of provisions, and as soon as the enimy heard his guns they fled into the woods. This Ting has gained a great character here for his conduct and courage. We parted from Robin's a little after three and betwixt 5 and 6 arrived att Dedham, a village within eleven miles of Boston, where we rested a little and drank some punch . . . . At 13 miles' distance from Boston is a range of hills called the Blue Hills, upon the top of one of which a gentleman has built a country house where there is a very extensive view. A quarter before eight we arrived in Boston. There I put my horses att one Barker's and took lodging att Mrs. Guneau's, a French woman, att the back of the Alms House near Beacon Hill, a very pleasant part of town situated high and well aired."

[Note: He was close to the town of Roxbury, where several of eighth-great-grandfather JAMES MORGAN's children were born,—18 May 1642, 3 Mar 1644, & 16 Mar 1645. Roxbury was annexed by Boston in 1868. It claims to be the birthplace of the revolutionary war hero, Joseph Warren. Eighth-great-grandfather REMEMBRANCE LIPPINCOTT was born 15 Mar 1642 in Dorcester, nearby—now part of Boston. A few of the younger members of this family were born in Boston, before their father, RICHARD LIPPINCOTT, created non-conformist problems with the Puritans and returned to England.where he joined the early Quakers. RICHARD was imprisoned in Plymouth, England, and after his release the family returned to America and settled in Rhode Island. REMEMBRANCE soon after married eighth-great-grandmother MARGARET BARBER of Boston. The families then moved to Shrewsbury, New Jersey. There are many BARBERs in the early Quaker records of Pennsylvania.]

"My landlady and I conversed about two hours. She informed that one Mr. Hughes, a merchant, that lately had been in Maryland, lodged att her house, which I was glad to hear, having had some small acquaintance with him . . . . I got up half an hour after 5 in the morning, and after breakfast I took a turn in the garden with Mr. Hughes, from whence we had a view of the whole town of Boston and the peninsula upon which it stands. The neck which joins this peninsula to the land is situated south west from the town, and at low water is not above 30 or 40 paces broad and is so flat and levell that in high tides it is sometimes overflowed. The town is built upon the south and southeast side of the peninsula and is about two miles in length, extending from the neck of the peninsula northward to that place called North End, as that extremity of the town next the neck is called South End. Behind the town are severall pleasant plains, and on the west side of the peninsula are three hills in a range, upon the highest of which is placed a long beacon pole. To the northward over the water is situated a pritty large town called Charlestown. We could see a great many islands out in the bay, upon one of which about three miles from town stands the Castle, a strong fortification that guards the entry of the harbour. Upon the most extreme island about 12 miles out is the light house, a high building of stone in form of a pillar, upon the top of which every night is kept a light to guide ships into the harbour. When a snow, brig, sloop, or schooner appears out at sea, they hoist a pinnace upon the flag staff in the Castle; if a ship, they display a flag . . . . I went to the Change or place of publick rendezvous. Here is a great building called the Townhouse, about 125 foot long and 40 foot broad. The lower chamber of this house, called the Change, is all one apartment, the roof of which is supported all along the middle with a row of wooden pillars about 25 foot high . . . . I dined att Withered's a taveren att the Change, and there heard news of the magazines att Placentia being blown up.

"Friday, July 20 . . . Att eleven a clock I went abroad with Mr. Hughes, and after taking a walk to the water side we went to Change at 12 a'clock where I delivered severall letters. I saw att Change some Frenchmen, officers of the flag of truce, with prisoners for exchange from Canso and of the privateer taken by Captain Ting. They were very loquacious, after the manner of their nation, and their discourse for the most part was interlaced with oaths and smutt.

"Sunday, July 22. After dinner I went to the English chapel .... A certain pedantick Irishman preached to us, who had much of the brogue. He gave us rather a philosophicall lecture than a sermon and seemed to be one of those conceited priggs who are fond of spreading out to its full extent all that superficial physicall knowledge which they have acquired more by hearsay than by application or study; but of all places the pulpit is the most impropper for the ostentations of this sort; the language and phraseology of which sacred rostrum ought to be as plain to the ploughman as the schollar. We had a load of impertinence from him about the specific gravity of air and water, the exhalation of vapours, the expansion and condensation of clouds, the operation of distillation, and the chemistry of nature. In fine it was but a very puerile physicall lecture and no sermon att all. There sat some Indians in a pew near me who stunk so that they had almost made me turn up my dinner. They made a profound reverence to the parson when he finished; the men bowed, and the squas curtsied.

"Tuesday, July 24th ... After dinner I went with Mr. Vans to an auction of books in King's Street where the auctioneer, a young fellow, was very witty in his way. 'This book,' says he, 'gentlemen, must be valuable. Here you have every thing concerning popes, cardinals, anti-christ, and the devil. Here, gentlemen, you have Tacitus .... He gives an account of that good and pious person, Nero, who loved his mother and kindred so well that he sucked their very blood.' ... We were called to the windows .. . by a noise in the street which was occasioned by a parade of Indian chiefs marching up the street with Collonell Wendal. The fellows had all laced hats, and some of them laced matchcoats and ruffled shirts, and a multitude of the plebs of their own complexion followed them.

"This was one Henrique and some other of the chiefs of the mohooks who had been deputed to treat with the eastren Indians bordering upon New England. When he first arrived att the place of rendevous, none of the eastren chiefs were come. However, he expressed himself to the commons to this purpose: 'We, the Mohooks,' said he, 'are your fathers, and you, our children. If you are dutifull and take up the hatchet against the French, our enemies, we will defend and protect you; but otherwise, if you are dissobedient and rebell, you shall dye, every man, woman, and child of you, and that at our hands. We will cut you off from the earth as an ox licketh up the grass.' To this some of the Indians made answer that what he said was just . . . 'it is true you are our fathers, and our lives depend upon you. We will always be dutifull, as we have hitherto been, for we have cleared a road all the way to Albany betwixt us and you, having cut away every tree and bush that these might be no obstruction. You, our fathers, are like a porcupine full of prickles to wound such as offend you; we, your children, are like little babes whom you have put into cradles and rocked asleep.' . . . These Mohooks are a terror to all round them and are certainly a brave warlike people, but they are divided into two nations, Protestants and Roman Catholicks, for the most of them are Christians; the first take part with the English, the latter with the French, which makes the neighbouring Indians, their tributarys, lead an unquiet life, always in fear and terrour.

"Wednesday, July 25. I [was] to go to Cambridge . . . but the weather proved too hot. I went to Change at 12 o'clock and heard . . . some distant hints of an intended expedition of the English against Cape Breton, which is a great eye sore to their fishing trade upon this coast.

"Thursday, July 26 . . . After dinner one Captain Tasker came in who had been att Canso when the French took it. He had a vessel there laden with provisions for which he had contracted with the French before the war broke out. When they carried him to Cape Breton, they were so generous as to pay him for his cargo of provisions and dismiss him . . . . I supped att Fletcher's . . . . the night being very dark and rainy, I had much adoe to find my way . . . to my lodging , , , , The streets of this town are very quiet and still a'nights; yet there is a constant watch kept in the town.

"Saturday, July 28th. I departed Boston this morning betwixt seven and eight o'clock, and crossing the upper ferry I came to Charlestown, a pritty large and compact town consisting of one street about half a mile long . . . . Departing Charlestown I passed thro' Mistick att 10 o'clock, a pritty large village about 4 miles north east from Boston . . . . At one o'clock I arrived att Marblehead, a large fishing town, lying upon the sea coast, built upon a rock and standing pritty bleak to the easterly winds from the sea. It lyes 18 miles N.E. from Boston and is somewhat larger than Albany but not so neatly or compactly built, the houses being all of wood, and the streets very uneven, narrow and irregular. It contains about 5000 inhabitants, and their commodity is fish. There is round the town above 200 acres of land covered with fish flakes, upon which they dry their cod. There are 90 fishing sloops always employed, and they deal for 34,000 pounds sterling prime cost value in fish yearly . . . . [Mr. Malcolm, the Church of

England minister] carried me round the town and showed me the fish flakes and the town battery, which is built upon a rock, naturally well fortified, and mounts about 12 large guns.

"Monday, July 30. Mr. Malcolm and I set out att eleven o'clock in the morning for Salem, which is a pritty town about 5 miles from Marblehead going round a creek, but not above two if you cross the creek. The town of Salem is a pritty place, being the first settled place in New England. In it there is one Church of England, one Quaker meeting, and 5 Presbyterian meetings. It consists of one very long street running nearly east and west. Upon the watch house is a grenadeer carved in wood, shouldering his piece."

He proceeded through Ipswitch, Newburry, and on Wednesday, August 1:

"I arrived in Portsmouth att 4 in the afternoon, which is a seaport town very pleasantly situated close upon the water and nearly as large as Marblehead. It contains betwixt 4 and 5 thousand inhabitants. There are in it two Presbyterian meetings and one Church of England, of which last one Brown, an Irishman, is minister, to whom I had a letter recommendatory from Mr. Malcolm . . . .

"Thursday, August 2d. I went and breakfasted with Mr. Brown, and after breakfast we waited upon Governour Wentworth who received me very civily and invited me to take a souldier's dinner with him, as he called it, att the fort. Att 10 o'clock we went by water in the Governour's barge to Newcastle, a small town two miles from Portsmouth, where the fort stands upon a little island. Opposite to Newcastle upon the other side of the water there is a village called Kitterick. The tide in these narrows runs with great rapidity and violence, and we having it in our favour and six oars in the barge, we were down att the fort in about 10 minutes. This fort is almost a triangle, standing on a rock facing the bay . . . . This fort mounts about 30 guns, most of them 32 pounders, besides 15 or 20 small arms for about 60 men, but kept in very bad order, being eat up with rust. Mr. Brown and I crossed the water att three a clock and rid nine miles up the country to a place called York. In our way we had a variety of agreeable prospects of a rocky and woody country and the ocean upon our right hand. We returned to the fort again a little after 7 o'clock. This province of New Hamshire is very well peopled and is a small colony or goverment, being inclosed on all hands by the Massachusets province to which it once belonged but has lately . . . been made a separate goverment from New England. The Provinces here are divided into townships instead of shires or countys. The trade of this place is fish and masting for ships, the navy att home [England] being supplied from here with very good masts. I observed a good many geese in the fort. The Governour took notice that they were good to give an alarm in case of a nocturnal surprize, mentioning the known story of the Roman capitol. We rowed back to town against the tide betwixt 8 and 9 att night."

[Note: Kitterick and York became part of the State of Maine when it gained its statehood. The township of York included Cape Porpoise (about 15 miles further on the coast), where ancestor, ROGER BARTON's father, sea captain EDWARD BARTON (born abt. 1593) was buried in 1671. ROGER's brother, EDWARD was reported to have been in Pemaquid, (coastal fingers of Maine) in the *Encyclopedia of the Early Settlers of New England*. This brother EDWARD died in 1688 in Westchester, New York, where ROGER BARTON also lived at that time. Their brothers WILLIAM and THOMAS remained in Massachucetts, and brother RUFUS went to Rhode Island, as mentioned earlier in PART II: STANDING FIRM.]

Traveler Dr. Hamilton returned to Boston then journeyed to Cambridge [Harvard] and back. He enjoyed Boston and wrote,

"I need scarce take notice that Boston is the largest town in North America, being much about the same extent as the city of Glasgow in Scotland and having much the same number of inhabitants . . . . it is considerably larger than either Philadelphia or New York, but the streets are irregularly disposed and, in generall, too narrow . . . . There were now above 100 ships in the harbour besides a great number of small craft tho now, upon account of the war, the times are very dead. The people of this province chiefly follow farming and merchandise. Their staples are shipping, lumber, and fish. The goverment is so far democratic as that the election of the Governour's Council and the great officers is made by the members of the Lower House, or representatives of the people. Mr. Shirly, the present Governour, is a man of excellent sense and understanding and is very well respected there. He understands how to humour the people and, att the same time, acts for the interest of the Goverment. Boston is better fortified against an enimy than any port in North America, not only upon account of the strength of the Castle but the narrow passage up into the harbour which is not above 160 foot wide in the channell att high water.

"There are many different religions and perswasions here, but the chief sect is that of the Presbyterians. There are above 25 churches, chapells, and meetings in the town, but the Quakers here have but a small remnant, having been banished the province att the first settlement . . . . The people here have latlely been, and indeed are now, in great confusion and much infested with enthusiasm from the preaching of some fanaticks and New Light teachers, but now this humour begins to lessen. The people are generally more captivated with speculative than with practicall religion. It is not by half such a flagrant sin to cheat and cozen one's neighbour as it is to ride about for pleasure on the sabbath day or to neglect going to church and singing of psalms . . . . I must take notice that this place abounds with pritty women who appear rather more abroad than they do att York and dress elegantly. They are, for the most part, free and affable as well as pritty. I saw not one prude while I was here.

"The paper currency of these provinces is now very much depreciated, and the price and value of silver rises every day . . . . Their money is chiefly founded upon land security, but the reason of its falling so much in value is their issuing from time to time such large summs of it and their taking no care to make payments att the expiration of the stated terms. They are notoriously guilty of this in Rhode Island colony so that now it is danger-ous to pass their new moneys in the other parts of New England, it being a high penalty to be found so doing. This fraud must light heavy upon pos-terity. This is the only part ever I knew where gold and silver coin is not commonly current.

"Friday, August 17. I left Boston this morning att half an hour after nine o'clock, and nothing I regretted so much as parting with La Moinnerie (his French friend), the most livily and merry companion ever I had met with, always gay and chearfull, now dancing and then singing tho every day in danger of being made a prisoner. Their temper is always alike, far different from the English who, upon the least misfortune, are for the most part cloggd and overclouded with mellancholly and vapours and, giving way to hard fortune, shun all gaiety and mirth. La Moinnerie was much concerned att my going away and wished me again and again 'une bon voy-age' and 'bon sante', keeping fast hold of my stirrup for about a quarter of an hour."

61

THE PROVIDENCE COLONY, ACROSS CONNECTICUT, NEW YORK TO MARYLAND

"Saturday, August 18. I set out [from Wrentham] . . . the weather being cloudy and close. I went by way of Providence, which is a small but long town situated close upon the water upon rocky ground, much like Marblehead but not a sixth part as large. It is the seat of goverment in Providence Colony [Rhode Island], there being an assembly of the delegates sometimes held here. About 4 miles N.E. of this town there runs a small river which falls down a rock about 3 fathom high, over which fall there is a wooden bridge. The noise of the fall so scared my horses that I was obliged to light and lead them over the bridge. At this place there are iron works. I breakfasted in Providence att one Angel's at the Sign of the White Horse."

[Note: Ancestor Captain LAWRENCE WILKINSON was born in Lanchester, Durham, England, about 1628. He was a lieutenant in the army of Charles I, during the English Civil War, and taken prisoner by the Scotch and Parliamentary troops at the surrender of Newcastle-on-Tyne, 22 Oct 1644. They deprived him of his ancestral estates. In the records of Durham we find the name "LAWRENCE WILKINSON Officer in Arms, Went to New England." Captain LAWRENCE WILKINSON married, in England, SUSANNAH SMITH and in 1652, with their young two year old son, SAMUEL, they sailed the Atlantic and settled in the lands given them in Providence, Rhode Island. SUSANNA was the daughter of CHRISTOPHER and ALICE SMITH, who also settled in Rhode Island. LAWRENCE was made a freeman in 1658; was a member of the Colonial Assembly which met at Portsmouth in 1659; deputy to the General court in 1673, and was a Captain of Provincial troops in the Indian wars. He died 9 May 1692, "full of years and honors". His son (ancestor) SAMUEL WILKINSON, born in 1650, like his father, also took a prominent part in public affairs. He took the oath of allegiance to Charles II, 1 May 1682; he was appointed constable, 12 Jul 1683. He was commissioned captain in the Rhode Island Militia, 4 Apr 1697, and took part in the early Indian wars. He was commissioned a justice, 3 May 1704, and was chosen a deputy to the Colonial Assembly, October, 1705; 27 Oct 1707; 25 Feb 1708, and 31 Oct 1716, and probably served continuously during the intervening dates. He was a surveyor, and in 1711 assisted in running the line between Rhode Island and Massachusetts, and was one of the commissioners appointed 14 May 1719 to settle the dispute over this boundary. He and his brothers, JOHN and JOSIAS, were soldiers in the Indian wars, and the historians of New England say, "fought valiantly." The records at Providence, and the later histories of that section make numerous reference to the public service of Captain SAMUEL WILKINSON. He died at Providence, 27 Aug 1727. Captain SAMUEL WILKINSON married PLAIN WICKENDEN, of Newport, Rhode Island, daughter of Rev. WILLIAM WICKENDEN, second pastor of the first Baptist Church in America. They had nine children.

Ancestor, their second son, JOHN WILKINSON, a Quaker, was born in 1677 and was raised at "Loquieses" the WILKINSON plantation in Providence, but moved to Hunterdon County, New Jersey, and then to Bucks County, Pennsylvania, where he was active in the Pennsylvania Assembly and Congress. JOHN's sister RUTH WILKINSON (born 1685) married WILLIAM HOPKINS, a descendent of the *Mayflower* HOPKINS, and they were the parents of STEPHEN HOPKINS (born about 1705), who was governor of Rhode Island from time to time and was one of the signers of the Declaration of Independence. STEPHEN HOPKINS' brother ESEK HOPKINS became the first Admiral of the Continental Navy at the opening of the Revolutionary War. (*New England Dictionary of Early Settlers; Wilkinson family records; Americana.*)]

From Dr. Hamilton's Journal, Saturday, August 18.

"I crossed Providence Ferry betwixt 10 and eleven o'clock, and after some difficulty in finding my way, I crossed another ferry about 4 miles eastward of Bristo'. I arrived in Bristo' att one o'clock and a little after crossed the ferry to Rhode Island . . . . I departed thence att 4 o'clock but was obliged to stop twice before I got to Newport upon account of rain. I went into a house for shelter where were severall young girls, the daughters of the good woman of the house. They were as simple and awkward as sheep, and so wild that they would not appear in open view but kept peeping at me from behind doors, chests, and benches. The country people in this island, in generall, are very unpolished and rude.

"I entered Newport betwixt seven and eight att night, a thick fog having risen so that I could scarce find the town when within a quarter of a mile of it . . . . I put up at Niccoll's att the Sign of the White Horse and, lying there that night, was almost eat up alive with buggs.

"Sunday, August 19. I called upon Dr. Moffat in the morning and went with him to a windmill near the town to look out for vessels but could spy none." A mill was grinding corn, "an instance of their not being so observant of Sunday here as in the other parts of New England.

"Thursday, August 23 . . . I found the people in Newport very civil and courteous in their way . . . . The Island is famous for making of good cheeses, but I think those made in the Jerseys as good if not preferable. In time of war this place is noted for privateering, which business they carry on with great vigour and alacrity. The Island has fitted out now 13 or 14 privateers and is dayly equipping more. While I stayed in this place they sent in severall valuable prizes. But notwithstanding this warlike apparatus abroad, they are but very sorrily fortified att home. The rocks in their harbour are the best security, for the fort which stands upon an island about a mile from the town is the futiest thing of that nature ever I saw. It is a building of near 200 foot square of stone and brick, the wall being about 15 foot high with a bastion and watch tower on each corner, but so exposed to cannon shot that it could be battered about their ears in ten minutes. A little distance from this fort is a battery of 17 or 18 great guns.

"They are not so strait laced in religion here as in the other parts of New England. They have among them a great number of Quakers. The island is the most delightfull spot of ground I have seen in America. I can compare it to nothing but one intire garden. For rural scenes and pritty, frank girls, I found it the most agreeable place I had been in thro' all my peregrinations. I am sorry to say that the people in their dealings one with another, and even with strangers, in matters of truck or bargain have as bad a character for chicane and disingenuity as any of our American colonys. Their goverment is somewhat democratick, the people choosing their governour from among their own number every year by pole votes. One Mr. GREEN is now governour; the House of Assembly chooses the Council. [In checking the Governors of Rhode Island, Governors GREEN and HOPKINS were usually elected at this time.] They have but little regard to the laws of England, their mother country, tho they pretend to take that constitution for a precedent. Collectors and naval officers here are a kind of cyphers. They dare not exercise their office for fear of the fury and unruliness of the people, but their places are profitable upon account of the presents they receive for every cargoe of run goods. This colony separated it self from New England and was formed into a different goverment thro' some religious quarrells that happened betwixt them. It is customary here to adorn their chimney pannells with birds' wings, peacock feathers and butterflys.

"Friday, August 24 . . . . I called at Dr. Moffat's . . . who entertained me for half an hour with his sun microscope which is a very curious apparatus and not only magnifys the object incredibly upon the moveable screen but affords a beautifull variety and surprizing intermixture of colours. He showed me a a small spider, the down of a moth's wing, the down of feathers, and a fly's eye, in all which objects, Nature's uniformity and beautiful design, in the most minute parts of her work, appeared. The doctor walked to the landing with me, and . . . we took leave of one another."

Across Connecticut to Rye, New York—
MORGAN, COOL, COLET, COOLEY, EATON

"I had a tedious passage to Connecticut. It being quite calm we were obliged to row most of the way. Our passage was more expeditious over Naragantzet Ferry, and there I had the company of a Rhode Islander all the way to Kingstown, where I dined att Case's in the company of some majors and captains, it being a training day. Betwixt Case's and HILL's I was overtaken by a gentleman of considable fortune here. He has a large house close upon the road and is possessor of a very large farm where he milks dayly 104 cows and has, besides, a vast stock of other cattle. He invited me into his house, but I thanked him and proceeded, the sun being low. I put up att HILL's about sunset and enquired there att the landlord concerning this gentleman. HILL informed me that he was a man of great estate, but of base character, for being constituted one of the committee for signing the publick bills of credit, he had counterfieted 50,000 pound of false bills and made his bretheren of the committee sign them, and then counterfeited their names to 50,000 pound of genuine bills which the Government had then issued. This piece of villany being detected, the whole 100,000 pound was called in by the Goverment and he fined in 30,000 pound to save his ears. But I think the fate of such a wealthy villain should have been the gallows, and his whole estate should have gone to repair the publick dammage. As one rides along the road in this part of the country there are whole hedges of barberries.

"Saturday, August 25th. I set off att seven o'clock from HILL's . . . . In this goverment of Rhode Island and Providence you may travell without molestation upon Sunday, which you cannot do in Connecticut or Massachusets province without a pass, because here they are not agreed what day of the week the sabbath is to be kept, some observing it upon Saturday and others upon Sunday."

He arrived at New London that evening and became acquainted with a Deacon Green, whose son visited him in the evening and tells him of

"one Davenport, a fanatick preacher there who told his flock in one of his enthusiastic rapsodies that in order to be saved they ought to burn all their idols."

They began it with a large pile of their favorite books and sang psalms and hymns over the pile while it was burning. Then they brought their

"fancy hoop petticoats, silk gowns, short cloaks, cambrick caps, red heeld shoes, fans, necklaces, gloves and other such aparrell, and what was merry enough, Davenport's own idol with which he topped the pile, was a pair of old, wore out, plush breaches. But this bone fire was happily prevented by one more moderate than the rest, who found means to perswade them that making such a sacrifice was not necessary for their salvation . . . which was lucky for Davenport who, had fire been put to the pile, would have been obliged to strutt about bare-arsed, for the devil another pair of breeches had he but these same old plush ones which were going to be offered up as an expiatory sacrifise.

"Monday, August 27. After visiting Deacon Green this morning and drinking tea with him and wife, he gave me a paquet for his son Jonas att Annapolis. The old man was very inquisitive about the state of religion with us, what kind of ministers we had, and if the people were much addicted to godliness. I told him that the ministers minded hogsheads of tobacco more than points of doctrine, either orthodox or hetrodox, and that the people were very prone to a certain religion called self interest.

"I left New London betwixt eight and 9 o'clock in the morning and crossed Hantick [Niantic] Ferry, or the Gutt, a little before ten. This is an odd kind of a ferry . . . The skeow that crosses here goes by a rope which is fixed to a stake att each side of the Gutt, and this skeow is fastened to the main rope by an iron ring which slides upon it, else the rapidity of the tide would carry skeow and passengers and all away. A little after I passed this ferry I rid close by an Indian town upon the left hand situated upon the brow of a hill. This town is called Nantique and consists of 13 or 14 hutts or wig-wams made of bark. I passed over a bridge in very bad repair . . . . I payed eight pence toll, which . . .is something more than a penny farthing sterling, and coming down to Seabrook upon Connecticut River, I waited there 3 or 4 hours att the house of one Mather before I could get passage. The wind blew so hard att northwest with an ebb tide which, the ferrymen told me, would have carried us out into the Sound had we attempted to pass."

[Note: It was further up the Connecticut River that our early Dutch relative PIETER CORNELISSON COOL, (PETER COLET), had been in charge of the Dutch Fort of Good Hope, (Hartford), when the British took the town of Saybrook and proceeded up the Connecticut River taking possession of the land surrounding the fort. As the overland trail was very dangerous and difficult, PETER tried to save Hartford for the Dutch, but without control of Saybrook and the Connecticut River, the Dutch soon returned to their lands on Long Island and the Hudson River. Uncle MILES MORGAN and a Benjamin Cooley came in 1636 with a group led by John Winthrop Jr. and settled north on the river in Springfield, Massachucetts. Many genealogists have tried to connect, without success, my COOLEY ancestors to Benjamim Cooley, instead of the Dutchman PETER COLET, pronounced much the same. In the treaty of Hartford, September 17, 1650, Stuyvesant lost Dutch New England to the British.]

"Mather and I had some talk about the opinions lately broached here in religion. He seemed a man of some solidity and sense and condemnd Whitefield's conduct in these parts very much. After dinner there came in a rabble of clowns who fell to disputing upon points of divinity as learnedly as if they had been professed theologues. 'Tis strange to see how this humour prevails, even among the lower class of the people here. They will talk so pointedly about justification, santification, adoption, regeneration, repentance, free grace, reprobation, original sin, and a thousand other such pritty, chimerical knick knacks as if they had done nothing but studied divinity all their life time and perused all the lumber of the scholastic divines, and yet the fellows look as much, or rather more, like clowns than the very riff-raff of our Maryland planters. To talk in this dialect in our parts would be like Greek, Hebrew, or Arabick.

"I crossed the ferry att 5 o'clock. This river of Connecticut is navigable for 50 miles up the country. Upon it are a good many large trading towns, but the branches of the river run up above 200 miles. We could see the town of Seabrook below us on the westeren side of the river. I lodged this night att one Mrs. Lay's, a widow woman, who keeps a good house upon the road about 6 miles from Seabrook. I had much difficulty to find the roads upon this side [of the] Connecticut River. They wind and turn so much and are divided into such a number of small paths." He passsed through Killingworth, Gilfoord, Branfoord and "I arrived in Newhaven att 5 o'clock, where I put up att one Monson's att the Sign of the Half Moon. There is but little good liquor to be had in the publick houses upon this road. A man's horses are better provided for than himself, but he pays dear for it."

[Note: In early New Haven THEOPHILUS EATON, born about 1619 in Stratford-on-Avon, England, was the first governor elected by the popular vote of landholders of the area. His second wife, ANNE (LLOYD) MORTON, had also been married previously. ANNE (LLOYD) MORTON (Yale Eaton) was excommunicated in a church/state court, because she would not renounce her belief that infant baptism was wrong, although she had been severely admonished to do so by her husband, the governor, and the Reverend John Davenport—[an ancestor of the fanatic preacher Davenport spoken of in Dr. Hamilton's New London report?] Their daughter ELIZABETH EATON married JOHN MORGAN, son of JAMES. Her story is in PART II]

Dr. Hamilton continues.

"Newhaven is a pritty large, scattered town laid out in squares, much in the same manner as Philadelphia, but the houses are sparse and thin sowed. It stands on a large plain, and upon all sides (excepting the south which faces the Sound) it is inclosed with ranges of little hills as old Jerusalem was according to the topographicall descriptions of that city. The burying place is in the center of the town just faceing the college [Yale], which is a wooden building about 200 foot long and three stories high, in the middle front of which is a little cupula with a clock upon it. It is not so good a building as that att Cambridge, nor are there such a number of students. It was the gift of a private gentleman [ELIHU YALE of England, see Part II: STANDING FIRM.]

"Wednesday, August 29th. I set out from Monson's a little after 7 o'clock and rid a tollerable good road to Millford . . . . I breakfasted in Millford att one Gibbs's, and while I was there the post arrived so that there came great crowds of the politicians of the town to read the news, and we had plenty of orthographicall blunders. We heard of some prizes taken by the Philadelphia privateers. Millford is a large scattered town situated upon a large pleasant plain . . . . [He proceeded through Stratford and Fairfield— the home of JOSEPH MORGAN and SARI—to Norwalk.] I dined at one Taylor's here. My landlord was an old man of 70. He understanding from my boy that I was a doctor from Maryland and having heard that some of the doctors there were wonder workers in practice, he asked my advice about a cancer which he had in his lip. I told him there was one Bouchelle in Maryland who pretended to cure every disease by the help of a certain water which he made, but as for my part, I knew of no way of curing a cancer but by extirpation or cutting it out . . . . While I was att Taylor's the children were frightened att my negroe, for here negroe slaves are not so much in use as with us, their servants being chiefly bound or indentured Indians. The child asked if that negroe was a coming to eat them up. Dromo indeed wore a voracious phiz (face), for having rid 20 miles without eating, he grinned like a crocodile and showed his teeth most hideously.

"Betwixt Taylor's and Norwalk I met a caravan of 18 or 20 Indians. I put up att Norwalk att one Beelding's, and as my boy was taking off the saddles, I could see one half of the town standing about him making enquiry about his master.

"Thursday, August 30. I left Norwalk att 7 in the morning and rid 10 miles of stonny road, crossing severall brooks and rivulets that run into the Sound, till I came to Stanford. A little before I reached this town, from the top of a stonny hill, I had a large open view or prospect of the country westward. The greatest part of it seemed as it were covered with a white crust of stone, for the country here is exceeding rockey, and the roads very rough, rather worse than Stonnington. I breakfasted att Stanford att one Ebenezar Weak's. In this town I saw a new church, which is now a building, the steeple of which was no sooner finished than it was all tore to pieces by lightning in a terrible thunder storm that happened here upon the first day of August in the afternoon. I observed the rafters of the steeple split from top to bottom, and the wooden pins or trunells that fastened the joints half drawn out.

"I rode a stonny and hilly road to Horseneck and overtook an old man who rid a sorrell mare with a colt following her . . . . He said he had been traveling the country for 3 weeks visiting his children and grandchildren who were settled for 50 miles round him. He told me he had had 21 sons and daughters of which 19 were now alive, and 15 of them married and had children; and yet he did not marry himself till 27 years of age and was now only 72 years old. This old man called in at a house about 2 miles from Horseneck where he said there lived a friend of his. An old fellow with a mealy hat came to the door and received him with a 'How d'ye, old friend Jervis?' So I parted with my company.

"I passed thro Horseneck, a scattered town, att half an hour after eleven a clock and passed over Rye Bridge att 12, the boundary of Connecticut and York goverment, after having rid 155 miles in Connecticut goverment. 'Farewell, Connecticut,' said I, as I passed along the bridge. 'I have had a surfeit of your ragged money, rough roads, and enthusiastick people.' The countrys of Connecticut and New England are very large and well peopled, and back in the country here upon the navigable rivers as well as in the maritim parts are a great many fine large towns. The people here are chiefly husbandmen and farmers. The staples are the same as in the Massachusets province. They transport a good many horses to the West Indies, and there is one town in this province that is famous for plantations of onions, of which they send quantitys all over the continent and to the islands, loading sloops with them. Many of these onions I have seen nearly as large as a child's head. It is reported that in Connecticut alone they can raise 50 or 60,000 men able to bear arms. One Mr. Law is present governour of the province. It is but a deputy goverment under that of New England or the Massachusetts."

Westchester County, New York—BARTONS

"Coming into York goverment I found better roads but not such a complaisant people for saluting upon the road, tho' in their houses they are neither so wild nor so awkward. It is to no purpose here to ask how many miles it is to such a place. They are not att all determined in the measure of their miles. Some will tell you that you are two miles from your stage. Ride half a mile farther, they'll tell you it is 4; a mile farther, you'll be told it is 6 miles, and three miles farther they'll say it is seven, and so on. I had a long ride before I arrived at Newrochell where I dined att the house of one Le Compte, a Frenchman, who has a daughter that is a sprightly, sensible girl. Coming from thence att 4 o'clock I put up this night att Doughty's who keeps house att Kingsbridge, a fat man much troubled with the rheumatism and of a hasty, passionate temper. I supped upon roasted oysters, while my land-lord eat roasted ears of corn att another table. He kept the whole house in a stirr to serve him and yet could not be pleased. This night proved very stormy and threatened rain. I was disturbed again in my rest by the noise of a heavy tread of a foot in the room above. That wherein I lay was so large and lofty that any noise echoed as if it had been in a church."

[Note: Westchester County, New York, included Rye, New Rochelle, Yonkers, Mamaroneck, White Plains and other birth places in my New York ancestrial records. Kingsbridge (Bronx) crossed over to Manhattan Island, or York Island, as Dr. Hamilton called it. In 1744, fifth-great-grandfather NOAH BARTON (b. abt. 1668), fourth son of ROGER BARTON, with his family, including his son—fourth-great-grandfather ELISHA BARTON (born 5 Oct 1729) . . . were living in Westchester County, New York. In the Barton and Hummell Family Histories page 79 it reads:

"NOAH BARTON, when well along in life sold all his holdings in Westchester Co., New York and went to New Jersey. Apparently NOAH died intestate but many of his descendants can be traced with prob-ability if not with certainty. NOAH was the most prominent [son of ROGER] of all. He became a Justice in Mile Square, near Yonkers, where he owned considerable land. He was one of the commissioners cho-sen by New York State to treat with Connecticutt commissioners concerning the disputed boundary lands known as the Oblong. When a mature man, NOAH decided that Perth Amboy, and not New York City, was to become the Metro, and sold all his holdings in Westchester County, New York and invested in Perth Amboy and became impoverished. He died apparently near Cranbury, Middlesex County. New Jersey. His daughter SUSANNAH BARTON married ZEBULON MORFORD and lived at Cranbury, which is near Morristown, New Jersey, where George Washington wintered his Continental Army. NOAH's will has not been found. He probably had sons—GILBERT, ELISHA, GEORGE and others. GILBERT kept the nearby famous White Horse Tavern on the Trenton Turnpike during the Revolution. And his son Lieutenant WILLIAM BARTON, was with Sullivan's Expedition against the 5-Nation Indians and left an historically valuable diary of the campaign. ELISHA, NOAH's second son, probably founded the Hunterdon, New Jersey, BARTON family. He built a fine brick Colonial house. GEORGE is the progeni-tor of those of Fulton and Bedford County, Penn." In 1744, fourth-great-grandfather ELISHA BARTON was 15 years old.]

From the Journal of Dr. Hamilton:

"Friday, August 31. I breakfasted att Doughty's. My landlord put himself in a passion because his daughter was tardy in getting up to make my choco-late. He spoke so thick in his anger and in so sharp a key that I did not com-prehend what he said. I saw about 10 Indians fishing for oysters in the gutt before the door. The wretches waded about stark naked and threw the oys-ters, as they picked them up with their hands, into baskets that hung upon their left shoulder. They are a lazy, indolent generation and would rather starve than work att any time, but being unaquainted with our luxury, na-ture in them has few demands, which are easily satisfied.

"I passed over Kingsbridge at 9 o'clock and had a pleasant ride to York. This small island is called York Island from the City of York which stands upon the south west end of it. It is a pleasant spot of ground covered with severall small groves of trees. About three miles before I reached York I saw the man of war commanded by Commodore Warren lying in Turtle Bay. This was a festival day with the crew. They were a roasting an entire ox upon a wooden spit and getting drunk as fast as they could, Warren having given them a treat. I was overtaken here by a young gentleman who gave me a whole paquet of news about prizes and privateering, which is now the whole subject of discourse. I met one Dutchman on the road who addressed me, 'May I be so bold, where do you come from sir?' I arrived in New York about eleven o clock and put up my horses at Waghorn's . . . . The table chat run upon privateering and such discourse as has now become so common that it is tiresome and flat . . . . We had a deal of news by the Boston papers and some private letters, and among other news, that the Dutch having declared war against France and the capture of some of the barrier towns in Flanders by the French, as also the taking of some tobacco ships near the capes of Virginia, which furnished matter for conversation all night."

Through New Jersey to Philadelphia

[Tuesday, Sept. 11] "I took boat along with Mr. Rhea from York to Elizabeth Town Point and had a pleasant passage making 15 miles by water in three hours. Mr. Rhea and I mounted horse and rid 12 miles farther after sun down. We passed thro' Elizabeth Town att 7 o'clock att night and arrived att Woodbridge att half an hour after eight. The country here is pleasant and pritty clear with a beautiful intermixture of woods. The roads are very good in dry weather. We put up att one Heard's where we supped.

"I was sorry to leave New York upon account of being separated from some agreeable acquaintance I had contracted there, and att the same time I cannot but own that I was glad to remove from a place where the temptation of drinking (a thing so incompatable with my limber constitution) threw it self so often in my way. I knew severall men of sense, ingenuity, and learning, and a much greater number of fops whom I chuse not to name, not so much for fear of giving offence as because I think their names are not worthy to be recorded either in manuscript or printed journals. These dons commonly held their heads higher than the rest of mankind and imagined few or none were their equals. But this I found always proceeded from their narrow notions, ignorance of the world, and low extraction, which indeed is the case with most of our aggrandized upstarts in these infant countrys of America who never had an opportunity to see, or if they had, the capacity to observe the different ranks of men in polite nations or to know what it is that really constitutes that difference of degrees.

"Wednesday, September 12. I was waked this morning before sunrise with a strange bawling and hollowing without doors. It was the landlord ordering his negroes with an imperious and exalted voice . . . . We set off at seven o'clock . . . passed thro' a place called Pitscatuay . . . . We crossed Raretin River and arrived in Brunswick att 9 o'clock. We baited our horses and drank some chocolate att Miller's. We mounted again att 10, and after riding 15 miles . . . we put up att Leonard's att Kingstown a little before one, where we dined. Here we met with an old chattering fellow . . . . He told us he had served in Queen Anne's wars and that he was born under the Crown of England, and that 18 years agoe he had left the service and lived with his wife. We asked him where his wife was now. He answered he supposed in hell, 'asking your honour's pardon, for she was such a pleague that she was fit for no body's company but the devil's.' We could scarcely get rid of this fellow till we made him so drunk with rum that he could not walk . . . . We took horse again . . . and at six arrived att Bond's in Trenton where we put up for all night.

"Thursday, September 13. This morning proved very sharp and cold. We set out from Trenton att 7 o'clock, and riding thro' a pleasant road we crossed Delaware Ferry a little before eight, where the tide and wind being both strong against us, we were carried a great way down the river before we could land. We arrived att Bristo' betwixt 9 and 10 a clock and break-fasted att Walton's. Setting out from thence we crossed Shammany Ferry att eleven a'clock. The sun growing somewhat warmer we travelled with ease and pleasure . . . . Before we went into town we stopped to see the works where they were casting of cannon, where I thought they made a bungling work of it, spoiling ten where they made one. [The LACEY's had ironworks further up the Delaware River.] We entered Philadelphia att 4 o'clock.

"Friday, September 14 . . . Att Philadelphia I heard news of some con-turbations and fermentations of partys att Annapolis concerning the elec-tion of certain parliament members for that wretched city and was sorry to find that these triffles still contributed so much to set them att variance, but I pray that the Lord may pity them and not leave them intirely to them-selves and the devil.

"Saturday, September 15 . . . I paid a visit to Dr. Thomas Bond . . . and dined att Cockburn's in company with two stanch Quakers, who sat att ta-ble with their broad hats upon their heads. They eat a great deal more than they spoke, and their conversation was only yea and nay . . . . Att 6 o'clock I went to the Governour's Club, where the Governour himself was present and severall other gentlemen of note in the place. The conversation was agreeable and instructing, only now and then some persons there showed a particular fondness for introducing gross, smutty expressions which I thought did not . . . become a company of philosophers and men of sense.

"Sunday, September 16 . . . I . . . went to the Presbyterian meeting in the morning . . . There I heard a very Calvinisticall sermon preached by an old holder forth whose voice was somewhat rusty, and his countenance a little upon the 4 square . . . . There were a great many men in the meeting with linnen nightcaps, and indecent and unbecoming dress which is too much wore in all the churches and meetings in America where I have been in, unless it be those of Boston where they are more decent and polite in their dress tho more fantasticall in their doctrines and much alike in their honesty and morals.

"I . . . in the afternoon, went . . . to the Roman Chapell where I heard some fine musick and saw some pritty ladys. The priest, after saying mass, catechised some children in English and insisted much upon our submitting our reason to religion and believing of every thing that God said (or, properly speaking, every thing that the priest says, who often has the impudence to quote the divine authority to support his absurditys) however contradictory or repugnant it seemed to our natural reason. I was taken with a sick qualm in this chapell which I attributed to the gross nonsense proceeding from the mouth of the priest, which, I suppose, being indigestible, bred cruditys in my intellectual stomach and confused my animal spirits. I spent the evening att the taveren with some Scotsmen.

"Wednesday, September 19. To day I resolved to take my departure from this town. In the morning my barber came to shave me and almost made me sick with his Irish brogue and stinking breath. He told me that he was very glad to see that I was after being in the right religion. I asked him how he came to know what religion I was of. 'Ohon! . . . as if I had not seen your Honour at the Roman Catholic chapell coming upon Sunday last' . . . . Taking horse at half an hour after three o'clock, I left Philadelphia and crossed Skuilkill Ferry att a quarter after four. I passed the town of Darby about an hour before sunsett. About the time of the sun's going down, the air turned very sharp, it being a degree of frost. I arrived in Chester about half an hour after seven. Here I put up att one Mather's, an Irishmann att the Sign of the Ship.

"Att my seeing of the city of Philadelphia I conceived a quite different notion of both city and inhabitants from that which I had before from the account or description of others. I could not apprehend this city to be so very elegant or pritty as it is commonly represented. In its present situation it is much like one of our country market towns in England. When you are in it the majority of the buildings appear low and mean, the streets unpaved, and therefor full of rubbish and mire. It makes but an indifferent appearance att a distance, there being no turrets or steeples to set it off to advantage, but I believe that in a few years hence it will be a great and a flourishing place and the chief city in North America.

"The people are much more polite, generally speaking, than I apprehended them to be from the common account of travellers. They have that accomplishment peculiar to all our American colonys, viz., subtilty and craft in their dealings. They apply themselves strenuously to business, having little or no turn toward gaiety (and I know not indeed how they should since there are few people here of independent fortunes or of high luxurious taste.)

"Drinking here is not att all in vogue, and in the place there is pritty good company and conversations to be had. It is a degree politer than New York tho in its fabrick not so urban, but Boston excells both for politeness and ubanity tho only a town."

South through Wilmington, Delaware—CANBY, BAKER, JARVIS

"Thursday, September 20th. I set out att nine o'clock from Mather's and about two miles from Chester was overtaken by a Quaker, one of the politest and best behaved of that kidney ever I had met with. We had a deal of discourse about news and politicks, and after riding 4 miles together we parted. I now entered the confines of the three notched road by which I knew I was near Maryland. Immediately upon this something ominous happened, which was my man's tumbling down, flump, two or three times, horse and baggage and all, in the middle of a plain road. I likewise could not help thinking that my state of health was changed for the worse upon it. Within a mile of Willmington I met Mr. Neilson of Philadelphia who told me some little scraps of news from Annapolis. I crossed Christin Ferry att 12 o'clock, and at two o clock I dined att Griffith's in New Castle."

[Note: Seventh-great-grandfather THOMAS CANBY moved to Wilmington, Delaware, in 1741. THOMAS CANBY was born 15 May 1667 in Thorne, Lincolnshire, England. His mother, MARY BAKER (Canby), died soon after his birth. His father, BENJAMIN CANBY was the youngest son in a royalist family and was without inheritance. THOMAS' mother, MARY BAKER (Canby), was a sister of HENRY BAKER, a Quaker, and an early adventurer who had been prospecting for land on the Delaware before William Penn's arrival. There were many of these, and western New Jersey was well settled with Quakers among the earlier Swedes before Penn's refuge and model state began.

Returning to England, BAKER sailed again for America in 1684 from Dolgelly in Wales (near Bristol) on the *Vine* of Liverpool. With him were his wife, four daughters, and two sons, also seven servants mentioned by name. Among these servants was registered his nephew, THOMAS CANBY, age 17, who was to work for his uncle for an indeterminate time to pay for his passage, and for the six months (presumably in England) he had "rested with him in his charge."

Uncle HENRY BAKER seems to have been a skinflint. Four years was the usual time an able-bodied man was supposed to work to pay off the five pounds paid for his transportation across the sea, but THOMAS' uncle persuaded the Quaker meeting, to which young THOMAS must have appealed, to bind the boy for five years from 15 Jun 1685, in addition to his year already passed as a servant; then he was to be given apparel and "what other things are allowed by law to minors so brought over."

HENRY BAKER, family, and servants arrived in Philadelphia on 17 Sep 1684, and took up land, which had probably been previously purchased, near Willow Grove, ten or fifteen miles out from Philadelphia. It was a wilderness then, uncleared and covered with a magnificent hardwood forest. Young THOMAS CANBY's name is listed in the Quaker records soon after his arrival, although he grew up in the Church of England. One record states, "He had a gift for the ministry," and he was clerk of the Buckingham Quaker meeting for nineteen years and held other offices there.

Two of his daughters, MARY and PHOEBE, were approved ministers of the meeting and licensed to travel and preach. His daughter, sixth-great-grandmother ELIZABETH CANBY, married THOMAS LACEY. They were the parents of ancestor BARBARA LACEY (who married JOSEPH WILKINSON). THOMAS LACEY was one of the partners of the iron mill on the Delaware River in Bucks County. THOMAS CANBY had talents for business and administration. He first married seventh-great-grandmother SARAH JARVIS, a sister of CHARLES JARVIS, the London artist and Painter to the King of England. One of THOMAS' descendants, CALEB HARLAN CANBY, married BETSY ROSS, who for many years was credited with making the first flag to bear the stars and stripes.

THOMAS and SARAH CANBY had a farm in the admirable Lunday tract in Buckingham Township. They had nine children when she died. He next married MARY OLIVER, a Welsh Quaker, and soon purchased 280 acres in Solebury, and added eight more children. His second wife died. Leaving this farm for two of his sons to care for, he moved to 444 acres near New Hope on the Delaware, and with Anthony Morris of Philadelphia remodelled a mill called Heath's Mill, and married a third wife, a widow, JANE PRESTON. They had no children. This farm was on the creek leading from the *Great Spring* to the Delaware at New Hope. It was a marvellous spring, perhaps 100 by 150 feet, clear as daylight in its deepest part.

The Governor had made THOMAS CANBY Justice of Peace for Bucks County in 1719, and he filled this office with some slight intermissions until 1741. In 1721, again in 1722, in 1730, 1733, and 1738, he was elected a member of the Provincial Assembly. Of his seventeen children, twelve were girls, and at least one son died young, which may account for the plenitude of CANBY blood and the scarcity of CANBY as a surname in the United States. His daughter JANE married THOMAS PAXSON and was the great-grandmother of Chief Justice EDWARD M. PAXSON of Philadelphia.

In 1741, THOMAS' son THOMAS, who married SARAH PRESTON was also a member of the Colonial Assembly. THOMAS Senior took out a certificate for his family to the Newark, Delaware, meeting, and set out with his wife, his son OLIVER (then twenty-five), and, with the THOMAS CANBY Junior family, went to the Brandywine near Wilmington, where the younger family remained. Probably THOMAS, Sr., in his seventy-third year, had been there before investigating the magnificent mill site—the finest in the Colonies. There is a surveyor's map of the land by Brandywine running from the present bridge site at the foot of the falls up through the properties on which the two old CANBY houses were afterward built. The map, which is dated February 22, 1741/42, clearly indicates a purchase, and is the land next to what is now Market Street, on which the second CANBY house was built much later.

The next year, ancestor THOMAS CANBY (Sr.) went back to his Solebury farm, which he had kept through his migrations, and died there 20 Nov 1742. OLIVER stayed behind, and THOMAS Junior was still there when OLIVER was married in 1744.]

Annapolis, Maryland

Dr. Hamilton's travel journal continued:

"Tuesday, September 25. I departed North East this morning att nine a clock. The sky was dark and cloudy, threatning rain. I had a solitary ride over an unequall gravelly road till I came to Susquehanna Ferry, where I baited my horses, and had a ready passage . . . . dined att my old friend Tradaway's, whom I found very much indisposed with fevers. He told me it had been a very unhealthy time and a hot summer. I should have known the time had been unhealthy without his telling me so by only observing the washed countenances of the people standing att their doors and looking out att their windows, for they looked like so many staring ghosts. In short I was sensible I had got into Maryland, for every house was an infirmary, according to ancient custome.

"Thursday, September 27. I set off from Mr. Hart's a little after nine o clock . . . . I met with some patients that welcomed me on my return. I arrived att Annapolis att two o'clock afternoon and so ended my perigrinations. In these northeren travells I compassed my design in obtaining a better state of health, which was the purpose of my journey. I found but little difference in the manners and character of the people in the different provinces I passed thro', but as to constitutions and complexions, air and government, I found some variety. Their forms of goverment in the northeren provinces I look upon to be much better and happier than ours, which is a poor, sickly, convulsed state. Their air and living to the northward is likewise much preferable, and the people a more gygantick size and make. Att Albany, indeed, they are intirely Dutch and have a method of living something differing from the English. In this itineration I compleated, by land and water together, a course of 1624 miles. The northeren parts I found in generall much better settled than the southeren. As to politness and humanity, they are much alike except in the great towns where the inhabitants are more civilized, especially att Boston."

THE EXILE OF THE ACADIANS

[Note: The oldest French colony in America was Acadia (Nova-Scotia.) On the 20th of May, 1755, a British squadron of 3,000 troops sailed from Boston to the Bay of Fundy. It had been determined by the leaders in this chess game (probably General Braddock in Alexandria, Virginia,) that these long settlers of France were too numerous to tolerate and needed to be gotten rid of. It took them about four days to overcome the two surprised French garrisons and round up the peasants like a herd of cattle into the Grande Pre Historical Site area—currently shown on our maps. Some of the peasants escaped into Canada, others into New Orleans, but those on the beach were forced onto ships and distributed into the English colonies without any special concern for their welfare. I have a third-great-grandmother, MARY SUSANNAH POYER, who married AARON WILKINSON—pioneers of Northumberland County, Pennsylvania. Her French great-grandparents may have found refuge in the Rombout area of Dutchess County, New York. The early census records show very few of that name: New York; New Jersey, and a few in New Orleans— many more of that name in Canada.]

CROSSROAD—THE FRENCH AND INDIAN WAR OR SEVEN YEAR WAR IN EUROPE

After Louisbourg fell to the Colonial English in 1745, Shirley of Massachusetts and his colonial troops wanted to extend the war up the St. Lawrence and claim all of Canada. However, powerful men in England began to fear that these Americans were becoming too self-reliant. The colonies felt greatly betrayed when a treaty was signed at Aix-la-Chapelle in 1748 returning Louisbourg and Cape Breton Island to the French in return for French concessions in Europe. Were they only pawns in a European chess game? The Hanoverian George I could never speak English and George II had a marked German accent.

The English colonies were increasing rapidly in numbers, doubling about every 25 years, while the population of Great Britain actually declined between 1720 and 1750. An estimate of the colonial population in 1750 was 1,260,000, and by 1770 it was believed to be 2,312,000—an increase of nearly 100%. The younger sons in England and America and the disconsolate of Europe moved westward—braving the dangers of the frontier for their personal desire to own property and feel independent. There were large numbers of Scots, Irish, Germans, and Scandinavians. The English colonies claimed that their land extended in parallel lines to the Mississippi River. The French had extended their fur trading and missionary activities westward—following the Mississippi and St. Lawrence Rivers inland. Building forts south and west, they explored and claimed the vast interior. The French were far less in number and were far less threatening to the large Indian population that resided there and enjoyed the fur trading.

Virginia claimed the lush Ohio River valley. Britain's George II decided to support his colonies in their westward drive for land with arms and ammunition. France's Louis XV sent additional troops to promote French rights. So, in 1753, the young 21-year-old Virginian surveyor, George Washington, began his military career as the newly appointed Governor Dinwiddie's deputy and official diplomatic envoy by carrying a warning paper drawn up in Williamsburg, Virginia, to the French General St. Pierre, at Presque Isle, on Lake Erie—a dangerous and arduous journey into the wilderness 500 miles away. Washington had personally prepared detailed papers and applied for this opportunity at this new governor's palace in Williamsburg. It was not only a mission of diplomacy, but also a mission of intelligence—spying and reporting on the strength of France and the Indians throughout the area. At Will's Creek near Cumberland (far-west Maryland), the seven-man delagation (that would increase to 15) set off north by northwest in freezing rain on November 11.

He left behind his memories that his sweetheart had refused to marry him, his lost desire to become a sea captain had ended with his continual seasickness during his trip to Barbados with his ailing brother Lawrence, who had returned home to die, and an independent minded, never satified mother.

After an arduous journey, which included Indian camps along the way, on 13 Decenber he finally was able to deliver the document that warned the French to withdraw from British Territory. The French officers held a council of war. While they were distracted, Washington's diary states it gave him

> "an opportunity of taking the dimensions of the fort and making what observations I could. . . . [he also learned from the Indians that the French were enlisting their help in hunting down "all our straggling traders." Demanding "Why" of the French commandant, "he told me the country belonged to them, that no Englishman had a right to trade upon their waters and that it had orders to make every person prisoner that attempted it."

He also learned that they had not only taken the hunters prisoners to Canada but had taken eight scalps, and that they would not withdraw their troops. Washington was concerned when the French kept delaying there answer to their Indian guide, and he took his men and slipped away down the river by canoe, which worked until the canoe became ice-bound on their fourth day. The French had followed them, but the French canoe overturned during their pursuit. Washington was

> "determined to prosecute my journey the nearest way through the woods on foot [actually on snowshoes]. I took my necessary papers, pulled off my clothes, tied myself up in a mach coat and, with my pack at my back, with my papers and provisions in it and a gun, set out with Mr. Gist fitted in the same manner."

After one day, they were attacked by "a party of French Indians which had laid in wait for us." They fired at Gist, but missed. Before the Indian could re-load, Washington seized him and took him away at gunpoint as a hostage, not releasing him until late at night—the two men trudged on without stopping. The Allegheny was not frozen over, but it was filled with large chunks of ice. They had only a poor hatchet to build them a raft. It took most of the day.

> "We got it launched and [climbed] on board of it and set off, but before we got half over, we were jammed in the ice. We expected every moment our raft would sink and we perish."

Washington set his pole, hoping the ice would pass, put it jerked him into the ten feet of water. He was able to grab hold of one of the logs of the raft, but it stayed in the middle. A small island was closeby, so they swam to it. On the island with frozen clothes and perhaps frozen toes and fingers, they slept through the night and were able to cross to the other side on the ice the next morning.

Washington rode into Williamsburg on 16 January 1755 arriving at the Governor's palace after a seventy-nine day mission. He didn't complain, but stated that there was only one day it didn't rain or snow incessantly. He concluded his writing by saying, "I hope it will be sufficient to satisfy your honor with my proceedings."

His final report was very detailed and well-done. Dinwiddie sent Washington's report along with his expert drawings and map of the Ohio country to London to the Board of Trade, where it had a great impact on British officials. The report was also printed in Williamsburg, creating much discussion among the Virginians—making Washington's exploits a sensation among his peers.

In March 1754, an English party, financed partly by the Washingtons, reached the confluence of the Allegheny and the Monongahela, where the Ohio River begins, and built a rough fort; but as the ice broke in the spring a fleet of

French boats swept down the river, overpowered the small company of men, rebuilt the fort and named it Fort du Quesne. (McKEES Rocks and McKEESport are nearby the location.)

At age 22 Washington was commissioned lieutenant-colonel and enlisted recruits at Alexandria. In April, under the authority of the governor of Virginia, Washington proceeded with his little frontier army to claim this fort and to repel all who interrupted the English settlement of that country. An older first in command officer was to join him with more troops and Indians. The roads were miserable; rivers without bridges, and provisions insufficient. They reached the Great Meadows of the Ohio on May 26 and were informed that the French were on the march to attack them. A stockade was immediately erected and named Fort Necessity. Washington, after conference with the Mingo chiefs, decided to strike the first blow. Two of their Indians discovered the hiding-place of the French and the small colonial army advanced. The French were on the alert and flew to arms. "Fire!" commanded Washington, and the first volley of a great war went flying through the forest. Jumonville, the leader of the French, and ten of his party were killed and twenty-one were made prisoners.

Washington returned to Fort Necessity and cut twenty miles of road in the direction of Fort du Quesne while he waited for the rest of the army with their reinforcements. Only one company of volunteers arrived and none of the Indians he had expected to join him came. His whole force numbered about 400 men. On 3 Jul 1754, the regiment of the French general De Villiers surrounded the fort and for nine hours, during a rain storm, the French poured an incessant shower of balls upon the heroic band in the fort. Thirty of Washington's men were killed, but the steady presence of Washington encouraged his men and they returned the fire with vigor. At length De Villiers, realizing his ammunition was being depleted, asked for a parley. On 4 July, the English garrison with Washington in command marched out of Fort Necessity and retaining all of their accouterments, they withdrew safely from the Ohio country, while the more numerous French soldiers and their Indian comrades watched.

Unsuccessful in stopping what they considered French intrusion, a congress of the American colonies assembled at Albany. Their object was two-fold: first, to renew the treaty with the Iroquois confederacy; and secondly, to stir up the colonial authorities to some sort of concerted effort against the French. This dignified and venerable group of men included Thomas Hutchinson of Massachusetts, STEPHEN HOPKINS of Rhode Island, Benjamin Franklin of Pennsylvania and others scarcely less distinguished. After a few days of consultation, the Iroquois, still disgruntled at the losses of the English, renewed their treaty and departed. This convention then took up the question of uniting the colonies in a common government, and Benjamin Franklin on 10 Jul 1754 brought before the commissioners the draft of a federal constitution. Copies were sent to the various colonies—Connecticut, rejected; Massachusetts, opposed; New York, adopted with indifference, and the English board of trade rejected it with disdain, saying that the Americans were trying to make a government of their own.

The British became concerned about all the long-established French colonists in Acadia (Nova Scotia). This territory had been given to the English by the treaty of Utrecht, made in 1713. British occupation of this area for 50 years was limited to a small English military government over the predominantly French settlers. In May 1755, a squadron with 3,000 British troops sailed from Boston and quickly brought all of Nova Scotia under the military control of the English. They then displaced more than 3,000 French settlers—known in history as the Acadians—and distributed them in limited numbers, helpless and half-starved, among the English colonies from New England to Georgia. Many of the Acadians escaped into French Canada and into French New Orleans. It is possible that our POYER ancestors were among these displaced persons, or perhaps part of the French army, as JACQUE POYER, born about 1666, was sent to Canada by Louis XIV much earlier, where he was sergeant of the troops at Fort Chambly, near Montreal. Some of his daughter's sons would later join with the Americans against the British in the Revolutionary War when the Continentals captured Montreal and the surrounding forts—then British. Early records show a few families of POYERs in Canada, New York, New Jersey, and Louisiana. Third-great-grandparents AARON WILKINSON and MARY POYER, daughter of JOSEPH and MARGARET POYER, were married in Northumberland County, Pennsylvania, about 1810.

Both countries still claimed they were at peace; but Louis XV sent 3,000 troops to Canada and the English sent General Edward Braddock to America with two regiments of regulars with orders to take Fort du Quesne from the French. On 8 Jul 1755, Braddock and his troops were ambushed, and George Washington, the only remaining officer, lead the flight of the British with his Virginians back to Philadelphia.

Early in August of 1755, Governor Shirley of Massachusetts set out from Albany with two thousand men. Their object was to take Fort Niagara from the French. After spending four weeks in Oswego preparing their boats, tempests prevailed, sickness broke out in the camps, the Indians deserted, and on 24 October they marched home.

Also in August, British General William Johnson proceeded from Albany up the Hudson. His object was to capture Crown Point and drive the French from Lake Champlain. They first built Fort Edward on the Hudson above Albany and then proceeded to Lake George, where they made camp, bringing up their artillery and supplies. However, the French commandant Dieskau at Crown Point didn't wait to be attacked. He advanced south with 1400 French, Canadians, and Indians to capture Fort Edward. General Johnson sent Colonel Williams and the chief of the Mohawks—Hendrick, with twelve hundred men to relieve Fort Edward. They were ambushed by the French and driven back to Johnson's camp on Lake George. Unsupported by their Indians, the French and Canadians attacked the camp. A battle ensued for five hours, until at last the English troops charged across the field and completed the rout. Nearly all of Dieskau's men were killed and Dieskau was mortally wounded. Two hundred and sixteen of the English were killed. The English remained and constructed Fort William Henry on their camp site, while the French fortified Ticonderoga.

As 1756 began, Governor Shirley of Massachucetts was given command of the English forces; Washington and his provincials repelled the French and Indians in the Shenandoah Valley, and Benjamin Franklin was chosen as colonel of the Pennsylvania volunteers, who built a fort on the Lehigh River and checked enemy advances.

In Europe, Empress Maria Theresa of Austria thought she saw an opportunity to extend her power and wrote a flattering letter to Madame de Pompadour, who was all-powerful in France, soliciting her influence in securing a Franco-Austrian league against England—but Maria Theresa's real purpose was to gain the aid of France when she renewed her war with Prussia. Elizabeth of Russia had been mortally offended by disparaging comments Frederick of Prussia (Germany) had made about her character twenty years prior, saying "she was too fat and orthodox, and did not have an ounce of nun in her composition." The Czarina, Elizabeth, joined quickly with Austria, but Louis XV delayed until the Austrian Empress offered him the portion of The Netherlands that had belonged to the Empire. Negotiations were quietly completed and everything was prepared to begin the war on Prussia in 1757. Frederick of Prussia discovered their plans, allied his country with England and began the European Seven Year War in September of 1756 by entering Saxony with his army. It would be in 1770 that Austrian Maria Theresa's very young daughter Marie Antoinette would marry the dull and very young dauphin of France, who would become Louis XVI upon the death of his father Louis XV four years later. Louis XVI was in his 20th year when he ascended to the throne of France.

In America, 1756, partly at the request of the friendly Indians who feared the French and their northern Indian allies, the governor of the Pennsylvania province built a fort in the Indian Territory on the banks of the Susquehanna at the point of junction of the northeastern and western branches of this river. It was built during the summer months and occupied by the soldiers of the Pennsylvania militia. It was named Fort Augusta and became one of the best and most important of the numerous frontier forts in Pennsylvania. Its strategic location was desired by the French in northwestern Pennsylvania who planned the destruction of the fort, but without success, throughout the entire war. Twenty years later the Pennsylvania troops again occupied this fort with diligence and it became a strong defense position for the Americans in interior Pennsylvania during the Revolution and added troops and supplies for the Sullivan Expedition.

Fourth-great-grandfather JOHN WILKINSON (born about 1755), son of JOSEPH and BARBARA LACEY WILKINSON of Hunterdon County, New Jersey, and Bucks County, Pennsylvania, may have been one of the Pennsylvania troops stationed there during the Revolution, as family records state that AARON, the son of JOHN and SUSANNAH WILKINSON, was born 23 May

1781 in Shamokin, Northumberland, Pennsylvania. This would be during the Revolutionary War, and Shamokin was the name of the Indian village that was located around Fort Augusta when it was built. Northumberland was first organized as a Pennsylvania county on 21 Mar 1772. As the white settlers came in and the Indians vacated the valley, the city became known as Sunbury. Present day Shamokin is a small Indian town in the eastern mountains, where high-grade anthracite coal was found. The history of Northumberland County lists AARON WILKINSON as one of the very early settlers in the valley.

Shikellamy, the great Indian chieftain who was the father of the half-breed Chief Logan, lived at Shamokin in 1728 when he was sent by the Six Nations to assert the right of the Iroquois over the conquered remnants of the native Pennsylvania Indians, which included the Delawares and others. Their earliest government records date back to 1728 when two Indian traders, Petty and Smith, were authorized to establish trade with the Indians of that region. A Moravian mission was established there in 1742 and marked the beginning of white records in that area.

The name Iroquois is the French name given to what the English called the Six Nations. The Indians called themselves Aquanuschiani, which meant 'United People.' The Six Nations were the Mohawk, Oneida, Onondago, Cajuga, Senneka and Tuscarora, who joined about 1713.

Rev. David Brainerd visited Shamokin in 1745 and in 1746. The following is a descriptive extraction from his journal:

"Sept. 13, 1745.—After having lodged out three nights, I arrived at the Indian town I aimed at, on the Susquehanna, called Shaumoking; one of the places, and the largest of them, which I visited in May last. I was kindly received and entertained by the Indians; but had little satisfaction, by reason of the heathenish dance and revel they then held in the house where I was obliged to lodge—which I could not suppress, though I often entreated them to desist, for the sake of one of their own friend, who was sick in the house, and whose disorder was much aggravated by the noise. Alas! how destitute of natural affections are these poor uncultivated pagans! although they seem some what kind in their own way. Of a truth, the dark corners of the earth are full of the habitations of cruelty. This town, as I observed in my diary of May last, lies partly on the east side of the river, partly on the west, and partly on the large island in it, and contains upwards of

50 houses, and nearly 300 persons; though I never saw much more than half that number in it. They are of three different tribes of Indians, speaking three languages, wholly unintelligible to each other. About one half of the inhabitants are Delawares, the others called Senekas and Tutelas. The Indians of this place are accounted the most drunken, mischievous, and ruffian-like fellows, of any in these parts; and Satan seems to have his seat in this town, in an eminent manner."

An Escape from the Indians

The following is an interesting narrative about the Indians and whites in the area of the Susquehanna written by the daughter of a Revolutionary soldier who was familiar with the facts:

"James Thompson lived, at the commencement of the revolutionary war, on a beautiful farm, near Spruce run, in White Deer township. On a contiguous farm lived a family named Young. One morning in March they were surprised by five Indians, who took James Thompson and Margaret Young prisoners. Thompson was a very active young man, and determined to rescue Miss Young, and make his own escape. On the second night of their captivity, while the Indians were asleep—each with his rifle, tomahawk, and scalping-knife, wrapped with himself in his blanket—Thompson found a stone weighing about two pounds, and kneeling down beside the nearest Indian, with his left hand he felt for his temple—his intention being to kill one, and, having secured his tomahawk, he thought he could despatch the rest successively as they arose. The darkness of the night, however, frustrated his plan; for, not seeing, he did no serious injury. The Indian bounded up with a fierce yell, which awoke the others, and springing on the young man—who had thrown his stone as far from him as he possibly could—would have put an end to his existence, had not the rest interfered and secured Thompson. The Indian immediately accused him of endeavoring to kill him—while he signified that he had only struck him with his fist—and nothing appearing to induce them to doubt his word, they were highly amused at the idea of an Indian making so terrible an outcry at any stroke a pale-face could inflict with his naked hand. He, however, although he had not an ocular, had certainly a very feeling demonstration that something weightier than a hand had been used—but was shamed into silence by the laugh raised at his expense. Our prisoners were now taken up the Susquehanna, crossed the river in a canoe, and proceeded up Loyal Sock creek. For five nights he was laid upon his back, with his arms extended and tied to stakes. On the seventh night, near the mouth of Towanda creek, the Indians directed Thompson and his companion, as usual, to kindle a fire for themselves, while they built another. By this means he had an opportunity of communicating to her his intention of leaving the company that very evening. She advised him to go without her. He expressed great unwillingness; but she overruled his objections, declaring that even did she now escape, she would not be able to reach home. Accordingly, in gathering the dry sticks which were strewn round, he went further from the circle, throwing each stick, as he found it, towards the fire, and then wandering slowly, though not unconsciously, still further for the next, until he had gone as far as he thought he could without exciting suspicion; then he precipitately fled. They were soon in pursuit; but were unable to overtake him; and he ran in such a quick, zigzag manner, that they could not aim straight enough to shoot him.

"He was obliged to travel principally at night; and in going down Loyal Sock creek, he frequently came upon Indian encampments, when he had either to wade the stream, or cross the slippery mountains, to avoid them. Sometimes he came to places where they had encamped. The bones of deer, &c, which he found at these places, he broke open, and swallowed the marrow. This, with the few roots he could find, was all the food he was able to procure. Once, when almost overcome with fatigue and loss of sleep, he thought of getting into a hollow tree to rest; but this would not do, for where he could get in a wild animal might also get, although naturally possessed of great courage, he did not like to be attacked in this manner, where he had no means of defence. In this way he reached the Susquehanna, where he found the canoe as they had left it. He entered it, and descended the river; but fatigue, and want of nourishment and rest, had so overcome him, that when he reached Fort Freeland—a short distance above where Milton now stands [and 16 miles above Sunbury]—he was unable to rise. He lay in the canoe until discovered by the inhabitants, who took him ashore; and by careful treatment he was restored to health. He afterwards received a pension from the United States, and died about the year 1838, in the 96th year of his age.

"The Indians, meantime pursued their course, taking Miss Young with them, to the neighborhood of Montreal, in Canada. She had frequently understood them to lament the loss of Thompson. As he was a fine active young man, they were keeping him as a subject upon which to exercise their cruelty. Miss Young was given to an old squaw, who wished to make her work sufficient to maintain them both; but an old colored man advised her to work as little as possible—and what she must do, she should do as badly as she could; 'for,' said he, 'if you work well, she will keep you for a slave,—but be lazy, and do your work wrong, and she will get tired of you, and sell you to the whites.' . . . She acted her part well; for when the corn was ready for hoeing, she would cut up the corn, and neatly dress some weed in its stead. The old squaw thought she was too stupid ever to learn—for, notwithstanding all the pains she had taken to teach her, she was still as awkward and ignorant as ever; and thinking her a useless burden, she sent her to Montreal, according to her wish, and sold her. Her purchaser was a man of some distinction, of the name of Young; and when he discovered her name, he began to trace relationship, and found they actually were cousins. This was a happy discovery. She lived almost as contentedly, in her cousin's family, as in her father's house. Some time after the conclusion of the war, she became very anxious to visit her friends in the United States. She came home, where she sickened and died soon after."

Back in the Colonies

In the summer of 1756 as the French and Indian War continued, NOAH BARTON and his family were living in Westchester County, New York, where he was justice of the peace and his son, fourth-great-grandfather ELISHA BARTON, had volunteered and was being trained for the northern campaign where the English were hoping to take Crown Point from the French.

[Note: Possibly our POYER ancestors and their close relations were in the French forts and villages above Crown Point on the Richeleau and St. Lawrence Rivers near the small town of Montreal, striving equally to preserve their lands (Frenchman JACQUE POYER was buried at Sorel, where the two rivers joined.) The Dutch COOLEY, COLET, relations were located from Albany and Schenectady on the north, down the Hudson River on both sides into New York City, Westchester county, Staten Island and Long Island. Many of their records are found in the Kingston Dutch Reformed Church records, where baptisms and marriages were recorded from as far away as Rochester, New York. Their friendship and knowledge of the Indians, as well as their military capabilities were invaluable in the upper Hudson River campaigns. Our MORGAN relations were scattered throughout Connecticutt, New York and New Jersey. In Pennsylvania, the anti-war Quakers were trying to avoid conflict. Our Quaker ancestors included the LIPPINCOTTs, CANBYs, VAN KIRKs, PRESTONs, and WILKINSONs, who lived in central New Jersey, and along both sides of the Delaware River into Trenton and Philadelphia. It is highly probable that at least a few of their sons or grandsons broke the rules of the Quakers and volunteered with the Pennsylvania provincials. The eleven McKEE brothers arrived from the British Isles and spread south and west into the Virginia and Pennsylvania frontiers and Indian Territory. THOMAS and his son ALEXANDER McKEE [older than our direct ancestor] were British officers and Indian agents who were sent early into frontier Pennsylvania.]

The Earl of Loudoun was appointed commander in chief of the British forces in America in the spring of 1756, and two battalions sailed for New York. On 17 May 1756, Great Britain, after nearly two years of actual hostilities, made a formal declaration of war against France. Lord Loudoun assumed his command in July. Meanwhile, the French appointed the Marquis of Montcalm to succeed Dieskau, and they quickly besieged and captured Oswego, obtaining 6 vessels of war, 300 boats, 120 cannon, and 3 chests of money for the French. During that same summer, the Delaware Indians in western Pennsylvania increased their savagery and killed or captured more than 1,000 people. In August, Colonel Armstrong, with 300 Pennsylvania volunteers, marched against the Indian town of Kittanning, and on September 8 defeated the Delawares with great losses. The village was burned and the Indians' fighting spirit was broken.

On 22 Apr 1756 Private ELISHA BARTON's name is mentioned with 47 others who went on the "Expedition to Crown Point" under the command of Major Nichols. Going through Albany and up the Hudson, they came to the "carrying place" on 14 August. Proceeding on foot, they arrived at Lake George 4 September. Josiah Walton wrote in his journal,

> "Sept. ye 8th, there was a scout of 700 men which met an army of French and Indians, which beat us back to the camp, and there fought some hours. The fight began four miles from camp."

These volunteers were dismissed on 4 Oct 1756, and the young man ELISHA returned to his home near Yonkers, New York. This quote was taken from a brief journal kept by Mr. Josiah Walton of Reading, during a campaign in the "Old French War."

On 20 Jun 1757, Lord Loudoun sailed from New York with an army of 6000 regulars to capture Louisburg. He was joined at Halifax by Admiral Holbourn, with a fleet of 16 men-of-war, and 5000 fresh troops from England, but, strangly, sailed back home without fighting.

Meanwhile, the daring Frenchman Montcalm advanced against Fort William Henry with more than 7,000 French, Canadians, and Indians. The English had 500 men at the Fort. For six days the French pressed the siege; the ammunition in the garrison was exhausted, and the French took possession of the fortress on 9 August. Unfortunately, the Indians, drunken from a quantity of spirits from the English camp, fell upon the prisoners and massacred 30 of them.

At the close of 1757, France possessed twenty times as much American territory as England. All the English had been driven from the Ohio valley and from the whole basin of the St. Lawrence. But in England, William Pitt was placed at the head of the British ministry and a new spirit was manifest in the conduct of the war. Loudoun was brought back to England and Abercrombie was appointed to succeed him in America with reliance on an efficient corps of subordinate officers: Admiral Boscawen in command of the fleet; General Amherst to lead a division; James Wolfe to lead a brigade; Colonel Richard Montgomery head of a regiment and young Lord Howe was next in rank to Abercrombie.

The English had three objectives planned for 1758: one to capture Louisburg, a second to take Crown Point and Ticonderoga, and third to retake Fort du Quesne from the French. On 28 May, Amherst, with ten thousand men, reached Halifax. In six more days the fleet was anchored before Louisburg; 21 July three French vessels were burned in the harbor and the town reduced to a heap of ruins. On 28 July Louisburg capitulated. Cape Breton and Prince Edward's Island surrendered to Great Britain, and the French garrison of 6000 men became prisoners of war.

On 5 July, General Abercrombie, with an army of 15,000 men, moved against Ticonderoga. On the morning of the 6th the English fell in with the picket line of the French. After a severe skirmish, the French were overwhelmed—but Lord Howe was killed in the attack. He was an older brother of British general William Howe of the Revolutionary War. On the 8th the English attempted to conquer Fort Ticonderoga. After a desperate battle of over four hours, the English were repulsed with a loss in killed and wounded of 1,916 soldiers—greater than any battle of the Revolution. The English retreated to Fort George and soon sent 3000 men against Fort Frontenac on Lake Ontario, which fell in two days to the English.

Late in the summer General Forbes, with 9000 men, advanced against Fort du Quesne. Washington led the Virginia provincials. On 24 November, they were within ten miles of Du Quesne. During that night the French garrison became alarmed, burned the fortress, and floated down the Ohio. On the 25th, the victorious army marched in, raised the English flag, and named it Pittsburgh to honor the great protector of the American colonies, William Pitt of the British parliment.

In 1759, General Amherst, now promoted to the chief commander of the

American forces, had nearly 50,000 British and colonial troops. The French army scarcely exceeded 7000. Three campaigns were again planned: General Prideaux was to conduct an expedition against Niagara; Amherst was to lead the main division against Ticonderoga and Crown Point, and General Wolfe was to capture Quebec.

The Niagara campaign began 10 July. On the 15th, General Prideaux was killed by a bursting mortar, and Sir William Johnson succeeded to the command. On the morning of the 24th the French army commanded by D'Aubry came in sight and a bloody battle ensued, in which the French were completely routed. On the next day Niagara capitulated, and 600 French prisoners of war were taken.

Meanwhile Amherst was marching with an army of eleven thousand men against Ticonderoga. The French partially destroyed the fortifications and abandoning Ticonderoga retreated to Crown Point. Five days later, they deserted Crown Point and intrenched themselves on Isle-aux-Nuix, in the river Sorel [Richelieu].

Earlier in the spring General Wolfe began his ascent of the St. Lawrence. His force consisted of nearly 8000 men with a fleet of 44 vessels. They arrived on 27 June at the Isle of Orleans, four miles below Quebec, and pitched camp at the upper end of the island, which gave him command of the river. On the night of the 29th, the English seized Point Levi, and from this position they reduced lower Quebec to ruins. Still, the fortress held out.

On July 9, Wolfe crossed the North Channel at low water and camped on the east bank of the Montmorenci. July 31, Montcalm and his French troops met them in battle and with severe losses the English returned to their former camp on the Isle. For several days Wolfe suffered from exposure and fatigue. A council of officers was called in, and Wolfe proposed a second assault, but was overruled, deciding to attack from the rear. Moving their camp to Point Levi, they found a way up the steep precipice and gained the Plains of Abraham behind the city.

On the night of September 12, the English entered their boats and dropped down the river to a place now known as Wolfe's Cove. Members of Wolfe's boat reported that as they went silently down the river, shadowed by the overhanging cliffs, Wolfe kept repeating the words of a stanza of Gray's Elegy:

"The boast of heraldry, the pomp of power,
And all that beauty, all that wealth e'er gave,
Await alike the inevitable hour
The paths of glory lead but to the grave."

With great difficulty the soldiers clambered up the precipice, dispersed the Canadian guard, and at dawn Wolfe collected his army for battle. Montcalm was amazed and hastened to retrieve his troops from the trenches and lower fortifications. After an hour's cannonade, Montcalm attempted to turn the English flank, but was beaten back. The Canadians and Indians were routed. The French regulars were thrown into confusion. Wolfe was leading the charge and was wounded in the wrist, and then struck again; but he continued on. At the moment of victory a third ball pierced his breast, and as he sank to the ground, the cry rang out,

"They run! They run!"

"Who run?" Wolfe asked.

"The French are flying everywhere," the officer replied.

And Wolfe's last remembered words were,

"Do they run already? Then I die happy."

French commander Montcalm who was attempting to rally his men was also mortally wounded.

"Shall I survive?" he asked his surgeon.

"But a few hours at most," was the reply.

DEATH OF WOLFE — DRAWN BY P. PHILIPPOTEAUX

Montcalm responded,

"So much the better, I shall not live to witness the surrender of Quebec."

The surrender of the citadel came five days later.

In the following spring of 1760 France tried to recoup their losses. A great battle was fought west of Quebec, but with reinforcements to the English, the French were driven back and on 8 September, Montreal surrendered and

Canada passed under the dominion of England.

The war continued on the ocean, and everywhere the English were victorious. On 10 Feb 1763, a treaty of peace was made at Paris, and all the French possessions in America east of the Mississippi were ceded to the English Crown and Guadeloupe was returned to the French. The Spanish, who had aided Austria and France in Europe, gave the upper inland parts of East and West Florida to the British.

This treaty had been strongly debated in the British Parliament. The English had captured Guadeloupe, the great French West Indies sugar island, as well as Canada, and if peace was to be made, they were required to return one or the other to the French. Guadeloupe would be a greater economic boon as sugar was more lucrative than the French fur trading. Parliament was also concerned about the troublesome American colonies that were becoming more demanding, and they feared an American revolution. The French in Canada made them more loyal subjects. Earlier Benjamin Franklin, in London, tried to allay their fears by suggesting that the colonies were so diversified and divided that they would never be able to unite against their mother country, and emphasized the importance of their colonial trade with England.

Franklin's premises were challenged by another pamphlet which read:

"I say the acquisition of Canada would be destructive, because such a country as North-America, ten times larger in extent than Britain, richer soil in most places, all the different climates you can fancy, all the lakes and rivers for navigation one could wish, plenty of wood for shipping, and as much iron, hemp, and naval forces, as any part of the world; such a country at such a distance, could never remain long subject to Britain; you have taught them the art of war, and put arms in their hands, and they can furnish themselves with every thing in a few years, without assistance of Britain; they are always grumbling and complaining against Britain, even while they have the French to dread, what may they not be supposed to do if the French is no longer a check upon them; you must keep a numerous standing army to over-awe them; these troops will soon get wives and possessions, and become Americans; thus from these measures you lay the surest foundation of unpeopling Britain, and strengthening America to revolt . . . it is no gift of prophecy, it is only the natural and unavoidable consequences . . . and must appear so to every man whose head is not too much affected with popular madness or political enthusiasm."

Still, the British chose to keep Canada, and the French rejoiced, glad for the sugar—and the coming revolution.

Unfortunately for the Indians, they had befriended the wrong side, and in May 1763, the greatest Indian uprising of the century, led by Pontiac, chief of the Ottawas, broke out. The Indians, deprived of their French allies, were still supported by the French settlers who assisted and encouraged them in raids and massacres on the western frontiers of Pennsylvania, Maryland, and Virginia. The British answer was the Proclamation of 1763, which attempted to separate the Indians from the white population in the colonies. It proclaimed that the entire region between the Alleghenies and the Mississippi was reserved for the Indian tribes, except for white traders who were to be licensed to sell goods to the Indians and buy the highly prized furs from them. Land speculation by the colonists was to stop and British soldiers were to be the enforcers.

This arrangement of appeasing the Indians against the more wealthy and influential colonial land speculators, small fur traders, and soldiers who had been promised some of this land for their war services might have seemed like a good solution to the British parliamentarians on an island across the Atlantic Ocean, but it was not satisfactory to the colonists, who soon ignored it, because it was unenforceable. The fighting force that put down Pontiac's rebellion and had the most casualties was largely made up of British regulars, not colonial volunteers. Garrison duty was very unpopular with the colonists, so mostly British regulars were sent to the posts beyond the mountains. Parliament proposed sending 7,500 British troops into the bordering forts of the west. Soldiers cost money. Who should pay for them and the past war debt, which had come about in defense of the colonists? Of course, Parliament and King George III, who ascended to the throne in 1760, chose to have the Americans pay, and they set about finding ways to accomplish this. On this side of the ocean, however, the colonists had no desire to pay for a European war or a standing army on their shores, especially when that army appeared like an occupational army sent to enforce tax payments and laws over which they had no control.

The French and Indian War treaty ended one of the most important wars in the history of mankind—a world war, involving the major powers of Europe that crossed an ocean into a new continent. The crossroads was reached with this British victory, and the old decaying institutions of the Holy Roman Empire with the monarchs of Europe would not prevail in this new land. The powerful laws, liberty, and language of the English people would be extended into this western continent. A new age was beginning and a new nation was about to be born—with all the pain and struggle still to be required of it for the formation of its new life.

Northern Theater of Operations

~ 63 ~

THE THRASHER's IN NORTH CAROLINA — DANIEL BOONE

The Shawnees knew the British had closed the frontier and when the Virginian soldiers of the French and Indian War were given land bounties and went with greater force into this territory, the Shawnees decided to resist and sought the aid of other tribes. The Iroquois Six Nations and the Cherokees remained loyal to the British, but the Mingos and Ottawas joined with the Shawnees. Lord Dunmore claimed Kentucky under Virginia's 1609 sea-to-sea charter and sent John Connolly to Pittsburgh, Pennsylvania, to maintain the right of white expansion westward. Connolly aroused and collected Virginians to aid him as he proceeded. Of course, atrocities on both sides resulted. Thirty-five miles west of Pittsburgh at Logan's Camp (Logan was a half-breed Indian, the son of Shilkellamy, the great Indian Chief of Shamokin, Pennsylvania) one Indian was killed and another captured, 27 Apr 1774. Three days later, Daniel Greathouse lured some Indians to a party at Logan's Camp and murdered six of them. Logan, who had befriended the whites, lost a brother and a sister in the slaughter.

Shawnee Chief Cornstalk had tried to negotiate peace, but Lord Dunmore had decided the best way was to drive the Indians out of Kentucky, and without summoning a new Assembly, declared war on the Indians. He illegally called up the colony's militia more than a month after the Militia Act had expired and rode west as the leader of fifteen hundred to 2000 frontiersmen to meet the hundreds of Cornstalk's warriors who had crossed the Ohio to stop them. The fighting continued until after a major battle on 10 Oct 1774. The Indian resistance collapsed. The Shawnees, Mingos and Delawares on the Kanawha sued for peace, but instead of joining them, Chief Logan sent a speech to Lord Dunmore, of which, young Tom Jefferson obtained a copy and included it in his *Notes on Virginia*. It reads in part:

"I appeal to any white man to say if he ever entered Logan's cabin hungry, and he gave him not meat, if he ever came cold and naked, and he clothed him not. During the course of the last long and bloody war, Logan remained idle in his cabin, an advocate for peace. Such was my love for the whites that my countrymen pointed as they passed and said, 'Logan is the friend of white men!' I had even thought to have lived with you, but for the injuries of one man . . . [who] last spring, in cold blood, and unprovoked, murdered all the relations of Logan, not sparing even my women and children. This called on me for revenge. I have sought it. I have killed many. I have fully glutted my vengeance. For my country, I rejoice at the beams of peace. But do not harbor a thought that mine is the joy of fear. Logan never felt fear. He will not turn on his heel to save his life. Who is there to mourn for Logan? Not one."

Jefferson, a young lieutenant in the Virginia militia, found Chief Logan inspiring and once proclaimed,

"I challenge the whole orations of Demosthenes and Cicero and of any more eminent orator if Europe has furnished anyone more eminent, to produce a single passage superior to the speech of Logan."

There is a land patent granted to JOHN THRASHER for 400 acres of land "lying and being in the County of Goochland on both sides of Buffalo River near the Blue Mountains." It was recorded 1 Feb 1738. Goochland County, Virginia—formed from Henrico County in 1728 [now Amherst County.] The patent is signed by William Gooch. JOHN received a second grant of 388 acres "in Goochland on both sides of Buffalo River" 20 Sep 1745. This JOHN THRASHER was a descendant of the early 1600s Elizabeth City THRASHERs. [See PART II] In 1761 he sold this land. About 45 miles north and east of Amherst is Monticello, the home of Thomas Jefferson, whose father's ancestors were early frontiersmen into Albemarle County.

JOHN THRASHER moved south after selling his property, 1761, and had a land patent on Hogan's Creek of 693 acres in Orange County, North Carolina—a very large county that was later split into several counties, including Guilford, Randolph, Surry, Rowan, Wilkes. His land was on the northern border of North Carolina in what is now Rockingham County, North Carolina, which borders Pittsylvania County, Virginia. In 1774, JOHN THRASHER was granted a patent for 130 acres in Halifax County, Virginia—east of Pittsylvania. He is on the tax list of Orange County, North Carolina, in 1754, so he probably had land there before the 1761 land patent. I believe fourth-great-grandmother ELIZABETH THRASHER was his daughter.

JOHN THRASHER married RUTH CLOUD. The CLOUDS were English Quakers and had come from Chester County, Pennsylvania. In 1746, JOSEPH CLOUD was granted a patent for 400 acres on Mill Creek at a place called Buffalo Camp in Pittsylvania County, Virginia. In 1748, ISAAC CLOUD patented 400 acres on Tomahawk Creek,

> "beginning at a Red Oak blazed 3 ways by a Buffalo Lick . . . near a Beaver Pond. Also 400 acres beg. at a Hollow Chestnut Tree in which s'd CLOUD and Smith us'd to camp on the Grounds between a Br. of Banister and Turkey Cock Creek."

In July 1770, RICHARD THRASHER gave an affidavit in a court held for Pittsylvania, which proved in court that ELIZABETH LAYNE was the eldest daughter of ISAAC CLOUD, who was the eldest son of JOSEPH CLOUD, and that the said CLOUD (ISAAC) had no living male heir; also that the CLOUDS were of the Province of Pennsylvania, in the County of Chester. [*History of Pittsylvania County — Maud Carter Clement.*]

[Note: The known sons of JOHN and RUTH CLOUD THRASHER are ISAAC, JOSEPH CLOUD, and JOHN THRASHER Jr. They also had MARY. There are no births or christening records for these children. The three sons were deeded the North Carolina land in the years 1784 to 1788. MARY had children with first names of THRASHER and CLOUD, which establish her as a daughter. In Pendleton County, South Carolina, in 1792, fourth-great-grandparents, WILLIAM and ELIZABETH THRASHER ALLRED were with ISAAC THRASHER and his family. Both of these families went to Franklin County, Georgia, for the land lotteries around 1800. JOHN THRASHER, Jr. and family were also there. Georgia's census did not survive the civil war, so the tax list is used. ELIZABETH was an older sister. ISAAC later went to Kentucky, then east Tennessee, where he died.

The brothers, ISAAC and JOHN (JR.) THRASHER married sisters, RUTH and SUSAN BARTON, daughters of DAVID and RUTH BARTON. This DAVID BARTON accompanied Daniel Boone on one of his early expeditions into Kentucky where DAVID was said to have been killed by the Indians in 1772. The name of DAVID BARTON is inscribed on a monument located at the original Boonesborough site, which is dedicated to the builders of Boonesborough and the famous "Wilderness Road." He may have been related to my Pennsylvania BARTON cousins—not established; but quite possible. His father was believed to be THOMAS BARTON.]

Daniel Boone was originally from Pennsylvania, of English parents, and was living in Rowan County, North Carolina, on the Yadkin River, in September

1773, when he moved his family to Kentucky, which was then still part of Virginia. RUTH BARTON, widow of DAVID BARTON and the JOHN THRASHER family were also living in North Carolina on the Yadkin River at this same time—southwest from JOHN THRASHER's Hogan's Creek property. Hogan's Creek empties into the Dan River.

With the Proclamation of 1763, the British closed the frontier at the crest of the Appalachians. The young lawyer, Thomas Jefferson, delivered a warning not to trespass on Indian Territory to Daniel Boone. But the temptation must have been too great for in the spring of 1769, backwoodsman Daniel Boone of North Carolina and a friend had found financial backing and supplies from a land speculator and slipped through the Cumberland Gap into the forbidden territory. They roamed through Kentucky, collecting furs and living off the land as the Indians did. They were captured by the Shawnees, but escaped by hiding in the extensive vegetation. Boone returned again in 1771. Two years later, emerging with a fortune in furs, Daniel Boone and his companion were ambushed near Cumberland Gap. All their furs, horses, and supplies were seized by the Indians and they went home empty-handed. If the story and date of DAVID BARTON is correct, they also went home with one less companion.

THREE SISTERS
Daughters of RICHARD FAUSETT and MARY McKEE

ELIZA McKEE FAUSETT
1808–1896

MARTHA SPENCER FAUSETT
1815–1873

AMANDA ARMSTRONG FAUSETT
1810–1885

MARRIED

JAMES RUSSELL IVIE

WILLIAM MILLIGAN
AND JOHN BUISH

MOSES MARTIN SANDERS

THE McKEES—AN INDIAN HERITAGE?

My mother, LILLIE IVIE CONDIE, lived in the Kimball Apartments in downtown Salt Lake City, Utah, for several years around 1967. While she was there, she took classes in genealogy and did research in the Family History Library—at that time it was called the Genealogical Society. During her research, she discovered in one of the books a statement that an ALEXANDER McKEE had married an Indian girl, and, with their many children, they had come from Pennsylvania and were among the early settlers of Tennessee. Since her third-great-grandfather was ALEXANDER McKEE, who had many children when he moved from Orange County, North Carolina, to Tennessee, she was very interested. However, time had run out. The library was closing. There were no copy machines in those days. She would come back tomorrow. The following day the book wasn't there, nor the day after; in fact, she was not able to locate it again.

When she told me about it, I commented that pictures of second-great-grandmother ELIZA McKEE FAUCETT (Ivie), his granddaughter, had always reminded me of the Indians. I had wondered if she had Indian blood. My mother laughed and said, "I never had to wonder about her. I just looked in the mirror."

She then told me that when she mentioned it to another descendant, her comment was,

"Oh no! ALEXANDER McKEE came straight from Ireland to Orange County, North Carolina. There's no Indian blood in our ancestry!"

Nevertheless, I have been open-minded to the possibility, and currently it seems quite probable.

Philadelphia, Pennsylvania, was one of the major ports for the Irish immigrants who began to come in large numbers about 1720. [New York City closed their port to them at times.] There are many ALEXANDER McKEES, McKEYS, McKAYS, MACKEYS and other variations in Chester, Buck, and Lancaster Counties. These counties were originally called Upland until William Penn arrived at New Castle, Delaware, 27 Oct 1682. During that winter, he divided and renamed them. Boundary disputes between Delaware, Maryland and Pennsylvania ensued in these early days, and the same land might have been shown in any of the three states.

[Note: The following land record is found in the printed record of Chester County, Pennsylvania: "WILLIAM CLOUD ye elder to ROBERT MACKEE, 100 acres on Branch of Namans Crk. Bethel Tp. with ye buildings and improvements upon ye same. Ye seventh day of ye Tenth month 1691."

At a Quarter Session Court held 12 Sep 1693, these 100 acres of land were seized for debt and sold by the Sheriff as the Estate of "ROBT. MEKEES, 100 acres lying on Namans Crk. Bethel Tp." This land lay in what is now New Castle County, Delaware.

JAMES and DANL. MACKE of White Clay Creek, and ROBT. MACKE of Octorora Creek petition through "Ye minister Craighead for parcels of land to settle on," (CCPCM-XIX-743). Thos. Craighead, a Presbyterian Minister, was a member of the New Castle Presbytery in January 1724. He was installed as pastor of the White Clay Creek Church on 22 Sep 1724.]

The following is from GEO. WILSON McKEE's 1890 publication *McKees of Virginia and Kentucky*":

"About 1738, ten or eleven brothers by the name of McKEE came to America & first settled in Lancaster County, Pa. Some writers say from five to ten or eleven sons of a McKEE who had borne a part in the defense of Derry came with the Scotch Presbyterians. Two of these, JNO. McKEE and ROBT. McKEE left Lancaster Co. and went to Kerr Crk. in what is now Rockbridge Co. VA, settling on part of Borden's grant. Some of the bros. settled near Wheeling, W. Va. and Pittsburg, Pa., while the others remained in Lancaster Co. Pa."

This ROBERT McKEE is the ancestor of Colonel JOHN McKEE, the Indian Agent to the Choctaw Indians of the Mississippi, Alabama Territory in the 1790s through the early 1800s. He had come from Rockbridge County, Virginia.

The early British government asked their young officers who were sent to the Indian territories to marry Indian girls. They felt this would help to unite the Indians with the British instead of the French. There is an ALEXANDER McKEE, born about 1665, in Antrim, Ireland, who married ELIZABETH

GORDON. He died in Lancaster, Pennsylvania, about 1740. His son was Capt. THOMAS McKEE, born about 1709, who married MARGARET, a Shawnee woman. They had a son, Colonel ALEXANDER McKEE, born about 1735, who also married a Shawnee maiden (see Ancestral File).

According to the book *The Mackeys and Allied Families*, this Colonel ALEX. MACKEY was a man of education and influence and for 12 years the King's Deputy Agent of Indian Affairs. He was also a most deep-dyed Tory (Loyalist). As an Indian trader, he acquired a wide reputation with the Indians and was active among them in the British interest. He was suspected of treason in dealings with the enemy by the colonists, who imprisoned him. He was put on parole in 1778, escaped to Detroit along with Samuel Girty, Matthew Elliott, and four others.

> "Thereafter these men were tireless instigators of many Indian raids among the inhabitants of the Frontier." (Dunaway: History of Pa. -158)

He is listed in England among the British officers serving in America: ALEX. MACKAY, (Hon.) Col. 65 Regt. 24 Mch 1764 and Col. 21 Regt. 18 Nov 1770. When the Revolutionary War ended,

> "ALEX. McKAY: Of Pa. at the peace accompanied by his family went from N. Y. to Shelburne, Nova Scotia, where the Crown granted him 50 acres, 1 town lot and 1 water lot."

He had a son, Capt. THOMAS McKEE, born in 1768 in Pennsylvania who married Therese Askin of Ontario, Canada. THOMAS died there in 1815. This son, along with Matthew Elliott, mentioned above, was with Tecumseh during the War of 1812, which is told in more detail in *PART IV: UNITED STATES ?*

But back in 1756, Captain THOMAS McKEE, the father of the Colonel, was

> "given orders to raise a Co. of 28 men in the pay of the province . . . as soon as your Co. is complete march to Hunter's Mill on the Sesquehannah and either complete the fort or build a new one as James Gilbreath shall advise." *Pa. Archv. S1-2-563.*
>
> "Capt. THOS. McKEE on the 30 June 1756 was instructed by Gov. Morris to conduct (an Indian) [from] New Castle's dtr. to Phila. with safety" (Ibid p. 684.)

This THOSAS McKEE, who married a Shawnee Indian girl, died in 1773, leaving a son ALEXANDER and *five other children* (Orphans Crt. Rec.) The names of these other children are not given. It is a possibility that one of them had a son ALEXANDER McKEE, who is my ancestor.

> "There were three routes of migration to the South. 'The Great Road' ran from Philadelphia through Lancaster and York to Winchester, thence up the Shenandoah Valley, crossing the Fluvanna at Looney's Ferry, thence to Staunton River and down the river through the Blue Ridge, thence Southward, crossing the Dan River below the mouth of Mayo River, thence still Southward near the Moravian Settlement to the Yadkin River just above the mouth of Reedy Creek . . . It was 435 miles." (Saunders: 4-22)

A second route branched off near Winchester, Virginia, and went east of the mountains to Charlotte, North Carolina, and into South Carolina and Georgia. The third route left Philadelphia and was called the Kings Highway as it followed a more coastal shipping route to Baltimore, Maryland; Norfolk, Virginia; coastal eastern North Carolina, and along the coast to Charleston, South Carolina. A large number of Scotch took this route, then came up the Cape Fear River into what is now Cumberland County, North Carolina. McKEE is also a Scotch name. The first route goes through Orange County, North Carolina, which is near the Dan River. It would be the most likely route for settlers into this area of North Carolina. We have McKEEs, THRASHERs, ALLREDs, FAUSETTs, and CLOUDs that mostly used this route.

[Note: In searching early land records in western North Carolina, we find several ALEXANDER McKEEs of other counties. There is also an ANN McKEE with 378 acres in Orange County—1745-65, where fourth-great-grandfather became a private during the Revolutionary War. The 1790 U.S. census places ancestor ALEXANDER McKEE in Orange County along with a WILLIAM McKEE. These records did not include additional information on them or their families; however, ALEXANDER's oldest daughter, MARY, married RICHARD FAUCETT the 28 Jan 1792 in Orange County, North Carolina; there were not any of his other children listed in the marriage records of this county.]

Fourth-great-grandfather ALEXANDER McKEE left Orange County, North Carolina, around the spring of 1793, with a land grant in Tennessee for his military service. Then, Tennessee was an extension of North Carolina. The same land records are shown in both states.

WILLIAM BEAN of Tennessee

In the early history of Tennessee, there was a British fort called Fort Loudon about 30 miles southwest of present day Knoxville.

"It had been built and occupied by the British in 1756. In 1760 it was surrendered to the Indians on condition that the troops and their families should be allowed to return to the eastern settlements, but most of them were treacherously massacred the morning after leaving the fort. In 1769 Capt. WILLIAM BEAN and his family built a cabin at the mouth of Boon's Creek. His son RUSSELL is claimed to be the first white child born in Tennessee. Within a few months a number of families from eastern North Carolina and Virginia located in the same vicinity. It was called The Watauga Settlement. These pioneers being far from the mother State, without government and without protection, in 1772 organized themselves into the Watauga Association, the purpose of which was to protect themselves and to dispense justice among the colonists. The Watauga Association was the foundation of the Commonwealth of Tennessee. Roosevelt says that these were the first white men of America to establish a free and independent community on the continent." See Tennessee in the *Americana*.

Captain WILLIAM BEAN was perhaps an early British officer in Fort Loudon. He may have followed orders and taken an Indian wife in an effort to establish peace with the Cherokees. This might have been why he survived and others were killed. It may also be why he was able to be the first to return with his family and build a cabin in 1769. An older daughter might have been the MARY BEAN, who married ALEXANDER McKEE. There were also other families of BEANs in this area of North Carolina, and a lot of *mights* in this paragraph.

[Note: ALEXANDER and MARY BEAN McKEE's oldest child JOHN was born about 1771. Their daughter MARY married RICHARD FAUCETT, the son of the Huguenot WILLIAM FAUCETT from Ireland, after they had been driven from France. Their story is told in "PART II: STANDING FIRM." My second-great-grandfather, JAMES RUSSELL IVIE married ELIZA McKEE FAUCETT, a daughter of RICHARD and MARY McKEE FAUCETT in Tennessee, June, 1824.]

THE WILL OF WILLIAM F. FAUCETT, BOOK A, P. 339.
DATED 28 SEP 1784, AND PROVEN 1785.

*"In the name of God Amen; The 28th of September in the year
of our Lord one thousand seven hundred and eighty four, I
WILLIAM FOSSETT of the County of Orange in the State of
North Carolina, farmer, being sick and very weak in body, bute of
perfect mind and memory, thanks be to God for ite, and calling to
mind the mortality of my body, and knowing that its appointed
for all men to die, do make and ordain this my laste Wille and
Testament, thate is to say, princaply, and first of all, I give and
recommend my Soul to God thate gave ite, and for my Body, I
recommend to the Earth, to be buried in a Christian and decente
manner ate the discretion of my Executors, nothing doubtting, bute
at the general resurrection ite shall receive the same again, by the
mighty power of God, and [touching my] worldly Estate, wherewith
ite hath pleased God to bless me in this life, I give, deliver, and
dispose of the same in manner and form following, that is to say, In
the first place I give and bequeath to MARGARETE my beloved
Wife my whole Estate [for] her lifetime; ate her death, also I give
my son WILLIAM the place he now lives on in paying to the Estate
70 pounds, and finding my daughter ELAN one Horse and Saddle,
oute of whate he oweth me. The remaining part to be equally
divided among my children, only WILLIAM to have twenty
pounds more than any of the reste, this and no other to by my laste
Will and Testamente, in Witness thereunto I have set my hand and
Seal this 28 day of September.*

his

William X Fossett

mark   Seal

Signed, sealed published, pronounced and do by these

DAVID FOSSETTE

RICHARD FOSSETTE

John Munstead (?)

Rebellion in North Carolina—the ALLREDs

On an early visit to the Family History Library in Salt Lake City, I found a thin orange colored volume entitled Orange County, North Carolina Records. Upon opening it, I discovered it was photo copies of Granville County Records. An explanatory insert at the front of these original photographed abstracts stated that the original records had been buried during the Revolutionary War to preserve them from being harmed by the British. Many of these records were moldy and completely unreadable. Other pages were only partially readable. It also stated that they were in the Granville Land Office records, because Orange County in these early days did not have a court house, so the people went to their old county seat at Granville, a larger county also at that time, until their Orange county court house was completed. (see next page)

According to Archibald F. Bennett's *The Allred Family in America* (about 1950) WILLIAM ALDRIDGE and JOHN ALDRIDGE were brothers, born abt. 1704 and 1706, in Wicomico, Northumberland County, Virginia. They were two of the children of WILLIAM ALDRIDGE and ALICE FALLIN, who were large land holders in that area, and they also had large debts, which placed them in the court records from time to time. Their grandparents were CLEMENT ALDRIDGE and ELIZABETH TILLS of Worstead, Norfolk, England, who were descended from an English Reverend ALDRIDGE.

The Virginian WILLIAM ALDRIDGE (1704) had three sons: WILLIAM, JOSEPH and NATHANIEL ALDRIDGE, who are the William, Joseph, and Nathaniel Aldridge in these land records in Orange, NC.

Brother Virginian, JOHN ALDRIDGE, was born 16 May 1706 and had four sons: THOMAS, WILLIAM, SOLOMON and JOHN. Bennett believed these sons Americanized their last name to ALLRED when they went to North Carolina and were the JOHN ALRID, SOLOMON ALRED, THOMAS ALRID and WM. ALLRED in these land records.

Archibald Bennett ("Mr. Genealogy") was the secretary of the Utah Genealogical Society at Salt Lake City, Utah. He was a very careful researcher [but not related to the ALLREDs] and his book was considered correct by most of the ALLRED family throughout the rest of the 20th century. His very sweet and lovely widowed wife lives across the street from my daughter ROXANNE in Salt Lake City, and is still busy writing her own books.

As the century ended, disagreement was expressed within the *Allred Family Organization*—the largest family organization in the United States, claiming 90,000 known descendants of these original North Carolina English immigrants. Currently, 2005, the organization is of the opinion that the ALLRED and the ALDRIDGE families are not related, and that the ALLRED family came down the Great Wagon Road from Chester County, Pennsylvania, where there are tax records of a SOLOMON ALLRED who went to North Carolina about 1752.

From my extentsive research, the ALLRED name is rarely found in the early northern U. S. records—only a few in the very early New England area; there are many named Aldrich.

[Note: The following records have been typed much like they were handwritten in the Orange County book. The cc and scc refer to the "chain carriers" in the surveys. I have included these records in this book to help explain the confusion within the ALLRED and Aldridge families in tracing their ancestorial lines. For those who are unacquainted with the term acre---640 acres equals one square mile.]

"ABSTRACTS — GRANVILLE PROPRIETARY LAND OFFICE

Page 12: Allrid, John   warrent   15 Mar 1755
640 acres on east side Deep R., on south of Mount Pleasant Run of Sandy Run; Includes his and Thomas Allrid's improvements; heretofore entered by John McDaniel.
     Entered   15 Mar 1755
     Surveyed   2 May 1755
     Deed   15 Mar 1756

Page 12: Aldridge, William   warrent   15 Mar 1755
640 acres on Mount Pleasant Run, a br. of Sandy Creek, Running into Deep River, the east side, Begin on the North end of a division line between him & Luke Smith.
     Entered   15 Mar 1755

Page 12: Husband, Herman   warrant   15 Mar 1755
640 acres on the head of a branch of Sandy Cr. called Mt. Pleasant on the east side of Deep R.

Including a cabin built by Soloman Alred & claimed by Zach. Martin.
    Entered   15 Mar 1755 "In Lieu of an Entry made the 14 Nov. 1754"
    Surveyed   2 May 1755

Page 21: Allred, Wm. [from index–no record found]
Page 22: McDaniel, John   warrint   5 Feb 1757
    640 acres on Sandy Cr., on his own place, on west side Haw River, near South of Alamance,
    provided it does not fall in McCullock's line, on the Haw R. tract.
    Entered   Feb. 1757
    *In lieu of McDaniell's warrant, now in Churton's Hands, the land being granted to
    John Aldridge."

Page 26: Alred, Solomon   warrent   7 Nov 1757
    640 acres on Bush Creek, includes improvements of Alexander McDaniel.
    Entered   7 Nov 1757
    Surveyed   15 Oct 1759
    Assigned to Luke Smith

Page 28: Aldridge, Joseph   warrent   1 Aug 1758
    640 acres on both sides Flatt river, joins John Cate's line. "The execution of the above warrant
    having been prevented by the late disturbances, I do hereby validate it for six month's longer ..."
        Edenton   20 Feb 1760
        Entered   14 Mar 1758
        Surveyed   29 Jul 1760
        Deed   Jan 1761

Page 31: Alred, Solomon   Survey   16 Oct 1759
    400 acres on both sides of the south of Sandy Creek, Begin on Deep River on Hopkin's line;
    George Julian, John Alred: cc

Page 32: Aldridge, Nathaniel   Entry   1 Feb 1760
    500 acres on the Bushey Fork of Flatt River, begin where Thomas Robison's line crosses
    So Fork on the North side, signed 'Nathaniel + Aldridge.'

Page 32: Aldridge, Nathaniel   warrant   1 Feb 1760
    500 acres on Bushey Fork of Flatt River.
        Surveyed   29 July 1760
        Deed   6 Feb 1761

Page 35: Aldridge, Nathaniel   Survey   29 July 1760
    220 acres on Bushey Fork of Flatt River, adj. Thomas Robinson; Joseph Aldridge,
    John Hague: scc

Page 35: Aldridge, Joseph   Survey   29 July 1760
    295 acres on both sides of Flatt R., joins John Cate; Nathaniel Aldridge, John Reedman: scc

Page 48: Aldridge, Nathaniel by James Watson Entry   21 Dec 1761
    700 acres on mouth of Reedy Br. Of Bruch Cr., waters of Deep R., near Cox's Road."

The family now believes that this SOLOMON was from Lancashire,
England, and his birth is recorded in the Church Records in Eccles Parish–12

Nov 1680. He was the youngest child of JOHN and ELLEN PEMBERTON ALLRED.

[Note: ELLEN died in 1684. A letter was found, dated 1695, which states that JOHN was in Manchester, England, with a second wife and three of his sons, OWEN, THEOPHILUS and SOLOMON. There were two daughters, MARY and ALICE. In the letter, JOHN asked his cousin PHINEAS PEMBERTON for financial help so he could bring his family to Pennsylvania. The letter also mentions an additional son of JOHN ALLRED, PHINEAS ALLRED, who has "gone to be a soldier." PHINEAS PEMBERTON was wealthy and politically well connected—close friend and ally of William Penn. PHINEAS' father, RALPH PEMBERTON, was the first cousin of ELLEN PEMBERTON (Allred). She was a member of the Quaker faith when she died and her death is recorded in their records in England. JOHN ALLRED was arrested several times for attending Quaker meetings in 1661; but he was also arrested during this time for attending Presbyterian meetings.

Two years prior to ELLEN's death in 1684, PHINEAS PEMBERTON; his wife and children; PHINEAS' father, RALPH; PHINEAS' father-in-law of his second marriage, James Harrison, and other members of their family sailed to Pennsylvania aboard the ship Submission, owned by William Penn. Their voyage is well documented in the ship's log, Pemberton family records, and other sources.

PHINEAS PEMBERTON kept detailed records of all business, religious, and family dealings and the family donated this collection to the Pennsylvania Historical Society in 1972. [See the Allred Family Newsletter, Summer 2003.] This is probably the family that gave their name to the town of Pemberton, New Jersey, about 30 miles east of Philadelphia with a present population of around 1,400. This is where Brigadier General JOHN LACEY built two iron mills and a forge after the Revolution and married ANTIS (Anastasia) BUDD REYNOLDS. The bride's father was Thomas Reynolds, who was married to Elizabeth Budd. They were prominent citizens of Pemberton, which was then known as New Mills.

The Allred Family Organization is continuing its research, even to the extent of doing DNA testing to prove the relationship to JOHN and ELIZABETH ALLRED in England and America.

According to the Allred Family Newsletter, SOLOMON ALLRED received a land grant in North Carolina in 1752 and had sons named THEOPHILUS, PHINEAS, JOHN, and SOLOMON. These are rather unusual names [except JOHN]; but they are quite common in the ALLRED descendants as are WILLIAM and THOMAS.]

There are several things of interest in the above Granville Land Records of Orange County, North Carolina, the boundaries of which included Randolph County at that time:

1. On page 12, John Alrid obtained his land from John McDaniel. On page 22, John McDaniel's land is referred to as being "granted to John Aldridge."

2. John Alrid and William Aldridge (the neighbor on the east of the 640 acres) have land warrants granted on the same day, 15 Mar 1755, showing they were probably well acquainted, or possibly related in some way. Brothers, cousins, and relatives in general went to new lands together for safety and companionship. This was the frontier.

3. Herman Husband was also there that same day. His land bordered west of JOHN ALLRED's with his son (ancestor) THOMAS ALLRED's inprovements on the east side. Husband's land included a cabin built by SOLOMAN ALLRED. This Herman Husband was a Quaker from Pennsylvania. In the historical accounts of North Carolina, Herman Husband was given the credit for instigating the War of the Regulators and was hanged. We find on other documents JOHN and THOMAS ALLRED's signatures with William Aldridge's signatures next to theirs on some of the petitions of the Regulators.

4. My fourth-great-grandfather was WILLIAM ALLRED. He married ELIZABETH THRASHER be-
    lieved to be the daughter of JOHN THRASHER of the previous chapter. His father was THOMAS
    ALLRED, the son of JOHN ALLRED.

I believe the ALLRED Family Orgnization is right, but I have included these records partly to explain the
difficulty of early American genealogical research and to help understand some already existing pedigrees.
If the ALLED and Aldridge families are not related, they appear to be very good friends and neighbors
with very similar given names.]

The following map shows the early areas of settlement in North Carolina,
and the approximate dates that these areas were settled. By 1765, the western
population of the state far outnumbered the eastern population; but they had
only two counties, while the east had nine counties. This gave the East a far
greater representation in the British North Carolina Assembly. As the Assembly
and Governor divided the western counties, they kept dividing the eastern, also,
always keeping a large majority of the Assembly in the east, even though some
eastern counties had a very small population.

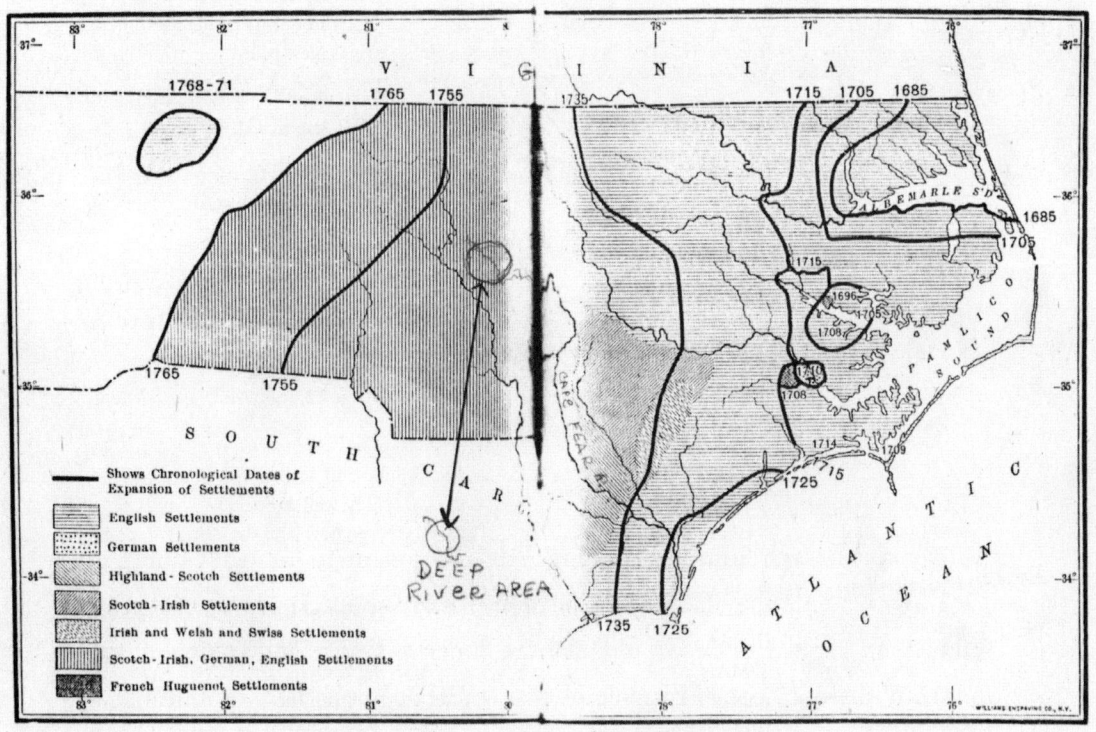

MAP OF EARLY SETTLEMENTS IN NORTH CAROLINA UP TO 1778
THE ALLRED ANCESTERS SETTLED BY THE DEEP RIVER.

The *under-construction* North Carolina capitol building, often called the "Palace," was in the east at New Bern (about 100 miles north of Wilmington on the Neuse River), where their newly arrived Governor Tryon from England would have his home. He had planned and was building it to be the finest in the Colonies. The time of construction and financial debt for construction kept growing and growing. Governor Tryon (1765-1771) needed more taxes to pay the debt; but much of his tax money somehow got diverted—somewhere. Most of the farmers were paying their taxes with pigs and produce. He needed cash to pay his thousands of pounds of debt. He asked the king for the right to print paper money—on credit. The King and Parliament in England wouldn't allow it. They wanted the colonies to be more self-sufficient, less materialistic, and send money to their coffers.

GOVERNOR'S PALACE, NEW BERN

A young lawyer, Edmund Fanning, Yale 1757, came to Orange County in 1761. By this time they had their courthouse at Hillsbourgh. He was soon assemblyman, register of deeds, judge of the Superior Court, and colonel of the militia. With the exception of assemblyman, these positions were appointments by the governor. As the people watched his wealth increase, a local bard, Rednap Howell, distributed this poem, which found great favor with the people:

"When Fanning first to Orange came
He looked both pale and wan,
An old patched coat upon his back,
An old mare he road on.
Both man and mare warn't worth five pounds
As I've been told;
But by his civil robberies
He's laced his coat with gold."

In his *History of North Carolina*, R. D. W. Connor describes Fanning:

"One need not think him deserving of all the infamy that has been heaped upon him to understand the sentiments of the people toward him. That he was a man of culture and more than average ability there can be no dispute. To his equals he was kind, hospitable, [and] considerate; to his inferiors, patronizing, supercilious, [and] overbearing. He despised the 'common people,' and they cordially reciprocated the sentiment. They believed that he had acquired his wealth, which he displayed with great ostentation, 'by his civil robberies.' Although on the evidence he may be fairly acquitted of the charge of deliberate and positive dishonesty, he was unquestionably guilty of abusing his official power and influence for the purpose of perpetuating an oppressive system and obstructing all efforts at reform. He was, indeed, the progenitor of the race of carpetbaggers."

Upon the recommendation of the assemblymen from each county, the governor, with council, appointed the local government leaders: county justices, sheriffs, registers and officers of the militia. There was a clerk of the pleas who farmed out the clerkships. Moreover these local officials controlled the Assembly. Multiple office-holding was legal.

1. NORTH CAROLINA CURRENCY, 1718   2. NORTH CAROLINA CURRENCY, 1776
3. EDMUND FANNING   4. MONUMENT TO THE REGULATORS

"Assemblymen were also generally clerks, justices, and militia colonels, who formed what in modern political parlance we call 'courthouse rings.' Where these 'rings' were composed of high-minded, patriotic men, as in most of the eastern counties, government was honestly administered; but in the 'back country' such officials were rare, local government was usually inefficient, often corrupt, and generally oppressive" [Ibid.]

Herman Husband's work, *Impartial Relations* reads as follows:

"Well, Gentlemen, it is not our mode or form of government nor yet the way of our laws, that we are quarreling with, but with the malpractices of the officers of our county courts, and the abuses we suffer by those that are empowered to manage our public affairs, this is the grievance gentlemen, that demands our serious attention. And I shall show you that most notorious and intolerant sources have crept into the practice of law in this country and I doubt not in other countries; though that does not concern us."

Husband, who quoted these words in 1770 to show the complaints of the people of Orange County, took them from an address given by George Sims in 1765 to the people of Granville County, North Carolina. Many of the "back country" counties had similar problems.

"At the August term, 1766, of the County Court at Hillsboro, a group of Sandy Creek men, inspired by the success of the Sons of Liberty in resisting the Stamp Act, issued an address calling upon the people to send delegates to a meeting at Maddock's Mill to inquire 'whether the free men of this county labor under any abuses of power or not.' The address was read in open court and the officers present, acknowledging that it was reasonable, promised to attend the meeting. On October 10, twelve delegates appeared, but no officers. Apparently under the influence of Edmund Fanning, who denounced the meeting as an insurrection, they had repented of their promise and sent a messenger to say that they would not attend because the meeting claimed authority to call them to an account. The delegates, therefore, were compelled to content themselves with a proposal that the people hold such a meeting annually to discuss the qualifications of candidates for the Assembly, to inform their representatives of their wishes, and to investigate the official acts of public officers. But public office-holders in 1766 did not acknowledge their responsibility to the people. Accordingly they threw all of their personal and official influence against the proposal, and the Sandy Creek men, discouraged at the lack of popular interest and support, abandoned their project.

"Though the agitation continued, no further organized opposition was attempted until the spring of 1768. Almost simultaneously a report reached Hillsboro that the Assembly had given the governor 15,000 pounds for a 'Palace' and the sheriff posted notices that he would receive taxes only at five specified places and if required to go elsewhere he would distrain at a cost of 2s. 8d. for each distress. The coincidence caused wide comment. The people declared they would not pay the tax for the Palace. They denounced the sheriff's purpose as a violation of the law and determined to resist it, organizing themselves into an association, which they later called *The Regulation*, in which they agreed:

'1. To pay no more taxes until satisfied that they were according to law and lawfully applied;

2. to pay no fees greater than provided by law;

3. to attend meetings of the Regulators as often as possible;

4. to contribute, each man according to his ability, to the expenses of the organization;

5. in all matters to abide by the will of the majority.'"

They then sent the officers a notice demanding a strict accounting, declaring that:

"as the nature of an officer is a servant of the publick, we are determined to have the officers of this county under a better and honester regulation than they have been for some time past."

This was received by the officers with an outburst of indignation. Fanning denounced the people for attempting to arraign the officers before

"the bar of their shallow understanding" and charged them with desiring to set themselves up as the "sovreign arbiters of right and wrong."

The officers were haughty and seized a Regulator's horse, saddle, and bridle, selling them for taxes. A storm of popular fury greeted this challenge. The Regulators rode into Hillsboro, rescued their comrade's property and fired several shots into Fanning's house. When this affair was reported to Fanning, who was absent attending court at Halifax, he promptly ordered the arrest of William Butler, Peter Craven, and Ninian Bell Hamilton, called out seven companies of Orange militia, and hurried to Hillsboro to take command. He immediately reporting the situation and his own actions to Governor Tryon and asked for authority to call out the militia of other counties, if it became necessary.

The governor accepted his subordinate's report at face value and authorized Fanning to use the Orange militia to suppress the insurrection, and further ordered the militia of Bute, Halifax, Granville, Rowan, Mecklenburg, Anson, Cumberland, and Johnston counties to be in readiness to respond to Fanning's call. Then he sent a proclamation to be read to the people, and offered to go, himself, to the scene of action, if Fanning desired his presence. The Governor's Council, declaried the Regulators guilty of insurrection and approved these actions of the governor.

In the meantime, the officers in Orange County became alarmed at the storm they had raised and offered to meet the Regulators to adjust their differences. To Fanning, they explained their offer as a subterfuge to gain time. The Regulators, however, accepted it in good faith and immediately made preparations for the meeting. They appointed a committee to collect data relating to the taxes and fees and required its members to take an oath to do justice between the officers and the people to the best of their ability.

Fanning was determined to prevent any such meeting. While the Regulators were making their preparations, he collected a band of armed men and swooping down upon Sandy Creek, arrested Butler and Husband on a charge of inciting to rebellion and hurried them off to prison at Hillsboro. At this high-handed act 700 men, many of whom were not Regulators, seized their guns and marched on Hillsboro to rescue the prisoners.

It was now the officers' turn to become frightened. They threw open the prison doors, released their captives, and hurried them off to turn back the mob. Along with them went Isaac Edwards, the governor's private secretary, who promised the people in the name of the governor that if they would peaceably disperse, go home quietly, and petition the governor in the proper manner, the governor would see that justice was done them. Since this promise was exactly in line with their own plans, which had been interrupted by the arrest of Husband and Butler, the Regulators accepted it gladly.

In spite of Fanning's opposition, they appointed a committe to prepare their case to lay before the governor. Governor Tryon, however, repudiated the promise of his secretary, saying Edwards had exceeded his authority. He refused to deal with the Regulators as an organization, demanded that they immediately disband, and expressed his hearty approval of Fanning's course. At the same time he stated for the information of the people the amount of poll tax due for the year 1767, promising to issue a proclamation forbidding the officers' taking illegal fees, and ordered the attorney-general to prosecute any officer charged in due form with extortion.

In July, 1768, Tryon went to Hillsboro hoping he might induce the people to submit to the laws. The Regulators, after meeting together, told him his proclamation forbidding the taking of illegal fees had had no effect, and they had decided to petition the Assembly. Other meetings were held and several communications, both verbal and written, passed between the governor and the Regulators. In one of them he told the Regulators that he was ever ready to do them justice and as evidence of it he had ordered the attorney-general to institute prosecutions against officers charged with extortion, one of whom was Colonel Fanning himself.

This brought more misunderstanding. The Regulators thought he meant immediate action. The governor planned slow legal action through his court system. He had hoped to placate the people, so he would not have to call in the militia when the trial of Husband and Butler began. When they were unwilling to give him their promise, he called for the support of the militia in the surrounding counties. This was somewhat difficult, for the people in these surrounding counties were in sympathy with the Regulators' principles. So Governor Tryon appealed to the preachers and won over the leading Lutherans, Presbyterians, and Baptists. He came up with 1,461 men, one-fifth of which were commissioned officers: six lieutenant-generals, two major-generals, three adjutant-generals, seven colonels, five lieutenant-colonels, and many majors, captains, aides-de-camp, and minor officers.

As many anticipated, Edmund Fanning, who was to be tried for extortion and who this army had come to protect, was to be in charge of the court, and Maurice Moore was the associate justice of the court. Both were in active command in the gathered militia. A council of war was held in Hillsboro by thirty-four officers with ranks exceeding that of major. Of these, six were members of the Governor's Council, eighteen of the Assembly (one-fourth of that body).

This was to be a fair trial?

The Regulators assembled. There were 3,700 of them that had come, hoping for justice. They were surrounded by an army that included an artillery company. All stood quietly as the court proceeded. Husband was tried and acquitted; Butler and two other Regulators were convicted and sentenced to fines and imprisonment. The governor chose to be lenient. He released the prisoners and suspended the payment of their fines, and later pardoned them, on the advice of the king. Fanning was tried for extortion and found guilty on five counts, but the judges held their judgement in reserve and no further action was taken on his case. He promptly resigned his office as register, but, of course, kept all his other offices. Everyone went home, and the governor's debt had increased. The Regulators were still plagued with Fanning and were not impressed with the court system, governor, or the eastern American leaders.

The Regulating spirit spread to other counties. In some of them it found expression in acts of violence. A band of about thirty men from Edgecombe County attempted unsuccessfully to rescue an insurgent leader who had been imprisoned in the Halifax jail. In Johnston County a mob attacked the county court. In Anson a hundred armed men entered the courthouse, broke up the sitting of the county court, drove the justices off the bench, and then entered into an oath-bound association to assist each other in resisting all efforts of the sheriff to collect taxes. They repented, however, on the advice of the Orange County Regulators and sought redress through a petition. There was also an organization in Rowan County attempting to resolve their court problems.

In the summer of 1769, the governor dissolved the Assembly and ordered the election of a new one. Husband campaigned, declaring,

> "the majority of our Assembly is composed of lawyers, clerks and others in connection with them, while by our own voice we have excluded the planter."

In Orange County, Husband and Pryor replaced Edmund Fanning and Thomas Lloyd. Other counties sent representatives that better understood the problems of the regulators. The Regulators had prepared and drafted their bills carefully and were ready for their presentation for consideration, when Speaker Harvey arose and presented the resolutions transmitted by the House of Burgesses in Virginia, which began:

> "Resolved, That the sole right of imposing taxes on the inhabitants of this his Majesty's colony in North Carolina is now and ever hath been legally and constitutionally vested in the house of Assembly. . . . Resolved, That all trials for treason or crime whatsoever committed in said colony by any person residing therein ought of right to be had and conducted in and before his Majesty's courts held within said colony . . . . We cannot without horror think of the new, unusual, and permit us to add unconstitutional and illegal mode recommended to your Majesty of seizing and carrying beyond seas the inhabitants of America suspected of any crime . . . ."

The North Carolina Assembly adopted the resolution, with the hearty approval of the regulators who had stood so strongly for representation by the people. This measure, as violent as it was unexpected, was a blow in the face of the governor. His pride was wounded. The House assured him of its steadfast confidence in his integrity and good intentions; but with great mortification he dissolved the Assembly. He then wrote to Lord Hillsborough in January, requesting to be relieved as governor. But before the dissolution the House zealously went about its business. The petitions of the inhabitants of the different western counties were read to the Assembly by Herman Husband. Many of their requests were excellent and had the support to pass. The unexpected dissolution of the Assembly was a great disappointment to those members of the Assembly who sympathized with the Regulators. A similar disappointment was felt generally by the people of the west. Their great hope for action in this Assembly was gone.

In February, 1770, the governor issued a proclamation for a new election of assemblymen. The leaders of the Regulators at once began their campaign for favorable candidates throughout the territory. However, as yet they had not paid their taxes. The sheriff of Orange County reported 1833 of them still delinquent for the year of 1766. For 1768, only 205 or about one-tenth had paid their taxes. On 13 March, the day after the election, Judge Moore, who was holding court at Salisbury, wrote to the governor that "there is no such thing as collecting the public tax or levying a private debt," and that civil process could not be executed among the Regulators. Early in April the governor therefore issued a proclamation commanding the enforcement of the law and requiring that all sheriffs obstructed in their office should attend the next meeting of the Assembly; then, remembering the rebellious action of the last Assembly, he postponed the meeting of the Assembly until November.

But postponing the Assembly did not postpone action by the people. At a general meeting of the Sons of Liberty of the six Cape Fear counties they resolved to adhere to non-importation; and as Rhode Island was in violation, they resolved to have no mercantile dealings with Rhode Island and added that

> "all merchants who will not comply with the non-importation agreement are declared enemies to their country." They further declared that every county throughout the colony were "firmly resolved to stand or fall with them in support of the common cause of American liberty."

Governor Tryon then had two groups of strong-willed people to deal with—The eastern Sons of Liberty, whose tentacles extended throughout all the colonies and his western Regulators, who were standing firm for reform and spreading discontent throughout the colony. With both groups, he felt powerless. Early in June the palace was so near completion that he left Brunswick and began his residence in his long-awaited mansion.

The superior court was scheduled to meet at Hillsboro in September. Chief Justice Howard was absent, so Judge Richard Henderson opened the court on Saturday, 22 Sep 1770. As he took his seat, a petition was presented to him by James Hunter, in which was declared:

> "The juries were illegally drawn and were prejudiced; the county justices were parties to the delinquencies of the sheriffs and other officers; that the officers still took illegal fees; that the sheriffs would not settle, and their bondsmen were insolvent; that justice was not administered in the courts, and that they had determined to obtain redress, but in a legal and lawful way."

Judge Henderson promised to make an answer to it on Monday. But as court opened on Monday, approximately 150 Regulators came into the courthouse armed with clubs and whips. They were lead by Husband, Hunter, Howell, Butler, Hamilton and Jeremiah Fields. Fields addressed the court, declaring that,

> "the Regulators did not propose to have the cases against their leaders postponed, but that the trials should proceed at once; and as they objected to the jurymen drawn for that court, they would have others appointed

who would not be prejudiced against their own party."

The judge attempted to reason with them and they withdrew, but some fell furiously upon an attorney, John Williams, who was just arriving in court. He succeeded in escaping with his life. They next seized Colonel Fanning, who had sought shelter on the bench, and they dragged him by the heels out of the door of the courthouse. He managed to escape and take refuge in a store, where the mob threw bricks, breaking the windows. Several of the group approached the judge. Hunter and others told him that he would not be hurt if he would stay until the end of the term, however, no lawyers would be allowed except the one for the prosecution. They also informed him that they would stay and see justice impartially done. Outside many of the "courthouse ring" were being severely whipped, some escaped. The judge agreed to stay, and court proceeded for four or five hours, and the rage of the crowd subsided a little. Hunter and his group allowed the judge to adjourn for the day and conducted him safely to his lodging. At ten o'clock that evening, the judge escaped through a back way into the woods and was able to make it to his home in Granville County.

Fanning finally surrendered to them. They allowed him his freedom, if he would "take to his heals and get out of their sight." They then destroyed his home and household effects. The store owners ran from town expecting the destruction of their property; but the broken windows and Fanning's belongings seemed to be the end of this type of violence. Judge Henderson reported to the governor. In retribution, on 12 November his barns and stables were destroyed, and two days later his home was burned down. Colonel Fanning had been able to regain his Assembly seat by the governor making Hillsboro a borough town, and rumors were afloat that the Regulators were planning to attack the Assembly in the same way as they had the court to prevent him from taking his seat as a member. Fanning and his group organized themselves and called their group the Redressers.

The Assembly met without problems from the Regulators on 5 December in their new Assembly Hall at New Bern. On 12 December, in England, Governor Tryon was given his transfer and was appointed as the new governor of the New York province. Efforts were made to bring forth legislation that would bring peace throughout the colony, before Governor Tryon left for his new post.

Colonel Fanning, as a very close friend of the governor and highly knowledgeable about Regulator problems, worked hard to prepare and pass the reasonable
legislation. Things were going quite well for the Regulators.

Unfortunately, in January 1771, Samuel Johnson, a strong eastern county
leader within the Assembly, introduced a bill that became known as the "Riot
Act." It read as follows:

> "If ten or more persons, being unlawfully, turmultuously and riotously as-
> sembled together, to the disturbance of the public peace, after being openly
> commanded by any justice or sheriff to disperse, should notwithstanding
> remain together one hour thereafter, they should be adjudged guilty of
> felony and suffer death."

It went further, and freed the sheriff and other public-minded individuals
from any responsibility if one of the rioters were killed. It gave the right of prosecution under this law to any court in the colony, with the right of the judge to
issue a proclamation to be put up at the courthouse and at each church or chapel of the county where the crime was committed, commanding the indicted
person to surrender himself to the sheriff within sixty days; and if the person
did not surrender himself according to the proclamation, he was to be deemed
guilty of the offence as if he had been convicted. It was made lawful for anyone
to slay any such outlaw. It authorized the governor to order out the militia, who
were to be paid for their services. And if any number of men should, in an armed
and hostile manner, oppose the military force raised under the act, they were to
be considered as traitors and treated accordingly. This "Riot Act" was to remain
in effect for one year.

While the Assembly was still in session, Regulator James Hunter had a letter
addressed to Judge Maurice Moore, who was a member of the Assembly, published in the New Bern *Gazette*. It was considered slanderous, and members of
the House felt that Herman Husband, also a member of the House, had put him
up to it. They formed a committee to investigate Assemblyman Husband, and
found him guilty of gross prevarication and falsehood, and sentenced him to be
confined by order of the house. Husband commented that there might be those
who would come to release him. The Assembly quickly adjudged him in contempt of the house, and he was immediately expelled. The governor, fearful for
his own safety if Husband were allowed to join his group, issued a warrant for

the apprehension of Husband, and they committed him to jail and continued to confine Husband until he could be tried.

On 15 Jan 1771, the riot act was passed. A week later the governor informed the Assembly that he had received intelligence that led him to suspect that the insurgents were preparing for some speedy act of violence—the liberation of Husband by force. All were in a flutter, and the Assembly finally dismissed to reconvene at a later date—May 10th. After Husband had been in jail a month, it was reported that the people of Orange County were assembling, and the governor appointed a special court under the riot act to be held by the Chief Justice on 22 February for the trial of Husband and other alleged criminals. In anticipation of an attempt at rescue, the governor ordered the militia of the neighboring counties to be in readiness to repulse the insurgent force. Wake, Johnston, and Dobbs counties prepared their militias for the event. On 8 February, however, the grand jury of the special court, having considered the bill preferred against Herman Husband for libel, found it not a true bill and Husband was discharged. Now free, he leisurely returned to the back country. His friends had assembled and were proceeding eastward when word came of his release. With this news, they retired to their homes and the militia disbanded.

On 11 March another special court convened at New Bern attended by the chief justice and Judges Moore and Henderson. This grand jury came up with "true bills" against the "insurgents" as being enemies to government, and to the liberty, happiness and tranquillity of the inhabitants of the province. Accused were Herman Husband, Hunter, Butler, the Hamiltons, James Few, poet Rednap Howell, and many other leaders of the Regulators—a total of 31 persons. The Hillsboro superior court was afraid for their personal safety, if court was held on 22 March.

Not content to leave his little kingdom in North Carolina without using his newly acquired "Riot Act" to bring this stubborn people into subjection, Governor Tryon, with the agreement of his Council, decided to subdue the Regulators by force of arms. He sought an army of two thousand, five hundred and fifty men from twenty-nine counties. Bute County at first refused to furnish a single man, since all of the eight hundred assembled declared themselves on the side of the Regulators. The Wake militia was almost the same, but 50 volunteers came forth. Later, some volunteers from Bute County supported them. General Waddell was placed in command by Tryon. The eastern colonial leaders, who but a few years before had opposed the Stamp Act, and who would in a few years be the leaders in the Revolutionary movement, were now eager to help Governor Tryon subdue a group of their own countrymen who were only struggling for their just rights. In fact, most of the leading men of the east were in the line of march. Colonel Frohock and Martin had negotiated a settlement with the Regulators and communicated it to the governor, who was marching with his men westward. But Governor Tryon felt the Regulators had gone too far. The power of the insurgents to overturn government was too apparent. The day for temporizing had passed. The authority of the law was now to be asserted. Colonel Forhock, who should have commanded the Rowan militia, was sarcastically excused by the governor.

General Waddell was collecting troops from the southern counties. With him was Colonel Shaw of Cumberland with a detachment of artillery. On 5 May, General Waddell with nearly three hundred men crossed the Yadkin near Salisbury, and went into camp at Pott's Creek. Finding himself confronted by a considerable number of "insurgents" he halted and threw up entrenchments. On 10 May, at a council of war, it was resolved that it was too hazardous to engage the enemy, who were reported to extend a quarter of a mile, seven or eight deep, with a large body of horsemen, extending one hundred and twenty yards, twelve or fourteen deep. It had also come to his attention that many of his own troops would not fight the Regulators, but rather, in case of a conflict, would join them. General Waddell prudently retreated and fortified himself at a post near Salisbury, where he remained until 28 May.

The general had another problem. The White brothers, James, William, and John, had blackened their faces and took possession of the powder wagons midway between Charlotte and Salisbury. They destroyed the wagons and exploded the powder in a tremendous display. Because of their blackened faces, the Whites became known as the "Black Boys." Such was the general feeling toward government that pervaded throughout that region. General Waddell found himself hemmed in by forces too powerful to contend with. Governor Tryon was more fortunate. His colonial troops from the east marched steadily forward.

While the army advanced, the inhabitants of the west were all astir. Every highway and byway was filled with men hurrying to the front. They came from Wachovia, Anson, Surry and from the foothills of the mountains at the rendez-vous between the Haw and the Deep Rivers, animated by a purpose to fearlessly resist oppression, and were not to be overawed by a show of power.

> "Probably no one thought of subverting government; no one thought of wresting the province from the dominion of the British Empire; they only thought that they would stand up openly and with their own strong hand prevent the operation of laws passed by the Assembly, which, under the circumstance of their situation and lives, they deemed unjust and found oppressive."

Many came unarmed, and but few probably realized that there was really impending a conflict involving life and death. They gathered in force between the Haw and the Deep Rivers, and learning of the governor's approach, went forth to meet him.

Tryon, hearing of their advance on 11 May marched from Hillsboro, crossed the Haw, and on the night of the 13th encamped on the Great Alamance. There he prepared for battle. Here he received word of the plight of General Waddell, who claimed he was surrounded by 2000 Regulators and had been forced to retire. He also learned that the rendezvous of the two forces of the Regulators was to be at Hunter's plantation of Sandy Creek. It was also reported to the Governor that the Regulators were preparing to attack his camp. Instead of an attack, however, around 6 o'clock he received a communication from them de-siring to know if he would hear their petition for a redress of their grievances. He laid the letter before a council of war, and informed the Regulators that he would return an answer by 12 o'clock the next day. Some of his men, who were sent out to reconnoiter, were captured by the rebels, tied to trees and severely whipped. When the messenger with the governor's letter of reply arrived at the Regulators camp, he felt he was insulted so severely that he returned to his own camp without delivering the letter.

Early in the morning 16 May, the forces being about five miles apart, the governor moved forward, and about 10 o'clock came within a half mile of the Regulator encampment, forming a line of battle. He then sent one of his aides, accompanied by the sheriff of Orange County, with a letter that required them to lay down their arms, surrender all of their outlawed leaders, and submit to the laws of the province. These terms were rejected with disdain. Then communication was sent for the exchange of the two prisoners held by the Regulators for the seven prisoners held by the governor. The rebels delayed and sent word that they would comply within an hour. The governor, suspecting that the delay was intended to enable the enemy to outflank him, determined to wait no longer and demanded that if they did not immediately lay down their arms, they would be fired on. "Fire and be d—d!" was the answer.

The governor gave the order, which was not immediately obeyed; so, rising in his stirrups and turning to his men, he called out, "Fire! fire on them or on me!" Accordingly, the artillery began the fire, and the action almost instantly became general.

There were about 1100 militia. The number of the Regulators has been variously estimated as being between 2000 and 4000; but a great number of them were unarmed and probably only a few expected to engage in battle. They were not organized, nor trained. They were resolute citizens rather than an army. Their chief commander was James Hunter. At the first fire many of them left the field, among them being the Quaker, Herman Husband. After the conflict had lasted about a half hour, the Regulators moved to the woods and fought behind trees. An account in a Moravian record reads,

> "many had taken refuge in the woods, whereupon, the governor ordered the woods to be set afire, and in consequence some of the wounded were roasted alive."

Another account observed that in the middle of May a fire would burn slowly, if at all.

It was said that one of the Regulators was taken prisoner and as he tried to escape the governor personally shot him down. Reports of the killed and wounded vary. Probably around 25 were killed on both sides with 30 to 60 of both Regulators and militia wounded. The rebels battled boldly for about two hours, but were driven from the field. The militia advanced but finding the enemy dispersed, returned to their original encampment, where the wounded of both sides were humanely cared for, and the dead were buried.

The ceremonies of the day were concluded by the hanging of the prisoner, James Few. The Moravians reported,

> "A certain young man, a fine young fellow, had been captured, and when given the alternative of taking the oath or being hanged he chose the latter. The governor wished to spare his life, and twice urged him to submit. But the young man refused . . . . With the rope around his neck, he was urged to yield but refused, and the governor turned aside with tears in his eyes as the young man was swung into eternity."

The governor had regarded Few, Hunter and Husband as outlaws under the "Riot Act." However, he had not legally complied with all the rules required by the nefarious "Act". He tried later to justify this action by saying that he did it for his men, who needed this show against the leaders of the Regulators after so many of them had been killed and wounded.

The next day the wounded were sent to the plantation of Michael Holt with a surgeon and medicine. A proclamation had been issued granting pardon to all who should come into camp, surrender up their arms, take an oath of allegiance to the king and an oath of obligation to pay their taxes, and to support and defend the laws of the land. Exceptions were made of the outlaws, the prisoners taken, and some fourteen others. Many now accepted these terms and submitted.

The following day the army marched to James Hunter's and destroyed his dwelling and outhouses. Then they took possession of Herman Husband's plantation, where they found a "large parcel of treasonable paper." The Regulators continued to come in and take an oath, but the exceptions now included the "Black Boys," Thomas Person, and some others that they had previously omitted. The outlaws were Husband, Hunter, Howell and Butler, and on their heads a price was set. Heavy rains, which had begun on 20 May continued eight days, creating pleurisies.

The army remained a week at Sandy Creek, then passed to Deep River, and on 1 June was in the Jersey settlement—on 4 June, at Reedy Creek. General Waddell's force joined the main army, and they marched to Wachovia, where they remained several days, and at Salem on 6 June they celebrated the king's birthday and the victory of the 16th. During the march, the houses and plantations of those who were outlawed were laid waste and destroyed, and their owners fled from the province. The insurgents having been quieted on the Deep and the Haw, and information being received that they were rising to the south and west, General Waddell was detached on 8 June with some 500 men and artillery to move into that section and suppress them, while the governor began his return movement. He reached Hillsboro on the 14th, where the cattle and horses were turned on the plantation of William Few, the father of James Few.

The governor had kept the prisoners with him to parade them along the way. Now they were to stand trial at Hillsboro, where the courts were waiting with open arms. The trials began on 14 June and lasted until the 18th, when twelve prisoners were sentenced to death on the charge of high treason. Six were immediately executed. The records of the court were not preserved. Four of those executed were Benjamin Merrill, Robert Matear, Captain Messer and James Pugh. Six were reprieved and later pardoned by the king. The melancholy spectacle of the execution was accompanied by a military parade. The governor attended with the entire army, and caused all of the prisoners to be brought to witness it.

The people were completely subdued, their leaders fled or taken, and they continued to come in and ask pardon, so that by 19 June more than 3,000 had submitted to the government and taken the oath to pay their taxes and obey the laws which Governor Tryon had exacted of them. Later, when General Waddell had made his report, giving the result of his excursion into the southwestern part of the province, the entire number who had taken the oath was 6,400, and about 800 guns had been turned into the government. Disarmed and subjugated, but not pacified, many of the people moved from the province, some passing the mountains and finding homes in the forests of the Holstein settlement.

On 30 Jun 1771, Governor Tryon embarked for New York, where he arrived on 7 July and assumed the administration of that state. He carried with him the goodwill of the leading men of the eastern part of the province, who commended his bravery and courage. The cost of the expedition to Hillsboro was 60,000 pounds. Treasurer Ashe issued notes, which he announced would be received by him in payment of taxes. These notes circulated as currency, relieving a little of the monetary problem which had helped to create the problem in the first place.

Our ALLRED relations participated and signed petitions; but they were never listed with the leaders. Their property bordered Herman Husband's, and undoubtedly the full force of these events involved them in many ways, which will be further addressed in later chapters. Fanning went to New York with his friend Governor Tryon, where they found that discontent and independent thinking did not end with the North Carolina state line.

~ 66 ~

SUGAR, STAMPS AND POWER—
COASTAL AMERICA RETALIATES

Returning to the mid-1760s and the unrest in coastal America after the French and Indian War:

For the past thirty years, the "Molasses Act" had rested undisturbed in the legislative records of England. It required a duty of sixpence a gallon on imported molasses from the West Indies sugar islands into the American colonial ports where the rum was manufactured, especially in New England. This rate was so high that the rum manufacturers could not pay it, and the British government had winked an eye as the bulk of the molasses was smuggled in. Without an army, the law was unenforceable. Many of the more wealthy New Englanders had built their moderate fortunes on this premise.

As the English Parliament contemplated how to meet their huge war debt, the "Molasses Act" was resurrected. They realized the sixpence (currently about 12 U.S. cents) a gallon was excessive and decided to lower the duty. After debate, the Sugar Act of 1764 settled for threepence, and they thought they had sweetened the deal by proclaiming that all "revenue" brought in was specifically reserved "for defending, protecting, and securing" the British colonies in America. The colonies might have tolerated this, since the duty involved only a small portion of the influential colonists, among them STEPHEN HOPKINS, the elected governor of Rhode Island; however, Parliament added the following clause to the Act, "it may be proper to charge certain stamp duties in the said colonies and plantations."

The uncollectible sixpence of the past three decades was far less threatening to the colonists than the threepence that was earmarked to provide funds for an army to collect it and perhaps a more comprehensive stamp tax. Adding to this already combustible fuel, Parliament took away the right of the colonists to try the offenders and gave the jurisdiction to the vice admiralty courts of the British fleet, which at this time was located in Halifax, Nova Scotia. All the seized vessels and cargoes were to be sent all the way to Halifax. Ultimately, this cost the British more money than it took in.

Western expansion had been stopped with the British Proclamation of 1763 which gave the newly acquired territory to the Indians. The colonists longed for the good old days, before the Paris treaty. The first response came from Massachusetts, where a committee of the town of Boston sent instructions to their newly elected members of the Assembly on how to deal with the recent British measures, especially the forthcoming stamp tax. These instructions were drafted by Samuel Adams, who belonged to an old Boston family, going back to the early seventeenth century. His father was a man of "ample fortune" who operated a brewery and was actively engaged in local politics, finally succeeding in getting himself elected to the Massachusetts assembly. Sam had studied law at Harvard but never finished. He inherited the brewery and one-third of his father's property but lost most of it. In short, until he was over 40 years of age, he was a failure in everything but politics.

Adams's instructions included:

"For if our Trade may be taxed why not our Lands? Why not the Produce of our Lands & every thing we possess or make use of? This we apprehend annihilates our Charter Right to govern & tax ourselves—It strikes at our British Privileges, which as we have never forfeited them, we hold in common with our Fellow Subjects who are Natives of Britain: If Taxes are laid upon us in any shape without our having legal Representation where they are laid, are we not reduced from the Character of free Subjects to the miserable State of tributary Slaves?"

In June, the Massachusetts assembly took the initiative to form an all-colonies movement. It called upon all the other colonies to protest both the sugar duty and the prospective stamp tax—with the emphasis on representation.

A special session of Rhode Island assembly appointed a committee of correspondence to confer with the other colonies on measures to obtain a repeal of the Sugar Act and to prevent passage of the Stamp Act. Its agent in London was instructed "to do everything in his power, either alone or by joining with the agents of the other governments, to effect these purposes." Realizing that they could do little alone, in October 1764, the Rhode Island assembly sent the following message to the Secretary of the Connecticut assembly:

"If all the Colonies were disposed to enter with Spirit into the Defence of their Liberties; if some Method could be hit upon for collecting the Sentiments of each Colony, and for uniting and forming the Substance of them into one common Defence of the whole, and this sent to England, and the several Agents directed to join together in pushing and pursuing it there in the properest and most effectual Manner, it might be the most probable Method to produce the End aimed at."

The General Assembly of New York worded their complaints stating that it was improper

"to impose Taxes upon the Subjects here, by Laws to be passed there" as calculated to "reduce the Colonies to absolute Ruin." The "Exemption from the Burthen of ungranted, involuntary Taxes, must be the grand Principle of every free State.—Without such a Right vested in themselves, exclusive of all others, there can be no Liberty, no Happiness, no Security; it is inseparable from the very idea of Property, who can call that his own, which may be taken away at the Pleasure of another?"

Pamphlets were written and distributed among the colonies by James Otis, Thacher, and others. The last pamphlet, published towards the end of 1764, was the work of STEPHEN HOPKINS, the governor of Rhode Island. It read:

"British subjects are to be governed only agreeable to laws to which them- selves have some way consented, and are not to be compelled to part with their property but as it is called for by authority of such laws." Anything less amounted to "the miserable condition of slaves." The Crown, it con- tended, had always treated the colonies as "dependent, though free, but now the scene seems to be unhappily changing."

To change it back again, HOPKINS suggested a distinction be made be- tween "matters of a general nature," such as commerce and credit, and the par- ticular matter of taxation. For this reason, he proposed a division of labor be- tween Parliament and the colonial legislatures, the former to take charge of the concerns common to the entire British empire and the latter "to take care of its interest and provide for its peace and internal government." HOPKINS chose to "pass by" the question of Colonial representation in Parliament and merely asked that the colonies be given notice of every new measure that affected their rights, liberties, or interests.

HOPKINS objected to the molasses tax on practical grounds and argued that Rhode Island was peculiarly dependent on foreign molasses and its own distilleries. When it came to the stamp tax, however, he could hardly control his rhetoric:

> "For it must be confessed by all men that they who are taxed at pleasure by others cannot possibly have any property, can have nothing to be called their own. They who have no property can have no freedom, but are indeed reduced to the most abject slavery."

HOPKINS scoffed at the idea that

> "the people in Britain have a sovereign authority over their fellow subjects in America." The British empire was an "imperial state, which consists of many separate governments each of which hath peculiar privileges," so that "all laws and all taxations which bind the whole must be made by the whole," not by the British people alone. The House of Commons had acted by virtue of "mere superiority and power."

The colonies, he protested, had always raised money requested by the Crown; this was the only constitutional way. One of the most striking allusions went back to the conquest of Canada in the Seven Years' War:

> "Hard will be the fate, yea cruel the destiny, of these unhappy colonies if the reward they are to receive for all this is the loss of their freedom; better for them Canada still remained French, yea far more eligible that it ever should remain so than the price of its reduction should be their slavery."

Early in 1765, Martin Howard Jr., of Rhode Island, expressed an opposing view to the publications of STEPHEN HOPKINS and James Otis. Like the others, Howard was a lawyer. He charged HOPKINS as having claimed that

> "the House of Commons have not any sort of power over the Americans." Howard presented a number of arguments in rebuttal that were endlessly repeated in the years to come. It was "the essence of government that there should be a supreme head" in this case Parliament. It represented "every British subject, wheresoever he be."

It could levy taxes as well as regulate trade. James Otis answered Howard's charges thus:

> "Is it to be believed that when a continent of 3000 miles in length shall
> have more inhabitants than there are at this day in Great Britain, France,
> and Ireland, perhaps in all Europe, they will be quite content with the bare
> name of British subjects, and to the end of time supinely acquiesce in laws
> made, as it may happen, against their interest by an assembly 3000 miles
> beyond sea . . . [or] that an admission of an American member would 'sully
> and defile the purity of the whole body'? One hundred years will give this
> continent more inhabitants than there are in the three kingdoms."

But Otis soon began to realize that others were seeking independence, not
representation in parliament. He softened his comments. Others came forward:
Delany of Maryland and Dickinson of Pennsylvania.

The ideological pamphlets of 1764-65 were not matched in quantity or
quality until 1774, the eve of the Revolution. Dickinson produced another out-
standing pamphlet in 1768, but he was never forgiven for refusing to sign the
Declaration of Independence. The great controversialists of 1764-65 were, with
few exceptions, unable to keep up with the onrushing revolutionary tide. Otis
slid behind in 1765. Fitch, after 11 years as governor of Connecticut, was defeated in 1766 and died a loyalist. Thacher died in 1765. Dulany dropped out
of active opposition to British rule and went through the Revolutionary War a
neutral. Only Governor HOPKINS of Rhode Island did not falter throughout
the revolutionary struggle.

In the summer of 1765 the battle of words moved into actions. A Boston
group, known as the Loyal Nine, would later, with increased numbers, be called
the Sons of Liberty. The Boston Nine included two distillers, two braziers or
brass fabricators, a house painter, a printer, a shipmaster and a jeweler. The
most prominent among them was John Avery Jr., the distiller or merchant, and
Benjamin Edes, the co-printer of the Boston Gazette, the paper to which James
Otis, Samuel Adams, and other radical figures contributed. A second group in
Boston was the ideological lawyers, which included the Adams brothers. Then
there was a third group. Its leader was Ebenezer Mackintosh, a fourth-generation
descendant of Scottish prisoners sent to the colonies by Oliver Cromwell. He
was a shoemaker by trade, but had molded his South End street fighters into a
disciplined, semimilitary organization. At the birthday celebration of the Prince

of Wales on 12 August, the Loyal Nine met and decided to have their own celebration two days later by staging a political protest—the hanging of two effigies
representing their locally appointed future stamp distributor, Andrew Oliver,
and the British minister they considered to be most responsible. 14 Aug 1765,
the effigies were hung from a big tree near the entrance of Boston. Orders were
given to take them down; but they remained there all day and in the evening they
were taken down by the instigators and carried at the head of a march through
the town. The mood turned ugly as the marchers, which included Mackintosh
and his South End street fighters, turned into a violent mob. They destroyed the
building they felt the stamps would be distributed from, and shouting "Liberty,
Property and No Stamps!" they continued on their way to Oliver's home, which
they severely damaged. They next proceeded to Lieutenant Governor Thomas
Hutchinson's dwelling, which escaped with little damage as a neighbor mistak-
enly reported to them that he was not at home. Oliver resigned as stamp distributor the next day.

Two days later the mob met again, this time destroying Hutchinson's home
and several others. Governor Francis Bernard fled to the fort at Castle William.
He wrote the next day to general Thomas Gage in New York,

> "The Mob was so general & so supported, that all civil power ceased in an
> instant, & I had not the least authority to oppose or quiet the Mob . . . .
> The Town of Boston is in possession of an incensed & implacable Mob; I
> have no force to oppose them; I know not whether I shall be able to pre-
> serve this Castle, which is threatened to be attacked, if the stamped papers
> from England should be, as is designed, placed here. The Garrison, when
> Compleat, amounts but to 60 men; & I dare not reenforce them out of the
> Country, for fear it should be the Means of betraying the place."

Mackintosh was arrested, charged with having led the mob in destruction
of Hutchinson's house, and discharged without a trial. Others were jailed but
Hutchinson wrote,

> "in the dead of night, a large number of men entered the house of the prison
> keeper; compelled him to deliver the keys, opened the prison doors; and
> set every man free who had been committed for this offence."

Bernard offered a reward of 300 pounds for information leading to the arrest of the actual leaders, but no one came forward, although hundreds must

have known who they were.

The violence was contagious. Newport, Rhode Island, followed Boston. Samuel Ward, the governor of Rhode Island was the only Colonial governor who refused to take the oath to enforce the Stamp Act. In 1775, in the Continental Congress, he was made Chairman of the Committee of the Whole, which from 1774 to 1776 sat daily, working without intermission in the cause of independence, but he was not privileged to sign the Declaration of Independence. John Adams says of him:

> "When he was seized with the smallpox he said that if his vote and voice were necessary to support the cause of his country, he should live; if not, he should die. He died, and the cause of his country was supported, but it lost one of its most sincere and punctual advocates."

[Note: Governor Ward's great-grandfather John Ward of Gloucester, England, was a cavalry officer in Cromwell's army. He came to this country after Charles II was restored on the throne—settling in Newport, Rhode Island. His son Thomas married Amy Smith, a granddaughter of Roger Williams.. Thomas's son Richard became Govenor of Rhode Island and had fourteen children, among them Samuel.]

In October 1765, two months after the Boston incidence, 2,000 people gathered in New York harbor to prevent the landing of stamps, but were outwitted by the British who waited until night, when the crowd had dispersed, to bring them ashore. Governor William Franklin of New Jersey informed his father, Benjamin Franklin, who was in London, that

> "it is said the Presbyterians of N. England have wrote to all their Brethren throughout the Continent, to endeavor to stir up the Inhabitants of each Colony to act as they have done, in hopes of thereby making it appear to the Ministry too difficult a Matter to call them to account for their late outrageous Conduct."

As the discontent spread throughout the colonies, no blood was shed, in part because the protestors did not meet with any opposition: governors fled to their forts, stamp collectors quickly resigned, and the British military was not prepared. General Thomas Gage had only 15 regiments available to him, which were spread throughout the areas which had formerly belonged to France. Previously, there had been no need for a display of force within the American colonies. Most colonists still thought they were protesting the Stamp Act; but the general feeling in the British ministry was that it went much deeper.

Benjamin Franklin in London tried to allay these fears and worked for peace. In America an initiative came from Massachusetts in June 1765, three months after the Stamp Act's final passage through Parliament and five months before it was slated to become effective. This initiative proposed the meeting of representatives from all the colonies in New York on 1 October, to consult together on the problems facing them.

This Stamp Act Congress met in New York from 7 Oct to 25 Oct 1765. It was attended by twenty-seven delegates from nine of the thirteen colonies. In the group were ten lawyers, ten merchants, and seven landowners. All were men of considerable property and high social position. They drew up three carefully worded documents—an address to King George III, a memorial to the House of Lords, and a petition to Parliament. The documents objected to the Stamp Act, the Proclamation of 1763 that prohibited settlement beyond the Allegheny Mountains to the Mississippi River, the Sugar Act of 1764, and the new vice admiralty court of Halifax. Still, they considered themselves to be loyal British subjects.

The merchants were very successful men who had carried on large-scale export and import business with the British and foreign markets. They owned their own ships and sent them anywhere in the world to buy, sell, or exchange cargoes. They had made fortunes during the Seven Years' War. In a sense they were a "mercantile aristocracy." They had close family ties, as their children often married into the family of another merchant. The landowners had vast tracts of land, not a small country farm. The ideological lawyers worked for these merchants. In London, the Americans had a formidable lobby of provincial agents, many of whom were British merchants. They threatened to cut off the very important American trade with England. It might be said that there were great personal economic reasons for this meeting in New York of the Stamp Act Congress; however, it never hurt to have economic interest coincide with political correctness—especially if funds and prestige were needed to support and unite the cause. These merchants at the congress were headed by ROBERT R. LIVINGSTON of New York, who had close family ties to the RENSSELAER and COOL families along the Hudson River.

This unprecedented political activity by the American merchants and lawyers was probably one of the greatest achievements in the prerevolutionary period of time. It crowned a movement that had developed with unusual speed. In a very short time and with little organization or planning, the Americans had proved themselves capable of: formulating a political program and platform; producing resolutions and pamphlets; bringing out mobs and rioters; creating a secret, militant organization—the Sons of Liberty; holding a congress to address the British government; organizing a mass boycott of British goods, and uniting the social strata from the lowest to the most elite in a common ideological cause.

In England, Lord Grenville complained about "giving birth to sedition in America" as being directed against him personally. Pitt followed these remarks with one of his most splendid defenses of American liberty:

> "The gentleman tells us, America is obstinate; America is almost in open rebellion. I rejoice that America has resisted. Three millions of people, so dead to all the feelings of liberty, as voluntarily to submit to be slaves, would have been fit instruments to make slaves of the rest." He went on, however, to say that parliament had their rights, too, and suggested the following be done: "It is, that the Stamp Act be repealed absolutely, totally, and immediately . . . because it was founded on an erroneous principle. At the same time, let the sovereign authority of this country over the colonies, be asserted in as strong terms as can be devised . . . that we may bind their trade, confine their manufactures, and exercise every power whatsoever, except that of taking their money out of their pockets without their consent."

And Parliament proceeded and did just that by enacting the Townshend Duties.

Northern Theater of Operations

THE POWER STRUGGLE CONTINUES—
THOSE REBEL AMERICANS

In April 1766, after the repeal of the Stamp Act, the American merchants were the honored guests of a "City feast" in London. The "Annual Register" reported,

> "The company last Wednesday at Draper's hall was very numerous, and the most brilliant almost ever seen in the city of London. It is said there were about 240 who dined, amongst whom were nine Dukes, and a very considerable number more of the nobility, and the members of the House of Commons, who honored the American merchants with their company."

In America, the colonists celebrated and built statues of William Pitt, while British merchants, manufacturers, ship captains with crews, ironworkers, shoemakers, window-glass makers and others who had been dependent on sales to the American colonies returned triumphantly to their work. They felt they had been saved from a devastating ruin. The Pennsylvania ambassador in London, Benjamin Franklin, hoped it was true—he was also the toast of London—and he with others hoped for the return to the status quo they had enjoyed before the war with the French and Indians.

But a major change had occurred. The Americans had flexed their economic muscles and found a weakness in their opponent. The threepence duty on imported molasses was reduced to one pence per gallon. However, the British still felt that the colonists should pay for the British soldiers which were sent to aid in the defense of their frontiers against French and Spanish colonists and the Indians.

Parliament came up with the Quartering Act in 1765, which required the colonial assemblies to provide and furnish quarters for British troops. The New York Assembly felt they were being asked to bear a disproportionate share of this burden with General Gage's headquarters and supporting troops stationed there. Many refused to submit, stating "we find it impossible to comply with what is now demanded." Noncompliance became the escape for the disagreeable laws, which would include the Townshend Acts. Pamphlets and letters began again. The wealthy Dickinson of Pennsylvania wrote:

> "These duties, which will inevitably be levied upon us—which are now levying upon us—are expressly laid *for the sole purpose of taking money*. This is the true definition of 'taxes' . . . . We are taxed without our own consent, expressed by ourselves or our representatives. We are therefore—slaves!"

When British chief minister Charles Townshend died in September 1767, his successor was Frederick North. He made political changes in the House of Commons and the Earl of Hillsborough, who had been Grenville's president of the Board of Trade, became the first Secretary of State for the colonies. Hillsborough remarked to Benjamin Franklin that Dickinson's Letters were "extremely wild." The political climate in London was shifting and the American rebels were becoming bolder. But still the desire to reconcile their differences prevailed throughout most of the colonies.

The full change came in January 1768, when North replaced Conway as leader of the House of Commons. Benjamin Franklin delayed his return home in order to get the repeal of the Townshend duties. He became increasingly more pessimistic. Both sides were prisoners of principles so often avowed that they could not retreat from them now. The Massachusetts Assembly lead in the anti-Townshend Acts movement, followed all through 1768 by the Assemblies of Virginia, New Hampshire, Rhode Island, Connecticut, New York, New Jersey, and Pennsylvania assemblies. Another united front was forming and only waiting for some provocative action on either side.

One of the most cherished colonial freedoms had been the freedom to smuggle. On 10 Jun 1768, the *Liberty*, a vessel owned by John Hancock, was seized by custom officers. John Hancock was considered the richest merchant in Boston and had inherited a large portion of his fortune from his father—both had been suspected of smuggling. The seized vessel was taken near a British warship, the

Romney, which had recently arrived in Boston harbor. A mob gathered onshore and attacked the customs officers, "not without wounds and bruises & a narrow escape with life," forcing them to flee to the Boston fort, Castle William—according to the report of Governor Bernard of Massachusetts.

Two British regiments were moved from Halifax to Boston. Gage was concerned that the British authorities might not approve of strong enough measures, and he implored them that they must

> "effectively quell the Spirit of Sedition, which has so long and so greatly prevailed here, and bring the People back to a Sense of their Duty . . . and . . . reduce them to their Constitutional Dependence, on the Mother Country."

In Boston, every effort was being made to prevent the quartering of troops from Halifax; but by early November, Gage reported that in six months the troops had restored peace and quiet in Boston.

However, Sam Adams had new fuel for insurrection. He contributed the following to the *Boston Gazette*:

> "Can any one be surprized, that when property was violently seized, under a pretence of law . . . by the aid of military power, a power ever dreaded by all the lovers of peace and good order . . . is it surprizing that such ill-timed, violent and unheard of proceedings, should excite the resentment even of the better sort of people in town? . . . In such Circumstances, while they have the spirit of freedom, they will boldly assert their freedom . . . . They are in the right of it to complain, and *complain aloud*. And they will complain, till they are redress'd, or become poor deluded miserable ductile Dupes, fitted to be made the slaves of dirty tools of arbitrary power."

Colonial imports from Great Britain fell to about half in 1769. The Americans hoped to boycott the goods until the duties were taken off. George Washington, one of the prime motivators in Virginia, thought that nonimportation was going to also encourage local manufactures and decrease the Colonial indebtedness to Great Britain. In 1765, STEPHEN HOPKINS had struck a similar note from Providence, Rhode Island, which was particularly hit bad at that time by the duty on molasses:

> "The genius of the people in these colonies is as little turned to manu-
> facturing goods for their own use as is possible to suppose in any people

whatsoever; yet necessity will compel them either to go naked in this cold country or to make themselves some sort of clothing, if it be only the skins of beasts." He had gone so far as to say, "Better for them Canada still remained French, yea far more eligible that it ever should remain so than that the price of its reduction should be slavery."

But the anti-Townshend movement was individualistic with each colony going off on its own. The merchants in Boston, New York, and Philadelphia had different interests. When New York dropped out in mid-1770, the movement began to fall apart. George Mason, neighbor of George Washington, realized that the fault had been with their lack of organization and a general plan. Benjamin Franklin saw that the British were caught in a quandary. They did not want the Townshend duties anymore, but they did not want to get rid of them to please the Americans.

The British garrison in Boston in early 1770 numbered 600, of whom only 400 could be used effectively. The civilian population numbered 16,000, according to Hiller B. Zobel, *The Boston Massacre*. He tells us that the British had enough troops in Boston to stir up strong resentment but not enough to contain it if it overflowed into violence. The British soldiers were not well paid and often took casual off-duty jobs to supplement their meager pay.

On 2 Mar 1770, private Patrick Walker walked by John Gray's rope works and the following dialogue precipitated what has become known as the Boston Massacre. The individuals by the name of GREEN and PRESTON might have been distantly related to our ancestors; but if so, I am not, as yet, aware of any connection.

"Soldier, do you want work?" asked ropemaker William Green.

"Yes, I do, faith," said Walker.

"Well," said Green, in a triumph of ready wit, "then go and clean my shithouse."

"Empty it yourself," said Walker.

After more similar exchanges, Walker swore that he would have revenge and swung wildly at the ropemakers. Nicholas Ferriter, a one-day employee, disarmed Walker. Humiliated, the soldier fled. In a few moments he was back, reinforced by eight or nine other soldiers. They were commanded by Captain

Thomas Preston. Someone, not Preston, shouted, "Fire!" and shots rang out from the outnumbered soldiers. Three townspeople died, two others were so badly wounded that they later died. Nine soldiers, including Captain Preston, were arrested and jailed. Within days, the Boston radicals had a pamphlet out, *A Short Narrative of the Horrid Massacre in Boston.* Boston was not the same. The two regiments were quickly moved to the island in the harbor—Castle William.

John Adams, Josiah Quincy Jr., and another lawyer defended Captain Preston at his trial in November 1770. In the still charged atmosphere, they were able to show that Preston had not ordered the troops to fire, and he was found not guilty. Six of the other soldiers on trial received the same verdict, and two more were released on a technicality. This was a triumph for the colonial lawyers who were willing to defend the British. But blood had been shed, and the question of who was right or wrong was lost in the minds of the colonists, who remembered it only as the *Boston Massacre!* And it has been nurtured as such ever since.

In January 1770, Lord North replaced Grafton as the formal head of the British government. He would remain in this position for the next twelve years. North encouraged the repealing of all the Townshend duties with the exception of the one on tea. Tea became the British stand for maintaining the last shred of British power to collect money from their American colonies. The colonies did not rebel against the duty on tea because it was so arduous; they rebelled against it because it had come to be viewed as a tax. England's parliament, in the colonial view, had the right to tax England, but not the American colonies who each had their own assemblies. Sam Adams spoke strongly against parliament and the king. Benjamin Franklin in London blamed parliament, but not the king. His feelings were more conciliatory. His son, William Franklin, was appointed by the British as governor of New Jersey. Benjamin's attitude may have delayed the revolution another five years, as the colonists tried to negotiate with the king instead of parliament for their rights. And tea continued to be smuggled in to avoid the duty.

During this period of political unrest, my direct northern American ancestors were in western New Jersey and across the Delaware River in Pennsylvania. ELISHA BARTON, with his father NOAH BARTON, had left Westchester

County, New York, for New Jersey. ELISHA had married JEMIMA VAN KIRK, daughter of the Dutchman HENRY VAN KIRK and DOROTHY MORGAN. They were living in Hunterdon County, New Jersey.

Also living in Hunterdon County was JOHN COOLEY who had left his Dutch cousins along the Hudson River and married ABIGAIL LIPPINCOTT the daughter of the Quakers SAMUEL LIPPINCOTT of New Jersey and MARY PRESTON, of Philadelphia.

JOSEPH WILKINSON of Hunterdon, New Jersey, and his brother JOHN WILKINSON of Bucks, Pennsylvania, cousins of STEPHEN and ESEK HOPKINS, had married daughters of the LACEY brothers, who owned the iron mill on the Delaware River near what would later be known as Washington's Crossing.

JOHN WILKINSON, the son of JOHN Sr., became a member of the Provincial Assembly in 1761 and 1762, and the magistrate of Bucks County in 1764. Although he was a Quaker, he took sides with the colonies. He became one of the deputies to the Provincial conference of 15 Jul 1774, a member of the convention of 15 Jul 1776, and represented Bucks County in the Assembly in 1776, 1781, and 1782. During the Revolution, he took an important part in the military affairs of his locality. He was known as Colonel JOHN WILKINSON and became involved in the Pennsylvania conventions.

THOMAS CANBY, also a Quaker, was the grandfather-in-law of BETSY ROSS, who is credited with making the first flag for the United States of America.

French descent JOSEPH POYER was either in Canada—perhaps at Sorel or Fort Chambley, near Montreal, or along the Hudson River, east of Ploughkeepsie in Dutchess County, New York.

In the south the IVIEs, originally from the Norfolk peninsula and the James River, were in southeast Virginia near the North Carolina border. Across this North Carolina border and further west were the ALLREDs, THRASHERs, McKEEs, and the more recent arrivals, the FAUCETTs—French Huguenots who had earlier fled to Ireland. In this area of North Carolina during the early 1770s, the less trumpeted War of the Regulators was taking place.

— 68 —

AWAKE! AWAKE, MY COUNTRYMEN!

Governor Tryon, formerly of North Carolina, did not remain long in New York before he felt the need to return to England where he advocated leniency for the colonies. Perhaps his recent participation in the War of the Regulators was bothering his conscience; more likely, he realized the unrest of the colonists in a broader sense. In Boston, it mattered very little that the exchange of insults between a colonial ropemaker and a British private in March 1770 had set off a chain of events that resulted in a colonial mob attack on a British sentry, and that British Captain John Preston and his men had been acquitted by a colonial jury of any fault in the resultant death of several Bostonians. The facts were submerged in the shouts and orations that proclaimed it as "The Boston Massacre!," which was commemorated annually in Boston from 1771 to 1783. In 1771, James Lovell, a prominent schoolmaster, proclaimed

> "Make the bloody 5th of March the aera of the resurrection of your birthrights which have been murdered by the very strength that nursed them in infancy."

In 1772, Dr. Joseph Warren gave the commemorative oration. He was a Harvard graduate and practiced medicine in Boston where he soon joined politically with some of his patients: Samuel and John Adams, James Otis, John Hancock and others. He declared:

> "Awake! Awake, my countrymen, and by a regular and legal opposition, defeat the designs of those who would enslave us and our posterity." Then he directed "the destruction of property, tarring and feathering, and intimidation" of the British or British sympathizers. He cried out against the "ruinous consequences of standing armies . . . the ready engines of tyranny and oppression." He recalled the day in 1770 "when our streets were

stained with the blood of our brethren—when our ears were wounded by the groans of the dying, and our eyes were tormented with the sight of the mangled bodies of the dead . . . . The voice of your fathers' blood cries to you from the ground, my sons scorn to be slaves! . . . May our land be a land of liberty, the seat of virtue, the asylum of the oppressed, a name and a praise to the whole earth, until the last shock of time shall bury the empires of the world in one common undistinguished ruin!"

British governors felt helpless against such rhetoric, and as these words arrived in London, the meaning could not escape even the more sympathetic.

In May 1773, British Parliament passed a Tea Act to rescue the East India Company from threatened bankruptcy. It was felt that five-sixths of the tea consumed in Massachusetts had been illegally smuggled into the colony and nine-tenths in Philadelphia and New York. The British planned to undersell the smugglers, drive out the Dutch competition, and benefit the American consumers. But they had underestimated the smuggling business in America, which

"was so universal, that the Smugglers Interest had engrossed so great a Power . . . it would have required ten British soldiers to protect every chest of tea." New York merchants warned that the smugglers were "a formidable body among the merchants, and will of themselves be able to raise a considerable mob, including a great number of retainer, such as boatmen, longshoremen, etc. who are all paid highly for their services."

And, of course, there was still a duty on tea. British Minister Lord North stated,

"Teas may be exported cheap enough to find a market in America, and preserve the duty. You will find a market in America, and preserve the duty. You will have your market and your revenue."

News of the Tea Act reached the colonies in October 1773. Meetings of merchants were held in New York and they spread the word and the unrest. What had started as a protest against the East India Company turned into a wide-spread revolt against paying any duty on tea. The opposition to the Tea Act might have been strong or weak; but the opposition to slavery (as the merchants chose to consider their position) could not be strong enough in the minds of the Americans. On 16 Dec 1773, at Long Wharf in Boston the planned "Tea Party" took place with between thirty and sixty men participating and as many as 2,000 people watching. The British stayed at Castle William at the entrance to Boston harbor, not choosing to add more flame to the fire. Shortly after, New York brewed their tea in their harbor, also.

In London, Boston was considered by Lord North as

"the ringleader of all violence and opposition . . . Boston has not only therefore to answer for its own violence but for having incited other places to tumults . . . They deny our legislative authority . . . . We must control them or submit to them . . . . Whatever may be the consequence, we must risk something; if we do not, all is over."

They closed Boston harbor, and in May 1774, replaced Governor Hutchinson with General Thomas Gage, who was to enforce this action and dissolve the Boston legislature. Bostonians called on the other colonies for help and in mid-June 1774, the decision was made to hold the proposed congress in Philadelphia on 1 September. All the colonies except Georgia voted to attend. Meanwhile 4,000 people marched into Cambridge and surrounded the house of Lt. Gov. Thomas Oliver of Massachusetts demanding his resignation. At first he refused; but finally broke down and wrote under their petition,

"My house being surrounded with four thousand people, in compliance with their commands I sign my name Tho. Oliver."

When the First Continental Congress met on 5 Sep 1774, there were sixty-four delegates present. Among those present were John Adams and Samuel Adams of Massachusetts; PHILIP LIVINGSTON and ROBERT R. LIVINGSTON of New York; STEPHEN HOPKINS of Rhode Island; John Dickinson and Joseph Galloway (Benjamin Franklin's former close associate) of Pennsylvania; Patrick Henry, Richard Henry Lee, Peyton Randolph and George Washington from Virginia. Young Thomas Jefferson was not a delegate; but he submitted a number of resolutions intended as instructions to the delegation. The proceedings were to be kept secret, for such an assembly was not approved by their mother country, Great Britain. Undoubtedly some of their words were disloyal if not treason. Letters and journals by the delegates have since been read and a fair consensus of the debates is known. Joseph Galloway presented a plan of reconciliation with Great Britain somewhat similar to Benjamin Franklin's plan of 1754. It was first favorably assented to by many of the delegates, including STEPHEN HOPKINS, who had participated somewhat in Benjamin Franklin's 1754 plan. However, Patrick Henry and Richard Henry Lee spoke strongly against it, which changed the whole tone of the congress and Galloway's plan was voted down and expunged from the record without delicacy. Joseph Galloway, along with Benjamin's son William Franklin, then governor or New Jersey—who agreed with Galloway—would later break their friendship with Benjamin Franklin when he returned from England and expressed his strong stand for independence. Both Joseph Galloway and William Franklin remained strong loyalists.

Congress adopted a nonimportation agreement to Great Britain beginning 1 Dec 1774. They halted all exports to Great Britain, Ireland, and the West Indies as of 10 Sep 1775. They set up an "Association" to enforce the economic sanctions against Great Britain and then decided to reconvene on 10 May 1775, if their grievances were not redressed by that time. They sent addresses to various groups, including King George. In general, they defended Massachusetts, denounced parliament, encouraged the inhabitants of the Province of Quebec to send delegates to the Second Continental Congress, and they still expressed a loyalty to King George.

British General Gage in Boston harbor wanted more troops sent. He was told,

> "The State of this Kingdom will not admit of our sending more Troops from Great Britain."

He was to depend upon his "fortitude & discretion" to deal with "the present critical situation of The King's Affairs in North America, and more particularly in New England." Gage returned the following ominous message,

> "The people would cool, was not means taken to keep up their enthusiasm. Truths or falsehoods equally serve the purpose for they are so besotted to one side that they will not believe or even hear what is said to convince them of their errors." Then he reported that a "secret determination," to be put into effect at the Second Continental Congress in 1775, "to form a complete government as they can and to have, as they say, a vast army in the field in the spring at the continental expense."

By this time, the British were getting alarming reports of arms being imported, although they had been prohibited. Word came to the British of "large quantities of Gunpowder exported from Holland to North America." and of "Americans purchasing large Quantities of Arms and Ammunition in the different Ports of Europe. The people of Rhode-Island have used the precaution to remove the powder, cannon, and other military stores from the fort at Newport, into the country. The people at Portsmouth, in New Hampshire, have done the like by their cannon and other military stores at the fort at New Castle, at the entrance of their harbour."

So, by the end of 1774, King George stated, "the dye is now cast." Still neither side wanted the responsibility of a hot war. And still, neither side wanted to show weakness in the face of the other's perseverance. As usual in such national disagreements, they spoke of peace and prepared for war.

[Note: ALEXANDER HAMILTON was born on Nevis, one of the British Virgin Islands in the Caribbean, but was brought up on the Danish island of St. Croix. His mother was RACHEL, whose mother was MARY FAUCETT, the daughter of a French physician—expelled from France with the other Huguenots. His father was James Hamilton, a ne'er-do-well Scotch soldier with a title. They were not married. Given into a loveless marriage by her father, she evidently was indiscreet, and her husband divorced her. Under the Dutch law, she was prohibited from a second marriage. RACHEL recognized early that her son was precocious. Through her persistence, the island unitedly sent her son to school in New York when he was twelve (or fifteen) years old. My ancestral tie, other than that our ancestral FAUCETTs were also French Huguenots who were expelled from France about the same time, was his later marriage to distant cousin ELIZABETH SCHUYLER, the daughter of general PHILIP SCHUYLER and his wife CATHERINE RENNSELAER. The stigma of his birth never left him. Long after HAMILTON's death, the aging John Adams referred to him in a letter to Thomas Jefferson as that "bastard Bratt of a Scotch Pedlar."]

Young ALEXANDER HAMILTON was admitted to King's College (predecessor of Columbia and now New York University) in the spring of 1774. At the age of seventeen, after only a few months of college, he began his political career as one of the revolutionary pamphleteers. In his first pamphlet he claimed to know what was behind the British insistence on maintaining the tax on tea. It was to enable the British House of Commons to have complete control over American lives and properties. He scorned any other.

"How ridiculous then it is to affirm, that we are quarreling for the trifling sum of three pence a pound on tea; when it is evidently the principle against which we contend." He later gave a deeper motive. "Jealousy would concur with selfishness; and for fear of the future independence of America, if it should be permitted to rise to too great a height of splendor and opulence, every method would be taken to drain it of its wealth and restrain its prosperity. We are already suspected of aiming at independence, and that is one principal cause of the severity we experience. The same cause will always operate against us, and produce an uniform severity of treatment."

In the end, HAMILTON did not want war. He was committed to the First Continental Congress and their decision on economic measures only—nonimportation and nonexportation. HAMILTON believed that Great Britain could not withstand them. America could not lose. The enemy was parliament!

The colonists of Massachusetts would not sit still and wait. With their port closed, their legislature dissembled, their government moved to Salem, and with 2,500 British troops in their Boston harbor, patience was not in their plans. While general Gage resided in Salem, Percy took command of the British troops in Boston on 5 Jul 1774. Before arriving in Boston, Percy wrote his father in England saying,

> "Surely the People of Boston are not Mad enough to think of opposing us." By August 1774 he wrote, "The people here are a set of sly, artful, hypocritical rascals, cruel, & cowards. I must own I cannot but despise them completely." Towards the end of November 1774, he felt that "nothing can secure the Colonies to the Mother Country, but the Conquest of them. The People here are the most designing, Artfull Villains in the World. They have not the least Idea of either Religion or Morality. Nor have they the least Scruple of taking the most solemn Oath on any Matter that can assist their Purpose, tho' they know the direct contrary can be clearly & evidently proved in half an Hour."

General Gage was prudent enough to know that his troops were not sufficient to control a land war and begged for thousands more; however, Lord Dartmouth of London insisted that he do something to show strength with those he already had. Percy urged him on and the taking of the colonist's ammunition arsenal at Concord, Massachusetts, became their objective—as well as the capture of revolutionaries Sam Adams and John Hancock.

On Tuesday evening 18 Apr 1775 at ten o'clock there was a knock on the door of Paul Revere's house on Boston's North Square. The unknown messenger whispered the name "Dr. Warren." Tall, fair, and blue-eyed Dr. Joseph Warren was thirty-four years old and rather handsome. He probably was only out-ranked as a colonial political leader by Samuel Adams and John Hancock. He was a good doctor, and extremely popular with the 15,000 residents of Boston. Paul Revere had been a close friend of the doctor for several years. They had both put on their Mohawk garb and heaved the tea into Boston harbor. They had both attended the unauthorized Provincial Congress of Massachusetts the previous Saturday. They had both returned to Boston, while Sam Adams and John Hancock, fearing a British arrest, had remained at the home of a kinsman, the Rev. Jonas Clark in Lexington, where they planned to remain until the Second Continental Congress met in May. With the messengers summons, Paul Revere journeyed quickly to the home of his friend Dr. Joseph Warren in Boston.

At Dr. Warren's, Revere recalled,

> "Dr. Warren . . . begged that I would immediately set off for Lexington, where Messrs. Hancock and Adams were, and acquaint them of the movement and that it was thought they were the objects . . . I found he had sent an express by land to Lexington, a Mr. William Dawes . . . [as an afterthought, he told him to alert the countryside.] I left Dr. Warren, called upon a friend and desired him to make the signals. [Which had been previously agreed upon—one if by land and two if by sea from the tower of the old North Church.]

> "I then went home, took my boots and surtout, went to the north part of the town, where I had kept a boat. Two friends rowed me across Charles River, a little to the eastward where the 'Somerset' man-of-war lay. It was then young flood, the ship was winding, and the moon rising.
>
> "They landed me on the Charlestown side. When I got into town I met Colonel Conant and several others. They said they had seen our signals. I told them what was acting and went to get me a horse. I got a horse of Deacon [John] Larkin. While the horse was preparing, Richard Devens, Esquire, who was one of the Committee of Safety, came to me and told me that he came down the road from Lexington after sundown that evening, that he met ten British officers, all well mounted and armed, going up the road."

The old North Church is still standing. The streets are very narrow, and the surrounding buildings very close together. We dropped Troy off to get the best picture he could of the tower—August 2001.

They had asked Devens where "Clark's tavern" was—leading Revere to suspect that they knew Adams and Hancock were at Clark's, but not knowing that it was a parsonage. Riding quickly through Charlestown, Revere went left on the short road through

Cambridge to Lexington. Suddenly, Revere saw two shadowy horsemen ahead. He recognized their British holsters and cockades. One started towards him while the other trotted up the road to head him off. Revere spun short about, raked his horse's flanks, and

"road a full gallop for Mystic Road." Over his shoulder he saw his pursuer's heavy charger stumble into a clay pond. "I got clear of him," Revere continued, "and went through Medford, over the bridge, and up to Menotomy. In Medford I awaked the captain of the minutemen. And after that I alarmed almost every house till I got to Lexington."

Adams and Hancock had previously received Devens' warning that a British patrol was heading toward Lexington and perhaps Concord, so they sent warning to Concord and posted nine minutemen around the parsonage as a guard; then they retired with instructions to Sergeant Munroe of the minutemen not to disturb them with any noise in the yard. When Revere trotted up and was rebuffed by the sergeant he shouted,

"Noise! You'll have noise enough before long. The regulars are coming out!"

Inside, John Hancock heard Revere's voice and called out,

"Come in, Revere. We are not afraid of you!"

Young Hancock was the wealthiest man in New England and, in contrast, fifty-two year old Samuel Adams actually despised money for the overbearing it gave those who possessed it. Hancock wanted to arm himself and fight the British. Adams didn't want to lose his wealthy and popular companion before he accomplished his long fought-for political position. They were both representatives to the Second Continental Congress. They were still debating when Dr. Warren's other messenger, William Dawes, arrived from Boston. Quickly, the two couriers resumed their journey to Concord. They were joined by Dr. Samuel Prescott of Concord, who had been courting Miss Milliken in Lexington.

About halfway between Lexington and Concord,

"the other two stopped at a house to awake the man. I kept along." said Revere. "When I had got about two hundred yards ahead of them, I saw two officers under a tree . . . . In an instant I saw four officers, who rode up to me with their pistols in their hands, and said . . . . 'If you go an inch further, you are a dead man!' . . . Dr. Prescott came up . . . we attempted to get through them, they . . . swore if we did not turn into that pasture, they would blow our brains out . . . . When we got in Dr. Prescott said to me, 'Put on!'. . . He . . . took a left, I turned to the right . . . towards a wood, intending when I had gained . . . that to jump my horse and run afoot."

The doctor, who knew the ground, jumped his horse over the low stone wall of the pasture and headed safely for Concord. William Dawes also escaped. Paul Revere was not that fortunate.

"Just as I reached it, out started six officers, seized my bridle, put their pistols to my breast, ordered me to dismount, which I did."

They questioned him. He told them his name and then informed them that the British would

"miss their aim," because he had alarmed "the country all the way up" from Boston.

Hoping to gain time and perhaps release, he lied that the British boats had run aground; by the time the delayed troops reached Lexington, he warned, five hundred men would fall upon them. This agitated the British, who had already collected four other countrymen who were riding in the night.

"We rode toward Lexington . . . . I was insulted by the officers . . . . When we got within about half a mile of the Lexington Meeting House, we heard a gun fired. The major asked me what . . . that was for. I told him to alarm the country."

The major, hoping to lose no time in joining and informing the advancing British troops, ordered the girths and bridles on the four countrymen's horses to be cut and the horses driven afield, and told the men to go home afoot. A little further, the sergeant's horse became tired. He appropriated Deacon Larkin's horse from Revere, and Revere was left to find his way on foot back to Jonas Clark's house, where he found Messrs. Hancock and Adams, whom he helped to find refuge in another home a distance away.

Revere's alert had brought Captain John Parker and his minutemen from their warm beds to the Lexington Common located in front of Buckman's Tavern to "consult what to do." Their consensus was that they were not strong enough to confront the British Army; however, they would try to protect their women and children, if the redcoats were to threaten them in any way. They had sent riders to spy on the British. Boston was 16 miles away. None had returned. It was a cold and clear night. They stamped their feet and blew on their stiff fingers. After about an hour of this, Captain Parker decided Revere was wrong and dismissed his troops, but warned them that they should assemble at the sound of the drum.

Earlier that evening, Lord Percy had left British General Gage's office to return to his home. Unrecognized, he casually joined a group of eight or ten men on the Common. One of them said,

"The British have marched, but they will miss their aim."

"What aim?" Percy asked.

"Why, the cannon at Concord," came the reply.

Percy quickly retraced his steps and informed the general that their plan was known. Gage, hoping that it was not commonly known, decided to proceed anyway.

They had been very secretive, not even telling any of their men, who had been quietly awaken from their sleep and had left silently without even the observation of their own sentries. A dog barked. It was killed instantly with a bayonet. They proceeded to the beach in the least inhabited part of town to board their boats with muffled oars. At Phip's Farm on Cambridge Marsh the men dropped overboard into shallow water. Lieutenant John Barker wrote in his diary,

> "After getting over the marsh, where we were wet up to the knees, we were halted in a dirty road and stood there till two o'clock in the morning waiting for provisions to be brought from the boats and to be divided, and which most of the men threw away, having carried some with them. At two o'clock we began our march by wading through a very long ford up to our middles."

Very soon, Colonel Smith sent Major Pitcairn ahead with six companies as an advance corps to secure the two bridges beyond Concord. Pitcairn had captured all but one of Parker's spies with a small advance guard as flankers. Shortly, he was met by the patrol that had taken Revere and was told that 500 men stood ready at Lexington to oppose their advance. Pitcairn slowed his advance and waited for Colonel Smith and his men to come closer. Paul Revere's whopper had found its mark and slowed down the enemy. Meanwhile, Colonel Smith had already sent for reinforcements from Boston. He had heard the distant musket shots and bells ringing. Lord Percy collected his army and ammunition, of which, Smith and Pitcairn had very little. They were not expecting the Americans to dare to fight them.

Twenty-three-year-old Sylvanus Wood heard the ring of the Lexington bell three miles away in Woburn. He wrote,

> "I immediately arose, took my gun, and with Robert Douglas went in haste to Lexington . . . . While we were talking [to Parker] a messenger came up and told the captain that the British troops were within half a mile.
>
> "Parker immediately turned to his drummer . . . and ordered him to beat to arms."
>
> As the men gathered Parker called out, "Every man of you who is equipped, follow me. And those of you who are not equipped, go into the meetinghouse and furnish yourselves from the magazine and immediately join the company. Parker led those of us who were equipped to the north end of Lexington Common, near the Bedford Road, and formed us in single file. I was stationed about in the center of the company.
>
> 'While we were standing, I left my place and went from one end of the company to the other and counted every man who was paraded, and the whole number was thirty-eight and no more. Just as I finished and got back to my place, I perceived the British troops had arrived on the spot between the meetinghouse and Buckman's, near where Captain Parker stood when he first led off his men."

Paul Revere, also, observed the British march into sight from a second-floor window. He was helping John Lowell carry off a trunk of John Hancock's papers, which papers were certainly not for the eyes of the British army. The two of them ran from the tavern with their burden as the early signs of dawn showed in the eastern sky.

Thomas Willard, who watched from a window in Daniel Harrington's house, testified later,

> "I . . . saw . . . about four hundred of Regulars in one body coming up the road and marched toward the north part of the Common . . . . As soon as said Regulars were against the east end of the meetinghouse, the commanding officers said something, what I know not. But upon that, the Regulars ran till they came within about eight or nine rods of about a

hundred of the militia . . . at which time the militia of Lexington dispersed . . . . Directly . . . an officer rode before the Regulars to the other side of the body and hallooed after the militia . . . . 'Lay down your arms, d—n you! Why don't you lay down your arms?'"

Sylvanus Wood told it this way,

"The officer . . . swung his sword and said, 'Lay down your arms, you d_____d rebels, or you will all be dead men! Fire!'

   "Some guns were fired by the British at us from the first platoon, but no person was killed or hurt, [the guns] being probably charged only with powder. Just at this time, Captain Parker ordered every man to take care of himself. The company immediately dispersed, and while the company was dispersing and leaping over the wall, the second platoon of the British fired and killed some of our men. There was not a gun fired by any of Captain Parker's company within my knowledge. I was so situated that I must have known it, had anything of the kind taken place before a total dispersion of our company."

As the Americans scurried for the protection of walls and trees, British Lieutenant Barker later reported,

"The men [British regulars] were so wild they could hear no orders."

They not only shot at the colonials, but also pursued them with their bayonets. Jonas Parker, an older cousin of the captain, stood his ground. When a British ball buckled his knees, he tried to reload, but died from the deep pierce of a Redcoat's bayonet. Major Pitcairn's "Cease fire!" order went unheeded. Finally he was able to reform his ranks just as Colonel Smith came into view with the main body. One regular had a slight leg wound.

Regrouped, the British fired a victory volley, struck up their band and marched sharply on to Concord. Sylvanus Wood reported,

"After the British had begun their march to Concord I returned to the Common and found Robert [Munroe] and Jonas Parker lying dead . . . near the Bedford Road, and others dead and wounded. I assisted in carrying the dead into the meetinghouse. I then proceeded toward Concord with my gun."

So ended the "Midnight Ride of Paul Revere," and the Revolutionary War began with the dawn. British General Gage had not intended to start it. He was only responding to Lord Dartmouth's admonishment to "do something" with the troops he had. The alarm set off by Dr. Warren had spread far and wide. Concord would be different than Lexington. Peace was no longer negotiable in the eyes of the revolutionaries, and the alerted minutemen throughout the countryside, muskets in hand, flowed to Concord.

— 69 —

CONCORD—THE SECOND CONTINENTAL CONGRESS BEGINS

All men and boys capable of carrying firearms were commanded by English law to enroll in the Crown militia. From ages sixteen to sixty they were expected to possess a firelock, a bayonet, and a quantity of ammunition. The alarm set off by Dr. Warren and carried by Paul Revere, William Dawes and Dr. Prescott spread quickly in every direction. Farmers, tanners, wheelwrights and clerks assembled rapidly in Concord with their arms.

British Lieutenant Barker described the redcoats' approach to Concord.

"We met with no interruption till within a mile or two of the town, where the people had occupied a hill which commanded the road. The Light Infantry were ordered away to the right and ascended the height in one line, upon which the Yankees quitted it without firing, which they did like-wise for one or two more successively. They then crossed the river beyond the town, and we marched into the town, after taking possession of a hill with a liberty pole on it and a flag flying which was cut down."

While the British officers refreshed themselves at the local taprooms, ad-vance companies marched on to secure the bridges that crossed the river, and with around 700 British troops in and about the town, a company of thirty-odd redcoats advanced about a half-mile toward the ever increasing rebels of around four hundred and fifty. Outnumbering the regulars, the colonials advanced slowly as a group towards the enemy, who quickly retreated, and sent into town for reinforcements. Neither side was eager to be guilty of the opening fire. At the bridge the redcoats started pulling up the planks. Colonial Corporal Amos Barrett recalled,

"Mager Buttrick said if we wair all of his mind he would Drive them away

from the Bridge, they should not tair that up, we all said we would go . . .
we wair all orded to Load and had stricked order not to fire till they fir firs,
then to fire as fast as we could, we then marched on . . . . Capt Davis had
got, I Be leave, within 15 Rods of the B. when they fir 3 gons one after the
other. I see the Balls strike in the River on the Right of me. As soon as they
fir them, they fir on us, their balls whisled well. we then was all orded to
fire . . . it is Straing that their warnt no more kild but they fird to high. Capt
Davis was kild and mr osmore and a number wounded. we soon Drove
them from the Bridge."

DRESSED AS A BRITISH GRENADIER, A (FORMER) BRITISH CITIZEN DESCRIBES THE BATTLE AT THE
CONCORD BRIDGE. THE TALL BEAR LIKE HAT GAVE THEM EXTRA HEIGHTH AND FIERCENESS—
PHOTO BY TROY RUSHTON, AUGUST 2001.

Three British regulars were killed; four officers and four privates were
wounded before the British retreated toward the town. They were not pursued.
The Americans returned to their wooded hill. British Colonel Smith joined his
retreating troops. Indecisive, as the ever increasing numbers collected in the
woods, and concerned that they might be surrounded and trapped in Concord,

Smith first crossed the bridge again without incident and then retreated and evacuated the town. About a mile out of town, where the road narrowed, the rebels attacked them. British Lieutenant Barker describes it,

> "we were fired on from all sides, but mostly from the rear, where people had hid themselves in houses till we had passed and then fired. The country was an amazing strong one, full of hills, woods, stone walls, etc., which the rebels did not fail to take advantage of, for they were all lined with people who kept an incessant fire upon us, as we did too upon them, but not seeing them . . . . We marched miles, their numbers increasing from all parts, while ours was reducing by deaths, wounds, and fatigue; and we were totally surrounded with such an incessant fire as it's impossible to conceive; our ammunition was likely near expended."

Lord Percy had been ordered to reinforce Colonel Smith with 1,000 more regulars stationed at Boston. Their fifes and drums loudly sounded *Yankee Doodle*, as they briskly marched triumphantly toward Roxbury. Royal Welsh Lieutenant Frederick Mackenzie recorded in this diary,

> "As we advanced, we heard the firing plainer and more frequent, and at half after two, being near the church at Lexington and the fire increasing we were ordered to form a line . . . . But by reason of the stone walls and other obstructions, it was not formed in so regular a manner as it should have been . . . . About a quarter past three, Earl Percy having come to a resolution of returning to Boston . . . our regiment received orders to form the rear guard . . . . we formed a line and remained in that position for near half an hour, during which time the brigade began their march . . . toward Cambridge. [Then] took the resolution of returning by way of Charlestown, which was the shortest road and which could be defended against any number of rebels . . . . Our men had very few opportunities of getting good shots at the rebels, as they hardly ever fired but under cover of a stone wall, from behind a tree, or out of a house, and the moment they had fired, they lay down out of sight until they had loaded again or the column had passed . . . . In the road indeed in our rear, they were most numerous and came on pretty close, frequently calling out 'King Hancock forever!' Many of them were killed in the houses on the roadside from whence they fired. In some of them seven or eight men were destroyed. Some houses were forced open in which no person could be discovered, but when the column had passed, numbers sallied out from some place in which they had lain concealed, fired at our rear guard and augmented the

numbers which followed us . . . . Many houses were plundered by the soldiers, notwithstanding the efforts of the officers to prevent it . . . Soldiers who stayed too long in the houses were killed in the very act of plundering by those who lay concealed in them . . . . Few or no women or children were to be seen throughout the day. As the country had undoubted intelligence that some troops were to march out and the rebels were probably determined to attack them, it is generally supposed they had previously removed their families from the neighborhood . . . [but] even women had firelocks. One was seen to fire a blunderbuss between her father and husband from their windows. There they three, with an infant child, soon suffered the fury of the day. In another house which was long defended by eight resolute fellows, the grenadiers at last got possession, when after having run their bayonets into seven, the eighth continued to abuse them . . . but a moment before he quitted this world applied such epithets as I must leave unmentioned."

Passing through Lexington the British column descended the high road to the "Foot of the Rocks" at Menotomy. Here eighteen hundred fresh colonial troops descended upon the harassed redcoats, and it was here that most of the fierce, bloody, close-quarter and house-to-house fighting of the day took place. The cornered British officers turned their cannon on the rebels with little results. In the frenzy, Lord Percy and his leaders lost control of their men. From one house, Deacon Joseph Adams had fled to a barn and was hidden in the hay. His wife lay in bed in the house. She later reported,

"divers of them entered our house by burning open the doors, and three of the soldiers broke into the room in which I then was laid on my bed . . . not having been to my chamber door from my being delivered in childbirth to that time. One of said soldiers immediately opened my [bed] curtains with his bayonet fixed and pointing . . . to my breast. I immediately cried out, 'For the Lord's sake, don't kill me!'

"One that stood near said, 'We will not hurt the woman if she will go out of the house, but we will surely burn it.'

"I immediately arose, threw a blanket over me, went out, and crawled into a corn-house near the door with my infant in my arms, where I remained until they were gone. They immediately set the house on fire, in which I had left five children and no other person; but the fire was happily extinguished when the house was in the utmost danger of being utterly consumed."

Further on at Cooper's Tavern, the owner stated later at the Provincial Congress,

> "The King's Regular troops . . . fired more than one hundred bullets into the house where we dwell, through doors, windows, etc. Then a number of them entered the house where we and two aged gentlemen were, all unarmed. We escaped for our lives into the cellar. The two aged gentlemen were immediately most barbarously and inhumanly murdered by them, being stabbed through in many places, their head mauled, skulls broke, and their brains beat out on the floor and walls of the house."

Passing on, Lord Percy, with better control of his troops, made a feint as if to enter Boston by way of Cambridge, then wheeled left in North Cambridge and marched for Charlestown. At sunset, half past six, the exhausted column staggered its last mile across Charlestown Neck toward the safety of Bunker Hill, which rose a hundred feet above the surrounding country. As darkness enclosed them and musket fire ceased, with the warship *Somerset* anchored in the nearby Charles River, the footsore, thirsty, hungry British regulars flung themselves down on the slopes of Bunker Hill for some much needed rest.

American Militia General William Heath was now the senior officer. He ordered the three thousand colonials

> "to halt and give over the pursuit, as any further attempt upon the enemy in that position would have been futile."

He posted a guard close to the Neck to watch the enemy and then ordered the militia

> "to march to the town of Cambridge, where below the town, the whole were ordered to lie on their arms."

John Jones had arrived in Concord too late for the fighting, but that night at Cambridge, protected by the walls of Harvard College, he wrote to his

> "Loving Wife, 'Tis uncertain when we shall return . . . . Let us be patient & remember that it is ye hand of God.'"

The famous 19 Apr 1775 with its "shots that were heard around the world" had ended. About eighteen hundred British regulars had marched to destroy some secreted rebel storage: seventy-three of them had been killed, two hundred were wounded or missing. Forty-nine Americans had died and forty-six were wounded or missing. Thus began the War of Independence, after rubbing each other the wrong way for ten years.

The Second Continental Congress Begins

One of the final decisions of the First Continental Congress had been to meet again in Philadelphia on 10 May 1775, if Great Britain had not redressed the American grievances. With the warning of Paul Revere and greatly recognizing their need to be in Philadelphia to unify the colonies, John Hancock and Samuel Adams had fled first to Woburn, then Billerica, and then moved on to Worcester on 24 April. Here they hoped to meet up with the other members of the Massachusetts delegation, Sam's country cousin John Adams, Robert Treat Paine, and Thomas Cushing, as well as an armed guard to protect them on their journey. It didn't happen. Hancock wrote a desperate letter back to Boston.

> "Who fired first? . . . Who commands our forces? . . . Are our men in good spirits? . . . Drive the British from Boston . . . Seize Castle William in the bay . . . . Where was Cushing? . . . We travel rather as deserters, which I will not submit to. I will return and join you, if I cannot travel in reputation. . . . How was the Provincial Congress going? Who was president? . . . Pray remember Mr. S. Adams and myself to all friends. God be with you."

SAMUEL ADAMS

John Hancock and Samuel Adams were greatly relieved a few days later when the two of them were joined by the other Massachusetts delegates, as well as those from Connecticut, Rhode Island, and New Hampshire. The local militia would journey with them until they were relieved of their duty by the next group of militia. Hancock's fear of being labeled as a leader of the hotheaded people of Massachusetts subsided as he came to realize that the news of the dire events of Lexington and Concord had preceded them and apparently had united the colonists. First cousin STEPHEN HOPKINS of Rhode Island joined with the group. He was one of the older delegates, but strong in his dedication to the cause.

At first twelve armed men accompanied the delegates, by the time the procession left Manhattan, where New York's delegation joined in, about two hundred militiamen accompanied the congressmen. Distant cousin-in-law ROBERT R. LIVINGSTON was with the New York delegation. On 6 May, when the parade arrived in New York City, which was still nestled at the southern end of Manhattan Island, a cacophony of bells rang out and another "amazing concourse of people" gathered, whether by horse, carriage, or foot, "trudging and sweating thro' the dirt" for an opportunity to shout "huzzah" at the Massachusetts representatives: "the doors, the windows, the stoops, the roofs of the plazas, were loaded with all ranks, ages and sexes." Another large crowd gathered two days later to bid them farewell, after a rather quiet Sabbath.

The march continued through the ancestral lands of Newark, Elizabethtown, Woodbridge, Brunswick, Princeton and Trenton, New Jersey, "rolling and gathering like a Snowball," until the parade arrived at Philadelphia on 10 May—the day of their scheduled meeting. Some two hundred "principal Gentlemen, on Horseback, with their Swords Drawn" met the delegations six miles outside the city and led the way into Philadelphia. It is likely that distant uncle JOHN WILKINSON, first cousin of STEPHEN HOPKINS was with this militia.

Delaware's Caesar Rodney reported,

"The Massachusetts delegate's entrance into the city was verry grand and Intended to show approbation of the Conduct of the good people of that Government, in the distressing situation of Affairs there."

Richard Henry Lee of Virginia observed that there had

"never appeared more perfect unanimity among any sett of Men than among the Delegates . . . all the old Provinces not one excepted are directed by the same firmness of union, and determination to resist by all ways and to every extremity."

General Gage's official report of Lexington and Concord did not reach London until 10 June; but the colonials' more favorable report, claiming self-defense, had been rushed across the Atlantic and arrived on 29 May. Benjamin Franklin quickly sailed for his home in America. The king and parliament had been skeptical of the colonist's report; but when Gage's report reached them and they considered their lack of military power, they tried to make a deal with

Catherine of Russia for twenty thousand Russian mercenaries. Catherine refused their request.

The British-held fort at Ticonderoga was captured on 9 May 1775—the day before the Continental Congress met—by the double initiative of the troops led by the disputing commanders, Vermont's Ethan Allen and Connecticut's thirty-four-year-old militia colonel and apothecary of New Haven, Benedict Arnold. The news of this conquest and the subsequent taking of Crown Point and St. John's on the Richelieu River did not reach the Continental Congress for another week. Congress, whose delegates had not been sent from their various colonies with the authority to declare independence, tried to explain these victories to London as an act of defense—an attempt to thwart the invasion of the British through Canada. There still seemed to be a hope that reconciliation with Great Britain might be possible. However, on the British islands across the Atlantic, when word finally reached them, the king and parliament felt it was pure unadulterated aggression by the foolish American colonists. These rebels needed to be humbled.

THE BATTLE OF BUNKER HILL—
CHOOSING A COMMANDING GENERAL

Meanwhile in Massachusetts, General Gage watched the growing rebel forces building entrenchments and redoubts under militia General Ward and Dr. Joseph Warren and his committee. By June, the colonials had about seventy-five hundred men from Massachusetts, Rhode Island, New Hampshire, and Connecticut settled in a ring west of Boston from Charlestown on the north to Roxbury on the south. Gage realized his troops were too weak to penetrate into New England, so he decided it was time to occupy and fortify the outlying heights of Dorchester and Charleston.

[Note: Ancestor, eighth-great-grandfather REMEMBRANCE LIPPINCOTT, was born in Dorchester one-hundred-thirty-three years prior to this event, 15 Mar 1642. He had married MARGARET BARBER of Boston in 1665. They had joined the Quakers and moved to Shrewsbury, Monmouth, New Jersey. Their grandson, sixth-great-grandfather SAMUEL LIPPINCOTT, had married sixth-great-grandmother MARY PRESTON according to the Philadelphia Quaker records on 7 Apr 1743. They had six children. After her death, SAMUEL married ELIZABETH RICE LANE. She bore him four more children. Their youngest was born in 1769 in Alexandria twp, Hunterdon County, New Jersey.]

As British General Gage prepared to move a detachment to Dorchester on 18 June and another as soon as possible toward Bunker Hill and Breed's Hill on the Charlestown peninsula, his plans became known in the rebel camp. To stop the British offensive, the Committee of Safety decided to ignore Dorchester and advance forward to Bunker Hill and Breed's Hill. The famous "Battle of Bunker Hill" occurred on 17 Jun 1775.

Colonist Peter Brown was of Captain Gridley's artillery company who attempted to fortify Breed's hill. Later, he wrote,

"We worked there undiscovered till about five in the morn, and then we saw our danger, being against eight ships of the line and all Boston fortified against us . . . . And about half after five in the morn, we not having about half the fort done, they began to fire . . . . They killed one of us, and then they ceased till about eleven o'clock, and then they began brisk again; and that caused some of our young country people to desert, apprehending the danger in a clearer manner than the rest, who were more diligent in digging and fortifying ourselves against them . . . . They fired very warm from Boston and from on board . . . It being about three o'clock, there was little cessation of the cannon roaring. Come to look, there was a matter of forty barges full of regulars coming over to us. It is supposed there were about three thousand of them and about seven hundred of us left not deserted, besides five hundred reinforcement that could not get so nigh to us as to do any good . . . till they saw that we must all be cut off . . . and then they advanced.

"When our officers saw that the regulars would land, they ordered the artillery to go out of the fort and prevent their landing if possible, from which the artillery captain took his pieces and went right off home to Cambridge as fast as he could, for which he is now confined and we expect will be shot for it.

"But the enemy landed and fronted before us . . . and after they were well formed, they advanced towards us in order to swallow us up. But they found a chokey mouthful of us, though we could do nothing with our small arms as yet for distance and had but two cannon and nary gunner. And they from Boston and from the ships a-firing and throwing bombs keeping us down till they got almost round us."

An officer of the advancing British troops described it thus,

"Our troops advanced with great confidence, expecting an easy victory . . . As we approached, an incessant stream of fire poured from the rebel lines. It seemed a continued sheet of fire for near thirty minutes. Our Light Infantry [was unable] to penetrate. Indeed, how could we penetrate? Most of our Grenadiers and Light Infantry the moment of presenting themselves lost three-fourths, and many nine-tenths, of their men. Some had only eight and nine men a company left, some only three, four, and five.

"On the left, Pigot was staggered and actually retreated. Observe, our men were not driven back; they actually retreated by orders."

American drummer boy Robert Steele was on Bunker Hill with Ephraim Doolittle's regiment. Years later he told a friend,

"I beat to 'Yankee Doodle' when we mustered for Bunker Hill that morning . . . the British . . . . marched with rather a slow step nearly up to our entrenchment, and the battle began. The conflict was sharp, but the British soon retreated with a quicker step than they came up, leaving some of their killed and wounded in sight of us. They retreated . . . and formed again . . . and a second battle ensued which was harder and longer than the first . . . . About the time the British retreated the second time, I was standing side of Benjamin Ballard, a Boston boy about my age, who had a gun in his hands, when one of our sergeants came up to us and said, 'You are young and spry, run in a moment to some of the stores and bring some rum. Major Moore is badly wounded. Go as quick as possible.'

"We . . . run as fast as we could . . . down to Charlestown Neck and found there was a firing in that quarter. We heard the shot pass over our heads . . . . We however immediately passed on and went into a store, but see no one there. I stamped and called out to rally some person and a man answered in the cellar below. I told him what we wanted, but he did not come up, nor did we see him at all. I . . . asked him why he stayed down cellar. He answered, 'To keep out of the way of the shot,' and then said 'If you want anything in the store, take what you please.'

"I seized a brown, two-quart, earthen pitcher . . . and filled my pitcher with rum . . . . Ben took a pail and filled with water, and we hastened back to the entrenchment on the hill, when we found our people in confusion and talking about retreating. The British were about advancing upon us a third time. Our rum and water went very quick. It was very hot, but I saved my pitcher and kept it for sometime afterwards."

When the American powder was gone, Peter Brown was among the last defenders. He told his mother,

"I was in the fort till the regulars came in, and I jumped over the walls and ran for about half a mile where balls flew like hailstones and cannons roared like thunder."

Lieutenant Samuel Webb of Connecticut said,

"The dead and wounded lay on every side of me. Their groans were piercing indeed, though long before this time I believe the fear of death had quitted almost every breast. They now had possession of our fort and four field-pieces, and by much the advantage of the ground . . . . Our orders then came to make the best retreat we could. We set off almost gone with fatigue and ran very fast . . . leaving some of our dead and wounded in the field."

Among the dead lay the beloved Dr. Joseph Warren. Although he had been voted to become a major general by the Provincial Congress three days before, he had not yet been commissioned. Throughout the hard-fought action at the redoubt, the doctor fought side by side with the men, who were heartened by his cold, debonair courage. A musket ball struck him in the back of his head just as the fort was overrun.

"He died in his best cloaths," said a British officer, "everybody remembered his fine, silk fringed waistcoat."

At five o'clock on the hot summer afternoon, the day was over. British General Clinton reported,

"A dear bought victory, another such would have ruined us."

General Howe reported to Gage that his men were far

"too much harassed and fatigued to give much attention to the pursuit of the rebels."

And at Cambridge, American Captain Peter Coburn of Dracut perhaps spoke for all when he sighed,

"I arrived at Cambridge About Sunset alive, tho much Tired and Feteogued. Blessed be God Theirfor."

Gage had gained his outpost, but the cost was disastrous. Of the 2,250 men engaged, 1,054, including 92 officers, had been hit by the fierce rebel fire. Two-hundred-twenty-six British died, among them Major John Pitcairn of Lexington infamy, whose son carried him dying from the field. One-hundred-forty Americans were killed and two-hundred-seventy-one wounded. Gage and Howe had had enough for the present. Clinton argued vainly with them to seize Dorchester Heights. The armies settled to inactivity.

The Colonies Unite and Choose a Commanding General

Meanwhile, westward in Philadelphia, John Hancock had been elected unanimously as president of the Second Continental Congress to replace re-tiring Peyton Randolph. He then aspired to be the general of the Continental Army—a much more exciting position for the thirty-plus-year-old delegate than haggling with other delegates and swatting flies in a hot Philadelphia conference room. Some delegates from Massachusetts suggested that congress adopt the New England militia and appoint General Ward as the commanding officer.

Armies were gathering in the various colonies. In Virginia—it was said —

every member of the House of Burgesses

"has clothed himself in homespun and has each on the breast of his coat these words wrote with needlework or painting, LIBERTY OR DEATH; and with this on his breast each member sits in the House of Assembly."

Charleston, South Carolina, has

"rather the appearance of a garrison town than a mart for trade."

In Philadelphia,

"Every man here without distinction is learning the use of arms, and even the Quakers have their companies."

Riflemen were called from the frontiers of Pennsylvania, Maryland, and Virginia. The volunteers were greater than the number called for, so a competition was set up:

"He took a board of a foot square and with chalk drew the shape of a moderate nose in the center and nailed it up to a tree at one hundred and fifty yards distance, and those who came nighest the mark with a single ball was to go. But by the first forty or fifty that fired, the nose was all blown out of the board, and by the time his company was up, the board shared the same fate." [Reported by John Harrower, an indentured servant teaching a plantation school.]

Congress worried about money, arms, and fortifying New York harbor, where most believed the British would strike hardest if they were forced from Boston. Ideas were profuse; agreement scarce. Some delegates still suggested sending someone to England to negotiate a peace settlement. John Adams, the rather plump country cousin of Samuel Adams, became anxious about these confusions. His fellow delegates from Massachusetts were split in their support for Hancock or Ward for the commanding general. He didn't want either one. He had his eye on a tall six-foot-four delegate from Virginia, Colonel George Washington.

In his diary he wrote:

"I walked with Mr. Samuel Adams in the State House yard for a little exercise and fresh air, before the hour of Congress, and there represented to him the various dangers that surround us. He agreed to them all, but said, 'What shall we do?'

"I answered him that he knew I had taken great pains to get our colleagues to agree upon some plan, that we might be unanimous; but he knew that they would pledge themselves to nothing; but I was determined to take a step which should compel them and all the other members of Congress to declare themselves for or against something. I am determined this morning to make a direct motion that Congress should adopt the army before Boston, and appoint Colonel Washington commander of it."

So when Congress assembled the morning 14 Jun 1775, (three days before the Battle of Bunker Hill), John Adams rose in his place and

"in as short a speech as the subject would admit, represented the state of the colonies .... I concluded with a motion, in form, that Congress would adopt the army at Cambridge and appoint a general; that though this was not the proper time to nominate a general, yet, as I had reason to believe this was a point of the greatest difficulty, I had no hesitation to declare that I had but one gentleman in my mind for that important command, and that was the gentleman from Virginia who was among us and very well known to all of us, a gentleman whose skill and experience as an officer, whose independent fortune, great talents, and excellent universal character, would command the approbation of all America and unite the cordial exertions of all the Colonies better than any other person in the Union. Mr. Washington, who happened to sit near the door, as soon as he heard me allude to him, from his usual modesty, darted into the library-room. Mr. Hancock, who was our President, which gave me an opportunity to observe his countenance while I was speaking on the state of the Colonies, the army at Cambridge, and the enemy, heard me with visible pleasure; but when I came to describe Washington for the commander, I never remarked a more sudden and striking change of countenance. Mortification and resentment were expressed as forcibly as his face could exhibit them. Mr. Samuel Adams seconded the motion, and that did not soften the President's physiognomy at all.

"The subject came under debate, and several gentlemen declared themselves against the appointment of Mr. Washington, not on account of any personal objection against him, but because the army were all from New England, had a general of their own, appeared to be satisfied with him, and had proved themselves able to imprison the British army in Boston, which was all they expected or desired at that time .... The subject was postponed to a future day. In the meantime, pains were taken out of doors to obtain unanimity, and the voices were generally so clearly in favor of Washington, that the dissentient members were persuaded to withdraw their opposition."

At supper time, Washington was addressed as "General" and told of his appointment by some of the delegates. He spent the evening preparing his reply.

When Congress convened the following morning, John Hancock, from the chair, informed Washington of his appointment and his wish that he accept their choice of him as general and commander in chief of the forces raised and to be raised for the defense of America. Colonel Washington bowed, took a paper from his pocket and read:

JOHN HANOCK

"Mr. President: Though I am truly sensible of the high honor done me in this appointment, yet I feel great distress from a consciousness that my abilities and military experience may not be equal to the extensive and important trust. However, as the Congress desire, I will enter upon the momentous duty, and exert every power I possess in their service, and for the support of the glorious cause: I beg they will accept my most cordial thanks for this distinguished testimony of their approbation . . . . As to pay, sir, I beg leave to assure the Congress that as no pecuniary consideration could have tempted me to have accepted this arduous employment at the expense of my domestic ease and happiness, I do not wish to make any profit from it; I will keep an exact account of my expenses; those I doubt not they will discharge, and that is all I desire."

Later to his friend, Patrick Henry, Colonel Washington sorrowfully said,

"From the day I enter upon the command of the American armies I date my fall and the ruin of my reputation."

Congress named two major generals who were to be his senior subordinates: Artemas Ward, general of the Massachusetts army, and Charles Lee, the gifted British veteran of American and foreign wars, recently settled in America, who would only accept the appointment if Congress agreed to indemnify him for "any loss of property which he may sustain by entering into their service."

Major Horatio Gates was made adjutant general. Distant-cousin-in-law PHILIP SCHUYLER, the rich Dutch descendant and former mayor of Albany described in a previous chapter, along with Israel Putnam of New England were made major generals. Eight brigadier generals were chosen. Among these was another distant-cousin-in-law, NATHANAEL GREENE, of Rhode Island. All eight brigadiers were from New England, except RICHARD MONTGOMERY of New York. Accepting his appointment as the admiral of the small Continental Navy was first-cousin ESEK HOPKINS, a slightly younger brother of STEPHEN HOPKINS.

On 23 June, George Washington mounted his horse for his long ride to find his army in the surrounding areas of Boston. Accompanying him were the generals Charles Lee and PHILIP SCHUYLER and two young men: Thomas Mifflin, his aide-de-camp, and Joseph Reed, his military secretary. It was a rainy day; still the Philadelphia Light Horse and some of the delegates escorted the party a distance on their way. PHILIP SCHUYLER remained behind in New York, as he was to command in that area. Washington and Charles Lee arrived at Cambridge 2 Jul 1775.

After appraising his forces, their camps, and their fortifications for two or three days, Washington wrote to his friend, banker Robert Morris in Philadelphia:

> "We found everything exactly the reverse of what had been represented.
> We were assured at Philadelphia that the army was stocked with engineers.
> We found not one. We were assured that we should find an expert train of
> artillery. They have not a single gunner."

General Charles Lee was placed over the left wing of the army. This pleased him. He was particularly impressed and pleased to have brigadier general NATHANAEL GREENE under his command. Greene commanded the Rhode Island forces. NATHANAEL GREENE was the youngest of the generals appointed by the Continental Congress. He is described as a

> "pleasant man, moderately tall and well set up, with a rugged candid face,
> eyes of bright blue, a full mouth deep-set, and a finely chiseled nose. He
> was a man of labor, one of the sons of a Quaker preacher who had reared

him to run the family flour, grist, and sawmills and forge. He had educated himself, especially in mathematics, history and political theory. Although a Quaker, he had come to believe in the necessity for resistance to the Crown and to support it at the cost of expulsion from the Society of Friends for forsaking pacifism. Resolutely he had served the Rhode Island Assembly in setting up military laws, and had enlisted in a local company.

"The husky ironmonger was genial but impetuous, and sensitive. When his friends and neighbors intimated that his stiff left leg, which gave him a decided limp, was a blemish to the company, NATHANAEL concealed his hurt and graciously volunteered to withdraw, but he was persuaded to stay. Only six months later, when the Assembly voted itself an army and sent it to Cambridge, NATHANAEL GREENE was unanimous choice as brigadier general in command. His talents, though undeveloped, were evidently recognized; he knew how to manage men, to husband resources, to exercise great patience and intelligent caution, and he believed in discipline." [*Rebels & Redcoats* by Scheer & Rankin]

Of General Washington's disappointment and near disgust with his New England army, young brigadier general NATHANAEL GREENE observed,

"His Excellency . . . has not had time to make himself acquainted with the genius of this people. They are naturally as brave and spirited as the peasantry of any other country, but you cannot expect veterans of a raw militia of only a few months' service. The common people are exceedingly avaricious; the genius of the people is commercial from their long intercourse with trade. The sentiment of honor, the true characteristic of a soldier, has not yet got the better of interest. His excellency has been taught to believe the people here a superior race of mortals, and finding them of the same temper and disposition, passions and prejudices, virtues and vices of the common people of other governments, they sink in his esteem."

Evidently GREENE knew his people. The majority of the men remained steadfast and devoted and stood behind their aristocratic general long after he came to proclaim his New England soldiers the "finest troops in the world." In the fall of 1775 Washington wrote to General SCHUYLER in New York,

"We mend every day, and I flatter myself that in a little time, we shall work up these raw materials into good stuff."

~ 71 ~

THE CANADIAN CAMPAIGN

While Washington was pulling together his Continental Army outside Boston, word came from Canada to the Continental Congress in Philadelphia that Sir Guy Carleton, military governor of Canada, was

"making preparations to invade these colonies and . . . instigating the Indian nations to take up the hatchet against them."

This worried Congress sufficiently that they instructed General PHILIP SCHUYLER to invade Canada if

"it will not be disagreeable to the Canadians."

Knowing that Carleton had less than eight hundred regulars to protect the whole Canadian province and that reinforcements from England would probably be unable to come before the icy St. Lawrence River thawed in the spring, Congress felt that if they took Montreal, Quebec, and the various forts, the Canadians and Indians would join with them.

SCHUYLER seemed to be an obvious choice. As a former mayor and distinguished landholder of Albany, he was very well acquainted with the Indians, the French, and the cold terrain. He is described as a tall, slight, pleasant-looking, brown-eyed, forty-two-year-old man. He appeared hearty and confident, which hid the fact that he had chronic ill health that made him moody, sensitive, and often indecisive. Trouble plagued him from the start. Enlistments were incredibly slow; supplies difficult. Ticonderoga was in "a perfectly defenseless state"—the garrison undisciplined and insubordinate. Nothing he could do seemed to hurry the carpenters building bateaux. These were troop boats that could be carried by the inhabitants from one river to another which were especially needed in the dividing mountains where the waters would switch, one side flowing north to the St. Lawrence, the other flowing into the Hudson. Fortunately, his second in command was the tall, slender, well-limbed brigadier general RICHARD MONTGOMERY, also of New York. With his "genteel, easy, graceful, manly address, he had the voluntary esteem of the whole army."

When he arrived from Albany and took charge of details, the expedition began to take shape. General MONTGOMERY was married to a sister of ROBERT R. LIVINGSTON.

SCHUYLER was ill in Albany when the spies reported that Carleton was ready to launch two heavily armed vessels at St. John's to defend the Sorel [Richelieu] River above Lake Champlain. Fearing to wait any longer, MONTGOMERY wrote SCHUYLER to come and take command as he pushed off shore his whole force in open batteaux toward Ile aux Noix, twenty miles below St. John's. SCHUYLER overtook him in a whaleboat in time for the landing on the fifth of September; however, he was so ill with a "bilious fever" that he was unable to continue and returned again to Albany, leaving his command to MONTGOMERY who promptly laid siege to the stockaded Canadian Fort St. John's, which had been reclaimed by the English.

The British garrison at the fort felt quite secure within their massive log walls and barricaded surroundings as the fall rains descended and drenched MONTGOMERY's troops as they dug their siege lines.

"Whenever we attempt to raise batteries, the water follows in the ditch," complained one. MONTGOMERY wrote,

"We have been like half-drowned rats crawling through a swamp." About half of his troops, "upwards of six hundred," were too ill to stand duty. After seventeen or eighteen days of this pelting rain with short rations, grumbling, and increased resentment, the brigadier wrote of his New Englanders, "The privates are all generals," and of his own New Yorkers, "The sweepings of the York streets."

To his highly concerned wife, the sister of ROBERT R. LIVINGSTON, He wrote,

"I must entreat the favor of you to write no more of those whining letters. I declare if I receive another in that style, I will lock up the rest without reading them. I don't want anything to lower my spirits. I have abundant use for them all, and at the best of times I have not too much."

At last the colonials were able to raise a gun battery north of the fort above the British works and the garrison surrendered. Moving north, Fort Chambly fell with very little combat. It was here that many of these French settlers, including fourteen of the MONTEEs, joined with the Americans against the English.

[Note: The female genealogical line of at least three of these MONTEEs was MARGUERITE POYER, daughter of JACQUES POYER and MARGUERITE DUBOIS. JACQUES was a young French soldier sent to Fort Chambly by Louis XIV in the latter 1600's. It is possible that fourth-great-grandfather JOSEPH POYER was a younger brother or a nephew to MARGUERITE POYER MONTEE and joined with the colonials at this same time. JACQUES POYER, a sergeant of the troops, was buried at Sorel near the St. Lawrence River on 7 Sep 1748. Many of his children were born in Chambly according to the Catholic records.

There is a record of a JOSEPH POIRIER [b. 1729] who married MARGUERITE TESSIER [b. 1743] the 12 Sep 1763, in Montreal. This was JOSEPH's second marriage.]

Unfortunately for the Americans, Ethan Allen, who had been disposed of his command of the Green Mountain Boys after taking Fort Ticonderoga, had joined this expedition and was sent ahead with Major John Brown and three hundred men to enlist other Canadians in Montreal. He brazenly disobeyed his orders and attempted to take the fortress. Several score of his men vanished when the garrison sallied. He was captured along with many of his men. He was insolent to the Montreal commandant, General Richard Prescott, when he was recognized and questioned. The general subsequently sent him in chains to England for trial. Allen irreparably hurt the colonist cause. His failure gave heart to loyal Canadians and discouraged those who might have joined with the Americans. The Indians were not impressed, either, and turned their strength to the victorious British.

When word of this foray reached General Washington, he declared to SCHUYLER,

"Colonel Allen's misfortune will, I hope, teach a lesson of prudence and subordination to others who may be too ambitious to outshine their general officers and regardless of order and duty rush into enterprises which have unfavorable effects to the public and are destructive to themselves."

When Montgomery's forces crossed the St. Lawrence north of Montreal on the windy morning of 12 Nov 1775, there were only 150 men in the garrison. Sir Guy Carleton and Prescott tried to get their men away in boats; but the Americans captured all of them except Carleton, who was able to slip away. The next destination was the strong fortified city of Quebec—the final conquest of

Canada. Benedict Arnold with another American force was already surrounding this city. They had been sent by General Washington as a diversionary expedition through Maine by way of the Kennebec River. Carleton would have to choose. He could defend Quebec and allow SCHUYLER's troops to advance relatively unimpeded or he could battle the advancing Americans and lose Quebec. He chose Quebec.

This "second front" had been concocted by Benedict Arnold while he stamped and fumed and waited for what he considered to be a miserly Provincial Congress at Watertown tediously studying each item on his expense account of 1,060 British pounds for his expenditures on his earlier victory at Ticonderoga. He presented his Canadian invasion plan to Adjutant General Gates who in turn presented it to Washington. Washington then talked it over with Arnold and impressed with his quick intelligence and tremendous energy chose him to lead the expedition.

He was given a force of about 1100 men, which included three rifle companies. Arnold placed DANIEL MORGAN in charge of these riflemen. DANIEL MORGAN was a thirty-nine-year-old northern wagoner hauling freight between remote settlements.

"He was a giant of a man, big-chested and bull-necked, with a plain, open, friendly face and a mighty temper. His education was negligible, but he had a fine, strong, understanding mind, and was a natural leader. He had fought in the Indian wars and his muscled back still bore the scars of 499 stripes, a miscount for twenty years ago. Recently he had been a farmer in Virginia's beautiful Shenandoah Valley. Big DAN MORGAN was his county's unanimous choice to lead its rifle company to Boston in 1775, and he had come to war with a personal grudge to settle with George III." [*Rebels & Redcoats*, p. 115]

Captain DANIEL MORGAN was tacitly considered second in command by the troops leaving for Quebec.

[Note: DANIEL MORGAN was probably distantly related to sixth-great-grandmother DOROTHY MORGAN. The MORGANs originate in Wales. DOROTHY MORGAN married Dutchman HENRY VAN KIRK in New Jersey, about 1723. Records show that DANIEL MORGAN was born in Hunterdon County, New Jersey.]

The riflemen were chosen but the other men volunteered. The siege on Boston was monotonous, so there were more volunteers than needed.

Preparations were rapidly made and a disappointed rifleman, Jesse Lukens, wrote to his Philadelphia friend on 13 Sep 1775,

> "Here I took leave with a wet eye. The drums beat and away they go as far as Newburyport by land, from there they go in sloops to Kennebec River, up it in batteaux, and have a carrying place of about forty miles over which they must carry on their shoulders their batteaux and baggage, scale the walls [of Quebec] and spend the winter in joy and festivity among the sweet nuns."

Through the lower inhabited part of the Kennebeck, it was a great adventure; but then the going became hard. Over sixty-five tons of supplies had to be hauled around the various falls on aching, raw shoulders; the long pointed batteaux, weighing four hundred pounds apiece, were carried by four men. Five Mile Falls was next, where the river fell thirty-four feet through rapids, "very dangerous and difficult to pass." Sometimes they "plunged over the head into deep basins." Often it rained. 1 October, the men's wet clothes were frozen "a pane of glass thick." Twenty-two year old Dr. Isaac Senter of New Hampshire wrote at the dangerous Norridgewock Falls:

> "By this time, many of our batteaux were nothing but wrecks, some stove to pieces, etc. The carpenters were employed in repairing them, while the rest of the army were busy in carrying over the provisions, etc. . . . We were now curtailed of a very valuable and large part of our provisions, ere we had entered the wilderness or left the inhabitants. Our fare was now reduced to salt pork and flour . . . a few barrels of salt beef remained . . . of so indifferent quality as scarce to be eaten."

Thirty-two miles north of Norridgewock Falls was the Great Carrying Place from the Kennebec to the Dead River. From the doctor's journal we read:

> "Saturday, 14th . . . The army was now much fatigued, being obliged to carry all the batteaux, barrels of provisions, warlike stores, etc. over on their backs through a most terrible piece of woods conceivable. Sometimes in the mud knee deep, then over ledgy hills, etc. . . .
>
> "Sunday 15th . . . Many of us were now in a sad plight with the diarrhea. Our water was of the worst quality . . . . No sooner had it got down than it was puked up by many of the poor fellows.
>
> "Monday 16th . . . We now found it necessary to erect a building for the reception of the sick . . . 19th . . . This carrying place was four miles . . . two

and a half of which ascending till we rose to a great height, then a sudden descent into a tedious spruce and cedar swamp, bog mire half knee high, which completed the other mile and half."

When Benedict Arnold reached the Dead River on October 16, he realized his error. He had thought the total distance to be 180 miles, which he felt could be done in twenty days. He brought food for forty-five days. By 24 October, they were less than half way, and provisions were almost totally lost or consumed. Colonel Green's division had eaten candles the night before "by boiling them in water gruel." Colonel Enos' division voted to return home leaving less than 700 men in near starvation to continue the expedition. Arnold with a guide, a small boat and sufficient men to carry it over the carrying places, boldly pushed ahead. He was hoping to find some French inhabitants and obtain food for his loyal soldiers. When word came back that he had found them and was well received, "unspeakable joy" brimmed over in all the camps. All provisions were pooled and each man received five pints of flour and about two ounces of pork to sustain him over the last 100 miles.

On 1 November, Dr. Senter wrote:

"Clean and unclean were forms now little in use. In company was a poor dog [who had] hitherto lived through all the tribulations [and who] became a prey for the sustenance of the assassinators. This poor animal was instantly devoured, without leaving any vestige of the sacrifice. Nor did the shaving soap, pomatum, and even the lip slave, leather of their shoes, cartridge boxes, etc., share any better fate."

They even ate the extra supply leather carried in their boats.

On 2 November, twenty-two-year-old private Abner Stocking wrote,

"When we arose this morning many of the company were so weak that they could hardly stand on their legs . . . . As I proceeded, I passed many sitting wholly drowned in sorrow, wishfully placing their eyes on everyone who passed by them, hoping for some relief . . . . My heart was ready to burst and my eyes to overflow with tears when I witnessed distress which I could not relieve."

On this same day Dr. Senter stated,

"We were scattered up and down the [Chaudiere] River at the distance of perhaps twenty miles. Not more than eight miles had we marched, when [we saw] a vision of horned cattle, four-footed beasts, etc. rode and drove by animals resembling Plato's two-footed featherless ones. Upon a nigher approach our vision proved real! Exclamations of joy! Echoes of gladness resounded from front to rear with a 'te deum.' Three horned cattle, two horses, eighteen Canadians, and one American. A heifer was chosen as victim to our wants, slain and divided . . . . Soon arrived two more Canadians in . . . canoes, ladened with a coarse kind of meal, mutton, tobacco, etc. Each man drew likewise a pint of this provender . . . . They proceeded up the river in order to the rear's partaking of the same benediction. We sat down, eat our rations, blessed our stars, and thought it luxury."

On 8 November, Private Melvin wrote in his journal,

"Marched six miles and came to Point Levi, on the River St. Lawrence, opposite Quebec."

On 13 and 14 November, Arnold had commandeered sufficient boats and canoes to take his army across the St. Lawrence to Wolfe's Cove. They then ascended to the Plains of Abraham within a mile and a half of the city. Carleton, after escaping the colonials in Montreal, had safely entered the city and now commanded a force of about twelve hundred regulars, militia, and seamen. Arnold, considering himself short of ammunition, cannon and small arms, retired twenty miles up the river to await the arrival of Montgomery's army. They arrived shortly. MONTGOMERY took command and together they plotted to take Quebec by storm in that fierce, sub-zero, windy Canadian winter, which had piled snow up to the second story of many of the houses.

At first they planned their attack for Christmas Day; but the fog lifted. They waited for more favorable surprise-attack weather. The army was split. MONTGOMERY took the southern approach. Unfortunately, a single cannon shot killed MONTGOMERY, two valuable young captains, his orderly sergeant and a private. This left Colonel Campbell, a less spirited officer, in command of Montgomery's troops. He retired them from action, leaving the British forces to concentrate on Arnold's northern approach.

Arnold had passed the Palace Gate unchallenged when they received a tremendous fire of musketry from the ramparts above. Boldly, Arnold led them down into the lower town, yelling to his men to come on. They advanced to a barricaded narrow street. Benedict Arnold stumbled with a bullet in his left leg. He reported,

"'The loss of blood rendered me very weak. As soon as the main body came up . . . . I returned to the hospital, near a mile, on foot, being obliged to draw one leg after me and a great part of the way under the constant fire of the enemy from the walls."

The giant DANIEL MORGAN later wrote a friend:

"I. . . took his place, for, although there were three field officers present, they would not take the command, alleging that I had seen service and they had not . . . . I ordered the ladder, which was on two men's shoulders, to be placed (every two men carried a ladder). This order was immediately obeyed and for fear the business might not be executed with spirit, I mounted myself and was the first man who leaped into the town among [the British gun captain] McLeod's guard [of fifty men] who were panic struck and after a faint resistance ran into a house that joined the battery and platform.

"I lighted on the end of a heavy piece of artillery which hurt me exceedingly and perhaps saved my life, as I fell from the gun upon the platform where the bayonets were not directed.

"Colonel Charles Porterfield, who was then a cadet in my company, was the first man who followed me. The rest lost not a moment, but sprang in as fast as they could find room. All this was . . . in a few seconds. I ordered the men to fire into the house and follow up their fire with their pikes (for besides our rifles we were furnished with long espontoons). This was done and the guard was driven into the street.

"I went through a sally port at the end of the platform, met them in the street, and ordered them to lay down their arms, if they expected quarter. They took me at my word and every man threw down his gun. We then made a charge upon the battery and took it and everything that opposed us, until we arrived at the barrier-gate [at the intersection of Sault-au-Matelot and Mountain Street] where I was ordered to wait for General Montgomery. And a fatal order it was, as it prevented me from taking the garrison, having already made half the town prisoners. The sally port through the barrier was standing open. The guard left it, and the people came running in seeming platoons and gave themselves up in order to get out of the way of the confusion . . . . I went up to the edge of the Upper Town with an interpreter to observe what was going on, as the firing had ceased. I found no person in arms at all. I returned and called a council of war of what officers I had for the greater part had missed their way and had not got into the town.

"Here I was overruled by hard reasoning: it was stated that if I went on I would break an order, in the first place. In the next . . . . I had more prisoners than I had men . . . if I left them, they might break out, retake the battery, and cut off our retreat . . . . General MONTGOMERY was certainly coming down the St. Lawrence and would join us in a few minutes, so that we were sure of conquest if we acted with caution. To these arguments I sacrificed my own opinion and lost the town."

Of course, the retreated army of the now dead General MONTGOMERY never arrived. The British regrouped and American Private George Morison reported,

"Betwixt every peal the awful voice of MORGAN is heard, whose gigantic stature and terrible appearance carries dismay among the foe wherever he comes . . . . We are now attacked in our rear . . . . They call out to us to surrender, but we surrender them our bullets and retreat to the first battery. Here we maintain ourselves until ten o'clock [in the morning], when surrounded . . . many of our officers and men slain, and no hope of escape, we are reluctantly compelled to surrender . . . having fought manfully for more than three hours. Tears of rage streamed down the bearded cheeks of Captain MORGAN, backed against a wall and daring a ring of the enemy to force his sword from his hand. Suddenly in the crowd in the noisy street he spotted a man in clerical garb. 'Are you a priest?' he cried. 'I am.' 'Then I give my sword to you. No scoundrel of those cowards shall take it out of my hands.' The fight for Quebec was over . . . . The Americans had lost about a hundred killed and wounded and four hundred prisoners." [*Rebels and Redcoats, p. 117*]

A British officer made this observation of the prisoners:

"You can have no conception what kind of men composed their officers. Of those we took, one major was a blacksmith, another a hatter. Of their captains, there was a butcher . . . a tanner, a shoemaker, a tavern-keeper, etc. Yet they all pretended to be gentlemen."

And Carleton treated them so. He sent a British Major to the American camp for their baggage, allowed them their own cook, allowed outdoor walks when the weather was warm, and tried to make their confinement endurable.

The wounded Arnold took command from his hospital bed, insisting on arming the hospital patients rather than retreating, if Carleton's army advanced. This Carleton declined to do. His troops waited comfortably in their warm houses with plenty of food for spring and the arrival of reinforcements from England, while Arnold and his men felt the full impact of the twenty-eight-below-zero weather and attempted to lay siege to a city much better prepared than they were. Congress sent the older, lethargic Gen. David Wooster to take command. He was soon replaced by General John Thomas, who soon decided to retreat to Sorel. His retreat took on greater speed when the thaw opened the St. Lawrence and the now reinforced 900 British troops sallied forth. It was perhaps more like a panic to Montreal.

Congress finally became aware of what they were losing in Canada and sent fresh troops under the command of the New Hampshire lawyer, John Sullivan, a self-made son of Irish indentured servants who had no love for the English. He met the British forces at Trois Rivieres and was brutally crushed. His discouraged soldiers trudged back and were joined by Arnold's Montreal garrison at St. John's. At Ile-aux-Noix, they contracted smallpox, malaria, and dysentary, and their bodies were tossed into huge pits in the center of each regimental camp until the survivors could push on to Crown Point. Here, only the Sixth Pennsylvania was left as an advance guard and the rest of the army of less than three thousand took quarters in Ticonderoga in early July 1776. It seemed at that time to many that bad luck and bad leadership had wasted five thousand men and a great deal of money.

[Note: Fourth-great-grandfather JOHN COOLEY or COLE, was captured at the battle of Three Rivers (Trois Rivieres) and was soon exchanged and joined again with the army. He was later a sergeant with the colonial German regiment. Fourth-great-grandfather JOSEPH POYER may have been with the Americans with his cousins from Fort Chambly, or, if his father was THOMAS POYER of Dutchess County, New York, his father's sickness and later death may have been the result of injuries sustain in these battles. Sons JOSEPH and his older brother would have been under 21-years-of-age. With the Pennsylvanians in this Canadian campaign were: fourth-great-grandfathers Captain ELISHA BARTON and JOHN WILKINSON, and their 26-year-old cousin, the future militia brigadier-general JOHN LACEY—the first young man to organize and enlist troops on both sides of the Delaware River north of Philadelphia.]

~ 72 ~

BACK IN BOSTON

While the Canadian campaign was progressing, General Gage was wise enough to realize that his troops were not sufficient to come at the more numerous colonial army. He waited for additional troops, while his army licked their wounds from Bunker Hill. One of their surgeons groaned:

> "I have scarce time sufficient to eat my meals . . . . The Provincials had either exhausted their ball, or they were determined that every wound should prove mortal; their muskets were charged with old nails and angular pieces of iron, and from most of our men being wounded in the legs, we are inclined to believe it was their design, not wishing to kill the men, but leave them as burdens on us."

Royal Attorney General Jonathan Sewall stated:

> "Death has so long stalked among us that he is become much less terrible to me than he once was. Habit has a great influence over that mystical substance, the human mind. Funerals are now so frequent that for a month past you met as many dead folks as live ones in Boston streets, and we pass them with much less emotion and attention than we used to pass dead sheep and oxen in days of yore when such sights were to be seen in our streets."

The British shot a lot of cannon balls at the Americans, which were mostly dodged and did little damage. An English officer wrote:

> "As far as I can guess from a matter not perfectly known, we at present are worse off than the rebels. In point of numbers they so far surpass us that we are like a few children in the midst of a large crowd. Trusting to this superiority, they grow daily more and more bold, menacing us most insolently; and we fear when the days shorten, and the dark nights come on, they'll put some of their threats in execution, unless other reinforcements and a fleet of war arrive soon. They know our situation, as well as we do

ourselves, from the villains that are left in town, who acquaint them with all our proceedings, making signals by night with gunpowder, and at day, out of church steeples."

But the Whigs who remained in Boston were far worse off than either the regulars or the Tories. John Leach a prominent Whig teacher of navigation, was jailed on false charges of spying. Confined in the Stone Gaol, on whose top floor lay the captured American Bunker Hill wounded, he recorded,

> "The poor sick and wounded prisoners fare very hard, are many days without the comforts of life. Dr. Brown complained to Mr. Lovell and me, that they had no bread all that day and the day before. He spoke to the Provost, as he had the charge of serving the bread; he replied they might 'eat the nail heads, and gnaw the planks and be damn'd.' . . . They have no wood to burn many days together. . . . Some of the limbs which have been taken off, it was said, were in a state of putrefaction, not one survived amputation."

On 26 Sep 1775, the British *H.M.S. Scarborough* arrived in Boston harbor; but instead of bringing the troops that the sincere, devoted servant of the king, General Gage requested, it brought a letter recalling him to London and the orders that Sir Guy Carleton was to command all British troops in Canada, and William Howe, all troops south of there, until Gage's return. Gage was not deceived. He knew as he sailed for home on 11 October that he would not return. His powerful political enemies in London had destroyed his command.

General George Washington was not without his problems, also. When the Continental Army came to Massachusetts in July, they had expected some brief encounters with the British and then some reasonable peace negotiations. Independence was not the common object in those days. But as the Continental Army entrenched and waited, so did Gage and his successor Howe wait. The English hoped to completely wear out the rebels' taste for resistance. On December 10, the enlistment of all Connecticut and Rhode Island troops would terminate and the homesick warriors planned to march home that day. On 31 December, all the other enlistments in New England expired. Unless something was done, Washington would be a general without an army. Twice he planned an attack on Boston; but his council of officers rejected his proposals, although on the second proposal in October the Congressional Committee was in camp and had expressed their strong approval for action. Enlistment beyond their terms went badly. As of 19 November, only 996 men of eleven regiments had agreed to continue service.

Washington wrote congress nine days later. On the same day he also wrote his friend Joseph Reed, the Philadelphia lawyer:

"Such a dearth of public spirit and want of virtue, such stock-jobbing and fertility in all the low arts to obtain advantages of one kind or another in this great change of military arrangement I never saw before, and pray God I may never be witness to again. . . . .And such a dirty mercenary spirit pervades the whole that I should not be at all surprised at any disaster that may happen. In short, after the last of this month, our lines will be so weakened that the minutemen and militia must be called for their defense; these being under no kind of government themselves will destroy the little subordination I have been laboring to establish . . . . Could I have fore-seen what I have and am likely to experience, no consideration upon earth should have induced me to accept this command."

Calling in the militia and minutemen was a great worry to General Washington. He had experience with militia in the French and Indian War. He wanted a Continental army he could train and depend upon. The militia were originally under the command of each colonial government and had been trained to defend their homelands when an emergency presented itself and then to go home to their farming and families. They were needed to patrol the vast New England coast line and prevent the British ships from raiding their farms and burning their towns. It was their duty also to control the Tories from de-structive activities, and were successful at this.

He complained:

"I fear I shall be under the necessity of Calling in the Militia and minute men of the Country to my assistance. I say I fear it, because, by what I can Learn from the Officers in the Army belonging to this Colony, it will be next to an impossibility to keep them under any degree of Discipline, & that it will be very difficult to prevail on them to remain a moment Longer than they Chuse themselves, it is a mortifying reflection to be reduced to this Dilema."

Nevertheless, he called them, and the Colonial governments responded quickly to help him. On 11 December, Washington responded to Congress,

"The militia are coming fast. I am much pleased with the alacrity which the good people of this province, as well as those of New Hampshire, have shown upon this occasion; I expect the whole will be in this day and to-morrow, when what remains of the Connecticut gentry who have not en-listed will have liberty to go to their firesides."

Two days later a report from camp reported,

"things wear a better complexion here than they have done for some time past. The army is filling up. The barracks go on well. Firewood comes in. The soldiers are made comfortable and easy."

Martha Washington arrived from Virginia to be with her husband. General Charles Lee was delighted with the militia and wrote to a friend,

"Some of the Connecticutians who were homesick could not be prevailed on to tarry, which means in the New England dialect to serve any longer. They accordingly marched off bag and baggage, but in passing through the lines of other regiments, they were so horribly hissed, groaned at, and pelted that I believe they wished their aunts, grandmothers, and even sweethearts to whom the day before they were so much attached at the devil's own palace."

"January 1, 1776, presented a great change in the American army. The officers and men of the new regiments were joining their respective corps; those of the old regiments were going home by hundreds and by thou-sands . . . . Such a change in the very teeth of the enemy, is a most delicate maneuver; but the British did not attempt to take advantage of it."

The above was from the journal of General Heath.

Washington was greatly relieved. He declared,

"Search the vast volumes of history through and I much question whether a case similar to ours is to be found; to wit, to maintain a post against the flower of the British troops for six months together, without [powder] and at the end of them to have one army disbanded and another to raise within the same distance of a reinforced enemy."

Colonial Victory at Boston

Word came early in January that the British were fitting out a Boston fleet whose object might be New York. General Lee was sent quickly to New York to put it "into the best posture of defense which the season and circumstances will admit of," using volunteers and whatever troops New Jersey could furnish. By 20 January, the strong and rugged Henry Knox was within twenty miles of the camp with his fifty-odd pieces of heavy artillery from captured Fort Ticonderoga. The tremendous guns had been dismounted by hand, floated in scows and boats the length of Lake George, and then brought over the snowy Berkshires and Massachusetts by sleigh. If these guns could be mounted on the lines-—if the lines could be extended to include the Dorcester hills, and if powder enough were available-—then said Colonel Moylan, "I do believe Boston would fall into our hands." Powder enough was the problem.

As news of a British evacuation kept trickling in, the general and his council concluded that the only way to get at Howe, before he should slip away, was to lure him out. And the way to do that was to seize Dorchester Neck. If they could then fortify its heights quickly, victory was a strong possibility, and a victory was needed, not only for the stagnant Continental Congress and the unification of the colonials, but also to discourage the whole British Empire and encourage some help from their enemies. All of Europe was watching.

There was still snow on Dorchester Heights. Colonel Rufus Putnam suggested that earthworks be built on top of the ground instead of dug into it. Construct them of fascines held in place by wooden frames they called chandeliers. Haul up bundles of hay. Cover the hay and fascines with earth and make parapets. The army went to work. fascines and chandeliers were built. Hay was screwed into great bundles. Wagons and carts were collected from the country. Solid shot and shell were brought up to the guns in easy range of Boston. Boats were assembled in the Charles River, if needed for a retreat. The militia was called up from the neighboring towns. On 28 February, Washington wrote to his wife's brother-in-law Burwell Bassett,

> "We are preparing to take possession of a post (which I hope to do in a few days, if we can get provided with the means) which will, it is generally thought, bring on a rumpus between us and the enemy."

Studying the tides, the weather, the circumstances, they decided to take their positions on Dorchester Neck on Monday night, 4 March. As a diversion, a cannonade was opened on Boston the night of the 2nd—eleven balls and thirteen solid shot. These were warmly returned by the British, but with little damage. It was repeated on the next night. On the night of the fourth, heavy American fire burst from Cobble Hill, Lechmere's Point and Lamb's Dam at Roxbury.

As darkness began to enshroud the city, General Thomas with three thousand chosen men started from Roxbury for the hills on Dorchester peninsula. They were followed by three hundred teams, hauling fascines, chandeliers, screwed hay, and barrels. They deposited their loads and returned for more. It was a clear night with a full moon.

General Heath wrote:

"The Americans took possession of Dorchester Heights and nearly completed their works on both the hills by morning. Perhaps there never was so much work done in so short a space of time. The adjoining orchards were cut down to make the abatis, and a very curious and novel mode of defense was added to these works. The hills on which they were erected were steep and clear of trees and bushes. Rows of barrels, filled with earth, were placed round the works. They presented only the appearance of strengthening the works, but the real design was, in case the enemy made an attack, to have rolled them down the hill. They would have descended with such increasing velocity, as must have thrown the assailants into the utmost confusion, and have killed and wounded great numbers."

Major John Trumbull recorded:

"Our movement was not discovered by the enemy until the following morning, and had an uninterrupted day to strengthen the works which had been commenced the night preceding. During this day we saw distinctly the preparations which the enemy were making to dislodge us. The entire water front of Boston lay open to our observation, and we saw the embarkation of troops from the various wharves, on board of ships, which hauled off in succession, and anchored in a line in our front, a little before sunset, prepared to land the troops in the morning.

"We were in high spirits, well prepared to receive the threatened attack. Our position[s], on the summits of two smooth, steep hills, were strong by nature, and well fortified. We had at least twenty pieces of artillery mounted on them, amply supplied with ammunition, and a very considerable force of well-armed infantry. We waited with impatience for the attack . . . . In the evening the Commander in Chief visited us and examined all our points of preparation for defense. Soon after his visit the rain, which had already commenced, increased to a violent storm, an heavy gale of wind, which deranged all the enemy's plan of debarkation, driving the ships foul of each other, and from their anchors in utter confusion, and thus put a stop to the intended operation."

The "finger of Providence," upon which Washington had relied before stopped Howe's attack and gave the Americans time to make their defenses on the heights so strong that they could not be forced. With American guns commanding a large part of the city and the harbor and the Colonial positions impregnable, Howe, who had been instructed by Dartmouth months before to abandon Boston, decided it was a great time to evacuate this city. A British deserter stated that Mr. Howe went upon a hill in Boston the morning after the Colonials had occupied Dorcester Neck and General Howe had made this exclamation:

> "Good G—! These fellows have done more work in one night than I could have made my army do in three months. What shall I do!"

On Sunday, 17 March, St. Patrick's Day, a newspaperman printed:

> "This morning the British army in Boston, under General Howe, consisting of upwards of seven thousand men, after suffering an ignominious blockade for many months past, disgracefully quitted all their strongholds in Boston and Charlestown, fled from before the army of the United Colonies, and took refuge on board their ships . . . . The joy of our friends in Boston, on seeing the victorious and gallant troops of their country enter the town almost at the heels of their barbarous oppressors, was inexpressibly great . . . . We are told that the Tories were thunder-struck when orders were issued for evacuating the town, after being many hundred times assured, that such reinforcements would be sent, as to enable the king's troops to ravage the country at pleasure . . . . Many of them, it is said, considered themselves as undone, and seemed, at times, inclined to throw themselves on the mercy of their offended country, rather than leave it. One or more of them, it is reported have been left to end their lives by the unnatural act of suicide . . . . To the wisdom, firmness, intrepidity and military abilities of our amiable and beloved general, his Excellency George Washington Esquire, to the assiduity, skill and bravery of the other worthy generals and officers of the army, and to the hardiness and gallantry of the soldiery, is to be ascribed, under God, the glory and success of our arms, in driving from one of the strongest holds in America, so considerable a part of the British army as that which last week occupied Boston."

On Monday, 18 March, Washington dispatched five regiments of foot and two companies of artillery to follow the rifle battalion already marching for New York. Rumors were rampant that Howe's army was sailing to Halifax; but Washington was convinced that his real destination was New York:

> "It is the object worthy their attention; and it is the place that we must use every endeavor to keep from them."

~ 73 ~

COMMON SENSE —A WAR OF WORDS

The Second Continental Congress had assembled with directions from all thirteen colonies that they were NOT to declare independence from Great Britain. They, therefore, spent many long hours in committees or as a whole trying to reach some form of reconciliation with their mother country. Each of the colonies had only one vote and in all their decisions they wanted unanimity. Different colonies sent different numbers of delegates; but a large number of delegates only added to the possibility of dissension within the colony regarding their one vote. Distressed with the slow pace and long hard hours, many delegates would go home for periods of time, leaving decisions to the more willing or ambitious workers.

John Adams wrote on 17 Jun 1775,

"America is a great, unwieldy body. Its progress must be slow. It is like a large fleet sailing under convoy. The fleetest sailors must wait for the dullest and slowest. Like a coach and six, the swiftest horses must be slackened, and the slowest quickened, that all may keep an even pace."

He and his cousin Sam Adams had wanted independence from the beginning of the Congress—they had dealt with, and instigated, British animosity for years. Each of the colonies had their own problems with their former Royal governors and assemblies. Thomas Jefferson had been slow to come to the Continental Congress, and when the individual colonies started to consider independence, he expressed regret that he had come. He wanted to be back in action in Virginia.

North Carolina's Sons of Liberty had created a great philosophical division between their eastern coastal region and the fast expanding western frontier (where many of my ancestors were) when these eastern colonials supported British Governor Tryon and joined his army in the "War of the Regulators" defeating their fellow North Carolinians. Tryon, when he was made Governor of New York, had been replaced with Governor Martin who had taken advantage of this division, giving amnesty and favor to the westerners in return for their "Oaths of Allegiance" to the Crown. Governor Martin promised Parliament and King George that this vast region would fight with the British, if they could take the coast.

Tryon did not stay very long in New York before he was called back to London as an advisor to parliament and the king regarding their rebel American colonies. When he returned to New York and his loyal Tory friends, he feared for his life and property; but Washington had instructed the New York militia to leave him alone, unless he became an active threat.

Benjamin Franklin's son William had curried favor with the British while his father was in London attempting to reconcile the colonial differences, and William was appointed governor of New Jersey. William remained a loyal subject to the king and was eventually imprisoned in Connecticut by the colonials for his activities. He was exchanged by the British in 1778 and remained loyal to the Crown.

Pennsylvania's John Dickinson of the Continental Congress had drafted the Olive Branch Petition to the king, which Congress had adopted and signed on 8 Jul 1775. Richard Penn, a former governor of Pennsylvania, with the colonial agent, Arthur Lee, delivered it to Lord Dartmouth, the King's Secretary for the American Colonies, "the first moment that was permitted us" on 1 Sep 1775, since George III had refused to receive it in person. When seeking an answer, they were told that since the king would not formally receive the petition on the throne, no answer would be given.

However, it would seem that the king had already answered, for on 23 August, he had issued a proclamation that said the Americans had "proceeded to open an avowed rebellion."

Then on 26 Oct 1775, in a speech to parliament, the king asserted that the American rebellion was

"manifestly carried on for the purpose of establishing an independent Empire. [The time had come] to put a speedy end to these disorders by the most decisive exertions." The British were to strengthen their naval and land forces and to consider "friendly offers of foreign assistance."

After some debate, parliament approved the king's speech and further passed a "Prohibitory Act" that prohibited all commerce with the thirteen North American colonies "during the continuance of the present Rebellion." The act declared the Colonial vessels and their cargoes, whether in harbor or at sea, forfeit to the Crown "as if the same were the ships and effects of open enemies." It also allowed the impressment of those vessels' officers and crews into the Royal Navy, in effect, forcing them to fight against their countrymen. Their commanders of the Royal Navy were given orders in the king's name "to proceed as in case of actual rebellion against such of the sea port towns and places being accessible to the king's ships, in which any troops shall be raised or military works erected." As a result, British Captain Henry Mowatt assembled the people of Falmouth (now Portland, Maine), accused them of rebellion, and gave them two hours, which was later extended until the next morning, to leave the town, which he brutally bombarded from 9:30 A.M. until sunset, driving "hundreds of helpless women and children" from their homes in a manner long since abandoned by "civilized nations."

Then 7 Nov 1775, Lord Dunmore, the Royal Governor of Virginia, issued a proclamation offering freedom to slaves who would join him and fight their masters, and so won more Virginians to the idea of Independence, as the historian Merrill Jensen put it, "than all the acts of Parliament since the founding of the colonies."

On 8 Jan 1776, news of George III's October speech was received by the Continental Congress, that also learned on that day that a British fleet had set sail with 5,000 troops and that "Ld. Dunmore has Destroyed the Town of Norfolk in Virginia."

Norfolk, of course, was where our original IVIE ancestors settled, beginning in 1613. The following is taken from the *Historical Register* from papers belonging to my mother, LILLIE IVIE CONDIE:

"Capt. WILLIAM IVY was born on the estate, which he afterwards inherited from his father, called 'Sycamore View,' and situated on Tanner's Creek, in the county of Norfolk. This estate, or a portion of it, is still in possession of his lineal descendants, having been transmitted from father to son for 170 years. Very early in the revolutionary war, having been brought up to the sea, Capt. IVY entered the naval service of the State, though not in his case for the reason assigned by Commodore Barron when he says that masters of vessels were compelled to enter the navy 'in order to obtain clothes suitable to their decent appearance in public,' for at that time Capt. IVY owned two plantations, and was in the habit of building vessels on them at his own cost. During the war, however, he suffered greatly from the depredations of the enemy—his residence, 'Sycamore View' being only about two miles from Hampton Roads. The houses on both of his estates were plundered and then destroyed by fire, together with his crops, after the deprecators had abundantly supplied themselves, and about sixty of his slaves were carried off by the British, and never recovered."

[Note: According to the research and pedigree compiled by Alice Granbery Walter of Virginia Beach, Virginia, a Capt. WILLIAM IVEY, born about 1702, was the son of seventh-great-grandparents, GEORGE IVY and ELIZABETH LANGLEY of Prince George County, Virginia. GEORGE inherited land in Norfolk from his father and Capt. WILLIAM IVY was mentioned in the will of eighth-great-grandmother ELIZABETH MASON THELABALL of Tanner's Creek, Norfolk, Virginia, and she described him as the son of GEORGE IVY. Since the Capt. WILLIAM IVY in the article was born in Norfolk, he was probably GEORGE's grandson. These original land patents were granted in the 1630s to 1680s, so the above article must have been written in the early or middle 1800s.]

In Congress, the "conservative" Robert Morris of Pennsylvania reported that the seizing of American ships and burning of colonial towns along "with numerous acts of wanton barbarity & Cruelty perpetrated by the British Forces has prepared Men's minds for an Independency, that were shock'd at the idea a few weeks ago." However, on 9 January, the day after the news of the burning of Norfolk reached Congress, James Wilson proposed that Congress once again "disavow any desire for Independence."

Such were the feelings and debate in the Philadelphian Second Continental Congress when this same day the Philadelphia press of Robert Bell distributed the first copies of *Common Sense*. It was copied anonymously, but later it became known that it was the work of Thomas Paine. Paine was a largely self-educated Englishman of no particular previous distinction, who first arrived in America on 30 Nov 1774. This pamphlet was not the writings of a polished aristocrat. John Adams later described his language as "suitable for an Emigrant from New Gate [the English jail], or one who had chiefly associated with such Company."

Paine argued that American freedom would never be secure under British rule, because "the so much boasted Constitution of England" was deeply flawed

with two major "constitutional errors" —
monarchy and hereditary rule. Monarchy
and hereditary rule made bad rulers even
of capable individuals by breeding arrogance, and by separating them from the
rest of mankind whose interests they
needed to know well. The ambitions
of kings and those who would be kings
caused civil and foreign wars that had
laid both Britain and "the world in ashes."
The only way to solve that problem was
to redesign the government, eliminating
monarchy and hereditary rule and expanding the "republican" element of the
British government which derived power

THOMAS PAINE

not from birth but from the ballot. The solution, then, was revolution—but
with plans for a new government. Americans could "form the noblest, purest
constitution on the face of the earth," one free of the errors that had dogged
mankind for centuries. "We have it in our power to begin the world over again
... [and affect the future of] all mankind."

Paine challenged the fears of the Colonials. Could the Americans hold out
against the British? Yes, since they had sufficient men and materials, a strength
that came from political unity, and the prospect of foreign aid. Would their
economy survive? Yes, American products "will always have a market while eating is the custom of Europe." He reminded the colonials of the king's willingness
to use Indians, slaves, and foreign mercenaries to defeat and subject them to the
whims of parliament and the king. He wrote,

> "No man was a warmer wisher for reconciliation than myself, before the
> fatal nineteenth of April, 1775, but the moment the event of the day was
> made known, I rejected the hardened, sullen-tempered Pharaoh of England
> for ever; and disdain the wretch, that with the pretended title of FATHER
> OF HIS PEOPLE can unfeelingly hear of their slaughter, and composedly
> sleep with their blood upon his soul. . . . How came the king by a power
> which the people are afraid to trust, and always obliged to check? Such a

power could not be the gift of a wise people, neither can any power, which needs checking, be from God . . . . Not one third of the inhabitants, even of this province, are of English descent. [He mentioned Holland, Germany, Sweden, and France.] Wherefore I reprobate the phrase of parent or mother country applied to England only, as being false, selfish, narrow and ungenerous . . . . The blood of the slain, the weeping voice of nature cries, 'TIS TIME TO PART.' Even the distance at which the Almighty hath placed England and America, is a strong and natural proof, that the authority of the one, over the other, was never the design of Heaven. The reformation was preceded by the discovery of America, as if the Almighty graciously meant to open a sanctuary to the persecuted in future years, when home should afford neither friendship nor safety. . . . But where says some is the King of America? I'll tell you Friend; he reigns above, and doth not make havoc of mankind like the Royal Brute of Britain. Yet that we may not appear to be defective even in earthly honors, let a day be solemnly set apart for proclaiming the charter; let it be brought forth placed on the divine law, the word of God; let a crown be placed thereon, by which the world may know, that so far as we approve of monarchy, that in America THE LAW IS KING. For as in absolute governments the King is law, so in free countries the law ought to be King; and there ought to be no other. But lest any ill use should afterwards arise, let the crown . . . . be demolished, and scattered among the people whose right it is."

"Common Sense for eighteen pence," appeared in advertisements in newspapers, taverns, "and at every place of public resort."

Paine estimated that some 150,000 copies had been sold in America alone. The pamphlet's style, the news of the King's October speech, the burning of Norfolk, Virgina, "struck a string which required but a touch to make it vibrate," the Reverend Ashbel Green testified.

"The country was ripe for independence, and only needed somebody to tell the people so, with decision, boldness, and plausibility."

Paine wanted to shift the focus of public debate from the prospects for reconciliation to deciding how an independent America should be governed. And that is what he did.

~ 74 ~

TRAVAILS OF THE BIRTH OF A NATION!

Heart and Hand Shall Move Together

"Indeed We Must All HANG Together,
otherwise We Shall most assuredly HANG Separately"
Benjamin Franklin, signing the Declaration of Independence

It is fortunate for all of us that when a child is born neither the mother nor the child can reverse the process of birth when the hard labor pains commence—the population might not have survived. So it was in America. In 1777, Thomas Paine wrote:

"America, by her own internal industry, and unknown to all the powers of Europe, was, at the beginning of the dispute, arrived at a pitch of greatness, trade and population, beyond which it was the interest of Britain not to suffer her to pass, lest she should grow too powerful to be kept subordinate."

And as the war dragged on, even British Lord North frequently stated that

"the advantages of the contest could never repay the expence."

To this King George III replied,

"The present Contest with America I cannot help seeing as the most serious in which any Country was ever engaged[;] it contains such a train of consequences that they must be examined to feel its true weight . . . step by step the demands of America have risen—independence is their object . . . should America succeed in that, the West Indies must follow them, not independence, but must for its own interest be dependent on North America; Ireland would soon follow the same plan and be a separate State, then this Island would be reduced to itself, and soon would be a poor Island indeed, for reduced in Her Trade, Merchants would retire their

Wealth to Climates more to their Advantage, and Shoals of Manufacturers would leave this Country for the New Empire."

The dye had been cast. As Thomas Paine said, "The Rubicon was passed."

He ended his pamphlet by advising,

"Let none other be heard among us, than those of a good citizen . . . and a virtuous supporter of the RIGHTS of MANKIND and of the FREE AND INDEPENDANT STATES OF AMERICA."

The struggle for power might have been delayed, but could not have been reversed. As King George III put it—"submit or triumph!" Both sides chose to triumph, regardless of cost.

As the idea of a republic started to mature within the thirteen colonies, questions started to be asked. If the people rule, who will be ruled? Athens and Rome had early republics that never survived. England even had its own commonwealth of the 1650s. It didn't survive. Can a republican nation survive? Would "Intestine Wars and Convulsions" among the colonies leave the Americans worse off than they were under a hostile king and parliament?

> John Adams argued that the creation of constitutions for the states could only be accomplished on "popular Principles and Maxims," which were "abhorrent to the Inclinations of the Barons of the South, and the Proprietary Interest in the Middle Colonies—thirteen Colonies under such a Form of Government as that of Connecticut . . . leagued together in a faithfull Confederacy, might bid Defiance to the Potentates of Europe if united against them."

[Note: It might be well to remember that at this time the American colonists had carried with them across the Atlantic many of the aristocratic ways of Europe. Large estates were entailed to the oldest sons. The more prominent, wealthy families had permanent family seats in the legislatures. Committees for safety, military leaders, and so forth, were usually taken from these same families. These people would often marry their cousins or other strong leaders.

One such family was the LIVINGSTONs of New York. Robert, the elder, was in Rotterdam, Holland, when his exiled (for non-comforming) Scottish father, the Reverend John Livingston died there. He decided to seek his fortune in America and arrived at Charlestown, Massachusetts, 28 Apr 1673. Since he had learned the Dutch language, he decided to settle in Albany, where he bought land in March 1675. Robert married ALIDA SCHUYLER (Van Rensselaer), born in Albany 28 Feb 1656. She was the widow of DOMINIE NICOLAS VAN RENNSELAER (died Nov 1678). ALIDA was the daughter of Philip Pieter Schuyler, the first mayor of Albany. Robert Livingston became the first town clerk. When Robert, the elder and first Lord of the Manor Livingston, died 1 Oct. 1728, he entailed his manor to his oldest surviving son—PHILIP, and 13,000 acres went to his son ROBERT of New York City.

This (son) ROBERT LIVINGSTON became the grandfather of ROBERT R. LIVINGSTON, who was on the Committee in charge of drafting the Declaration of Independence. He never signed the document, as he had other duties in New York at the time. He became Chancellor of the state of New York in 1777. When George Washington became the first president of the United States, ROBERT R. LIVINGSTON gave him his oath of office. ROBERT R. LIVINGSTON's wife was a great-granddaughter of Phillip Pieter Schuyler and a granddaughter of STEPHEN VAN RENNSELAER. She was descended on the Livingston side from ROBERT LIVINGSTON, the nephew of ROBERT LIVINGSTON, the elder.

ROBERT R.'s sister JANET, born 27 Aug 1743, married General RICHARD MONTGOMERY 4 Jul 1773. He was the commanding general that was killed in the battle for Quebec, 31 Dec 1775. They had no children.

PHILIP, the Second Lord of the Manor, also had a "princely manor" in New York City. He was described as handsome, dashing and gay and had "a winning way with women, and went about breaking hearts promiscuously." He was a member of the New York bar. He married on 19 Sep 1707, CATRINA VAN BRUGH, whose mother was SARA CUYLER, the daughter of HENDRICK and ANNETJE SCHEPMOES CUYLER, the original progenitors from Holland. This is the PHILIP characterized in the previous chapter from the journal of Dr. Hamilton's in Albany in 1744.

Their first son, ROBERT, was born in Albany 16 Dec 1708. He became the Third Lord of the Manor of Livingston in 1749, when his father died. This ROBERT occupied the family seat in the New York legislature from 1737 until 1758. He is described as being too old when the Revolutionary War broke out; but he had four sons who were "active for liberty." However, this elderly man placed at the disposal of the Committee for Safety his "Iron mines and Foundry." He became practically impoverished by war debts—even wondering where his next meal would come from. He died at home in Clermont, New York, in November 1790.

ROBERT (son of PHILLIP) married first Maria Thong, or Tong, whose maternal grandfather was Rip Van Dam, who was president of the council. ROBERT's second wife was GERTRUDE VAN RENNSELAER (Schuyler), daughter of patroon KILEAEN VAN RENNSELAER [son of JEREMIAS and Maria Van Cortland RENNSELAER, also mentioned in Dr. Hamilton's travels]. GERTRUDE was the widow of ADONIJAH SCHUYLER, whose will was probated on 28 May 1762. ROBERT had 13 children by his first wife. Their first three children died quite young—not married. The fourth child of ROBERT and Maria Thong was Colonel PETER ROBERT LIVINGSTON. Their fifth child, MARY LIVINGSTON, married JAMES DUANE, 21 Oct 1759. The Honorable JAMES DUANE was a member of the Provincial Congress in April 1775 and a delegate to the Second Continental Congress on 10 May 1775, in Philadelphia, where he tried very hard to preserve alliances with England. ROBERT and Maria Thong's sixth child, WALTER LIVINGSTON, was also a delegate to the Provincial Congress in 1775. He was a member of the New York Assembly in 1777, 1778 and 1779. He was their Speaker in 1778-79. He was a member of the Continental Congress in 1784 and Commissioner of the U.S. Treasury in 1785. ROBERT and Maria Thong's seventh child was ROBERT CAMBRIDGE LIVINGSTON. Their twelfth child JOHN was the only loyalist, and their youngest son was HENDRICK, who was born in New York City, 8 Jan 1753, and died unmarried 20 May 1823.

The LIVINGSTON descendants have remained active in New York and U. S. politics through the years. Among the many, ELEANOR ROOSEVELT, b. 11 Oct 1884, who was the favorite niece of President TEDDY ROOSEVELT and the wife of FDR, was also a descendant of the LIVINGSTONs on her mother's side. [FDR was a fifth-cousin of TEDDY ROOSEVELT.] TEDDY's mother was MARTHA BULLOCK, of Georgia. The son of ROBERT IVEY, WILLIAM A. IVEY, married FLORIDA BULLOCK, 10 Mar 1852, in Georgia, which gives him a shirt-tail family-in-law connection to President TEDDY ROOSEVELT.

None of my direct ancestors appear to be the recipients of entailed lands in New England, Virginia, or New York, at the time of the Revolutionary War. The 'younger sons' of these northern ancestors had moved into western New Jersey and eastern Pennsylvania, which spared them from some of the New England fighting. My direct southern ancestors were in southern Virginia and north-central North Carolina. These northern direct ancestors were probably not part of the strong 'proprietary interest' of the middle colonies spoken of by John Adams, nor were the Southerners the land 'Barons of the Southern Colonies' he referred to. However, it appears that they were not so distantly related to some of these groups that they would not have felt some of the impact the war had on them. Certainly they had read "Common Sense." Those who were Quakers were faced with an additional decision regarding their religion's strong feelings for peace at any price and the Quaker's general dislike of any controlling central government. It is beyond the scope of this book to know or attempt to guess the true feelings of my ancestors; but with uncle JOHN WILKINSON as a member of the Pennsylvania Congress who belatedly voted for independence; with their first cousin STEPHEN HOPKINS' long stand for independence and his signature on the final document; with nephew JOHN LACEY first to recruit volunteers for George Washington along the Delaware river; with great-grand-parents ELISHA BARTON enlisting first as an ensign and being promoted to captain, and fourth-great-grandfather JOHN COLE, or COOLEY, the captured enlisted private at Three Rivers, who was promoted to sergeant; it would seem that most of my northern relations were willing to do whatever they could to stand for independence from Great Britain.]

Virginia consents

On Wednesday, 15 May 1776, the one hundred and twelve members of Virginia's colonial government sent their unanimous instructions to their delegates in the Second Continental Congress.

"Forasmuch as all the endeavours of the United Colonies, by the most decent representations and petitions to the King and Parliament of Great Britain, to restore peace and security to America under the British Government, and a reunion with that people upon just and liberal terms, instead of a redress of grievances, have produced from an imperious and vindictive Administration increased insult, oppression, and a vigorous attempt to effect our total destruction. By a late act, all these Colonies are declared to be in rebellion, and out of the protection of the British crown; our properties subject to confiscation; our people, when captivated, compelled to join in the murder and plunder of their relations and countrymen; and all former rapine and oppression of Americans declared legal and just. Fleets and Armies are raised, and the aid of foreign troops engaged to assist these destructive purposes. The King's representative in the Colony hath not only withheld all the powers of Government from operating for our safety, but, having retired on board an armed ship, is carrying on a piratical and savage war against us, tempting our slaves, by every artifice to resort to him, and training and employing them against their masters.

"In this state of extreme danger we have no alternative left but an abject submission to the will of those overbearing tyrants, or a total separation from the Crown and Government of Great Britain . . . . Resolved, unanimously, That the Delegates appointed to represent this Colony in General Congress be instructed to propose to that respectable body to declare the

United Colonies free and independent States; absolved from all allegiance to, or dependance upon, the Crown or Parliament of Great Britain, and that they give the assent of this Colony to such declaration, and to whatever measures may be thought proper and necessary by Congress for forming foreign alliances, and a confederation of the Colonies . . . . Provided, that the power of forming Government for the regulation of the internal concerns of the Colony, be left to the respective Colonial Legislatures.

"Resolved, unanimously, That a Committee be appointed to prepare a Declaration of rights, and such a plan of Government as will be most likely to maintain peace and order in this Colony, and secure substantial and equal liberty to the people.

"Edmund Pendleton, President"

Some distant cousins were in the Virginia Assembly at Williamsburg. Many of the IVIEs of Norfolk and Sussex Counties joined the Continental Army and gave aid in other ways to the cause. Two-years-old, third-great-grandfather ANDERSON IVIE had been born in Virginia on the 29 Mar 1774, according to the census records and his tombstone in Missouri.

Pennsylvania consents

The Assembly of Pennsylvania sent the following instructions to their Delegates in Congress on 8 June 1776:

"Gentlemen: When, by our instructions of last November, we strictly enjoined you, in behalf of this Colony, to dissent from, and utterly reject any proposition, should such be made, that might cause or lead to a separation from Great Britain, or a change of the form of this Government, our restrictions did not arise from any diffidence of your ability, prudence, or integrity, but from an earnest desire to serve the good people of Pennsylvania with fidelity, in times so full of alarming dangers and perplexing difficulties.

"The situation of publick affairs is since so greatly altered, that we now think ourselves justifiable in removing the restrictions laid upon you by those instructions . . . . We therefore hereby authorize you to concur with the other Delegates in Congress in forming such further compacts between the United Colonies, concluding such treaties with foreign Kingdoms and States, and in adopting such other measures as shall be judged necessary for promoting the liberty, safety, and interests of America; reserving to the people of this Colony the sole and exclusive right of regulating the internal government and police of the same.

"The happiness of these Colonies has, during the whole course of this fatal controversy, been our first wish; their reconciliation with Great Britain our next. Ardently have we prayed for the accomplishment of both. But if we must renounce the one or the other, we humbly trust in the mercies of the Supreme Governour of the Universe, that we shall not stand condemned before His throne if our choice is determined by that overruling law of self-preservation, which His divine wisdom has thought fit to implant in the hearts of His creatures."

On 24 Jun 1776, the Provincial Conference of Pennsylvania met, read, reread, considered and with the greatest unanimity of all the Members, agreed to and adopted the following Declaration:

"Whereas, George the Third, King of Great Britain, Etc., in violation of the principals of the British Constitution, and of the laws of justice and humanity, hath, by an accumulation of oppressions unparalleled in history, excluding the inhabitants of this, with the other American Colonies, from his protection; and whereas he hath paid no regard to any of our numerous and dutiful petitions for a redress of our complicated grievances, but hath lately purchased foreign troops to assist in enslaving us, and hath excited the savages of this country to carry on a war against us, as also the negroes to imbrue their hands in the blood of their masters, in a manner unpractised by civilized nations; and hath lately insulted our calamities, by declaring that he will show us no mercy until he has reduced us: And whereas the obligations of allegiance (being reciprocal between a King and his subjects) are now dissolved on the side of the Colonist, by the despotism of the said King, insomuch that it now appears that loyalty to him is treason against the good people of this country: And whereas not only the Parliament, but, there is reason to believe, too many of the people of Great Britain, have concurred in the aforesaid arbitrary and unjust proceedings against us: And whereas the publick virtue of this colony (so essential to its liberty and happiness) must be endangered by a future political union with, or dependance upon, a Crown and nation so lost to justice, patriotism, and magnanimity:—We, the Deputies of the people of Pennsylvania, assembled in full Provincial Conference, for forming a plan for executing the Resolve of Congress of the 15th of May last, for suppressing all authority in this Province derived from the Crown of Great Britain, and for establishing a Government upon the authority of the people only, now, in this publick manner, in behalf of ourselves, and with the approbation, consent, and authority of our constituents, unanimously declare our willingness to concur in a vote of the Congress declaring the United Colonies free and independent States, provided the forming the Government, and the regulation of the internal police of this Colony, be always reserved to the people of the said Colony; and we do further call upon the nations of Europe, and appeal to the great Arbiter and Governour of the Empires of the World, to witness for us that this declaration did not originate in ambition, or in an impatience of lawful authority, but that we were driven to it, in obedience to the first principles of nature, by the oppressions and cruelties of the aforesaid King and Parliament of Great Britain, as the only possible measure that was left us to preserve and establish our liberties, and to transmit them inviolate to posterity.

"Ordered, That this Declaration be signed at the table, and that the President deliver it in Congress."

Great-uncle JOHN WILKINSON was a deputy to the Conference and represented Bucks County in the Pennsylvania Assembly in 1776, 1781 and 1782. He chose military service and was granted the rank of lieutenant colonel. For these choices he was disfellowshipped from the Quakers. He died in 1782 of natural causes and is listed among the deaths of the Revolution. His Quaker friends consented to have him buried in their Quaker cemetery, where he was interred with great honor.

New Jersey follows Virginia

The New Jersey legislature read and filed the Virginia instructions to their delegates on 12 Jun 1776, and then took a very radical step. It arrested the colony's governor, William Franklin, the loyalist son of Benjamin Franklin. Then it voted to form a new state government, and elected a new slate of Congressional delegates favorably disposed toward independence, and on 22 June, it adopted briefer and more equivocal instructions for its congressmen than those of Virginia. Their congressmen were directed to join with delegates from other colonies

"in the most vigorous measures for supporting the just rights and liberties of America," including, if they considered it "necessary and expedient for this purpose . . . . declaring the United Colonies independent of Great Britain, entering into a Confederacy for union and common defence, making treaties with foreign nations for commerce and assistance" and taking "such other measures as . . . appear necessary for these great ends."

"When in the course of human events it becomes necessary . . . . "

ROBERT R. LIVINGSTON had been assigned to the committee to draft the Declaration of Independence along with Thomas Jefferson, John Adams, Benjamin Franklin, and Roger Sherman of Connecticut. Seventeen days later, on 28 June, the committee presented it to Congress, which promptly tabled the report. They wanted a unanimous endorsement of the colonies. By then only Maryland and New York had failed to allow their delegates to vote for Independence. That night Maryland fell into line.

But the war did not wait for Congress's decision. On 9 June, according to intelligence Washington received, a British fleet of 132 ships sailed from Halifax, Nova Scotia, under General William Howe. Two days later President Hancock urged Massachusetts, Connecticut, New York, and New Jersey to send their militia as soon as possible to New York City, which Howe was expected to attack within the next ten days. Howe's voyage took longer than Congress anticipated; but on 29 June, Washington reported the arrival of some fifty British ships of sail at Sandy Hook on the New Jersey shore near the entrance to New York harbor. This number doubled in the next few days.

[Note: Sandy Hook is close to Shrewsbury, Monmouth, New Jersey, where the LIPPENCOTTs were among the largest chartered landholders for over 100 years (1669). They had multiplied handsomely and were very numerous in New Jersey. They were Quakers, and therefore their participation in this war was limited. A few were loyalists.]

Washington was making "every preparation" for the attack, but he reported he was "extremely deficient in arms . . . and in great distress for want of them." By 1 July, Congress also learned that another fifty-three British ships were outside Charleston, South Carolina, and that the American army had been forced to evacuate Canada. This placed a great deal of stress on the delegates. The outcome of this war would decide whether they would be remembered as the founders of a nation or be hanged by the British as traitors.

A newspaper letter signed "Republicus" and dated 29 June, argued

"I would . . . choose rather to be conquered as an independent State than as an acknowledged rebel." The time had come for Americans "to call ourselves by some name," for which he proposed *the United States of America.* That new nation could only be helped by independence, "and every man that is against it is a traitor."

So it was on 1 July, congress again resolved itself into a committee of the whole "to take into consideration the resolution respecting independency." The 2 July vote was affirmative for twelve of the colonies. Only New York resisted.

On 3 July, the British landed on Staten Island, and since the New Jersey militiamen were helping defend New York, this threatened the Jersey coast. Congress asked Pennsylvania's Committee of Safety to send as many troops as it could to help defend Monmouth County, New Jersey—home of the LIPPINCOTTs. The troops from *Bucks*, Berks, and Northampton counties of Pennsylvania were sent to the bordering northern area of New Brunswick, New Jersey.

As the British proceeded to bring the greatest fleet and largest army ever assembled in North America into action against the Americans, Congress devoted the greater part of two days to revising the draft of the Declaration of Independence. Wars, it understood, were not won by ships and sailors and arms alone. Words, too, had power to serve the cause of victory. It struck out 500 words [leaving 1,337] of Thomas Jefferson's carefully written draft, adding softer wording in places—much to his consternation. The document was approved but not signed on 4 July, as it needed to be rewritten—beautifully. The Declaration was signed on 2 August.

As cousin STEPHEN HOPKINS of Rhode Island signed the Declaration, he stated,

"My hand trembles but my heart does not."

According to family records, his mother RUTH WILKINSON (Hopkins) was born 31 Jan 1685, and he was born in 1707, so he was sixty-nine-years-old. He had remained strong for independence after the publication of his first pamphlets in 1764-5, not faltering as all the other early pamphlet writers had done. From the short biography of STEPHEN HOPKINS, Rhode Island, in the book, *The Signers of the Declaration of Independence* by Robert G. Ferris and Richard E Morris, they add:

"This signer, the second oldest next to Benjamin Franklin, [was] afflicted with palsy . . . . Before, during, and after a comparatively brief stretch of congressional service, he occupied Rhode Island's highest offices and fostered the cultural economic growth of Providence . . . a farmer and a surveyor, he married at age 19. Five years later, he plunged into politics:

STEPHEN HOPKINS

moderator of the first town meeting; town clerk; president of the town council; justice of the peace; justice and clerk of the Providence County court of common appeals; legislator, and speaker of the house. In 1742, after starting a merchantile-shipping enterprise with his brother ESEK, he moved back to Providence and broadened his political activities, including the legislature, assistant and chief justice of the Superior Court and ten-times Governor—representing Rhode Island at various intercolonial meetings. He was a good friend of Benjamin Franklin and John Adams.

"In 1762, he helped to found the influential Providence Gazette and Country Journal. Two years later, he contributed an article entitled "The Rights of the Colonies Examined," which criticized parlimentary taxation and recommended colonial home rule. It was issued as a pamphlet the next year, and it was widely circulated throughout the colonies and Great Britain. He sat on the committee that prepared the Articles of Confederation and the Continental Navy, to which, his brother ESEK was appointed commander in chief.

"He acted as first chancellor of Rhode Island College (later Brown University).

"In 1774, he authored a bill enacted by the Rhode Island legislature that prohibited the importation of slaves into the colony—one of the earliest anti-slavery laws in the United States.

"HOPKINS' health compelled him to retire from national service a few months after he signed his famous signature, although he remained somewhat active within his state. He died in 1785, at the age of 78."

The conflicting loyalties that had weakened the American war effort for the past year were over. A call could finally go out for men to fight "for the Defence of the Liberties and Independence of the United States," as a late 1776 recruiting poster put it. JOSEPH BARTON of Sussex County, New Jersey, wrote to his cousin HENRY WISNER of Newton, New Jersey, 9 Jul 1776:

"Now we know what to depend on. For my part, I have been at a great stand. I could hardly own the King and fight against him at the same time; but now these matters are cleared up. *Heart and hand shall move together.* We have had great numbers who could do nothing until we were declared a free State, who are now ready to spend their lives and fortunes in defence of our country. I expect a great turn one way or the other before I see you again."

Celebrations were held throughout the colonies as the Declaration of Independence was read. A "leaked copy" was read in Philadelphia on 4 July. The official document was read at Philadelphia, Easton, and Trenton on 8 July, and finally made its way to distant Georgia in August. In place after place all "portable signs of royalty" were destroyed. The king's arms or pictures of the king or the Crown on public buildings, coffeehouses and tavern signs, even in churches, were ripped down, trampled, torn, or otherwise broken to pieces, then consumed in great bonfires before crowds of people who responded with "repeated huzzas." In New York City a crowd pulled down a gilded equestrian statue of George III that had been put up in 1770: "the IMAGE of the BEAST was thrown down," one observer reported, "and his HEAD severed from his Body." Later the monument was sent to Litchfield, Connecticut, where local women converted its lead contents into bullets. Pennsylvania's Committee of Safety sent letters by an express rider "to the Counties of Bucks, Chester, Northampton, Lancaster, and Berks, Inclosing a Copy of the said Declaration, requesting the same to be publish'd on Monday next, at the places where the Election for Delegates are to be held." Each colony spread the word to their people.

But the document was soon set aside. They had a war to fight; and when peace returned,

"the whole country was miserably exhausted by the exertions and sufferings incident to the arduous struggle, and all became earnestly engaged . . . in repairing their wasted fortunes."

It would be exactly fifty years later that John Adams, the *heart* that had unceasingly pushed for Independence, and Thomas Jefferson, the *hand* that had drafted the document of Independence, would both die on the same day, 4 Jul 1826. Both older men had ardently hoped that with their illnesses, they might survive until this anniversary.

ROBERT R. LIVINGSTON, who had been on the drafting committee for the document with Thomas Jefferson, became known as the "Chancellor of New York State" and later became a partner of Robert Fulton in his inventing and development of the steamship enterprise. Robert Fulton had married WALTER LIVINGSTON's daughter. ROBERT R. died on 26 Feb 1813.

Of the 56 men who signed and pledged *"Our lives, fortunes, our sacred honor"* many sad stories can be told. Their names were not published at first, but the British marked down every member of Congress suspected of having put his name to treason. All of them became objects of vicious manhunts. Some were taken. Some had narrow escapes. All who had property or families near British strongholds suffered greatly.

Notes on some of the Signers;

PHILIP LIVINGSTON, who added his signature to the final document, was the fifth son of PHILIP LIVINGSTON, second lord of the Livingston Manor, and his wife was Catherine Van Brugh. He was born in 1716 at his father's townhouse in Albany. He received his degree from Yale (1737) and joined wih the import business in New York harbor. He had five sons and four daughters, and lived mainly in his townhouse on Manhattan Island. He built a fortune during the French and Indian War as a trader-privateer, and built a 40-acre estate on Brooklyn Heights overlooking the East River and New York Harbor. He opposed the aristocratic ruling class of the colony, giving much of his energy and financial support to philanthropic and humanitarian endeavors, and was a strong proponent of religious freedom. He stood with the Whigs against their royal governor and attended the Stamp Act Congress. He was defeated when the Tories took over the legislature in 1769, but managed to maintain political activity. In 1775 he won election to the committee of one hundred that governed New York City temporarily until the first provincial colony met later in the year. Chosen as one of the delegates to the Second Continental Congress, he divided his time between Philadelphia and New York. With the British attack on Long Island, Washington used his home on Brooklyn Heights as his headquarters until it became necessary to abandon the island (27 Aug 1776). The British were quick to occupy this home and turn it into a hospital for their injured soldiers. In Manhattan, his home became the barracks of the Royal Navy. LIVINGSTON and his remaining household, moved quickly north to Livingston Manor on the Hudson River. He was absent on the roll call days in Philadelphia, 1-2 Jul 1776; but signed the "Declaration of Independence" with the others on the second of August. His fortune in Long Island and New York in ruins, and having given additional lines of credit on his remaining property to sustain the nation, PHILLIP, in poor health at age 62, still in congress, then at York, Pennsylvania, in 1778, died and was buried in Prospect Hill Cemetary in that city.

Francis Lewis, New York delegate, saw his home plundered and his estates in Harlem completely destroyed by British soldiers. Mrs. Lewis was captured and treated with great brutality. Though she was later exchanged for two British prisoners through the efforts of Congress, she died from the effects of her abuse.

William Floyd, another New York delegate, was able to escape with his wife and children across Long Island Sound to Connecticut, where they lived as refugees without income for seven years. When they came home, they found a devastated ruin.

Louis Morris, the fourth New York delegate, saw all his timber, crops and livestock taken. For seven years he was barred from his home and family.

John Hart of Trenton, New Jersey, risked his life to return home to see his dying wife. Hessian soldiers rode after him, and he escaped in the woods. While his wife lay on her deathbed, the soldiers ruined his farm and wrecked his homestead. Hart, 65, slept in caves and woods as he was hunted across the countryside. When at last, emaciated by hardship, he was able to sneak home, he found his wife had already been buried, and his 13 children taken away. He never saw them again. He died a broken man in 1779, without ever finding his family.

Judge Richard Stockton, a New Jersey delegate signer, had rushed back to his estate and family, who had found refuge with friends, but a Tory sympathizer, betrayed them. Judge Stockton was pulled from bed in the night and brutally beaten and thrown into a common jail, he was deliberately starved. He was released as an invalid, when he could no longer harm the British cause. He returned home to find his estate looted and did not live through the revolution. His family was forced to live off charity.

Robert Morris, merchant of Philadelphia, delegate, and signer, met Washington's appeals and pleas for money year after year. He made and raised arms and provisions which made it possible for Washington to cross the

Delaware at Trenton. In the process he lost 150 ships at sea, bleeding his own fortune and credit nearly dry.

George Clymer, Pennsylvania signer, escaped with his family from their home, but their property was completely destroyed by the British in the Germantown and Brandywine campaigns.

Dr. Benjamin Rush, also from Pennsylvania, was forced to flee to Maryland. As a heroic surgeon with the army, Rush had several narrow escapes.

John Martin lived in a strongly loyalist area of Pennsylvania. When he stood strong for independence, most of his neighbors and some of his relatives ostracized him. A sensitive and troubled man, many believed this action killed him. When he died in 1777, his last words to his tormentors were; "Tell them that they will live to see the hour when they shall acknowledge it [the signing] to have been the most glorious service that I ever rendered to my country."

William Ellery, Rhode Island delegate, saw his property and home burned to the ground. Thomas Lynch, Jr., South Carolina delegate, had his health broken from privation and exposure while serving as a company commander in the military. His doctors ordered him to seek a cure in the West Indies and on the voyage he and his young bride were drowned at sea.

Edward Rudedge, Arthur Middleton and Thomas Heyward, Jr., the other three South Carolina signers, were taken by the British in the siege of Charleston. They were carried as prisoners of war to St. Augustine, Florida, where they were singled out for indignities. Exchanged at the end of the war, they found their large landholdings and estates had been completely devastated.

The New Jersey signer, Abraham Clark, gave two sons to the officer corps in the Revolutionary Army. They were captured and sent to that infamous British prison hulk afloat in New York harbor known as the hell ship *Jersey,* where 11,000 American captives were to die. The younger Clarks were treated with a special brutality because of their father. One was put in solitary and given no food. With the end almost in sight, with the war almost won, the British offered him his sons' lives if he would recant and come out for the King and parliament. The utter despair in this man's heart, must reach out to all of us with his answer, "No!"

Of those 56 who signed the Declaration of Independence, nine died of wounds or hardships during the war. Five were captured and imprisoned with brutal treatment. Several lost wives, sons or entire families. Two wives were brutally treated. All were the victims of manhunts and driven from their homes. Twelve signers had their homes completely burned. Seventeen lost everything they owned. Yet none defected or went back on his pledge.

With so many relatives in North Carolina during this period of time and the War of the Regulators relatively recently ended, I was curious to know who their "signers" were and a little more about them. There were three of them Joseph Hewes, William Hooper, and John Penn, none of them were born in North Carolina.

Joseph Hewes was born in 1730 on an estate near Princeton, New Jersey. He was brought up strictly as a Quaker. Choosing to be a merchant, rather than follow his well-to-do father in farming, he moved to Philadelphia, where he learned and thrived as a merchant. Seeking additional opportunity for himself, he moved to the seaport of Edenton, North Carolina, around 1760. Just before his planned wedding, his intended bride suddenly died. He remained a bachelor throughout his life. As a member of the North Carolina assembly (1766-75), the committee of correspondence (1773), and the provincial assemblies (1774-75), he helped the Whigs overthrow the royal government, and was a strong supporter of nonimportation measures, although it meant personal financial loss.

At first he was against separation from England, but as Richard Henry Lee of Virginia presented his June 7 indpendence resolution, John Adams recalled that at one point in the debate a transformation came over Hewes. "He started suddenly upright, and lifting up both his hands to Heaven, as if he had been in a trance, cried out, 'It is done! and I will abide by it.'"

As a key member of the marine committee, Hewes and John Adams were key men in establishing the Continental Navy. They locked horns in the appointment of the Commander in Chief. Hewes wanted John Paul Jones, an experienced seaman from Scotland that had recently immigrated to Virginia. John Adams had already raised a stir in New England by nominating George Washington of Virginia as Commander in Chief of the Army. He stubbornly insisted that this major naval officer must come from New England. ESEK

HOPKINS, brother of STEPHEN, was his choice. Hewes reluctantly submitted. Tired and overworked, Hewes in Congress at Philadelphia, died shortly before his fiftieth birthday (1780.)

William Hooper was born in Boston, Massachucetts, in 1742. His father was a clergyman first of the Congregational Church, and later of the Anglican. He was very desirous that his son receive an exceptional education and choose the church as his occupation. Hooper graduated from Harvard, but preferred a different career, studing law under the rebel James Otis. Tired of his unhappy family relationship and seeking better legal opportunities, he moved to Wilmington, North Carolina, where he married after several years and sired two sons and a daughter. Politically ambitious, he became the deputy attorney general (1770-71.) This was during the time of Royal Governor Tryon, whom he encouraged and supported in his cause against the Regulators, even accompanying him across North Carolina to the battlegrounds of Alamance, in Orange County. Perhaps memories of this sad occasion softened his heart, for within a few years he changed direction and opposed the Royal government. Elected to the state assembly 1773-1775, the assembly attempted to attach to a new court act a clause by which the colony could confiscate American property owned by debtors, including inhabiants of Great Britain. When the Royal Governor Martin blocked the bill, a four-year struggle for the control of the colony ensued. Hooper championed the cause of the assembly, and rose to a position of leadership among the Whigs. In a letter to a friend dated April 1774, Hooper prophesized the Colonies' break with Great Britain—the earliest known prediction of independence, which won him the epithet of "Prophet of Independence." He helped set up the colonial government and was elected as a delegate to the Continental Congress. When the British invaded North Carolina, he moved his family into Wilmington for safety, but it fell to the enemy while he was away on business in January 1781. Separated from his family for more than ten months, he was dependent on his friends in Edenton for food and shelter and was often destitute. He became violently ill with malaria. They nursed him back to health. When the British moved their army north into Virginia, evacuating Wilmington, he returned home and found everything in ruins and his family escaped into Hillsborough. Joining them, the family remained there. In 1788, he campaigned vigorously for the ratification of the Federal Constitution. He was not well accepted by the people politically. His aristocratic attitude and lack of faith in the common people undermined his popularity. He became ill and despondent and died two years later in 1790, in his late forties.

John Penn, the third member of the group, was born in Caroline Countly, Virginia, about 1740. His father was a well-to-do farmer, and he inherited his estate when he died. He was eighteen years old. Discontent, he decided to improve his meager education, and encouraged by his relative, EDMUND PENDLETON, the well-known lawyer of the area, he was given the use of his library and within three years of self-study he was admitted to the bar, and successfully practiced law in his district. He married and was the father of three children. In 1774, he moved to Granville County, North Carolina, settling near Stovall. He was elected to the provincial assembly and a few weeks later to the Continental Congress (1775-80). He was one of sixteen signers who also signed the Articles of Confederation. It is said that he rarely disputed with others, was peaceable by nature, very efficient, and discreet. On one occasion he was challenged to a duel on a personal matter by the President of Congress, Henry Laurens of South Carolina. He accepted the challenge, but on the way to the event he convinced Laurens that they should bury their differences and they returned to their homes. Late in 1780, he was called to return back to North Carolina by their legislature to sit on a three-man board of military affairs in conjunction with their governor. Under his leadership, the board soon assumed control of all military affairs, much to the resentment of the governor and his council. Within a year, they convinced the assembly to disband the board. Penn was offered an appointment on the governor's council, but his health was poor and he declined the offer. Devoting his last years to his law practice, in 1788 he died while in his late forties.

Glory was not their object when they signed their names and pledged:

"And for the support of this Declaration
with a firm reliance on the protection of divine providence,
we mutually pledge to each other
our lives, our fortunes and our sacred honor."

CANADA, LONG ISLAND, NEW YORK CITY—LOST

Benjamin Franklin had been a very busy man. On 2 Apr 1776, the seventy-year-old man had been sent by the Continental Congress on a secret mission up the Hudson River with Maryland's Congressman Samuel Chase, wealthy Charles Carroll, his cousin John Carroll [a Jesuit priest], and a Prussian officer. They were to evaluate the Canadian situation and use their best efforts to convince the Catholic French-Canadian settlers to join with the largely Protestant American Colonists in their struggle against Great Britain. In 1763, the French King Louis XV would never have agreed to the treaty which relinquished Canada to the British had he not felt that in doing so the Americans would lose their fear of France and gain the strength they needed to fight for their own independence against France's hated rival across the English Channel. The French statesman, Vergennes, stated, when he signed the document,

> "There now! We have arranged matters for an American rebellion in which England will lose her empire in the West."

Charles Carroll was a devout Catholic who spoke fluent French and his cousin John Carroll had spent 25 years in France as a Jesuit priest. Benjamin Franklin had only a second-grade formal education; however, through intense self study, his inventive mind, his publications, and his foreign diplomacy, he had been given honorary degrees from Harvard, William and Mary, and Yale, and a doctorate from the University of Edinburgh, after which he was always addressed as Dr. Franklin. While he represented the colonies in England, he gained many European admirers. They saw him as a philosopher, a patient, wise, and immensely practical man with a delightful sense of humor and a rare ability for thoroughly relishing almost everything he did.

Thomas Jefferson wrote of him many years later,

"I served with George Washington in the legislature of Virginia before the Revolution and during it with Dr. Franklin in Congress. I never heard either of them speak ten minutes at a time, not to any but the main point which was to decide the question. They laid their shoulders to the great points, knowing that the little ones would follow of themselves."

A few years later, Dr. Franklin wrote to a friend,

"I do not find that I grow any older. Being arrived at seventy, and considering that by traveling further in the same road I should probably be led to the grave, I stopped short, turned about, and walked back again; which having done these four years, you may now call me sixty-six. Advise those old friends of ours to follow my example; keep up your spirits, and that will keep up your bodies."

In April 1776, Benjamin Franklin's home town of Philadelphia was the largest city in the colonies and second only to London in the British Empire. New York had a population of 27,000 and was the second largest colonial city. It had the major harbor and was the key to the Hudson River, which was the major inland shipping and trading route with a back door to Canada. If Canada remained British, the logical way to launch a British second front was from the north through Canada to Montreal, then south up the Richelieu [or Sorel] River to Lake Champlain; then retake Crown Point and Fort Ticonderoga. If these were secured, Albany and the Hudson River were at great risk for the Americans, especially if the British were able to control New York City and its harbor. British control of the Hudson River would isolate New England from the other colonies, which added up in the minds of many as "divide and conquer."

So when the British army evacuated Boston harbor in March, Washington felt certain that New York would be their next target. He had sent Gen. Charles Lee earlier, in January, to raise an additional army in Connecticut and New York, stop Tory activities, and to begin the fortifications—in the city, Long Island, Staten Island, and the Highlands. Then when the last British ship had sailed out of Boston harbor, he hastened to bring the bulk of his Continentals with him to New York and to increase the fortifications along this northern route to Canada.

Major General Charles Lee had arrived on the fourth of February; the same day that Sir Henry Clinton arrived in New York harbor with the British fleet.

Governor Tryon of New York, former British governor of North Carolina during the grievous "War of the Regulators," was surrounded by a large number of Tories who had sought his favors through the preceding years. He was disappointed that the British ships had only arrived to pick up supplies for the invasion of Charleston, South Carolina. He had hoped for an early military occupation of New York City with relief from the persecution of his loyalist constituents by the Americans. Tryon had twice dismissed the New York assembly in unsuccessful attempts to get more of his friends elected. As the fleet sailed south, General Charles Lee instigated much harsher laws and imprisoned many loyalists who refused to take an oath of allegiance to the rebel cause.

When the British plans for conquest of South Carolina became known to the Continental Congress, they sent General Lee south with his army to prevent the British landing, leaving Major General SCHUYLER in command of the Middle Department—New York, New Jersey, Pennsylvania, Delaware, and Maryland. SCHUYLER stayed north in Albany and assigned Brigadiers William Thompson and Lord Stirling to command in Southern New York.

Lee arrived too late in the south. Charleston had been successfully defended by Moultrie; however, the ambitious Charles Lee was quick to take the personal credit and was called the "Hero of Charleston." He returned to New York where he connived to arrange and manipulate events and people toward his aspiration to replace George Washington as Commander in Chief.

New York and the Hudson Valley had many conservative, landed aristocrats—they included Dutch, Swedes, Scots, Huguenots, Germans, and Scotch-Irish who for financial reasons might support England. When Franklin's party arrived in New York City in April, one of them observed,

"The city was no more the gay, polite place it used to be esteemed: but was become almost a desert [except] for the troops."

As fear grew among its people that the anticipated attack by huge British forces would be accompanied by a naval bombardment, thousands of the residents fled, both Tories and Whigs—perhaps as many as one-third of the population, and when the British did arrive in June 1776, many additional citizens evacuated leaving about 5,000.

On 3 April, Franklin and party with a wind from the northeast sailed up the Hudson, past the immense estates of a handful of families, among them the SCHUYLERs, LIVINGSTONs, and RENSSELAERs. The settlements extended inland no more than 100 to 150 miles, where they were blocked by the Appalachians. This was the most densely populated area of the continent, and yet it contained an average of only eighteen individuals per square mile (without, the figure ranged from two to eighteen).

On 7 April at seven-thirty in the morning, the group was greeted at the Albany dock by Major General PHILIP SCHUYLER and his "2 daughters (BETSY and PEGGY,) lively, agreeable, black-eyed girls," as Charles Carroll described them. Distant cousin-in-law SCHUYLER was described by author Richard M. Ketchum as

> "tall and slender, with an imperious manner and an erect, commanding experience and hands-on knowledge that came from managing a huge estate that composed a virtually self-sufficient community. He knew carpentry and construction, boat-building, and farming, and had been a merchant of grain and timber. He was a child of the frontier, knew the Indians, had considerable influence with them, was fluent in the Mohawk tongue, and had fought in the French and Indian War. But in two respects he differed from the commander in chief. Lacking the physical strength and toughness demanded by wilderness fighting, he was often sickly, and because he was frequently absent from his military duties on that account his enemies unjustly accused him of cowardice. A more important contrast between the two was that SCHUYLER lacked Washington's steely determination, his utter will to win, his resolve never to give up.
>
> "It was SCHUYLER's misfortune, despite his considerable abilities and experience and what seemed unflagging devotion to the patriot cause, to be intensely disliked by New Englanders. Some of the animosity was ethnic: his eastern neighbors of predominantly English descent considered him a Dutchman and thought that reason enough to hate him. Another factor was a polished, urban manner that was often taken to be haughty, aristocratic, or downright snobbish. A Connecticut chaplain, writing to his wife, described the general as haughty and overbearing, noting that `he has never been accustomed to seeing men that are reasonably well taught and able to give a clear opinion and to state their grounds for it, who were not also persons of some wealth and rank."

The New Englanders were also resentful because of boundary disputes, which had nothing to do with General SCHUYLER.

But our very distant cousin-in-law SCHUYLER was a very generous and hospitable host. The commissioners spent two pleasant days in Albany before their host and his family took them by wagon thirty-two miles to the general's summer home at Saratoga, which is now Schuylerville, New York. There, he took them on a tour of his estate, whose bottomland and mills for grain, lumber, hemp, and flax were of particular interest to Charles Carroll. The next day SCHUYLER bade his guests farewell and departed with Brigadier General John Thomas who was heading for Quebec. SCHUYLER would travel with the General as far as Lake George and remain there to expedite the transport of military stores and supplies for the troops.

Four days later, Franklin and party left CATHERINE R. SCHUYLER and her daughters behind and the comforts of Saratoga and faced the bitter wintery cold and rugged route that rose to the summit where the run-off water began to change its course from south to north and flow into Lake Champlain, then to the Richelieu River, which drained into the St. Lawrence River. Between the landing at the north end of Lake George and Fort Ticonderoga by Lake Champlain, a distance of three-and-a-half miles, the water levels drop 200 feet. The baggage was loaded into wagons to avoid the spectacular waterfall, then each boat was lifted out of the water with a hoist and let down into a special carriage that was drawn overland by six oxen to the water of Lake Champlain. Thirty-five to fifty men then lifted the boat off the carriage to launch it. Ticonderoga is an Indian name meaning "between the two great waters."

The commissioners noted that this fort, which was much superior to any they had passed, was in no condition to withstand attack by a professional army. Charles Carroll, seeing the place for the first time, was aghast and described it as "ruinous"—with "a few pieces of cannon mounted on one bastion, more for show . . . than service." Of course, most all the cannon and ammunition that was there when the fort was taken by Ethan Allen and Benedict Arnold had been removed to fight the British in Boston.

Messengers going south with letters met them. There was a letter for Gen. SCHUYLER from Benedict Arnold which Benjamin Franklin took the liberty of opening, thus discovering that 786 of his 2,505 men at Quebec were sick, and that the enlistments of 1,500 would expire on April 15. This further convinced the commissioners that the likelihood of their army succeeding in the conquest of Quebec was "extreamly problematical."

On 24 April, the "heartily tired" commissioners were on their way north on Lake Champlain, sometimes under sail and sometimes with oars. They passed a naked landscape on the west bank, which had been stripped of trees for firewood and timber to construct and maintain Fort Ticonderoga. Fifteen miles north they stopped at Crown Point. The once important fort and barracks was in ruins, accidentally burned by the English [when they earlier had possession] and blown up when the fire reached the powder magazine. As they proceeded on, they saw a few fields under cultivation in lonely settlements. They passed the Narrows and Split Rock, where the great inland lake begins to widen.

Charles Carroll was awed by the majesty of the distant snow-capped mountains—Adirondacks to the west, Green Mountains on the east—and was made further aware of their great height when he saw them later from Montreal, over eighty miles away. Of Lake Champlain, he concluded that if America "should succeed and establish liberty thro'out this part of the country," the lands bordering the lake would become very valuable, since they would participate in the great trade that was bound to be carried on between Canada and New York.

The Richelieu River began at the old French fort Ile aux Noix. Nearby was a house owned by Colonel Moses Hazen. Carroll wrote,

> "There is scarcely a whole pane of glass in the house. The window shutters and doors are destroyed and the hinges stolen. In short, it appears a perfect wreck."

But the company stopped long enough to dispatch a messenger to Montreal to arrange for carriages for the last part of their trip to Montreal.

Colonel Moses Hazen had acquired a seigniory, or feudal estate, from the British, but when Montgomery's army came through this area in 1775, Hazen chose to join with them in their conquest of Canada. Montgomery made him a Colonel with the charge to raise a regiment of Canadians. According to the recorded land claims awarded to the Canadians after the Revolution, most of them list their service in Colonel Hazen's regiment. Included in these records are the MONTEEs whose mother was a POYER and perhaps an older sister of our fifth-great-grandfather JOSEPH POYER, who may also have been with Colonel Hazen. Charles Carroll had little to say about the area surrounding Fort Chambly where JACQUES POYER had been stationed as a French soldier during the reign of Louis XIV, and where many of his children were born. He described it as flat and rather poorly drained land. Of the two-wheeled carts the Canadians call "cale` chs," he wrote, "I never travelled thro' worse roads, or in worse carriages."

On 29 April the travelers reached their final destination, the island-city of Montreal. They were surprised to find Brigadier General Benedict Arnold awaiting them with a grand reception of

> "a great body of officers, gentry, &c" welcoming them in grand military style with an artillery salute and full military honors. They were then taken to Arnold's elegant headquarters to meet a smaller group of well-wishers. In another room they "unexpectedly met . . . a large assemblage of ladies, most of them French," and all of them married to Englishmen friendly to the American cause. Tea time arrived with another round of conversation, and "an elegant supper, which was followed with the singing of the ladies, which proved very agreeable" except for their fatigue, as told by the Priest John Carroll. He was impressed with the French women, who had a "softness of manner [which] is charming." He was also charmed by Benedict Arnold's polish and poise, saying that , "an officer bred up at Versailles could not have behaved with more delicacy, ease, and good breeding."

Unfortunately, the next day the reality of the colonial situation set in with a vengeance. A steady stream of angry creditors confronted them, who had waited long with the expectation that they would be paid for supplies and services they had granted to the American army—and they wanted cold, hard cash, not promises or paper money. Franklin advanced 353 lbs in gold from his own purse and the commissioners wrote Congress for 20,000 additional pounds which they said would be necessary just to continue the war, much less effect a union with Canada. Arnold emphasized that the army had no hope without a major influx of men and money, as the British fleet would be at Quebec as soon as the ice broke.

Shortly, they heard from General John Thomas, who had preceded them with replacement troops for Quebec. He wrote that nearly half of his men had smallpox, while one-third of the remaining army was preparing to leave, because their enlistments had expired along with their enthusiasm. Powder was running short; provisions were on hand for only six days, and the residents in the vicinity were unwilling to help.

On 5 May at least 15 British ships were sighted entering the St. Lawrence. They disembarked the next day. The next morning two columns advanced against Thomas' pitiful, yet long enduring siege army. It was too much. The panic-stricken men ran down the roads as fast as they could move. The British pursued them for nine miles.

Realizing that the entire Continental army would be driven out of Canada within a few weeks and his health rather poor from the journey, Dr. Franklin decided to return to Philadelphia. Father Carroll decided to accompany him. Charles Carroll and Samuel Chase remained for nearly three weeks to help bolster the army morale and leave such military orders and papers as they felt might be helpful. But help was then impossible. A garrison of four hundred Americans at a post called the Cedars was surprised and surrendered.

When the two commissioners arrived at Fort Chambly they found, "all things in much confusion, extreme disorder and negligence, our credit sunk and no money to retrieve it with." What remained of the army was turning into an undisciplined mob "without order or regularity, eating up provisions as fast as they were brought in." General Thomas contracted smallpox and resigned his command. He was blinded from the disease and died on 2 June.

[Note: Inoculation was in question at this time. Those who were inoculated would get a milder disease; however, they would give it to others not inoculated in a more virulent form. In Marblehead, Massachusetts, the citizens were convinced it was spreading the disease and they burned the hospital.]

Thomas was succeeded by the Irish general from New Hampshire, John Sullivan, who had brought 1400 fresh troops. The newly arrived British Major General John Burgoyne with four thousand British regulars were elated to see

"the Rebels . . . flying before us in the greatest Terror." A Connecticut officer who saw the Americans at Crown Point reported that the fragmented regiments from New Jersey, Pennsylvania, New York, and New England were "not an army but a mob . . . the shattered remains of twelve or fifteen very fine battalions, ruined by sickness, fatigue, and desertion, and void of every idea of discipline or subordination."

Fourth-great-grandfather, JOHN COOLEY, enlisted 3 Feb 1776. He was sent as a messenger to Three Rivers (Trois-Rivieres) on 8 Jun 1776, and was taken prisoner at Hollander's Creek. He was among those who were exchanged later, and he became a sergeant in the Colonial German Regiment 16 Jul 1776. Quite a few Germans had settled in the Hunterdon County, New Jersey area, including the early Peter Rockefeller. JOHN COOLEY (or COLE) was made an Ensign in the Pennsylvania 10th Regiment on 4 Dec 1776. Fourth-great-grandfather ELISHA BARTON is listed in the Pennsylvania Archives, also— first as an ensign in the eighth class roll of Capt. Patrick Campbell's Company.

On 9 June, Carroll and Chase were back in New York delivering their sad story to Generals Washington, Horatio Gates, and Israel Putnam. While in Philadelphia, on 10 June, Benjamin Franklin was appointed to the committee in Congress to prepare the Declaration of Independence. He signed that document on 2 Aug 1776, as did Carroll and Chase, well aware of the terrible failure in Canada, the lack of finances, the shortage of supplies and the British forces that were collecting in New York harbor. When Franklin declared as he signed, "Indeed we must all hang together, otherwise we shall most assuredly hang separately," it was not just a cute parlor joke. It was *treason* in his old city of London, where he had been the American minister and he knew it.

This photo is taken from a small portion of the original much larger oil painting of the *Signing of the Declaration of Independence* by artist John Trumbull, who was much more familiar with these men than we are. It depicts Thomas Jefferson with his appointed committee standing with him as he hands the completed document to John Hannock in front of all the men who would later sign it.

(LEFT TO RIGHT) JOHN ADAMS, RODGER SHERMAN, ROBERT LIVINGSTON, THOMAS JEFFERSON, AND BENJAMIN FRANKLIN.

The original agreement for independence was reached on 4 Jul 1776, but the document at that time included many corrections by the larger representitive group assembled from all the original thirteen colonies. It was given then to Thomas Jefferson to copy on beautiful paper with his magnificent handwriting into the final document that was signed by 53 members on 2 Aug 1776. It should be noted that Chancellor of New York, Robert Livingston, was not present at this signing, because of other duties.

I am not as familiar with Rodger Sherman as I am with the accomplishements of some of the others; so I would like to mention two of his personal accomplishments. First, he signed all three of the important founding documents: *The Articles of Confederation; the Declaration of Independence, and the United States Constitution.* Only one other man can claim that distinction—Robert Morris, one of the wealthiest merchants of Pennsylvania in the Colonies.

Second, this great *patriot* from Massachusetts and New Haven, Connecticut, (and strong contributor to Yale) that *"sees beyond the years"* in 1787 conceived and introduced the Connecticut *Great Compromise* which broke a dead-lock between the large and small states by presenting the duel legislative system for the constitution of our federal government. One body would represent the majority of the people; the other would give equal representation to all the states throughout the nation.

[Note: As an example of what might have happened to our nation, if the compromise had not been established, is what has happened in our present state in Nevada and the most significant "Why" my husband ran for the state legislature. Shortly before 1964, the United States Supreme Court of our nation did what I consider to be some illegal legislation of their own when they said that the states could not follow this same system in their individual state constitutions. So by 1964 all states had to reapportion all their state governments to conform to their mandate of majority rule. Our Lincoln County ended up with no representation at all from our very large area of land, and it had nearly destroyed our whole county economy by 1968 as all we had was being taken legally away from us. Approximately 50 years later, the whole state is now a city-state—and can be controlled completely by our now much larger and continually growing city of Las Vegas—for more information see Volume I— Part II: STANDING FIRM.]

On 23 April, Washington had only eighty-three hundred men fit for duty. He sent the greater number of them with General NATHANAEL GREENE to Long Island and spread the rest on Manhattan wherever he felt the need. He greatly missed the thousands that had been sent to Canada. More troops from New York, New Jersey and Pennsylvania were entreated to enlist and their militias were called for.

New York City was not Boston. An old-time church property, which was still called "the holy ground," was definitely unholy ground, now. Colonel Baldwin, whose duty it was to patrol this area, wrote home to his wife.

"The whores (by information) continue their employ, which is becoming very lucrative. Their unparalleled conduct is a sufficient antidote against any desires that a person can have that has one spark of modesty or virtue left in him . . . . I . . . with my guard of escort, have broke up the knots of men and women fighting, pulling caps, swearing, crying, "Murder!" etc., hurried them to the Provost Dungeon by half dozens . . . some are punished and some get off clear—Hell's work."

General Washington gave an order and another soldier wrote,

"The gin shops and other houses where liquors have been heretofore retailed within or near the lines . . . are strictly forbidden to sell any for the future to any soldier in the army and the inhabitants of said houses near the lines are immediately to move out of them; they are to be appropriated to the use of the troops . . . . If any soldier of the army shall be found disguised with liquor, as has been too much the practice heretofore, the General is determined to have him punished with the utmost severity, as no soldier in such situation can be either fit for defense or attack."

News of the Declaration of Independence would not reach England until late August. But in America, Washington assembled his troops and it was read to them on 9 July at 6 P. M. Following the reading he remarked,

"The General hopes that this important event will serve as a fresh incentive to every officer and soldier to act with fidelity and courage, knowing that now the peace and safety of his country depend, under God, solely on the success of our arms, and that he is now in the service of a State possessed of sufficient power to reward his merit, and advance him to the highest honors of a free country."

The Continentals roared three cheers. After dismissal, many joined in the destruction of the gilded statue of King George III on Broadway. Lieutenant Isaac Bangs of the Massachusetts militia observed,

"Last night the statue on the Bowling Green representing George Ghwelps alias George Rex was pulled down by the populace. In it were four thousand pounds of lead and a man undertook to take ten ounces of gold from the superfices, as both man and horse were covered with gold leaf; the lead we hear is to be run up into musket balls for the use of the Yankees, when it is hoped that the emanations from the leaden George will make . . .. deep impressions in the bodies of some of his red-coated and Tory subjects."

The colonials were by no means totally united. With Tories still anxiously awaiting the British occupation, a fearful Governor Tryon of the New York colony moved his home and headquarters to the Royal Fleet; and as the fence sitters saw the arrival and disembarkment of the ever increasing British soldiers on Staten Island without any colonial resistance, and the dreaded Hessian warriors started to appear, loyalist support increased daily. There was a rumor of a plot to kill General Washington. The Army had been in New York for two months when this supposed "vile attempt was discovered;" but no evidence of the conspiracy was ever discovered.

[Note: By checking the wills and other probate records of New York for this period of time, we find that JOSEPH and SARAH BARTON's grandchildren inherited "all the land of SAMUEL HOLMES of the South Quarter of Richmond Co., yeoman." Richmond County is Staten Island. His will was dated 9 Jul 1778 and proved 19 Oct 1779. JOHN MORGAN, whose wife was CATHERINE LAKERMAN, the daughter of Abraham Lakerman, Gentleman of the County of Richmond is mentioned 25 Mar 1734. On 17 Jan 1774 a will is proved in which Barent Slaght of Staten Island leaves a considerable amount of his estate to "ABRAHAM COLE, COLES COLE, STEPHEN COLE, JACOB COLE, DANIEL COLE, Mary, wife of WILLIAM LAKERMAN, all children of my brother, ABRAHAM COLE, deceased . . . and my nephew PETER COLE, son of my brother, ISIAC COLE, deceased." The son COLES COLE is especially interesting, since it gives us an additional link in establishing that our JOHN COOLEY may indeed be the JOHN COLE shown in the Pennsylvania revolutionary war records, and descended from a Dutch ROBERT COLES with the various Americanizations of the Dutch names. This same will leaves an equal share to "CHRISTIAN, wife of HEZEKIAH WRIGHT, Esq. and to CATHERINE, wife of JAMES Lequin." The original Long Island settler, ROBERT COLES married MERCY WRIGHT, whose English father NICHOLAS WRIGHT drowned in Queens County, Oyster Bay where NATHANIEL COLES and his son NATHANIEL COLES Jr's descendants were still living. NICHOLAS WRIGHT had a very large family with more daughters than sons. There are records indicating that some of the descendants of ROBERT COLES still owned property in Oyster Bay.

Ancestor Captain ELISHA BARTON's brother, GILBERT BARTON, is said to have owned a tavern in Trenton, New Jersey, where the rebels would often gather throughout the Revolutionary War years. Trenton was a village of about 100 homes when it was occupied by the Hessian soldiers.

The VAN KIRKs, MORGANs, LIPPINCOTTs, PRESTONs, WILKINSONs, LACYs, have been mentioned earlier and were still residing in Philadelphia and Bucks Counties, Pennsylvania, or across the Delaware in Hunterdon County, New Jersey. "Washington's Crossing" left Bucks County, Pennsylvania, and crossed into Hunterdon County, New Jersey.

The female descendants had other surnames, but of course, are equally related. Our possible ancestor DEBORAH UNDERHILL married ROBERT COLES in the 1600s. A will of NATHANIEL UNDERHILL of Boroughtown, Westchester County, proved on 1 Dec 1775 left his daughter HELENA, wife of JAMES MORGAN 200 British pounds. He named 3 sons, 4 daughters and several grandchildren.

These ancestral lands of Long Island, Staten Island, Manhattan Island, Westchester County [Bronx and White Plains], Monmouth County and other central New Jersey Counties, Bucks, Philadelphia and other southeastern counties of Pennsylvania comprise the major area of action for General George Washington and the troops he personally commanded for the next seven years. Both the British and the Americans invaded, occupied, retreated, and fought desperate battles, often back and forth across this territory. Many died. Soldiers foraged the fields, destroyed, burned, and occupied homes. The Hessians were especially brutal and raped many of the women. The Frenchman Lafayette was especially popular with the colonials. Our great-grandmother MARY CATHERINE BARTON [Ivie] named one of her sons JOHN LAFAYETTE IVIE. Her partiality might also indicate that her grandmother MARY SUSANNAH POYER [Wilkinson] was of French descent, as the name implies.

I have capitalized the name of SAMUEL HOLMES, because he may be part of my ancestrial connections to ABRAHAM LINCOLN, who genealogists say— I am his sixth cousin, four times removed through our common ancestor O. HOLMES.]

Long Island lost

But back in New York harbor after the Declaration of Independence had been signed, little had gone well for the colonials. The British and German troops had populated Staten Island with their thousands of tents and crowded New York harbor with the world's largest navy. But Howe was waiting. Perhaps forty-eight-year-old Sir William Howe was hoping the colonials would surrender when they realized the magnitude of the forces against them. He had not approved of this war. His brother, George Augustus, 3rd Viscount Howe, had been very popular with the colonies in the French and Indian War, and had died during the 1758 attack on Fort Ticonderoga. Sir William had served with Wolfe at the head of the light infantry, storming the Heights of Abraham, when the British had taken Quebec from the French. He had opposed parliament's colonial policy and even told his parlimentary constituents that he would not accept a command in America. But he did what he was ordered and trained to do, and usually did it very well. Still, at times, when he delayed, there were those who remembered his former sympathy for the Americans. And they wondered. Howe, however, was making well-organized plans.

On 22 Aug 1776, at dawn, Howe began ferrying his troops from Staten Island to the southwest shore of Long Island under the covering guns of four frigates that were anchored in Gravesend Bay in The Narrows. By 8:00 o'clock there were over 4,000 British and Hessian troops under Generals Cornwallis and Clinton making the crossing. Hand's 200 Pennsylvanian Continentals pulled back to Prospect Hill, burning anything they thought the enemy might use. By noon, there were 15,000 well-supplied redcoats on Long Island. The waiting war of nerves continued three more days until German General Heister landed a little to the east with two more brigades of grenadiers. They quick-marched the four miles inland to Flatbush to join Cornwallis and his ten battalions. There was little American resistance. The British then occupied the old ancestral lands and hamlets of Gravesend, New Utrecht, Flatbush, and Flatlands. To their north was a ridge of hills, the Heights of Guan, extending northeasterly nearly across the island. This ridge with its four roads at the passes separated the 21,000 British from most of Washington's 7,000 colonial forces—Washington would later increase these forces several thousand when he came from Manhattan Island. There would be 9,500 troops with their equipment evacuated from Long Island on the evening of 29 August.

General NATHANAEL GREENE had been put to bed with a raging fever on 15 August and was replaced on Long Island by colonial General Putman. Putman chose to command his troops at the lower swampy Narrows pass, near where the enemy troops had landed. Putman believed the British would attempt to make their main approach to Brooklyn along this route. He gave Sullivan command of the higher passes. Sullivan took center with his troops between the Flatbush and Bedford roads, and gave Lord Stirling command at his right. The German Hessians were assembled south of these two passes. The extreme western left toward the Jamaica pass was entrusted to Colonel Samuel Mile's Pennsylvania Regiment of Stirling's brigade, but the actual Jamaica pass was not guarded, only patrolled by a horse guard of five young officers who were to report any enemy movement. A highly concerned General Washington crossed over from Manhattan and took command of the troops waiting behind the lines to defend Brooklyn Heights and to fortify any of the passes when the British made their forward thrust through one of them.

An enlisted man recalled,

"I saw [General Washington] walk along the lines and give his orders in person to the colonels of each regiment . . . . I also heard Washington say, 'If I see any man turn his back today, I will shoot him through. I have two pistols loaded, but I will not ask any man to go further than I do. I will fight so long as I have a leg or an arm.' Then he told them the time had come when they must be freemen or slaves . . . all that is worth living for is at stake."

However, English General Howe conducted a few skirmishes at the three western passes, while at night three Tory loyalists directed the bulk of his army eastward to the Jamaica Pass, where they silently captured the five patrolling officers and advanced without incident through the Pass. Sullivan heard their signal shots the morning of August twenty-seventh, and realized that the enemy was at his rear. He was trapped with the vast British army behind him and the Hessians coming up the passes from the south with bayonets, with which the Americans were unprepared to combat. Many were butchered.

An American soldier wrote to his family,

"General Sullivan I believe is taken prisoner; the last I heard of him, he was in a corn field close by our lines with a pistol in each hand, and the enemy had formed a line each side of him, and he was going directly between them. I like to have been taken prisoner myself; crossing from the lower road to the Bedford, I came close upon the advanced party of the enemy. I very luckily got within the lines time enough to give the alarm or I believe they would have been in upon us in surprise, for we had not at that time above two thousand men in our lines."

By eleven o'clock the British had cleared the ridge of all the rebels except Stirling's Marylanders and Delawares on the west. A rifleman wrote:

"the main body of British, by a route we never dreamed of, had surrounded us, and driven within the lines or scattered in the woods, all our men except the Delaware and Maryland battalions, who were standing at bay with double their number. Thus standing, we were ordered to attempt retreat by fighting our way through the enemy, who had posted themselves and nearly filled every road and field between us and our lines . . . . Our men fought with more than Roman valor. We forced the advanced party which first attacked us to give way, through which opening we got a passage down to the side of a marsh, seldom before waded over, which we passed, and then swam a narrow river, all the while exposed to the enemy's fire . . . . The whole right wing of our battalion, thinking it impossible to march through the marsh, attempted to force their way through the woods, where they, almost to a man, were killed or taken . . . . Most of our generals on a high hill in the lines, viewed us with glasses, as we were retreating, and saw the enemy we had to pass through, though we could not. Many thought we would surrender in a body without firing. When we began the attack, General Washington wrung his hands, and cried out 'What brave fellows I must this day lose!'"

By early afternoon, most of the continentals who were able to escape the cruel bayonets and merciless fire of the thousands of redcoats and Hessians that had ascended the ridge had found some safety in the Brooklyn defenses. They anxiously waited for Howe to storm these lines; but he drew back and halted. Night came. They waited. There was no night attack. The morning of August twenty-eighth arrived—still no movement from Howe's forces. That afternoon a cold northeast rain fell and continued into the night. The next morning, as the rain continued, the continentals could view the preparations of the British on the regular approaches. Ankle deep in water with little protection in their light clothing, the Americans still rejoiced. The northeasterly wind was preventing the Royal Navy from entering the East River, which could cut off all possible retreat to New York City.

Young Connecticut adjutant Major Benjamin Tallmadge described the situation.

> "General Washington was so fully aware of the perilous situation of the division of his army, that he immediately convened a council of war, at which the propriety of retiring to New York was decided on. After sustaining incessant fatigue and constant watchfulness for two days and nights, attended by heavy rain, exposed every moment to an attack by a vastly superior force in front, and to be cut off from the possibility of retreat to New York by the fleet which might enter the East River, on the night of the twenty-ninth . . . Washington began recrossing his troops from Brooklyn to New York."

This was a great undertaking with formidable obstacles. However, in spite of the difficulties, the Commander in Chief was prepared, and at ten o'clock, the troops began to retire from the lines in such a manner that no space was left in the front lines. As one regiment left their station on guard, the remaining troops moved right and left filling the vacancies, while General Washington took his station at the ferry.

Talmadge further explained:

> "It was one of the most anxious, busy nights that I ever recollect; and being the third in which hardly any of us had closed our eyes in sleep, we were all greatly fatigued . . . As the dawn of the next day approached, those of us who remained in the trenches became very anxious for our own safety, and when the dawn appeared there were several regiments still on duty. At this time a very dense fog began to rise and it seemed to settle in a peculiar

manner over both encampments. I recollect this peculiar providential occurrence perfectly well, and so very dense was the atmosphere that I could scarcely discern a man at six yards distance.

"When the sun rose, we had just received orders to leave the lines, but before we reached the ferry, the Commander-in-Chief sent one of his aides to order the regiment to repair again to their former station on the line. Colonel Chester immediately faced to the right about and returned, where we tarried until the sun had risen, but the fog remained as dense as ever.

"Finally, the second order arrived for the regiment to retire, and we very joyfully bid those trenches a long adieu. When we reached Brooklyn ferry, the boats had not returned from their last trip, but they very soon appeared and took the whole regiment over to New York, and I think I saw General Washington on the ferry stairs when I stepped into one of the last boats that received the troops. I left my horse tied to a post at the ferry. The troops having now all safely reached New York, and the fog continuing as thick as ever, I began to think of my favorite horse and requested leave to return and bring him off. Having obtained permission, I called for a crew of volunteers to go with me, and guiding the boat myself, I obtained my horse and got off some distance into the river before the enemy appeared in Brooklyn.

"As soon as they reached the ferry, we were saluted merrily from their musketry and finally by their fieldpieces, but we returned in safety. In the history of warfare, I do not recollect a more fortunate retreat. After all, the providential appearance of the fog saved a part of our army from being captured, and certainly myself among others who formed the rear guard."

Charles Stedman, an officer in the British army who had been a former student at the College of William and Mary in Virginia, commented,

"Driven to the corner of an island, hemmed in within a narrow space of two square miles, in their front . . . near twenty thousand men, in their rear, an arm of the sea a mile wide . . . they secured a retreat without the loss of a man."

Although London praised General Howe for his brilliant occupation of Long Island, Sir George Collier, in his cabin aboard the ship *Rainbow* harbored at New York, waited bitterly for Howe to continue the war and sarcastically recorded:

"The having to deal with a generous, merciful, forbearing enemy, who would take no unfair advantages, must surely have been highly satisfactory to General Washington, and he was certainly very deficient in not expressing his gratitude to General Howe for his kind behavior towards him. Far from taking the rash resolution of hastily passing over the East River . . . and crushing at once a frightened, trembling enemy, he generously gave them time to recover from their panic,—to throw up fresh works,—to make new arrangements,—and to recover from the torpid state the rebellion appeared in from its late shock.

"For many succeeding days did our brave veterans, consisting of twenty-two thousand men, stand on the banks of the East River, like Moses on Mount Pisgah, looking at their promised land, little more than half a mile distant. The rebel's standards waved insolently in the air from many different quarters of New York. The British troops could scarcely contain their indignation at the sight and at their own inactivity."

But British General Howe explained that he had routed the entire American line along the heights with under 400 casualties, whereas the Americans had 1,097 lost. He reasoned that defeating the rest of the rebels on Long Island would not have defeated the entire colonial army, and "The most essential duty I had to observe was, not wantonly to commit his majesty's troops, where the object was inadequate. I knew well that any considerable loss sustained by the army could not speedily, nor easily, be repaired." Perhaps that explains his careful, conservative approach.

While the battle for Long Island was taking place, New Jersey was conducting an election for a new governor to replace William Franklin, the loyalist son of Benjamin Franklin. The winner was another of those extremely distant and perhaps questionable cousins, the tall slender militia general WILLIAM LIVINGSTON. He was a staunch supporter of the revolution, George Washington, and the war effort, especially militia assistance. His sarcastic writings directed at the British government soon earned him the distinction of being included in their list of the treasonably most wanted.

Two hundred continentals, commanded by Lieutenant Colonel HENRY LIVINGSTON, remained on Long Island and were directed by Washington to "pursue every step which shall appear to you necessary and Judicious, for annoying and harassing the Enemy, and to prevent their foraging," The colonel tried to enlist the help of the islanders, but found them reluctant and frightened. He disarmed several Tories and retreated with his men to the mainland in the

RETREAT OF THE AMERICANS FROM LONG ISLAND

first week of September. From the safety of the mainland they would on occasion return and harass the enemy in whatever way the opportunity presented.

Manhattan Island defended

On 14 Mar 1776, the young orphaned revolutionary student of King's College [Columbia] ALEXANDER HAMILTON, whose mother was a granddaughter of the exiled French Huguenot physician Dr. FAWSETT, was found to be qualified in cannons—after much reading, politicking, and military drilling—and was therefor appointed as a captain of an artillery unit. Uniforms weren't provided for the men he enlisted, so he used his small savings or borrowed to buy sharp-looking clothing for himself and all his men. He took the cost of his soldier's uniforms out of their pay. It is said that through his life he followed Polonius' direction, "Costly thy habit as thy purse can buy." His artillerymen wore blue coats with cuffs and facings. His company's first assignment was guarding the colonial records, relieving continental troops for further duty.

Captain HAMILTON set a precedent by persuading the New York Congress to promote from the ranks to fill vacancies in the officer corps. He recommended that Thomas Thompson, the first sergeant, be made a lieutenant; he "has discharged his duty in the present station with uncommon fidelity . . . and expertness . . . and his advancement will be a great encouragement . . . to my company in particular, and will be an animating example to all men of merit to whose knowledge it comes." After some inquiry, the Provincial Congress ordered the promotion and published the new rule it had adopted in the newspaper.

HAMILTON's artillery was one of Lasher's Independent Companies which constructed the principal fort for the defense of Manhattan Island. The Bayard's Hill redoubt overlooked the city and mounted twelve six-pounders and was manned by two commissioned officers, four noncommissioned, and twenty privates. HAMILTON and company were there during the battle of Long Island, and they remained and were part of the 5,000 troops that Washington kept on lower Manhattan—9,000 were at King's Bridge, at the northern extremity, where Washington expected the attack, and 6,000 were in the space between, which included Fort Washington.

An exhausted George Washington was "entirely unfit to take pen in hand," for more than twenty-four hours after his return from Long Island. On the morning of the thirtieth he reported a guess of a loss of from 700 to 1000 men killed or taken. In spite of all of his persuasions, he continued, writing,

> "The check our detachment sustained . . . has dispirited too great a proportion of our troops and filled their minds with apprehension and despair. The militia, instead of calling forth their utmost efforts . . . in order to repair our losses, are dismayed, intractable, and impatient to return [to their homes.] Great numbers of them have gone off, in some instances almost by whole Regiments, by half ones, and by companies at a time."

Lewis Morris Jr. wrote to his father General Morris of Westchester County who was at the Continental Congress at that time.

> "As for the militia of Connecticut, Brigadier Wolcott and his whole brigade have got the cannon fever and very prudently skulked home. Such people are only a nuisance and had better be in the chimney corner than in the field of Mars. We have men enough without them who will fight and

whose glory is the defense of their country—Colonel Hand's regiment plunder everybody in Westchester County indiscriminately, even yourself has not escaped. . . . Jimmy DeLancey, Oliver, and John, after giving their parole, are gone off to the enemy and their house is plundered, and hers and Mrs. Moncrief's clothes were sold at vendue. Seabury has likewise eloped, and Mrs. Wilkins has very industriously propagated that you had fled to France. Such brimstones will certainly meet their desert."

General GREENE wanted to evacuate the city of New York and then burn it, as he felt it impossible to retain, and it would give the British too comfortable a foothold in America. Congress wanted it defended.

Washington wrote them that inevitably it must be abandoned, and explained further,

> "It was impossible to forget that History, our own experience, the advice of our ablest friends in Europe, the fears of the enemy, and even the declarations of Congress demonstrate that on our side the war should be defensive. It has even been called a war of posts; that we should on all occasions avoid a general action or put anything to the risk, unless compelled by a necessity, into which we ought never to be drawn."

After a harmless bombardment of the shifting enemy vessels, the officers voted on the twelfth of September to evacuate the entire island except Fort Washington, where 8,000 troops were to remain. They hoped to secure the Hudson River with the help of Fort Constitution on the Jersey side of the river. But the decision was late. Off Kip's Bay on the evening of the thirteenth, Private Martin wrote,

> "We heard a heavy cannonade at the city, and before dark saw four of the enemy's ships that had passed the town and were coming up the East River; they anchored just below us . . . . the next night [the fourteenth], under the command of the Lieutenant Colonel . . . . we arrived at the lines about dark . . . . Every half-hour, they passed the watchword to each other, 'All is well.' I heard the British on board their shipping answer, 'We will alter your tune before tomorrow night—'and they were as good as their word for once! . . . As soon as it was fairly light, we saw their boats coming out of a creek or cove on the Long Island side of the water, filled with British soldiers. We kept the lines till they were almost leveled upon us, when our officers, seeing we could make no resistance, and no orders coming from any superior officer and that we must soon be entirely exposed to the rake of their guns,

gave the order to leave the lines.

"In retreating we had to cross a level, clear spot of ground, forty or fifty rods wide, exposed to the whole of the enemy's fire. And they gave it to us in prime order. The grapeshot and language flew merrily, which served to quicken our motions . . . . We saw a party of men, apparently hurrying on in the same direction with ourselves. We endeavored hard to overtake them, but on approaching them we found . . . they were Hessians. We immediately altered our course [to] the main road leading to King's Bridge.

"We had not long been on this road before we saw another party, just ahead of us, whom we knew to be Americans. Just as we overtook these, they were fired upon by a party of British from a cornfield, and all was immediately in confusion again. I believe the enemy's party was small, but our people were all militia, and the demons of fear and disorder seemed to take full possession of all and everything on that day. When I came to the spot where the militia were fired upon, the ground was literally covered with arms, knapsacks, staves, coats, hats . . . " Washington, on Harlem Heights to be nearer King's Bridge, had mounted and ridden at a gallop toward the point of attack in the vicinity of Murray's Hill. He desperately attempted to halt their flight and rally them. "Take the walls!" "Take the cornfield!"

Colonel George Weedon of the newly arrived Virginia regiment witnessed the encounter from King's Bridge, and wrote,

"though General Washington was himself present . . . they were not to be rallied, till they had got some miles. The General was so exasperated that he struck several officers in their flight, three times dashed his hat on the ground . . . . It was with difficulty his friends could get him to quit the field, so great was his emotions. He however got off safe."

Seventeen officers and 350 men were lost, most of them captured; but the Hessians zealously cut the rebels down. British General Howe arrived at Murray's Hill at two o'clock and called a halt to await his reinforcements, which did not land until about five.

According to the Surgeon's Mate James Thacher, Mrs. Robert Murray of Murray's Hill was a middle-aged Quaker mother of twelve children and a friend of the rebel cause.

"It so happened that a body of . . . British and Hessians were at the same moment advancing on the road, which would have brought them in immediate contact with General Putnam before he could have reached the turn into the other road. Most fortunately the British generals, seeing no prospect of engaging our troops, halted their own and repaired to the house. Mrs. Murray treated them with cake and wine, and they were induced to tarry two hours or more, Governor Tryon frequently joking her about her American friends. By this happy incident, General Putnam by continuing his march, escaped an encounter with a greatly superior force which must have proved fatal . . . . Ten minutes, it is said, would have been sufficient for the enemy to have secured the road at the turn and entirely cut off General Putnam's retreat. It has since become almost a common saying among our officers that Mrs. Murray saved this part of the American army."

~ 76 ~

THE CHASE, RHODE ISLAND, NEW JERSEY—LOST

The British took New York City; but once more the Americans got away. According to Admiral Howe's secretary, Serle, who had watched from shipboard,

> "The King's forces took possession of the place, incredible as it may seem, without the loss of a man."

But the British celebration was short-lived. The next day, 15 Sep 1776, Washington retreated to the high natural plateau of Harlem Heights and ordered construction of three lines of defenses: GREENE with 3,300 men along the southern defensive line; Putman was next with 2,500 men, which included many who had bolted the day before, and Spencer in the rear with 4,200 Connecticut and Pennsylvania troops.

On 16 September, Washington sent Lieutenant Colonel Thomas Knowlton with 150 Connecticut rangers on a predawn reconnaissance of the enemy lines. They followed the ravine called the Hollow Way and scaled the heavily wooded, rocky Morningside Heights. They ran into the dreaded Black Watch regiment at West 106th Street and Broadway and got off eight volleys before they escaped with ten men wounded—Highlanders in pursuit. Between noon and 1 P.M. in a wheat field at West 120th Street heavy fighting broke out, and the Scotch Highlanders only escaped a crushing defeat by the arrival of the British light infantry and the Hessians. The Americans chased them south; but with the arrival of an additional 5,000 enemy troops, Washington called off the attack.

He wrote to General PHILIP SCHUYLER at Albany,

> "This little advantage has inspired our troops prodigiously. They find that it only required resolution and good officers to make an enemy (that they stood in too much dread of) to give way."

On Friday night about 10:00 P.M., 20 September, British Lieutenant Fredrick Mackenzie was called from his bed by a sentry. New York City was on fire! Later he wrote in his diary:

"On going to the window I observed an immense column of fire and smoke and went and called General Smith . . . . I dressed myself immediately and ran into town, a distance of two miles, but when I got there the fire had got to such a head, there seemed to be no hopes of stopping it, and those who were present did little more than look on and lament the misfortune. As soon as buckets and water could be got, the seamen and the troops, assisted by some of the inhabitants, did what they could to arrest its progress, but the fresh wind and the combustible nature of the materials of which all the houses were built rendered all their efforts vain.

"From a variety of circumstances which occurred, it is beyond a doubt that the town was designedly set on fire, either by some of those fellows who concealed themselves in it since the 15th . . . or by some villains left behind for the purpose. Some of them were caught by the soldiers in the very act of setting fire to the inside of empty houses at a distance from the fire . . . One or two . . . who were found in houses with firebrands in their hands were put to death by the enraged soldiery and thrown into the flames . . . . No assistance could be sent from the army 'til after daybreak, as the general was apprehensive the rebels had some design of attacking the army.

"It is almost impossible to conceive a scene of more horror and distress . . . . The sick, the aged, women, and children, half naked were seen going they knew not where, and taking refuge in houses which were at a distance from the fire, but from whence in several instances driven a second and even a third time by the devouring element, and at last in a state of despair, laying themselves down on the Common.

"The terror was increased by the horrid noise of the burning and falling houses, the pulling down of such wooden buildings as served to conduct the fire . . . . the rattling of above one hundred wagons sent in from the army . . . constantly employed in conveying to the Common such goods and effects as could be saved; the confused voices of so many men; the shrieks and cries of the women and children; the seeing the fire break out unexpectedly in places at a distance, which manifested a design of totally destroying the city . . . . The appearance of the Trinity Church, when completely in flames, was a very grand sight, for the spire being entirely framed of wood and covered with shingles, a lofty pyramid of fire appeared, and as soon the shingles were burnt away, the frame appeared with every separate piece of timber burning . . . the whole fell with a great noise."

The burning of New York City was not the act of George Washington, he wrote to his brother Lund,

"Providence, or some good honest fellow, has done more for us than we were disposed to do for ourselves . . . . [However] enough remains to an-swer" the purpose of the British.

The young captain, Nathan Hale, formerly a schoolteacher, was captured during these stressful times by the British. Mackenzie mentions him in his diary:

"A person named Nathaniel Hales [sic], a lieutenant in the rebel army and a native of Connecticut, was apprehended as a spy last night [September 21] upon Long Island. And having this day made a full and free confession to the Commander-in-Chief of his being employed by Mr. Washington in that capacity, he was hanged at eleven o'clock in front of the park of artil-lery. He was about twenty-four years of age and had been educated at the College of New Haven in Connecticut. He behaved with great composure and resolution, saying he thought it the duty of every good officer to obey any orders given him by his Commander-in-Chief, and desired the specta-tors to be at all times prepared to meet death in whatever shape it might appear."

Washington apparently knew little or nothing of Nathan Hale's mission un-til he learned of Hale's death from Howe's aide, Captain John Montresor, during a prisoner exchange with his famous words, "I only regret that I have but one life to give to my country."

Evidently Captain Hale had volunteered when Colonel Knowlton, who had been killed on the battlefield, asked for a man to enter New York on behalf of headquarters to try to determine Howe's activities and possible plans.

Washington waited for Howe's attack on Harlem Heights for nearly a month, while his army seemed to be falling apart. Straggling, plundering, malingering, desertion, etc., brought about many General Orders that seemed almost futile. He begged Congress to provide inducements to "gentlemen of abilities to en-gage to serve during the war," and to hurry plans for a standing army.

Back in Canada

In Canada, General Carleton was now General *Sir* Guy Carleton. He had been knighted for his persistence in holding Quebec through the long winter months until the ice broke and the fresh supply of troops arrived that had routed the Americans from Canada all the way back to Fort Ticonderoga. Carlton's advance had been stopped at Fort St. Johns, where he waited for more troops and dismantled a square-rigged three-master known as the *Inflexible*. They hauled the pieces around the rapids on the Richelieu and reassembled it on Lake Champlain in 28 days. And, in spite of the grumbling of the local shipwrights who constantly reminded them that "winter comes here early; nothing will come of the expedition this year," they assembled a collection of ships and two hundred bateaus.

But General SCHUYLER with the aid of a very creative Benedict Arnold had been assembling their own makeshift fleet. The two fleets met off Valcour Island where Benedict Arnold once more showed his valor and resourcefulness in meeting the superior forces of the enemy. It was a British victory; but their advance had been ruinously delayed for the weather had turned and for twenty days strong gale winds stopped the British ships.

Carleton's spies had been led to believe that there were 20,000 rebel soldiers at Fort Ticonderoga. With his chief of artillery, Major General William Phillips, he reconnoitered near the fort and felt that it was truly too strongly held to attack. A siege would be required. Phillips wanted to set up a winter garrison at Crown Point. Although he was an excellent soldier, he had not experienced the ice and cold that Sir Guy Carleton had dealt with the previous winter. "I still fear a dreadful winter," Carleton countered. He left orders in St. Johns and Montreal for building ships, floating batteries, gun boats and cannon, two ships of 20 guns each for an early spring attack and pulled back to Quebec to await the spring thaw.

[Note: Sixth-great-grandmother BARBARA LACEY WILKINSON's young nephew, JOHN LACEY had enlisted his soldiers early in Buck's County, Pennsylvania, and across the Delaware in Hunterdon County, New Jersey. He had been given the rank of captain and was placed under the command of Colonel Anthony Wayne who was commanding at Fort Ticonderoga that winter. Their relationship was not without its conflicts and he later requested a change. When he was about twenty five years of age he became a brigadier general in the New Jersey militia. He left a journal of his escapades.]

Colonel Wayne was not as strongly prepared that winter as Carleton had been led to believe. Wayne informed General SCHUYLER that he was unable even to post pickets for lack of men. He was losing troops by the score to a malady that combined chills and fever, aching joints, nausea, and loss of appetite and was called "camp distemper." Some men froze to death in their tents, and hardly a day passed without a fatality caused by exposure to the cold in these most primitive conditions. Wayne complained that he was short of staff officers and was obliged to serve as combination quartermaster, engineer, and commandant, and "worried with Wretches applying for Discharges or Furlows . . . until I am a mear Skeleton . . . the fort . . . will be an easy prey to the Enemy for want of proper Supplies to maintain an Army in the Spring—owing to a Supineness somewhere."—referring probably to Congress in Philadelphia, where General SCHUYLER had been writing incessantly for men and supplies.

Wayne, a formerly prosperous tanner, surveyor, and Pennsylvania legislator, had been fearless in battle when he had led a battalion to Canada in '76 in relief of the rebel army and he fought valiantly against the three-to-one odds near Trois Rivieres. After the Americans had lost half their men, they were forced to retreat, pursued by Indians and Canadian irregulars, "almost devoured by musketoes of a monstrous size and innumerable number" as they were chased through the "most horrid swamps." His men had gone bravely forward in meeting the enemy on Lake Champlain that fall, and had been able to retain Fort Ti, as it was often called. But with the desperate situation of his men at the fort, he had a daily reminder of its vulnerability. On 25 March, while seeking more militia troops in Massachusetts, he reported that Indians led by a British officer had ambushed and killed a number of his troops and taken twenty-one prisoners by Lake George, which ensured in his opinion that the enemy, which were rumored to be gathering at Montreal and St. Johns, would soon know of "the debilitated state of their garrison." So, he continued, "rouze your field and other officers from their lethargy. . . . There is not one moment to spare." Similar to the cries of George Washington, there was little response.

[Note:In the New York Historical Society's Abstracts of Wills, City of New York, Vol 36, p 100, is the will of THOMAS PIRE (or POYER), of Rumbouts precinct, Dutchess County. It was dated 1 Jan 1777. He named his beloved wife, MARGARET, and six children: SARAH, MARGRET, THOMAS, JOSEPH, HANNAH and JACOB. The will is signed "Thomas Poyer." This will was proved on 3 May 1783. [Six years later.] The will mentions his "oldest son, THOMAS, if he be of age" indicating that son THOMAS was under 21 years 1 Jan 1777. With a dying father and six children, did any of these young POYER sons participate as soldiers in the Revolutionary War? Was the dying middle-aged father, THOMAS POYER's "being sick" the result of injuries or disease as a soldier in the Canadian campaign? Was his son JOSEPH my ancestor? The time was right. Canadians who joined with the Americans were excommunicated from the Catholic Church and not allowed to stay in Canada, unless they repented of their supposed error. The major battles of the Revolution had not extended into Dutchess County, yet; but an able bodied man would probably fight, and war was nearby with plenty of disease.]

Westchester County, New York

In Harlem Heights, as the days rolled into weeks, Washington wrote his brother John,

> "Fifty thousand pounds should not induce me again to undergo what I have done." And in a letter to cousin Lund he told him in confidence, "I never was in such an unhappy, divided state since I was born . . . I cannot have the least chance for reputation . . . and to be told . . . that if I leave the service all will be lost, is, at the same time that I am bereft of every peaceful moment, distressing to a degree."

Howe waited until 12 October to make his move. He passed up the East River under the cover of a heavy, warm fog and landed his advance force of around 4,000 on Throg's Neck, which peninsula was often called Frog's Neck by the natives. It was east and somewhat behind Washington's lines and about equal distance to King's Bridge, four miles away. Some of seventh-great-grandfather ROGER BARTON's descendants were still living in the area of Westchester and Eastchester. The Neck at high tide became an island and was separated from the mainland by a creek with marshy borders. There were two approaches: at the lower end was a causeway and wooden bridge over the milldam at Westchester village and at the upper end there was a ford. Both were guarded. At an enormous pile of cordwood on the west side of the creek, General Heath placed a small guard of thirty riflemen. Another detail watched the fording place. Heath reported,

> "The troops landed at Frog's Neck and their advance pushed towards the causeway and the bridge at Westchester Mill. Colonel Hand's riflemen took up the planks of the bridge as had been directed and commenced a firing with their rifles. The British moved towards the head of the creek, but found here also the Americans in possession of the pass."

Both sides were reinforced before evening. For several hours, behind a pile of wood, thirty riflemen held up, with field pieces, the advance of the four thousand British troops, who could have cut off Washington's only retreat, if they had not been stopped.

General Charles Lee, back from South Carolina on the 14th, was given command of the troops north of King's Bridge. Washington and his generals, including Sullivan and Sterling, who had been exchanged, assessed Howe's action, and decided, in opposition to Congress, that Manhattan Island could no longer be held. However, General GREENE felt he could hold Fort Washington and Fort Constitution on both sides of the Hudson River. General Washington finally conceded; but removed his greater army of 13,000 troops twenty miles along the west side bank of the little Bronx River to the village of White Plains, which they felt they could defend and stop the British attempt to surround them. They were encumbered by a lack of wagons, which would load, journey, unload, and return for more equipment and supplies. It took four days, and on 23 October they were able to set up headquarters in the village.

To deter the advance of the British from Throng's Neck, Washington sent Colonel John Glover, the feisty little redheaded fisherman who had so ably brought the continental army safely from Long Island, with a mixed brigade of eleven hundred men to Pell's Point to protect the American rear from the enemies advance. Early on the morning of the 18th, Colonel Glover mounted a hilltop near Eastchester to look down the Sound with his spyglass. He focused in on

> "a number of ships in the Sound under way. In a very short time saw the boats, upward of two hundred sail, all manned and formed in four grand divisions."

Quickly, the colonel marched about 750 of his men with three field pieces to oppose the landing of the British troops. Glover confessed,

> "I would have given a thousand worlds to have had General Lee or some other experienced officer present to direct or at least to approve of what I had done."

He "looked around," but "could see none," so he led his troops forward, disputing the ground so ferociously that Howe lost three more days and another chance to stop the American retreat.

On the 20th Howe was encamped on a short line from Eastchester to New Rochelle. By the 25th he was within four miles of White Plains. A British officer reported,

> "The rebels in our front supposed not to be above two thousand, their sentries and ours very near, and no firing from our side or theirs. An officer observed that they marched off with great composure the last evening and in much better order than he had ever seen them when he first came to the

ground, and behaved more like soldiers than he had ever known them to do before."

Before dawn on 27 October, American brigade major Benjamin Tallmadge reported,

"We learned that the enemy was in full march directly in front of us. General Spencer . . . immediately made the necessary disposition to receive the enemy, having the river Bronx on our right and between us the troops on Chatterton's Hill. At the dawn of day, the Hessian column advanced within musket shot of our troops, when a full discharge of musketry warned them of their danger. At first they fell back, but rallied again immediately, and the column of British troops having advanced on our left made it necessary to retire. As stone walls were frequent, our troops occasionally formed behind them and poured a destructive fire into the Hessian ranks. It, however, became necessary to retreat wholly before such an overwhelming force.

"To gain Chatterton's Hill, it became necessary to cross the Bronx, which was fordable at that place. The troops immediately entered the river and ascended the hill, while I being in the rear and mounted on horseback endeavored to hasten the last of our troops . . . . By the time I reached the opposite bank of the river, the Hessian troops were about to enter it and considered me as their prisoner. As we ascended the hill, I filed off to the right, expecting our troops on the hill would soon give them a volley."

Tallmadge's volley was delivered, and he escaped.

The British had decided that Chatterton Hill must be taken. Howe marched eight regiments and a dozen fieldpieces to an eminence a half mile away, while much of the British army watched. According to Heath's report:

"A part of the left column, composed of British and Hessians, forded the river and marched along under the cover of the hill, until they had gained sufficient ground to the left of the Americans . . . . When they briskly ascended the hill, the first column resumed a quick march. As the troops which were advancing to the attack ascended the hill, the cannonade on the side of the British ceased, as their own men became exposed to their fire if continued . . . . This led some American officers . . . to observe the British were worsted . . . but a few minutes evinced that the Americans were giving way. They moved off the hill in a great body, neither running, nor observing the best order. The British ascended the hill very slowly."

They arrived at its summit, formed and made no attempt to pursue the Americans.

With the loss of the hill, Washington lost the day. Howe did not press him, only cannonaded a short while. Washington drew in his right and moved his sick, wounded, and baggage to the high ground of North Castle, while the British Army dug fortifications. For several days, "the two armies lay looking at each other." The Americans bound the cornstalks remaining in the fields from the summer's harvest into fascines to protect their works.

During the night of 4 Nov 1776, American sentinels reported the rumble of the wheels of the British gun carriages—evidence that the British were leaving Westchester County and apparently returning to New York City. Maybe New Jersey and ultimately Philadelphia would be Howe's objective. This was a relief to the Connecticut militia guarding their borders; but New Jersey's "Flying Army" militia was mostly at Fort Washington on Manhattan Island. Many of the Pennsylvanian troops were at Ticonderoga, where Generals SCHUYLER and Gates were sparing for control, and much of the New York militia was guarding the Hudson Highlands.

Fort Washington and Fort Lee

By 10 November, Washington had chosen to split his army, leaving General Charles Lee to command the 7,000 troops at White Plains, NATHANAEL GREENE with 3,500 soldiers was still at Fort Washington and Fort Constitution (known soon as Fort Lee) and as Washington crossed the Hudson River below Stony Point with about 2,000 men, he left Heath at Peekskill with about 4,000 men to protect the Highlands. He felt that he could recruit additional militia in New Jersey and Pennsylvania to support his army in their lands. It was a desperate spread and dilution of his army; but there was so much land to protect. Unfortunately, many of the militia decided to go home and much of the continental army had enlisted only until 31 December.

Suddenly, it became clear what the enemy's first objective was—Fort Washington. A Hessian officer said of it:

> "The enemy had erected a fort on a high rocky elevation, which seemed fortified by nature itself, which they called Fort Washington. Human skill had also been employed to make it very strong. Without possession of this

fort, we could not keep up communication with New York, nor could we think of advancing any further, much less get quiet winter-quarters."

A total of eight thousand were to take place in the assault, including forty-seven hundred Hessians who had just arrived from Europe—commanded by Wilhelm von Knyphausen. Serving under him was Colonel Rall, who would later command at Trenton, plunder the countryside and rape the New Jersey women. Rall didn't speak English. The two led the murderous charges up the hill to displace the Americans and occupy Fort Washington.

One of the major reasons for the British diversion from White Plains and their rapid attack on Fort Washington was caused by the desertion and betrayal of Pennsylvanian, William Demont, who was an adjutant stationed at Fort Washington. On 2 November, he had craftily left the Fort with all its plans and fortifications and given them to the enemy. British Lieutenant McKenzie wrote:

> "He says the rebels remaining on this island amount to about two thousand men, who . . . are to retire into Fort Washington and defend it to the last extremity, having therein two months provisions, many cannon, and plenty of ammunition. He says there are great dissensions in the rebel army, everyone finding fault with the mode of proceeding, and the inferior officers, even ensigns, insisting that, in such a cause, every man has a right to assist in council and to give his opinion. They are much distressed for clothing. The people from the Southern colonies declare they will not go into New England, and the others that they will not march to the Southward. If this account is true in any degree, they must soon go to pieces."

William Demont plead with the British for cash for his treasonable act. They finally gave him sixty pounds, and he escaped to London.

After the cruel assault and surrender of the Fort, British McKenzie described their American prisoners:

> "The rebel prisoners were in general but very indifferently clothed. Few of them appeared to have a second shirt, nor did they appear to have washed themselves during the campaign. A great many of them were lads under fifteen and old men, and few had the appearance of soldiers. Their odd figures frequently excited the laughter of our soldiers."

But the laughter did not extend across the Hudson at Fort Lee, where General NATHANAEL GREENE wrote his friend Henry Knox,

"I feel mad, vexed, sick and sorry. Never did I need the consoling voice of a friend more than now . . . . This is a most terrible event; its consequences are justly to be dreaded."

Washington had sent word to commander Mcgaw to hold out until dark and they would find a way to get his soldiers into New Jersey. The messenger returned with the word that Mcgaw had been forced to capitulate.

Even Washington's adjutant general, Joseph Reed, without hesitation, condemned his personal friend NATHANAEL GREENE and his Commander in Chief in a letter to General Charles Lee:

"If a real defense of the lines was intended, the number was too few; if the fort only, the garrison was too numerous by half. General Washington's own judgment seconded by representations from us would, I believe, have saved the men and their arms, but unluckily, General GREENE's judgement was contrary. This kept the General's mind in a state of suspense till the stroke was struck. Oh! General—an indecisive mind is one of the greatest misfortunes that can befall an army. How often have I lamented it this campaign."

The Americans had lost around 2500 men. If they were not killed in the assault, they were put in the antiquated, over-crowded British prison ships or the old goal at New York City, where they rotted, with very few concerns from the enemy.

With Fort Washington in the hands of the enemy the need for Fort Lee was questionable. It was important "in conjunction with that on the other side of the river," so Washington proposed that the soldiers and all supplies and equipment be evacuated as rapidly as possible. But with the exception of the gunpowder, the decision was too late. The British were knocking on their doors. On 20 November, during a cold, rainy night, Howe landed 4,000 soldiers under the command of Lord Cornwallis. They were discovered by an American officer riding patrol, which turned and galloped down to the fort and shook GREENE out of his bed to make his report. GREENE rapidly put his men under arms, and leaving kettles boiling and tents standing, fled to join General Washington, who was gathering his troops in the village of Hackensack. The Americans had lost many cannon, three hundred irreplaceable tents, hundreds of muskets, thousands of shot, shell, and cartridges, and over a thousand barrels of flour.

One of the British contemptuously reported:

"On the appearance of our troops, and in a few moments after we reached the hill near their entrenchments, not a rascal of them could be seen. They have left some poor pork, a few greasy proclamations, and some of that scoundrel 'Common Sense' man's letters, which we can read at our leisure, now that we have got one of the "impregnable redoubts" of Mr. Washington's to quarter in . . . . We intend to push on after the long-faces in a few days."

The British reported that of the dead they found near Fort Washington

"many were without shoes or stockings and several were observed to have only linen drawers on with a rifle or hunting shirt, without any proper shirt or waistcoat. They are also in great want of blankets."

The clear, balmy fall weather had now turned to freezing winter rain. This was not agreeable to the 3,000 poorly clad Americans as they continued south to the Aquackinack Bridge, across the Passaic River, and on through the miry, broken roads to Newark, New Jersey. They now had few tents and had lost their picks and shovels to make fortifications.

The Race west across the Delaware River

Washington called on General Lee to join him with 3,500 of his continentals, leaving two brigades to guard their stores until their time ran out, when he assumed they would go home. An insubordinate Lee stubbornly delayed. Washington left Newark on the twenty-eighth, as Cornwallis' troops began their entrance on the other side of town. A cry for help was made to New Jersey Governor WILLIAM LIVINGSTON and to the Continental Congress. Very few could be recruited. The British were offering amnesty to all the fence-straddlers that would join them. The loyalists were delighted to welcome the invaders. The Continental Congress was considering their move to Baltimore, Maryland. The Maryland and the New Jersey militia left Washington the day after he reached Brunswick.

The scouts reported the enemy to be within ten miles the next day. Once more, they were on the move. At Princeton, Washington waited only long enough to write Congress that Lee had not yet joined him and then posted Sterling with two brigades to slow Cornwallis' advance. He then moved on with his army to the small village of Trenton, where he hoped to cross the Delaware River and gain safety for his remaining men and supplies.

For some unexplained reason, Cornwallis stopped his close pursuit at Brunswick, and Washington was able to cross the river with all the sick, wounded, baggage, and supplies. He collected or destroyed all the boats for seventy miles north to gain control of the river, then returned to New Jersey with the intent to join Sterling at Princeton and meet the enemy. But Sterling had already begun his retreat, so Washington joined with the Delaware troops at the rear and, with a select group, proceeded to destroy bridges, cut down trees and do such other encumbrances that would slow the approach of the enemy. At dusk their last boat crossed the Delaware River into Pennsylvania, as Cornwallis' advance troops arrived on the eastern bank only to discover there were no boats.

Howe was so confident that he sent Clinton with 6,000 soldiers by ship to take Rhode Island. They met the Rhode Island militia of around 1,000 men, overwhelmed them and, on 8 December, settled around their major seaport of Newport. This enemy occupation would remain for three years in the homeland of General NATHANAEL GREENE and our relatives: the BARTONs; WILKINSONs; WILBURs; SMITHs; TALLMANs, and HOPKINS.

First cousin, STEPHEN's brother, ESEK HOPKINS, in command of the Continental Navy had been ordered to protect the Chesapeake and Narragansett Bays, but had instead sailed to the Bahamas and seized two poorly defended forts. He was able to acquire British weaponry—cannon, mortars, and their ammunition—that required two weeks to load aboard his six newly commissioned warships. He then sailed northward to Narragansett Bay. Before he could reach land, early in April of 1776, his flotilla was forced to battle with the twenty-gun British warship *Glasgow*. Since they approached her one by one, the British warship was able to ruin each American vessel and proceed on into the bay, while the Americans stumbled into their harbor at New London, Connecticut. Five months later, HOPKINS was censured by a court-martial board and his commission was later revoked. He would be replaced by one of his daring young officers, John Paul Jones.

The Americans had smaller armed privateer vessels that were suitable for their protection against pirates and to harass the enemy, and they had been helpful in the French and Indian War. Newport, Rhode Island, was ideally situated for this variety of activity and was a 'thorn in the side' of the British naval activity and their foraging along the coast. Closing this port gave some comfort to the enemy anchored in nearby New York harbor.

The delinquent, cocky American General Charles Lee finally obeyed orders and crossed the Hudson River with his part of the Continental Army on 4 December and moved toward Morristown, New Jersey, arriving a few miles southwest on 12 December. That night he slept at a tavern three miles from his camp, accompanied by his guard and some of his military family.

The next morning, while General Sullivan marched onward with the overdue continental army, Lee dallied in his dressing gown and slippers to write a few dispatches. One was to his friend General Horatio Gates to whom he confided,

> "The ingenious maneuver of Fort Washington has unhinged the goodly fabric we had been building. There never was so d—ed a stroke. 'Entre nous', a certain great man is most d—ably deficient. He has thrown me into a situation where I have my choice of difficulties: if I stay in this province I risk myself and army, and if I do not stay, the province is lost forever. . . . In short, unless something which I do not expect turns up, we are lost."

Lee then dressed, sent for his horses and would have been mounted and gone within 10 minutes, when around 10 o'clock they were surprised by about fifty horsemen, who came from the wood and orchard, surrounded the house and fired upon it, according to Lee's aide-de-camp, William Bradford Jr. He continued,

> "Lee looked out of the window to see how the guards behaved and saw the enemy twice with his hanger cut off the arm of one of the guards crying for quarter. The guard behaved well, fired at first, but were rushed upon and subdued. The general saw then that they must submit and after walking the chamber perhaps ten or fifteen minutes, told his aide-de-camp to go down and tell them General Lee submitted."

A Whig newspaper reported,

> "The enemy showed an ungenerous, nay, boyish triumph after they had got him secure at Brunswick, by making his horse drunk, while they toasted their king till they were in the same condition. A band or two of music played all night to proclaim their joy for this important acquisition. They say we cannot now stand another campaign. Mistaken fools! to think the

fate of America depended on one man. They will find ere long that it has no other effect than to urge us on to a noble revenge."

Although William Shippen Jr. cried, "Oh! what a d—ed sneaking way to being kidnaped, I can't bear to think of it."

Washington received the news with regret. He wrote Congress,

"Our cause has . . . received a severe blow."

Of Congress, Lee had recently written, they "seem to stumble at every step. I do not mean one or two of the cattle, but the whole stable."

Thomas Paine, who had written the pamphlet *Common Sense* which had aided greatly in uniting the colonies, had volunteered for service and was with the army as they crossed the Jerseys. His new pamphlet, *The American Crisis*, now appeared on the Philadelphia streets. It was snatched up by the populous, and often quoted, especially this cry that seemed to emanate from the very heart of Washington and his army:

> "These are the times that try men's souls: The summer soldier and the sunshine patriot will, in this crisis, shrink from the service of his country; but he that stands it NOW deserves the love and thanks of man and woman. Tyranny, like Hell, is not easily conquered. Yet we have this consolation with us, that the harder the conflict, the more glorious the triumph."

General Sullivan arrived with Lee's forces the same day, 20 December, that General Gates arrived from Ticonderoga with six hundred men—all that still remained from the seven regiments. This gave Washington about 7,500 soldiers—at least, until December 31st, when many enlistments would be completed. One young brigade major related,

> "You ask me our situation. It has been the Devil, but is to appearance better. About two thousand of us have been obliged to run d—ed hard before about ten thousand of the enemy. Never was finer lads at a retreat than we are . . . . No fun for us that I can see. However, I cannot but think we shall drub the dogs. Never mind, all will come right one of these days."

This was the belief of George Washington, as well, and incessantly they harassed the Hessians across the Delaware.

Perhaps it was Lee's capture or the effort it would take to follow Washington into Pennsylvania; but on 14 Dec 1776, British General Howe issued general orders closing the campaign, and personally retired comfortably into the arms of the wife of his commissary of prisoners, Joshua Loring, in New York City. To his 14,000 troops strung out from Burlington, New Jersey, on the Delaware River, north through Bordentown, Trenton and Pennington, then across New Jersey through Princeton to Staten Island, he gave the following order:

> "The Commander-in-Chief calls upon the commanding officers of corps to exert themselves in preserving the greatest regularity and strictest discipline in their respective quarters, particularly attending to the protection of the inhabitants and their property in their several districts."

He gave General Cornwallis leave to return to England for a visit with his wife, who was not well. Colonel von Donop was given about 3,000 troops of Hessians and Highlanders—about half was stationed at Trenton and the other half at Bordentown. These veterans, who considered plundering, raping and terrorizing part of the prize of victory, ignored this part of the British commander's order. The devastation was appalling.

The loyalist Charles Stedman reported,

> "No sooner had the army entered the Jerseys than the business . . . of plunder began. The friend and the foe . . . shared alike. The people's property was taken without being paid for or even a receipt given . . . . The British army foraged indiscriminately, procuring considerable supplies of hay, oats, Indian corn, cattle, and horses, which were never or but very seldom paid for . . . . The people of the Jerseys were well effected to his Majesty's government . . . . But when the people found that the promised protection was not afforded them, that their property was seized and most wantonly destroyed, that in many instances their families were insulted, stripped of their beds with other furniture—nay, even of their very wearing apparel— they then determined to try the other side, trusting . . . .at one period or other, [to] receive compensation for the supplies taken from them for the use of the American army.

> "And it is but justice to say that the Americans never took anything from their friends but in cases of necessity, in which cases they uniformly gave receipts for what they did take, always living as long as they could upon their enemies and never suffering their troops to plunder their friends with impunity. But at the same time, it is to be noticed that the American troops were suffered to plunder the loyalists and to exercise with impunity every act of barbarity on that unfortunate class of people, frequently inflicting on them scourges and stripes."

In mid-December an American patrol on the Pennsylvania side of the Delaware River heard a group of women calling for help. They rowed over and discovered that the group of women had all been raped, including a 15-year-old girl. Colonel Johann Gottlieb Rall, whose 1,600 Hessian troops had slaughtered Americans as they tried to surrender on Long Island and on the slopes of Fort Washington, was left in command at Trenton. He had a reputation for rape and plundering that even worried British General Lord Howe. His secretary, Ambrose Serle, reported:

> "It is impossible to express the devastations which [they] have made upon the houses & country seats of some of the rebels. All their furniture, glass, windows, and the very hangings of the rooms are demolished or defaced. This with the filth deposited in them makes them so offensive . . . that it is a penance to go into them."

It is not hard to understand why many of the fence-straddling New Jersey farmers took down the loyalist red ribbons from their doors and started ambushing the Hessian patrols and British scouting parties that risked leaving the safety of their Trenton fortress. It has been said that there were a few less German soldiers on colonial soil every day. The New Jersey, New York, and Pennsylvania citizens came to know, as had Boston, the terror associated with an army of occupation. They may have dreamed of life as it had been, but reality was now upon them. Their seven-year reality of war, with hunger, disease, and devastation surrounding them, included everyone—men, women, children, and even the supposed neutral Quakers.

[Note: Such was the life of our ancestors, New Jersey friends, and relations, as their lands were occupied by one army or the other throughout the remainder of the long war. Direct ancestors ELISHA BARTON, JOHN COOLEY, JOSEPH POYER, and JOHN WILKINSON were with the continental army; but their families resided in Hunterdon County, New Jersey or across the Delaware River in Bucks County, Pennsylvania at his time. GILBERT BARTON, ELISHA's older brother, owned a tavern in Trenton, where the Whigs and revolutionaries would meet, discuss events, and plan. Washington crossed the Delaware on Christmas night, 1776, very close to the BARTON, COOLEY and WILKINSON lands on both sides of the river.]

77

VICTORY OR DEATH, NEW JERSEY RECLAIMED

Colonel John Fitzgerald, one of Washington's aides, wrote the following account:

"Dec. 23 — Orders have been issued to cook rations for three days. Washington has just given the countersign, 'Victory or Death.' He has written a letter to General Cadwalader at Bristol, which he has entrusted to me to copy. He intends to cross the river, make a ten-mile march to Trenton, and attack Rall just before daybreak. Ewing is to cross and seize the bridge crossing the Assumpink [on the road south to Bordentown]. Putnam and Cadwalader are to cross and make a feint of attacking Donop [at Bordentown] so that he cannot hasten to Rall's assistance.

"Dec. 24 — A scout just in says that the Hessians have a picket on the Pennington road half a mile out from Trenton, and another at Dickenson's house on the river road.

"Dec. 25 — Christmas morning. They make a great deal of Christmas in Germany, and no doubt the Hessians will drink a great deal of beer and have a dance tonight. They will be sleepy tomorrow morning. Washington will set the tune for them about daybreak. The rations are cooked. New flints and ammunition have been distributed. Colonel Glover's fishermen from Marblehead, Massachusetts, are to manage the boats just as they did in the retreat from Long Island.

"Christmas, 6 p.m. — The regiments have had their evening parade, but instead of returning to their quarters are marching toward the ferry. It is fearfully cold and raw and a snowstorm setting in. The wind is northeast and beats in the faces of the men. It will be a terrible night for the soldiers who have no shoes. Some of them have tied old rags around their feet; others are barefoot, but I have not heard a man complain. They are ready to suffer any hardship and die rather than give up their liberty. [A nineteen-year-old officer, Major JAMES WILKINSON, noted in his journal that footprints down to the river were 'tinged here and there with blood from the feet of the men who wore broken shoes.'] I have just copied the order for marching. Both divisions are to go from the ferry to Bear Tavern, two miles. They will separate there; Washington will accompany GREENE's division with a part of the artillery down the Pennington road. Sullivan and the rest of the artillery will take the river road.

"Dec. 26, 3 A.M. — I am writing in the ferry house. The troops are all over, and the boats have gone back for the artillery. We are three hours behind the set time. Glover's men have had a hard time to force the boats through the floating ice with the snow drifting in their faces. I never have seen Washington so determined as he is now. He stands on the bank of the river, wrapped in his cloak, superintending the landing of his troops. He is calm and collected, but very determined. The storm is changing to sleet and cuts like a knife. The last cannon is being landed, and we are ready to mount our horses.

"Dec. 26, noon — It was nearly four o'clock when we started. The two divisions divided at Bear Tavern. At Birmingham, three and a half miles south of the tavern, a man came with a message from General Sullivan that the storm was wetting the muskets and rendering them unfit for service. 'Tell General Sullivan,' said Washington, 'to use the bayonet. I am resolved to take Trenton.' It was broad daylight when we came to a house where a man was chopping wood. He was very much surprised when he saw us.

"'Can you tell me where the Hessian picket is?' Washington asked. The man hesitated, but I said, 'You need not be frightened; it is General Washington who asks the question.' His face brightened, and he pointed toward the house of Mr. Howell. It was just eight o'clock. Looking down the road I saw a Hessian running out from the house. He yelled in Dutch and swung his arms. Three or four others came out with their guns. Two of them fired at us, but the bullets whistled over our heads. Some of General Stephen's men rushed forward and captured two. The others took to their heels, running toward Mr. Calhoun's house, where the picket guard was stationed, about twenty men under Captain Altenbrockum. They came running out of the house. The captain flourished his sword and tried to form his men. Some of them fired at us, others ran toward the village.

"The next moment we heard drums beat and a bugle sound, and then from the west came the boom of a cannon. General Washington's face lighted up instantly, for he knew that it was one of Sullivan's guns.

"We could see a great commotion down toward the meetinghouse, men running here and there, officers swinging their swords, artillerymen harnessing their horses. Captain Forrest unlimbered his guns. Washington gave the order to advance, and we rushed on to the junction of King and Queen streets. Forrest wheeled six of his cannon into position to sweep both streets. The riflemen under colonel Hand and Scott's and Lawson's battalions went upon the run through the fields on the left to gain possession of the Princeton Road. The Hessians were just ready to open fire with two of their cannon when Captain [William] Washington and Lieutenant [James] Monroe with their men rushed forward and captured them.

"We saw Rall coming riding up the street from his headquarters, which were at Stacy Potts' house. We could hear him shouting in Dutch, 'My brave soldiers, advance!'

"His men were frightened and confused, for our men were firing upon them from fences and houses and they were falling fast. Instead of advancing they ran into an apple orchard. The officers tried to rally them, but our men kept advancing and picking off the officers. It was not long before Rall tumbled from his horse and his soldiers threw down their guns and gave themselves up as prisoners.

"While this was taking place on the Pennington road, Colonel John Stark from New Hampshire, in the advance on the river road, was driving Knyphausen's men pell-mell through the town. Sullivan sent a portion of his troops under St. Clair to seize the bridge and cut off the retreat of the Hessians toward Bordentown. Sullivan's men shot the artillery horses and captured two cannon attached to Knyphausen's regiment.

"Dec. 26, 3 P.M — I have been talking with Rall's adjutant, Lieutenant Piel. He says that Rall sat down to a grand dinner at the Trenton Tavern Christmas Day, that he drank a great deal of wine and sat up nearly all night playing cards. He had been in bed but a short time when the battle began and was sound asleep. Piel shook him, but found it hard work to wake him up. Supposing he was wide awake, Piel went out to help rally the men, but Rall not appearing, he went back and found him in his nightshirt.

"'What's the matter?' Rall asked.

"Piel informed him that a battle was going on. That seemed to bring him to his senses. He dressed himself, rushed out, and mounted his horse to be mortally wounded a few minutes later.

"We have taken nearly one thousand prisoners, six cannon, more than one thousand muskets, twelve drums, and four colors. About forty Hessians were killed or wounded. Our loss is only two killed and three wounded. Two of the latter are Captain [William] Washington and Lieutenant [James] Monroe, who rushed forward bravely to seize the cannon.

"I have just been with General Washington and GREENE to see Rall. He will not live through the night. He asked that his men might be kindly treated. Washington promised that he would see they were well cared for.

"Dec. 27, 1776 — Here we are back in our camp with the prisoners and trophies. Washington is keeping his promise; the soldiers are in the Newtown Meeting House and other buildings. He has just given directions for tomorrow's dinner. All the captured Hessian officers are to dine with him. He bears the Hessians no malice, but says they have been sold by their Grand Duke to King George and sent to America, when if they could have their own way, they would be peaceably living in their own country.

"It is a glorious victory. It will rejoice the hearts of our friends everywhere and give new life to our hitherto waning fortunes. Washington has baffled the enemy in his retreat from New York. He has pounced upon the Hessians like an eagle upon a hen and is safe once more on this side of the river. If he does nothing more, he will live in history as a great military commander."

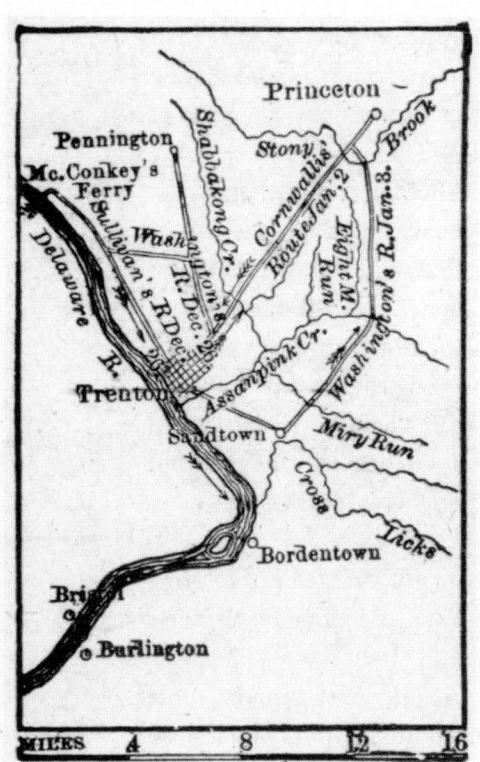

BATTLES OF TRENTON AND PRINCETON, 1776–1777

The Knyphausen regiment had tried to fight there way out, although their commanding officer, Major von Dechow, had also been fatally wounded and, seeing the other officers surrender, had given his men the same order. His officers refused and led their men across the freezing, shoulder-deep Assumpink Creek, with heavy snow still falling. They were surrounded on the far shore and shelled by artillery. General Arthur St. Clair shouted to a Hessian captain,

"Tell your commanding officer that if you do not surrender immediately, I will blow you to pieces."

The Hessians said they would if they could keep their swords and their baggage. The two officers shook hands, and galloped off to find Washington. Major WILKINSON reported the capitulation. Washington grasped his hand and with a rare smile declared, "Major WILKINSON, this is a glorious day for our country!"

[Note: This was Major JAMES WILKINSON, who was born in Benedict, Maryland, in 1757. He became a colonel and an aide to Horatio Gates, and then a brigadier general. His relationship to our WILKINSON family has not been established and is probably quite distant. My direct Quaker ancestor named AARON WILKINSON was born 23 May 1781 in Pennsylvania. The name James doesn't appear in my WILKINSON line.]

Captain ALEXANDER HAMILTON and his artillery men had been part of Washington's continental army as they were pursued across New Jersey by Cornwallis. He had posted his two field pieces on high ground to delay the enemy and kept up a fusillade while the Americans proceeded to Princeton. A veteran officer

"noticed the youth, a mere stripling, small, slender, almost delicate in frame, marching . . . with a cocked hat pulled down over his eyes, apparently lost in thought, with his hand resting on a cannon, and every now and then patting it, as if it were a favorite horse or a pet plaything."

HAMILTON was under the command of General GREENE on the upper road as they entered Trenton on that morning of 26 December. HAMILTON planted his battery on the high ground at the head of King Street and Captain Thomas Forrest similarly commanded the length of Queen Street. The enemy, in close ranks, was torn to pieces, and Colonel Rall fell from his horse, mortally wounded. Some believe this event brought HAMILTON to the attention of General Washington, who within a few weeks requested him as his aide-de-camp with a promotion to Lieutenant Colonel. HAMILTON had turned down two lesser generals, previously, because of his desire to actively command his own men; but he accepted General Washington's proposal. A great friendship developed between the two men. Washington returned across the Delaware with 900 prisoners.

Embarrassed by the Trenton attack, Cornwallis left his ship and his luggage and with a picked force of his best grenadiers and light infantry sped across New Jersey to join von Donop's Hessians in a retaliatory attack. Washington was determined to meet him, although his troops were rapidly diminishing. He offered a bonus of ten dollars. None of them moved forward to volunteer. With one last appeal, in a soft voice, he pleaded,

"You have done all I asked you to do, and more than could be reasonably expected. But your country is at stake, your wives, your homes and all that you hold dear. You have worn yourselves out with fatigues and hardships, but we know not how to spare you. If you will consent to stay only one month longer, you will render that service to the cause of liberty and to your country which you probably never can do under any other circumstance."

He closed by saying,

"This is the crisis which is to decide our destiny."

Then he rode off to one side for their decision.

At first, no one moved. Then one stepped forward. A few more followed. By the end of the day only the sick and unable held back. 1,200 men had accepted the bounty and remained. Now it was necessary to find the cash. Fortunately, Robert Morris of the Continental Congress had the money they had been able to extract from the Quaker Philadelphians. It seems that the Quakers who would not turn out to drill at the weekly musters would instead pay a day's wages in cash. Congress sent him this money and also a resolution giving him authority to take "whatever he may want for the use of the Army." This was an open authorization for his men to loot loyalist and Quaker property.

On 2 Jan 1777, the army of Cornwallis was arriving with a far superior force on the east side of Assunpink Creek. On the west side, Washington saw that he had left himself no place to retreat, if things went against him the next day. He also observed that Cornwallis planned once more to rest his troops before attacking. That night the American campfires burned brightly as men continued to pile on logs and move deliberately in front of them in clear view of the enemy. The pounding and digging of new fortifications rang loudly across the creek for the British ears. Silently the padded wheels of the artillery moved north and then northeast with the main body of Washington's army—well behind the campfires of both armies. With the news of the victory at Trenton spreading through the countryside, eager Pennsylvania and New Jersey recruits and militia volunteers began to flock to the American standard and joined Washington's army as they flanked the British and moved quietly to attack the British rear guard at Princeton.

A sergeant who had re-enlisted at Trenton and moved forward with General

Hugh Mercer's troop described his early sunrise events:

"Reaching the summit of a hill near Princeton, we observed a light-horse-man looking towards us . . . General Mercer, observing him, gave orders to the riflemen . . . to pick him off . . . But at that instant, he wheeled about and was out of their reach.

"Soon after this, as we were descending a hill through an orchard, a party of the enemy who were entrenched behind a bank and fence, rose and fired upon us . . . We formed, advanced, and fired upon the enemy. They retreated eight rods to their packs . . . I advanced to the fence on the opposite side of the ditch which the enemy had just left, fell on one knee, and loaded my musket with ball and buckshot. Our fire was most destructive. Their ranks grew thin and the victory seemed nearly complete, when the British were reinforced. Many of our brave men had fallen, and we were unable to withstand such superior numbers of fresh troops. I soon heard General Mercer command in a tone of distress, 'Retreat!' He was mortally wounded and died shortly after . . . I ran for a piece of wood at a distance where I thought I might shelter.

"At this moment, Washington appeared in front of the American army, riding towards those of us who were retreating, and exclaimed, 'Parade with us, my brave fellows, there is but a handful of the enemy, and we will have them directly.' I immediately joined the main body . . . . The British were unable to resist this attack and retreated into the College [now Princeton University], where they thought themselves safe. Our army was there in an instant, and cannon were planted before the door, and after two or three discharges, a white flag appeared at the window and the British surrendered. They were a haughty, crabbed set of men, as they fully exhibited while prisoners on their march to the country.

"In this battle, my pack, which was made fast by leather string, was shot from my back and with it went what little clothing I had. It was, however, soon replaced by one which had belonged to a British officer and was well furnished. It was not mine long, for it was stolen shortly afterwards."

The Battle of Princeton was over in less than an hour; but it was one of the most savage battles of the war and extremely dangerous to the fearless General Washington, whose life was perhaps preserved only by the dense smoke from the gunfire as he led his troops forward. For the first time, American troops were charging from three sides against regular British troops and keeping up an incessant fire. The spectacle unnerved the British, who turned in panic and bolted from the field. When the Americans realized what they had done, they broke into a cheer and joined General Washington as he momentarily led the pursuit to Princeton. He shouted over his shoulder, "It's a fine fox chase, boys." Among the troops was the Philadelphia Light Horse. The British lost heavily, nearly four hundred killed, wounded, or taken prisoner. Washington lost only forty-four men; but General Hugh Mercer had been cut down by the British bayonets, and the handsome, athletic Colonel Haslet of the Delaware troops died with a bullet in his brain.

The story is that ALEXANDER HAMILTON's battery of artillery was the one that lined up their cannons at Nassau Hall at Princeton, where the British had sought refuge, and that it was one of his cannon balls that passed through and beheaded the portrait of George II hanging in the college chapel. The British inside, who surrendered, have variously been numbered between sixty and two hundred. British General Cornwallis swung back quickly for Princeton when he discovered that morning at Trenton that Washington had duped him once more. Washington would not hazard his exhausted troops to a general action against him. He had his army break the bridge over the Millstone to halt Cornwallis' advance, and then moved his troops northward to Somerset with Morristown, New Jersey, as his ultimate destination. Cornwallis moved on to Brunswick to protect that post.

The village at Morristown was a difficult position for the enemy to attack. There were large swamps that guarded each side of the eastward approach. Then there were the barriers of Long Hill and the First and Second Watchung Mountains. In this secure village, Washington could watch British movements in New York, guard the roads connecting New England with Philadelphia, and move to any threatened point. His army arrived on Monday, 6 January, "At five P.M. and encamped in the woods, the snow covering the ground." Headquarters was at Jacob Arnold's Tavern on the north side of the village green.

One of Howe's British officers admitted that they had "been boxed about in Jersey as if we had no feelings." In ten lustrous, demanding days the redcoats had been driven into a few square miles of New Jersey at Amboy and Brunswick. Howe had pulled back all his outposts to New York. Never again would the British try to hold large portions of the countryside. Their concept had changed to an occupation of the coastal cities. The countryside, where most of the Americans lived, belonged to George Washington and that newly proclaimed country, the United States of America, which now became more than a joke on the European Continent.

When Benjamin Franklin, the American emissary to the court of King Louis XVI at Versailles, announced the twin American victories at Trenton and Princeton, the French dispatched four shiploads of guns together with the best gunpowder in the world, developed by chemist Antoine Lavoisier, to America. The French and Spanish had already been sending money quietly to the colonies. All of this was to be used against their eternal enemy, the English, whose great burden of debt from their seven-year war with France was one of the major underlying causes of their difficulties in America.

The elderly Franklin had arrived in France with his two grandsons on 3 Dec 1776. Congress had sent him on another secret mission—secret, because his life would have been forfeited had he been captured by the British navy. Benjamin Franklin was very high on the British list of "Most Wanted," and a long sea voyage exposed him dangerously to the enemy. It was not his desire to "hang separately." He joined two other American commissioners in their efforts to procure a French alliance. The Court of France had welcomed the witty and jovial diplomat with open arms. The rather dull Louis XVI had been crowned on 10 May 1774. He was wise enough to turn most of his duties over to Vergennes and other courtiers. On the Continent, these were the days of the Austrian musician Mozart, who was born in 1756 and died in 1791. The gaiety of the courts hid the poverty and unrest of the populace, who were also watching this American revolution. King Louis XVI and Queen Marie Antionette would loose their heads to the guillotine the 21 Jan 1793.

78

THE GENERALS' AMBITIOUS INTRIGUES AND PREPARATIONS

Gentleman Johnny Burgoyne

"I wish nothing but good," proclaimed English King George III, "therefore anyone who does not agree with me is a traitor and a scoundrel."

Lord George Germain, the British Secretary of State for the Colonies in America, agreed wholeheartedly with the king and the death of those rebellious colonial subjects. Burgoyne had returned to England with more in mind than the welfare of his family that winter. It was not surprising then that Major General Johnny Burgoyne, upon arriving in England in early December, approached the office of Lord George with the letter from General Sir Guy Carleton, which reported Carleton's withdrawal from Crown Point. He was tired of his subordinate roll in America, first under General Gage and then Carleton. He wanted his own command.

Finding Germain with a sympathetic ear, Burgoyne requested an audience with the king to put forth his plan to divide the colonies with a strong early drive from Canada to Crown Point. His army would take Fort Ticonderoga and then advance with speed toward Albany. A second army would proceed further to Lake Ontario, enlist the strong support of the Indians and Loyalists there, then proceed eastward across New York by land to Albany arriving at approximately the same time as the first army from Fort Ti. While this

BRITISH GENERAL JOHN BURGOYNE

was being done, General Howe and his British Army in New York City would move north, up the Hudson River and arrive at Albany from the south, thus separating New England from the middle and southern colonies. The rebellious New Englanders would then become an easy prey; loyalists from the middle and south colonies would join with the British, and the war would soon be over. Of course, they would need a more aggressive and daring General than Sir Guy Carleton—one who knew America, like himself. The maneuvering, audacious officer hit the right notes and was granted his desired visit to George III. His plan was soon agreed upon and preparations begun.

First he needed an additional army to take with him. Officers were not too difficult. Their commissions could be bought and advancements were almost perfunctory; however, the young rank and file was more difficult to enlist in England than in America, for they lacked the American's motivation of freedom and independence. The usual method to entice these soldiers in Europe was to grant bounties or impressment. The creative Burgoyne began plastering his original posters in Northhampton, starting a trend that was copied by other nations for years.

> *"You will be mounted on the finest horses in the world, with superb clothing and the richest accoutrements; your pay and privileges are equal to two guineas a week; you are admired by the fair, which, together with the chance of getting switched a buxom widow, or of brushing a rich heiress, renders the situation truly enviable and desirable. Young men out of employment or uncomfortable, 'There is a tide in the affairs of men, which, taken at the flood, leads on to fortune.' Nick in instantly and enlist."*

His quote from Shakespeare and adventurous approach had great appeal and, as enlistments flooded in, he was authorized to enlist two additional troops. Instead of floggings, he advised his officers to treat these enlisted men as "thinking beings" instead of spaniels "trained . . . by the stick." His troopers were soon fondly calling him "Gentleman Johnny."

General Charles Lee

Back in America, Washington's troops had diminished to a new low of about 1,000 men at Morristown. Smallpox was a problem and inoculations were ordered. Unknown to Washington, the captured and generously cared for General Charles Lee was traitorously conspiring with his British captors. After brazenly informing their officers of the mistakes the British had made at Westchester and White Plaines, he prepared detailed plans for the capture of Philadelphia by sea, the enemy occupation of Annapolis and Alexandria, and the resulting division of the north and south colonies in a more southerly fashion. This traiterous scheme, dated 29 Mar 1777, was given to Admiral Lord Howe's secretary; but Lee's participation would not be discovered by the Americans until the war had ended and the British were willing to share their documents. General Washington was still regretting the loss of this crafty general.

General Horatio Gates and General SCHUYLER

In Fort Ticonderoga, the American General Horatio Gates was plotting against Albany's General SCHUYLER, making secret trips and meetings with Samuel and John Adams, who with most of the New Englanders disliked SCHUYLER and accused him of cowardice, because his health and his great efforts in obtaining supplies had not allowed him to fearlessly lead his troops into battle. SCHUYLER decided to run for Governor of New York; however, he lost. The powerful New York delegation in Congress, of course, strongly favored their relative and friend, SCHUYLER. At Washington's suggestion SCHUYLER remained the controlling general of Northern operations. General Washington was well aware that Gates' ambition extended beyond SCHUYLER's position, and that the Adams cousins were becoming progressively disenchanted with his own leadership.

DANIEL MORGAN

One year before, DANIEL MORGAN had taken command in the Battle of Quebec as asked to by his superior officers, when Benedict Arnold was wounded and MONTGOMERY was killed. The company was at last captured and he and his fellow officers had been treated with dignity by British General Sir Guy Carleton in Quebec. MORGAN, after refusing offers by the British to become one of their officers, was exchanged about one year after his capture, probably on 31 Dec 1776. He enlisted 400 riflemen and joined with George Washington.

DANIEL MORGAN was born in Hunterdon County, New Jersey, in 1736. DANIEL MORGAN, a first cousin of Daniel Boone, left Hunterdon County in 1753 and went to Virginia, where he served under General Braddock as a teamster, and had been whipped without mercy by the British, which he deeply resented. He was afterward engaged in Indian warfare and served in Pontiac's War and Lord Dunmore's War. In 1775 he entered the army of the colonists and commanded a company of riflemen under General Washington, and thus on to Quebec with Benedict Arnold, where he was captured.

[Note: Sixth-great-grandmother <u>DOROTHY</u> MORGAN married sixth-great-grandfather HENRY VAN KIRK in New Jersey about 1723. They were Quakers and lived in Hopewell, Hunterdon County, New Jersey, and six children were born to them between 1724 and 1737. DOROTHY died, and HENRY later remarried Sarah, 24 Feb 1772. HENRY died before his will was probated 3 Apr 1776 at Hopewell, Hunterdon County, New Jersey. Their daughter, our fifth-great-grandmother JEMIMA VAN KIRK, married ELISHA BARTON [later a Captain], also of Hunterdon County, New Jersey, where they built a beautiful colonial style home. DOROTHY is believed to have had at least three brothers, BENJAMIN, ABRAHAM, and JOSEPH MORGAN. DANIEL's ancestor is believed to be a different line, but, at least, the two MORGANS, DOROTHY and DANIEL, shared the same New Jersey county during his early life.]

British General Howe

In New York City, Mrs. Elizabeth Loring unknowingly continued to contribute to the American cause by her endearing entertainment of British General Howe. In March, when Howe was awarded the esteemed Order of the Bath, English Justice Jones lashed out against him.

> "This month was remarkable for the investiture of General Howe with the Order of the Bath, a reward for evacuating Boston, for lying indolent upon Staten Island for near two months, for suffering the whole rebel army to escape him upon Long Island and again at the White Plains, for not putting an end to rebellion in 1776 when so often in his power, for making such injudicious cantonments of his troops in Jersey as he did, and for suffering ten thousand veterans under experienced generals to be cooped up in Brunswick and Amboy for nearly six months by about six thousand militia under the command of an inexperienced general."

British Major General Richard Prescott

Then there was British Major General Richard Prescott, commander of forces in Rhode Island. He was reported to have left his headquarters for a Mr. Overing's house, near Newport, "to lodge there that night with some of his whores."

The news story was:

"Thursday evening last a party of Thirty-eight men [plus seven volunteers] ... under the command of Lieutenant Colonel WILLIAM BARTON ... went in five boats from Warwick Neck with a view to take Major General Prescott ... whose headquarters were then at a house about four miles from Newport. The Colonel and his party ... about twelve at night ... got to Prescott's quarters undiscovered. A sentinel at the door hailed, but was immediately secured and the party instantly breaking the doors and entered the house took the general in bed. His aide-de-camp leaped from a window in his shirt and attempted to escape, but was taken a few rods from the house. The party soon after returned to their boats with the prisoners." [10 Jul 1777.]

The London press added the following poetry:

> *"On General Prescot being carried off naked,*
> *'unanointed, unanealed'*
> *What various lures there are to ruin man;*
> *Woman, the first and foremost all bewitches!*
> *A nymph thus spoil'd a General's mighty plan,*
> *And gave him to the foe—without his breeches."*

This WILLIAM BARTON was probably a descendant of seventh-great-uncle RUFUS BARTON of Rhode Island, which would make him a third cousin to our fifth-great-grandfather ELISHA BARTON. WILLIAM was born in Warren, Rhode Island, 26 May 1748. He died in Providence, Rhode Island, 22 Oct 1831. He joined the American army soon after Bunker Hill.

Genenerl Prescott was quickly taken to General Washington in New Jersey. Washington rejoiced in General Prescott's capture. He now had a prisoner to exchange for General Charles Lee. This exchange would not take place until April, 1778. BARTON received a sword from Congress and was promoted to colonel. He was afterwards a member of the state convention which adopted the federal Constitution.

Washington had Prescott thrown in a jail for felons, because he had been led to believe that Lee was being treated that way. He knew that Ethan Allen had been carried to England in chains, when he was taken prisoner in Canada.

Brigadier General JOHN LACEY

Philadelphia was the capitol of the United States of America and was the largest city. Congress, of course, convened at Independence Hall. The Delaware River was Philadelphia's shipping route to the Atlantic Ocean. In Europe, the capture of a capital city with its rulers would often mean the end of the hostilities, and a time for peace negotiations. Howe had no desire to occupy the countryside again. He wanted Philadelphia and, he hoped, a victorious end to this war. The Pennsylvanians realized the importance of fortifying the Delaware River against a sea attack by the British. They were concerned for more than just Philadelphia. This river bordered the colonials' major iron mills, which were so very important to their war effort.

One of these iron mills on the Delaware was owned by the brothers THOMAS and JOHN LACEY. THOMAS' daughter, BARBARA, married JOSEPH WILKINSON of Hunterdon County, New Jersey. It is believed that they are my fifth-great-grandparents. Their nephew was Brigadier General JOHN LACEY of the New Jersey militia. He had been the first to raise troops in the county for the Continental army in his county, and as their Captain, they were placed in Wayne's regiment in January 1776.

"During the march northward to invade Canada by way of Lake George and the Sorel, which began April 26th, Colonel Wayne detached Captain JOHN LACEY, of the Third Company, and placed it under the command of Captain Moore until July 13. This action of Wayne has been severely criticized by LACEY and his friends, and was ascribed to Wayne's arbitrariness and to an undue friendliness to Moore . . . . At the battle of Troise Rivieres, on June 8, the Pennsylvania troops, with Maxwell's New Jersey regiment, bore the brunt of the attack, and were barely able to hold back the advancing Britiah until our army was extricated from its dangerous position and commenced its rapid retreat. Wayne's three companies lost more heavily than any regment in this attack, and formed the rear-guard until they reached the "Camp at Sorel," where their commander said,

'Their spirited conduct in bravely attacking and sustaining the fire from both great and small arms of an enemy more than ten times their number merits his highest approbation." They arrived at Ticonderoga July 9, "without shoes or stockings and almost in rags." Generals Sullivan and Trumbull "spoke of the Pennsylvainia regiments at the beginning of the campaign as the elite and flower of the army." ["Jones Campaign"]

Their enlistments expired in January 1777, and LACEY changed to the militia. The general's parents,

"JOHN LACEY, Jr. married JANE CHAPMAN in 1746. Since the father ran the family mill, the son, JOHN, also worked in the mill from an early age, learning the fundamentals of the operation. [Son] JOHN, born 1754, enlisted in the army at the beginning of the Revolutionary War. This act was in contravention of his Quaker Faith from which he was quickly disunited. He began his service as a Captain in the 4th Pennsylvania Battalion which served at Fort Ticonderoga and in the drive into Canada. He was promoted to the rank of Lieutenant Colonel in 1777 and sent to White Moose, Pennsylvania. On January 9, 1778, he was promoted to the rank of Brigadier General and, later, transferred to Hatboro [Pennsylvania]. From here, he was moved to Trenton and then discharged in October 1781." [*Lacey Township: Its People and Its Growth (GS US/CAN 914.948/01 H21)*]

Hatboro is about 20 miles north of Philadelphia.

"It was between the Red Lion and Dunk's Ferry that General LACEY destroyed a large quantity of forage in the beginning of March, 1778, to prevent its falling into the hands of the British while in possession of Philadelphia." [*The Red Lion Inn*]

He was only 27 years old and unmarried when he was discharged.

The Journal of Miss Sally Wister, reads:

"Almost adventureless, except General LACY's riding by, and his fierce horse disdaining to go without showing his airs, in expectation of drawing the attention of the mill girls, in order to glad his master's eyes. Ha! ha! ha! One would have imagin'd that vanity had been buried within the shades of N. Wales. LACY is tolerable; but as ill luck would order it, I had been busy, and my *auburn ringlets* were much dishevell'd; therefore I did not *glad his eyes,* and cannot set down on the list of honors receiv'd that of a bow from Brigadier-General LACY. Fifth Day, Night, June 18th."

[Note: At the time of the Revolution the Delaware River was the most important waterway for the majority of our direct BARTON ancestors and their posterity—who lived from Wilmington, Delaware, up past Philadelphia, and on to the north past Washington's Crossing—in both Hunterdon County, New Jersey, on the east side, and Bucks and Philadelphia Counties, Pennsylvania, on the west side.]

The best engineers with great numbers of the Pennsylvania and New Jersey colonists were heavily engaged during the winter of 1776-77 in fortifying the Delaware River with forts, cannon, underwater barriers, and any deterrent they could imagine that would protect Philadelphia and their iron supply. It was sufficiently well done that Howe decided to forget New Jersey and go by sea to capture Philadelphia. He sent the British fleet south to the Chesapeake Bay, then north past the Potomac River to Elkton for a southwest approach.

Lieutenant Colonel (uncle) JOHN WILKINSON

"With the inception of the struggle for redress of the grievances caused by oppressive acts of the British Parliament and ministry, JOHN WILKINSON became one of the most active patriots of Bucks county . . . . He was appointed, August 25, 1775, lieutenant-colonel of the Third Battalion, Bucks County Associators, and on re-organization of the Assembly became one of its most important members, serving on the committees to consider and draft 'Such laws as it will be necessary should be passed at this session;' one of the committees to consider an act for remitting the sum of 200,000 pounds in Bills of credit, for the defence of the State, and for providing a fund for sinking the same by a tax on all estate real and personal; and was constantly on important committees. He was commissioned September 3, 1776, by the Supreme Executive Council, a justice of the peace and judge of the Court of Common Pleas of Bucks county, and filled many other important positions. His military service as Lieutenant-Colonel of militia was probably not very extensive, as his time must have been pretty fully occupied with the duties of the several positions he held in the civil department of the state and county." US/CAN 974.8 D2c 1978 v.2

Fifth-great-uncle JOHN WILKINSON was a brother of Fifth-great-grandfather JOSEPH WILKINSON who married BARBARA LACEY.

From *The Pennsylvania Gazette, 19 June 1782,* the obituary notice of Colonel Wilkinson reads:

"On Friday the 31st ult. departed this life, at Wrightstown in the county of Bucks, JOHN WILKINSON, Esq., in the seventy-first year of his age, after a long, painful illness and on the Sunday following his remains were interred in the Friend's burying ground; the funeral being attended by a very large concourse of people of all denominations. Mr. Wilkinson was a man of very reputable abilities, and of sound judgment, scruptiously just in all his transactions, free from bigotry, as to religion or party, and a friend of merit wherever it was found. As a companion, a friend, a neighbor, a master, a husband, a father, a guardian to the orphan and widow, his life was amiable, and exemplary. He served his people in different important offices with fidelity and applause, under the old constitution as well as the new. His conduct in the present Revolution was such as entitled him to the peculiar esteem of all his friends of the country, but it drew on him the rage of the enthusiastic bigots.

"He mingled not in idle strife and furious debates, but lived as became a Christian, studying peace with all men. His principles led him to believe that defensive war was lawful. He was strongly attracted to a republican form of government, and the liberties of the people, and when Great Britain, by her folly and wickedness, made it necessary to oppose her measures from Judgment and principle, he espoused the cause of his country. He was unanimously chosen a member of our convention and afterwards served in the Assembly with zeal and integrity becoming a freeman and a Christian.

"This unhappily aroused the resentment of the Society with which he was connected so that one committee after another were dealing with him and persecuting him to give a testimonial renunciation of what they were pleased to consider errors of his political life, though there was no rule of the meeting which made his conduct a crime. This demand he rejected although as tending to belie his own conscience at length, worried with their importunities, weakened by the growing infirmities of age, and fondly hoping that his country might dispense with his services, he consented to promise that he would hold no other appointments under the constitution.

"This seemed to be satisfactory for a time, but, when Sir William Howe began his victorious march through Pennsylvania, a more pressing sense of duty urged his brethren to renew their visit, while his dear son lay dying in his house, and to demand an immediate and peremptory renunciation of his past conduct.

"Provoked by this indecent and unfeeling application, he gave them a decisive answer, and preferred the honest dictates of his conscience to his membership in the meeting, and he was, for his patroitism alone, formally expelled as unworthy of Christian fellowship. The testimony of the meeting against him on this occasion was heretofore published in this paper. We trust he is now in those mansions where the wicked cease from troubling and the weary are at rest."

[Note: He is included with our nation's list of American soldiers who were killed or died in the Revolutionary

War. His "dear Son, who lay dying in his house" was JOHN WILKINSON, the only son of MARY LACEY WILKINSON. She had five children. The other four were girls. MARY died and the Colonel remarried HANNAH HUGHES in 1769—they had one son, ELISHA (b. 1772 in Bucks, Pennsylvania) and 3 daughters. I have been especially interested in the young JOHN WILKINSON (md. 1763 to JANE CHAPMAN b. 12 Sep 1736 at Wrightstown, Bucks, Pennsylvania) who "lay dying," (Howe's victory in Pennsylvania was September through November of 1777) because third-great-grandfather AARON WILKINSON's (b. abt 1781) father was also JOHN WILKINSON, born about 1755 of Bucks County, Pennsylvania. Family records show AARON's mother as SUSANNAH with no last name.

It appears that fifth-great-uncle JOHN WILKINSON was born at his father's estate in Hunterdon County, New Jersey. The family moved on to Bucks County, Pennsylvaia, where the older son JOHN inherited the family estate in Bucks and the younger son JOSEPH inherited their lands in Hunterdon County, New Jersey. Family records are very sketchy and it has been my finding that many records are not accurate, so two cousins with the same name from the same county require careful consideration. I have sometimes wondered if AARON's father JOHN died during the Revolution, since there appears to be so little information about him and our records show AARON (1781) as his only child. AARON is also shown in the history of Sunbury, Northumberland, Pennsylvania, as an early settler. Fort Augusta, located at this strategic junction of the Western and Northern branches of the Susquehanna River, was garrisoned during the Revolution. The countryside and Sunbury were settled after the war.

JANE CHAPMAN, wife of the dying young JOHN WILKINSON, was a first cousin to her husband. Her mother MARY WILKINSON was an older sister of JOHN and JOSEPH WILKINSON. Mary Wilkinson married Joseph Chapman and the IGI records four children: Joseph b. 1731; Mary b. 1733; Jane b. 1736; and Margaret b. 1739, all of Wrightstown, Pennsylvania. So far, I haven't any death records for JANE or her children.

To further confuse us all, Brigadier General JOHN LACEY's mother was another JANE CHAPMAN. She married JOHN LACEY Jr. in 1746 when the other JANE was only 10 years old.]

General Washington and his militia

With the continental army at Morristown for the winter and the British army in New York, Staten Island and Amboy, hostilities between the two did not sleep under the cover of the winter snows. Washington's strategy against the enemy was clear, he "would not suffer a man to stir beyond their Lines, nor suffer them to have the least Intercourse with the Country." The general coordinated the continentals and militia to attack exposed British posts and foraging parties, raid enemy supplies, and cut all communication between the enemy and the country. He urged Generals William Heath and Samuel Parsons to launch raids from Connecticut against enemy positions on Long Island. Small parties of continentals and militia were ordered to collect all the livestock and wagons, prevent the British from stockpiling supplies for the coming months, and hopefully delay their opening of the campaign in the spring. He established advance parties to watch for enemy movement. As he explained to General Heath,

"This would Oblige them to forage, with such large covering parties, that it would in a manner harass their Troops to death . . . by keeping four or five hundred Men far advanced, we not only oblige them to forage with parties of 1500 and 2000 to cover, but every now and then, give them a smart Brush."

The Americans were successful at times. The New Jersey militia forces were particularly effective. In late January, General Philemon Dickinson and four hundred militia soldiers plunged through an icy stream, attacked and defeated an equal number of enemy foragers near Somerset Courthouse, and captured nine prisoners, forty wagons, and about one hundred horses. On 1 February, a foraging party of two thousand British soldiers emerged near New Brunswick, and ran into a colonial foraging party of five hundred continental light infantry under the command of Colonel Charles Scott and a party of 200 militia. In the ensuing battle, the redcoats eventually retired after suffering about 100 casualties with the loss of their wagons and hay, while the American wounded or killed was 24 or less. Anticipating a British search for supplies, the rebels would hide through the night and ambush the enemy foragers the next morning. At times the Americans would disguise themselves as farmers and drive a herd of cattle near the British lines to bait them into a trapped position.

On 8 February, General Cornwallis led forth a foraging party of 1,750 British and German troops. Near Quibbletown, they ran into American riflemen, who stubbornly held their ground until British artillery forced their retreat. But the skirmish continued throughout the day until Cornwallis returned behind his British lines. In the middle of February, a British party of about 1600 tried to surround a rebel party within ten miles of Amboy. The Americans retreated with little loss; then as the enemy marched back toward Amboy, the Americans tried to surround them, and firing continued all the way back.

On 18 February, a party of 250 New Jersey militia joined 50 Pennsylvania militia to attack a loyalist regiment about three and a half miles south of New Brunswick. They surprised the loyalists, captured about sixty of them, killed four, and wounded one. The New Jersey militia had one man killed. The Pennsylvania militia increasingly joined with the New Jersey militia and the continentals. Major General Israel Putnam sent a party of 500 Pennsylvania militia into Monmouth County to secure a pile of provisions collected there by local loyalist, resulting in some skirmishes. Putnam also sent Pennsylvania riflemen to the coast near New Brunswick to effectively snipe at passing boats.

Similar small battles and skirmishes were taking place in New York and western Connecticut, and this type of confrontations continued through the spring. Since the continentals were so few, Washington relied greatly on his militia in all these states; however, his enlistments increased greatly when spring arrived. Although our ancestors were apparently now in New Jersey and Pennsylvania along the Delaware River and not in the immediate area of all these encounters, they had close relations that were in the middle of it all. Can you imagine what it would be like to live in this area with two armies trying to survive on your land? It might be well to remember, at this time, the LIPPINCOTTs of Shrewsbury and Freedom, New Jersey. Some of them were loyalists and may have been part of the enemy in those skirmishes in Monmouth County. Very few LIPPINCOTTs, although they were numerous in New Jersey, are listed with the DAR records—whether for Quaker religious reasons or loyalist attachments, I could not say.

An army-in-waiting in deep-frozen Canada

Sir Guy Carleton was not only the general in charge of the Canadian military but he was also the governor of the Canadian province, living in Quebec "in a great degree of elegance, and as absolute in his government as possible." His army was quartered in the homes in Montreal and the many tiny villages on both banks of the frozen St. Lawrence River. In nineteen of these villages were the 2,222 German soldiers that had reinforced the British after the American siege of Quebec had been broken and the rebels had fled in front of the pursuing soldiers of the Crown.

The Americans usually referred to these Germans as Hessians, because Landgrave Friedrich II of Hesse-Cassel was the first German sovereign to provide troops to the British—sending throughout the Revolution thirty thousand of them. They were mostly young men whose services, in this age of absolutism, had been sold and then taken from their feudal serfdoms to fight in America by their various dukes, princes, landgraves, and margraves in their cold fortress castles. To enrich his own treasury, the duke would receive from the British treasury 7 pounds and 4 shillings for each soldier or his replacement. If the young serf was killed, the same amount was paid. If he was wounded, only half as much would be paid, which meant that the young soldier was worth more to the duke dead than wounded. This procedure explains partly why desertions from the German troops were quite high in America.

It was in February 1776 that they were marched from their homelands and the first division of Brunswick troops passed in review before His Serene Highness Duke Carl and their commanding officer, Major General Friedrich Adolf Baron von Riedesel. Then, after a twelve-day march through the little towns with flags waving, bands playing, and the troops singing their favorite hymns, they arrived at Stade, where they were again reviewed and counted by King George III's agent as they were boarded on thirty-four ships—first to England and then the New World.

The crossing would take about six or seven weeks. The common soldier was crowded below deck where they had to endure the stench of vomit and unwashed bodies and the crude sanitary facilities, with bunks for three men stacked tightly in a space five feet high and seven feet wide. They were fed rock-solid hardtack, crawling with weevils, and given drinking water that was green with algae. Some suffered from scurvy and other diseases. It has been said that 130 to 200 would be ill on arrival to America for every shipload of 900 to 1000 men.

Then there was the fury of the gales of the North Atlantic. A German officer described one experience. He was about to fall asleep one night and was awakened by a powerful movement of the ship, strong thunderclaps, and lightning, so he went up on deck to find that

> "a violent wind was blowing with a mighty roar and deafening noise, that suddenly became so strong that we could hardly furl our sails , , , , The sea rose violently . . . and rendered the wind's deafening noises even more terrible. Each foaming wave . . . resembled a fiery mountain in the dark night rolling forward with utmost speed and threatening to swallow up everything."

On their journey, the fleet of young German soldiers was joined by another convoy of forty-two transports, escorted by two frigates, which had left from Cork, Ireland on 8 Apr 1776. These contained five companies of the regiment of Major John Dyke Acland who was accompanied by his wife, his manservant, her maid, and their dog. His wife of five years had insisted on the adventure. She was Lady Christian Harriet Caroline Fox-Strangways, the daughter of Stephen, the 1ˢᵗ Earl of Ilchester. The couple had been given estates in Devonshire and Somerset counties in England, the lands of our TUCKER ancestors. She kept a journal of their exciting experiences.

John Dyke Acland, whose father was a baronet with large land holdings in Devon and Somerset, had purchased a seat in the House of Commons to denounce Lord North for his reluctance to tax the colonists. Then as a colonel of a Devonshire militia regiment, he signed an address to the king, promising support against those despised, seditious "Enemies of your Majesty's Government and this Constitution," and urged use of militia to support the regular army, pledging to raise as many as a thousand West Country men himself. This was against Lady Acland's circle of friends and relations, who were Whigs. Her cousin Charles James Fox was one of the sharpest thorns in the side of George III, who had declared, "That young man has so thoroughly cast off every principle of common honour and honesty that he must become as contemptible as he is odious." Kinsman Fox foresaw that the Devonshire militia would "alienate the King from the people, to imbue their hands in the blood of their fellow-subjects," and remarked that such men ought not to be trusted with weapons.

Aboard the 20-foot, 709-ton East Indian *Kent*, the better accommodated Lady Harriet described her sea voyage. Two hours out of Cork a northwest gale carried away the *Kent's* mizzen sheet and the topmast of another transport, and she saw her brother, Captain Stephen Strangways, on board the ship being carried by the soldiers, leaning over the side, "very sick." A week later another gale overturned her bureau, smashing glass and china, and the next day huge swells caused the ship to heel over so far it was impossible to see the topmasts of vessels less than a quarter mile away. She recorded long weeks of fog, gales, clear and very cold days. They sighted porpoises, penguins (probably puffins), and "mountains of ice." They had an epidemic of the measles and several men died of mysterious fevers. They had a brush with rebel privateers, and on 10 May they sighted Cape Breton Island. The weather was "monstrously cold," accompanied by snow and sleet, and three ships ran aground. They entered the St. Lawrence on 18 May, where they saw whales "spouting water to a great height," and a week later they rowed to shore on Filbert Island.

She wrote of her encounter with,

"the first American ground we had ever stept on . . . . It is easy to conceive how happy we were once more to feel terra firma under us, many of us having never been 3 days together at sea before. The hills rose immediately from the shore magnificently bold, clothed with the most beautiful trees, silver firs, larch, sycamore & many other plants with which we were un-acquainted . . . the variety & the luxuriancy of the verdure, & the strength of the vegetation . . . the neatness of a forest where no underwood but the clearest & most odoriferous plants could be seen, almost persuaded us that the scene was a creature of the imagination, or that we were walking on magic ground."

On 27 May 1776, they dropped anchor below Quebec, seven weeks after leaving Ireland. Of all the German soldiers who came to this New World, less than half of the 30,000 rented, voiceless pawns would return home to their families. This could be attributed to casualties in battle, disease, and desertion. One of their Brunswick officers described their plight. Painfully isolated in a strange land, where letters from home could take two or three years to be delivered, these Brunswickers

"found themselves far from the Fatherland and kinfolk, and in an unknown country, in which they—with Englishmen, Hanoverians, Hessians, and other German troops, were to do battle for England's supremacy and wage a successful campaign against the native-born of the land, who were familiar with every road and lurking-place, and who were striving for their independence."

For men who did not want to be there in the first place and who were given no personal reward, it was not an enviable situation.

But this fleet of soldiers had arrived after Quebec's siege was lifted and the Americans had fled. There was a great deal of time through the summer and winter for sight-seeing. The majestic waterfalls, mountains, rivers and lakes with almost uninterrupted forest inhabited with brilliantly colored birds, moose, beaver, black bear, bison, wolves, foxes, large wildcats, martens, turkeys, snow-shoe hares, raccoons, woodchucks, skunks, passenger pigeons that darkened the sky when they flew over by the millions, and Lake Champlain filled with huge salmon, all delighted them. However, they regretted the terrifying blacksnakes, rattlesnakes, and the clouds of voracious mosquitoes "that almost devoured us," along with insects known to Americans as no-see-ums. They were outfitted with snowshoes, called "raquets," when winter arrived and the snow was already over three-feet deep in early December.

These things were bearable; but "our greatest enemies" are the Canadian people, wrote Julius Friedrich Wasmus, a Brunswick surgeon, who had left behind his wife and two children that February.

> "They call us the German dogs . . . and would like to do away with us if they could."

He attributed much of this animosity to the Catholic priests and their fanaticism; they preached against the Protestants from Germany, saying that

> "if females were so unfortunate as to become pregnant from such heretics, they would bring all such types of animals into this world as wolves, dogs, cats, and the like."

Much to the discomfort of these same priests, when these unwanted events did take place, the offspring proved to be "fair little boys and girls,"—much to the great satisfaction of surgeon Wasmus. Wasmus also noted with disgust that Canadian "men are the women's slaves inasmuch as they have to do all the work," and how in the cities, the wives dressed extravagantly in the French or English fashion, "looking like high-ranking ladies."

He saw the men as strong and healthy, while the women, who spent their days inside were sickly, not attributing this in any way to the fact that they bore fifteen or sixteen children.

However, Lady Harriet liked the Canadian people from the moment she set her foot on the land. She imagined that she saw in them

> "the outlines of original society, excepting that being descended from ancestors who had lived in a polished country they had left behind them the barbarity which generally attends the first stages of primitive manners."

She was impressed with their good health, cleanliness, comfortable dress, self-sufficiency, and willingness to share food and drink with her party.

All of them were fascinated by the American Indians, which they observed for the first time. Wasmus wondered if they might possibly be descendants of the lost Jewish tribes, whom they resembled "in ceremonies, positions, and gestures." He described a number of Hurons and Iroquois as big, strong, well-built men, whose color was a brownish yellow. Lieutenant James Hadden was at a

"Congress of Savages" in Montreal. He added to this description with,

> "In the hair a feather was fastened for each scalp they had taken. They wore rings and other decorative objects in their ears, which were slit, and a silver ring hung from the nose. Their attire consisted of a blanket and breech clout, covering their private parts, but at important dances and on this occasion some were totally naked.... Painted with vermilion and other brilliant colors, they were a fearsome sight indeed, especially when carrying their arms, consisting of a wooden ball fixed to a handle, a tomahawk or hatchet, scalping knife, and musket, all of which they used with deadly skill."

The women were "far from tempting," the Lieutenant noted, being covered with grease as protection against mosquitoes and flies. They wore no ornaments—only blankets and leggings or moccasins, with their long black hair tied in a club with red or blue cloth. The Europeans were quick to learn that the Indians were fond of spirits, which was likely to make them berserk, and that they were "cunning and treacherous," constantly demanding gifts of such items as silver bracelets, gold-laced hats, and arms of all sorts. General Burgoyne was heard to say that "a thousand Savages brought into the Field cost more than 20,000 Men." Still they were valued as guides and as a psychological weapon, since most whites were aware of their uncanny ability to move silently and quickly through the most difficult terrain, using trees, leaves, streams, and other natural features as guideposts. They could tell a man's nationality from his footprints and follow a trail through underbrush in the dark by their acute sense of smell. Hadden noted regretfully, that

> "the ... most mischievous and treacherous Nations are those who are nearest & mix most with the Europeans: they acquire only our Vices & retain their ferocity."

On 31 Dec 1776, exactly one year after the rebels had been defeated in Quebec, Governor Carleton staged a commemoration of his victory and triumph. On that chilly morning eight captured Canadians who had joined with the Americans were standing outside the cathedral with ropes around their necks—tied in the hangman's loops. Inside was a solemn thanksgiving service with Te Deum Laudamus sung for the liberation of the city and Canada. The captured Canadians were to plead forgiveness of God and country at the proper time. If properly humble, Protestant Sir Guy had arranged to have the Roman

Catholic archbishop forgive them, and they would be allowed to stay in Canada and retain full fellowship with the church. There was an assembly midmorning followed by a tribute to Carleton, where eight companies of Canadians fired cannon, lit bonfires, and shouted "vive le Roe!" This was followed with more religious services, the firing of guns from windows by enthusiastic local citizens, and a dinner for sixty at three in the afternoon.

That evening the officers of the armies filed through a lane of pine torches that lighted the entrance to the auberge as jingling sleigh bells signaled the arrival of Quebec's gentry, dressed in their finest and wrapped in furs. They were all here for the banquet and fancy ball celebrating the city's liberation and the incoming New Year, when even more glorious victories were expected. General Carleton arrived amid a thunderous vivat, and an original cantata was sung to him. But to the regret of many, John Acland and his popular wife were not present. The major had contracted a fever, and Lady Harriet had traveled "to attend him upon his sickbed in a miserable hut at Chamblee."

Chambly was the fort near Montreal that possible ancestor JACQUE POYER had been sent to as a soldier by Louis XIV about 100 years previously. The births of many of his children are recorded in the records of their Catholic priest. Perhaps some TUCKER relations from Devonshire were there with John Acland and his Devonshire regiment.

There were other parties through the winter. There was skating for miles on frozen rivers. Twelve soldiers standing at attention succumbed to frostbite. Wolves came slinking out of the woods in search of food. It was a melancholy landscape,

> "broken only by trees, which appear planted in the snow." Brigadier Johann Specht noted that from mid-November until May 6 they were "completely cut off not only from every communication with Europe but also with the rest of our neighboring American provinces."

This was not totally true. In April, the twice escaped Tory Captain Samuel McKay, a half-pay officer of the Royal American Regiment, was leading a scouting party of Indians near Lake George when a group of American recruits was spotted. At dawn McKay's men surprised the thirty sleeping Americans at Sabbath Day Point, tomahawked four of them, wounded their officer, and took twenty-one captive. McKay and party were tracked down and attacked by Benjamin Whitcomb and his rangers. However, McKay returned safely to Canada and reported that the Americans were preparing for a British attack on Ticonderoga, and also a false rumor that Howe had taken Philadelphia.

"I now find that there is a bad Wind Blown up." Chief Cornstalk

In October 1775, Maquachake Chief Cornstalk made the following address to the assembled commissioners from Virginia at the Fort Pitt treaty council:

> "Brothers, I imagined all Matters were settled last fall and that we were as one People. I now find that there is a bad Wind Blown up. I know not from whence it has Arisen but I desire the White People will search into it. I hope they will not let that Interrupt the Good work we are now about. If we are Strong and finish the good work we have begun our Children now Growing up will live in peace but if we regard what wicked or foolish People do it may be an Impediment to our living in Friendship"

Earlier in Lord Dunmore's war, Cornstalk had counseled against fighting; but his voice along with those of the older chiefs had been drowned out by the young warrior's clamor for war.

> "Our People at the lower Towns have no Chiefs amongst them," the Shawnees told ALEXANDER McKEE, "but all are Warriors."

In the end Cornstalk had no choice but to follow them. During the daylong conflict at Point Pleasant in 1774, Virginian troops heard his voice ringing out over the noise of the battle, urging his warriors to stand firm.

In early November 1776, Cornstalk sent the following address to Congress in Philadelphia via GEORGE MORGAN, the American Indian Agent at Fort Pitt:

> "When God created this World he gave this Island to the red people and placed your younger Brethren the Shawnees here in the Center—Now we & they see your people seated on our Lands which all Nations esteem as their & our heart—all our Lands are covered by the white people, & we are jealous that you still intend to make larger strides—We never sold you our Lands which you now possess on the Ohio between the Great Kenhawa & the Cherokee, & which you are settling without ever asking our leave, or obtaining our consent—Foolish people have desired you to do so, & you have taken their advice—We live by Hunting & cannot subsist in any

other way—That was our hunting Country & you have taken it from us. This is what sits heavy upon our Hearts & on the Hearts of all [Indian] Nations, and it is impossible for us to think as we ought to do while we are thus oppress'd . . . . Now I stretch my Arm to you my wise Brethren of the United States met in Council at Philadelphia—I open my hand & pour into your heart the cause of our discontent in hopes that you will take pity on us your younger Brethren, and send us a favorable Answer, that we may be convinced of the sincerity of your profession."

In February 1777, Cornstalk with many other chiefs met with MORGAN to reassure him of their desire for peace and neutrality in what they considered to be an American civil war; but reminded him that the chiefs could do little if the Mingoes corrupted their young warriors.

"They will not listen to me—when I speak to them they will attend for a Moment & sit still whilst they are within my Sight.—at night they steal their Blankets & run off to where the evil Spirit leads them."

Cornstalk decided to move closer to the Delawares where, he said, they would be safer from the Mingo threats.

On 6 Oct 1777, Captain Matthew Arbuckle, commanding at Fort Randolph on the Kanawha, informed Edward Hand that he had detained two Shawnees who came into the fort professing friendship and asking for information. A few days later he added Elinipsico, son of Cornstalk, when he came to the Fort to inquire why his friends were being detained. Aarbuckle resolved to detain "as many as fall into my hands" as hostages to ensure the Shawnees' good behavior. When Cornstalk arrived with two other Shawnees, Red Hawk and Petalla, he added them to his prison, saying, "I am well satisfied the Shawanese are all our enemies."

On 10 Nov 1777, claiming retaliation for the killing of a white man near the fort, members of a militia broke into the cabin where they were being held prisoners and killed all of them—Cornstalk and his son, as they forced there way through the door, and Red Hawk was put to death as he tried to escape up the chimney; "the other Indian was shamefully mangled."

The governors of Pennsylvania and Virginia rapidly sent letters of regret to the Shawnees; GEORGE MORGAN conveyed the deep sorrow of Congress, and Patrick Henry gave a public oration denouncing the murders. General

Hand sadly stated,

> "If we had anything to expect from that Nation it is now Vanished." But the Maquachakes still valued peace and according to White Eyes did "not take it so much to Heart that their Chief at the Canhewa is killed, but take hold to the Chain of Friendship & mind nothing else." They migrated to the Delawares and they themselves were "determined to sit still and preserve their women and Children, and think of nothing but peace."

In some ways these events portrayed the attitude that prevailed with the Indians in the west and the south. The older chiefs sought neutrality and peaceful existence; but human weaknesses, youthful ambitions and distrust in general prevailed. There were three European nations vying for the lands of America: the British, French and Spanish. That vast, only slightly populated, western land with all its resources that lay beyond the thirteen small colonies and extended to the Pacific Ocean was an enormous temptation to all three. The French wanted Louisiana that extended north and west of the Mississippi. The Spanish kept the possession of Florida, which extended through the coastal regions to the eastern side of the Mississippi River, and, of course, Texas and the territory to the west and south were Spanish. The British had Canada and a determination to bring their rebel subjects back into their power and extend their dominions westward. To all three, civilization was European and the Indian population and African slaves were only tools or obstacles to be dealt with and used in their quest for domination and power. Even the white American colonists were looked upon as inferiors—subjects, not equals, in their European feudal minds.

All three European nations tried to buy the Indian's loyalty with liquor, provisions, guns, and trinkets. All three were constantly trying to stir up their hatred against the white colonists by telling them how the land belonged to the Indians and that the Americans were taking their lands. This didn't work so well with the Stockbridge, Massachusetts, Indians. They remembered the British and had fought with them in the French and Indian War. They had been the great Mahican nation of New England and now they were reduced to this small town and were being forced to sell even this to pay their debts. They would fight with the Americans against these oppressive redcoats. It is unfortunate that while they gave their all for liberty, their wives were still being forced to sell their lands in payment for the bare necessities of food and shelter. Some colonists became rich in the process, especially those that gave them credit for alcoholic beverages. The Indian community of Stockbridge with their own city council and legislative representitives of twenty years ago became a white community, and the Indians moved to West Stockbridge or further west to join other Indian tribes.

From the [GEORGE] *Morgan Letterbook 1776* we read:

"If our father is allied to the Americans, why do these allow us to be in want of everything; must we die together with our wives and children while rejecting the offers which the English make to us? . . . On the one hand we are forgotten, abandoned, on the other hand we are solicited and at times threatened by the English; in such a situation what can we do, what ought we to do?"

In this particular instance, the Indians gave their loyalty to the French. In the south many moved to Spanish Florida and became the Seminoles. The majority of the northern and western tribes took the rich British bribes and influenced the southern tribes to join with them. They thought the British would win and give them back their lands; so they fought against the struggling poorer Americans. There was great distress when the Americans burned their villages in retaliation for the Indian brutality towards them and then claimed their lands, which they gave or sold to American war veterans to pay part of the debts of the new nation.

[Note: The ALEXANDER McKEE mentioned earlier was not our fourth-great-grandfather of Orange County, North Carolina, who joined with the colonists as a young private. This ALEXANDER McKEE was the son of Captain THOMAS McKEE, a British soldier and Indian agent who had been sent early to the American frontier. These soldiers had been asked by the British to take Indian wives to further peace between the two nations, so THOMAS McKEE married a Shawnee girl, the mother of ALEXANDER and at least four other children and lived in Pennsylvania. This ALEXANDER McKEE became an Indian agent with loyalty to King George and his Indian heritage. He organized and led the Indians against the Americans during the Revolution. He was eventually taken prisoner by the colonists; then exchanged by the British and given land for his family in Nova Scotia. Tecumseh, the great American Indian chief of the War of 1812, grew up near ALEXANDER McKEE's village in Ohio and played with his son THOMAS McKEE when they were children.

At this time, I am not aware of the relations and ancestors of the Indian agent, GEORGE MORGAN. Like DANIEL MORGAN, he may be connected to fifth-great-grandmother DOROTHY MORGAN, if not closely, then in Glaumorgan, Wales, where all the MORGANS appear to have originated.]

79

"THIS ARMY MUST NOT RETREAT!"
GENTLEMAN JOHNNY BURGOYNE

When Burgoyne arrived in Quebec on the *H.M.S. Apollo* on 6 May 1777, he was welcomed by the thunderous, deafening collisions of huge chunks of ice that crashed down the St. Lawrence from the Great Lakes. His first order of duty was to inform former superior officer General Sir Guy Carleton that he was taking his place.

Johnny's friend, Simon Fraser, who was to be one of the brigadier generals on the campaign, commented that it came as a coup de foudre, a thunderclap, and required all Burgoyne's tact and understanding

> "to do business with a proud, austere, narrow-minded man, disappointed in all his views of ambition, environed by flatterers, Dependants & Sycophants, possessing for some time a degree of power not far inferior to that anciently given to a Roman Dictator."

But Fraser underestimated Sir Guy, who showed courtesy and coopera-tion with a high sense of duty. Burgoyne wrote to an army friend in London: Carleton

> "has received me and the orders I brought in a manner that, in my opinion, does infinite honour to his public and private character."

But accepting his military orders with politeness did not stop Carleton from submitting his resignation as governor to London stating that he had been treated with "Slight, Disregard and Censure," and he suggested that Germain was a fool to think large numbers of Canadians would volunteer, and he criti-cized the colonial secretary's policy of employing Indians.

After six weeks in Quebec, with the full co-operation of Carleton,

Gentleman Johnny was ready to begin his offensive. Sir Guy had handed him an army of over 8,300, which included 600 artillerymen for a train of 138 guns, 650 Canadian and Tory auxiliaries, 400 Indians of the Six Nations, and a main force of 3,700 well-trained British regulars supported by 3,000 Germans serving under thirty-nine-year-old Baron Friedrich Adolph von Riedesel, a very experienced, intelligent, aggressive soldier dedicated to strict discipline. About 3,500 soldiers would remain in Quebec, including the invalids, under the command of General Carleton. Another army, composed of 200 regulars, 200 provincials, 300 to 400 Germans and an expected 400 to 500 Indians, was to be led by Lieutenant Colonel Barry St. Leger to Niagara, and from there across Lake Ontario to Oswego. From that point they were to go inland, capturing the American forts, as they gained strength and numbers from the supposed loyalists and Indians that were waiting with open arms for the shipload of promised bounty.

There is a case-study history of loyalist JOHN PETERS, who may or may not be an ancestor or relative of great-grandmother MARY CATHERINE BARTON's second husband, LYMAN PETERS, who was born in Vermont, and came west from Michigan during the California Gold Rush days. He is believed to have ancestors from Connecticut. JOHN PETERS was born in Connecticut in 1740 to a well-to-do family whose ancestors included Oliver Cromwell's chaplain—one of the regicides who took part in the trial and execution of King Charles I of England. JOHN had graduated from Yale and with his family first settled in Piermont, New Hampshire, and later moved to Moortown on the west bank of the Connecticut River, where he had large land holdings, a house, saw and grist mills, and a farm in the New Hampshire Grants. This land was claimed, at that time, by the New York colony, whose royal governor appointed him justice of the peace, colonel of the militia, judge of probates, county registrar, clerk of the court, and judge of the court of common pleas. He wrote: "Here I was in easy circumstances as independent as my mind ever wished,"

He was selected by two local counties as a delegate to the First Continental Congress, but as he traveled south and passed through his hometown of Hebron, he and his uncle SAMUEL were mobbed by American "Governor Trumbull's Liberty Boys" because they suspected JOHN and SAMUEL were loyal to the crown. After much verbal abuse, they were released.

Uncle SAMUEL concluded that "the bankrupts, dissenting teachers, and smugglers meant to have a serious rebellion, and a civil and religious separation from the Mother Country." He decided to return to England, but he persuaded his nephew, JOHN, to go on to Congress and take the pulse of the delegates there. JOHN did, and after deciding that "nothing short of independence would satisfy them," he refused to swear that he would not reveal what went on in Congress.

On his way home he was attacked and mistreated by three mobs before he reached Moortown, where another mob threatened to kill him as "an enemy of Congress" under suspicion of dealing with Governor Carleton in Canada. On orders of Eleazer Wheelock, president of Dartmouth College, and three justices of the peace, he and a group of Church of England members were beaten and dragged through water and mud before being jailed, where they were held until they sickened and several died.

That was only the beginning. PETERS was scorned and abused by his neighbors, and even his own father turned against him, saying that his uncle SAMUEL had "taught him bad principles." Finally JOHN PETERS was allowed to go to Canada with some rebel troops, where he acted as a double agent. He was in Montreal with Benedict Arnold when Benjamin Franklin and the other commissioners arrived. He was taken prisoner by Sullivan's men near Sorel, escaped, and after returning to Canada, joined with Carleton's army as it pursued the Americans up Lake Champlain in the fall of 1776.

That spring of 1777, he was told by two rebel deserters that his property in the Grants had been confiscated, that he was branded as an outlaw. His wife and eight children had been turned out of their home and "sent off in a sleigh with one bed to Ticonderoga, 140 miles through the woods, snow storms, and bad roads," where they arrived more dead than alive. General Anthony Wayne treated them kindly and in April sent them on their way to Canada, but they were conveyed to a deserted house and left there for eighteen days before being discovered by a passing British ship and taken to Fort St. Johns—"miraculously in good health," PETERS added, "but naked and dirty." By the time he was reunited with his family and had taken them to Montreal, he was ready to seek revenge. That month he began to recruit men for a regiment and signed on with

Burgoyne, who named his unit the Queen's Loyal Rangers. But PETERS never came close to filling his ranks.

Burgoyne was also unhappy with only 400 instead of the 1,000 Indians he had requested to be recruited by the Chevalier St. Luc de la Corne and Charles Langlade. New Englanders placed these two on the top of their list of devils. Frenchman Langlade had planned and executed the ambush and destruction of General Edward Braddock's army on their way to the Forks of the Ohio in 1755. Frenchman St. Luc was born in Quebec in a wealthy, influential family and had gone into the western Indian country at the age of 21. His participation in the frontier wars was endless disasters for the English colonists. He was with a war party that torched all the isolated houses in Deerfield, Massachusetts, and took a number of scalps. He raided Albany, Schenectady, and Saratoga, and once surprised and destroyed a British wagon train, which yielded eighty scalps and sixty-four prisoners. He was in Montcalm's army in 1757, where he led 1800 Indians and was in charge of escorting a number of English prisoners when the savages discovered liquor in a fort they captured. The drunken captors erupted in an orgy of brutality, butchering over sixty-nine prisoners. He bought and sold slaves and by 1760 was believed to be one of the wealthiest men in Canada. He spoke four or five native languages and was one of the most successful Indian recruiters of his day. Now, at age 66, his influence over the Indians was undiminished.

It was a clear morning on 20 Jun 1777, as Burgoyne bid farewell to Carleton with full honors at Cumberland Head, north of Valcour Island. Carleton would return to Quebec and his army of occupation. Burgoyne set sail in a mile-long flotilla up the Richelieu River to the sparkling blue waters of Lake Champlain and Crown Point. Here he stopped about eight miles north of Fort Ticonderoga to establish magazines and hospitals, repair batteaux, and issue ammunition. Then on 30 June with his General Orders "This Army must not retreat!" still ringing in their ears, he moved his army to within four miles of the American fortifications.

British General William Howe makes his own plans

The following day, on 1 Jul 1777, Howe withdrew his troops from New Jersey to Staten Island. He was tired of playing "cat and mouse" with George

Washington the cat. He was also very unhappy with the orders from Germain in London to proceed North up the Hudson and give that upstart Johnny Burgoyne the credit for subduing the rebels. He was tired of trying to deal with the New York\New Jersey countryside. He wanted the capitol—Philadelphia. He praised the traitorous General Charles Lee and his plans for its capture, added his own modifications, and trusted that his conquest of Philadelphia would give him greater honors than a trek up the Hudson. The command to move north up the Hudson, from a man an ocean away, who had never been to America, was, he felt, more suited to a naval operation with Clinton at the helm—after he had removed Washington's army out of the mountains and into the lower countryside. So, he sent letters to London and Quebec announcing that he would move his army north—later in the summer—after he had taken Philadelphia.

A few days later, Howe began to load between fifteen and eighteen thousand soldiers with supplies on his ships. His loyalist chronicler, Thomas Jones, watched him spend the next

> "fortnight in dailiance with Mrs. Loring, while his troops were lying on board the transports crowded together in the sultry heat of summer."

Washington had spies on Staten Island, but he could not decide which way to go with his army. He thought at first Howe would head up the Hudson, when he was told that the troops were embarking onto the ships. It seemed logical. They would go north. Then it was reported that supplies were being loaded for a much longer voyage. Where? He sent messengers to the eastern states and others south—Virginia? Charleston? Then while the fleet remained in the harbor, he received word that Burgoyne was advancing rapidly toward Ticonderoga. The shuffling of his troops began—northward and into the highlands by West Point. Howe was still in the bay. Where? Then Howe was reported sailing out of the harbor—south.

When the British fleet was spotted off Maryland, still heading south, he camped his army on the borders of the Neshaminy River in Bucks County, Pennsylvania. [The home land of uncle, Lt. Col. JOHN WILKINSON]. Then word reached Washington that the British fleet had entered Chesapeake Bay and was going north, evidently heading for Philadelphia. Washington was somewhat relieved to at least know Howe's destination. The enemy had passed by the Delaware River, knowing it was highly fortified.

A new major general had been added to Washington's army, the young nineteen-year-old French Marque de Lafayette, who had offered to serve without pay. He was so willing, charming and convincing that Congress had commissioned him a major general, although he had only been a reserve captain in the French army and had never fired a musket in combat. Washington was equally impressed with him, and invited him to his camp and to accompany him as the army marched to Philadelphia to view the city. It was nearly the end of August and the armies of Howe and Washington were still preparing for battle.

But first, there is much to be said about Generals Gentleman Johnny Burgoyne, Baron Riedesel, PHILIP SCHUYLER, Horatio Gates and the Colonels Benedict Arnold and DANIEL MORGAN, who were not playing "cat and mouse."

~ 80 ~

"I HAVE BEAT ALL THE AMERICANS!"
KING GEORGE III

Major General Arthur St. Clair

Major General Arthur St. Clair arrived on 12 Jun 1777 at Fort Ticonderoga. He was the fifth to be given command of this fort since the rebels acquired it shortly after the battle of Concord. General Horatio Gates was his immediate superior; but Gates was so impressed with his own importance and comfort that he had convinced Congress that he needed to reside in the more sophisticated Albany. Of course, he never mentioned his personal ambition, which was to first downplay SCHUYLER and George Washington to his own advantage with Congress and rise to the office of commander in chief of the Continental Army. To do this would require more ambience than he could manage at an isolated fort in the wilderness.

A Scot by birth, St. Clair had first come to America as a loyal British soldier with the "Royal American Regiment" and fought with distinction at Louisbourg and the capture of Quebec. He was with the light infantry under William Howe when Wolfe took the city from the French. After the French and Indian War ended, he stayed in America, and with the fortune he had acquired from his mother and his wife's vast holdings, he purchased 4,000 acres in the rolling hill country of Pennsylvania's Ligonier Valley, becoming the largest landholder west of the Appalachians.

When the Revolutionary War began, this handsome, nearly forty-year-old St. Clair first became colonel of a militia battalion, then colonel of the 2nd Pennsylvania Battalion, which joined in the Canadian advance to Quebec and more rapid retreat of the previous year. He then fought with honor under George Washington in the Battle of Trenton and helped engineer the escape and the following attack on Princeton. He had distinguished himself sufficiently that he was recommended and promoted to major general. Congressman James Wilson of Pennsylvania wrote the promotional letter with his new assignment the middle of May saying, "the important Command of Ticonderoga is destined for you next campaign. I presage it a Theater of Glory."

St. Clair, whose name was pronounced Sinclair, inwardly questioned this "Theater of Glory." He remembered the Fort Ti of last year as being a dilapidated ruin, short of manpower, arms, provisions, and every item of equipment. Yet, he also knew that its loss would be a blow to the new nation's pride as well as its sense of security. Then, too, John Hancock had told him there was "no probability of an active campaign.," and his own superior, Major General Horatio Gates, had claimed to have superior knowledge and the "strongest assurance from Congress that the King's troops were all ordered round to New York, leaving only a sufficient number to garrison their forts" in Canada. He believed them and decided to take his young eleven-year-old son with him to give him a taste of military life and "to superintend his education."

This chestnut-haired Scot general with the determined chin found Ticonderoga quite different from the Ti he had left behind in 1776. Colonel Jeduthan Baldwin, the army's engineer, and Lieutenant Colonel John Trumbull, the twenty-year-old son of the Connecticut governor and a Harvard graduate, had prepared plans for the defense of the old French fort that had been built to face a southern army—not a northern army from Canada. They wanted an additional fort built on Rattlesnake Hill to the south (later called Mount Independence) across the narrow point of Lake Champlain and water barriers to prevent ships from passing southward. There would be a long, floating rope bridge crossing the water between the two forts—later called the Great Bridge and Boom. Trumbull also wanted fortifications on Sugar Loaf Hill (later called Mount Defiance), which was more difficult to reach, but a higher prominence, on the west of South Bay. Colonel Baldwin was given permission to proceed with the water barrier, the fort on Rattlesnake Hill, and the Great Bridge and Boom by both SCHUYLER and Gates. Somehow the fortification on Sugar Loaf Hill, although explored, was either ignored or forgotten. Work had proceeded under Colonel Baldwin and was not yet complete when Major General St. Clair arrived on 12 June.

Although the workmanship was excellent, if not complete, St. Clair was quick to determine that his army of approximately 2,500 New Englanders would not be capable of manning all of it. It would require 10,000 soldiers, with more artillery, ammunition and food supplies. He sent correspondence urgently requesting these additions. Washington had discovered that the New Englanders fought better as a unit without the central states battalions and militia of New York, New Jersey, Pennsylvania and even the Canadians, who were now under his personal command. This, also, placed most of both armies closer to their own homelands. This bitter animosity was evidently a two-way street. A Pennsylvania captain had commented, when he heard of the imminent arrival of these troops the previous year,

> "unless they are better than the greater part of those that … have been here before . . . they had better stay at home. No man was ever more disappointed respecting New Englanders than I have been. They are a set of low, griping, cowardly rascals."

According to the report of HENRY BROCKHOLST LIVINGSTON to his father, the governor of New Jersey, the Pennsylvanians would as soon fight the Yankees as the British.

Unfortunately for SCHUYLER the New England soldiers included him in their antagonism, because of New York Dutch/New England land disputes in the past, his more aristocratic demeanor and the health problems that had not allowed him to lead his men into Canada the previous year. Gates was more to their liking; but he was not so well known, especially in battle. St. Clair's call to arms was sent into New England.

While St. Clair was still in a state of preparation, Burgoyne was preparing his letter to be sent to the colonists of New England, who he called

> "the harden'd Enemies of Great Britain and America," (whom he considered to be one and same). He offered open arms, restoration of their rights, and security to loyal subjects of the king. He ended with a threat to the American rebels. "I have but to give stretch to the Indian Forces under my direction, and they amount to Thousands" and the King's enemies could now expect to meet "the messengers of justice and of wrath … devastation, famine, and every concomitant horror."

This pompous manifesto, which he had hoped would intimidate and bring fear to the enemy, only created a reaction in the Americans which was about equally divided between ridicule and anger. The few inhabitants of this isolated area, who had been selling their cattle to the British for cash, drove their live-stock away, out of the reach of this advancing army.

The next day he delivered a speech to his "Congress of Indians," in which he urged them to go forth, and "strike at the common enemies of Great Britain and America, [these] disturbers of public order, peace and happiness, destroy-ers of commerce, parricides of state." . . . He recognized their custom of taking scalps as "badges of victory," but under no circumstances were they to scalp any-one who was innocent, or still alive, even though wounded or dying. The braves cheered. But they knew they would be paid by the scalp. How would Burgoyne know if it was a scalp of a woman, child, or a man, living or dying?

On 17 June, eighteen-year-old American soldier John Whiting was shot in the head, stabbed in the throat, neck, and stomach and then scalped, while strolling on a road to the sawmills near Fort Ti. His companion, John Batty, was wounded in three places, but somehow survived by playing dead while an Indian stripped him of his clothes and scalped him. After the Indians disap-peared into the woods, he was able to hobble back to the fort—screaming for help and covered with blood. He was carried to their hospital. Other terrorizing incidents occurred and St. Clair believed that the enemy must be approaching, or the Indians would not be so bold.

On the 18th General SCHUYLER arrived from Albany to check out the fort and was amazed at what he found. Much of the work was incomplete—especially the barriers to the ships. The men were "miserably clad and armed . . . many are literally barefooted, and most of them ragged," without blankets. Some had only sharp pointed poles with no bayonets. Many of their huts had been burned for firewood last winter. St. Clair decided that with his shortage of men, he would hold on to Fort Ti as long as he could and then evacuate his men across the Great Bridge to Mount Independence on Rattlesnake Hill. SCHUYLER concurred and suggested he also should plan for a further retreat, if necessary.

Burgoyne asked the Indians to bring him two prisoners for questioning. On 17 June, they brought in a retired British soldier, Scotchman James MacIntosh. He had lived near Fort Ti for many years. He was very knowledgeable and communicated fluently about its outworks, the position of its cannon, the number of troops on hand, and about anything else Burgoyne cared to ask—less helpful about the new fort.

At 4:00 A.M. on 24 June, the order for the general march was beaten, and the British troops boarded their batteaux and rowed out from Cumberland Bay. Out in front were the Indians in birchbark canoes with their war paint and feathers. Then came the advance corps—regulars in their scarlet coats, white breeches, and waistcoats; light infantry in black leather caps and red waistcoats; the grenadiers, whose tall heavy black bearskin hats gave them extra height and a more fearsome look; the Canadians in Indian costume, followed by gunboats with the artillerymen in blue.

Their largest ship, the 384-ton *Royal George* with twenty-six guns that had been built in St. Johns through the winter and the three-masted, twenty-two gun ship, the *Inflexible*, which had been brought from Quebec, torn down and then reassembled at St. Johns, followed in their wake towing large booms that would reach from one side of the lake to the other and prevent the rebels from going north. These were followed by the smaller ships, the *Maria* and *Carleton*, then the first British brigade. Three cutters were next in line—each bearing a general—Burgoyne, artillery general Phillips, and the German general Riedesel. The second British brigade was next, followed by the Germans with their own styles of uniforms. To the south they could see the small watch boats of the rebels as they would approach and then scamper away to make their fearful reports to General Arthur St. Clair at Ticonderoga.

St. Clair had been warned the previous day by one of his most reliable scouts, Sergeant Heath, that the Indians were as thick as their famous mosquitoes, that he had seen five British ships, as well as encampments on each side of Gilliland's Creek, and that there was "a vast number of batteaux and some gondolas." Because of the Indians, he had not been able to get closer than six miles. To this disagreeable report the general had responded,

> "We are infallibly ruined" unless reinforcements arrive. No doubt his contingency plan for total retreat took on more meaning, and perhaps, Washington's retreats to save his army were strongly considered. He wrote SCHUYLER, "No army was ever in a more critical situation than we now are."

On 27 June, 150 fresh troops arrived from Massachusetts, and a number of cattle had been brought in from Pawlet. He sent Colonel Seth Warner to the New Hampshire Grants to round up all the militia he could locate.

For two days nature gave her ominous warning. The dark lake was lit by shattering streaks of lightning followed by the cracking blasts of thunder that echoed, into the heights of the stately Adirondacks, as fierce winds delivered the downpour of torrential storm clouds. Burgoyne and his troops huddled in their tents, until finally on 30 June, he gave his order:

> "The army embarks tomorrow, to approach the enemy. We are to contend for the King and the constitution of Great Britain, to vindicate Law, and to relieve the oppressed—a cause in which His Majesty's Troops and those of the Princes his Allies, will feel equal excitement. The services required of this particular expedition are critical and conspicuous. During our progress occasions may occur, in which, not difficulty, nor labour nor life are to be regarded. This Army must not Retreat."

The wind shifted to the south, favoring the rebels and delaying the British armada for a week or more. The American sentries increased their diligence and one night a shot rang out and a body was heard dropping forcefully to the ground, only to be discovered as one of their cows. St. Clair decided it was time to send his eleven-year-old son home. He felt this was enough "taste of army life." He also removed his most debilitated soldiers—those who could not possibly carry a gun and who would become a burden to feed and care for and to evacuate under gunfire. There had been a rough measles epidemic. Most of them could stay and hopefully be helpful.

Then the winds had calmed and silently the British soldiers invaded the woods and started the torturing slow process of surrounding and outflanking the enemy in an unfriendly domain. The Germans went east into the shadows behind Fort Ti. Fraser with some of the artillery took the longer route to the west, staying out of the range of the enemy guns. The gun ships moved in from the lake waters north of Fort Ti. St. Clair still planned to make a fair show at Ticonderoga, then quietly pull the bulk of his army across the Great Bridge and Boom into Mount Independence, where he planned to face the enemy.

As British General Fraser and his men trudged up the assent of Mt. Hope on the west, they became aware of a higher peak that appeared to command a view of both Fort Ti and Mount Independence. Captain Craig with forty light troops and several Indian scouts were sent to reconnoiter. By midnight they were back. They had reached its height, and found the view "very commanding ground." This was Sugar Loaf Hill or the Mt. Defiance that John Trumbull had suggested should be fortified by the Americans. It was a terrible struggle up the almost perpendicular ascent; but the British were determined. By heaving and pushing throughout the night and with the help of "most the cattle belonging to the army" two twelve-pounders from the gun ship *Thunderer* reached the very top, while a detail of four hundred men cleared the road and constructed a battery. It might have been a total surprise to the colonial army had not some Indians lit a fire on the heights that revealed to the rebels what was going on.

It was a forlorn group of commanding American officers that met to determine what should be done. They had captured a British regular in a skirmish the previous day. He had refused to furnish any information, however, that evening a roughly dressed Irishman was thrown into his cell and loudly accused of being a spy for the British. He just happened to have a bottle in his possession, which he amiably shared with his young companion. The two spoke freely to each other, and before the morning the disguised Lieutenant Andrew Hodges Tracy of Stevens's artillery battalion was able to report a great deal about the enemy positions, number of troops, their objectives, and so forth, to American Major General St. Clair.

The rebel officers now counted their able regular troops at 2,089 plus the artillery, 124 unarmed artificers, and about 900 militia that had just arrived, but could only stay a few days, as they had come so quickly they hadn't been able to collect extra clothing and sustenance. The Americans now knew they were outnumbered 4 to 1. They also knew the Germans were moving, though slowly, through the tortuous swamp on the east and that Burgoyne desperately wanted to surround and capture the whole rebel army. The British had already cut off escape on the route to Lake George and the Germans on their more difficult advance were steadily closing the route to the east. The river south was still open, but not for long. And now, with British artillery able to proceed with what they likened to call a turkey shoot from Mt. Defiance, the American officers Fermoy, Poor, Paterson and Long did not hesitate to unanimously agree with St. Clair that it would be less glorious, but far more prudent, to save the army than to make a magnificent display that would only end in death or capture. Without a dissenting vote, it was agreed that a retreat into the open countryside east of the Mount "ought to be undertaken as soon as possible, and that we shall be very fortunate to effect it."

Lieutenant Colonel Udney Hay was told to prepare to move the invalids and stores by boat and forbidden from disclosing any reason to anyone. He was shocked at the order but reported that St. Clair had observed that if he defended the fort,

> "he would save his character and lose the army." But if he retreated, "he would save the army and lose his character ... which he was determined to sacrifice to the cause in which he was engaged."

Evidently he was aware of how Congress would later view this evacuation and ruin his reputation as an officer.

The movement of the army from Ticonderoga to Mount Independence had been well planned and moved forward rather quickly and silently. The loading of the boats was much more confusing—there were not enough boats and much would be left behind, even some of the wounded. After dark, as the main army tramped out to the east and south on what was little more than a trail through the heavy timber, the disorder and confusion increased. Strict orders of secrecy were maintained, and even BROCKHOLST LIVINGSTON, who was acting as an aide to St. Clair and passed orders on to the various officers, had no idea why they were given or what their ultimate destination and purpose would be. He had hoped for the fulfillment of his dream, which was "an Opportunity of being present at a Battle in which I promise myself the pleasure of seeing our arms flushed with victory." This dream seemed to be fading as the orders more and more indicated retreat.

At 3:00 A.M., 6 July, twelve hours after the officers had determined to evacuate the army, Colonel Pierce Long was charged with the safe delivery of the two hundred boats laden with cannon, gunpowder, stores, baggage, invalids and his own regiment by water, south to Skenesborough. He was to assume command there until St. Clair and his main body marched overland and caught up with him. His final destiny was to be Fort Edward and General SCHUYLER.

Colonel Ebenezer Francis was given the most dangerous command of the rear guard—450 handpicked men from several regiments. They were expected to fight to the finish to keep the enemy away from the main army.

While St. Clair was still trying desperately to organize his troops for the hard journey south and east, without warning, flames shot up from a building on Mount Independence, illuminating the whole scene to any enemy eyes that were on watch. The French officer, Fermoy, had disobeyed orders to extinguish all lights of any kind and had set his own quarters ablaze. Realization that the British would now know of their retreat brought fear to an already confused militia, who ran off on the road to Hubbardton followed by some equally nervous continentals. St. Clair followed them and was finally able to bring order to his troops and send them single file down the small trail. He then returned to the final organization of his army on the Mount.

By 4:00 A.M. St. Clair was on his way with his army. His aide, the young son of the New Jersey governor WILLIAM LIVINGSTON, described his feelings in a letter:

> "thro pathless woods, and over mountains where no vestige of Human foot remained," with neither bed nor blankets, only what food he could scrounge, and depressed of "the Misfortunes of my Country—all our Dependence & hopes on Tyconderoga are now blasted—Our Frontiers are open and a merciless, Savage Foe let loose on defenceless inhabitants." Later he wrote to his sister Susan in New Jersey, "The Enemy with you had some glimmerings of humanity left—Those with us have none—Murder, Scalping, and plunder stain their steps everywhere."

The rear guard under Col. Francis had collected "every living thing" from Fort Ticonderoga before crossing the floating bridge and damaging it as much as they dared in the darkness. The troops wondered what had caused the General to turn tail and run without putting up a fight. They were sullen and angry, but formed up in excellent order behind their able commander. Francis had chosen four men to remain behind at great risk. They were assigned to man the already loaded cannon and fire it at the bridge when the enemy crossed it in pursuit. They were then supposed to destroy the cannon and put fire to all remaining supplies by lighting the powder that had been generously distributed throughout Mount Independence. During the resulting confusion, they were to escape into the woods and join the rest of the rear guard. Unfortunately there was a problem. When the enemy cautiously crossed the bridge and carefully looked for snipers, they found these four men at their posts, linstocks lighted and ready to fire, but beside them was an empty cask of Madeira. They were all four drunk and had passed out. The unlit gunpowder still silently surrounded the vast quantity of powder and supplies.

Colonels Ebenezer Francis, Seth Warner, and Nathan Hale— all of New England

The small, narrow trail between Mount Independence and Hubbardton was to bear the almost continuous weight of the tramping feet of four armies that sixth day of July, 1777. In the lead was St. Clair followed by the smaller rear guard that kept increasing in numbers as they picked up the stragglers, the frightened and the ill from the first and much larger army. About four or five miles behind the rear guard was Fraser's British army, who were followed by Major General Friedrich Adolph Baron von Riedesel and his German troops. All of them would pass through the approximately three-acre clearing with "a small indifferent Logg house" called LACEY's Camp—St. Clair's original destination. It was about sixteen miles from Mount Independence and ten miles from Castle Town, which became the final destination for St. Clair on that day, when he was informed by the inhabitants of Hubbardton that "a large number of the enemy and Indians" were at Hubbardton, two miles away. He felt secure in meeting them; but was concerned about reinforcements from the rear. LACEY's Camp undoubtedly got its name from Brigadier General JOHN LACEY, who with a lesser title was stationed earlier at Fort Ticonderoga under Colonel Anthony Wayne. This was the first real clearing along the route and was above the swampy northern end of Lake Bomoseen.

St. Clair and his troops climbed to the 1,300 ft. summit of Sargent Hill then followed the rough trail that descended to Sucker Brook and rose to the flat plateau where Farmer Selleck's cows had been grazing the day before in the small settlement of nine widely scattered homesteads, which was called Hubbardton after its first occupant of 1774, Thomas Hubbard. The Sellecks had deserted their land heading for Massachusetts with their personal belongings and livestock when several of their neighbors had been captured by the reported "enemy and Indian" raiding party, which had also moved on. It was one o'clock. The exhausted army had been on the rough road for nine hours. Some had food, others nothing. One of their cattle was slaughtered and the general allowed a brief rest before he pushed them onward the additional six miles to Castle Town. He sent a courier back with orders to the three rearguard colonels to continue their march and not delay until they reached a position a mile from his camp.

Unfortunately, Colonel Seth Warner, who had been given command said, "No." He believed his men were too exhausted when they reached Selleck's farm. He felt they deserved a night's rest before moving on. Seth had fought to the end at Breed's Hill and had been with the retreat from Canada. Connecticut born, Warner had moved to Bennington at age 29. He was over six feet tall, lean, and strong—a favorite with the rugged men of the New Hampshire Grants, whom he and Ethan Allen had led in the brutal border disputes with the New Yorkers before the revolution. Both men had been declared outlaws by the New York legislature, with a reward offered for their capture. When Allen captured Fort Ti from the British after the battle of Concord, Warner was in charge of his rear guard. With the need for daring and capable officers, much was forgiven and forgotten about the two men. When the Green Mountain Boys reorganized in 1775, they ousted Ethan Allen and left Lieutenant Colonel Warner in command. He had experience and knowledge of this country; but St. Clair was not aware of his stubborn determination to be his own boss when he placed him in charge.

Colonel Nathan Hale, not the young spy who had been captured and hung by the British in New York, had also fought at Breed's Hill. He was later commissioned colonel of the 2nd New Hampshire Regiment and served under Washington in New York and New Jersey. He was in his early thirties, a capable and well-liked officer. His troops with most of the stragglers would camp below by Sucker Brook, where the British would first arrive along the trail.

The tall and imposing Colonel Ebenezer Francis had left behind a wife and five small children at Beverly, Massachusetts, when he came to Fort Ticonderoga to lead one of the regiments. Three of his brothers were also officers during the Revolution. He drove his men hard and expected a great deal from them. His troops admired him and took great pride in being considered by many as the best-trained, best-disciplined outfit under St. Clair. They bivouacked to the right and north of Warner in the woods, where they could block the enemy, if they came from that direction. As he retired that night to perhaps a very troubled sleep, he was unaware that within three miles at LACEY's Camp lay Fraser and his first-rate troops of the British army.

It had been daybreak on that 6 July before General Burgoyne's friend Fraser and his men realized that all the rebel activity of the previous evening—including Fermoy's burning house lighting the whole fort—meant that the Americans were actually evacuating and in retreat. Three American deserters had come into their lines and reported it early that morning. Fraser suspected momentarily that it was a trap to get him closer to their grapeshot, but quickly sent a message to Burgoyne and ordered his men to turn out immediately. It was delightful when they discovered the Great Bridge mostly intact as they crossed and then found the four drunken American soldiers who had perhaps grown tired of waiting for the sleeping British army, found the Madeira and neglected their duty of final destruction. Had his army been alerted more rapidly, perhaps the American's greeting would have been more spectacular. But Fraser's army was fresh and rapidly on the trail with all the enthusiasm of the victorious to push forward when Burgoyne triumphantly ordered them to pursue his lost enemy. He then ordered Riedesel to lead his own regiment and Breymann's company and follow Fraser toward Hubbardton.

The British fleet had quickly broken through the boom and was soon on its way to Skenesborough, where the Americans had sent their boats earlier in the night. The self-satisfied Generals Burgoyne and Phillips were on board. The 62nd Regiment would take over Mount Independence while the Prinz Friedrich troops secured Fort Ticonderoga.

At LACEY's Camp, British General Fraser had his men rested and ready to march at 3:00 A.M. that 7 Jul 1777. It was dark, so they moved slowly. Two hours later, as they neared the saddle of Sargent Hill, their Indian and Tory scouts were spotted by the rebel pickets whose shots rang out before they quickly retreated. Fraser called a halt, appraised his situation, and decided to push forward without the slower Germans, confident his superior troops would prevail over the demoralized colonials. He had Major Grant's 24th regiment followed by Major Lindsay, Earl of Balcarres, and his ten companies of elite light infantry, then Major John Acland's ten companies of husky grenadiers with their tall hats. Acland's troops were recruited from the Somerset and Devonshire English counties and had spent the winter in Canada near Fort Chambly.

The young sixteen-year-old fifer Ebenezer Fletcher was with American Colonel Nathan Hale's troops at Sucker's Creek. He observed that the American camp was

> "all in a very unfit posture for battle," with the men cooking, eating, packing up their gear. About seven o'clock someone shouted, "The enemy are upon us!"

He whirled around and saw pickets running for their lives with British behind them, forming their line of battle through the tangle of underbrush and trees. British Major Grant climbed upon a stump to better view the situation, ordered his men to fire and without another word fell to the ground—killed instantly by an American volley that cut down twenty of the British. But the redcoats advanced, bayonets bared that sliced stomachs open and stabbed horror into the minds of young men in their first battle. Fletcher fired his rifle, reloaded—a misfire. Reloaded again, took aim—he felt an excruciating pain in his back. His uncle, Daniel Foster, saw that he was hit and carried him away from the action, placing him behind a large tree, where another wounded soldier was crying in agony. Fear and extreme loneliness encircled young Ebenezer as he watched his uncle and comrades being forced back—up toward the plateau of Selleck's farm. Frantic with the realization that he was bleeding, faint, and entirely on his own, the terrified boy crawled thirty-five feet in extreme pain and hid behind a big log, where he lay motionless in the midst of Barcarres's light infantry of British regulars who would leap over his log in the pursuit of his uncle and friends of the New Hampshire Regiment.

On the plateau above were the troops of American Colonel Ebenezer Francis who had prepared to march south when General St. Clair had sent early scouts to inform them that the British fleet had arrived at Skenesborough and captured their supplies with the small encampment of sick and wounded they had sent by boat from Fort Ti, and he ordered them to take a circuitous route to the Hudson, where they would meet SCHUYLER. There was a shout and a quick reversal of direction when a few redcoats were seen emerging from the far trees across Farmer Selleck's field. They were within firing distance—thirty or forty yards. Francis' troops open fired, took the British by surprise, disorganized their tattered lines and sent them plunging down the hill, leaving behind their wounded and dead. Among the British dead was Lieutenant Haggit, who was shot between the eyes, and handsome young Lieutenant Douglas, the son of a colonel. The wounded Douglas was being carried away—shot in the heart.

British Brigadier General Fraser kept his cool. He rallied his troops for an organized frontal attack and sent some of Balcarres' light troops with Acland and his grenadiers to head off the Americans and prevent them from reaching the Castle Town road. He then dispatched a messenger to German General Riedesel urging his speedy reinforcement.

St. Clair heard the distant shots, knowing it meant trouble. He sent his two aides—Lieutenant Colonel HENRY BROCKHOLST LIVINGSTON and Isaac Dunn to ride to Ransomvale and order the militia regiments there to reinforce his rear guard at Hubbardton. The order was delivered with great speed to Colonel Bellows. Unfortunately, his troops refused to obey. LIVINGSTON wrote,

> "An unaccountable panic had seized his men, and no commands or intreaties had any effect on them."

The two aides despaired and rode toward the ensuing battle.

While Lord Balcarres formed new lines with his light infantry, steadfast Colonel Ebenezer Francis regrouped his colonials behind the fortifications on the rise and fearlessly awaited the new attack of the enemy. Lord Balcarres was most fortunate that morning. A musket ball that could have shattered the upper bone of his left leg was diverted by a flint in his pocket; the barrel of his fusil and the lock was shot off while it was in his hand, and he later counted ten holes in his clothing made by gunfire. In a letter to his sister Margaret he wrote,

> "You may observe on this occasion I am not born to be shot whatever may be my Fate."

His American opponent, the equally conspicuous Colonel Francis, was not as prosperous. Talking to his captains—moving up and down his lines—rallying and encouraging his troops—then withdrawing to the log fence—somewhere in the battle a musket ball hit his right arm and it hung helpless at his side. Still, he would not quit.

The battle continued, perhaps an hour. Major Acland's grenadiers pushed Warner's Green Mountain Boys before them closing in on the left. On the right the Germans arrived in force. The gunsmoke was so thick they could not distinguish the enemy from their countrymen. Ebenezer Francis shouted to his troops not to shoot—they were hitting their own men. His words were followed by a volley from the enemy and Colonel Francis fell dead. His friend Captain Greenleaf mourned,

> "the Brave & ever to be Lamented Colo Francis, who fought bravely to the Last . . . rec'd the fatal wound thro' his Body Entering his right breast, he drop'd on his face."

Without their leader to spur them on, the American soldiers scattered and ran for their lives up the cliffs behind Hubbardton Brook. The battle was over. Among the British observers who came to view the body of the courageous and cool enemy warrior, Colonel Ebenezer Francis, was Lieutenant Digby of the 53rd Regiment of British Grenadiers who noted, "his figure . . . was fine" and even in death "made me regard him with attention."

When the British buried their dead after the gunsmoke had dispersed, they buried Colonel Francis with their own men. The other forty or more dead Americans were left unburied. One officer on the burial detail reported

> "the wolves came down in numbers from the mountains to devour the dead, and even some that were in a . . . manner buried, they tore out of the earth." The crows and other vultures took their turn at the cleanup, along with millions of flies and a stench that "was enough to have caused a plague"

and left the bones that bleached in the sun and lay there until after the Treaty of Paris was signed—three years later.

Colonel Seth Warner escaped with his Green Mountain Boys and eventually joined St. Clair. Colonel Nathan Hale with about 300 other Americans was captured. They suffered greatly with the wounded as they were returned to prison at Fort Ti. The young fifer, Ebenezer Fletcher was discovered under his log and included with the prisoners. He later escaped and returned alone and hungry to his home in Ipswich, New Hampshire—but only until he had completely recovered. He then returned to his company to complete his three year enlistment as a soldier.

The British had lost Major Grant, and Major John Dyke Acland was wounded along with twelve other officers. Acland wrote his beautiful wife, Lady Harriet, at Montreal and asked her to once again join him, while he recuperated. She immediately left to care for him with one servant and their dog, Jack, and arrived safely at Mount Independence on 18 July. She recorded in her journal a storm on the lake that almost drove her boat onto the rocks.

BROCKHOLST LIVINGSTON and Isaac Dunn, the aides of General St. Clair, who had set off personally on a gallop in the direction of the gunfire, were too late. Captain Chadwick and about thirty men were rapidly approaching them with the news that the battle was lost and all were in retreat. The guns were now silent, so they hastened to Castle Town to report to their commander. St. Clair had additional problems. Two of his Massachusetts regiment's enlistment times had expired. He remonstrated with them; but, according to LIVINGSTON, their looting and disorderly conduct "obliged the General a day or two afterwards to dismiss them from the army with disgrace." Collecting his remaining army, St. Clair hastened to Manchester hoping to find supplies and then join with SCHUYLER. His troops increased as the march progressed with the valiant men of the rearguard who had escaped the enemy.

It would be two months before General John Burgoyne's letter of triumph in Ticonderoga reached England. When it arrived, His Majesty George III joyfully rushed into Queen Charlotte's chambers and shouted,

"I have beat them! I have beat all the Americans!"

Unfortunately for his Royal Highness, by that time there was a different sort of letter that needed to be sent across the Atlantic.

It would be two years before Major General St. Clair was vindicated through a court-martial in which he was acquitted. In the meantime his name was bantered and associated with SCHUYLER's name by those who looked for scapegoats. In congress, John Adams commented in a letter to his wife, Abigail,

"We shall never be able to defend a post until we shoot a general."

The name of the general was not included in the letter; but at that time it wasn't Adam's favorite, General Horatio Gates. Gates was priming himself to escape any association of his name with the loss of Ticonderoga. He had been appointed, but had neglected, to command and prepare its defenses before St. Clair arrived. At his side, helping with all his maneuvering, was the equally ambitious JAMES WILKINSON, whom Gates had chosen as his deputy adjutant general.

⟿ 81 ⟿

SCHUYLER, STARK—
AND BENEDICT ARNOLD DOES IT AGAIN!

Fort Anne—Indians—Fort Edward

PHILIP SCHUYLER received word of the American evacuation of Fort Ticonderoga on 7 July, as he was traveling with a small detachment between Saratoga and Fort Edward. The informant had no details or the whereabouts of St. Clair and his soldiers. With great concern, the general immediately sent a courier to find his army and to have them join him at Fort Edward. Another courier was to take SCHUYLER's own desperate letter and requests for more troops and supplies to George Washington without delay. Perhaps his anxiety for his men, his reputation, his home at Saratoga and his great concern for Albany came through with too much despair. It read:

> "My prospects of preventing them from penetrating is not much. They have an army flushed with victory, plentifully provided with provisions, cannon, and every warlike store. Our army, if it should once more collect, is weak in numbers, dispirited, naked, in a manner destitute of provisions, without camp equipage, with little ammunition, and not a single cannon."
> He begged for all kinds of supplies, men and cannon and ended by saying,
> "The country is in the deepest consternation."

SCHUYLER then hurried on to Fort Edward with his small detachment, where he sent numerous dispatches with orders, requests and encouragement to his soldiers, friends, neighbors and relations seeking aid wherever he could find it. His wife's relation, Colonel HENRY VAN RENSSELAER, with 400 fresh New York militiamen were sent from Fort George to join the "genteel, amiable" Colonel Pierce Long in his battle against Burgoyne at Skenesborough.

Another relation, PHILIP VAN RENSSELAER, received a message in Albany requesting immediate delivery of musket balls and cartridge paper.

Washington, still waiting for Howe's direction of attack, received SCHUYLER's letter and was shocked by "an event of chagrin and surprise, not apprehended, nor within the compass of my reasoning." He responded by sending SCHUYLER the troops under Glover and John Nixon; Generals Benjamin Lincoln and the feisty Benedict Arnold to inspire the New Englanders, and he would later add to that list weeks later by sending DANIEL MORGAN and his crack riflemen. He, of course, reported the event to Congress, who were horrified and immediately took steps to release SCHUYLER from his command and to have him replaced as rapidly as possible. When Washington requested not to make the choice of the new General, they appointed General Horatio Gates and gave him authority almost equal to that of George Washington. But Gates was not in a hurry after his appointment on 4 August. He dawdled so long on his trip from Philadelphia that he did not reach Albany until 19 August. By this time, the tide of the war was already turning toward the Americans. Much of the thanks belonged to SCHUYLER, who was decisive and tireless in his efforts.

When Colonel HENRY VAN RENSSELAER and his four hundred militia joined Colonel Long at Fort Anne, he had with him the remaining troops of his six hundred New Hampshiremen and Captain James Gray's Company, who had been stationed at Skenesborough to await further orders. The Americans had dumped much of their vast food supplies in the bay and set fire to the blockhouse and abandoned many supplies on shore. The American boats were destroyed, either by enemy fire or by the spreading inferno, which had enveloped a nearby sawmill, storehouses, barracks, and ironworks, then jumped to the surrounding forest and was out of control, as were Long's and Gray's men who were hotly pursued by the British into the woods, up Wood Creek and were assembling at old Fort Anne.

Deputy Adjutant General JAMES WILKINSON was to later write in his *Memoirs* that Colonel Long made three bad mistakes: he failed to drive his men hard enough to gain proper speed on the voyage south; he neglected to move his men and guns to the high bluffs that commanded the narrows below, which could have at least delayed Burgoyne, and he seriously underestimated the skill of a formidable enemy.

On the morning of 7 July, Burgoyne had ordered his 9th Regiment under Lieutenant Colonel John Hill to march by land and reconnoiter the enemy strength and position at Fort Anne. The 20th and 21st Regiments were to carry or drag fifty batteaus over the carrying place to Wood Creek to get men and guns to Fort Anne by water, which became impossible as the forest fire blazed toward them. Colonel Hill found his road slow and tortuous, but was able to advance about ten miles and sent out his pickets. Unfortunately for the British, Captain Gray was out on a scouting mission with 150 men and 17 rangers and ran into Hill's pickets about one-half mile from the fort. The pickets retreated and a brush with the enemy occurred that lasted about four hours. One of Gray's men was killed and three were wounded.

At dawn the next morning, an American deserter showed up at Hill's camp. He informed them that the rebels now had over 1,000 men. Colonel Hill was deeply concerned and sent a rider back for reinforcements. In the resulting confusion, the American deserter spy slipped away and returned to Fort Anne to report happily that the enemy camp consisted of only 200 soldiers. Long and Colonel VAN RENSSELAER soon advanced with what the British called "a heavy and well-directed fire." The British retreated up the ridge and held out for two hours until their ammunition was nearly gone. They were about to surrender when loud Indian war whoops rang out. It was a signal that reinforcements were about to arrive. The British shouted out three cheers. The unfortunate Americans pulled back. Their ammunition was also nearly gone. They took with them the prisoners the British had taken the day before, their dead and their wounded. Lieutenant Colonel HENRY VAN RENNSELAIR was among the wounded. He had been shot in the hip—a wound that would trouble him throughout the rest of his life. Sadly the war whoops were only a ruse. Burgoyne's quartermaster, Captain John Money, had been sent with a party of Indians to help Hill; but the Indians didn't like facing live bullets or fighting like the English insisted. They had all deserted the captain. It was Captain Money, all by himself, that had made the blood-curdling yells. Both sides claimed victory, and maybe they were both right—or wrong, as both armies retreated.

With the British pulled back to Skenesborough, SCHUYLER had sent orders that his men were not to pursue them but to saw and chop down giant pines to block the rutted trail south and dam the small streams to create water barriers. The trees were piled crisscross in such a manner that the British could not drag them over to the side of the trail but had to chop and saw a great deal to proceed further down this mosquito-infested boggy carrying place that required the redcoats to heft their boats on their shoulders or drag them to the next waterway. All colonials were ordered to vacate their homes, remove their animals and burn their fields. They deliberately pulled down bridges and spread the fire within the forest to delay Burgoyne with his guns and thousands of trained soldiers. A woman who had been captured the previous day and was now back in camp reported that a much larger British army was coming by land and would soon arrive to join Burgoyne. The American officers conferred and decided to pull back to Fort Edward with their forces, so Fort Anne and the neighboring ridge so desperately fought for lay deserted by both. The wounded were sent on to Albany. St. Clair had collected his men and by a circuitous route, also arrived at Fort Edward.

Meanwhile, Gentleman Johnny Burgoyne, who had not personally encountered this fiery enemy, delayed his "seize the moment" to obtain the victory that he had promised King George. He waited for all the thirty wagonloads of his belongings, and then those of his favored officers to be moved ashore to the old stone house of loyalist Mr. Skene. They gambled, drank Madeira and port. He dallied with his mistress, secure that he had conquered the bedraggled, fleeing Americans. He thought of St. Leger's army joining him at Albany and Howe's large troop ships arriving up the Hudson. He probably even considered his future in the king's court in London—maybe a baronetcy, and of replacing General Howe. But SCHUYLER's army's chopping and sawing continued into the nights, and the British soldiers grew tired of swatting mosquitoes and sinking in mud.

After the troops sent by George Washington arrived at Fort Edward, word came on 25 July that British Colonel St. Leger with his soldiers had landed on the shores of Lake Ontario and had advanced with their loyalists and over 1,000 Indians to Fort SCHUYLER, or Stanwix, as it was previously called, where they were laying siege. General SCHUYLER was confident that the fort was well supplied with food and could hold out long enough that he could send them an additional 500 men. Most of his officers advised against it, expressing their fear that it would weaken their army; but Benedict Arnold wanted to lead them and expressed great confidence. SCHUYLER gave the order and Arnold was on his way with 950 troops from the Massachusetts continentals eagerly joining him. Benjamin Lincoln had been sent eastward to find St. Clair and his army, take command and collect more New Englanders. St. Clair was to return and report to Washington and Congress.

But while the rebels and redcoats licked their wounds, collected their armies and jostled for position, the Indians who had come from Canada with St. Luc and Langlade, anxious to obtain the bounty offered by the invaders did not sit idly by waiting for the command of an indolent British general. The American surgeon, James Thacher, treated several survivors of Indian scalping, and reported the following about their procedure:

> "with a knife [the Indians] make a circular cut from the forehead, quite round, just above the ears, then taking hold of the skin with their teeth, they tear off the whole hairy scalp in an instant, with wonderful dexterity. This they carefully dry and preserve as a trophy, showing the number of their victims. And they have a method of painting on the dried scalp, different figures and colors, to designate the sex and age of the victim, and also the manner and circumstances of the murder."

One Hessian officer commented,

> "Our Indians . . . behaved like hogs. When it comes to plundering, they are on hand every time."

A rebel paymaster with SCHUYLER's army wrote a relative,

> "It is believed the Tories have scalp'd many of their countrymen, as there is a premium from Burgoyne for scalps . . . . One hundred Indians in the woods do as much harm than a thousand British troops. They have been the death of many brave fellows."

After being rewarded a barrel of rum by Burgoyne and consuming it, a frenzied war party captured an American captain with nineteen of his men and returned with three other scalps. They requested the right to keep three of the prisoners, roast two of them and eat them in front of the third and then send him back to the rebels to report their atrocities and what others might expect.

Burgoyne refused, but paid his bounty. His surgeon Wasmus wrote:

> "I pity the first Americans that fall into their power; it will be a horrible feast for them . . . The Savage resembles a tiger that is only moved by blood and prey."

In all fairness to the Indians, it is said that the scalping knives that were found were manufactured in London.

However, the story that struck fear and horror into the hearts of the Middle Colonies and the New Englanders was the story of Jane McCrea, fiancee of a loyalist militiaman, Lieutenant David Jones, who had joined with PETERS in his American Volunteer Corps. Jane was one of seven children born to a Presbyterian minister in New Jersey. After both her parents died, she moved to the Fort Edward area to live with her brother, John, who was a colonel in the New York militia. This twenty-two year old beauty with extremely long reddish hair fell in love with the young local man David Jones. They became engaged to be married; but his strong loyalist feelings took him northward to join PETERS and his loyalist army. When the British army advanced to Skenesbourgh, her brother John decided to move his family to Albany, and hoped she would go with them. But she chose to remain with an elderly widow woman, who was a cousin of British Brigadier General Simon Fraser.

These two women remained behind when SCHUYLER evacuated the bulk of his army from Fort Edward. They probably felt a certain degree of safety because of their loyalist and British connections. On 23 July, there was an unexpected Indian attack on the remaining look-out scouts at Fort Edward. It was reported in a letter,

> "We have just had a brush with the Enemy at Fort Edward in which Lt. Van Vechten was most inhumanly butcher'd and Scalped, two Serjeants and two privates were likewise killed and Scalped—one of the latter had both his hands cut off."

Warned that the Indians were coming, the ladies attempted to go through a trap door and hide in the cellar; but they were discovered and taken with the other prisoners, probably in spite of their protests. They became separated and an argument arose between two young Indians regarding which one would claim Jane as his prisoner. In anger, one of them shot her, mutilated her, and took her scalp, adding it to Lt. Van Vechten's scalp. It is said that her shocked young lieutenant, David Jones, recognized her long beautiful reddish hair when the Indians were dancing with their trophies that evening at Burgoyne's head-quarters. The widow arrived at the British camp also. She had been stripped of her clothing, and it is said that she was so large that her cousin, General Fraser, covered her with his own greatcoat, because they could not find any suitable clothing large enough to cover her for awhile. But she was totally devastated with the loss of her young companion.

Burgoyne wanted to execute the young Indian that had killed Miss McCrea; but he was advised against it by many of his officers who felt the other Indians might return to Canada or join forces with the Americans. The "young Lady of Beauty & Family," as she was described by SCHUYLER's aide, BROCKHOLST LIVINGSTON, in his journal,

> "had proved of service to the Country. Many of the Inhabitants who had resolved to stay in consequence of Burgoyne's Proclamation & submit to the terms of the Victor, are now determined to a Man to disregard his promises."

Years later the grandniece of the broken-hearted David Jones wrote:

> "He was so crushed by the terrible blow and disgusted with the apathy of Burgoyne in refusing to punish the miscreant . . . that he and his brother . . . asked for discharge and were refused, when they deserted—he having first rescued the precious relic of his beloved from the savages—and retired to this Canadian wilderness, which he had never been known to leave, except upon one mysterious occasion many years before."

Jane McCrea's murder, of course, was only one of many similar incidents, which also spread through the frontier—some involving far more people; but her story was told more often, probably because she was a young girl, the ro-mance, and because it showed that the Indians cared little about the gender, age, or whether the victim was a Whig or a Tory. The Indian problem became so great that SCHUYLER moved all of his army to Fort Miller on 29 July and then ordered another withdrawal on 30 July to Saratoga.

Joseph Brandt was an attractive young Indian Chief that had been taken to London and educated and trained by them. He spoke wonderful English and dressed fashionably. He had now returned to the area of Lake Ontario and had been given a beautiful home with lands for his wife and family. He was greatly admired by his Indian people, especially the young braves. They joined with him in his raiding parties of the white western settlers, who counterattacked and burnt the Indian villages. By the time British St. Leger arrived on the shores of Lake Ontario with his soldiers and his shipload of promised blankets, knives, guns, food, liquors, and trinkets, Joseph Brandt had collected a sizeable army of over 1,000 Indians, who with their families waited with outstretched arms as the bounty ship was unloaded. The British had their army of Indians; but they also had their dependent families, which, like Esau of old, had sold their liberties for a mess of pottage.

Burgoyne was concerned. General William Howe at New York City had not sent him any message confirming his plans. The couriers between the two British armies were not getting through the American lines. Several had been sent with small letters concealed in silver bullets, which they were to swallow— if they were caught. But the rebels were on the alert. If that was suspected, they gave them emetics until they vomited and when the messages were found they hung them as spies. But General George Washington was equally concerned about Howe's plans. They had spotted his fleet sailing north on Chesapeake Bay and we left him in the previous chapter camped with his troops twenty miles north of Philadelphia on the meadows by the Neshaminy River. [fifth-great-uncle Lieutenant Colonel JOHN WILKINSON's estate was 15 miles north of Philadelphia on the Neshaminy.] At last, it was now evident that Philadelphia was Howe's object and that he would proceed up the Chesapeake and then over-land toward the capitol city. General Washington rejoiced that he would have time to place his army between their approach and Philadelphia.

Washington now had around 12,000 soldiers and a new officer the nine-teen-year-old French boy, the Marquis de Lafayette. The young Marquis was tall and thin with an agreeable but not attractive face. He had big shoulders, a large thin nose, and reddish-brown hair that was thinning and pulled back from his receding brow. Watching him, Washington was pleased to discover that he had acquired a useful and trustworthy officer at this critical time.

A letter had finally gotten through from General Howe to Burgoyne on Sunday, 3 August. There was excitement and curiosity in the camp, but when the usually talkative, gregarious general said nothing, not even to his staff or General Riedesel, it was unnerving to an army that had come to know him quite well.

Howe had written the letter on 17 July, with his troops sweltering in the July heat below deck, waiting to sail for the Chesapeake. He congratulated Burgoyne on his capture of Ticonderoga; he reported that Washington had sent 2,500 troops with Sullivan to Albany, and then he dropped his bombshell:

> "My intention is for Pennsylvania, where I expect to meet Washington, but if he goes to the northward contrary to my expectations, and you keep him at bay, be assured that I shall soon be after him to relieve you. After your arrival at Albany, the movements of the enemy will guide yours; but my wishes are, that the enemy be drove out of this province before any operation takes place in Connecticut. Sir Henry Clinton remains in the command here [in New York], and will act as occurences may direct. Putnam is in the highlands with about 4000 men. Success be ever with you."

The reality of this letter burst the bubble of Burgoyne's vain imaginations, and awakened within him the difficulties before him. His supply line from Canada was uncertain and slow—he could barely meet the needs of his army. Pasture land had been burnt. His animals needed food. St. Leger would probably still meet him in Albany; but his army was small compared to the 6,500 rebels mentioned in the letter. Ticonderoga was fine; but it took soldiers to maintain it and guard the prisoners. Some of his Indians were deserting—uncomfortable with his stronger control of their activities, since the Jane McCrea affair.

The afternoon of 4 August, German General Riedesel was surprised by a visit from General Burgoyne, who had prepared a plan he intended to give to Lieutenant Colonel Friedrich Baum for a foray into Vermont. He wanted Baum to proceed to Manchester, where he was to test the

> "affections of the country, to disconcert the councils of the enemy, to mount Riedesel's dragoon, to complete PETERS' corps, and to obtain large supplies of cattle, horses and carriages."

And in addition to this awesome fete, the lieutenant colonel was to proceed on to Rockingham, near the Connecticut River, where he was to wait for his Indians and light troops to return from a scouting mission to the north, after which he was to head south to Brattleboro and then make haste to Albany to join with the main army—all within a fortnight. While doing this he was to collect carriages, wagons, and oxen, plus 200 horses with saddles and bridles for the dragoons, and another 1300 horses that were to be roped together in strings of ten—each string of horses was to be led by an unarmed man from PETERS' corps and conducted to Burgoyne's force.

This excursive trip to Rockington and then to Albany was more than 200 miles and through the extremely rugged Green Mountains. Burgoyne stated that Baum could use his own judgement whether to attack Seth Warner and his army, if they didn't run away when he approached.

The German General said, "No!"

Either Baum should go foraging for horses and cattle or he should go prepared to fight, but not both. The detachment was not strong enough, experienced enough, or capable of achieving all those goals. Besides, Rockingham was too far away, and so was Manchester, and Baum spoke little English. But the tall Burgoyne looked down at his short confederate and tapping his epaulette said,

"My friend, I intend to kill two flies with one blow."

He then explained that he was about to advance to Saratoga and that General Benedict Arnold (who he believed to be in command of the American army at that time) wouldn't dare send troops to help the rebels in Vermont, especially since St. Leger is now laying siege at Fort Stanwix on the Mohawk River. Arnold would have to send reinforcements there.

Under protest, Riedesel wrote out Burgoyne's instructions for Baum, and the British General took them to his headquarters for further study. Several days later, just before Baum was scheduled to leave, Burgoyne learned that the Americans had a large supply depot at Bennington, which was not heavily guarded. He got on his horse, rode to Baum's camp and verbally changed his orders, telling Baum to forget Manchester and Rockingham and go to Bennington for supplies and horses. He later said he had planned it this way from the beginning, not wanting anyone to know his secret plans; but Major General Riedesel said he doubted it.

Bennington and John Stark

Unknown to either Burgoyne or SCHUYLER, on 18 July of that summer of 1777, the New Hampshire legislature voted to "raise a brigade, and our friend Stark, who so nobly sustained the honor of our arms at Bunker Hill, may safely be entrusted with the command, and we will check Burgoyne."

They then proceeded to make him a brigadier general, adding that he was to be

"always amenable . . . to the General Court or Committee of Safety" of New Hampshire—not answerable to Congress or the Continental Army. They "had lost all confidence in the General officers who had the command at Tyconderoga . . . they would not turn out nor be commanded by such officers."

They also knew that John Stark was their man and the only way to get him was to let him operate outside Congressional authority.

Stark was described by Richard M. Ketchum in his exceptional book *Saratoga* as

"proud, touchy, difficult, cantankerous, contrary, ornery, determined, and as independent as a hog on ice . . . . But never mind his disposition: he was a superb soldier and leader of men and knew as much about frontier warfare as anyone you could find . . . . After serving with distinction at the battle of Trenton, Stark figured he was entitled to a promotion. But when new brigadiers were appointed by Congress in February of 1777, John Stark's name was not on the list, and to make matters worse, that of Enoch Poor, another New Hampshire colonel, was . . . . In March he resigned, announcing that 'I am bound on Honour to leave the service, Congress having tho't fit to promote Junr. officers over my head.'"

This mostly new frontier state of New Hampshire was cash poor and could not finance the expedition. Fortunately, the speaker of the General Court, John Langdon, gave them seventy hogsheads of Tobago rum to be sold, plus $3,000 in cash—secured by a loan on his household plate. He was one of the few wealthy men who were not loyalist in the state.

Stark agreed immediately and within six days almost 1,500 men signed up to follow him. That was over ten percent of the males over sixteen in the whole state. To outfit them he needed to collect ammunition, bullet molds, cannon, wagons, food, camp kettles, and numerous necessities. Then it was on to Manchester, where General Lincoln was collecting his army. On 6 August, a farmer from Lyndeboro in the Grants, who was with General Benjamin Lincoln at Manchester, wrote to his wife,

> "We have made us tents with boards, but this moment we have had orders to march for Bennington and leave them and from thence we are to march for Albany to join the Continental Army and try to stop Burgoyne in his career .... P.S. August 7th. A few minutes after I finished my letter, there was a considerable turn in affairs, by reason of General Stark arriving in town. The orders we had for marching was given by General Lincoln. What passed between Lincoln and Stark is not known, but by what we can gather .... Stark chose to command himself. I expect we shall march for Bennington next Sabbath,"

For the information of those not closely acquainted with the geography of this area, the road from Manchester to Bennington, which is in the southwestern corner of Vermont, borders the Green Mountain range on the east and goes south-southwest through Arlington (9 miles) and continues in the same direction another 10 miles to Bennington. The main route turns to the west at Bennington and continues a little to the south for another 33 miles to the Hudson River, just above Albany. Stillwater, where SCHUYLER had at that time moved his army, is about 14 miles northward on the Hudson from this junction. This was probably the easiest way to join the army of Lincoln with that of SCHUYLER. Presently Bennington has a population of about 17,000 people. At that date of August 1777, it consisted of a meetinghouse with maybe fourteen dwellings.

Although General Lincoln felt that John Stark was insubordinate when in no uncertain terms he told Lincoln to inform SCHUYLER that he, John Stark, "considered himself adequate to the command of his own men," and handed Lincoln copies of his commission and his orders, Lincoln did not object when he told him he planned to take his troops to Bennington and protect the supply depot there, and then use his soldiers to harass Burgoyne from the rear. However, Lincoln left by horseback to confer with SCHUYLER, leaving Colonel Seth Warner in charge of his men. Warner remained behind with his soldiers as they watched Stark and his army march determinedly southward, leaving Manchester for Bennington about the same time that the German officer Baum began his journey with his men toward the same destination.

From Brigadier General John Stark's point of view, he accomplished several of his objectives in this plan. Probably, first and foremost in his thinking was that Bennington gave him a position that his men could protect Vermont and New Hampshire against any attempt Burgoyne, the Indians and the loyalists might make toward the east and the homelands of his troops. Were they not there, and had they gone west with Lincoln when he moved his army toward Albany, there would have been no major American deterrent, as he had enlisted nearly all the remaining men that would be effective in their defense. From this position, he could also force Burgoyne to use soldiers to defend his supply route and Fort Ticonderoga. And, of course, he also preserved his dignity and his individual control of his men, which they had been promised when they joined.

German Colonel Baume was at Fort Miller, eight miles south of Fort Edward, on 11 August, when he ordered his troops to begin the march to Bennington, as Burgoyne had personally ordered just shortly before. This left General Fraser to command Burgoyne's advance troops now at Fort Miller. The heavily equipped Germans were slow movers, and the rugged terrain with crude roads additionally slowed their usual lethargic advance. On the morning of the 14th, they reached Van Schaick's Mill on the Walloomsac near the Hoosick. At nine o'clock, after a brief brush with a detachment of Stark's troops from Bennington, he wrote Burgoyne:

> "By five prisoners taken here, they agree that fifteen hundred to eighteen hundred men are in Bennington, but are supposed to leave it on our approach. I will proceed so far today as to fall on the enemy tomorrow early .
> ... People are flocking in hourly, but want to be armed. The savages cannot be controlled; they ruin and take everything they please."

When Stark heard the news of the approaching enemy force, he hurriedly sent a message to Seth Warner and his troops to hasten and join him. Stark aroused all the men he could find to go to the aid of his detachment at the mill. About five miles from Bennington, he met them in retreat with the Germans in hot pursuit. He quickly deployed for battle, but the enemy "halted on a very advantageous hill or piece of ground." Stark withdrew about a mile toward Bennington to make his stand; but neither army advanced.

The morning of the 15th arrived in a fury of wind and heavy rain. Baum discerned that the Americans had no intention of fleeing before him, so he busied his men building fortifications and in sending the collected oxen and horses toward Burgoyne, while he awaited the supplies and reinforcements he was expecting to arrive soon. Burgoyne had sent Lieutenant Colonel Heinrich von Breymann with 550 Brunswick Grenadiers to the rescue. They had slouched forward through the muddy, rain drenched roads at the pace of ½ mile per hour, covering eight miles on 15 August. The determined Stark sent out patrols in spite of the forbidding weather, and the German surgeon, Wasmus wrote:

> "Every 40 paces a man is standing behind a tree," and that throughout the day thirty Canadians and Indians were shot, including two chiefs. A letter arrived at 11:00 P.M. that evening from Breymann informing Baum of his location and requesting help with the ammunition wagons that were bogged down in the mud. Baum's German Lieutenant Glich wrote of the torment of rain that washed down their ditches faster than they could build them . . . . Night came . . . . They were "not very comfortable . . . and . . . impressed with a powerful sense of impending danger . . . All was perfectly quiet at the outposts . . . for several hours before sunrise. So peaceable . . . that our leaders felt warmly disposed to resume the offensive, without waiting the arrival of the additional corps."

Throughout that day, American Brigadier General Stark had collected a lot of information about the enemy from his patrol and the local inhabitants who had brazenly pretended loyalist attachments, even obtaining guns from the enemy, and then falsely reporting a vast loyal population that planned to join with the King's Army. Stark had also collected more men—mostly the militia companies from Vermont and Berkshire County, which included the fiery Thomas Allen, who had strongly complained about evacuating Fort Ticonderoga. That night Allen emphatically told Stark that if the Massachusetts militia didn't get to fight they would never answer another call on them again. Stark sent him to get some rest and promised him that if the Lord sent sunshine the following day and they did not get fighting enough to suit them, he would never call on them again. John Stark knew that his rebels outnumbered Baum's troops. He knew of their fortifications. He decided to split his army into three divisions, surround the enemy and attack from all sides at a set signal. He gave his soldiers a "short but animated address" as he had done at Bunker Hill and included the long remembered,

> "There are the redcoats and they are ours, or Molly Stark sleeps a widow tonight."

German Lieutenant Glich and this soldiers were at an early breakfast when,

"Our people were recalled to their ranks in all haste . . . From more than one quarter, scouts came in to report that columns of armed men were approaching, though whether with friendly or hostile intention, neither their appearance nor actions enabled our informants to ascertain . . . . During the last day's march our little corps were joined by many of the country people, most of whom demanded and obtained arms, as persons friendly to the royal cause. How Colonel Baume became so completely duped as to place reliance on these men, I know not, but having listened with complacency to their previous assurances, that in Bennington a large majority of the populace were our friends, he was somehow or other persuaded to believe that the armed bands, of whose approach he was warned, were loyalists on their way to make tender of their services to the leader of the king's troops. Filled with this idea, he dispatched positive orders to the outposts that no molestations should be offered to the advancing columns, but that the pickets retiring before them should join the main body, where every disposition was made to receive either friend or foe. Unfortunately for us, these orders were but too faithfully obeyed. "About half past nine o'clock, I, who was not in the secret, beheld, to my utter amazement, our advanced parties withdraw without firing a shot, from the thickets which might have been maintained for hours against any superiority of numbers, and the same thickets occupied by men whose whole demeanor, as well as their dress and style of equipment, plainly and incontestably pointed them out as Americans.

"I cannot pretend to describe the state of excitation and alarm into which our little band was now thrown. With the solitary exception of our leader, there was not a man among us who appeared otherwise than satisfied that those to whom he had listened were traitors . . . . We . . . stood about half an hour under arms, watching the proceedings of a column of four or five hundred men, who, after dislodging the pickets, had halted just at the edge of the open country, when a sudden trampling of feet in the forest on our right, followed by the report of several muskets, attracted our attention. A patrol was instantly sent in the direction of the sound, but before . . . it had proceeded many yards from the lines, a loud shout, followed by a rapid though straggling fire of musketry, warned us to prepare for a meeting the reverse of friendly. Instantly the Indians came pouring in, carrying dismay and confusion in their countenances and gestures. We were surrounded on all sides: columns were advancing everywhere against us, and those whom we hitherto trusted as friends had only waited till the arrival of their support . . . in advancing . . . . If Colonel Baume had permitted himself to be duped into a great error, it is no more than justice to confess that he exerted himself manfully to . . . avert its consequences . . . the troops lining the breastworks replied to the fire of the Americans with extreme celerity and considerable effect. So close and destructive . . . was our first volley that the assailants recoiled . . . and would have retreated, in all probability . . . but ere we could take advantage of the confusion produced, fresh attacks developed themselves, and we were warmly engaged on every side . . . It was at this moment, when the heads of columns began to show themselves in rear of our right and left, that the Indians, who had hitherto acted with spirit and something like order, lost all confidence and fled . . . . The vacancy, which the retreat of the savages occasioned, was promptly filled up by one of our two fieldpieces, whilst the other poured destruction among the enemy in front, as often as they showed themselves in the open country. . . . In this state . . . we continued upwards three quarters of an hour . . . when an accident occurred, which at once . . . exposed us, almost defenceless, to our fate.

"The solitary tumbril, which contained the whole of our spare ammunition, became ignited and blew up with a violence which . . . caused a momentary cessation in firing, both on our side and that of the enemy . . . . The American officers, guessing the extent of our calamity, cheered their men to fresh exertions. They rushed up the ascent . . . in spite of the heavy volley which we poured in to check them, and finding our guns silent, they sprang over the parapet, and dashed within our works. For a few seconds, the scene which ensued defies all power of language to describe. The bayonet, the butt of the rifle, the saber, the pike were in full play; and men fell, as they rarely fall in modern war, under the direct blows of their enemies. But such a struggle could not . . . be of long continuance. Outnumbered, broken . . . our people wavered and fell back, or fought singly and unconnectedly, till they were either cut down at their post . . . or compelled to surrender."

It was half past four on that fateful day that Breymann's relief army reached Van Schaick's Mill, not knowing that Baum had already been defeated. They encountered some of Stark's men whom they drove back in a running fight toward the battlefield. Fortunately, Colonel Seth Warner arrived with his men in time to aid the tired and disorganized army of John Stark. Warner directed a Captain Stafford to take a redoubt that was occupied by about 250 loyalists. Included in this redoubt was Lieutenant Colonel JOHN PETERS of the

Queen's Loyal Rangers, and he had with him the loyalists that had been collected around Cambridge. PETERS had been able to raise 600 men after his enlistment in Canada and on his journey south with Burgoyne. Assigned to General Alexander Fraser's advance party, they had fought in every skirmish except Hubbardton, and PETERS said his troops had been killed off faster than he could muster new recruits and only 150 remained. PETERS' physical condition was not the best. He suffered from fever and chills and was lame from a wound of the previous day.

Rebel Captain Stafford discovered a ravine in which they were able to conceal themselves from the loyalists as they approached. Unfortunately, it ended directly below the enemy redoubt. To the surprise of both the rebels and Tories they were suddenly facing each other at very close quarters. Stafford was leading his troops, and as he turned to order the charge, he fell with the first shots and was to discover a musket ball had gone through his foot. He jumped up, saw a redcoated man racing across a distant field and shouted, "They run! They Run!" Suddenly, the uncontrollable preacher Thomas Allen appeared at the breastworks demanding that the enemy surrender in the name of Congress, which was responded to by another volley of fire, which then brought the rebels scampering up the hill and leaping over the earthworks before the loyalists could reload.

When PETERS saw a man taking careful aim at him, he fired. The rebel reloaded, ran closer, and shot, shouting as he approached, "Peters, you d... Tory. I have got you!" and he bayoneted PETERS in the left breast just as PETERS finished reloading his gun. He recognized him as

"A rebel Captain, Jeremiah Post by name, an old schoolmate and playfellow, and a cousin of my wife."

PETERS fired, and later stated,

"though his bayonet was in my body I felt regret at being obliged to destroy him."

PETERS' rib had deflected the bayonet, so his wound was not serious. He escaped; but his corps lost seventy-five percent of his recruits.

The reputed proud courageous Breymann reported to Burgoyne:

"The troops did their duty, and I know of no one who doubts this fact. After our ammunition was all expended, and the artillery in consequence ceased firing, nothing was more natural than to suppose that the enemy would be encouraged to renew his attack . . . . In order, therefore, not to risk anything (as I was unable to return the enemy's fire, my ammunition being exhausted), I retreated on the approach of darkness, destroyed the bridge, had as many of the wounded as possible brought thither that they might not be captured, and, after a lapse of half an hour . . . pursued my march and reached Cambridge toward twelve o'clock at night. Here, after taking precautionary measures, I remained during that night, and marched thence at daybreak of the seventeenth of August to the camp."

According to Stark's report of the affair, thirty Americans were killed and forty wounded. He claimed 207 Germans found dead, a large number wounded, and 700 prisoners. The Germans admitted to the loss of 596 men, exclusive of the losses of the British units. A week later, a farmer from Lyndeboro wrote home:

> "We do not know how many we have killed. Our scouts daily find them dead in the woods. One of our scouts found, the beginning of the week, twenty six of the enemy lying dead in the woods. They stank so they could not bury them . . . The wounded Hessians die three or four a day. They are all in Bennington Meeting House, which smells so it is enough to kill anyone to be in it."

Among the captured was the German surgeon, Wasmus, whose medical services were demanded by the wounded Americans; but whenever possible he aided his mutilated countrymen as the prisoners were marched or taken to Boston. A somewhat disheartened Burgoyne minimized the loss in his report to Germain by reporting,

> "about 400 men" killed or captured, with the rebel casualties at more than double that. He continued by attempting to somewhat share the blame by saying, "I hope circumstances will be such that my endeavours may be in some degree assisted by a co-operation of the army under Sir William Howe."

With this encouraging American victory, Congress refused to censure Stark for insubordination, and in October they made him a continental brigadier general. This didn't last long however, when he stubbornly refused to co-operate on one occasion.

British Brigadier (temporarily) St. Leger had landed at Oswego with around four hundred British, German, and Tory troops from Montreal on 25 July. He was met by Joseph Brandt, whose Indian name was Thayendanegea, who had enlisted and brought with him over 1,000 Indian braves, eager to help regain their lands from these American rebels. In one day they were ready to march eastward. All were confident as they marched without incident to the height of the divide, or great carrying place, that separated the western flowing waters from those that began and descended eastward down the Mohawk River that joined with the Hudson River near Albany. Located at this strategic spot was Fort Stanwix, or Fort SCHUYLER (as it was called at that time). It had been built during the French and Indian War and was not in best repair, so SCHUYLER had sent the tall, twenty-eight-year-old Colonel Peter Gansevoort and his Third New York Regiment to reoccupy and refurbish it in April.

The Colonel was warned by American friendly Indians of St. Leger's approach, and he immediately evacuated the women, children, and incapacitated, and then prepared to defend this star-shaped fort with his 750 men. His 2nd in command Lieutenant Colonel Marinus Willett wrote for his eastern newspapers on Sunday, 3 August, the following:

> "The enemy appeared in the edge of the woods, about a mile below the fort, where they took post, in order to . . . cut off the communication with the country . . . They sent in a flag, who told us of their great power, strength, and determination, in such a manner as gave us reason to suppose they were not possessed of great strength sufficient to take the fort. Our answer was a determination to support it.
>
> "All day on Monday we were much annoyed by a sharp fire of musketry from the Indians and German riflemen, which, as our men were obliged to be exposed . . . killed one and wounded seven. The day after, the firing was not so heavy, and men under better cover, all the damage was, one man killed by a rifle ball.
>
> "Wednesday morning there was an unusual silence . . . About eleven o'clock three men got into the fort, who brought a letter from General Harkaman, of the Tryon County Militia, advising us that he was at Oriska (eight miles from the fort) with part of his militia, and proposed to force his way to the fort for our relief."

Somehow, St. Leger discovered the approach of this rather wealthy Dutchman, whose name was Nicholas Herkimer, with his quickly assembled

800-man army; so the British general sent Joseph Brandt and his Indians to ambush them where the road dipped through a ragged defile about six miles east of the fort. Herkimer arrived about ten o'clock, and suddenly St. Leger's Indians were upon them—whopping and firing at their rear. Herkimer astride his great white horse turned and started toward the firing. Almost immediately he was fired upon and he and his mount fell toward a brook which ran in the bottom of the ravine. He had a bad wound in his leg; but he was placed astride his saddle at the foot of a beech tree. Here he lit his pipe and sat puffing it "with his sword drawn, animating his men." The gory fight lasted six hours. The attackers weakened and then withdrew. Herkimer had lost between 150 to 200 men killed and many prisoners were taken. They were not in any position to move toward the fort, so they retreated with their wounded general on a litter back down the Mohawk River about forty miles to Fort Dayton.

When Benedict Arnold arrived at Fort Dayton with his nine hundred and fifty Massachusetts Continentals, on 21 August, he was reinforced by a hundred of "old Honikol's" militia. Herkimer's leg had been amputated by an inexperienced surgeon who was unable to stop the bleeding. As he died, he took up his old German Bible and read the Thirty-eighth Psalm,

"My wounds stink and are corrupt because of my foolishness."

He had died the same day that Stark's men were fighting east of Bennington.

At Fort Dayton, Benedict Arnold learned that St. Leger had around 1,700 men who were laying siege to Fort Stanwix [Fort Schuyler] and that they were within 150 yards of the fort. Many of his officers advised him to wait for additional reinforcements; but he would not hear of it. He had known when he accepted this command that it would not be easy, and SCHUYLER had given him more men than he should spare for this daring enterprise with Burgoyne within a one day forced march to Albany. Washington was preparing to meet Howe— he would parade through Philadelphia on 24 August on his way to meet the enemy.

Arnold and his men had taken quite a few loyalist prisoners on their way. Among them was a distant cousin of General SCHUYLER named Hon Yost Schuyler, who was a nephew of General Herkimer. When his relatives pleaded for his release, Benedict Arnold struck a deal with them.

It seems that Hon Yost was a man that was given to speaking in unknown tongues and because of this, the Indians felt he had supernatural powers—a prophet who spoke for the Great Spirit. Arnold would set the young man free, if he would travel to the British lines outside Fort Stanwix and do his best to convince the Indians that there was a very large American army approaching. To insure his cooperation, Arnold held his father and brother hostage—with the threat of hanging, if he proved to be a traitor. Hon Yost enthusiastically agreed, and shot some bullets through his coat to give the appearance that he had just escaped from the rebels. He enlisted the help of a number of Oneida Indians who were friendly to the American cause to corroborate his story and left immediately.

Arriving at St. Leger's camp, he informed the Indians of Arnold's enormous army that was very close behind him. He claimed to have observed that the Americans were not hostile to the Indians, but if they continued with the British, they must unquestionably take their share of whatever calamities might befall their allies. When he was asked by a British officer to be more specific, he rolled his eyes, stared up at the treetops and seemed to convey the idea that they were more numerous than the leaves above. With that, St. Leger's Indians decided to leave. St. Leger tried to dissuade them, offering them liquor to get them drunk, but they refused. He offered to put them at the rear, but they charged him with a design to sacrifice them for his own safety. The British commander wrote that they

> "grew furious, seized upon the officers' liquor and clothes, and became more formidable than the enemy."

Without the help of their Indians, St. Leger's army quickly withdrew from their siege lines toward Oswego with such haste through the forest that they left their tents, cannon, and stores behind. It was said that none of them wanted to be in the rear, for their Indians were killing the stragglers. Several of the Oneida Indians who had traveled with Hon Yost, joined at the rear of the fleeing army and at proper intervals would call from various places, "They are coming!" to speed up their departure.

Hon Yost Schuyler met Benedict Arnold and his army 22 miles from the fort on 23 August. He reported his mission a success. Arnold arrived the next day and found the enemy totally vanished. He sent a pursuit detachment after them, and a few arrived at Lake Oneida in time to see their boats on the distant horizon. Leaving two militia regiments to support the garrison, he took his Massachusetts continentals to rejoin the army on the Hudson, where they found they had a new commanding officer, General Horatio Gates.

BENJAMIN FRANKLIN

GENERAL GEORGE WASHINGTON
OF THE AMERICAN REVOLUTION

PHILIP SCHUYLER

BENEDICT ARNOLD

ARTHUR ST. CLAIR

HORATIO GATES

GOVERNOR GEORGE CLINTON
NEW YORK

JOHN STARK
NEW HAMPSHIRE

GOVERNOR JOHN TRUMBULL
CONNECTICUT

82

Maneuvering and Manipulating
for Position

O n Sunday, 10 August, General SCHUYLER was stopped at his Albany
home by a courier from Congress, while he was in the process of mounting his horse to join his troops at Stillwater. This was the same day that German
Colonel Baume had left with his troops toward Bennington. The courier brought
him a copy of two resolutions passed by that body and signed by President John
Hanock. The first one, which he had expected and probably welcomed, called
for an inquiry into the loss of Fort Ticonderoga. The second one had some very
unwanted implications. Generals SCHUYLER and St. Clair were to report to
General Washington's Headquarters. This resolution implied a court-martial
trial for each of them. It also necessitated that he leave the command of the
Northern Army at a time when the battle for Albany, and perhaps the fate of the
country, could not be postponed much longer, with Burgoyne's Headquarters
now at the home of his friend and Saratoga neighbor, William Duer. The British
general was only waiting for his supplies before his major attack on the rebel
army. No mention was made of SCHUYLER's replacement or when, whoever
he was, he would arrive. St. Clair was quick to comply, and left on the 12th of
August. SCHUYLER refused to leave until the new commander arrived. This
was not a time to leave an army unattended.

Other letters arrived from Philadelphia. A letter to Josiah Bartlett from a
member of the New Hampshire delegation, Nathaniel Folsom, read:

"The loss of Ticonderoga hes given grate unEasyness: Generall
SCHUYLER and Sant Caire aire ordered to head Qurters in order for
an inquirey into thaire Conduckt . . . . General Gates is ordered to take

Comemand in the northern Department."

The appointment of the ubiquitously-manipulating Gates to replace him was very unsettling to SCHUYLER. Then his friend, William Duer, wrote him, that SCHUYLER's enemies in Philadelphia had done so much "to blast your character" and blame him for the loss of Fort Ticonderoga—that nothing his supporters might say could "stem the torrent of calumny." To add to the insult SCHUYLER felt, he learned several days later that Congress had given his old rival, Horatio Gates, their endorsement and had instructed the states of New Hampshire, Massachusetts, Connecticut, New Jersey, New York, and Pennsylvania to dispatch as many of their militia as General Gates thought necessary for the defense of the region—a right SCHUYLER had always been denied.

The poor general was totally crushed and unable for several days to speak to anyone about "the Indignity of being relieved of the command of the army at a time when an Engagement must soon take place." Still, he was too proud and responsible to go south until his successor arrived to take command.

The troops were not in the best health. There was the familiar "camp disorder," some had smallpox, and many were still experiencing the fever and ague. One soldier commented that this was not surprising considering that they were sleeping on "the bare Ground cover'd with Dew without Blankets having a few boards for Cover." Brigadier General John Nixon was severe enough, or perhaps important enough, that he was sent to the hospital at Albany.

SCHUYLER moved his army south from Stillwater to the "Sprouts," the name given to the little islands at the mouth of the Mohawk River. He begged Massachusetts and New York to send him more militia. He posted detachments along the south bank of the Mohawk River to prevent a British crossing. Then finally to his delight, he was able to send the glorious news abroad of the defeat of Baum's army at Bennington. He also felt a personal triumph when the news arrived later that St. Leger was fleeing and that his beloved Fort SCHUYLER, or Fort Stanwix, was now safe. His trust in Benedict Arnold had been justified.

When Horatio Gates completed his leisurely journey and arrived on 19 August to take over the command, he had inherited all the time and effort that had gone into the weakening of an enemy, who instead of triumph, now realized they could face defeat, and who were hungry and worn, also. Their troops were diluted by the defense of a long supply line that didn't seem to be able to bring in all that was needed. Their Indians were vanishing into the night, not desirous of belonging to the losing side, a little like football fans that leave the game early when their team doesn't appear to be winning. Carleton refused to send more men. William Howe was going another direction. But they were still hoping, for a few more days, to be joined by St. Leger. Although SCHUYLER's rivals would not care to admit it openly, Major General NATHANAEL GREENE was quick to attest,

> "the foundation of all the Northern success was laid long before [Gates's] arrival there" and that Gates appeared "just in time to reap the laurels and rewards."

Like the football player that rests throughout the game, enters in time to receive the winning football in the end zone, and is carried triumphantly off the field with all the honor—but then, I guess, he did catch the ball in the right place at a very crucial time.

SCHUYLER felt further disappointment when Gates ignored him—not socializing nor inviting him to his gathering for a council of war in which he invited all the continental officers and even the brigadier of the Albany militia. The kindly Gouverneur Morris of the New York Provincial Congress even commented:

> "The new commander-in-chief . . . may, if he please, neglect to ask or disdain to receive advice. But those who know him will, I am sure, be convinced that he needs it."

It became pointedly clear to the former commanding officer that Gates had no desire for his personal knowledge of the hidden roads and fords of the countryside in which he had spent his life, nor any of his battle plans that could be favorably initiated. With some reluctance, he mounted his horse and returned to his home in Albany to prepare further for his journey to Philadelphia and what he assumed would be a court-martial.

Gates, however, was quick to capitalize on the popularity of the two heroes of the day, when their east and west victories became known. He made every effort to smooth Stark's animosity and tried to bring him with his militia to his main army at the mouth of the Mohawk. DANIEL MORGAN and his riflemen had entered the camp on the 30th of August, and when Benedict Arnold arrived on the 31st, Gates gave him command of his left wing and included MORGAN's riflemen under him. The rather weary, despairing army started to spark with life. Enlistments increased daily as new hope spread through word of mouth, letters and newspapers. George Washington was elated by the "great stroke struck by Stark near Bennington," and a member of his official family wrote a friend:

> "I give you joy from the Bottom of my Heart on Account of the fortunate and Signal stroke given by Old Stark, and also the threshing the Enemy got at Fort SCHYULER. There was a cloud in the North, but I really think matters in that Quarter look well just now. I trust Burgoyne will be severely mauled."

Those last days of August were very hot and hardly a day passed without deserting Tories and Germans coming into the American camp, now with approximately 6,000 soldiers. With all this increased strength coming in daily, which would approach a total of 12,000 troops within the next few weeks, Gates determined to advance up the Hudson to a spot three miles north of Stillwater on 8 September. The place was called Bemis Heights, because the man Bemis had a tavern near the Hudson below them. Here the Hudson curved between mountainous, irregular banks. The plateau was two or three hundred feet above the river with deep ravines and creeks rushing, turning and dropping toward the great river. This was where Gates ordered the talented young Polish engineer, Colonel Thaddeus Kosciuszko, to build his fortifications to meet Burgoyne.

Gates planned to personally command his right wing, composed of the continentals under General John Glover, General John Paterson, and Colonel John Nixon. They would defend the river, the narrow level plain and the high ground that bordered it. The Massachusetts regiments under General Ebenezer Learned and the New Yorkers under Colonel JAMES LIVINGSTON were to defend the center. Benedict Arnold got the rugged mountainous left command. He had his New Hampshire regulars, New Yorkers, the Connecticut cavalry militia that arrived 28 August and 1 September, DANIEL MORGAN's riflemen and Lieutenant Colonel Henry Dearborn's Light Infantry.

Meanwhile the General "Gentleman Johnny Burgoyne" was experiencing the same old problems of rough roads, food and provender shortages, and a plague of dysentery, as well as an increase in desertion. Discipline became harsher. An unlucky German musketeer named Fasselabend had joined with the Americans and then had been captured when the American vessel he was on was captured at Skenesborough. He was chosen to be the example of what would happen if anyone else was captured as a deserter. Riedesel's entire German regiment and the army's picket guard were paraded to witness his execution by firing squad. Two men convicted of robbery received 1000 lashes each. Burgoyne worried about sabotage, so he ordered the careful guarding of the bridge of boats that Fraser's men had constructed across the Hudson lest "ill-designing people" might "injure it." Indians were offered rewards for capture of the deserters and were told to scalp any turncoats they killed. Then a reward was offered for the apprehension of any person who induced men to desert. Rations were tightened.

Still he presented a bold exterior. In writing to a friend in England, he admitted that the rebels had driven off all the livestock that might give them fresh meat, forcing them to rely on salt rations—a minor inconvenience not worth worrying about. He commented on the rapids in the Hudson that would force them to use ground transport, yet that would not interfere with his determination to

> "try the Countenance of Mr. Gates." The rebels, he continued, "pretend to be in spirits and threaten us a drubbing, but on the approach of the red Coats I rather believe it will be as usual. They will find they can take up better ground in the rear." He mentioned as evidence of the good spirit of his army that the ladies had no intention of leaving: "Lady Harriet Acland graces the advanced Corps" and Baroness Riedesel was with the Brunswick troops. Morale was excellent and they had "frequent din'ees and constantly musick." All in all, it would be difficult to imagine a more exciting and pleasurable adventure—"a lively Camp, good weather, good Claret, good musick and the enemy is near . . . a little fusillade during dinner does not discompose the Nerves of even our Ladies."

On 10 September, he left his headquarters at William Duer's home and moved south. He now had provisions for four weeks, but he planned to be in Albany by the 13th. It was a beautiful day as the British Army crossed the Hudson on the "bridge-of-boats" to begin their journey on the west side of the Hudson.

From there they would march by land until they discovered the enemy. Their Indian scouts had abandoned them and they really didn't know where those rebels were.

Further south near Wilmington, Delaware, on Brandywine Creek, on this same day of 10 September, George Washington was preparing to meet British General William Howe in what he thought would be a European style battle, which he expected would occur on the following day.

In Philadelphia, on Sunday 24 August, John Adams had written to his wife Abigail,

"The rain ceased, and the army marched through the town between seven and ten o'clock. The wagons went another road. Four regiments of light horse, Bland's, Baylor's, Sheldon's and Moylan's. Four grand divisions of the army and the artillery . . . marched twelve deep and yet took up above two hours in passing by. General Washington and the other general officers with their aides on horseback. The colonels and other field officers on horseback.

"We have now an army well appointed between us and Mr. Howe, and this army will be immediately joined by ten thousand militia, so that I feel as secure as if I were at Braintree, but not so happy. My happiness is nowhere to be found but there. . . . The army . . . I find to be extremely well armed, pretty well clothed, and tolerably disciplined . . . . There is such a mixture of the sublime and the beautiful, together with the useful, in military discipline that I wonder every officer we have is not charmed by it. Much remains to be done. Our soldiers have not quite the air of soldiers. They don't step exactly in time. They don't hold up their heads quite erect, nor turn out their toes so exactly as they ought. They don't all of them cock their hats; and such as do, don't all wear them the same way."

John Adams may have felt safe that day; but within a few weeks, Congress would meet in another location as the last of the congressmen fled from Philadelphia to safer quarters, while the redcoats entered Philadelphia.

For that same day, 24 August, the enemy began landing their army six miles below Head of the Elk, which was the closest landing to Philadelphia for ships navigating up the Chesapeake. From here they would need to cross Brandywine Creek, which flowed by Wilmington and then emptied into the Delaware River. The most popular crossing of the Brandywine was at Chadd's

Ford. Washington planned to meet the British at that point. [Recall that our LACEY ancestor, THOMAS CANBY and his son, years before, built a large mill on the Brandywine near Wilmington.]

On 22 July, Howe had crowded 17,000 of his best troops aboard 267 ships with their horses, artillery, and supplies when he sailed from New York harbor. Five weeks later, the British army was not in shape for a quick move. They had sweltered below deck in woolen uniforms, first in New York harbor, then on their journey. They needed rest. Most of their horses had broken their legs in transit and were dead. They would need to buy more from the countryside—at least enough for the officers to ride and to pull their heavy wagons with their ammunition, cannon and other supplies. It was September before they began their march to the north.

83

BRANDYWINE—
"AWFUL WAS THE SCENE TO BEHOLD!"

We often think of the Revolutionary War as being composed of Englishmen on both sides. This was not really the case. Genealogists should consider that by 1777, America was a mixture of many nationalities and among their soldiers were Czechs, Poles, Hungarians, Swiss, French, Greeks, Danes, Swedes, Italians, Bohemians, Dutch, Germans, Scots, Irish, Scots-Irish, Africans, and Indians. There were Protestants, Catholics, and Jews from many countries. The following are just a few examples.

The Scots-Irish and Sweds were the original settlers west of the Dutch in the New Jersey area. Thousands of Scots-Irish came to America in the 1770s when the linen-weaving industry collapsed in Ulster. Many of them migrated first to Liverpool and London, where they worked for wages and lived in slums before they left England in disgust, and then came to America. By 1776 an estimated 300,000 had arrived. Many Scots-Irish, like Patrick Henry, who became the first governor of Virginia, and Charles Thomson, who organized Philadelphia's Sons of Liberty, took active roles in the earliest protests against the British. Others, like John Rutledge, took part in the Continental Congress's debate over independence. Still others, like Henry Knox, Washington's chief of artillery, fought all through the eight years of this long war.

The Scots-Irish were only a little more numerous than the German immigrants. By 1776, at least 225,000 Germans of at least 250 different Protestant sects migrated to America in the wake of European religious wars. These were quite numerous in the western New Jersey and eastern Pennsylvania area. Many of them left behind the constant warfare of Europe only to march off to the war for America, some with clergy men like Frederick Muhlenberg. Other Germans came to fight beside the Americans, most famed was the Baron von Steuben, a Prussian professional soldier who drilled the American troops at Valley Forge into a tightly disciplined, highly maneuverable army. Steuben stayed in the new United States after the Revolution. So did 12,562 of the 29,875 German soldiers brought mostly against their will to fight on the British side. These hated, so-called Hessians were rented to the British to fight in America by their landgraves in Hesse-Hanau and Brunswick. About 30 years earlier, some had served in Scotland when, under the Hessian Duke of Cumberland, they had bayoneted the clans at the bloody Battle of Culloden in 1745. Their presence helped to account for the widespread support of the American Revolution by the Scots and Scots-Irish immigrants.

Polish American sailors in the crew of the American ship *Bonhomme Richard*, fought under the famous Scottish American captain, John Paul Jones, throwing grenades into the powder magazine of the British man-of-war *Serapis* until it exploded and sank. Greek knights journeyed to America and fought as volunteers under the French Marquis de Lafayette in Virginia. Two regiments of Italians were recruited in Italy and fought under the French flag at Yorktown.

An estimated 7,500 blacks fought under Washington, more than double that number fought on the British side. Both sides offered them their freedom. The Jews of Charleston, South Carolina, marched off in the Jews Company to defend their city against invading British and German forces. Colonel Mordecai Sheftall acted as commissary general for the southern Continental Army and was held prisoner on a British prison ship with his sixteen-year-old son for two years in horrible conditions and very little food. Young American Jewish David Salisbury Franks became Benedict Arnold's aide-de-camp all through the tough Canadian Quebec campaign and then joined with a Massachusetts regiment.

In my personal early American ancestry we find many Dutch, French Huguenots, perhaps French Canadian, perhaps Indian, and maybe some with Irish, Scotch, and German lineage, although the English predominate.

On 11 Sep 1777, when the Battle of Brandywine was about to commence, we may have had several direct ancestors participating. If our genealogical records are correct, forty-seven-year-old Captain ELISHA BARTON (mostly of

English descent) of Rareton, Amwell twp, Hunterdon, New Jersey, was with the Continental Army. He probably was serving under General. Anthony Wayne and his Pennsylvanians. His Dutch American wife was JEMIMA VAN KIRK, who was born about 1733 and grew up in Hopewell, Mercer, New Jersey. Her father was Long Island/Dutch. Her mother was DOROTHY MORGAN of New England/Welch descent.

Dutch/English extract Second Lieutenant JOHN COOLEY, of Alexandria twp, Hunterdon, New Jersey, had enlisted with the continentals 23 Feb 1776, when he was twenty-nine-years-old. He had been captured with the Pennsylvanians in the Battle of Trois-Rivieres in Canada on 8 Jun 1776. Upon release he reenlisted as a sergeant in an American German Regiment on 16 Jul 1776. He was promoted to Ensign on 4 Dec 1776, and to second lieutenant 30 Apr 1777. He served as a wagoner in Pennsylvania and New Jersey. On 11 Jul 1778, he served with the 10th Pennsylvania Regiment as a Supernumerary. His Quaker wife was ABIGAIL LIPPINCOTT, born 28 Oct 1753 was descended from English SAMUEL LIPPINCOTT of eastern New Jersey, and English MARY PRESTON, formerly of Philadelphia.

JOHN WILKINSON, father of third-great-grandfather AARON WILKINSON and son of English ancestry JOSEPH WILKINSON and BARBARA LACEY was born about 1754 in Bucks County, PA. Little is known of his participation in the war, although his uncle and cousins were highly involved in spite of their Quaker beliefs. He may have been killed, since he seems to have only the one child, born during the war. His grandfathers, JOHN WILKINSON and THOMAS LACEY, had large land holdings in Wrightstown and Buckingham, Bucks, Pennsylvania, and also had land in Hunterdon County, New Jersey. His twenty-three-year-old cousin JOHN LACEY Jr. had been promoted to the rank of lieutenant colonel in 1777 and had been sent to White Moose, Pennsylvania. On 9 Jan 1778, he was promoted to the rank of a militia brigadier general and, later, transferred to Hatboro. From there he was moved to Trenton. [After the war ended when he was twenty nine years old, General LACEY, married ANTIS (Anastasia) BUDD REYNOLDS, whose father was Thomas Reynolds, a prominent citizen of Pemberton, New Jersey.] Uncle JOHN WILKINSON was a lieutenant colonel, but had lessened his participation, because of his Quaker religious beliefs. However, with William Howe's landing, the threat to Philadelphia and "his young son [JOHN] laying dying," he chose to actively participate, and was excommunicated because of it.

French-Canadian or perhaps Huguenot JOSEPH POYER may be the young perhaps eleven-year-old son of THOMAS POYER of Rumbout's Precinct in Dutchess County, New York. If so, his father THOMAS POYER recorded his will, "being sick," 1 Jan 1777. His sons were both underage at that time, JOSEPH being the younger of the two. The will was not proven until the 3 May 1783. Perhaps the rather young father THOMAS was severely injured in some battle or diseased in the Canadian campaign, or maybe he was with Washington at Trenton. Anyway, he recorded his will at that time, recovered (perhaps reenlisted), but died six years later. Then, again, perhaps our ancestor is the young private, JOSEPH POULIER, who enlisted as a private in Canada in Loiseau's company, LIVINGSTON's Regiment; or maybe he is a son or grandson of JACQUE POYER, the French soldier stationed at Fort Chambly by Louis XIV. About fourteen of JACQUE's grandchildren, the MONTEEs of Montreal, joined with the Americans and were with Hazen's Company under the command of General Sullivan at Brandywine.

It is unfortunate that our ancestors did not leave us journals, but this recap may give us a few clues as to where they might have been during this battle.

At Chadd's Ford, Washington established his center with General NATHANAEL GREENE's army; however, he reserved the command for himself. He posted Wayne's Pennsylvanians on the brow of a hill near Chadd's house, a little above the ford, and Weedon's and Muhlenberg's Virginians directly east of the ford. Maxwell's eight hundred light troops of Lincoln's division he placed across the Brandywine on the southern bank nearest the enemy. Knox and his artillery were supporting his center position.

The right wing was composed of three divisions on the east bank of the stream, spread from Brinton's Ford to Painter's Ford. Stirling was on the extreme right, which included Col. Hazen's company at the furthest position; Stephen was below him and Sullivan, who was over the whole right wing, commanded closest to Washington at Brinton's Ford. Sullivan posted pickets beyond the wing, having been warned by Washington that Howe might attempt to surround the army and attack from the rear as he had on Long Island.

The left wing was posted on the steep, rough heights at Pyle's Ford, where there was little fear that the enemy would attempt to cross. Armstrong was given this command with 1,000 Pennsylvania militia.

British General William Howe watched the early morning positioning of the enemy and made his own plans. He sent General Knyphausen and his 5,000 Hessian veterans straight against the center of the American lines, while he marched 7,500 crack British troops fifteen miles up the Brandywine with Cornwallis second in command. It was a foggy, rainy day. Sullivan and his troops didn't see them go by, and when they were warned by the local residents of the redcoat's stealth approach, he didn't believe them. His scouts had reported to the contrary and he felt that the Quakers would favor the British and were attempting to trick him.

Meanwhile, Knyphausen hit hard at Maxwell's 800 troops that were west of the Brandywine and was able to force their retreat across the Brandywine; but his troops didn't follow them. Instead they took up their position on the high ground in the woods, out of the range of the American cannon fire, but close enough to the river to kill any rebels that attempted to cross. This lasted for several hours, and finally Washington got the message that they were only toying with him, and that the real battle would soon come from the north and rear. Accompanied by Lafayette, he hastened to warn Sullivan and change his plans. But Sullivan already knew. He had heard shots from the rear, and with these shots Knyphausen also began his offensive. The real battle had begun, almost. It was about 4:30 in the afternoon.

GREENE was given command at Chadd's Ford, and Washington, Lafayette and staff snatched up a neighborhood farmer, Joseph Brown, to guide them with all speed to the right wing battle that was said to be near Birmingham Meeting House. A friend of Brown recorded the following:

> "Brown was an elderly man and extremely loath to undertake that duty. He made many excuses but the occasion was too urgent for ceremony. One of Washington's suite dismounted from a fine charger and told Brown if he did not instantly get on his horse and conduct the General by the nearest and best route . . . he would run him through on the spot. Brown thereupon mounted and steered his course direct towards Birmingham

Meeting House with all speed, the General and his attendants being close at his heels.

"He said the horse leapt all the fences without difficulty and was followed in like manner by the others. The head of General Washington's horse, he said, was constantly at the flank of the one on which he was mounted, and the General was continually repeating to him, 'Push along, old man. Push along, old man.'"

Back at Chadd's Ford, loyalist Stephen Jarvis, with the Queen's Rangers wrote:

"The Fourth Regiment led the column and the Queen's Rangers followed, the [American] battery playing upon us with grapeshot which did much execution. The water took us up to our breasts and was much stained with blood before the battery was carried and the guns turned upon the enemy.

"Immediately after our regiment had crossed, two companies (the Grenadiers and Captain McKay's) was ordered to move to the left and take possession of a hill which the enemy was retiring from and wait there until further orders. From the eminence we had a most extensive view of the American army, and we saw our brave comrades cutting them up in great style."

So at Chadd's Ford, Wayne and Maxwell's valiant soldiers were forced to retreat, losing their cannon, while the militia downstream withdrew with very few problems. Wayne's Pennsylvanians continued to slow the crossing and engage the enemy until Washington arrived after dark and organized the retreat to Chester.

But up the Brandywine Creek at Birmingham Meeting House, Cornwallis had once again lost his edge. At 4:30 P.M., he was behind the American lines in excellent position, one mile from closing them in, when he called a halt. His men, he felt, needed a late lunch, so he stopped the action for a whole hour. This gave Washington a chance to reinforce the battered right wing with Weedon's Virginians. General GREENE was sent ahead with Maxwell's and Stephen's regiments. Their arrival had been accomplished by an incredible double-time march through thick underbrush and fog. They traveled from Chadd's Ford to the meeting house in only forty-five minutes and although there was still much confusion, they were mostly prepared and had filled in the exposed right when Cornwallis ended his lunch hour. Washington and Lafayette rode fearlessly to the front lines, encouraging their men and left Sullivan in charge of the coordination of the troops. Washington again proved bulletproof under intense enemy fire; but the French General Lafayette was shot in the thigh and fell from his horse. Maxwell protected the American artillery that blasted the charging British with extreme accuracy. This murderous battle continued over an hour until dusk when Washington slowly and neatly disengaged and retreated. It was considered a British victory, because they claimed the field; but Washington's army was still intact and blocking Howe's advance to Philadelphia.

A British officer wrote his report of the battle:

"What excessive fatigue. A rapid march from four o'clock in the morning till four in the eve, when we engaged. Till dark we fought. Describe the battle. T'was not like those of Covent Garden or Drury Lane . . . . There was a most infernal fire of cannon and musquetry. Most incessant shouting, 'Incline to the right! Incline to the left! Halt! Charge!' etc. The balls plowing up the ground. The trees cracking over one's head. The branches riven by the artillery. The leaves falling as in autumn by the grapeshot . . . . The misters on both sides showed conduct. The action was brilliant. Mr. Washington retreated . . . and Mr. Howe remained master of the field . . . A ball glanced about my ankle and contused it. For some days I was lifted on horseback in men's arms."

It was estimated that Washington lost between twelve and thirteen hundred men—killed, wounded, and missing. One of the MONTEEs in Hazen's Company from Canada had been killed. The Americans thought that Howe's loss would be greater; but their losses actually amounted to only 89 killed, 488 wounded, and 6 missing.

A young Quaker of the neighborhood, Joseph Townsend, had watched the day's fighting from behind the British lines and when the fighting ended he and his companions braved the dangers and ventured over to the field to

"take a view of the dead and wounded, as we might never have such another opportunity . . . awful was the scene to behold—such a number of fellow beings lying together severely wounded and some mortally—a few dead but a small proportion of them, considering the immense quantity of powder and ball that had been discharged. It was now time for the surgeons to exert themselves. . . . Some of the doors of the meetinghouse were torn off and the wounded carried thereon into the house to be occupied for an hospital . . . . The wounded officers were first attended to . . . . After assisting in carrying two of them into the house I was disposed to see an operation performed by one of the surgeons, who was preparing to amputate a limb by having a brass clamp or screw fitted thereon a little above the knee joint. He had his knife in his hand, the blade of which was . . . circular . . . and was about to make the incision, when he recollected that it might be necessary for the wounded man to take something to support him during the operation. He mentioned to some of his attendants to give him a little wine or brandy . . . to which he replied, 'No, doctor, it is not necessary, my spirits are up enough without it.'

"He then observed 'that he had heard some of them say there was some water in the house, and if there was he would like a little to wet his mouth.' As I was listening . . . one of my companions . . . mentioned that it was necessary to go . . . as they were fixing the picket guards and if we did not get away . . . we should have to remain within the lines . . . during the night. I instantly complied."

In the American camp, although wounded in the leg, Lafayette, with an improvised bandage covering his wound, set up a guard at Chester Creek to help bring order out of the confusion that accompanied their night flight. Captain Enoch Anderson of the Delawares, who had fought on the right, remembered that he saw

"not a despairing look nor did I hear a despairing word. We had our solacing words always ready for each other, 'Come boys, we shall do better another time,' sounded throughout our little army."

Weedon, who had covered the retreat, stated that

"such another victory would establish the rights of America, and I wish them the honor of the field again tomorrow on the same terms."

Congress voted thirty hogsheads of rum to the army,

"In compliment . . . for their gallant behavior," and neither the general nor his men were blamed for failure.

It would be two weeks before the British started their march to take Philadelphia. In the meantime, Washington, who worried more about his ammunition and supplies that had been given them by the French and were stored at Reading and Valley Forge than he did about the hundreds of empty houses now in the nation's Capital, sent his aide, Colonel ALEXANDER HAMILTON, with a party of cavalry under Captain Henry Lee to destroy flour stored in mills along the Schuylkill. This was accomplished only minutes before a British detachment galloped upon them. HAMILTON and four men that were with him jumped into a barge under their fire, which killed one of his companions and wounded another.

Directly upon landing, HAMILTON sent a note to President John Hancock:

"If Congress have not yet left Philadelphia, they ought to do it immediately without fail; for the enemy have the means of throwing a party this night into the city."

Congress responded quite rapidly and moved their activity to Lancaster. But the British were slower than HAMILTON believed at that time. He was able, by using Washington's emergency powers, to impress blankets, shoes, and horses from the citizens. But the citizens gave only a little in spite of his exhortations; however, he did get all of the public stores off safely.

LEADERS FOR
GREAT
BRITAIN

LORD GEORGE GERMAIN

JOHN BURGOYNE

LADY HARRIET ACLAND

JOHN DRAKE ACLAND

SIR WILLIAM HOWE

SIR HENRY CLINTON

BARRY St. LEGER

GENERAL SIMON FRASER

SIR GUY CARLETON

BARON von RIEDESEL

BARONESS von RIEDESEL

~ 84 ~

THE BATTLE OF FREEMAN'S FARM

While Howe's army was maneuvering and preparing to occupy Philadelphia, Burgoyne had begun his southward march to meet General Gates and his American army, after which "Gentleman Johnny" desperately hoped to occupy Albany, as he had promised King George. His advance troops crossed the Hudson on his bridge of boats on 13 September to the west side of the Hudson without incident. They were followed two days later by the Brunswickers, who brought up the rear. Then they broke up the bridge and let it float downstream. Burgoyne had voluntarily cut off his supply line from the north; but perhaps he feared leaving a bridge for the Americans to harass his rear, or a path for deserters to take. Word had come to him that some Americans were moving in from the east toward Fort Ti. His Indian scouts were gone. As his approximately 6,000 troops marched south with all their equipage and about 300 women and camp followers, they were not the cocky self-assured army that arrived at Fort Ticonderoga. These men in their sweat-stained, faded uniforms were tired and hungry and unaware of the location of the enemy. Then, on the 16th, the advance guard heard the distant tap of morning drums. Burgoyne halted to reconnoiter; unsure, he moved slowly forward the next morning to a spot about four miles from Gates camp—Van Vechten's Cove, still not seeing any rebels.

Burgoyne's army had started out marching with three columns, but found it necessary to resort to single file along the river bank. The Americans had broken up the roads, destroyed the bridges and left barriers wherever they could. The British remained at the Cove for two more days, sending out crews to repair bridges. During one night, the tent of Major John Acland and Lady Harriet caught fire. She wrote in her journal that their trusty Newfoundland dog, Jack

Catch, overturned a candle and started the fire and "we were in great danger of being burned to death." The pregnant Lady Acland escaped under the tent in the rear, unbeknownst to her husband, Major Acland, who dove into the flames to rescue her. His face and body were quite badly burned before he was saved by one of his aides.

The next day, 16 September, they marched further south and set up camp fifty yards from the Hudson River at SCHUYLER's homeland at Saratoga. Although Burgoyne had issued strict orders that no one was to leave camp for any reason, a group of hungry men and women stole away to look for food. Fourteen were killed, wounded, or missing, which quickly led to the assumption that the Americans were nearby and would also now know of their approach. Burgoyne was furious. He tightened his guard and sternly reminded them that "the life of the Soldier is the property of the King." He further declared that henceforth a man caught beyond the advanced sentries would be instantly hanged.

Autumn had almost officially arrived. The leaves on the trees were beginning to show their beautiful colors. The nights were much cooler. The food supply was very limited. In the American camp, General John Glover described Burgoyne's situation:

> "I think matters look fair on our side & I have not the least doubt of beating or compelling Mr. Burgoyne to return back at least to Ticonderoga, if not to Canada. His situation is dangerous, which he must see & know if he is not blind, and if he is not strong enough to move down to fight us, he cannot remain where he is without giving us a great advantage."

The American army had been growing. They now had about 12,000 troops, which included the artillery, engineers, and cavalry. New Hampshire's Major Henry Dearborn, who commanded their light infantry companies and had been placed under Benedict Arnold's command, observed that Gates's arrival put "a New face upon our affairs;" however, BROCKHOLST LIVINGSTON, who was now with Benedict Arnold's staff, observed that their recent successes had a lot to do with the growing number of troops, as did the knowledge that Burgoyne "has got himself into such a situation that he can neither retire or advance without fighting." Certainly winning is more fun than losing, and as Burgoyne camped at Saratoga, the rebel army in general was enthusiastic and mentally ready for a fight in their now fortified position at Bemis Heights, at least it seemed that way on the surface. Unfortunately, old slights, rivalries, suspicions, and unrestrained pride were creating a division.

After SCHUYLER left his home in Saratoga and occupied his abode at Albany, he kept in touch with the affairs of the northern army by corresponding with his former secretary, Richard Varick, who was now deputy commissioner general of musters. Varick did not hide his strong alliance to SCHUYLER, whom he wrote saying, "I wish . . . we had a commander who could see a little Distance before him without Spectacles." He would make bitter innuendos and sneers about Gates to members of the General's staff, which, of course, were reported.

When Benedict Arnold renewed his friendship with Varick, who had so capably supplied him with his little fleet on Lake Champlain the previous year, Gates became suspicious of Benedict Arnold's loyalty to him, also. Then when, against the wishes of Gates, Arnold invited HENRY BROCKHOLST LIVINGSTON (who had accompanied SCHUYLER to Albany and had been waiting to go south with him) to join his staff, General Gates' antagonism increased. This was not smoothed when Major General Arnold added as an aide̅ Livingston's cousin, MATTHEW CLARKSON.

Nineteen-year-old MATTHEW CLARKSON had been wounded about the end of July when he was trying to force back an Indian attack near Moses Creek. A ball had hit him in the neck, gone through his windpipe, and exited on the other side. He had recovered in time to accompany Arnold on his journey to Fort Stanwix. JAMES WILKINSON, a trusted aide of Gates, was quick to communicate freely and enlarge the situation. He wrote to St. Clair, "General Gates despises a certain pompous little fellow [i.e., Arnold] as much as you can." (WILKINSON had also accompanied Arnold in his march to Quebec.)

The insidious behavior erupted. General orders issued by WILKINSON assigned three New York militia regiments to John Glover, assigned to the right wing. Arnold exploded—these were his men! It placed him "in the ridiculous light of presuming to give Orders I had no right to do, and having them publickly Contradicted." Surely WILKINSON made a mistake.

Gates countered, "No!" The order was his—an oversight that he would correct (but never did.) Arnold assumed correctly he was being punished for engaging LIVINGSTON on his staff. BROCKHOLST LIVINGSTON thought himself insulted by a major and fought an inconclusive and bloodless duel. In the 4th New York regiment of another cousin, HENRY BEEKMAN LIVINGSTON, a quarrel broke out and a soldier Samuel Hemenway plunged a knife into the neck of Dudley Broadstreet, severing his jugular vein.

But General Horatio Gates had another problem with his heroes. On September 15th, John Stark arrived at camp. His men had been waiting for over a month to aid Gates in his battle against Burgoyne; but three days after General Stark arrived, his New Hampshires marched off. They claimed they had enlisted for only two months and they wouldn't stay an hour longer. So at midnight they broke camp. They were going home. But in all fairness to the State of New Hampshire, new troops were enlisted and were on their way—but they had only made it to Bennington when Stark and his men left.

Gates had formerly been a British officer. He knew the ugly results that accompanied a British bayonet charge. He appreciated the discipline and training of the approaching army. He preferred to keep his men secure behind what he considered to be excellent fortifications, and wait for the enemy to come to him. However, the fearless Benedict Arnold pointed out to him that the enemy should not be allowed to seize the initiative. He reminded him that if the enemy moved onto the heights instead of making a frontal attack along the river road, they might be able to outflank the rebel army and position their cannon above them, blasting holes in the American earthworks. Arnold wanted to attack them in the woods, where he felt the colonials would have the advantage. He felt that an organized bayonet charge would be quite difficult in the surrounding rugged terrain. As a final plea he mentioned that if all else failed, they could then return to their fortifications and renew the battle. Gates finally relented enough to allow him to use DANIEL MORGAN's elite riflemen with the support of Dearborn's Light Infantry to move out on the left and slow down any advance the British might take in that direction. He also ordered Arnold to keep his main force in reserve.

So in the early morning 19 September with the eerie fog hanging thick, the gigantic DANIEL MORGAN and his riflemen took to the dense woods beyond the middle branch of Mill Creek and spread out. About 300 of them, under a

Pennsylvania captain named Van Swearingin, prodded toward a ten- or twelve-acre clearing around an abandoned cabin—the remains of the farm of a man named Freeman. As the fog lifted around 10 o'clock, they took almost invisible positions behind the rail fence and in the trees that allowed as much vision as possible of the northern approach of the British through the woods in the ravine and hills beyond. But if they were nearly invisible, so was Burgoyne's army.

Gentleman Johnny Burgoyne and his scouts had reconnoitered sufficiently to decide against an approach along the river road. They had discovered Freeman's Farm, also. It gave a commanding view of the American fortifications—an excellent place for their cannon. Fraser's troops were stealthily approaching the northwestern side of the field. Burgoyne took command of the central troops, and they were drawing near on the northeastern side where the old cabin was. The German Riedesel was to guard the river and advance to the southeast, where he would be available, if needed, to storm the heights. It was very much like the feared plan that Benedict Arnold had described to Gates as a possible enemy approach.

As the advance pickets under Forbes of the British army stumbled through the trees upwards, toward the farm, MORGAN's riflemen were quick to spot them. They aimed, waited for more to emerge into the open area, and then fired, especially at the officers, with devastating effect—routing the astonished redcoats. The few British survivors staggered back into the woods, the motley Americans in pursuit. Suddenly, to the horror of the riflemen, the main line of the British army emerged from the woods into full view. The pursuers quickly went into reverse and scattered—literally for their lives.

Gates's adjutant, Colonel JAMES WILKINSON had been sent to the field to find out what was happening. He later wrote:

> "I crossed the angle of the field, leaped the fence, and just before me on a ridge discovered Lieutenant Colonel Butler with three men, all treed. From him I learned that they had 'caught a Scotch prize,' that having forced the picket, they had closed with the British line, had been instantly routed and from the suddenness of the shock and the nature of the ground, were broken and scattered in all directions . . . . I then turned about to regain the camp and report . . . when my ears were saluted by an uncommon noise which I approached and perceived Colonel MORGAN, attended by two

men only, who with a 'turkey call' was collecting his dispersed troops."

He added that the old wagoner was so upset he was in tears, thinking his corp was ruined.

Captain Van Swearingin was wounded and, along with twelve other rebels, was taken by Fraser's Indians, who began to strip him and steal his pocketbook. Fraser's batman rescued him from the Indians and took him to Fraser for interrogation; but it was quite unsuccessful as the Captain refused to cooperate—even when they threatened to hang him. He calmly replied, "You may if you please." The general was impressed and rode away leaving him in custody with the other prisoners and gave orders that he was not to be ill-treated. Fraser's troops included Acland's grenadiers, Balcarres's light infantry battalions, and Fraser's own 24th regiment. These were supported by two German regiments under Lieutenant Colonel Breymann. Preceding all of them, in the most exposed front, were the remaining Indians, Canadians, and the loyalists under PETERS and Jessup.

The skirmish, which lasted about forty minutes, then became an unorganized free-for-all with the Americans seeking their leader, the British scurrying to join the main line, and both sides retrieving their dead and wounded. Some of the redcoats became overly excited when Fraser's troops put in an appearance and shot without orders, killing some of their own men. Burgoyne's adjutant had sufficient presence of mind to order a cannon shot, which stopped this unneeded killing. All the British picket officers were killed or wounded, including Forbes, whose wounds still permitted him to rally his troops. One of the dead was Canadian Captain David Monin, whose eleven-year-old son was fighting next to him at the time.

Back in his "small hovel" behind the American lines, General Horatio Gates was informed that "the whole British Force and a Division of Foreigners" were about to attack, so he ordered General Poor to dispatch more men in support of MORGAN. About 900 men took off at once—Joseph Cilley's 1st and Alexander Scammell's 3rd. Cilley went to the left in hopes of flanking the enemy. Scammell went straight ahead through the woods towards the farm. Benedict Arnold had already ordered his reserve troops forward and he was in the middle of the fray. One of Dearborn's men saw him "riding in front of the lines, his eyes flashing, pointing with his sword to the advancing foe, with a voice that rang clear as a trumpet that electrified the line."

It was said that he cantered up to a picket guard from the 8th Massachusetts under Major William Hull, called for volunteers, and sent about 300 of them forward to aid General Poor. The official report of the early skirmish and the following major battle that began about 2:00 P.M. and ended with darkness did not even mention that Arnold participated, because Gates, who never left his "hovel" refused to even say that Benedict Arnold had done anything, nor would he send him more troops from his line when the battle became heavier and Arnold had desperately requested fresh troops—most of Phillips' artillerymen and the German's under Riedesel had scaled the heights from the river, since the two officers correctly felt that Gates would not attack from that direction. Horatio Gates feared the arrival of their infantry and artillery along the river route and held much of his army in reserve behind his fortifications where he still expected an attack. Toward the end of the day, Gates sent in Learned's brigade; but he refused to allow Arnold to direct its movements. Without effective leadership, they blundered too far left into Fraser's outposts and mostly wasted their ammunition in achieving nothing.

General John Glover recalled,

"Both armies seemed determined to conquer or die. One continual blaze without any intermission till dark, when by consent of both parties it ceased. During which time we several times drove them, took the ground, passing over great numbers of their dead and wounded. Took one field-piece, but the woods and bush was so thick, and being close pushed by another party of the enemy coming up, was obliged to give up our prize. The enemy in their turn sometimes drove us. They were bold, intrepid, and fought like heroes, and I do assure you, sirs, our men were equally bold and courageous and fought like men fighting for their all."

Alexander Scammell, whose 3rd New Hampshire regiment was in the thick of it, facing five field pieces and the center of the main British line, saw the resplendent British General John Burgoyne on horseback directing his troops. It was later falsely reported that the general had been shot from his horse and carried off—killed or badly wounded. Captain Charles Green, an aide-de-camp of

General Phillips, who was delivering a message to Burgoyne, had been mistaken for the British general, because he had equipped his horse with a very conspicuous and beautiful lace saddle cloth. The sharpshooter thought he had gotten Gentleman Johnny.

British Lieutenant Digby wrote that

"General Burgoyne was every where and did every thing [that] could be expected from a brave officer." His description of the battle was, "an explosion of fire . . . the heavy artillery, joining in concert like great peals of thunder, assisted by the echoes of the woods, almost deafened us with the noise . . . . This crash of cannon and musketry never ceased till darkness parted us, when they retired to their camp, leaving us masters of the field; but it was a dear bought victory if I can give it that name, as we lost many brave men.

"During the night we remained in our ranks, and tho' we heard the groans of our wounded and dying at a small distance, yet could not assist them till morning, not knowing the position of the enemy, and expecting the action would be renewed at daybreak. Sleep was a stranger to us, but we were all in good spirits and ready to obey with cheerfulness any orders the general might issue before morning dawned."

To make matters worse the wolves were out there tearing the flesh of dying men, and their blood-chilling howls were heard all night.

Burgoyne had lost six hundred men, twice the casualties of the Americans. Still he was quite content and wrote to his commander at Fort Ticonderoga:

"We have had a smart and very honorable action, and are now encamped in front of the field, which must demonstrate our victory beyond the power of even an American newswriter to explain away."

The dawn of 20 September arrived. A thick fog rolled over the ground and completely masked the enemies from each other. The British began their burial detail with Lieutenant Anburey in command. He later recalled:

"I . . . observed a little more decency than some parties had done, who left heads, legs, and arms above ground. No other distinction is paid to officer or soldier than that the officers are put in a hole by themselves. Our army abounded with young officers . . . and in the course of this unpleasant duty, three of the Twentieth Regiment were interred together, the age of the eldest not exceeding seventeen.

"This friendly office to the dead, though it greatly affects the feelings, was nothing to the scene in bringing in the wounded . . . . They had remained out all night, and from the loss of blood and want of nourishment, were upon the point to expiring with faintness: some of them begged they might lay and die, others again were insensible, some upon the least movement were put in the most horrid tortures, and all had near a mile to be conveyed to the hospitals."

He further observed,

"I am fearful the real advantages resulting from this hard-fought battle will rest on that of the Americans, our army being so much weakened by this engagement as not to be of sufficient strength to venture forth and improve the victory, which may, in the end, put a stop to our intended expedition; the only apparent benefit gained is that we keep possession of the ground where the engagement began."

Anburey had only praise for

"the courage and obstinacy with which the Americans fought . . . [Those characteristics] were the astonishment of everyone, and we now become fully convinced they are not that contemptible enemy we had hitherto imaged them, incapable of standing a regular engagement, and that they would only fight behind strong earthworks."

Burgoyne considered resuming the battle, but decided against it, although, according to British Lieutenant Digby, both Generals Fraser and Phillips wanted to continue their momentum of the previous day. Digby figured Burgoyne had decided against it because the hospitals were so full and the army's provisions inadequately protected. The Americans were in confusion and short on ammunition; Gates would not take the immediate initiative. Time was in his favor.

Sunday morning, 21 September, a courier arrived at Burgoyne's camp with a coded message from Sir Henry Clinton. It read,

"You know my good will and are not ignorant of my poverty [of troops]. If you think 2000 men can assist you effectually, I will make a push at [Fort] Montgomery in about ten days. But ever jealous of my flanks if they make a move in force on either of them I must return to save this important post. I expect reenforcement every day. Let me know what you would wish."

It was dated 12 September. This rather vague letter gave new hope to the British general, who had so carefully planned on help from the south. He would wait for Clinton and build more fortifications, including a large redoubt and a boat bridge across the Hudson. Trees could be heard falling near the American camp. They were building a bridge, also, with the large amount of lumber that was sent them by SCHUYLER from Albany. Lieutenant Digby wrote,

"I suppose seldom two armies remained looking at each other so long without coming to action."

It would last for two-and-a-half weeks.

~ 85 ~

PHILADELPHIA—FORT TICONDEROGA—
GERMANTOWN

Robert Morton, a teen-age Tory, was among the thousands who watched from the streets, windows, and roofs as the British marched in. He described it as follows:

> "About eleven o'clock A.M., Lord Cornwallis with his division of the British and auxiliary troops, amounting to about three thousand, marched into this city . . . to the great relief of the inhabitants who have too long suffered the yoke of arbitrary power, and who testified their approbation of the arrival of the troops by the loudest acclamations of joy.
>
> "Went with Charles Logan to headquarters to see his Excellency General Sir William Howe, but he being gone out, we had some conversation with the officers, who appeared well disposed towards the peaceable inhabitants, but most bitter against and determined to pursue to the last extremity the army of the United States.
>
> "The British army in this city are quartered at the Bettering House, State House, and other places, and already begin to show the great destruction of the fences and other things, the dreadful consequences of an army, however friendly. The army have fortified below the town to prevent the armed vessels in our river coming to this city, likewise have erected a battery at the Point.
>
> "This day has put a period to the existence of Continental money in this city."

After the Battle of Brandywine on 11 September, Washington first collected his army at Chester, but highly concerned about his vast store of guns and ammunition that had been sent him from France and were stored north at Reading and Valley Forge, he realized he could not allow the enemy to cut off his supplies. To him, they were more important than Philadelphia. So on the morning of the twelfth, he withdrew from Chester, crossed the Schuylkill River, and made camp near Germantown. Then he began to fear that Howe might try to out-flank his right and close off the western country. To prevent this, on the morning of the fifteenth, he took the initiative and crossed to the west of the Schuylkill and placed his army between Howe and Swedes Ford, where he expected Howe would try to cross the river.

Howe advanced toward him the next day and the two armies faced each other. Suddenly they were struck with a violent storm that had been brewing for several days—rain from the northwest, then northeast, with a wind that blew colder and colder.

"It came down so hard that in minutes we were drenched and sank in mud up to our calves," recorded a Hessian officer. Guns and ammunition were useless.

American General Knox moaned, "a most terrible stroke."

Not even a bayonet strike was possible in the quagmire. Howe maneuvered his army in such a way in the next two days that Washington feared for both flanks, so on the nineteenth, Washington once more crossed the Schuylkill at Parker's Ford. He detached Anthony Wayne's division of fifteen hundred men with four field pieces and gave him instructions to remain behind and harass the rear of the enemy—especially if Howe should decide to cross the river.

Wayne posted his men in a forest clearing by the Paoli Tavern, near his own home and three miles from the British lines. Howe was quick to locate their position and, around midnight on the twentieth, he sent Major General Sir Charles Grey with three battalions to surprise the sleeping continentals. There was to be no firing—only bayonets. The redcoats cut down fifty rebel soldiers and took one hundred as prisoners before Wayne could get the rest of them off into the rainy woods and finally to safety at Chester.

Howe then reversed his main line during the night and slipped down the river. He crossed at Farland and Gordon's Fords and walked into Philadelphia without any opposition. Once more he had successfully diverted General Washington. Sir William placed his main army near Germantown, about 3,000 troops in Philadelphia and another 3,000 across the Delaware in New Jersey.

But Washington still had his supplies; his strong defenses on the Delaware that controlled their seaport; an army that was resting and growing daily, and Howe would find it difficult to feed his troops. When Benjamin Franklin was told in Paris that Howe had captured Philadelphia, he said,

"No! Philadelphia has captured Howe!"

Major General Benjamin Lincoln, Colonel John Brown and Ft. Ticonderoga

Major General Benjamin Lincoln, still in Vermont, had 2,000 troops to harass Burgoyne's rear and guard against any further attempt by the enemy in that direction. When John Stark was in Bennington, the two of them put their heads together and as they saw it, the surest way to prevent the British General from putting all his force against Gates was to threaten his flank and rear, forcing him to leave sizable detachments between his main army and Fort Ticonderoga and requiring him to send more troops as escorts with his supply wagons. Lincoln also pointed out that this would further restrain the loyalists in that region, all of which was very close to Stark's original plan when he met Baum at Bennington.

By 7 September, Lincoln had collected a supply of flour for his men and marched north to Manchester, then fifteen more miles further north to Pawlet, where he felt protected by some almost impassable mountains. Here, the scouts brought him word that the garrison at Fort Ti was widely dispersed and probably off guard. Lincoln decided to try a surprise attack. He detached three colonels; Brown, Woodbridge, and Johnson, and gave each of them 500 men. He would stay behind with the balance of his men. Their orders were to "annoy, divide and distract the enemy."

Brown had the most difficult assignment. "Without risking too much," he was to cross over the narrows, attack the landing at the north end of Lake George, release any American prisoners he found there, destroy the enemy's boats and supplies and, if he could, attack Fort Ticonderoga. Woodbridge was to go to Skenesborough, which Burgoyne had evacuated, where he would cover Brown's line of retreat, while Johnson would threaten Mount Independence in support of Brown and make an actual attack if the situation warranted.

Colonel Brown had graduated from Yale in 1771. He had settled in Pittsfield, Massachusetts, and was sent to Canada by the Massachusetts Committee of

Correspondence to plan for a way to capture Ticonderoga from the British in 1775. Part of his plan was to send Ethan Allen and his Green Mountain Boys as soon as the committee approved it. Unfortunately, this placed him in the middle when Benedict Arnold a little later chose to do the same thing—with Arnold as the leader. But their real animosity developed when Brown brought charges against Arnold for alleged misdemeanors in Canada. Brown had been so hard hit in retaliation that he recognized a weakness in the daring Arnold that others had failed to perceive. He flatly stated,

> "Money is this man's God, and to get enough of it he would sacrifice his country."

Brown described his September adventure into the enemy stronghold and explained that after an all-night march he reached the heights above Lake George landing on 17 September, reconnoitered to assess the situation, arose with his men before dawn on the following morning, and attacked the posts at the landing and at Mount Defiance. He recorded, "In a few minutes we carried the place." A British naval officer credited Brown's smooth operation to his careful reconnaissance; but a more easily identifiable cause was that the British sentinels carelessly let a party of the rebels approach, assuming they were Canadians on a work detail hauling supplies between the two lakes. The guards were seized and the Americans were able to surround the camp and enter the enemies tents before anyone discovered them.

Simultaneously, at Mount Defiance, Captain Ebenezer Allen ascended "a craggy Precipice under the Fire of the Enemy" and overran the sergeant's guard in six minutes. Allen's men suffered no casualties, while they killed or wounded a number of the enemy and took 20 prisoners.

They were just beginning. Brown's men fanned out and liberated the American captives; they rounded up a number of British troops in a barn between the camp and the landing place; they seized a group of naval officers and men at the end of the landing; they boarded a vessel carrying three six-pounders, and then ran toward a barn about a mile from the fort, where they took more prisoners. The Frenchmen at the Fort failed to hear the commotion, because of the noise of the waterfall. This allowed the Americans to surprise a company of British troops there and free more rebels.

Amazingly, Brown's raiders released 118 Americans who had been "confined, fatigued and dejected to such a degree that one could scarcely conjecture what they were. They come out of their Holes and Cells with Wonder and Amazement," Brown said, "indeed the Transition was almost too much for them."

In addition, the Americans were able to capture twelve British officers, 143 regulars, 119 Canadians, several hundred stands of arms, and a large quantity of baggage.

But that was not all. After they had captured 150 bateaus in Lake Champlain and another fifty vessels in Lake George, Brown sent a message under a flag of truce to the British commandant, demanding a surrender of Ticonderoga and Mount Independence in "the strongest and most peremptory terms."

But the British brigadier responded,

"The garrison intrusted to my charge I shall defend to the last. I am, Sir, your humble servant. H. Watson Powell, Brig. Genl."

Brown bombarded them with their captured cannon for quite awhile. He realized he was not prepared to storm the forts, so he proceeded to destroy the wagons and all but twenty boats in Lake George. He burned the stores near Ticonderoga, sent off the cattle and horses, and with four hundred men boarded a small schooner and several gunboats armed with five cannon and sailed north toward the enemy posts at the other end of Lake Champlain. Unfortunately, "an unluky Circumstance happened." That night a violent storm arose and in the resulting confusion, a British prisoner was able to escape and warn the garrison at Diamond Island of the approach of Brown's men. After losing some of his gunboats to the heavier cannon on the Island, Brown "thought Proper to retreat," and he burned the remainder of his small boats and headed for Skenesborough.

When the news of this attack on Fort Ticonderoga reached the American lines at Bemis Heights, a thunderous cheer arose that resounded as far as the British camp. This was followed by a thirteen gun salute. Burgoyne and his troops wondered about the celebration, until a few days later, when an escaped prisoner informed them of the Americans' successful attack on Fort Ti. The British vulnerability in the north helped the British General to further realize that he must attack Gates and go south.

While most of the Americans were delighted, Benedict Arnold was not particularly happy with the news from the north. His jealous nature would not allow him to rejoice in the success of his bitter personal enemy, who he considered to be a rival—Colonel John Brown. And to add to his dejection, Gates had taken away his command—totally. The general had given his left wing to the new hero, Major General Benjamin Lincoln. Arnold considered joining George Washington, but his men begged him to stay and help them meet Burgoyne. The fearless Arnold had their trust.

Washington surprises the British at Germantown, 4 Oct 1777

His Excellency, General Washington, was not pleased with himself that Howe had been able to slip past him into Philadelphia. He felt his army quite capable of meeting the enemy immediately; but his council of war advised against it. Then, on 28 September he called another council in for debate. He had more information. Howe's total army did not exceed 8,000 men; McDougall had arrived from Peekskill with 900 men; William Smallwood came with 1100 Maryland militia, and 600 New Jersey militia under David Forman were expected. He now had 11,000 troops. Still, the council advised him to wait. However, he moved his army closer to the enemy, to a point where Skippack Creek crossed Skippack Road. Here, they intercepted two letters that indicated that a sizable portion of the British army had been sent as a detachment to try and open the Delaware River as a port. His officers finally agreed to attack, and they moved to within fifteen or sixteen miles of Germantown and made their careful plans—perhaps too intricate, for communication between four columns became very difficult.

Sullivan's and Wayne's divisions with General Thomas Conway were to make the frontal attack on the enemy camp; GREENE's and Stephen's divisions, with Mc Dougall's brigade in front, were to advance against the enemy's right; Smallwood's Maryland and Forman's New Jersey militia were to go even further than GREENE and approach the enemy right from the rear. Against the Schuylkill River, John Armstrong was to attack the enemy left from the rear. Stirling remained in camp with Francis Nash, and William Maxwell's troops as reserves. The army was to leave the evening of October 3rd on the sixteen-mile march to within two miles of the enemy. At exactly 5:00 A.M., they were to bayonet the pickets without firing a shot and then move to attack as soon as possible. Since their uniforms were precarious, every man was to have a piece of white paper in his hat to distinguish friend from foe.

British patrols reported the American advance to Howe about three in the morning, and he put his whole force under arms. But a British officer on outpost duty at Biggenstown was unaware of Washington's approach until the first attack struck. He wrote:

"General Wayne commanded the advance and fully expected to be revenged for the surprise we had given him [at Paoli]. When the first shots were fired at our pickets, so much had we all Wayne's affair in remembrance that the battalion was out and under arms in a minute.

"At this time, the day had just broke, but it was a very foggy morning and so dark we could not see a hundred yards before us. Just as the battalion had formed, the pickets came in and said the enemy were advancing in force. They had hardly joined the battalion when we heard a loud cry of, 'Have at the bloodhounds! Revenge Wayne's affair!'" And they immediately fired a volley.

"We gave them one in return, cheered, and charged . . . It was very weak: it did not consist of more than three hundred men and we had no support nearer than Germantown, a mile in our rear. On our charging, they gave way on all sides but again and again renewed the attack with fresh troops and greater force. We charged them twice, till the battalion was so reduced by killed and wounded that the bugle was sounded to retreat. Indeed had we not retreated at the very time we did, we should all have been taken or killed, as two columns of the enemy had nearly got round our flank. But this was the first time we had retreated from the Americans, and it was with great difficulty we could get our men to obey our orders.

"The enemy were kept so long in check that . . . two brigades had advanced to the entrance of Biggenstown, when they met our battalion retreating. By this time General Howe had come up and seeing the battalion retreating, all broken, he got into a passion and exclaimed, 'For shame, Light Infantry. I never saw you retreat before. Form! Form! It's only a scouting party.'

"However, he was soon convinced it was more than a scouting party, as the heads of the enemy's columns soon appeared. One coming through Biggenstown with three pieces of cannon in their front immediately fired with grape at the crowd that was standing with General Howe under a large chestnut tree. I think I never saw people enjoy a discharge of grape before, but we really all felt pleased to see the enemy make such an appearance and to hear the grape rattle about the commander-in-chief's ears after he had accused the battalion of having run away from a scouting party. He rode off immediately full speed, and we joined the two brigades that were now formed a little way in our rear, but it was not possible for them to make any stand against Washington's whole army, and they all retreated to Germantown, except Colonel Musgrave."

British Lieutenant Colonel Thomas Musgrave of the Fortieth Regiment took his quarters with twenty of his men in the large stone home with two upper floors that belonged to Pennsylvania Chief Justice Benjamin Chew, when he felt nearly surrounded by Sullivan's column. They slammed the doors and shutters tight and took post behind them.

Sullivan's troops had outpaced General Washington, who was accompanied by his thirty-two-year-old Adjutant General Timothy Pickering, originally from Salem, Massachusetts. When the sound of considerable small arms fire was heard through the "most horrid" morning fog, Washington said to his companion,

"I am afraid General Sullivan is throwing away his ammunition. Ride forward and tell him to preserve it."

Pickering spurred forward and delivered the message to Sullivan, three or four hundred yards beyond Chew's house. He later wrote,

"At this time I had never heard of Chew's house and had no idea that an enemy was in my rear. The first notice I received of it was from the whizzing of musket balls across the road, before, behind, and above me, as I was returning after delivering the orders to Sullivan.

"Instantly turning my eye to the right I saw the blaze of the muskets, whose shot were still aimed at me . . . Passing on I came to some of our artillery who were firing very obliquely on the front of the house. I remarked to them that in that position their fire would be unavailing and that the only chance of their shot making any impression . . . would be . . . firing directly on its front. Then . . . passing on I rejoined General Washington, who, with General Knox and other officers . . . were discussing . . . whether the whole of our troops then behind should . . . advance, regardless of the enemy in Chew's house, or first summon them to surrender. General Knox strenuously urged the sending of a summons . . . he said, 'It would be unmilitary to leave a castle in our rear.'

"I answered, 'to summon them to surrender will be useless. We are now in the midst of the battle and its issue is unknown. In this state of uncertainty and so well secured as the enemy find themselves, they will not regard a summons. They will fire at your flag.'

"However, a flag was sent with a summons. Lieutenant [Colonel Matthew] Smith of Virginia, my assistant in the Office of Adjutant General, volunteered his service to carry it. As he was advancing, a shot from the house gave him a wound of which he died."

The angry Americans determined to tear Musgrave from his stronghold. With their three-pounders they knocked open the doors and fired away at the upper windows. The infantrymen tried to force their way in. After losing a half-hour, Washington ordered his continentals to stay out of range of the house and by-pass it.

The confusion and mistakes increased. GREENE arrived at his position on the enemy right a half-hour late; his guide had been led astray. When he did meet the enemy's advance, he drove through almost to the center of the enemy line with great success. However, Adam Stephen, drunk at sunup and hearing the cannon and musket fire around Chew's house, guessed Sullivan was in trouble and turned back to help him. He met Stephen's division coming down to the main battle. Stephen's men mistook Wayne's for the enemy and volleyed. Wayne fired back promptly. Both groups broke and fled, and the seed of panic began.

No officer on the field was ever able to explain why it was that what appeared to be an American victory swiftly turned into a rout. General Weedon reported:

"Our men behaved with the greatest intrepidity for three hours, driving them from their camps, fieldpieces, stone walls, houses, &c. Trophies lay at our feet, but so certain were we of making a general defeat of it that we pass them by in the pursuit and by that means lost the chief part of them again, for when the unlucky idea struck our men to fall back, the utmost exertions to rally them again was in vain, and a few minutes evinced the absolute necessity of drawing them off in the best manner we could."

Some blamed the fog and smoke; some thought it was Stephen's and Wayne's fault; some blamed GREENE for his late arrival; Washington and others thought the delay at Chew's house was an issue; some believed it was the fresh troops that Howe brought in; but Private Joseph Martin explained it this way,

"The enemy were retreating before us until the first division that was engaged had expended their ammunition. Some of the men, unadvisedly
calling out that their ammunition was spent, the enemy were so near that
they overheard them, when they first made a stand and returned upon our
people, who, for want of ammunition and reinforcements, were obliged to
retreat which ultimately resulted in the rout of the whole army."

The American soldiers moved slowly as they retraced their steps and then
trudged further north to Pennypacker's Mill to encamp, a total march of twenty-
four miles. Most of the men had been twenty-four hours without food. Private
Martin claimed he had been "tormented with thirst all the morning, fighting
being warm work."

Washington lost about eleven hundred men including prisoners, and
Howe's loss was about half as many. General Weedon thought that "though the
enterprise miscarried, it was worth the undertaking," and General Washington
believed it "rather more unfortunate than injurious."

But Howe was still in possession of Philadelphia, and he turned his thoughts
to opening up the Delaware River. His ships with their most needed supplies,
troops and ammunition must have passage into this Quaker city, if he was to
survive the winter.

Burgoyne surveys Gates with 1700 of his Redcoats—7 Oct 1777

Sir Henry Clinton did take 3,000 British troops to the highlands, but he
informed General Howe it would be only long enough to destroy the cannon
at Forts Clinton and Montgomery. He felt this should be his diversion to help
Burgoyne. Surely Burgoyne did not expect him to go to Albany. Burgoyne had
said that a diversion would be of great use, and that would be that. He was back
in New York on 11 October and found out that General Howe was requesting
the troops that had arrived recently from Great Britain. He needed reinforcements to open up the Delaware River. Burgoyne was only a diversion, he felt, to
win his prize of the Capital of the United States.

A desperate "Gentleman Johnny" was beginning to get the same message
and wondering if London had intended it that way in the beginning. Baron
and Baroness Riedesel didn't like their situation. They both expressed themselves to Burgoyne that they felt a retreat to Ticonderoga was the best plan. The

Americans had continued with their fortifications and were well fortified on the river route. Any delay in the retreat used up more supplies. But his general's answer was an absolute, "No!" He would take Albany as directed. His pride and honor were at stake.

Burgoyne wanted to leave a few hundred men to guard the river and take the rest of his army into battle close to where they had met the enemy before, and where they had now constructed two redoubts. Riedesel asked what would happen if the Americans then chose to advance along the river and cut them off from any retreat? Burgoyne settled on the idea of taking his generals to reconnoiter the enemy with 1,700 troops to protect the generals. The Baroness was concerned when the call to arms came early on the 7th. She was planning to have all the officers to her place for dinner that night. Between 10 and 11 o'clock, the redcoats marched off with ten fieldpieces accompanying the officers: Burgoyne, Fraser, Phillips, Riedesel, Breymann, Balcarres, and Acland. They proceeded stealthily, hoping to surprise the enemy.

Several hours later in the American headquarters, Colonel John Brooks, of Massachusetts, remembered that Arnold was among the officers dining with Gates, and

> "While at table, we heard a firing from the advanced picket. The armies were about two miles from each other. The firing increasing, we all rose from the table; and General Arnold, addressing General Gates, said, 'Shall I go out and see what is the matter?'
>
> "General Gates made no reply, but upon being pressed, said, 'I am afraid to trust you, Arnold.' To which Arnold answered, 'Pray let me go. I will be careful, and if our advance does not need support, I will promise not to commit you.' Gates then told him he might go and see what the firing meant."

But he sent General Lincoln to accompany him. They returned to report in about a half-hour.

Evidently, Gates also sent his aide, JAMES WILKINSON, on his own recognizance, for he wrote in his memoirs:

> "On the afternoon of the 7th of October, the advanced guard of the center beat to arms . . . . On reaching the guard where the beat commenced, I could obtain no other satisfaction, but that some person had reported the

enemy to be advancing against our left.

"I proceed over open ground, and ascending a gentle acclivity in front of the guard, I perceived about half a mile from the line of our encampment several columns of the enemy, sixty or seventy rods from me, entering a wheat field which had not been cut and was separated from me by a small rivulet; and without my glass I could distinctly mark their every movement. After entering the field they displayed, formed the line, and sat down in double ranks with their arms between their legs. Foragers then proceeded to cut the wheat or standing straw, and I soon after observed several officers mounted on the top of a cabin, from whence with their glasses they were endeavoring to reconnoiter our left, which was concealed from their view by intervening woods. Having satisfied myself . . . that no attack was meditated, I returned and reported to the general, who asked me what appeared to be the intentions of the enemy.

"'They are foraging, and endeavoring to reconnoiter your left and I think, sir, they offer you battle.'

"'What is the nature of the ground, and what your opinion?'

"'There front is open, and their flanks rest on woods, under cover of which they may be attacked; their right is skirted by a lofty height. I would indulge them.'

"'Well, then, order on MORGAN to begin the game.'

"I waited on the colonel, whose corps was formed in front of our center, and delivered the order. He knew the ground and inquired the position of the enemy.

"They were formed across a newly cultivated field, their grenadier's [under *plain, rough* Major John Dyke Acland] with several fieldpieces on the left, bordering on a wood and a small ravine formed by the rivulet . . . their light infantry [under General Simon Fraser] on the right, covered by a worm fence at the foot of the hill . . . thickly covered with wood; their center composed of British and German battalions [under youthful Major the Earl of Balcarres]. Colonel MORGAN with his usual sagacity proposed to make a circuit with his corps by our left, and under cover of the wood to gain the height on the right of the enemy and from thence commence the attack, so soon as our fire should be opened against their left.

"This proposition was approved by the general, and it was concerted that time should be allowed the colonel to make the proposed circuit and gain his station on the enemy's right before the attack should be made on their left. Poor's brigade was ordered for this service, and the attack was commenced in due season on the flank and front of the British grenadiers, by the New Hampshire and New York troops. True to his purpose, MORGAN at this critical moment poured down like a torrent from the hill and attacked the right of the enemy in front and flank. Dearborn, at the moment when the enemy's light infantry were attempting to change front, pressed forward with ardor and delivered a close fire, then leaped the fence, shouted, charged, and gallantly forced them to retire in disorder; yet, headed by that intrepid soldier, the Earl of Balcarres, they were immediately rallied, and reformed behind a fence in rear of their first position."

Out in front, once more, with Poor's brigade was Alexander Scammell and his men. Acland's grenadiers held a position on a rise above them. They opened up on the rebels, firing muskets and grapeshot. But it seems to often happen when gunners shoot downhill, their aim was too high. Acland thought he saw the rebels falter and ordered a bayonet charge; but before they could bring it about, rebels emerged from the surrounding woods in great numbers—rushing the flank and front of the British. A German artilleryman described it as firing at the big men in bearskin hats with white belts crossed over their faded red coats, firing, reloading, and firing again, literally mowing down the shocked grenadiers, who were swept away by the ferocious charge. Major Acland was down, wounded in both legs and was carried off on Captain John Shrimpton's broad back.

JAMES WILKINSON had been sent to the rear to order up ABRAHAM TEN BROECK's New York militia, which contained about 1800 men. [TEN BROECK was a descendant of the RENSSELAER line.] He returned to the battle to find "a scene of . . . horror and exultation" where the grenadiers had been. In a space of twelve or fifteen square yards, he saw eighteen of them dying, and three officers propped against trees, two of them mortally wounded.

WILKINSON joined the rebels in their pursuit of the enemy, jumping around the dead and wounded, and then heard a voice call out from the corner of a rail fence,

"Protect me, sir, against this boy."

The young thirteen or fourteen-year-old soldier was about to pull the trigger when WILKINSON stopped him and asked the officer for his rank.

"I had the honor to command the grenadiers," was the reply.

WILKINSON realized it was Major Acland. Captain Shrimpton, who had been carrying him, had become winded from the extra exertion and Acland had told him to leave him and save himself. WILKINSON asked him how badly wounded he was, and he replied,

"Not badly, but very inconveniently. I am shot through both legs."

He then asked for help to go to the American camp. He was hoisted onto the orderly's horse and led away to Gates' headquarters.

When Balcarres regrouped his men behind the rail fence, Dearborn's light infantry swept in from the rear. Down the hill they ran, leaping over a fence, shouting at the top of their lungs, and Balcarres' startled troops broke ranks and ran for their redoubt. Dearborn's men had not fired a shot. The British left and right wings were in full retreat and only fifty-two minutes had passed since the first shot of the battle had been fired.

As a highly concerned Burgoyne watched from his main center line, he sent Sir Francis Carr Clerke with an order to bring off the guns, but before the aide could deliver the message he was shot and taken prisoner. The British left was now without artillery or a leader and the retreat of the grenadiers exposed the adjacent wing of the center under von Speth. As they waited for Learned's brigade to approach within range, the Germans saw a man in the blue uniform of an American general riding a bay horse with great speed. He was racing up to the front line of the marching men, shouting for them to follow him. It was Benedict Arnold.

It seems that Arnold could not sit quietly as ordered with a battle raging so very near. His personal enemies said he had been drinking heavily. He had borrowed the horse from a Connecticut friend and galloped toward the sound of the guns. At the rear of Learned's command were several Connecticut militia regiments. Shouting to the nearest group, he asked whose outfit it was.

"Colonel Lattimer's, sir," was the reply. Arnold grinned.

"My old Norwich and New London friends," he shouted.

"God bless you!" they cheered as he spurred his horse forward toward the head of the brigade.

When General Gates discovered that Arnold had dashed off, he assumed he was drunk and sent young Major John Armstrong to order his return.

[Note: Major Armstrong would later marry ALIDA the young sister of Chancellor ROBERT R. LIVINGSTON, on 19 Jan 1789. He would become a U.S. Senator in 1801; a minister to France in 1810; a brigadier general in the War of 1812, and the Secretary of War in 1813.]

Arnold saw the messenger coming and outran him. Armstrong stayed at the rear of the troops, having no desire to follow someone who

"behaved more like a madman than a cool and discreet officer."

Arnold yelled at the three leading regiments to follow him—fortunately the mild-mannered Learned raised no objection to the usurping of his command. A cheer went up from the men; they broke into a run and charged up the slope toward Speth and his Brunswickers, who were fearlessly waiting for them. The Americans had brought some small fieldpieces with them and were reloading and firing as rapidly as possible. The whole line of battle seemed enveloped in smoke and flame, and it was nearly impossible to discern what either side was doing. The rebels made no progress, and the determined Germans refused to be moved. Then, Balcarres's troops were moved back to the redoubt by MORGAN's men, and Speth saw that with three sides exposed to the enemy, he could not risk being surrounded, so he ordered his men to fall back.

The mounted Burgoyne was very conspicuous in his scarlet coat with its gold epaulets, but amazingly he was not hit. One horse had been shot out from under him; he had a bullet hole in his hat, and another had torn his waistcoat. His close friend, Brigadier Simon Fraser, was also very visible on his beautiful grey horse, riding along his lines, calmly reassuring his men of the light infantry and his own 24th Regiment.

MORGAN, perhaps at Arnold's suggestion, called to his experienced sharpshooter, Tim Murphy, to get rid of the man on the grey horse. Murphy climbed a tree and took aim. His first shot hit the horse's crupper, the strap looped under the tail; his second shot went through the horse's mane—just behind the ears. Fraser was urged to get away; but he refused. The third shot hit him in the stomach. Two junior officers took a place on each side and helped him to stay mounted, while his horse was led back to safety at their camp.

British Lieutenant Digby was to write that the loss of Fraser "helped to turn the fate of the day," and added that he was the only wounded officer they were able to take back to camp.

At the same moment that Fraser was shot, General ABRAHAM TEN

BROECK marched into view with his 1800 fresh soldiers. That was it. With Fraser gone and more rebels arriving, Burgoyne knew he had to get whatever was left of his reconnaissance force into the safety of their lines and ordered Phillips and Riedesel to cover the retreat. But the retreat was far from orderly. Off they went—into the woods, into the Balcarres's and Breymann's redoubts; but these were being "furiously assailed" by the dynamic leadership of one man—Benedict Arnold.

The two redoubts anchored the right of the British entrenched camp. Between the two redoubts a group of Canadian irregulars occupied several cabins near the road to the river. Somehow Arnold had picked up parts of Paterson's and Glover's commands, and he lead them forward with a waving sword to assault the stronghold manned by Balcarres's light infantry and the 24th Regiment, as well as the other redcoats who had sought safety there. They stormed through the surrounding abatis, facing heavy musket fire and grapeshot. But the redoubt gave the inhabitants a clear vision and the rebels were forced back to find the protection of the woods.

Arnold looked to his left, Learned's brigade was moving to the extreme right of the British lines where Breymann commanded. He spurred his horse and without any hesitation he galloped between the American and British lines, exposed to the gunfire of both armies. He emerged near the cabins occupied by the Canadians. With Learned's men he quickly cleared them out, picked up additional soldiers, and headed for the unprotected rear of the Breymann redoubt. MORGAN's men were already attacking from the front; Arnold's charge took the outnumbered Germans completely by surprise. But riding around behind the redoubt, Arnold was shot in his bad leg, his tan horse was killed, and as it fell, his wounded leg was pinned to the ground beneath the animal. The battle had ended for this redoubt, as well as for Arnold.

Breymann had been killed—some say by his own men, because he had sabered several of his men to keep them at their posts. Captain Benjamin Warren and troops from the 7th Massachusetts took possession of their cannon and the stored baggage. An American was about to bayonet the German who had shot Arnold; but the wounded general called out, "Don't hurt him! He only did his duty."

Major Armstrong had finally caught up with Arnold. However, his order to have him return was no longer needed. Several of his friends from the Connecticut militia helped pull him from under his horse and made a litter of blankets slung between two poles. They took him to a field hospital, where he absolutely refused to have his mutilated leg amputated.

For three months, Arnold remained in an Albany hospital, not certain that he would ever walk again. In January he sat up for the first time; but the wound reopened. It was late May 1778 before he was able to rejoin the continental army with his seniority restored.

Unlike Burgoyne, General Gates never stepped beyond his headquarters. His contributions to this actual battle were to order MORGAN to circle around the British right—after MORGAN suggested it—and then to send out additional detachments while the fighting ensued, not necessarily where they were most needed. Of course, Burgoyne had finally been greatly outnumbered, but the victory clearly belonged to Arnold, MORGAN, Dearborn, the New Hampshire continentals, the thousands of militiamen who came when they were most needed, and most assuredly to those hardy survivors of Ticonderoga, Hubbardton, Bennington, and others, who had worn out the enemy during their long, humiliating retreat, including those who had given their very lives for the freedom and liberty of their nation and future posterity.

The British had lost 184 killed, 264 wounded, and 183 taken prisoner—for a total of 631 men, of whom 31 were officers. The Germans had 94 dead, 67 wounded, and 102 captured, which brought the total of Burgoyne's lost men at 894—more than half of his 1700 reconnaissance troops. The Americans estimated that they had 30 killed and 100 wounded.

The British would not find rest that night. When Burgoyne arrived at his camp that evening, the attack on the Balcarres redoubt was still flaring—sheets of flame from the cannon and muskets silhouetted the men on both sides in the evening dusk. A heartsick Burgoyne ordered his camp guards to defend their post to the last man—which gave them an eery feeling and recognizance of their desperate situation. At 1 o'clock that night, the general ordered his camp to quietly leave their positions and evacuate everything to the confines of the Great Redoubt they had so recently constructed on the heights above the river.

The petite Baroness Riedesel's dinner party had been replaced by the care of their wounded friend, General Simon Fraser. She wrote in her memoirs:

"About three o'clock in the afternoon . . . they brought in to me upon a litter poor General Fraser . . . . Our dining table which was already spread was taken away and in its place they fixed up a bed for the general.

"The general said to the surgeon, 'Do not conceal anything from me. Must I die?'

"The ball had gone through his bowels . . . . Unfortunately, however, the general had eaten a hearty breakfast, by reason of which the intestines were distended and the ball, so the surgeon said, had not gone . . . between the intestines but through them. I heard him often amidst his groans exclaim, 'Oh, fatal ambition! Poor General Burgoyne! My poor wife!'

"Prayers were read to him. He then sent a message to General Burgoyne begging that he would have him buried the following day at six o'clock in the evening on the top of a hill which was a sort of redoubt."

Madame Riedesel had other wounded to care for and she had invited a sorrowful Lady Harriet Acland to stay with her. The Baroness described the captured wounded officer, Major Acland, as

"a rough fellow who was drunk almost every day, but, nevertheless, a brave officer."

Fraser died at 8 o'clock the next morning. The Americans arrived in force and gave an appearance of continuing the battle, but didn't. Gates was waiting, again.

One American stated,

"there were other and less expensive means of reducing his foe than by blood and carnage."

But as the British mourners tramped up the hill that evening to bury Fraser as he had requested, the enemy balls barraged them, one fell close enough to shower dust on the chaplain, and they were outraged that their enemies—"with an inhumanity peculiar to Americans"—fired on the group of graveside mourners, which procession included Burgoyne, Phillips, Riedesel, and their aides, in addition to Fraser's company. But in fairness to the Americans, they probably didn't know what the enemy was doing. The shelling on that day accomplished very little—a British artilleryman was killed and a horse. On the American side, a British ball shattered the leg of Major General Benjamin Lincoln.

Back at Gates's headquarters, Burgoyne's aide, Sir Francis Carr Clerke, who had been shot and captured by the Americans, was asking his surgeon,

> "Doctor, why do you pause? Do you think I am afraid to die?" and was then told that his wound was fatal. Burgoyne described him as a "useful assistant, an amiable companion, an attached friend." When WILKINSON had returned from the battle, he found Gates arguing with the young man, trying to convert him to the ideals of the Revolution. The dying Clerke held his own, and when Gates left the room in anger, Sir Francis asked WILKINSON if he had ever heard "so impudent a son of a b_____."

After dark that evening, Burgoyne went into full retreat, leaving many tents standing and fires kindled to deceive the enemy. He was unhappily aware that his

> "defeated army [should] retreat from an enemy flushed with success, much superior in front, and occupying strong posts in the country behind."

It was either retreat or surrender. He chose the former, and still hoping that Sir Henry Clinton might arrive with help, he insisted that the heavy artillery be brought along. It was a slow, discouraging exodus. The batteaux with the supplies and baggage had to move upstream against the current. The army advanced only six or seven miles, and Burgoyne was able to get some rest in General SCHUYLER's lovely home at Saratoga.

From Madame Riedesel's memoirs, the next morning:

> "On the tenth at seven o'clock in the morning, I drank some tea ... and we now hoped from one moment to another that we would again get under way. General Burgoyne in order to cover our retreat caused the beautiful houses and mills ... belonging to General SCHUYLER to be burned .... Thereupon we set out ... but only as far as another place not far from where we had started. The greatest misery and the utmost disorder prevailed in the army. The commissaries had forgotten to distribute provisions .... There were cattle enough but not one had been killed. More than thirty officers came to me who could endure hunger no longer. I had coffee and tea made ... and divided among them all the provisions with which my carriage was constantly filled, for we had a cook who, although an arrant knave, was fruitful in all expedients, and often in the night crossed small rivers .... to steal from the country people sheep, poultry, and pigs. He

would then charge us a high price for them, a circumstance, however, that we only learned a long time afterward.

"The whole army clamored for a retreat and my husband promised to make it possible, provided only that no time was lost. But General Burgoyne, to whom an order had been promised if he brought about a junction with the army of General Howe, could not determine upon this course and lost everything by his loitering. About two o'clock in the afternoon, the firing of cannon and small arms was again heard, and all was alarm and confusion."

The firing she heard came from the north. American General Stark had captured Burgoyne's guard at Fort Edward and thrown up an entrenched camp north of the fort to hold the road from there to Fort George. Brigadier General John Fellows with 1,300 Massachusetts militia were entrenched at Saratoga. When Burgoyne sent his army in their direction, Fellows rushed his troops across a rather shallow ford of the Hudson to a high bluff on the east side. Burgoyne sent troops north about twelve miles where they were to bridge the river and prepare for the army to follow. Gates's army followed them in pursuit in the afternoon, much to the distress of the baroness, who thought it improper to fire on their work parties. She took refuge in a house behind Burgoyne's lines as soon as Gates's army appeared. She describes their condition:

"On the following morning the cannonade again began, but from a different side. I advised all to go out of the cellar for a little while, during which time I would have it cleaned, as otherwise we would all be sick. They followed my suggestion, and I at once set many hands to work, which was in the highest degree necessary; for the women and children being afraid to venture forth had soiled the whole cellar.

"I had just given the cellars a good sweeping and had fumigated them by sprinkling vinegar on burning coals and each one had found his place prepared for him, when a fresh and terrible cannonade threw us all once more into alarm. Many persons, who had no right to come in, threw themselves against the door. My children were already under the cellar steps and we would all have been crushed if God had not given me strength to place myself before the door and with extended arms prevent all from coming in .... Eleven cannon balls went through the house and we could plainly hear them rolling over our heads."

She spent six awful days in her shelter, in which she nursed the wounded, comforted the dying, cheered the anxious wives, and cared for her own children. One of these anxious wives was Lady Harriet Acland, whom the baroness convinced to leave the British camp and join her husband behind the enemy lines to take care of him. Burgoyne was astounded when Lady Acland asked for passage. He later wrote,

> "After so long an agitation of the spirits, not only exhausted by want of rest but absolutely want of food, and drenched in rains for twelve hours together, that a woman should be capable of such an undertaking as delivering herself to the enemy, probably in the night, and uncertain of what hands she might first fall into, appeared an effort above human nature."

But she did go—setting off on the Hudson River in the dark of night in a boat, accompanied by the Reverend Brudenell, her maidservant, and her husband's wounded valet.

Sometime between midnight and 1:00 A.M. the sentinels alerted Henry Dearborn that two boats were coming down the river. The rain was pouring down in a torrent. The approaching boats were beating a parley on a drum. Dearborn hailed them to ask who they were. "A flag of truce from General Burgoyne," came the reply, and Dearborn allowed them to come ashore. They handed him an unsealed note addressed to General Gates and signed by General Burgoyne. Dearborn read the note,

> "Lady Harriet Ackland, a lady of the first distinction by family rank, and personal virtue" was so concerned about her husband that he was entrusting her to Gates's care so that she might join the major. He invited the very pregnant lady to go to his house and stay until morning. He further informed her that her husband's wounds were not serious. Dearborn had the fire lit for her, her baggage brought in, and she remained in bed until morning, when one of Gates's aides and Dr. Brown arrived to take her to headquarters. Gates promised the Aclands safe passage to Albany and New York after Acland recuperated. They arrived in New York on 2 Jan 1778, and from there, I suppose, they returned to their estates in Somerset and Devonshire, England—the home of our TUCKER ancestors. Many of their enlisted soldiers, perhaps some of our English relatives or friends from those counties, would not be as fortunate."

Back in the British camp, Brigadier Specht commented,

> "'The rain fell until midnight, afterwards, a cold wind arose; it started to

freeze hard. Our men, who had to camp in the open, spent a very bad night.' The Baroness Riedesel was soaked to the skin and lying on some straw with her children when General Phillips came up. 'Why don't we retreat while there is still time?' she asked, and added that her husband was prepared to cover the retreat and see everyone to safety."

He told her that he admired her fortitude; but Burgoyne was too tired, and wanted to spend the night there and give the generals a supper. According to her journal, it was quite a carousing occasion and Burgoyne was certainly in no mood to proceed until he knew what the rebels were up to near Fort Edward.

The artillery barrages were increasing in intensity, the batteaus were under constant attack, and every day brought more skirmishes. On the night of the 11th an entire picket guard of Germans, except for their officer, a sergeant, and the drummer, left their posts and went over to the rebels. At 10 o'clock on the night of the 12th, General Riedesel sent a message to Burgoyne requesting marching orders. To his dismay, the reply only postponed the retreat. They were then surrounded on three sides by the rebels. In the morning they were completely surrounded. By 13 October the Americans had taken 120 prisoners and received 160 deserters, and all the while

> "numerous parties of American militia . . . swarmed around . . . like birds of prey," British Sergeant Lamb complained that the "Roaring of cannon and whistling of bullets from their rifle pieces were heard constantly by day and night."

One of the officers participating on the American side was MORGAN LEWIS, who was born 16 Oct 1754, the son of Francis Lewis, a signer of the Declaration of Independence. On 11 May 1779, he would marry GERTRUDE LIVINGSTON, another sister of Chancellor ROBERT R. LIVINGSTON.

[Note: His short history states that he was prominent in the Revolution, especially at the surrender of General Burgoyne at Schuylerville, N.Y., [Saratoga] as well as Chief Justice of the N.Y. Supreme Court; Governor or New York, 1804-07, and that he was a Major General—although that was undoubtedly not the case in 1777, unless he was a New York militia general. He died 7 Apr 1844.]

That afternoon of the 13th at 3 o'clock, Burgoyne summoned all the generals and regimental commanders for a "solemn council of war." He announced to them that in his opinion it was impossible to attack the rebels or sweep around them to Albany. He added, that even if they could defeat the Americans, they hadn't enough food even to reach Fort Edward. The only possibility of escape in his opinion was for each man to make his own way individually to Ticonderoga.

General Phillips came out strong against this suggestion. He felt it was all very well for a few Indians or frontiersmen; but it was absurd to think that four or five thousand men could accomplish it on their own. Hunger, misery, attack by rebel forces, the onset of rainy weather—there were a dozen reasons it could not be contemplated. It would result in chaos. Even now the army's right and center was untenable should the enemy attack. They had supplies for only five days, and when they were gone, it would be even worse.

Burgoyne then asked them three questions: one—in the history of war had any armies in their situation surrendered? Yes! was the unanimous reply; two—was it dishonorable to capitulate in their situation? This brought a negative answer; three—was this army in such a fix that surrender was necessary? This question took more discussion; but in the end, Burgoyne produced a surrender document, saying if his terms proved acceptable to Gates, a capitulation would "save the army for the King, who could then use it for other purposes."

Whereupon it was agreed that surrender was the only way out, and a drummer, Major Griffith Williams' fifteen-year-old nephew, George Williams, was sent to Gates's lines with a message that General Burgoyne wished to have one of his field officers discuss "a matter of high moment" the next day. If acceptable, a truce would be in effect meanwhile. Gates agreed, and the shelling ended. Madame Riedesel wrote:

> "they spoke of capitulating, as by temporizing for so long . . . our retreat had been cut off. A cessation of hostilities took place, and my husband, who was thoroughly worn out, was able for the first time in a long while to lie down upon a bed."

Young George Williams is reputed to be the last survivor of the battle. He died in 1850 at the age of eighty-eight years.

JOHN PETERS, who had commanded the Queen's Loyal Rangers and had fought in every action but Hubbardton, spoke to General Phillips prior to the surrender and was asked why he was still there; why hadn't he gone north?

PETERS replied sensibly that he wasn't leaving without orders to do so, for fear of being accused of desertion by the British. He got his orders, and with about thirty-five of his men he made a scary escape through the rebel-infested woods, and they were able to make their way across the country to Lake George and then go by boat to Montreal and Quebec. On 8 November, British General Powell evacuated Fort Ticonderoga and Mount Independence, and by December the Hudson\Champlain waterway from New York to Canada was clear of all enemy troops.

At 10:00 on the morning of the fourteenth of October, Major Kingston, Burgoyne's adjutant general, met with Gates's aide, Colonel JAMES WILKINSON, who tried to blindfold him. He protested, then finally consented, if they used his own handkerchief. He was then conducted the final mile to Gates' headquarters.

86

THE DIFFICULT SURRENDER OF
A PROUD GENERAL

The morning of 12 October, Gates wrote a letter to John Hanock, president of Congress, to report "the great Success of the Arms of the United States in this Department" on 7 October 1777. He detailed the cannon, arms and ammunition, and baggage taken in the "very warm and bloody" battle. He listed the principal enemy officers captured—the artillerist Major Williams, Major Acland, and Burgoyne's aide Clerke. Simon Fraser, leading the "Flying Army" of the enemy, had been killed. He mentioned that desertion "has taken a deep Root in the Royal army, particularly among the Germans who come to us in Shoals." His own wounded included "the Gallant Major General Arnold," and then he praised the performance of MORGAN's riflemen and Dearborn's light infantry as key factors in the victory. Strangely, he never sent any report to George Washington. It has been speculated by some historians that Gates could now praise Arnold, since his wound placed him out of any immediate competitive position, and that Gates was becoming more open and serious in his attempts to undermine George Washington.

When the blindfolded British deputy adjutant general arrived in Gates's tent on the 14th and the blindfold was removed, Kingston said,

"General Gates, your servant."

"Ah, Kingston, how do you do?" was the amiable reply.

Kingston then read from a paper the proposals from Burgoyne, who reminded Gates that he was prepared to meet him a third time, but now—aware of the rebels' superiority in numbers and the disposition of those troops—he felt justified "to spare the lives of brave men upon honorable terms." If Gates concurred, he proposed a cessation of the fighting while they discussed preliminary terms.

Then, to the amazement of both Kingston and WILKINSON, Gates reached in his pocket and produced a paper with the conditions to which Burgoyne must agree. Basically, the terms were unconditional surrender, which began with some humiliating remarks about the condition of the British army and ended with the demand that the troops must ground arms in their camp and march out as prisoners. The truce was to last until sunset, before which time Burgoyne must reply. As the blindfolded Kingston was led back by WILKINSON, he boasted of the proud record of their army and decried the insult of the terms demanded.

Burgoyne called his officers to a second council. They unanimously agreed

"that they would rather die than accept such dishonorable conditions." There was no way that they would ground arms in their camp and surrender as prisoners of war. "If General Gates does not mean to recede from the first and sixth articles of his proposal, the treaty [is] to end and hostilities immediately to commence."

At sunset Kingston was sent back with Burgoyne's own terms; to march out of camp with the honors of war and ground arms at the bank of the Hudson at command of their own officers. The officers would retain their swords and equipment, the soldiers their knapsacks; and the army was to march to Boston, where they would be properly fed and sheltered before embarking for England. The only condition imposed was that they were not to serve in North America again during the present war. The Canadians were to be allowed to return home, and non-combatants were to be treated as British citizens, plus many other minor provisions favoring the British.

To the astonishment of all, Gates signed the proposal only adding that

"This capitulation to be finished by two o'clock this day and the troops march from their encampments at five."

It seems that while he had waited for Burgoyne's reply to his demands, a letter had arrived at his headquarters telling him of Sir Henry Clinton's success at the Highland forts and his advance with a fleet of twenty sails heading for Esopus (by Kingston). It did not tell him the number of troops, or that Clinton had presently returned to New York. The rapid signing and the speed demanded in the surrender made Burgoyne suspicious, and he asked for a postponement, which Gates granted. Once again, he felt that Sir Henry Clinton would come to his rescue, and he stalled. It was not until 19 September, with the unanimous demands of his officers and a demand by Gates that they comply within ten minutes, that Burgoyne finally signed the surrender document.

The next morning, Burgoyne dressed with care, putting on his gorgeous scarlet coat with shining gold braid and a hat fitted with plumes—a uniform he had kept spotless for his planned triumphal entry into Albany and all the glorious honors of the victorious. He must shortly visit with all his officers. It was difficult to hold back his tears, and at times, he stopped speaking to regain control of his voice, as he explained his reasons for the surrender and the lack of any of the help that had been promised. Not far away, the Baron Riedesel was assuring his own men that the surrender was no fault of theirs or of their lack of courage. He collected all their regimental flags and later gave them to the Baroness, who sewed them inside a pillow to be taken secretly back to Brunswick.

It was 10:00 o'clock—the time to go. Sergeants shouted orders; ranks were closed, shuffled and closed again. The troops stood at attention as company and regimental officers inspected their ranks. It was a final parade for Burgoyne's army, who in spite of everything that had happened were fond of their general. Sergeant Lamb observed:

> "He possessed the confidence and affection of his army in an extraordinary degree, that no loss or misfortune could shake . . . not a voice was heard throughout the army to upbraid, to censure or blame their general."

British William Digby of Balcarres's light infantry was much depressed, but he had enough respect for the enemy that his journal entry for that day had an extra-large heading: "A day famous in the annals of America." Yet he noted that the regimental drums lost the magic to excite him, while the grenadiers' march "seemed . . . as if almost ashamed to be heard on such an occasion . . . . Tears filled his eyes."

JAMES WILKINSON arrived to escort the general with his troops. As they approached the big field next to the Hudson River, Burgoyne asked if the river was fordable here. WILKINSON wondered if he still might have plans of escaping and said that it was, "but do you observe the people on the opposite shore?"

"Yes," was the sad answer. "I have seen them too long."

They forded Fish Creek, swollen with the heavy rain, and rode past the blackened remains of PHILIP SCHUYLER's house and outbuildings, then on toward Gates's headquarters about a half-mile away.

In the American camp a chaplain had delivered a Thanksgiving sermon. He had taken his text from the prophet Joel:

> *"But I will remove far off from you the northern army,*
> *and will drive him into a land barren and desolate*
> *with his face toward the east sea."*

Protocol called for young WILKINSON to introduce the two generals; but they were previously acquainted. Thirty years before in England the two lieutenants appeared on the roster of the regiment they were joining as numbers 15 and 16. Gates was the son of a boatman on the Thames and had become disillusioned about his advancement in a world where family and connection were so very important. He had sailed for America to begin a new life. WILKINSON described their meeting,

> "General Gates, advised of Burgoyne's approach, met him at the head of his camp, Burgoyne in a rich royal uniform, and Gates in a plain blue frock. When they had approached nearly within sword's length, they reined up, and halted. I then named the gentlemen, and General Burgoyne, raising his hat most gracefully, said, 'The fortune of war, General Gates, has made me your prisoner,' to which the conqueror, returning a courtly salute, promptly replied, 'I shall always be ready to bear testimony, that it has not been through any fault of your excellency.' Major General Phillips then advanced, and he and General Gates saluted, and shook hands with the familiarity of old acquaintances. The Baron Riedesel and the other officers were introduced in their turn."

As the British army filed into the field, the two generals stood by and watched; then the two faced each other, and without a word, Burgoyne drew his sword and handed it to Gates, who received it with a bow and promptly returned it to its owner. It was now time for the men in the ranks to meet. They had laid down their military arms, and with fife and drums beating they paraded past the American troops that lined each side of the road.

A German officer described the rebels,

"not a one of them was regularly equipped. Each one had on the clothes which he was accustomed to wear in the field, in the tavern, the church, and in everyday life . . . they stood in an erect and a soldierly attitude. All their muskets had bayonets attached to them, and their riflemen had rifles."

Another commented,

"We were utterly astounded, not one of them made any attempt to speak to the man at his side . . . [they were] so slender, fine-looking, and sinewy, that it was a pleasure to look at them." He was awed "that Dame Nature had created such a handsome race!"

In Europe the Prussian army required that a man be at least five feet tall to be accepted in the military, the average probably about five-foot-five. The majority of these Americans were five-eight to five-ten, and a number were taller still—"far ahead of those in the greater portion of Europe." Almost all carried pouches and powder horns slung over their shoulders and stood, right hand on their musket, the left hanging by their side, with their right foot placed slightly forward.

But what most impressed the defeated soldiers in Burgoyne's ranks was that

"not a single man gave any evidence or the slightest impression of feeling hatred, mockery, malicious pleasure or pride for our miserable fate . . . . [On the contrary] it seemed rather as though they desired to do us honor."

Lord Francis Napier was to write,

"They behaved with the greatest decency and propriety, not even a Smile appearing in any of their Countenances, which circumstance I really believe would not have happened had the case been reversed."

An American newspaper reported:

"General Gates invited General Burgoyne and the other principal officers to dine with him. The table was only two planks laid across two empty beef barrels. There were only four plates for the whole company. There was no cloth, and the dinner consisted of a ham, a goose, some beef, and some boiled mutton. The liquor was New England rum, mixed with water, without sugar; and only two glasses, which were for the two Commanders-in-Chief; the rest of the company drank out of basins. The officer remarked, 'The men that can live thus, may be brought to beat all the world.'"

"After dinner, General Gates called upon General Burgoyne for his toast, which embarrassed General Burgoyne a good deal; at length, he gave 'General Washington;' General Gates, in return, gave 'the King.'"

The British General was convivial and complimented his former foe by saying that he envied him his inexhaustible supply of men; "like the Hydra's head, when cut off, seven more spring up in its stead."

The Baroness von Riedesel had fearfully waited, not knowing the fate of her children and herself. At length a messenger arrived from her husband asking her and the children to join him in the American camp. Upon arrival, she was thankful to find—in contrast with her experience in London—that

"nobody glanced at us insultingly, that they all bowed to me, and some of them even looked with pity to see a woman with small children there."

When she reached the officers tent, a handsome man approached her carriage, lifted out her three daughters and kissed them, then helped her step down, saying,

"You are trembling. Don't be afraid,"

He led her to the dinner party, where she found her husband and saw Burgoyne and Phillips chatting genially with Gates. Burgoyne came over and reassured her, telling her that her suffering had now come to an end. When she observed that they were about to eat, she was uncomfortable, because there was no place for her or her children. But just then, the man who had first welcomed her and escorted her to the dinner approached her and said kindly,

"It would embarrass you to take dinner with all these gentlemen; come to my tent with your children and although I can only give you a frugal meal, it will be given gladly."

The frugal meal delighted her. It consisted of a delicious smoked tongue, beefsteaks, potatoes, and good bread and butter; and she wrote that nothing had tasted better. Her gracious host turned out to be none other than Major General PHILIP SCHUYLER, who had not been able to resist being present at a surrender he had worked so hard to obtain.

After they had eaten, SCHUYLER invited her with her children to stay at his home in Albany, as their guest. The baron told her to accept the invitation and they were soon on their way. When SCHUYLER met Burgoyne, the general expressed his regret at the destruction of his property, to which the former told him to think no more about it; that it was "the fate of war."

As the sun was setting, the Generals Burgoyne, Phillips, and Riedesel rode off toward Stillwater, escorted by some well dressed Connecticut dragoons. With the group was SCHUYLER's aide, Richard Varick, who had received orders to find for Burgoyne "better quarters than a stranger might be able to find." And so he did, as the general entered a "very elegant house," he was astonished to be greeted by CATHERINE RENSSELAER SCHUYLER, the wife of the Major General, and her family. She was later to say that Burgoyne was not eager to leave the SCHUYLER home. Instead of going at once to Boston he stayed with his hosts for five days—a difficult time, since his presence created "a great deal of trouble with her servants."

If the captured general presented an irritant to the servants, it might have been related to the fact that it was while he was abiding at the home of his former combatant, he was obliged to write his report of his entire Canadian campaign to parliament and the king. However he might write this letter, it would not be received with the hoped for adoration he had dreamed of, or even with a hint of forgiveness. He knew his actions would be closely scrutinized by the Germans, his own officers and men, as well as the London nobility and their courts. The letter must be written in such a way as to place the blame on their lack of support. He began by reminding them of the rigors of the march, the defection of the Indians, the desertion or timidity of the Canadians, and the failure of "other armies" to cooperate. His force had been reduced to 3,500, of whom less than 2,000 were British. They were surrounded by 16,000 rebels and had provisions for only three days. When the British army crossed the Hudson, "the peremptory tenor of my orders and season of the year admitted no alternative." He reminded them of his victory at Ticonderoga and their victorious advance and then concluded by stating that it was now up to His Majesty George III, his fellow officers, the public (especially the "respectable parts of my country") to decide whether he was to be praised or condemned.

It would be 2 Dec 1777, that London received their first official news. It came from Carleton in Quebec, who told of "the total annihilation . . . of Burgoyne's army," and Walpole stated, the king "fell into agonies on hearing this account, but the next morning, at his levee to disguise his concern, affected to laugh and be so indecently merry that Lord North endeavoured to stop him."

Francis Rush Clark, declared that Howe was to blame—his measures "have cost Great Britain America."

Burgoyne's friend Charles James Fox rose and spoke in the House of Commons to attack Lord George Germain calling him

"an ill-omened and inauspicious character . . . unfit to serve the Crown."

But the British nation was not the only European nation that was waiting for the results across the Atlantic Ocean. Jonathan Loring Austin, a prominent merchant and the owner of a privateer, boarded a fast sailing packet ship in Boston harbor on 31 October. He was carrying dispatches with the official word of Burgoyne's surrender. His destination was to be the official court of Benjamin Franklin at Passy, France. The local parson, who was to give him the assurance of a successful voyage, made it clear in his prayer that whatever the Lord chose to do with the messenger, he might at least see that those important papers reached their destination. An unguaranteed Austin arrived safely on the shore of Nantes and galloped off toward Paris. He arrived with his dispatches at Passy around noon on 4 December.

The commissioners who had heard rumors of his approach awaited his arrival. Before he could dismount Benjamin Franklin asked,

"Is Philadelphia taken?" To which he replied,

"Yes, sir."

Franklin clasped his hands as if he had heard of a death in the family and turned to go inside. Austin was quick to add,

"But sir, I have greater news than that. GENERAL BURGOYNE and his whole army are prisoners of war!"

Austin described the effect as "electric."

The commissioners were later to report to the United States Continental Congress that the news

"occasioned as much general Joy in France as if it had been a Victory of their own troops over their own Enemies."

One of the joyous Frenchmen was Caron de Beaumarchais, the agent who had been channeling French arms and money to the rebels through the dummy corporation of Hortalez & Cie. He was so excited to get to Paris with the news that his carriage was overturned and his arm injured. It has been said that part of his rush was to use this "inside information" for his own advantage, before it became public knowledge. It is also said that an important British spy with his own speculative purposes dashed off to London for this same reason.

When the news became generally known, everyone in France from Louis XVI on down openly rejoiced that an entire army of their enemy George III had been forced to surrender to his much despised rebels. France spoke quickly of an alliance with the United States with official recognition of this new nation. His Majesty Louis XVI sent his foreign minister with a communique to Passy on 17 December that he

> "was determined to acknowledge our Independence and make a Treaty with us of Amity and Commerce." He also promised to support America's insurrection and its independence "by every means in his power."

On 6 February the treaty was signed at the foreign ministry; but the actual ceremonial day of triumph for the three commissioners that had worked so hard for it was on 20 Mar 1778—one week after Britain and France were officially at war. On that day, the three commissioners, Arthur Lee, Silas Deane, and Benjamin Franklin, were to be presented in a grand gala affair to the king of France. They were to arrive first at the apartment of Vergennes, where a large crowd awaited their arrival. Lee and Deane arrived according to protocol wearing the prescribed formal dress. Benjamin Franklin, true to his character and knowing the effect it would make in this vain-glorious setting, arrived without wig nor sword, only a plain brown velvet suit with white stockings. His white hat was under one arm, his hair hung loose and his spectacles were perched on his nose. The courtiers generally agreed that nothing they had seen was so dramatic as the republican simplicity they witnessed that day.

> Louis XVI welcomed them cordially and with unusual care and grace stated,

> "Firmly assure Congress of my friendship. I hope that this will be for the good of the two countries."

Franklin replied,

"Your Majesty may count on the gratitude of Congress and its faithful observance of the pledges it now makes."

While Spain refused to join the alliance, they furnished secret subsidies to the Americans via Hortalez & Cie. It did not declare war on Britain until 1779. In Prussia, the Grand Duke of Tuscany declared in favor of the Americans, and persuaded the King of Prussia not to permit the German troops bound for America to cross his kingdom.

Ralph Izard, a wealthy South Carolinian in Paris observed in his report to the Congressional Foreign Affairs Committee that

"one successful battle will gain us more friends & do our business more effectually than all the skill of the ablest Negotiators."

The defeated Burgoyne, after his five day stay at the SCHUYLERs, joined his army as they trudged the long miles to Boston. Hannah Winthrop, a local resident of Cambridge, described their November arrival in a letter to her friend Mercy Warren:

"Last Thursday, which was a very stormy day, a large number of British troops came softly through the town via Watertown to Prospect Hill. On Friday we heard the Hessians were to make a procession in the same route. We thought we should have nothing to do with them, but view them as they passed. To be sure, the sight was truly astonishing. I never had the least idea that the Creation produced such a sordid set of creatures in human figure—poor, dirty, emaciated men, great numbers of women, who seemed to be the beasts of burden, having a bushel basket on their back, by which they were bent double; the contents seemed to be pots and kettles, various sorts of furniture, children peeping through gridirons and other utensils, some very young infants who were born on the road, the women bare feet, clothed in dirty rags; such effluvia filled the air . . . had not they been smoking all the time, I should have been apprehensive of being contaminated by them.

"After a noble looking advanced guard, General J[ohnny] B[urgoyne] headed this terrible group on horseback. The other G[enerals] also, clothed in blue cloaks. Hessians, Amspachers. Brunswickers . . . followed on. The Hessian G gave us a polite bow as they passed. Not so the British. Their baggage wagons [were] drawn by poor, half-starved horses. But to bring up the rear, another fine, noble-looking guard of American brawny, victorious yeomanry, who assisted in bringing these sons of slavery to terms;

some of our wagons drawn by fat oxen, driven by joyous-looking Yankees closed the cavalcade.

"How mortifying is it? They in a manner demanding our houses and colleges for their genteel accommodation. Did the brave G[eneral] Gates ever mean this? . . . Is there not a degree of unkindness in loading poor Cambridge, almost ruined before this great army seem[ed] to be let loose upon us . . . . It is said we shall have not less than seven thousand persons to feed in Cambridge and its environs, more than its inhabitants. Two hundred and fifty cord of wood will not serve them a week. Think then how we must be distressed . . . . I never thought I could lie down to sleep surrounded by these enemies. But we strangely become enured to those things which appear difficult when distant."

When word of the surrender finally reached General Washington on 18 October—by a courier from Albany, not from Gates, he was unhappy with the terms of surrender. He pointed out that even though the same soldiers never returned to America, they would replace others that would. But Washington was not in charge, Congress was—however, they agreed. They listened to the complaints from the people of Boston; the insulting complaints from Burgoyne that his officers were not given the accommodations they had agreed upon; a series of other complaints, and they delayed ratifying the document. Finally in 1779 the prisoners were marched from Boston to Charlottesville, Virginia. Thomas Jefferson, living nearby, wrote,

"I cannot help feeling a most thorough mortification that our Congress should have permitted an infraction of our public honor."

Part of his mortification might have been that his Virginians didn't want that many prisoners of war in their homes, either.

Burgoyne with his staff officers had returned to London nine months earlier—still technically a prisoner of war on parole until he was exchanged officially for over 1,000 American prisoners that were held by the British. In London, he was elected by the opposition to the House of Commons, but his military career was ended.

The bibliography for Part III: *Rebellion*
can be found at the end of Part IV: *United States ?*

~ Index for Part III ~
Rebellion

[Note: Maiden names are used for women, if known.]

Part IV

UNITED STATES ?

Brookie Condie Swallow

Contents

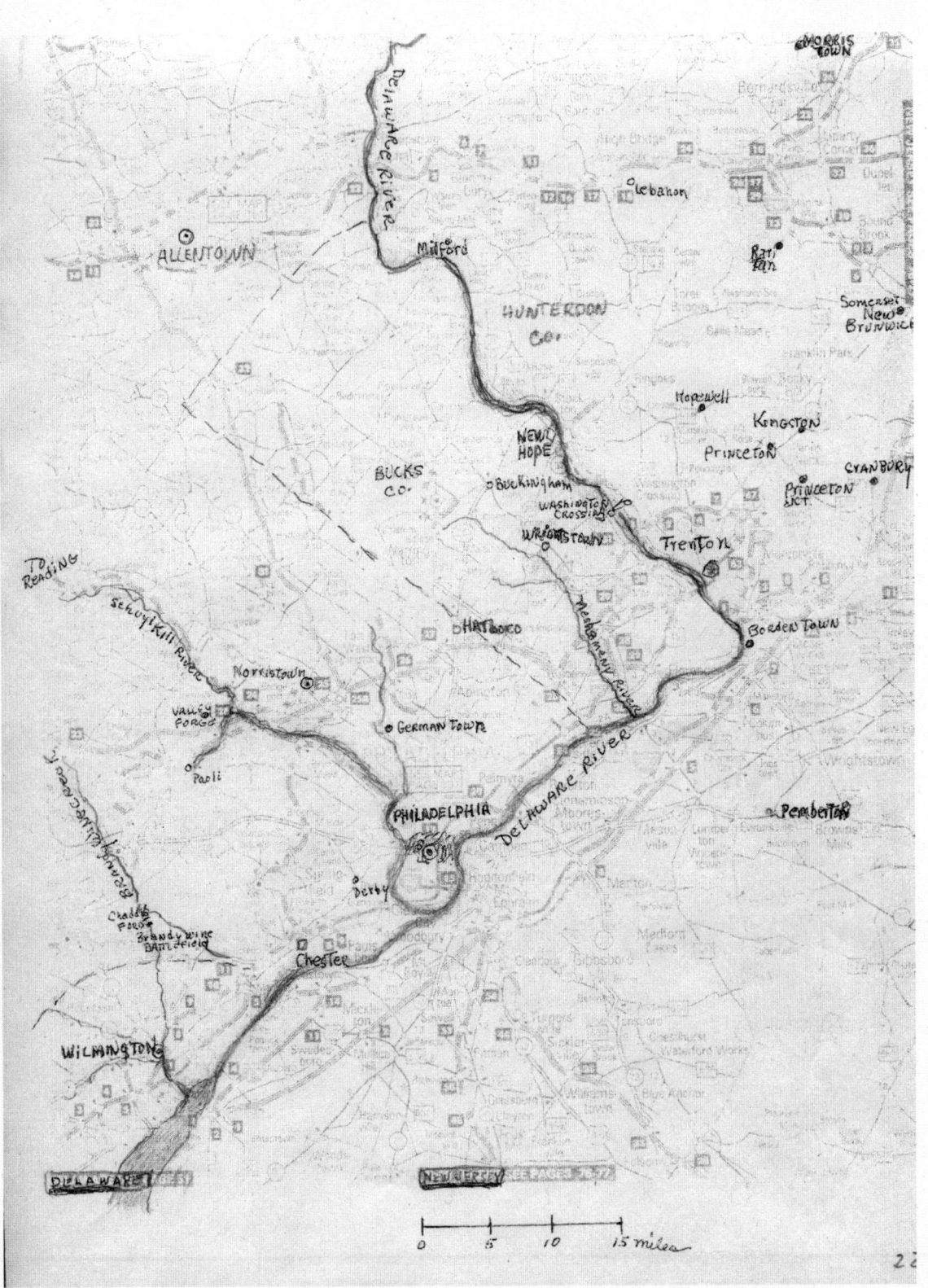

DELAWARE RIVER

ALLENTOWN

Milford

HUNTERDON CO.

MORRIS TOWN

Lebanon

Rari tan

Somerset New Brunswick

Hopewell

Kingston

Princeton

CRANBURY

NEW HOPE

BUCKS CO.

Buckingham

Washington Crossing

Wrightstown

Princeton JCT.

Trenton

TO READING

Schuylkill River

Neshameny River

Borden Town

Norristown

HATBORO

VALLEY FORGE

German Town

Brandywine River

Paoli

Philadelphia

Delaware River

Darby

Pemberton

Chadds Ford

Brandywine BATTLEFIELD

Chester

WILMINGTON

DELAWARE SEE

NEW JERSEY SEE PAGES 74-77

0   5   10   15 miles

2

87

THE PHILADELPHIA STORY

Thadeusz Kosciuszko, the impoverished son of Polish gentry, fled his homeland after he tried to elope with the daughter of a French nobleman who ordered his arrest. He escaped to Paris where he studied at the French royal military academy, Ecole Millitaire, and at the royal artillery and engineering school at Mezieres—specializing in river and harbor defense. Here he was taught the techniques of the great seventeenth-century French engineer Vauban. He arrived in Philadelphia in 1776 as a volunteer military engineer. Congress commissioned him as a colonel of engineers for the Northern Department; but before he could ride north, Benjamin Franklin, who at that time was in charge of the defense of Pennsylvania, commandeered the talents of the young engineering genius. Together they planned an elaborate network that was supposed to impede a British naval attack on Philadelphia. More than 5,000 men from the area, or about one out of five Philadelphians, including many freed blacks, joined in this project. It began in the summer of 1776 and lasted until Howe's British attack came through Maryland in October of 1777. However, prior to October, as was mentioned previously, Kosciuszko was taken north by General Gates to plan his river fortifications at Bemis Heights.

On the New Jersey side, just opposite our present-day site of Philadelphia International Airport, they laid out two forts on the marshy banks of the Delaware

River—Fort Billings and the higher Fort Mercer (named after the brave Hugh Mercer, who had been killed in the battle at Princeton). Across the mile wide river from Fort Mercer on the Pennsylvania side was Fort Mifflin. This highly fortified area, which included both land and highly sophisticated river barriers, had been considered sufficiently ominous that Howe had bypassed the Delaware River and gone further south to the Chesapeake to make his sea approach to the capital city. The work of building and manning these forts had been left more to the partisan militia of both New Jersey and Pennsylvania, which included older male citizens, freeing the younger men for the major battles. Many of our PRESTON, WILKINSON, BARTON, VAN KIRK, COOLEY, CANBY, LACEY, LIPPINCOTT and JARVIS relations were undoubtedly among them, and also contributed heavily to their financial support.

To these forts, Washington sent Colonel CHRISTOPHER GREENE, a tough Rhode Islander, probably related to the GREENE side of our RUFUS BARTON relations and a descendant of the original Thomas Greene that came with Roger Williams over a century before. The colonel was given two companies of Rhode Island Continentals, mostly blacks who had been promised their freedom—if they survived the war.

The British needed this part of the Delaware River to allow the world's finest navy to support their vast occupational army. On 11 October, one week after the battle of Germantown, Lord Howe and Cornwallis began their land-sea attack. Two thousand of Cornwallis' best regulars encircled Fort Billings, which was down river—the weakest of the three forts. It was garrisoned with only 250 men and six cannon, all of which faced the river and were quite useless against the land attack. During the night the New Jersey militia garrison spiked the guns so the enemy could not use them. They blew up the bakehouse, barracks, and stockade before retreating to Fort Mercer, where the Pennsylvania Navy had stationed galleys with 18-pound cannon at the foot of the bluffs.

Howe then ordered a land attack on Fort Mercer. Cornwallis entrusted this attack to Count Karl Emil von Donop, the British (Hessian) commander who was defeated at Princeton. He was given three battalions of Hessians and 1,000 redcoats. They ferried across the Delaware and marched to Deptford to rest for the night. Seeing the arrival of this army, a fleet-footed American, Jonas Cattell, ran the nine miles from Deptford to Fort Mercer to warn Colonel CHRISTOPHER GREENE, who was expecting an attack by water. That night the mostly black garrison, joined by the 250 New Jersey militia from Fort Billings, heaved and pushed the great guns around to the land side—and prepared their trap. Colonel GREENE placed sharpshooters in the outer works and backed them with two heavy guns placed inside the double embarkment with fallen trees and brush in front of them—double-loaded with grapeshot and canister.

Around noon on 22 October, the Hessians marched down the Deptford Road with drums beating and bugles blaring. They fanned out and formed a cordon that extended from the swamp to the plain south of the fort. Von Donop proudly dismounted his brown stallion and, handing the reins to an aide, told him to carry this message to GREENE.

> "The King of England orders his rebellious subjects to lay down their arms, and they are warned that if they stand the battle, no quarters whatsoever will be given."

GREENE yelled back his reply,

> "We'll see King George damned first. We want no quarters and we'll give none."

Von Donop then ordered simultaneous attacks against both the north and south walls. From the south the Hessians axed through the abatis and then bayoneted their way through a small line of skirmishers in the south ditch, in spite of the heavy, well-aimed musket fire from the black garrison inside. They then charged the walls, where a few made it to the top before they were shot down.

On the north side the American trap was set. At the first volley, the American skirmishers fired and then dropped back. Charging and huzzahing loudly, the Hessians ran though the breastworks and into the outer fort, then on toward the tall north wall of the fort. Then the trap sprang. Yanking away trees and brush, the hidden gun crews fired again and again. This was followed by the fort cannons and the shrewd crossfire from the marksmen on the parapets. Shot at close range, von Donop staggered and fell along with scores of his troops and fifteen other officers. From below, the river gunboats fired against the Hessians attempting to climb the west wall, on the river side. They mowed down the German grenadiers.

In fifteen minutes, the battle was over. The surviving Hessians ran back to the woods, throwing their cannon in the creek, and then, pausing only to make stretchers for their wounded officers, they fled back to Woodbury. They left 414 dead and dying on the field, in the ditches, and within the fort. Von Donop was carried by the Americans to the Whitall house nearby, where he died slowly and painfully. He told the young French engineer, Chevalier Mauduit, who had planned the trap,

> "I am content. I die in the hands of honor itself. It is finishing a noble career early, but I die the victim of my own ambition and the avarice of my sovereign."

Only twenty-four Americans had been killed or wounded, nineteen of them when a cannon was carelessly swabbed by its crew and exploded while being fired.

To support von Donop's land attack, Sir William Howe had ordered six men-of-war to maneuver through the heavily tree-spiked river barrier to the south. Here they dueled all day with the Pennsylvania Navy's 75-foot heavily armed row galleys. Toward evening, the British squadron opened up a two-hour broadside bombardment of Fort Mercer. Between them and the New Jersey shore was a narrow channel. When the British commander, Captain Francis Reynolds, aboard the 64-gun flagship *Augusta*, ordered two ships up the channel to prevent the highly maneuverable Pennsylvania galleys from reinforcing Fort Mercer, high winds broke loose, and the British vessels were unable to go forward, or even backwards. That night the *Augusta* and the sloop-of-war *Merlin* were swept aground. At dawn, the remaining men-of-war and their longboats tried to free the grounded ships under the fire of the Pennsylvania Navy and the gunners of Forts Mercer and Mifflin. Half the redcoats aboard the vessels were killed. An American cannonball struck the *Augusta*'s powder magazine, and Captain Francis Reynolds and his crew jumped into the river. It was noon when the *Augusta* blew up.

Washington could hear the blast at Whitemarsh and most of the windows were shattered in Philadelphia, three miles away. Tom Paine, at Washington's side, recorded a "report as loud as a peal of one hundred cannon at once." Thick smoke rose "like a pillar" and spread "from the top like a tree."

British General Howe ordered the Merlin scuttled.

The third fort, Fort Mifflin, on the Pennsylvania side of the Delaware River, had been built five years earlier by the British, under the command of Captain Joh Montresor, a Swiss-born military engineer. He had retired from the army and was living in New York City when the Revolution began. It was he who had planted the false maps of his exploration of the Maine backwoods on Benedict Arnold. He had also paid loyalists to retrieve the head of the equestrian statue of King George III, which the Americans had displayed on a spike outside a Bronx tavern, and had arranged to send it back to London to show Parliament the depth of the defiance of the American colonists against their King. Lord Howe decided to lay siege to this fort that had pounded on his navy for over a month with its 18-pounders and commanded Montresor to destroy this fort he had labored so hard to build. The forty-day siege began on 10 October—the same day the British had marched on Fort Billings down the river.

Montresor protected his cannon with earthworks, which he continued to build closer and closer to the fort, and proceeded to reduce the fort with fierce cannonades. British troops stormed the American positions on the two marshy islands adjoining the fort. This was unfortunate for the Americans as it stopped Kosciuszko's plan of defense, which was to break holes in the dikes along the river and flood the low-lying land—making the fort an island.

Fort Mifflin was commanded by the Marylander, Colonel Samuel Smith, and a French artillerist-engineer, Major Andre de Fleury, who wrote regularly in his journal. At first they were very confident and at night over a thousand men would be rotated across the river between Fort Mifflin and Fort Mercer. Colonel Smith was wounded, and they rowed him across to Fort Mercer. After 10 November, the cannonade became so heavy that the men couldn't sleep. If they went into their shattered barracks, it was death from the bombs that hit with regularity. Most could only doze minutes at a time sitting upright against the walls. Fleury wrote in his journal:

> "At 2 o'clock: The direction of the fire is changed—our palisades suffer—a dozen of them are broke down.
> "Eleven at night: The enemy keep up firing every half hour. General Varnum [now at Fort Mercer] promised us fascines [buckets filled with earth] and palisades [the spiked poles] but they are not arrived and they are absolutely necessary.

"Nov. 14: Daylight discovers us a floating battery of the enemy, placed a little above their grand battery and near the shore . . . . The fire of the enemy will never take the fort. It may kill us men but this is the fortune of war, and all their bullets will never render them master of this island . . . . We must have men to defend the ruins of the fort. Our ruins will serve us as breastworks. We will defend the ground inch by inch, and the enemy shall pay dearly for every step."

That night at high tide, the British "floating battery" was towed to within forty yards of the fort. It included the *Vigilant,* which had its masts sawed off to make it lighter, armed with four 24-pounders; next was the light sloop-of-war *Fury,* armed with six 18-pounders with its rigging crowded with Royal Marine sharpshooters. They bombarded the weak west side of Fort Mifflin, while some of the British fleet sailed up the river to the barriers. This included the 64-gun *Somerset,* along with the *Isis, Roebuck, Pearl,* and *Liverpool,* which commenced a barrage into the flattened remains of the fort. After four broadsides from the *Vigilant,* Fort Mifflin's remaining parapets and gun carriages were smashed. Their guns were broken to bits and the gun platforms totally destroyed. Every twenty minutes, another thousand shots smashed into the dilapidated remains in one of the heaviest bombardments in American history. The Americans lowered the Stars and Stripes to send up a blue flag of distress, while the enemy cheered loudly. This was not surrender, but a call for help.

That night, when the bombardment stopped, the Americans were out of large guns, their ammunition was depleted, and their blockhouses and palisades were splintered into ruins, so their officers ordered Fort Mifflin evacuated. Boats were brought from Fort Mercer and 250 wounded men were taken off while the other 200 set fire to the wreckage before leaving.

The next morning, when the British grenadiers stormed the fort, they found only a small herd of sheep and a few oxen to greet them. There were dead bodies everywhere. In the barracks, they discovered one man, who was alive, but disgustingly drunk. He claimed that he was a loyalist and had been an American prisoner. The British believed him and gave him a bounty and a British uniform. Later that winter he deserted and joined Washington at Valley Forge, giving him detailed information about the British defenses.

It was late November when Washington began his eleven-day, 30-mile march from Whitemarsh to the much lionized Valley Forge. Two weeks later the garrison from Fort Mercer was evacuated and joined with his forces. The British did not follow or hinder them. The Delaware River by Philadelphia was now British, and the extensive barriers could be safely and tediously removed, while the officers and their troops planned their exciting winter entertainment in the capital city with the remaining loyalists. In one record of Brigadier General JOHN LACEY, it stated that he was stationed at White Moose and then at Hatboro, Pennsylvania, just north of Philadelphia. I have not been able to locate White Moose.

88

THE CONWAY CABAL

In the beginning, John Adams and his cousin Samuel Adams had recognized that if their efforts for independence succeeded, they would need the support of more than the New England colonies. They recognized that Virginia was the strength of the southern states and that it was still far enough north that the middle colonies would not feel neglected. They also saw in George Washington a leader who seemed to unite rather than push for his personal ambition. For these reasons, they went against their own Bostonian, John Hancock, who desperately wanted to command the army, and nominated Washington for the post. He was given great authority, but Congress reserved the right of approval and advancement of other officers.

Through the past two years, the Adams cousins kept their strong positions in Congress, while most of the others who had so strongly supported George Washington found the routine tedious and personally unrewarding, and sought other areas of leadership within their more exciting state governments. Thomas Jefferson had gone to Virginia to rewrite the oppressive British Virginia laws to conform to republican law; Benjamin Franklin, Silas Deane, and Arthur Lee had been sent to France; ROBERT LIVINGSTON went to New York and eventually became chancellor. John Hancock returned to Massachusetts and became governor. Some had died. Only four or six members of the original Congress remained (histories differ).

Washington was extremely involved in the overall military of the new nation. He needed to command, feed, clothe, and give moral support to the whole continental army; direct the activities of the partisan militia; keep in close touch with the various state governments in addition to the Continental

Congress; and try to bring about a united effort for independence against the world's greatest military power. He looked for aid wherever he could find it—the cities, the countryside, foreign aid. Congress was far from having the finances to support all of the new nation's needs. Petty jealousies between the states, as well as individuals, abounded.

The American victory at Saratoga was viewed in Europe as a great military success for George Washington for he was the Commander in Chief. He had weakened his own forces against Howe to send the necessary generals and troops to support the northern army and at the same time had kept Sir William and his greater army contained within the cities of New York and Philadelphia with significant losses in their men, ammunition and supplies. He had met the British forces on the battlefield in European combat style and had shown sufficient skill to impress their military leaders. To them, he had lost some ground, but his army was still intact and certainly far from defeated. Much of Europe hated England—to help General Washington and humble the British seemed quite proper. The American soldiers and most citizens of the United States were inclined also to view the situation in the same way. Washington was considered their leader and hero. Any successful victory against the enemy was his victory, since he was ultimately in charge of all military operations. He was also someone in whom they could put their trust for he exhibited personal qualities of bravery, intelligence, and noble character.

His increasing popularity, however, began to worry some of his former friends and supporters. Whether it was from jealousy, envy, ambition, a fear for their own acceptance by the people, or a sincere belief, the story was secretly generated that George Washington was trying to take over the nation and to make himself a king. To add to his terrible physical struggles with his impoverished army that winter at Valley Forge, the trusting Washington was to find out in the next few months that he had strong opposition in his own ranks and that his adversaries included Samuel Adams, Dr. Benjamin Rush, Richard Henry Lee, and John Adams—all of them members of the Continental Congress. His two original aides were also highly involved—Thomas Mifflin, who went with him as an aide-de-camp to Cambridge, had become the Chairman of the Board of War, and the handsome Joseph Reed, who had also accompanied him there as his military secretary, was now a leading Pennsylvania politician. This plot to unseat Washington has become known in history as the Conway Cabal. Of course, Major General Horatio Gates of New England was involved.

Brigadier General Thomas Conway from whom the cabal received its name had commanded a brigade at Germantown in conjunction with the armies of Generals Sullivan and Wayne. The three generals were assigned the northern frontal attack. Conway did well and Sullivan thought him far exceeding in military knowledge over "any officer we have." He had arrived from France in May at Washington's headquarters in Morristown. Conway was an Irishman who had married a French countess, and he had come with a letter of recommendation from Silas Deane promising him a high commission.

Washington had not been as impressed with him as Sullivan had reported. On the 17 October he had written Richard Henry Lee, whom he still believed to be his friend,

> "General Conway's merit . . . as an officer and his importance in this army exists more in his own imagination than in reality, for it is a maxim with him to leave no service of his own untold, nor to want anything which is to be obtained by importunity."

Conway wanted to be made a major general. Washington felt there were 23 other brigadier generals with much longer service and who were far more deserving, among them Benedict Arnold. Lee reported back that it was likely Conway would be elected adjutant general to succeed Timothy Pickering, whom Congress was planning to appoint to the Board of War—an election that rankled Washington as he would have to work directly with this strutting peacock, Conway.

28 Oct 1777, the 21-year-old aide of General Gates, Colonel JAMES WILKINSON, arrived at Reading, Pennsylvania, from Gates' headquarters near Saratoga. He had been given orders by Gates to take his detailed report of the victory and surrender at Saratoga straight to Congress at York—deliberately bypassing and thus snubbing Commander in Chief Washington. Not able or willing to keep his mouth shut, young WILKINSON revealed to Stirling's aide that Brigadier General Thomas Conway had written secretly to Gates and that the letter had included the following,

"Heaven has been determined to save your country, or a weak General and bad counsellors would have ruined it."

The rumor flourished in the tap rooms of the countryside.

It was finally passed on to George Washington by General Stirling in a letter that arrived at his headquarters at Whitemarsh on a very busy day two weeks later.

On that day of 8 November, General Washington had written letters to the President of Delaware to procure clothing for his Delaware troops; to the New Jersey Governor, WILLIAM LIVINGSTON, to ask for militia reinforcement for Red Bank; to Congress with news and a request for more money; to the commanders involving the defense of Forts Mifflin and Mercer; to Colonel Theodorick Bland, who was planning to quit the service; to Brigadier General Thomas Nelson about another problem. He had then held a council of war about the Delaware forts and the advisability of attacking Howe, whose defense of Philadelphia was weakened by his attack on the forts. The news that this already irritating Thomas Conway had added a personal attack on his ability as a general to Horatio Gates was quite frustrating—the remark was not only disloyal, but treasonous.

Washington slept on it and sent Conway a brief letter the next day directly confronting him with what he had heard; but he sent it through normal channels—so all his general officers knew its contents. Conway wrote back to deny the charges and added that he was willing to have his original letter given to General Washington; then on 14 November, he sent his resignation to Congress. Had they accepted it, the matter could have ended; but they passed it on to Thomas Mifflin and the Board of War for further discussion, knowing he was an active participant in the plot to unseat Washington. Mifflin started the bandwagon in Congress that promoted Conway to major general with the position of inspector general of the continental army. At the same time, acting on the wishes of General Gates, they promoted JAMES WILKINSON to brigadier general for carrying the victory letter to Congress. Other radicals joined in and Pennsylvania attorney general Jonathan Dickinson Sergeant wrote a letter to Congressman James Lovell that

"thousands of lives and millions of property are yearly sacrificed to the inefficiency of the commander-in-chief. Two battles he has lost for us by two such blunders as might have disgraced a soldier of three months' standing."

A week later he further blamed America's problems on Washington by writing General Gates at Albany,

"We want you in different places . . . . What a situation we are in!"

The promotion of WILKINSON to a brigadier perhaps ruffled the officers more than Conway's appointment to a staff position, for his was a command position. Nine brigadiers complained of both promotions to Congress and General GREENE wrote his personal protest. Upon WILKINSON's elevation, they agreed with John Laurens that

"there is a degradation of rank and an injustice to senior and more distinguished officers when a man is so extraordinarily advanced for riding post with good news. Let Congress reward him with a good horse for his speed, but consecrate rank to merit of another kind!"

When General Washington had been informed on 18 October at Whitemarsh by the Albany courier of Burgoyne's surrender, he was delighted and had his men fire a thirteen-gun salute. With the forts on the Delaware under attack and Philadelphia and New York much more vulnerable, Washington counseled with five major generals and ten brigadiers and they chose to send ALEXANDER HAMILTON, Washington's aide, to Albany with instructions:

"you are chiefly to . . . point out, in the clearest and fullest manner, to General Gates, the absolute necessity . . . for his detaching a very considerable part of the army at present under his command, to the reinforcement of this."

HAMILTON was to use discretion, for it stated,

"If . . . you should find that [General Gates] intends, in consequence of his Success, to employ the troops under his command upon some expedition, by the prosecution of which the common cause will be more benefited than by their being sent down to reinforce this army, it is not my wish to give interruption to the plan."

HAMILTON set out on 30 October, riding sixty miles a day to travel the 250 miles to Albany on his mission of great trust. About half-way, he met DANIEL MORGAN and his troops on their way to join Washington. At Fishkill, he ordered Putman, in Washington's name, to send most of the continentals, keeping 1600 militia.

At Albany, Gates protested. Sir Henry Clinton might come up from New York and capture Albany, "the finest arsenal in America." Then there was Ticonderoga. How could he retake that fort if he was left without his full army? Gates decided he would send him Patterson's brigade. HAMILTON objected. It was

> "by far the weakest of the three now here, and does not consist of more than about six hundred rank and file fit for duty."

Two hundred could not be counted because their enlistment would expire before they could reach Washington. The young aide therefore felt

> "under the necessity of desiring, by virtue of my orders" from General Washington, that Glover's brigade be substituted for Patterson's, and "if agreeable to you, you will give orders accordingly." After further remonstration, Gates finally agreed to send Glover's brigade along with Patterson's. In his draft letter to Washington, Gates had crossed out the resentment he felt in Washington's giving "Dictatorial power, to one Aid de Camp sent to an Army 300 Miles distant."

Returning down the river, HAMILTON was pleased that he had found boats for Patterson's brigade and that Glover's troops were following on the east bank. However, he was soon to discover that Israel Putnam had ignored the orders he had given him from Washington. Poor's men had mutinied. There had been no pay for six or eight months. A captain had killed a soldier and was himself shot. New York's governor, George Clinton, came to help HAMILTON. He loaned him five or six thousand dollars to pay the men and they marched along. Putman held Warner's militia at Peekskill

> "to aid in an expedition against New York . . . at this time the hobby-horse of General Putnam." HAMILTON described it as "a suicidal parade against New York" and reported that Putman's conduct "gives general disgust."

He wished Putnam recalled from command, stating that Governor Clinton would support it. In all this, HAMILTON became quite ill and could not join Washington for another three weeks.

But the American troops were much too slow. Having opened the Delaware, the British reinforced General Howe in Philadelphia. The advantage for the Americans had passed. In Albany, Gates no longer needed an army. The British had evacuated Fort Ticonderoga, and the threat from New York had dissipated with the mass movement of troops to Philadelphia. Sir William Howe sent his resignation to London. He was tired of this war, and Philadelphia was already short of food with housewives begging and stealing British provisions. By spring he would be replaced by Sir Henry Clinton.

Horatio Gates received a warning from Mifflin that Conway's thrust at Washington "should not have been entrusted to any of your Family," for the injurious quotation had been conveyed to headquarters, and Washington had taxed Conway with it, and he stated further that some of Gates's best friends might suffer—probably including himself. Gates became very defensive and begged Conway "to let me know which of the letters was copied off. It is of greatest importance, that I should detect the person who has been guilty of that act of infidelity." But he never waited for a reply, for when WILKINSON returned to Albany he quoted Gates as saying,

> "I have a spy in my camp since you left me! Colonel HAMILTON had been sent up to him by General Washington . . . . he purloined the copy of a letter out of that closet . . . Colonel HAMILTON was left alone an hour in this room, during which time, he took Conway's letter out of that closet and copied it, and the copy has been furnished to Washington."

To avoid personal blame, WILKINSON tried to implicate another one of Gates's aides, Robert Troup, a close friend of ALEXANDER HAMILTON who had spent time with him when he was in Albany. But Gates would not have it. HAMILTON was the villain. Gates would compel Washington to admit it and both HAMILTON and Washington would be disgraced.

His first letter to his commander in chief read,

> "I conjure your excellency, to give me all the assistance you can, in tracing out the author of the infidelity which put extracts from General Conway's letters to me into your hands . . . . It is . . . in your . . . power to do me and the United States a very important service, by detecting a wretch who may . . . capitally injure the very operation under your immediate direction."

He then added that he was sending a copy of his letter to the President of Congress.

In his reply, Washington simply stated that it was WILKINSON, Gates's own confidant, who had babbled at Reading and whose indiscretion had reached him via Stirling, "from motives of friendship."

Then he added that until he learned that Gates was searching for an offender, he had supposed that Gates had meant to warn him against

"a dangerous incendiary.... Genl. Conway. But, in this, as in other matters of late, I have found myself mistaken."

With that, Gates then claimed that the paragraph quoted was

"spurious . . . a wicked forgery."

He insisted that the letter said nothing about a weak general or bad counselors. He then asked that the faithless WILKINSON be punished.

Washington answered with a rather long letter that asked questions. Why had Gates admitted Conway's stricture, and later denied that it existed? If Conway's letters were innocent of reflections on the commander in chief, why had Gates not produced them? Then he added that he was willing to bury their correspondence in silence, "and as far as future events will permit, oblivion."

Responding to the harsh words of his general, young WILKINSON challenged Gates to a duel and said that he would have the blood of Sterling. Gates plead for forgiveness and Sterling just ignored him.

Since he was no longer needed at Albany, Gates returned to his friends in Congress, now at York, Pennsylvania, where the newspapers applauded him with honors and Congress appointed him the president of the new board of war. Washington won the ballot in Congress by one vote, when his enemies tried to replace him with Gates. John Adams was not present for this vote. He had been appointed to go to France to replace Silas Deane as a Commissioner. Deane had been recalled by Congress—suspected by Arthur Lee of growing wealthy at the expense of the United States.

After serving very uncomfortably as Inspector General for a month or so, Thomas Conway was challenged to a duel by Pennsylvania general John Cadwalader, who shot him in the face. He survived and shortly resigned and returned to France. Mifflin resigned from the Board of War. The Conway Cabal had fallen flat on its face; but George Washington and ALEXANDER HAMILTON had been awakened through the winter of 1777—1778 to a new view of what it means to some people to be loyal, trustworthy, and/or a close friend. The idealism and trust of both men for constancy in the political arena was somewhat shaken.

89

VALLEY FORGE

D r. Albigence Waldo, the surgeon from Connecticut who recorded his journey to Quebec with Benedict Arnold in Part Three: REBELLION, tells
about the life of the ordinary soldier at Valley Forge:

"Dec. 14th [1777]. — Prisoners and deserters are continually coming in. The
army who have been surprisingly healthy hitherto—now begin to grow
sickly from the continued fatigues they have suffered this campaign. Yet
they still show spirit of Alacrity & contentment not to be expected from
so young troops. I am sick—discontented—and out of humour. Poor
food—ard lodging—cold weather—fatigue—nasty cloaths—nasty cookery—vomit half my time—smoak'd out of my senses—the devil's in't—I
can't endure it—why are we sent here to starve and freeze—what sweet
felicities have I left at home;—a charming wife—pretty children—good
beds—good food—good cookery—all agreeable—all harmonious. Here,
all confusion—smoke and cold—hunger & filthyness—a pox on my bad
luck. Here comes a bowl of beef soup—full of burnt leaves and dirt, sick-
ish enough to make a Hector spue,—away with it boys—I'll live like the
chameleon upon air.

"Dec. 18th.—Universal thanksgiving—a roasted pig at night. God be
thanked for my health which I have pretty well recovered. How much better should I feel, were I assured my family were in health—but the same
good being who graciously preserves me—is able to preserve them—&
bring me to the ardently wish'd for enjoyment of them again.

"Dec. 26th.—The enemy have been some days [on] the west [of
the] Schuylkill, from opposite the city to Derby—there intentions not
yet known. The city is at present pretty clear of them. Why don't his
Excellency rush in & retake the city, in which he will doubtless find much
plunder?—Because he knows better than to leave his post and be catch'd
like a . . . fool cooped up in a city. He has always acted wisely hitherto—his

conduct when closely scrutinised is uncensurable. Were his inferior generals as skillfull as himself—we should have the grandest choir of officers
ever God made.

"Dec. 28th.—Yesterday upwards of fifty officers in Gen. GREENE's division resigned their commissions—six or seven of our regiment are doing the like today. All this is occasion'd by officers families being so much
neglected at home on account of provisions.

"The present circumstances of the soldier is better by far than the officer—for the family of the soldier is provided for at the public expence if
the articles they want are above the common price—but the officer's family, are obliged not only to beg in the most humble manner for the neces-
saries of life—but also to pay for them afterwards at the most exhorbitant
rates—and even in this manner, many of them who depend entirely on
their money, cannot procure half the material comforts that are wanted in
a family—this produces continual letters of complaint from home.

"Dec. 31st.—Adjutant Selden learn'd me how to darn stockings—to
make them look like knit work—first work the thread in a parallel manner,
then catch these over & over as above.

"1778. January 1st.—New year. I am alive. I am well. Huts go on briskly,
and our camp begins to appear like a spacious city. Bought an embroidered
jacket.

"How much we affect to appear of consequence by a superfluous
dress,—and yet custom—(that law which none may fight against) has
rendered this absolutely necessary & commendable. An officer frequently
fails of being duly noticed, merely from the want of a genteel dress.

"Sunday, Jan. 4th.—Properly accouter'd I went to work at masonry—
none of my mess were to dictate me—and before night (being found with
mortar & stone) I almost compleated a genteel chimney to my magnificent
hut—however, as we had short allowance of food & no grogg—my back
ached before night.

"I was call'd to relieve a soldier tho't to be dying—he expir'd before I
reach'd the hutt. He was an Indian—an excellent soldier—and an obedient
good natur'd fellow. He engaged for money, doubtless, as others do, but he
has served his country faithfully. He has fought for those very people who
disinherited his forefathers.

"8th.—Unexpectedly got a furlow, Set out for home."

Early in the year of 1778, at the time when Washington's former aide,
Thomas Mifflin, had resigned in disgrace as the chairman of the board of war

from his involvement in the Conway Cabal, the army suffered from Mifflin's terrible lack of management of the Quartermaster and Commissary departments and was in a pitiful condition:

> "the property of the continent dispersed over the whole country; not a encampment, route of the Army, or considerable road but abounds with wagons, left to the mercy of the weather and the will of the inhabitants .... Not less than three thousand spades and shovels and a like number of tomahawks have been lately discovered and collected in the vicinity of the camp .... In the same way a quantity of tents and tent-cloth, after having laid a whole summer in a farmer's barn . . . was lately discovered and brought to the camp by a special order from the General."

Mifflin's mismanagement of the commissary had deprived the troops of their much-needed food. The soldiers slept on the frozen ground, and a sick soldier died in their huts for lack of straw to lay on—straw was available, but there were no wagons to carry it. According to the Congressional Committee report,

> "Almost every species of camp transportation is performed by men, who without a murmur, patiently yoke themselves to little carriages of their own making, or load their wood and provisions on their backs."

To the post of Quartermaster General, Washington assigned his trusted General NATHANAEL GREENE. He accepted somewhat graciously, but protested,

> "Who ever read of a quartermaster in history?"

He insisted on appointing his own assistants and keeping his field command. His diligence brought great improvement and Washington was pleased—feeling his army would be able to take to the field in the spring adequately furnished. The Commissary Department was improved—but not handsomely in this famished, stripped country—by the appointment of the solid Jeremiah Wadsworth of Connecticut. He replaced Joseph Trumbull, who had become ill months before and returned home, leaving his post to his highly-incompetent junior officers. In February, for four days, the army cried,

> "No meat! No meat!"

About the end of February 1778, the Baron von Steuben of Prussia arrived in camp. He had been a captain and aide-de-camp on the large staff of Frederick

the Great, and presented himself as a volunteer that would perform any role Washington
would assign him. He spoke German and
French, but not English. Fortunately, both
ALEXANDER HAMILTON and John
Laurens spoke fluent French, and Washington
was able to use their talents to communicate with his newly-arrived officer as well
as earlier with General Lafayette, who had
quickly learned to speak the English language. General Washington had been in the

BARON FREDERICK WILLIAM
OF STEUBEN

process of reforming his army and needed a drillmaster. Steuben was his wise
choice for he dutifully trained the soldiers in precision marching and maneuvers that would greatly help to prevent the confusion that had been experienced
at Brandywine and Germantown. He was well-liked by the men, although a
perfectionist, and when the ineffective Thomas Conway resigned, the baron
was promoted to major general and given Conway's office of inspector general
where he accomplished important economies in management throughout the
army. Washington added a hundred chosen men to the baron's guard to aid him.
One of these inspectors was perhaps a distant cousin, FRANCIS BARBER,
who had been HAMILTON's old teacher.

[Note: Our BARBER ancestral line of Boston in the mid-1600s (eighth-great-grandmother MARGREATT
BARBER b. 1651) needs further research. In 1665, she married REMEMBRANCE LIPPINCOTT (b.
15 Mar 1642 in Dorchester by Boston.) His father, RICHARD LIPPINCOTT was a nonconformist and
moved back to England, became a Quaker, and after being imprisoned in Plymouth, England, for his religion, he returned to Rhode Island and then became a charter member of the first English settlers in
Shrewsbury, Monmouth County, New Jersey. There are quite a few BARBERs in the early Quaker records
of Philadelphia and vicinity as well as LIPPINCOTTs and PRESTONs.]

As spring arrived, the name of the captured General Charles Lee came into
conversation more frequently among the officers at Valley Forge. According to
Elias Boudinot, Commissary of Prisoners,

"General Washington called me into his room and in the most earnest
manner entreated of me, if I wished to gratify him, that I would obtain the
exchange of General Lee, for he was never more wanted by him than at the
present moment and desired I would not suffer trifles to prevent it."

Of course, Washington was not aware that the traitorous Charles Lee had conspired with the enemy and even drawn up plans to help the British take Philadelphia. This was not known until thirty years after the war had ended.

To make the exchange, Boudinot was able to offer British General Richard Prescott, who had been captured in Rhode Island by one or our distant cousins, Colonel WILLIAM BARTON, with a few of his men about eight months before. WILLIAM was a descendant of a distant uncle, RUFUS BARTON, of Rhode Island. Lee was to leave the enemy lines on Sunday morning, 5 April, under parole. Washington sent a party of horsemen under his aide, Colonel Meade, to escort him to camp.

Boudinot detested the prisoner Charles Lee and wrote in his journal:

"The General, with a great number of principal officers and their suites, rode about four miles on the road toward Philadelphia and waited until General Lee appeared. General Washington passed through the lines of officers and the army who all paid him the highest military honors to Headquarters, where Mrs. Washington was and there he [General Charles Lee] was entertained with an elegant dinner, and the music playing the whole time. A room was assigned to him back of Mrs. Washington's sitting room and all his baggage was stowed in it. The next morning he lay very late and breakfast was detained for him. When he came out, he looked dirty, as if he had been in the street all night. Soon after I discovered that he had brought a miserable dirty hussy with him from Philadelphia (a British sergeant's wife) and had actually taken her into his room by a back door, and she had slept with him that night."

ENCAMPMENT AT VALLEY FORGE,
1777–1778

90

THE BATTLE OF MONMOUTH COUNTY, NEW JERSEY

In one of the genealogies of the LIPPINCOTT family, it states that there were more LIPPINCOTTs in New Jersey in the 1700s than any other surname, except Haines, because they had so many male descendants. It further stated that they were settled largely in Monmouth and Burlington Counties. In checking the D.A.R. records, very few LIPPINCOTTs were found, which leads one to believe that their Quaker antiwar beliefs were very strong, or they were loyalists. One loyalist, Captain RICHARD LIPPINCOTT, is often included in the history books in the trials that followed the Battle of Yorktown, Virginia.

[Note: This Captain RICHARD LIPPINCOTT was born in 1745, and died in 1820. He married HESTER BORDEN on 3 Apr 1770. She was the daughter of Thomas and Mary Edwards Borden of Burlington County, whose ancestors were also very early New Jersey settlers. He was either a third or fourth cousin to fourth-great-grandmother ABIGAIL LIPPINCOTT, wife of fourth-great-grandfather JOHN COOLEY of Hunterdon County, New Jersey. RICHARD and HESTER had one child, ESTHER, who married George Taylor Dennison. Captain RICHARD LIPPINCOTT was undoubtedly with the British when the Battle of Monmouth County was fought. It is well to remember that when the Revolution began, the population within all of the colonies was about 350,000, but it increased quite rapidly. This number divided by the 13 colonies suggests there were only 27,000 people in each state—of course, it wasn't an even division. Most of Georgia was claimed by the Indians. Inland South Carolina had few towns.

Fourth-great-grandmother ABIGAIL LIPPINCOTT was a second-great-granddaughter of the original charter landowner RICHARD LIPPINCOTT. Fifth-great-grandparents DOROTHY MORGAN and HENRY VAN KIRK were married in 1723 in Freehold, New Jersey, within a few miles of the location of the Monmouth County battlefield. They moved to Hopewell, New Jersey, (12 miles northwest of Princeton,) where they raised their family. DOROTHY died prior to the revolution—before 1770, and HENRY died before 3 Apr 1776 in Hunterdon County, New Jersey. Their daughter JEMIMA VAN KIRK married American Captain fourth-great-grandfather ELISHA BARTON of Hunterdon County, where the gigantic Colonel DANIEL MORGAN was born. Our early BARTONs, MORGANs, and VAN KIRKs originated in New England, Westchester County, New York, and the east and west sides of Long Island.]

The British general, Sir William Howe, sent his resignation to London early in the winter of 1777-8. The devastating news of Burgoyne's defeat at Saratoga had arrived only shortly before. The Crown was quite willing to accept his resignation and gave his command to General Henry Clinton, who had been assigned to the occupation of New York and Rhode Island. By this time, France had declared war on England and had committed part of their navy to aid the Americans. With this French naval strength moving toward America, the British defeat at Saratoga and the resulting increase in American troops surrounding the capital, King George III and his ministry had no desire to fight another land battle and ordered Henry Clinton to evacuate Philadelphia as soon as possible—hoping to avoid an American/French trap.

Britain's former governor of New York, William Tryon, who was earlier the governor of North Carolina when the 1771 Battle of the Alamance (Regulators) occurred, strongly suggested that the Carolinas were vulnerable and much more loyal to the king. The British also took a look at the French naval base in the West Indies, St. Lucia, and decided it should be a primary naval objective. Clinton was ordered to embark 5000 men immediately for St. Lucia and 3000 for Florida to protect that flank of the British position. New York harbor was to be retained, if possible. The prized Rhode Island harbor was to be saved as a retreat, if needed, and, as a last resort, they were to retreat to Halifax. The rest of their vast army was to be shipped to South Carolina, where Clinton was to lead a strong attack on the southern city of Charleston.

When word arrived in Philadelphia of General Howe's release, his officers decided to honor him with a gala celebration and appointed the young debonair Captain John André to make the arrangements. Expenses were not spared to make it the greatest pageant imaginable. A Hessian observer stated,

> "The great English shop of Coffin and Anderson took in 12,000 [pounds] sterling for silk goods and other fine materials, which shows how much money was lavished on the affair, and how elegantly the ladies were dressed."

Some were appalled at the "folly and extravagance of it." But one of the young loyalist girls that attended wrote,

> "we never had, and perhaps never shall have so elegant an entertainment in America again."

With summer approaching, Washington now had 11,000 to 12,000 troops at

Valley Forge, and he had in addition Maxwell's brigade of 1300 and Dickinson's militia of 800, who were already in New Jersey. DANIEL MORGAN and his 600 riflemen had been sent to join Dickinson in harassing the enemy. Not wanting to confront Washington's army, or engage in a naval battle with the French, the British retreated across New Jersey on 17 Jun 1778, surprising the Americans, who planned to do battle. According to reports by ALEXANDER HAMILTON, the enemy was estimated at 10,000 men with a superior cavalry, but impeded with 1500 wagons and carriages of loyalists fleeing Philadelphia and numerous camp followers.

The following day, General Charles Lee, now second in command because of tenure, led the first contingent across the Delaware River at Coryell's Ferry, (from New Hope, Pennsylvania, to Lambertville, New Jersey). From here the army marched on to one of our ancestral hometowns—Hopewell (a few miles northwest of Princeton), where they rested a day and held a council of war. Washington posed the question. Should the Americans just continue to heckle the enemy or should they initiate a major battle? D'Estaing's French fleet was already on the coast. With the capture of Burgoyne's troops, only Clinton's remained. Should they attempt to end the war on their own, or wait for a combined force with the French?

ALEXANDER HAMILTON recorded their answers. General Charles Lee wanted to allow the enemy to cross New Jersey unhampered—Americans could not match trained European soldiers in pitched battle, then wait patiently for French assistance. Knox, Stirling, and others would not give the British free passage—1500 troops should be advanced to add to the attachments already harassing Clinton's left flank and rear, while the main army was watchful of events. This was the opinion of the council, signed by all but Wayne, who wanted to bring on a stand-up fight. Accordingly, the order was given and Brigadier General Charles Scott was sent with 1500 troops to join MORGAN and Dickinson. A small party of foot soldiers under General Cadwalader and cavalry under Lieutenant Colonel Anthony White also joined them.

HAMILTON was indignant. In a letter to his friend Boudinot, he declared that the conclusion of the council

"would have done honor to the most honorable society of midwives, and to them only. The purport was that we should keep at a comfortable distance from the enemy, and keep up a vain parade of annoying them by detachment."

Lafayette and GREENE had reluctantly joined with the majority; but after the council ended, they joined with Wayne and wrote individual letters to Washington urging him to disregard the timid advice.

The next day, June 25th, Washington made his own decision, after it was evident that the British were taking the shortest route to the sea, which took them through Monmouth Court House (Freehold). Prompt action was required or the enemy would escape them. He ordered Lafayette forward with 1000 troops under Wayne. He was to take command of all the detachments near the enemy—about 4000 soldiers. HAMILTON was delighted to be sent with Lafayette as liaison officer. General Lee first agreed, then vacillated and asked for his right as commander. He then reversed his decision; but when additional troops were added, he again changed his mind and demanded the honor. Washington conceded with further instructions that he should aid any design formed by Lafayette as his subordinate.

HAMILTON reported,

"The enemy in marching from Allentown had changed their disposition and thrown all their best troops in the rear. This made it necessary . . . to reinforce the advanced corps. Two brigades were detached for this purpose, and the General, willing to accommodate General Lee, sent him with them to take command of the whole advanced corps, which rendezvoused the forenoon of the twenty-seventh at Englishtown, consisting of at least five thousand rank and file, most of them select troops. General Lee's orders were, the moment he received intelligence of the enemy's march, to pursue them and to attack their rear.

'This intelligence was received about five o'clock the morning of the twenty-eighth, and General Lee put his troops in motion accordingly. The main body did the same. The advanced corps came up with the enemy's rear a mile or two beyond the [Monmouth] Court House. I saw the enemy drawn up and am persuaded there were not a thousand men—their front from different accounts was then ten miles off. However favorable this situation may seem for an attack, it was not made, but after changing their position two or three times by retrograde movements, our advanced corps got into a general confused retreat and even rout would hardly be too strong an expression. Not a word of all this was officially communicated to the General [Washington]."

Washington, who was leading the main army further back, was met by a fifer who told of a retreat. The general was incredulous. He had heard little firing. He sent aides forward to discover the truth. Shortly they galloped back to report that enemy light infantry and grenadiers were pursuing out of the woods and would be upon him in fifteen minutes.

HAMILTON wrote,

"the General rode forward and found the troops retiring in the greatest disorder and the enemy pressing upon their rear . . . . [He met Lee with angry words east of the church.] He instantly took measures for checking the enemy's advance, then rode back and formed his own men on the high ground, Stirling on the left, GREENE on the right, himself and Lafayette in the center . . . . America owes a great deal to General Washington for this day's work; a general rout, dismay, and disgrace would have attended the whole army in any other hands but his. By his own good sense and fortitude he turned the fate of the day. Other officers have great merit in performing their parts well, but he directed the whole with the skill of a Master workman . . . . he brought order out of confusion, animated the troops and led them to success."

HAMILTON did not speak of his own action on the field, which included the posting of troops to protect American artillery in danger of capture. He was incapacitated when his horse was wounded and fell. A fellow aide reported HAMILTON

"was incessant in his endeavours during . . . the whole day—in reconnoitering the enemy and in rallying and charging."

American artillery and thrusts of infantry, especially under Wayne, drove enemy dragoons, grenadiers, and guards under Cornwallis back over the ground of Lee's retreat. It was a very hot day, around 96 to 100 degrees, and the heavily coated enemy was especially vulnerable to heat stroke. (This was the day of "Molly Pitcher" and her heroism.) Darkness closed on the longest and hottest day of battle. Washington and his troops lay on the field they had won that night, intending to continue the assault at dawn. But Clinton's orders were of a different nature—evacuation. His troops quietly slipped away under the cloak of darkness and were not pursued.

Of the day, General Anthony Wayne wrote RICHARD PETERS,

"The victory of that day turns out to be much more considerable than at first expected . . . by the most moderate computation their killed and wounded must be full fifteen hundred men of the flower of their army. Among them are numbers of the richest blood of England. Tell the Philadelphia ladies that the heavenly, sweet, pretty redcoats . . . have humbled themselves on the plains of Monmouth . . . and have resigned their laurels to rebel officers who will lay them at the feet of those virtuous daughters of America who cheerfully gave up ease and affluence in a city for Liberty and peace of mind in a cottage."

The following morning, while the Americans were burying their dead, Washington received a letter from General Charles Lee.

GENERAL ANTHONY WAYNE

"Sir: From the knowledge I have of your Excellency's character, I must conclude that nothing but the misinformation of some very stupid, or misrepresentation of some very wicked person could have occasioned your making use of such very singular expressions as you did on my coming up to the ground where you had taken post: they implied that I was guilty either of disobedience of orders, of want of conduct, or want of courage. Your Excellency will, therefore, infinitely oblige me by letting me know on which of these three articles you ground your charge that I may prepare for my justification, which I have the happiness to be confident I can do, to the Army, to the Congress, to America, and to the world in general."

The letter continued on demanding his right to reparation and ending with his inability to believe that Washington's remarks were a "motion of your own breast, but instigated by some of those dirty earwigs who will forever insinuate themselves near persons in high office."—referring to Generals Wayne and Charles Scott.

A furious Washington hurriedly wrote the following reply and sent it back by Colonel Fitzgerald:

"Sir: I received your letter (dated through mistake the 1st of July), expressed as I conceive, in terms highly improper. I am not conscious of having made use of any very singular expressions at the time of my meeting you, as you intimate. What I recollect to have said was dictated by duty and warranted by the occasion. As soon as circumstances will permit, you shall have an opportunity, either of justifying yourself to the army, to Congress, to America, and to the world in general, or of convincing them that you were guilty of a breach of orders and of misbehavior before the enemy on the 28th instant, in not attacking them as you had been directed and in making an unnecessary, disorderly and shameful retreat. I am, etc."

Lee sent two more letters and Washington answered the third by putting him under arrest for:

"disobedience of orders in not attacking the enemy, misbehavior before the enemy, disrespect in his letters to the Commander-in-Chief."

The military court sat several days, while the army began their march northward. Witnesses for the prosecution included Washington's aides, John Laurens and ALEXANDER HAMILTON. Lee was defended weakly by his own aides. In the end, he was suspended from any command for twelve months. Laurens felt he was entitled to challenge Lee to a duel for his expressions abusing the Commander in Chief and HAMILTON was to be his second. Lee's second was Major Evan Edwards. Two pistols were supplied each of the combatants and they approached each other, firing at will. Lee was wounded; but he protested that he wanted to renew the duel. The seconds objected, and they published a declaration that the demands of honor had been met. Other duels were threatened with Lee, but they were averted. Charles Lee died in 1782—only a few friends stood by him.

The actual losses for the Battle of Monmouth Court House were 250 British and Germans dead, and only 72 Americans. The British reported 59 dead of sunstroke, the Americans, 37. But the British had escaped, first to Sandy Hook (probably through or very near the original LIPPINCOTT ancestral home of Shrewsbury, New Jersey, and by 5 July they were in New York and preparing quite hastily for their embarkment on Admiral Howe's fleet of ships and their sea journey to South Carolina, while Washington described the march of his troops as an "inconceivably distressing march," twenty miles to Brunswick through deep, hot, sandy, red and yellow dust, almost without a drop of water.

The troops recuperated in Brunswick that week,

Private Elijah Fisher, a new member of General Washington's guard, recorded their celebration of 4 Jul 1778:

> "We Selebrated the Independence of Amarica. The howl army paraded
> . . . . the artilery Discharged thirteen Cannon. We gave three Chears &c.
> At Night his Excelency and the gentlemen and Ladys had a Bawl at Head
> Quarters with grate Pompe."

The men were given a double allowance of rum for the day. Many a man rededicated himself to the cause of freedom. Philadelphia was extravagant and burned powder in salute and fireworks, as did many other cities. Down in Charleston, South Carolina, a man proclaimed,

> "I would Willingley renounse all my Most Neair and Deair Connections
> on Earth for my Darling libertey."

And perhaps, his words would soon be put to the test with the British army almost ready to embark to that very location.

Benedict Arnold in Philadelphia

Because Benedict Arnold's wounded leg was still somewhat debilitated, Washington appointed him as the military governor of Philadelphia. Arnold found the city very dirty but in fair condition, considering the vast army that had occupied it, but with the quick return of Congress to their capitol city, he also found himself in the middle of the intrigue that had threatened General Washington the previous winter. Joseph Reed, one of the first two aides assigned to Washington in May 1775, was now president of the Supreme Executive Council of Pennsylvania. He hated the noble aristocracy of the English governors who had ruled in colonial America and was determined to prevent any military takeover of the United States government. He still believed that the genteel Washington was deliberately gaining the public support to make himself king. He believed that Benedict Arnold, as Washington's favorite, was sent to Philadelphia to prepare for such an event. The rugged, individualistic Arnold was insisting on absolute discipline from a more laid-back militia, which was interpreted by Arnold's opponents to be a distinctively English trait.

Reed had been brought to power by moderate men; but then he deserted them to lead the radical attack of his old friends, including Robert Morris, Silas Deane, and now especially Benedict Arnold. These attacks were by print and by mobs in the city's streets. Soon the Philadelphians began to take sides and moderation disappeared. A left-wing party that became known as the Radical Whigs emerged that opposed the right-wing party, the Republicans, whose leaders bore the brunt of the radical attack.

Arnold was criticized for his friendships with loyalist merchants, for his extravagant style of living, even for his attempt to distance himself from the fighting and verbal slander between the two parties. In a letter to General GREENE at Washington's headquarters, General Cadwalader reported that Arnold was "unpopular among the men in power in Congress, and among those of this state in general." He considered this campaign against Arnold as unfounded and the circulating charges against him in the city "too absurd to deserve a serious answer."

Reed kept digging and felt he had found proof that Arnold had allowed the private use of Pennsylvania's hired Conestoga wagons to haul the ship's cargo of Charming Nancy from New Jersey into Philadelphia. To this charge, he added Arnold's attempt to issue a passport to help Hannah Levy, the daughter of a wealthy Jewish Loyalist merchant, to join her family in New York City despite the Pennsylvania council's objections. He charged Arnold, under Pennsylvania law, to appear before the council and testify. Arnold refused, saying he was appointed by George Washington and would be accountable only to him.

Reed then demanded of Congress that Arnold be removed from command in Pennsylvania "until the charges against him are examined." Congress appointed a special committee to investigate. An unhappy Reed wanted control. If this proceeded, it forced him to admit publically that a congressional committee had more power than that of his own council; but if he backed down, Arnold would be acquitted.

Reed finally determined to add a new threat. He was in charge of raising troops and levying Pennsylvania's taxes, so he now added that if Congress refused to oust Arnold, allowing him "to affront us without feeling any marks of your displeasure," Pennsylvania would think long and hard about cooperating with Congress in the future. He was especially cognizant of the burden this would put on Washington, who depended heavily on the troops of the Pennsylvania Line and also the use of Pennsylvania's precious Conestoga wagons for the bulk of his transport.

Then early in February, 1779, Reed and his council somehow discovered that Arnold was planning a journey to visit Washington in his New Jersey headquarters, and then planning to go further into New York State to Kingston to confer with their revolutionary leaders, General PHILIP SCHUYLER, again, commander of the Northern Department, and James Duane, William Duer, and Gouverneur Morris, who had suggested that "the gentlemen of the State of New York" give Arnold a reward for his services in defense of their state, during the Canadian campaigns of 1775, 1776, and 1777. They proposed that he be given one of the two large loyalist manors, either the one at Skenesboro at the foot of Lake Champlain or Johnson's Hall on the Mohawk, where he could colonize his former troops as a buffer against further attacks from Vermont or Canada. Arnold preferred Skenesboro, but wanted to pay for it; however, he hoped the price would not be prohibitive.

As Arnold prepared to leave Philadelphia for his appointments, Reed and his council were furious. They didn't want him to escape their jurisdiction before they could prepare their final charges. So on 2 February 1779, the day before he was to leave the capitol city, Reed rushed eight charges to the printers, and on 3 February the proclamation was made public, just as Arnold's luggage was placed in his carriage and Major Clarkston bid him farewell. The proclamation stated that Arnold had granted illegal passes to loyalists, had closed the shops of Philadelphia so that he could make sizable purchases of foreign goods, had imposed degrading services on militiamen, and had used public wagons to transport private property. Arnold's "discouragement and neglect" of patriotic persons and his "different conduct toward those of another character" were "too notorious to need proof or illustration." As long as Arnold remained in command in Pennsylvania, they would not pay the army's costs and would call out the militia only in "the most urgent and pressing necessity." No more would the militia do Arnold or his staff's bidding.

Reed dispatched copies of the charges to every state and its congressional delegation and to Washington's headquarters at Morristown, New Jersey.

According to Arnold, the first he knew of them was when his aide Matthew Clarkson overtook him on the road with a copy of the Pennsylvania packet, which included the proclamation. At this point, he had two choices—to return to Philadelphia and face the charges or press forward to Washington's headquarters. He chose the latter, hoping for Washington's support. But in the eyes of many Philadelphians, he was fleeing north to join with the British.

Reports of the happenings at Washington's headquarters were differently reported; however, the result was that Arnold returned to Philadelphia to face these charges and General SCHUYLER received a letter from Arnold cancelling the meeting with the New York group. In Philadelphia, the issue became larger than the charges against Benedict Arnold. Reed wanted his pound of Arnold's flesh; but state rights and federal jurisdiction over the state of Pennsylvania became the real issue. The charges were sweat over by the original congressional committee, sent to Congress in favor of Arnold, and accepted by Congress, except the Pennsylvania delegation, who threatened to become an independent state. They formed a new committee and disregarded the findings of the first committee. They finally agreed to send the matter to George Washington with instructions that he was to hold the trial. Washington recognizing the need to keep the unity of the nation, at least until the war ended, delayed the trial and sent a rather short, terse notice to Arnold to that effect, not giving any reason, but promising another letter explaining his reason.

Realizing that this delay would put him out of the battles as well as Philadelphia and not receiving the promised explanatory letter, Arnold wrote Washington the following letter:

> "If your Excellency thinks me criminal, for heaven's sake let me be immediately tried and, if found guilty, executed. I want no favor; I ask only justice. If this be denied me by your Excellency, I have nowhere to seek it but from the candid public before whom I shall be under the necessity of laying the whole matter. Let me beg of you, Sir, to consider that a set of artful, unprincipled men in office may misrepresent the most innocent actions and, by raising the public clamor against your Excellency, place you in the situation I am in. Having made every sacrifice of fortune and blood and become a cripple in the service of my country, I did not expect to meet the ungrateful returns I have received from my countrymen; but as Congress have stamped ingratitude as a current coin, I must take it. I wish,

your Excellency, for your long and eminent services, may not be paid in the same coin. I have nothing left but the little reputation I have gained in the army. Delay in the present case is worse than death."

He was very close to telling the truth when he said he had nothing left. In his three-and-one-half years as an army officer, he had received no salary nor had he been compensated by the government of Massachusetts for his expenses. On the same day that Washington sent him notice that his trial was to be delayed, he was also notified that these Massachusetts accounts were being sent to the Board of War for further scrutiny. It is said that he still had money, but his capital was in continental currency that had depreciated to one-sixtieth its 1777 value. His reputation was in total jeopardy as it was flaunted across the new nation. He was to ask himself: without Washington's approval, what did he have? Sometime early in May 1779, with full approval of his new wife Peggy, Arnold made contact with her close British friend, the fashionable Captain Andre`, and offered his service to the enemy.

It was early in the year of 1780 before Washington allowed the trial to proceed. Junior officers conducted the trial. Washington still trusted Arnold and excused himself from the proceedings, although he was often found listening outside the door. Four of the charges were dropped by Congress before the trial. Of the four remaining, he was charged with only two, and his punishment was to be a reprimand by the Commander in Chief, George Washington. The general called his actions reprehensible, imprudent, and improper. In those days, when duels were fought over less insulting words, Arnold was mortified that his honor was in any way questioned by this man he felt he had so faithfully served.

In defense of the position of Reed and his radical Whigs, it might be well to acknowledge that when Arnold first arrived in Philadelphia in June 1778, he established himself in the mansion vacated by Howe and attempted to become a social somebody. He employed a housekeeper, a coachman, a groom, and seven other lesser servants. His fine carriage with four handsome horses and liveried attendants was seen frequently by everyone throughout the city. He hosted fabulous dinners that were the talk of the town. He took advantage of every available financial opportunity. To add to all of this, he expensively courted the popular, young, strong-willed Margaret Shippen, known as Peggy, even though he was still supporting a sister and three boys by his first marriage. They were married, and he then had an expensive wife who was a close friend of the British officers during the enemy occupation. To the conservative Quakers of Philadelphia and the returning patriots, who loved freedom and liberty, all of this was, indeed, reprehensible, imprudent, and improper.

~ 91 ~

SAVAGERY ON THE FRONTIERS—
GEORGE ROGERS CLARK

When Burgoyne surrendered in October 1777, the Indians had been quick to desert his army and return to the safety of Canada, which extended along both sides of the St. Lawrence River and the Great Lakes. This included the British held Fort Niagara on Lake Ontario, where it joins the eastern tip of Lake Erie. Here the Seven Nation Iroquois and the Pennsylvania Delaware had gathered to obtain the shipload of bounty the British had promised them in return for their enlistment against the Americans. The British had also promised that the Great King in London would restore additional lands to each of them. The Americans could do neither of these things. As a basically bankrupt nation, they needed to preserve their own homes and acquire new lands for their rapidly expanding population. Whatever meager finances they could obtain were needed to sustain their own army, and when that was insufficient, their men were promised this deserted Indian land—when the war ended. So, they burned the vacated Indian villages and were very anxious to claim the extended territory. The states of Virginia and North Carolina claimed all the land that extended west to the Mississippi River.

The Shawnees of the Ohio River valley were a fiercely independent tribe. They had resisted Christian missionaries and absolutely refused to trust either the British or the Americans—stubbornly attempting to hold to their traditions and refusing to "treat" with the white man, unlike the Seven Nation Iroquois or the Delaware Indians. Captain ALEXANDER McKEE's mother was a Shawnee, the wife of Captain THOMAS McKEE, an earlier British Indian agent that had lived in the area of Lancaster and Chester Counties of Pennsylvania.

ALEXANDER had also married a Shawnee girl. When the Revolution broke out, he lived with his family at Crooked Nose's Town westward from the Scioto-Ohio River valley near the Great Miami River. Here he operated a trading post—as well as maintaining his demeanor and title as a British officer.

[Note: At this same time, my younger fourth-great-grandfather ALEXANDER McKEE was residing in Orange County, North Carolina, where he would soon become a private in the continental army, which later entitled him to receive land in the former Indian territory of Sumner County, Tennessee. And, if he was a descendant also of Captain THOMAS McKEE and married MARY BEAN, who might have had some Cherokee Indian blood, he might very well have considered himself quite worthy in several ways to receive this remuneration of land.]

Residing at the main Scioto Shawnee's chief town of Chillicothe [Ohio] was a twelve-year-old Shawnee named Tecumseh, or Shooting Star. Like Captain McKEE, he had mixed parentage. Some have claimed that his mother was half-Creek Indian and half-white. His Shawnee father was also reported to have some white blood. Tecumseh was born in Tennessee; but his family had been forced to move northward—first into West Virginia, then to Fort Pitt, then on into the Ohio valley. This reportedly handsome, young, light-skinned Indian would within a few decades wage the greatest battles against American expansion that the new nation would experience. But in 1778 and until the Peace Treaty at Paris, he would follow, watch, and grow into manhood until he became, in the view of many, the greatest Indian warrior of all times.

While George Washington again wondered where the embarking thousands of the British army were headed as they sailed away from New York harbor that summer of 1778, after the battle at Monmouth County Courthouse, the Virginians, with Patrick Henry as governor, became anxious about their far western lands in the Ohio valley. They had sent the young, twenty-four-year-old George Rogers Clark, who had come to them with information and a plan, on an expedition into the territory. Clark had surveyed hundreds of miles in this western part of their state. He had previously helped the Kentuckians organize a government and become recognized as a Virginia colony. He was extremely supportive of the United States and a dedicated foe of British Colonel Hamilton, who had been sent to occupy Fort Detroit, located on the northwestern end of Lake Erie at the southern tip of Lake Huron. Hamilton had been assigned by his king to

"assemble Indians . . . and employ them in making a diversion and exciting an alarm upon the frontiers of Virginia and Pennsylvania."

Clark, whose younger brother William Clark would later explore the Louisiana Territory with Meriwether Lewis, had detailed his plan to the Virginia Assembly in January 1778. They commissioned him as a lieutenant colonel of a Virginia militia with authority to raise troops among the extremely small white population of Kentucky. They gave him 1,200 British pounds and allowed him to draw supplies from Fort Pitt. Secretly he was empowered to take the British post in the French town of Kaskaskia, which was located at the mouth of the Ohio River as it joins the Mississippi River in what is now southern Illinois. If successful, they were to proceed to the northeast and challenge British Colonel Hamilton and, if possible, take Fort Detroit.

So on 24 Jun 1778, Colonel Clark set out for Kaskaskia with a flotilla of flatboats carrying 175 frontiersmen from Kentucky, and four days later entered the mouth of the Tennessee River. They floated and rowed to the ruins of the old French fort, Massaic, around ten miles south. Here they hid their boats. To surprise the enemy, they must proceed by land.

The following morning they were joined by a group of hunters from Kaskaskia and began their 120-mile journey through the Shawnee National Forest area of today. The Clark expedition came in sight of their destination on the evening of 4 July. That night the hungry and exhausted soldiers, who had run out of supplies two days earlier, procured boats and ferried across the river to the sleeping town that consisted of two hundred and fifty houses and a stone fort. Dividing his little force, Colonel Clark surrounded the town, "broke into the fort," and took Kaskaskia without firing a shot.

> "Nothing could excel the confusion these people seemed to be in . . . being taught to expect nothing but savage treatment from the Americans. Giving all for lost . . . they were willing to be slaves to save their families."

[Note: This was taken from a letter Clark wrote to his close friend GEORGE MASON of Williamsburg, a member of the Virginia Assembly. This GEORGE MASON should not be confused with Washington's close friend and neighbor, also George Mason. This GEORGE MASON's grandfather was a brother to ELIZABETH MASON on my family tree.]

In this letter, Clark continued to relate how the French townspeople "fell into transports of joy" when they learned that France and the United States were now official allies and that these fierce-looking Americans would not harm or molest them in their persons, property, or religion if they took an oath of fidelity to the state of Virginia.

The colonel sent a detachment of sixty men on borrowed horses to capture Cahokia, which was sixty miles north—across the Mississippi River from the friendly Spanish post of St. Louis. Father Pierre Gibault of Kaskaskia volunteered to go to Vincennes (located on the Wabash River, which separates the southern parts of our present day states of Illinois and Indiana). He returned on the 1st of August to report that he had been completely successful in winning over the French inhabitants. Two other French posts joined with the Americans. Clark immediately sent Captain Leonard Helm to occupy Vincennes and its well supplied Fort Sackville and to take command of the French militia there, while he remained at Kaskaskia organizing the government of the Virginia County he called Illinois, convincing his troops to remain and extend American influence among the thousands of Indians.

When word came to British Colonel Hamilton at Fort Detroit of the American intrusion into the Ohio River territory, he took 500 men, which included 300 Indians, and marched the many difficult miles southwest to Vincennes. They arrived in a snow storm on 17 December and retook the fort, capturing the Americans, who consisted of Captain Helm and three soldiers.

Clark sent Francis Vigo to spy on Vincennes. He was an Italian fur trader and businessman of St. Louis who had gallantly given cash and joined with the Americans in their fight for liberty. He allowed himself to be captured, escaped and then returned to Kaskaskia where he informed Colonel Clark that

> "Mr. Hamilton had weakened himself by sending his Indians against the frontier ... that he had not more than eighty men in garrison, three pieces of cannon and some swivels mounted, and that he intended to attack this place [Kaskaskia] as soon as the winter opened [in the spring]."

With this information, George Rogers Clark decided to take the initiative and attack Vincennes. He thought the enemy

> "could not suppose ... we should be so mad as to attempt to march eighty leagues through a drowned country in the depth of winter, that they would be off their guard and probably would not think it worth while to keep out spies."

Clark was to later confess,

> "At this moment I would have bound myself a slave to have had five hundred troops."

He built a large row galley and armed it with six light guns. In February 1779, he manned it with forty-six men and sent it up the Ohio and Wabash Rivers where they were to take station

"ten leagues below the post Vincennes and wait until further orders."

He felt that the surrounding land would be flooded in this season of the year and that the only way Hamilton would be able to move his artillery would be by boat. So, if the British discovered his approach by land with his one-hundred-seventy men and Hamilton tried to escape down the Mississippi, the men on the galley were to attack and take them prisoners.

Clark wrote,

"We set out on a forlorn hope indeed. For our whole party with the boat's crew consisted of only a little upwards of two hundred. I cannot account for it, but I still had inward assurance of success and never could, when weighing every circumstance, doubt it."

It was an extremely difficult trek through that "drowned country" with cold, muddy prairies and ankle-deep water in the lowlands spreading and deepening near the mouth of the Little Wabash to a continuous lake five miles across, which was broken only by the bare branches of trees rising over the crystal surface. Of the journey, Clark wrote in his memoirs,

"My object now was to keep the men in spirits. I suffered them to shoot game on all occasions and feast on them, like Indians' war dances, each company by turns inviting the other to their feasts, which was the case every night . . . . Myself and principal officers hailing on the woodsmen, shouting now and then, and running as much through the mud and water as any of them . . . . Thus insensibly without a murmur was those men led on to the banks of the Little Wabash, which we reached the thirteenth, through incredible difficulties far surpassing anything any of us had ever experienced."

Clark said he

"viewed the sheet of water for some time with distrust."

Then, overcoming his fears, he ordered his men to build a great canoe and a platform above water on the eastern shore where they ferried their supplies. They then swam their horses across and loaded them. The men followed, splashing through three and four feet of water to the far branch of the river where they pitched their tents.

> "They really began to think themselves superior to other men and that neither the rivers or seasons could stop their progress. Their whole conversation now was what they would do when they got about the enemy and now began to view the main Wabash as a creek and made no doubt but such men as they were could find a way to cross it. They wound themselves up in such a pitch that they soon took Vincennes, divided the spoil, and before bedtime, was far advanced on their route to Detroit."

They were indeed remarkable men for their provisions were spoiled, the usually available game had moved to higher ground and the main Wabash River lay between their camp and Vincennes. Four days later they reached the bank of the Embarrass River. The weak had been stumbling and the valiant pushing them onward through the waist-deep water, only to be told at this time by their scouts that the Embarrass had flooded the whole nine miles of country between them and the Wabash. Vincennes was on its eastern shore. They moved onward with resolution, led by their intrepid colonel. That night, they found some murky ground for their camp from which the flood waters had receded.

At dawn, they heard for the first time and were "amused by the morning gun from the British garrison" at Vincennes. Within a short distance they were on the banks of the Wabash and viewed the continuous flooding that extended beyond the eastern bank. Undaunted, Colonel Clark plunged into the freezing, shoulder-high water and beckoned his men to follow. He told it this way,

> "[The men] ran from one to another, bewailing their situation. I viewed their confusion for about one minute, whispered to those near me to [do] as I did, immediately took some water in my hand, poured on powder, blacked my face, gave the war whoop, and marched into the water without saying a word. The party gasped and fell in, one after another, without saying a word, like a flock of sheep. I ordered those that was near me to begin a favorite song of theirs. It soon passed through the line and the whole went on cheerfully."

They were able to shoot a deer and divide it between the hungry men. Still, seven or eight miles of submerged land lay between them and their destination.

Pushing through breast-high water, on the twenty-third of February, the small American army arrived at a hill that gave them a sight of the French town of Vincennes. Here, Clark sent a letter to the inhabitants that announced his presence and his intention of taking the post that night with instructions that they stay indoors. He then personally led his men through the water to the higher ground surrounding the town and paraded them around and around the small hills, hoping that the enemy would believe he had over 1,000 soldiers. They entered the town about eight o'clock and took possession, while a company of fourteen went to fire on the fort.

From the diary of one of Clark's captains,

> "Smart firing all night on both sides. The cannon played smartly, not one of our men wounded . . . fine sport for the sons of Liberty."

Around eight in the morning, Colonel Clark sent a flag to Hamilton demanding unconditional surrender, which Hamilton refused with disgust. The firing continued until early afternoon, when the British colonel requested a parley in the church. They couldn't agree, so he returned to the fort.

During the afternoon, according to Hamilton's report, a party of Indians returning from a scout were attacked by Clark's men and two were killed and one was wounded.

> "The rest were surrounded and taken bound to the village where being set in the street opposite the fort gate, they were put to death, notwithstanding a truce at that moment existed . . . . One of them was tomahawked immediately. The rest, sitting on the ground in a ring, bound, seeing by the fate of their comrade what they might expect, the next on his left sung his death song and was in turn tomahawked. The rest underwent the same . . . . One only was saved by the intercession of a rebel officer who pleaded for him, telling Colonel Clark that the savage's father had formerly saved his life . . . Colonel Clark, yet reeking with the blood of these unhappy victims, came to the esplanade before the fort gate, where I had agreed to meet him and treat of the surrender of the garrison. He spoke with rapture of his late achievement, while he washed the blood from his hand stained in this inhuman sacrifice."

Clark admitted his act. He said that he hoped that the execution of the redmen before their friends would persuade them that the English could not or would not give them the protection they had been promised. Kentuckian Captain Joseph Bowman casually reported,

"We . . . brought the Indians back to the main street before the fort gate, there tomahawked them, and threw them into the river."

Colonel Henry Hamilton chose surrender and imprisonment, rather than risk the lives of anymore of his men, but he insisted on including in the articles of capitulation an article relating his reasons for giving up his post: the remoteness from succor, the state and quantity of provisions, the unanimity of officers and men on its expediency, the honorable terms allowed, and lastly his confidence in a generous enemy. At ten o'clock, 25 Feb 1779, the surrender was complete and the American flag was raised once more over Fort Sackville.

George Rogers Clark, who seemed so hardened in his treatment of the Indians, was indeed generous with the British. The enlisted men were paroled and the officers marched off for Virginia, where Hamilton was confined. Thomas Jefferson, then governor of Virginia, replacing Patrick Henry, made an investigation into Henry Hamilton's background, and found that Hamilton was guilty of offering rewards for scalps but none for prisoners, thus encouraging the Indians to slay their white captives. For a long time, Jefferson refused to exchange Henry Hamilton, who had become known as "the Hair Buyer," for fear of his influence and the evil he might again arouse on the frontier.

Clark claimed for Virginia all the surrounding territory—an area that amounted to more than half the size of all the original thirteen colonies put together. He was able to successfully bind the Indians of the area to the American cause; but he was never able to fulfill his commitment and dream to acquire Fort Detroit, probably because Virginia would no longer support his effort. They seemed to be more concerned with land speculation in the extended Virginia territory. But there was also another impediment—the independent, unconquered Shawnee Indians of the Ohio territory, where Tecumseh's family and Captain ALEXANDER McKEE resided.

Residing in Old Chillicothe was the formidable Indian War Captain Blackfish who, encouraged by the British, led the first Shawnee raids into Kentucky during 1777 and 1778. On a snowy day in February 1778, he had captured Daniel Boone and twenty-seven of his companions while they gathered salt on the Licking River. They brought them to their Shawnee towns, where their homes and gardens were very clean by frontier standards. Boone and a few escaped, others were adopted and some were eventually purchased by the

British and released. A young sixteen-year-old, Benjamin Kelly, who remained with the Indians five years and then became a Baptist minister, reported in 1821 that he had been adopted by Blackfish and lived in a house near a spring in Old Chillicothe. He claimed that Tecumseh and his older brother, known as the Prophet, were his foster brothers.

After dark, on the evening of 29 May 1779, Kentuckian Captain Joseph Bowman with 300 men quietly stole into Old Chillicothe. A lone Indian came out on the street and was quickly shot by one of the Kentuckians. Within minutes the town became a battleground. Many of the Indians fled; but Blackfish and his remaining warriors made a counterattack to defend the women and children who had escaped and had barricaded themselves in one of the council houses, where they could see their homes being torched by the invaders. It was a long night that lasted until the Americans became concerned that Indian reinforcements were fast approaching. Seven Indians were killed or fatally wounded, including Blackfish, whose wounds became infected and he died about six weeks later. Savagery and depredations continued on both sides.

In 1780, the British finally responded to the cries of the Indians for vengeance. British Captain Henry Bird, of the 8th Regiment of Foot, tramped south with about 1,000 soldiers. Included were 100 Shawnee Indians mustered by Captain ALEXANDER McKEE at Pekowi. They invaded Kentucky in June of that year and returned with about 350 American prisoners, men, women and children. Other skirmishes followed with the release of most of the prisoners.

By August of that same year, Colonel George Rogers Clark collected an army of 1,000 men and, bringing a six-pounder along, crossed over the vast territory and burned Old Chillicothe to the ground. As most of their warriors were with the British in Fort Detroit, the inhabitants fled into Pekowi sending riders for help, while the Americans destroyed their homes and crops. However, Clark was quick to follow them and when his artillery opened fire upon Pekowi, they again took flight to the east. They were able to escape to Wakatomica, and Clark gave up the chase and went home. The refugees had lost their homes and food for the winter. Clark reported 14 of his men killed and 13 wounded. The Indians said that six of their men were killed and others wounded, with a man and woman taken prisoners—the woman had been killed with her stomach slashed open.

The next spring found the Shawnee Indian women building new villages and planting crops somewhat to the northwest on the west bank of the Great Miami River. The Kispokos joined in this cluster of towns, which had regrouped around McKEE's trading post, which was located on a creek about two-and-a-half miles southeast of the site of modern Bellefontain. But these inveterate enemies of the western settlers were not allowed to live happily ever after. In the last campaign of the Revolution, in November 1782, Clark, with another army, destroyed Standing Stone and neighboring settlements, which included Louis Lorimier's trading post, New Pekowi, and Willstown. Seventeen Indians were killed or captured. Captain ALEXANDER McKEE led a war party from Wakatomica to harass Clark's retreat, but the Americans were too strong and the Shawnee withdrew after losing a few of their men. It is possible that this was when the Americans captured Captain McKEE, for the records claim he was taken as a prisoner to New York City. The British bargained for him in an exchange, and he and his family were given land in Nova Scotia. His son THOMAS McKEE later became the British Indian agent at Fort Malden across the Detroit River on the Canadian side.

While McKEE had chosen to support the cause of the Shawnee and the British, Indian agent GEORGE MORGAN worked hard with Patrick Henry and Thomas Jefferson to create peace between the Virginians and all the Indians in this Ohio territory claimed by Virginia. MORGAN left a valuable journal of his activities with these Indians and some mention is given in other chapters of this book.

The Wyoming Valley of Northeastern Pennsylvania

The British had 400 soldiers garrisoned at Fort Niagara, the old French fort they had captured in 1759 during the French and Indian War. This fort was a very busy and strategic place during the Revolutionary War. It was here that the Delawares of Pennsylvania, the Six-Nation Iroquois, Hurons, and other pro-British Indians had gathered to obtain the bounty King George had shipped from England to bribe the tribes to fight against their colonists. Loyalists found refuge in this area around Lake Ontario, also.

In the [Governor] Haldimand Papers, 21762:136, Lieutenant Colonel Mason Bolton reported in June 1778,

"Scalps & Prisoners are coming in every day which is all the News this Place affords." In 1779, at an Indian council, Seneca chief Sayengeraghta, who was also known as Old Smoke, was reported (in these same papers 21779:21) as instructing the Hurons, "It is also your Business Brothers to exert yourselves in the Defense of this Road by which the King, our Father, so fully supplied our Wants. If this is once stopt we must be a miserable People, and be left exposed to the Resentment of the Rebels, who, notwithstanding their fair Speeches, wish for nothing more, than to extirpate us from the Earth, that they may possess our Lands, the Desire of attaining which we are convinced is the Cause of the present War between the King and his disobedient Children."

To retain this active support of the Indians, the 500 pounds per annum at the beginning of the Revolution had increased to 100,000 pounds per annum by 1781. This was very expensive for the British, who often turned to the local merchants to supplement their shortages. The local merchants made huge profits, especially, from the sale of rum, and according to some of the scathing, discontent soldiers they "cheated the army blind" every chance they got. In the winter months between November 1778 and March 1779, there were 7,365 Indians, of whom 4,700 were women and children, who received provisions and clothing from Fort Niagara.

Major John Butler and his son, Walter, lead the loyalist rangers, supported by the Indians from Fort Niagara, in their exploits as they raided hundreds of miles of frontier white settlements, where they pillaged, burned and scalped the American inhabitants. It was early in June 1778 that a large force from Fort Niagara traveled the three-hundred-plus miles into the Wyoming valley of Pennsylvania, where Mayor Butler reported taking 227 scalps and only five prisoners. One of the stories that were spawned from this attack, called the Wyoming Massacre, told of a half-breed Seneca called Queen Esther who arranged fifteen prisoners in a ring, and, while circling them, she sang a dirge as she tomahawked them one by one. This raid was followed by a joint Loyalist-Iroquois raid on German Flats on the Mohawk River, below Utica, in September. Then, in November of that same year, they advanced further into the Cherry Valley, only fifty miles west of Albany.

That winter, George Washington decided to spare part of his continental army to attack the Iroquois in their homelands around the Finger Lakes and the

Genesee Valley of western New York, as soon as the spring weather permitted, with the order to destroy their homes and crops, and force the Iroquois to deplete the rations of the British at Fort Niagara.

He chose a frontiersman, Major General Sullivan, to lead this expedition. He gave him a force of 2,500 continentals at Easton, Pennsylvania (on the Delaware River a few miles north of the northwestern border of ancestral Hunterdon County, New Jersey.) General James Clinton of New York was to march from Albany with 1,500 New York continentals to the headwaters of the Susquehanna River at Otsego Lake and then float his forces down the river to rendezvous with Sullivan at Tioga. Colonel Daniel Brodhead joined Sullivan with 600 continentals from Fort Pitt in southwestern Pennsylvania, also. This gave Sullivan a total force of 4,600 Continentals, or about one-third of Washington's regulars. He was to take artillery with him. Washington had been an Indian fighter during and since the French and Indian War; he realized that the Indians had never had to face cannon on a battlefield and felt strongly about the advantage this would give Sullivan. He further instructed Sullivan that his men were to attack with bayonet and war whoop, "with as much impetuosity, shouting and noise as possible."

This was not an easy campaign to put together. It was 27 Aug 1779, when Sullivan's combined expeditionary force of 4,000 (Brodhead's troops from Fort Pitt had turned back, because they didn't have shoes) finally began to move north along the Delaware with nine fieldpieces, including four 6-pounders, four 3-pounders and a small portable mortar that was called a "grasshopper." Some of the officers were unhappy with the artillery.

Major Jeremiah Fogg recorded,

"The transportation appears to the army in general as impractical, and [as] absurd as an attempt to level the Allegheny Mountains."

However, there was a reversal of this opinion two days later when the artillery was cheered with acclamation. It seems that Chief Joseph Brandt, with over 1,000 Indians, with Butler's 250 Loyal Rangers and 15 British redcoats, had prepared an ambush for Sullivan's advancing army, and were waiting silently while Sullivan's continentals struggled up the narrow, steep Chemung Valley defile toward the Indian village of Newtown. Fortunately, for Sullivan, he had brought along several Oneida Indian scouts. One of them climbed a tree on a 700-foot hill and spotted painted Indians crouching behind a breastwork of logs which was camouflaged with green branches. This was one of the largest forces ever gathered by the Iroquois.

Sullivan immediately stopped his column and detached a strong flanking force to attack their hilltop position from the rear. He then positioned his artillery and fired on the breastwork with solid shot, grapeshot and iron spikes. The startled Iroquois held their position for about one-half hour—until they heard shots coming from behind and believed the enemy to have out-flanked them. Most ran, followed by the Loyal Rangers. On the hilltop the Indians struggled one-on-one with the continentals until Joseph Brandt signaled them to retreat. Three Americans were killed and thirty-six were wounded. Twelve Indian men and one woman died, who were scalped by the whites. The number of Iroquois who were wounded is unknown.

The "Battle of Newtown" terrorized the Indians. Although their losses were relatively small, they refused to fight again in force against the Americans. Sullivan and his army proceeded to follow orders and scorched the Indian lands and homes from Elmira to the St. Lawrence River and then southwest into the Genesse country. They raided and burned Indian settlements in the Mohawk Valley, on the west side of Seneca Lake, and on both sides of Cayuga Lake. These settlements were not the teepee villages shown in Western movies. These Indians, in over a hundred cases, had large and elegant homes, even the smaller were made of wood with glass windows. Their crops were well tended with some corn reported as having eighteen-foot stalks. Their barns were filled with corn, pumpkins, and other supplies. At Aurora, the army destroyed 1,500 peach trees. It is estimated that in all, Sullivan's army demolished forty Indian villages and 160,000 bushels of corn as well as immense quantities of other vegetables and fruits.

Marching back to Elmira, the Americans celebrated their 500-mile expedition with a large fireworks display and ox roast. A bull and a barrel of rum were furnished to each brigade. When they arrived at Tioga a few days later, they put on war paint, and led by an Oneida sachem, joined in a war dance with each step ending with a whoop. After destroying their stockades, they returned to the Wyoming Valley above Easton, Pennsylvania. They had lost only forty of their men, and had brought an ancient civilization to their knees. The culture of the Iroquois Confederacy was gone. Fort Niagara became the Iroquois's only means of support and a proud, independent people became the great burden for the British that Washington had hoped for, as they ate British food supplies and used British ammunition to kill the meat that they needed for survival. After the war ended, these new lands would be given to pay the huge national debt to the soldiers and were sold to the ever-increasing Europeans that crossed a vast ocean in search of a better, freer way of life.

[Note: It is very probable that some of our ancestors and relations were with these troops, because of the near proximity of their homes. JOHN WILKINSON, father of third-great-grandfather AARON WILKINSON, is shown in our pedigree chart as being from Hunterdon County, New Jersey, or from Bucks County, Pennsylvania. These WILKINSONs were early settlers in the Pennsylvania County of Northhumberland, where the Susquehanna River's northern and western branches join at Sunbury, south and west of the Wyoming Valley. These early settlers first arrived after the Revolution had ended. The old Fort Augusta is located at this spot and was garrisoned during the war. The BARTONs, the COOLEYs (both of Hunterdon County), and the POYERs probably came before 1800. John D. Rockefeller's grandfather was also an early settler in that valley. One township is named Rockefeller. John D.'s father and mother left the area and moved north to Tioga, New York, where he was born. We have a distant aunt who lived in this area that married Hiram Rockefeller. They didn't have any children that we know of.]

The younger sons of many New Englanders, also, moved into these western New York and Pennsylvania lands. It was 1815 before the impoverished Joseph Smith family came from the Connecticut River region of Vermont and New Hampshire to the more fertile lands above the Finger Lakes of New York to a town called Palmyra. Joseph Smith Jr. was a fifth-generation American. His ancestor Robert Smith came to America from Kirton, England, in 1636, and settled in Topsfield, Massachusetts—about 23 miles north of Boston. His great-grandfather, Samuel, who died in 1785, was proclaimed a Revolutionary War hero upon his death. New England was not large enough, nor productive enough for all of the ever-increasing posterity of liberty-loving, independent Americans. More land was desperately needed.

[Note: My early SMITH ancestors, twelfth-great-grandfather CHRISTOPHER SMITH and family arrived in America in 1652 with their daughter SUSANNA SMITH, who was married to LAWRENCE WILKINSON. They were from Lancester, Durham, England (located above Yorkshire County). LAWRENCE, who was an officer in the army of King Charles I, had lost his English lands when Cromwell came to power and Charles I was beheaded. They settled in Providence, Rhode Island. LAWRENCE and SUSANNA were also the great-grandparents of STEPHEN HOPKINS, who signed the Declaration of Independence. This is a different SMITH ancestral line than that of Joseph Smith Jr.]

∼ 92 ∼

THE WAITING GAME—
"WHO CAN I TRUST NOW?"

Rhode Island

Washington was unaware of London's orders to their new commanding general, Sir Henry Clinton, to move their offensive south to Charleston, South Carolina, with additional troops sent into the West Indies with the possible invasion of the French islands after the French alliance with the United States and declaration of war on the English. British General Clinton had withdrawn from Philadelphia, because they feared the French fleet could stop supplies to their troops and allow the Americans to surround and capture them. London gave him orders to retain New York City, if possible, but to evacuate to Rhode Island first and then to Halifax, Nova Scotia, if necessary. Sir Henry was not to launch any major offensive in the north—only defend their harbors and harass the enemy. General Washington, however, expected a major offensive action by the British and moved his troops closer to the Hudson River on 30 Jun 1778, after the battle of Monmouth Court House. He dismissed the militia, who were in large numbers already going home. MORGAN and Maxwell's troops remained behind to protect the New Jersey coast until the British troops sailed and then they were to join Washington's continentals.

General Gates, in the Highlands on the Hudson, assigned New York Governor George Clinton to take command at West Point, while he moved his main troops to White Plains, New York., and called on the Connecticut governor to send in their militia to join him. He hoped to feign an attack on New York City and expected the British to launch a major battle in defense of the city, but the British sat still on Manhattan, Staten, and Long Islands.

The second week of July, the French fleet was spotted just off Sandy Hook, New Jersey, and Maxwell's troops were sent south to join them, accompanied by aides Laurens and HAMILTON. They were to proceed to the flagship of the French Vice Admiral Charles Hector, Count d'Estaing, to arrange for signals, to furnish pilots, and to coordinate the efforts of both countries. It was a disappointment to both the Americans and the French—the large French vessels were too deep for the New York harbor.

D'Estaing wrote Congress:

"Both officers and crews were kept in spirits, notwithstanding their wants and the fatigues of service, by the desire of delivering America from the English colors, which we saw waving on the other side of a simple barrier of sand upon so great a crowd of masts. The pilots procured by Laurens and Hamilton destroyed all illusion. These experienced persons unanimously declared that it was impossible to carry us in. I offered in vain a reward of fifty thousand crowns to any one who would promise success. All refused, and the particular soundings which I caused to be taken myself too well demonstrated they were right."

With that, the attack on the British in New York was abandoned, and the French fleet set sail for the second objective—the port at Newport, Rhode Island. Washington immediately sent Lafayette with two crack brigades to Providence, followed in two days by a much larger expedition of continentals. The brusk frontiersman, General Sullivan, was to be in command. He was to divide them into two divisions with Lafayette commanding one and Rhode Islander General NATHANAEL GREENE was to command the other. John Hancock made his first appearance as a military officer and brought with him 5,000 militia from the New England states.

The French fleet arrived on 29 July, while Sullivan was still collecting his troops, so 10 August was chosen as the date for the coordinated attack. As Sullivan advanced into northern Rhode Island, he discovered that the British works had been abandoned. The French had disembarked 4,000 troops to the west on Conanicut Island. Then in the distance to the west d'Estaing spotted the approach of at least thirty vessels of Howe's British fleet. Concerned that his men might be trapped and, probably preferring a sea battle, he re-embarked his men and confronted the approaching array of sea power.

Sullivan continued his advance with 10,000 men to within two miles of British General Robert Pigot's lines of 6,200, north of Newport. Lieutenant Colonel Paul Revere and his son, Captain Paul, were among Sullivan's militia troops. The optimistic colonel wrote home:

> "I am in high health and spirits and so is our army. The enemy dare not show their heads . . . . It seems as if half Boston was here. I hope the affair will soon be settled . . . . I trust that All-wise being who has protected me will still protect me and send me safely to the arms of her whom it is my greatest happiness to call my own. Paul is well, sends duty and love to all."

But the battle at sea was interrupted by a gale of hurricane ferocity. Both British and French ships were severely damaged. Howe hobbled back to New York for repairs, and to the disheartenment of Sullivan and his generals, d'Estaing determined to proceed to Boston harbor for his repairs, without leaving any of his soldiers to join with the Americans. General GREENE is quoted as saying,

> "the devil has got into the fleet; they are about to desert us! . . . To evacuate the island is death. To stay may be ruin!"

And as they watched the French fleet vanish beyond the horizon on the twenty-fourth, 5,000 militia vanished with them.

Washington, at White Plains, foresaw another problem and sent a message to the hot-tempered General Sullivan.

> "Should the expedition fail, through the abandonment of the French fleet, the officers concerned will be apt to complain loudly. But prudence dictates that we should put the best face upon the matter and to the world attribute the removal to Boston to necessity.
>
> "The reasons are too obvious to need explaining. The principal one is that our British and internal enemies would be glad to improve the least matter of complaint and disgust against and between us and our new allies into a serious rupture."

But Sullivan had not waited to hear from his general. What was obvious to Washington was not obvious to Sullivan, who lashed out at the French in his orders on the twenty-fourth and concluded by saying that he

> "yet hopes the event will prove America is able to procure with her own arms that which her allies refused to assist her in obtaining."

An offended Lafayette and other advisers persuaded Sullivan to issue a retraction, which he begrudgingly did. However, he continued his insulting words that went forth across the countryside and America became indebted to the diplomacy of John Hancock, who was now back in Boston. He and the leaders in Boston were ever gracious to the French admiral, even to the extent of blaming the death of a high-born French lieutenant on the

> "secret enemies of our cause and the British officers [prisoners from Saratoga] in the neighborhood of this place are endeavoring to sow the seeds of discord as much as possible between the inhabitants. . . . and the French."

When Sullivan was alerted by Washington that British Admiral Sir Richard Howe (Black-Dick) had put out to sea again with reinforcements for Rhode Island, Sullivan began his evacuation early on 28 Aug 1778. By daylight, Pigot was after him. A battle ensued, and to the credit of Sullivan, his lines held. Sullivan's right was pounded upon by four British gunships; but an all-Negro Rhode Island regiment stood firm against the artillery and the Hessians until the battle broke. That night Sullivan evacuated his army.

Once more, John Glover and his Massachusetts Marbleheaders, who fought with Sullivan on his left, were successful in delivering an army by boat from an island to the safety of the mainland. Sullivan proudly reported,

> "Not a man was left behind, nor the smallest article lost."

He further reported 30 Americans killed, 137 wounded, and 44 missing. The British statistics were 38 killed, 210 wounded, and 12 missing. The next day, the British fleet brought in 5,000 troops to reinforce the garrison at Newport, Rhode Island. Washington spread his army of over 16,000 soldiers from Danbury, Connecticut, to the defenses of the Hudson River—waiting. His time was spent trying to placate the French and create harmony between the two nations, and goodwill was established. Without sea power, Washington wouldn't attack either port, and Sir Henry Clinton refused to enter into any major offensive land battle.

As flour became scarce in New England while the Bostonians tried to feed the French fleet and the British prisoners from Saratoga, as well as themselves and the American army, the prisoners were moved to Virginia. In November, Washington established his winter headquarters at Middlebrook, New Jersey, and took up his own residence at the house of John Wallace—still considering Sir Henry as being "indecisive and foolish."

[Note: Cousins to our ancestors in Rhode Island were undoubtedly greatly disturbed by the physical occupation of the British in Rhode Island during the Revolutionary War. STEPHEN HOPKINS, who signed the Declaration of Independence and had been governor of the state several times, of course, had his family there. His mother was RUTH WILKINSON, a sister of my ancestor JOHN WILKINSON, who moved to Hunterdon County, New Jersey, and then to Bucks County, Pennsylvania. The WILKINSON's original family came from England after Cromwell's army beheaded Charles I and took possession of their English lands. They had a plantation near Providence, in the area where the American army had collected.

JOHN and RUTH's father, ancestor SAMUEL WILKINSON married PLAIN WICKENDEN, who was born in Newport, Rhode Island, before her parents moved to Providence. The WICKENDENs have a numerous posterity, also. Many of the BARTONs and the GREENEs lived nearby, including Colonel WILLIAM BARTON, who lead the party that captured British Major General Richard Prescott, who was exchanged for American General Charles Lee. General NATHANAEL GREENE was related only through marriage. One of RUFUS BARTON's daughters had a son named NATHANAEL GREENE, a cousin.

Across the Sakonnet River to the east of Newport, close to the border of Massachusetts, was Little Crompton and Triverton. This was where my original American eleventh- and twelfth-generation great-grandparents of WILBORs, TALLMANs, and SMITHs arrived in the mid-1600s. They were mostly Quakers with large families—many of their descendants remained there. Their descendent, ninth-generation grandmother HANNAH WILBOR or WILBORE was born in Little Crompton. She had eleven brothers and sisters. She married ancestor WILLIAM LIPPINCOTT and moved to Shrewsbury, New Jersey. The WILBORs came from Braintree, Essex, England—a few miles from where my husband's [GROVER SWALLOW's] ancestors came from two and one-half centuries later—Stebbing, Essex, England.

On the northeast side of the Newport Island is Portsmouth. This is where twelfth-generation ancestors PHILLIP and ANN HILL were married in the year of 1627. They had a huge posterity that had spread throughout Rhode Island and the other colonies.]

Winter of 1778-79 and Stoney Point

In September 1778, British Major General Sir Henry Clinton had around 17,000 soldiers stationed in New York City and on Long Island, Staten Island and Rhode Island. In addition he had the 8,000 troops he was preparing to embark for the West Indies as London had ordered. These sugar cane islands were very important commercially to England, and with the French fleet moving south, a strong defense was imperative. He kept about 4,000 men in Rhode Island, and about 13,000 in or around New York—over half of which were Germans and loyalists.

[Note: The 13,000 men included the American Loyalist Corpe under Major General William Tryon, the former British governor of North Carolina during "The 1771 War of the Regulators." Ancestor JOHN ALLRED owned land bordering the land of Herman Husband, the leader of these Regulators. Tryon had insisted on the execution of Husband. Shortly after, the British king sent Tryon to New York to be the governor of that state. The lawyer of Orange County, North Carolina, Fanning, intensely disliked by the Regulators, went with Tryon to New York, where he became one of Tryon's lieutenants. The British replaced Tryon in North Carolina with a kinder, gentler man, Governor Martin, who befriended the

Regulators, asking only that they take an oath of allegiance to their British king. Because of his friendship and the oath, Martin believed this part of North Carolina to be loyalist. Perhaps some of our southern ancestors were, because their children, second-great-grandparents JAMES RUSSELL IVIE and ELIZA McKEE FAUSETT IVIE, named one son WILLIAM FRANKLIN and another son MARTIN.]

Tryon's loyalists in New York had been very active in supporting the British. They were stationed that fall on Long Island, with their headquarters at Oyster Bay—the homeland of ancestor NATHANIEL WRIGHT. Tryon wanted to make major raids on the Americans; however, Sir Henry limited his activities to mostly foraging into Connecticut to obtain food and other supplies that were needed for his large army. This, of course, created many skirmishes.

On 22 Sep 1778, Major General Charles Cornwallis took five thousand British soldiers across the Hudson at Paulus Hook and camped between New Bridge and Fort Lee two days later. At this same time, Lieutenant General Knyphausen went up the east side of the Hudson with about three thousand troops. He camped near Dobb's Ferry. He was to attract Washington and watch his actions, while Cornwallis looted the New Jersey countryside of their fall harvest. British possession of this strategic ferry prevented Washington from being able to quickly join his divided army, which was on both sides of the Hudson. Cornwallis was also close enough that he could join with the Germans, if Washington made a major attack. However, Washington chose to remain aloof of any major battle; but he sent a continental brigade to the west side of the Hudson to support the militia parties north of the British in New Jersey, and then he ordered Brigadier General William Maxwell to move his continental brigade from Elizabethtown toward Hackensack to support the New Jersey militia in that area. He moved Brigadier General James Clinton's continental brigade to Peekskill, near West Point, to protect this vital area. He warned Brigadier General Charles Scott, commander of the Light Infantry Corps in Westchester County, to be alert for any movement of Knyphausen's corps, especially if they tried to slip past him and march up the Hudson.

Brigadier General William Winds took command of about six hundred New Jersey militia who mustered near Cornwallis's column, while an Orange County militia regiment assembled and entered northeast New Jersey to restrain British foragers. New Jersey Governor WILLIAM LIVINGSTON and the Council of Safety called out all the militia of the six nearest counties to join Maxwell, and the New York Assembly ordered the Orange County officers to collect their militiamen as necessary. But the militia acted mostly the role of defenders and kept their distance. Only limited fighting occurred, to the disappointment of Sir Henry.

Then British General Clinton was informed that a large body of militia with a regiment of continental dragoons was near Tappan (New York/New Jersey border, near the Hudson.) Orders were given, and Major General Charles Grey led a detachment from Cornwallis' force in New Jersey to try to capture them on the night of 27 Sep 1778, while the 71st Regiment and Lieutenant Colonel Simcoe's Rangers from Knyphausen's column crossed the Hudson River to stop their retreat. Fortunately for the Americans, three deserters warned part of the militia. Simcoe's Rangers were three hours late in their crossing. The militia to the north escaped, unharmed. Unfortunately for the Americans, Colonel George Baylor and his continental dragoons were surprised by General Grey and very few of them escaped death or capture—at least seventy were killed, wounded or captured, along with many of the militia that were accompanying them. The British reported one man killed.

For awhile the militia surged in numbers and Washington sent Lord Stirling to coordinate the New Jersey forces. Then by 6 October, only around 400 militiamen remained of the 1,600 two days earlier. Cornwallis had received reinforcements and his 6,200 men continued their foraging with little interruption. Washington warned Stirling to maintain only a defensive position with his limited army.

Finally, Sir Henry Clinton decided to withdraw his troops from the New Jersey countryside. Consider for a moment how it would be for the colonists in the eastern—north and central—New Jersey and southern New York. They had first one army and then the other crossing their lands—foraging anything that was useful or edible—for years. Clinton's ships with the 8,000 soldiers were loaded and ready to sail south. The countryside was bare. Winter was fast approaching. Knyphausen returned to King's Bridge, and American General Charles Scott with his Light Horse Corp extended their territory to take control of Dobb's Ferry. Major military operations for 1778 came to a close; but the raiding, burnings, and harassing of the enemy continued through the winter, with Tryon's Loyalists scourging Long Island, the New York, and Connecticut coastal towns, where General I. Putman was sent to support the local militia under Governor Trumbull and the Connecticut Council of Safety. Strong improvements in West Point's fortification progressed rapidly, under the Highland's commander, General McDougall.

During the month of January, British food was scarce, A Hessian officer, Major Baurmeister, told of the efficiency of the American patrols. He wrote:

> "Their patrols are good, cautious and quickfooted. Enjoying the affection of the residents, they know all our movements."

The British were gratified when their ship arrived loaded with provisions the end of January,

The hatred between the Rebels and loyalists was vicious. If loyalists were captured, they were usually hanged for treason. In March, 650 loyalists raided near Middletown and surprised an American regiment at the LIPPINCOTT charter town of Shrewsbury, New Jersey. Then, during the early morning hours of 27 Apr 1779, about 800 British soldiers entered Monmouth County. The continentals retreated quickly, until the militia could assemble. About 150 militiamen arrived around 3 P.M. to watch the British retreat to their boats, although a brief skirmish ensued. The *New Hampshire Gazette* reported that the British usually launched such raids in the night and then fled before the militia could muster. If the militia ever assembled even half the number of the British, the militia would be "sufficient to drub them." After fleeing, the article continued, the British

> "then magnify in their lying Gazettes, one of those sheep-stealing nocturnal robberies, into one of the Duke of Marlborough's victories in Flanders."

While most of his army wintered at Middlebrook, New Jersey, during a much milder winter than Valley Forge, Washington was called to Philadelphia by Congress. They wanted to help him plan his 1779 summer campaign. Congress had passed the Articles of Confederation in the winter of 1777; but the thirteen colonies had been very slow to ratify them. Each colony was still claiming individual authority and greatly minimizing the power of the federal government.

General NATHANAEL GREENE wrote after his visit to Boston:

> "The local policy of all the states is directly opposed to the great national

plan; and if they continue to persevere in it, God knows what the consequences will be. There is a terrible falling off in public virtue since the commencement of the present contest. The loss of morals and the want of public spirit leaves us almost like a rope of sand.... Luxury and dissipation are very prevalent. "

Also greatly alarmed, Washington wrote to Congressman Gouverneur Morris of New York:

"Can we carry on the war much longer? Certainly no, unless some measures can be devised and speedily executed to restore the credit of our currency, restrain extortion, and punish forestallers."

Forestallers were those rascals who with previous knowledge bought up supplies needed by the army and sold them at advanced prices. His letter continued,

"Without these can be effected, what funds can stand the present expenses of the Army? And what officer can bear the weight of prices that every necessary article is now got to? ... The true point of light then to place and consider this matter in is not simply whether Great Britain can carry on the war, but whose finances (theirs or ours) is most likely to fail."

When Washington arrived in Philadelphia in December 1778, he wrote:

"I have seen nothing since I came [to Philadelphia] to change my opinion of men or measures, but abundant reason to be convinced that our affairs are in a more distressed, ruinous, and deplorable condition than they have been in since the commencement of the war. If I was to be called upon to draw a picture of the times and of the men, from what I have seen, heard, and in part know, I should in one word say that idleness, dissipation, and extravagance seem to have laid fast hold of most of them. That speculation, peculation, and an insatiable thirst for riches seems to have got the better of every other consideration .... That party disputes and personal quarrels are the great business of the day whilst the momentous concerns of an empire, a great and accumulated debt, depreciated money, and want of credit ... are but secondary considerations ... while a great part of the officers of your army from absolute necessity are quitting the service and the more virtuous few ... are sinking by sure degrees into beggary and want."

However, when Washington returned in mid-February to his headquarters at Middlebrook, he found his army in better spirits than he had anticipated.

Gen. Henry Knox and his indefatigable wife had dancing parties that lasted far into the night. Washington joined heartily into the festivities. Spring arrived. Sir Henry did not stir. Then on 31 May, while Washington was finishing his orders to Sullivan for his Indian campaign, he received word that the British had marched into White Plains. The campaign for 1779 had opened.

To Washington, this movement into White Plains meant that the British were pushing forward toward his fortifications at West Point in another attempt to claim the Hudson River. He had already ordered St. Clair's division to Springfield and Stirling's and De Kalb's to Pompton. McDougall had five continental brigades and two North Carolina regiments in the Highlands. The general shifted his whole army toward the protection of West Point. While marching northward with his troops, he was informed that 6000 British had already taken the little fort at Verplank on the east side of the Hudson, King's Ferry, and the unfinished fort at Stony Point on the west side of the river.

> "All we can do," he confessed to Horatio Gates, "is to lament what we cannot remedy and to prevent a further progress on the river and to make the advantage of what they have now gained as limited as possible."

With this in mind, he placed his army between the British position and West Point at the rough and rocky Smith's Cove—a difficult but excellent defense position.

But General Sir Henry Clinton had other objectives in his plans. Lord George Germain had sent him explicit orders from London:

> "bring Mr. Washington to a general and decisive action at the opening of the campaign," or failing that, force him into the Highlands or the Jerseys to allow the inhabitants of the open country freedom to follow their inclinations, which the London War Office thought would result in their return to the Crown.

Clinton was also told to employ two corps of four thousand each against the New England seacoast and in Chesapeake Bay. Substantial reinforcements were promised, but had not yet materialized.

London's first demand, without reinforcements, was impossible in Sir Henry's judgment, and he would only promise Germain to send 2500 soldiers to the Chesapeake Bay region of Virginia and Maryland. To maneuver Washington's

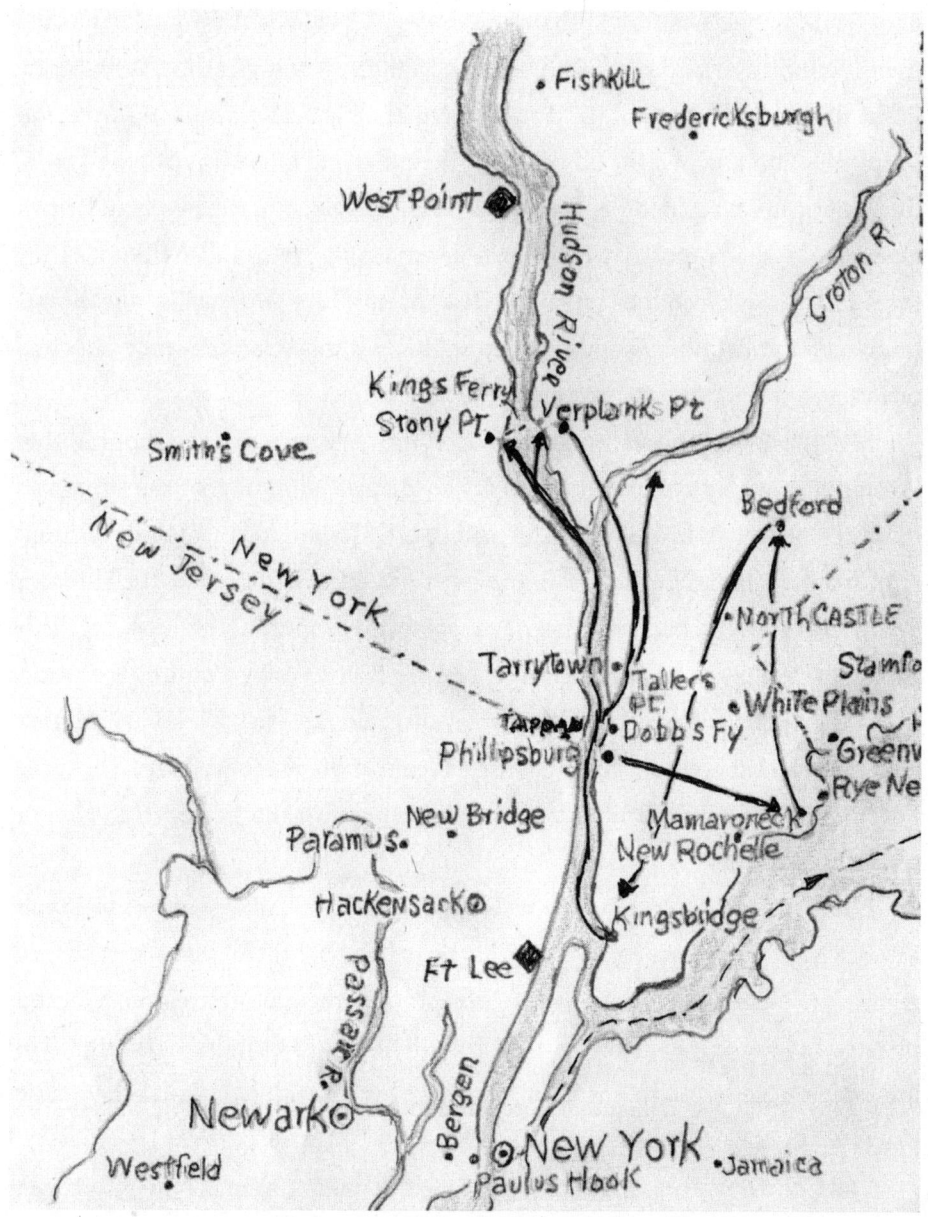

army into the Highlands, he started up the Hudson River on 28 May with one corp while a second corp was to go overland led by Simcoe's Rangers. Out in front of these Rangers, scouting and skirmishing, was Lieutenant Colonel Banastre Tarleton, who in the coming few years would lead the mounted troops that would fiercely devastate the southern colonies.

The Americans who garrisoned Stony Point quickly realized the impossibility of defending their position as the large army approached. They quickly burned their fortifications and ran. Stony Point was taken without a shot. With Stony Point under their control, the British fired their cannon across the river on Verplank's Point. When the first shot hit their fort and killed three of their men, the Americans evacuated the fort only to run straight into the overland British General Vaughan's forces, which were approaching from Taller's Point. They forced them back into the fort, where the seventy-four Americans quickly surrendered. The British claimed that throughout all this operation they only had one casualty.

Sir Henry kept his army at the forts until the end of June, hoping that Washington would come south and try to retake them; or that the promised reinforcements would arrive, and he could push forward to West Point. Without reinforcements from England, Clinton felt he could not proceed up the Hudson. So by 1 Jul 1779, he had withdrawn his major forces south to Phillipsburg. This gave him a midway position about 24 hours from Stoney Point at the north or, to the south, his occupied territories surrounding New York City. He left a garrison to occupy and build a strong fortification at Stony Point, This gave Washington the opportunity he had been hoping for, and he began to plan to retake the forts.

But the British general had more ideas in mind. He had sent orders to Tryon for an amphibious expedition by his loyalists to attack the Connecticut coastal region. If Washington brought his army to aid this coastal region, Clinton planned to intercept the American army with his forces from Phillipsburg, hoping a major battle might ensue in what Clinton considered a more favorable place.

The Connecticut coastal battles began with a quick 200-man raid of Fairfield, JOSEPH MORGAN's home, on 30 June. They set fire to several houses and barns, then escaped back to their boats before the militia could collect. On 5 July, Tryon arrived at New Haven with about 2500 soldiers. They marched into the city in two divisions. One approached from the west, and Tryon led the division that approached from the east. The militiamen collected at a bridge that separated the east and west British columns. The fighting continued for two days, while more and more militia kept arriving. The minutemen were able to hold the bridge. Tryon, fearing the ever increasing number of militia, decided it was time to leave. He embarked his corps on the evening of the 6th, leaving behind the smoldering ruins of several of New Haven's fine buildings. In this two day battle, the British lost around eighty men, while the militia lost about fifty.

[Note: New Haven was the later 1600s home of our MORGAN ancestors and relations, including the early governor, THEOPHILUS EATON and his wife, ANNE MORTON YALE EATON, whose grandson may have been the original financier of Yale University.]

Washington kept his army in their protective position in the Highlands, leaving this defense to Connecticut Governor Trumbull and his state militia. He had already alerted John Glover and his Massachusetts brigade, who were en route from Rhode Island to New York to aid Trumbell, if they were needed. He also ordered Brigadier General Samuel H. Parsons to Connecticut, to organize and command the scattered militia collecting along the coast.

On 8 July, Tryon's loyalists landed again near Fairfield. Fairfield's small militia force fired on them continually with their less than effective cannon and from their homes. On the morning of July 9th, the raiders burned most of the town, under the constant fire of the Americans, then hurried back to their boats before the additional militia could assemble.

During these raids, Sir Henry had moved his mobile corps of 7000 men from Phillipsburg to Mamaroneck, New York, the old original lands of ancestors ROBERT COLE and ROGER BARTON. He felt this to be an even stronger position to fight Washington and closer to aid and support Tryon in his coastal endeavors. From this point, he proceeded closer to the Connecticut border and advanced his troops to Bryam's Bridge. As pleas reached Washington regarding this further threat, Washington sent Major General William Heath towards Connecticut with two continental brigades, and the Massachusetts militia were called for additional support.

Despite all this mounting opposition, Tryon with his men returned only briefly to Huntington, Long Island, for supplies and then returned to Connecticut. He landed near Norwalk with his troops on July 11th. Major General Oliver Wolcott, who is related to the controversial BENJAMIN COOLEY line, of Springfield, Connecticut, had 700 militia ready to fight; but he retreated inland a little and waited until Parsons with his 150 continentals arrived. The loyalists advanced through Norwalk with little opposition from the local militia until they met Wolcott, who had increased his numbers to about 1100—Tryon estimated them to be around 2000 in number. They stopped the advancing British in their tracks. The fighting continued back and forth through the twelfth. Tryon retreated back to Norwalk, burned the town to the ground, and embarked to the safety of his ships.

Washington praised the militia and continentals for their orderly and brave defense of Norwalk. Even

> "if the opposition they give is not absolutely effectual, it serves to discourage the enemy and make them sick of such excursions."

While this fighting was going on, Sir Henry had moved his army toward Kingsbridge, then marched them north to Bedford, New York, and burned that town before Heath and his continentals arrived. This placed the British within 15 miles of Stamford; but instead of marching on into Connecticut, they turned back to Kingsbridge. Sir Henry was becoming more protective of his scattered army.

Tryon was quickly preparing for another coastal raid when orders came from Clinton to cancel the expedition and return to New York, because "all the militia of the country was assembling in arms." The raiding parties had too many casualties for the paltry results. Clinton was becoming discouraged.

Washington, who had stayed fixed in the Highlands, felt some humiliation at his own position. His army needed action, and the country needed a boost in morale. He, with Captain Alan McLane's partisans, had reconnoitered Stony Point. Washington determined to retake it from the British. For this purpose, he recalled Major General Anthony Wayne from his retirement to take command of a hand-picked Light Infantry. Wayne was a soldier's soldier and noted for his daring and action. They decided on a sudden night attack.

On the morning of the 15th, Wayne drew up his troops, all carefully picked veterans—all tall, young and muscular. They were well drilled, fully equipped, and provisioned for dress parade. After inspection, instead of dismissing the corps, he ordered a march westward from camp. The curiosity of these uniformed men increased as they passed Bear Mountain on a back road and then turned south on a rough trail. They puffed up and over the crest of Degaffles Rugh and down through the rocky woodlands on the other side. They felt stifled in the hot, humid summer heat. The afternoon brought them though the deep forest ravines of the Donderberg, and after dark they arrived at the farm of Mr. Springsteel, which was a mile and a half from their destination—the enemy at Stony Point.

After all had arrived, Wayne called his colonels into council and told them his plans. The scouts had done an excellent job. Wayne had a map of the Point with everything well marked: the abatis, the redoubts, the sally ports. British Lieutenant Colonel Henry Johnson had a garrison of nearly seven hundred soldiers. The Point was a promontory jutting a half-mile into the Hudson and rising a hundred-and-fifty feet above the water. The swift, unruly Hudson River surrounded the Point on three sides. On its inland side it fell off jaggedly to a marsh over which a causeway led to the Point and the ferry on its north side. At high tide, the Point became an island.

Wayne assigned his main attacking column to the south side. They would approach from a sandbar and hoist themselves up the steep cliff. They were to have bayonets, but no musket shots. His second column was to take the north side. Hardy Murfree's North Carolinians were to come in straight across the causeway with rifle fire. They were the diversion that would draw the enemy fire and allow the soldiers with their bayonets to climb up from the north and south. When the columns had formed, paper was passed out to every American to

> "fix a piece . . . in . . . his hat or cap as an insignia to be distinguished from the enemy."

When the bayonets were fixed and charges drawn, except those of Murfree's men, Wayne addressed his troops:

> "The distinguished honor conferred upon every officer and soldier who has been drafted to this corps by his Excellency, George Washington, the credit of the States they respectively belong to, and their own reputations, will be such powerful motives for each man to distinguish himself that the General cannot have the least doubt of a glorious victory. He hereby engages to reward the first man who enters the works . . . . But, should there be any soldier so lost to a feeling of honor as to retreat a single foot, or skulk in the face of danger, the officer next to him is immediately to put him to death that he may no longer disgrace the name of soldier, or the corps, or the state to which he belongs."

While his men ate their evening rations, Wayne wrote a letter to his closest friend, Dr. Sharp Delany, to be received only in the event of his death. He committed to his friend papers covering his side of his bitter difference with his despised rival, General St. Clair, who might attack his name after death, and he asked Delany to see to the education of his little son and daughter, for

"I fear that their mother will not survive this stroke."

He then set his quill aside and calmly ate his supper, after which he went out to give the signal for his men to advance.

The New York Journal later reported:

"The detachment marched in two divisions, and about one o'clock came up to the enemy's pickets who, by firing their pieces gave the alarm and . . . ran to the fort, from every quarter of which in a short time they made an incessant fire upon our people. They, with fixed bayonets and uncharged pieces, advanced with quick but silent motion through a heavy fire of cannon and musketry till, getting over the abatis and scrambling up the precipices, the enemy called out, 'Come on, ye d____d rebels! Come on!' Some of our people softly answered, 'Don't be in such a hurry, my lads. We will be with you presently.'

"And accordingly, in a little more than twenty minutes from the time the enemy first began to fire, our troops, overcoming all obstructions and resistance, entered the fort. Spurred on by their resentment of the former cruel bayoneting which many of them and others of our people had experienced and of the more recent and savage barbarity of plundering and burning unguarded towns, murdering old and unarmed men, abusing and forcing defenceless women, and reducing multitudes of innocent people from comfortable livings to the most distressful want of the means of subsistence—deeply affected by these cruel injuries, our people entered the fort with the resolution of putting every man to the sword. But the cry of 'Mercy! mercy! Dear Americans, mercy! Quarter! Brave Americans, quarter! Quarter!' disarmed their resentment in an instant, insomuch that even Colonel Johnson, the commandant, freely and candidly acknowledges that not a drop of blood was spilled unnecessarily. Oh, Britain, turn thy eye inward, behold and tremble at thyself."

Inside the second abatis, Wayne had fallen with a scalp wound.

"Carry me up to the fort, boys!" he had shouted. "Let's go forward!"

With two of his men supporting him and his forehead bloody, he stumbled victoriously into the fort. When the fort was securely in his hands, Wayne turned the British cannon on the *Vulture,* which was anchored in the river nearby, and then onto the British works across the river at Fort Verplank. The *Vulture,* to avoid the cannon, dropped downstream. It continued to fire on the fort; but its balls fell short and were not returned by the Americans. Wayne's special detachment of Light Infantry had captured 543 men, 3 servants, and 15 cannon. His men had killed 63 of the redcoats with the bayonet. The Americans had 15 dead and 84 wounded.

Washington arrived at Stony Point on the 17th of that hot day in July 1779. He was accompanied by Generals GREENE and Steuben. They inspected the works and decided that their army was not sufficient to garrison the two forts and hold them against the full force of the British army. So the next day the Light Infantry carried off supplies worth around $158,000. This was converted into cash, which was divided amongst the victors as prize money. With the Americans gone, the British quickly reoccupied the lost forts and ordered stronger fortifications to be built.

Baron von Steuben was delighted to learn that the fort had been taken without musketry. It was he who had taught the Americans the art of the bayonet. He coached Captain Henry Archer, an aide to General Wayne, on the behavior he should exhibit in Philadelphia when he took the news of the victory to Congress. Archer wrote back:

> "I came into the city with colors flying, trumpets sounding, and heart elated, drew crowds to the doors and windows, and made not a little parade, I assure you. These . . . were Baron Steuben's instructions and I pursued them literally, though I could not help thinking it had a little of the appearance of a puppet show."

An editorial in the *New Hampshire Gazette* read:

> "It demonstrates that the Americans have soldiers equal to any in the world, and that they can attack and vanquish the Britons in their strongest works. No action during the war, performed by the British military, has equalled this 'coup de main.'"

Washington considered this attack's greatest advantage to be the good effect it had on the American people and his troops and the proportionate depression of "the spirits of the enemy." But perhaps even he did not realize the full impact that it had on Sir Henry Clinton. The British General was completely discouraged—to the point of considering the possibility of resigning and returning back to England. American Major Henry Lee led a partially successful raid against the British post on Powle's Hook on the 18th—opposite the lower end of Manhattan Island. Washington moved his army to West Point, awaiting the enemy which never arrived. With no reinforcements from England, British General Clinton counted his losses in Connecticut and at Stony Point and dared not make an offensive move. With both Generals unwilling to begin a major battle, the campaign for 1779 came to a close—although neither of them really knew it.

G+B OLD RHINEBECK

[SEE PHOTO ON OPPOSITE PAGE]

In 2004, GROVER and I accompanied our daughter and her husband, HYRUM HAYNES with their two children on a motor trip through the eastern United States. One of HYRUM's "must see" destinations was the home of his former B.Y.U. roommate, whose father had owned at that time the *Old Rhinebeck Aerodrome and Museum* in Dutchess County, New York, by the Hudson River. We scheduled some individual air flights over the Hudson River and vicinity in the old biplane after the air show. It was a beautiful sunny day, and HYRUM took our picture before the show began. We watched from the bleachers while the pilots preformed the daring antics of years ago, including a staged World War I battle against the German monoplane. Just before their final act, it started to rain. It was not a sprinkle, but a downpour of water, and it wouldn't quit—so much for our planned flight over the Hudson.

With limited space at his old roommate's home, he had arranged for Grover and I to spend the evening and night at the home of his roommate's mother, Nadine. Her husband had died several years before and she had sold her interest in the *Aerodrome*. A few of her friends were at dinner, including her husband's brother, who was the pilot of the biplane. He was close to our age, and I asked him if he planned to retire. He laughed and said,

"Why? Where else can you have so much fun, and get paid for doing it?"

That evening I asked Nadine about the Rombout Precinct of Dutchess County. It wasn't shown on any maps or histories I had found, and my possible ancestor THOMAS POYER's will, written 1 Jan 1777 and proved 3 May 1783, had said he was "of the Rombout Precinct." Nadine hadn't heard about it, but worked as a volunteer in the Dutchess County Historical Library. After we retired that night, she worked on her computer far into the night and before we left in the early morning, she presented us with a quarter-inch stack of papers, showing the historic homes and the history of the Rombout Precinct, or Patent.

"In 1682, Francis Rombout and Gulian Verplanck jointly filed a petition for a land grant and permission to buy from the Indians a fertile tract on the east bank of the Hudson extending from Fishkill almost to Poughkeepsie, later known as the Rombout Patent or Precinct. . . . They say that Rombout bargained with the Indians for '*all the land he could see*'; he thereupon climbed to the top of Mount Becon to extend his outlook. . . . [The] Patentees sat at one side of a table while the Wappinger chiefs sat opposite. A round sum of Royals—a Royal equaled a half-sovereign— was laid on the board as the purchase price. This the Indians repeatedly pushed back, saying 'More, More!' until the bargain satisfied them. The deed of sale, dated 1683, was then duly drawn, witnessed and executed. . . . Stephanus Van Cortlandt had also been admitted to a third share in the purchase."

Francis Rombout, a Huguenot born at Hesselt in Flanders, sailed as super-cargo on a ship bound for New Netherland as a mere lad in 1654. He had to sue the captain for his wages—by "his energy, determination and love of justice, he prospered as a merchant, and it was said he imported the first table linen used in America. His home and orchard were on Broadway, New York City. He joined

473

the Dutch Reformed Church, and after the restoration of English control, he was Mayor of New York City, succeeding Stephanus Van Cortlandt in that post.

"By his third wife, Helena Teller Van Ball—daughter of William Telleer, one of the Patentees of Schenectady—Francis Rombout had a daughter Catheryna, born in 1687. To her he willed his house in Broadway and 'his land in the Wappins" —his third share in the Rombout Patent. . . . In November 1703 [Catheryna] married Roger Brett, of Somersetshire, a young Lieutenant in the British Navy . . . . Determined to live in the country and develop her land in the Rombout Patent., Madame Brett and her husband, in the summer of 1708, mortgaged their city house 'for 240 pounds current money.' In 1707 the Rombout Patent had been partitioned into three long, narrow parcels, each containing a stretch of river front, and water privileges by adjointure to the two creeks, the Fish Kill and Wappingers.." Lot Number One, in the drawing, fell to Madame Brett, while the Verplanck heirs got Lot Number two, just to the north of them, on the river and on Wappingers Creek "in the middle"; the third or northernmost Lot, on the river and the upper part of Wappingers Creek, went to the Van Cortlandts.

"By this division the Bretts possessed the fertile valley of the Fish Kill, a broad stretch along the river, and 'the north side of Wapingers Creek from its mouth to beyond the present site of Wapingers Falls.' On the banks of the Fish Kill, which gave them a valuable water power, they built a mill and a dwelling. . . . For many years the people of Dutchess and Orange Counties depended largely "upon this mill for their daily bread.' At one time all roads thereabouts seemed to lead 'to Madame Brett's Mill.'"

In 1710, when the Lutheran church of the German Palatines was established across the Hudson at Newburgh, she was accustomed to canoe across the river on Sundays to attend service. In 1743, she sold the mill property to her kinsman Abraham de Peyster.

"In 1726 Lieutenant Brett met a tragic death; returning from New York, the boom of his boat knocked him overboard just as he was entering the mouth of the Fish Kill."

Madame Brett continued to manage the property, even riding horseback daily around her land, until shortly before her death in 1764 when she divided the property among her heirs. In the eastern land of the Patent, which extended to the Connecticut border, she gave refuge to the Quakers who were driven from Connecticut and Massachusetts. The town of Pawling still has many Quakers, who are very anti-nuclear in their politics. Perhaps some Huguenot refugees, French Canadians, and Acadians also found refuge in her land, since her father had been a Huguenot as a child.

GULIAN VERPLANCK

"This home belonged to Gulian Verplank, who was one of the partners of the ROMBOUT Patent. It was built sometime between 1730 and 1750. The larger addition in the rear was added in 1804. During the Revolutionary War, the house served as headquarters for Baron von Steuben, the Prussian who, as a major general wrote the drill manual for the Continental army. After the war, a group of Revolutionary officers came together at Mount Gulian, as the house is called, and formed the Society of the Cincinnati, the first veterans' organization in the United States. " [Dutchess County Historical Society]

Major general Baron von Steuben probably enjoyed living in this area among the Dutch, French, and Germans for he didn't speak English.

Winter at Morristown, 1779-80

October, 1779, was a month of great activity in British occupied New York. Sir Henry Clinton withdrew his men, cannon, equipment, and supplies from the forts at King's Ferry to the occupied territory of the New York harbor. Two days later, he evacuated Rhode Island. Then he began preparations to transfer a large number of his troops into his ships. The warmer southern states, specifically Charleston, South Carolina, seemed right for a major attack. American General

Benjamin Lincoln was there with 2,000 continentals he had recruited. Two IVEY relations are listed in General Lincoln's muster records. Captain CURTIS IVEY, who would later be a legislator in North Carolina, and REUBEN IVEY, listed as a musician.

The French fleet had unsuccessfully tried to help General Lincoln dislodge the British from Savannah, Georgia. But the hurricane season arrived and the fearful French fleet departed for the West Indies. With the French fleet at a distance, Sir Henry collected 7,600 British soldiers and set sail for Charleston, South Carolina, on 26 Dec 1779. He felt they would have the help of many loyalists—especially to the west in North Carolina, where many of their loyal Scotch had quite recently settled. Former British Governor Martin, also, promised them the loyalty of the defeated "regulators" in the Orange and Randolph Counties of North Carolina. They had several years previously given their "oath of allegiance" to King George III. These are the counties where the ALLRED, FAUCETT, McKEE and THRASHER ancestors resided at that time.

As Washington saw the British preparations for winter in progress, he followed suit. He left a strong force at West Point and then chose Morristown, New Jersey, as his main winter quarters at a somewhat mountainous section known as Jockey Hollow. The construction of the huts for his men began in earnest with General NATHANAEL GREENE directing the positions for his brigades. General Horatio Gates, who had refused to command the troops that terrorized the Indians during the past summer, was anxious to lead the troops south to reinforce those of Benjamin Lincoln at Charleston, so Washington gave him the opportunity to proceed. DANIEL MORGAN had trouble with an injured leg and went to his home in Virginia.

Washington arrived in Morristown on 1 Dec 1779, in the middle of "a very severe storm of hail and snow all day." He took his quarters in the large white house of the recently widowed Mrs. Theodosia Ford. The commander in chief's guards arrived four days later, tented on the frozen ground for six days, and then moved into the huts they had built on the land southeast of the house. The weather became harsher every day as one snowstorm after another piled the snow higher and higher. The northern winds howled through the forest of oak, walnut, and chestnut bringing with it a brutal northern coldness that froze the water of the Hudson River into thick ice between Staten Island and the mainland—about 2000 yards. This allowed the British to supply their troops by sleigh. Even the heaviest of cannon crossed the frozen Hudson without incident.

The less fortunate barefoot Americans attempted to warm their half-frozen bodies by huddling together. Dr. James Thatcher, recorded in his daily journal their misery in this below zero weather:

> "No man could endure its violence many minutes without danger of his life. Several marquees were torn asunder and blown down over the officers' heads in the night, and some of the soldiers were actually covered while in their tents and buried like sheep under the snow . . . . We are greatly favored in having a supply of straw for bedding. Over this we spread our blankets, and with our clothes and large fires at our feet, while four or five are crowded together, to preserve ourselves from freezing. But the sufferings of the poor soldiers can scarcely be described. While on duty they are unavoidably exposed to all the inclemency of storms and severe cold. At night they now have a bed of straw on the ground and a single blanket to each man. They are badly clad and some are destitute of shoes . . . . The snow is now from four to six feet deep, which so obstructs the roads as to prevent our receiving a supply of provisions . . . . we are frequently for six or eight days entirely destitute of meat, and then as long without bread. The consequence is, the soldiers are so enfeebled from hunger and cold as to be almost unable to perform their military duty or labor in constructing their huts."

Joseph Martin, the young Massachusetts lad, who had enlisted at the beginning of the war when he was a few months less than sixteen years old, later recalled,

> "We were absolutely literally starved. I do solemnly declare that I did not put a single morsel of victuals into my mouth for four days and as many nights, except a little black birch bark, which I knawed off a stick of wood, if that can be called victuals.
>
> "I saw several . . . men roast their old shoes and eat them, and I was afterwards informed by one of the officers' waiters that some of the officers killed and ate a favorite little dog that belonged to one of them."

Many described the winter as worse than Valley Forge—two years before. Spring finally arrived. The weather was better; but relief from hunger and sparse clothing hadn't been as prompt.

On 10 May, Washington was greatly elated when Lafayette arrived from France, after having been gone for over a year. The news he brought was equally welcome. Six French ships of the line and six thousand troops were on their way to Rhode Island. They had been instructed by Louis XVI to accept Washington as their commander and do his bidding. But as his hopes for the summer campaign rose to a much higher plane, his immediate problems increased. His troops had stooped to mutiny against their officers for the first time in this long war.

Joseph Martin described the event:

"On the twenty-fifth, a 'pleasant day,' the men spent most of their times on the parade "growling like soreheaded dogs." Finally, "At the evening roll call they began to show their dissatisfaction by snapping at the officers and acting contrary to their orders. After their dismissal from the parade, the officers went as usual to their quarters, except the Adjutant who happened to remain, giving details for next day's duty to the orderly sergeants, or some other business, when the men (none of whom had left the parade) began to make him sensible that they had something to train. He said something that did not altogether accord with the soldiers' ideas of propriety. One of the men retorted. The Adjutant called him a mutinous rascal or some such epithet and then left the parade.

"This man, then stamping the butt of his musket upon the ground . . . in a passion, called out, 'Who will parade with me?'

"The whole regiment immediately fell in and formed. We had made no plans for our future operations, but while we were consulting how to proceed, the Fourth Regiment, which lay on our left, formed and came and paraded with us. We now concluded to go in a body to the other two regiments that belonged to our brigade and induce them to join with us . . . . We did not wish to have anyone in particular to command, lest he might be singled out for a court-martial to exercise its clemency upon. We, therefore, gave directions to the drummers to give certain signals on the drums. At the first signal we shouldered our arms; at the second, we faced; at the third, we began our march to join with the other two regiments, and went off with music playing.

"By this time, our officers had obtained knowledge of our military maneuvering, and some of them had run . . . and informed the officers of these regiments of our approach and supposed intentions. The officers ordered their men to parade as quick as possible without arms. When that was done they stationed a camp guard . . . between the men and their huts, which prevented them from entering and taking their arms . . . . Colonel

Meigs of the Sixth Regiment exerted himself to prevent his men from obtaining their arms, until he received a severe wound in his side by a bayonet in the scuffle . . . . Colonel Meigs was truly an excellent man and a brave officer . . . . It was dark and the wound was given, it is probable, altogether unintentionally . . . . When we found the officers had been too crafty for us, we returned with grumbling instead of music, the officers following in concert. One of the men in the rear calling out, 'Halt in front,' the officers seized upon him like wolves on a sheep and dragged him out of the ranks . . . but the bayonets of the men pointing at their breasts as thick as hatched teeth compelled them quickly to relinquish their hold of him. We marched back to our own parade and then formed again. The officers now began to coax us to disperse to our quarters, but that had no more effect upon us than their threats. One of them slipped away into the bushes, and after a short time returned, counterfeiting to have come directly from headquarters. Said he, 'There is good news for you, boys. There has just arrived a large drove of cattle for the army.' But this piece of finesse would not avail. All the answer he received for his labor was, 'Go and butcher them.' The rest of the officers, after they found that they were likely to meet with no better success . . . walked off . . . to their huts.

"While we were under arms, the Pennsylvania troops, who lay not far from us, were ordered under arms and marched off their parades, upon, as they were told, a secret expedition. They surrounded us, unknown to either us or themselves (except the officers); at length . . . . they inquired of some of the stragglers what was going on among the Yankees. Being informed that they had mutinied on account of the scarcity of provisions, 'Let us join the Yankees. They are good fellows and have no notion of lying here like fools and starving.' Their officers needed no further hinting. The troops were quickly ordered back to their quarters . . . . We knew nothing of all this for some time afterwards.

"After our officers had left us to our own option, we dispersed to our huts and laid by our arms of our own accord, but the worm of hunger knawing so keen kept us from being entirely quiet. We, therefore, still kept upon the parade in groups, venting our spleen at our country and government, then at the officers, and then at ourselves for our imbecility in staying there and starving . . . for an ungrateful people who did not care what became of us . . . . While we were thus venting our gall against we knew not who, Colonel [Walter] Stewart of the Pennsylvania Line, came to us and questioned us respecting our unsoldierlike conduct . . . . We told him . . . that we had borne till we considered further forbearance pusillanimity, that the times, instead of mending, were growing worse, and finally, that we were determined not to bear or forbear much longer. We were unwilling to desert the cause of our country when in distress, that we knew her cause involved our own, but what signified our perishing in the act of saving her when that very act would inevitably destroy us, and she must finally perish with us.

"'Your officers,' said he, 'are gentlemen. They will attend to you. I know them. They cannot refuse to hear you. But . . . your officers suffer as much as you do. We all suffer. The officers have no money to purchase supplies any more than the private men have . . . . Besides . . . . you know not how much you injure your own characters by such conduct. You Connecticut troops have won immortal honor the winter past by your performance, patience, and bravery, and now you are shaking it off your heels. But I will go and see your officers and talk with them myself.' . . . This Colonel Stewart was an excellent officer, much beloved and respected by the troops of the Line he belonged to. He possessed great personal beauty. The Philadelphia ladies styled him the 'Irish Beauty.' Our stir did us some good in the end, for we had provisions directly after."

Lafayette wrote to Joseph Reed in Philadelphia:

"An Army that is reduced to nothing, that wants provisions, that have not one of the necessary means to make war, such is the situation wherein I found our troops and however prepared I could have been to this unhappy sight by our past distresses, I confess I had no idea of such an extremity."

That same day, General Washington wrote to Joseph Jones, the Virginia Delegate in Congress:

"Certain I am, that unless Congress speaks in a more decisive tone; unless they are vested with powers by the several states, competent to the great purposes of war, or assume them as a matter of right; and they and the states respectively act with more energy than they hitherto have done, that our cause is lost."

To add to Washington's desolation, word arrived from South Carolina that Charleston had capitulated to the enemy. On 11 May 1780, surrounded completely by the British on sea and land and with no possible way of escape, Benjamin Lincoln surrendered. Five thousand continentals, militia, and armed citizens with all their arms and ammunition had been captured. The fate of Gates with his reinforcements was still unknown.

ALEXANDER HAMILTON and distant cousin
ELIZABETH SCHUYLER

The winter of 1779-80 was much more congenial to ALEXANDER HAMILTON than it was to the freezing infantrymen. He with his fellow aide and friend, John Laurens, had made a plan for the enlistment of the slaves in the south into the continental army. John Laurens had grown-up in South Carolina and his father was now representing the state in Congress. HAMILTON had spent his early childhood on the slave islands of the West Indies. They were both highly aware of the problems of slavery, and with the fall of Savannah and Augusta, Georgia, to the British, they determined to initiate their plan, if possible.

Laurens had written his father, then the president of Congress:

"we have sunk the African[s] and their descendants below the standard of humanity, and almost render'd them incapable of that blessing which equal Heaven bestow's upon us all." [We should] bring slaves to freedom by "shades and degrees."

Laurens wanted to go to South Carolina and try to repel this successful British invasion (1780) of his state. With the current shortage of troops, what more suitable than to enlist slaves and give freedom to those who survived the war? Washington's first reaction was negative; but Laurens planned to stop in Philadelphia and seek the approval of Congress.

HAMILTON gave him a letter to take to the current President John Jay with the intent of persuading Congress to take several battalions of slaves, if enlisted, into continental pay. HAMILTON wrote,

"I have frequently heard it objected to the scheme of embodying negroes; that they are too stupid to make soldiers. This is far from . . . a valid objection, that I think their want of cultivation (for their natural faculties are as good as ours), joined to [their] habit of subordination . . . will enable them sooner to become soldiers than our white inhabitants. Let officers be men of sense and sentiment . . . " Habitual contempt for Negroes made men "fancy many things that are founded neither in reason nor experience," and the clutch at valuable property "will furnish a thousand arguments to show the . . . pernicious tendency" of a measure that sacrificed selfish interest. [The proposal required owners to contribute slaves in proportion to the numbers they possessed.] He added that Washington well knew that the enemy would arm slaves if the Americans did not do it, giving them "their freedom with their swords."

The Americans should use this method to animate the courage of those enrolled and open the door to emancipation of those who remained.

Congress sent Laurens on his way to South Carolina with the recommendation that South Carolina and Georgia should raise 3000 Negro troops under white officers; the continent would recompense masters for the slaves thus serving and freed at the war's end. Laurens was a member of the South Carolina legislature; but after making repeated attempts in that body, he was unsuccessful—army officers, they said, were jealous of their honor, apt to "find quarrel in a straw" and invoke the "code duello." [You will recall that Laurens had challenged General Charles Lee to a duel after Lee's Monmouth County debacle and disparagement of George Washington. HAMILTON went as Laurens' second.]

Back in Morristown, New Jersey, HAMILTON had his own ambitions. His greatest desire was to command his own troops in the South. Washington would not agree. His second wish, with his fluency in speaking French, was that Laurens might convince Congress to send him to France as secretary to the American minister at Versailles; but, again, Washington convinced him to stay—not wishing to loose the services of this most trusted aide.

The unattached, handsome young HAMILTON attracted the local young ladies, and his attentions were bestowed upon Cornelia Lott and another neighborhood girl whose first name was Polly. Then, everything changed when Congress sent a committee to assess the crisis at Morristown. Included in this committee was Major General SCHUYLER, who brought his wife CATHERINE (RENSSELAER). They joined their two oldest daughters who had come to visit their aunt, the wife of the surgeon-general of the Middle Department, John Cochran, who resided at Morristown near Washington's headquarters.

SCHUYLER's eldest daughter, ANGELICA, had earlier eloped and married John Barker Church; but the dark-eyed ELIZABETH was quite available, and a romance quickly developed between the young couple—ALEXANDER and ELIZABETH. In March 1780, they were engaged to be married with the whole-hearted blessing of her parents. General SCHUYLER wrote his consent:

"You cannot my dear Sir be more happy in the connection you have made with my family than I am. Until the child of a parent has made a judicious choice his heart is in continual anxiety; but this anxiety was removed the moment I discovered on whom she had placed her affections."

He had known and respected HAMILTON throughout the war, in spite of those who would call him a bastard because his parents were unwed at his birth.

[[Note: His mother's ancestry was the French Huguenot physician whose surname was FAWSETT. When driven from France, he went to the West Indies and married his daughter (early records say MARY, later research says RACHAEL) to a merchant who had no love for her, which resulted in a divorce. HAMILTON's father was a young Scotch military officer stationed on the island. There was a law that would not allow a divorced woman to remarry.]]

ELIZABETH and ALEXANDER would have preferred to be married soon at Morristown; but her parents, who deeply regretted the elopement of her older sister, objected. They wanted the wedding to take place in the family mansion at Albany. So with the immediate military problems to be resolved and the summer campaign rapidly approaching, the young couple agreed to wait. They were married in Albany in the SCHUYLER drawing room on 14 Dec 1780. ELIZABETH was 23 years old and the groom was just under twenty-six.

Sometime during the month of March, HAMILTON was sent to Amboy to try to arrange for a prisoner exchange with the British. It was unsuccessful, as were many previous attempts.

HAMILTON wrote ELIZABETH during their long engagement:

"I love you more and more every hour. The sweet softness and delicacy of your mind and manners, the elevation of your sentiments, the real goodness of your heart—-its tenderness to me—the beauties of your face and person—-your unpretending good sense and that innocent simplicity and frankness which pervade your actions, all these . . . place you in my estimation above all the rest of your sex . . . You engross my thoughts too entirely . . . You not only employ my mind all day, but you intrude on my sleep. I meet you in every dream."

On another occasion he wrote,

"Do you soberly relish the pleasure of being a poor man's wife? . . . I cannot . . . forbear entreating you to realize our union on the dark side and satisfy . . . your self, how far your affection for me can make you happy in a privation of those elegancies to which you have become accustomed." If she could not contemplate bitter with sweet, "we are playing a comedy of all in the wrong, and you should correct the mistake before we begin to act the tragedy of the unhappy couple."

The marriage would last until his death twenty-six years later. She remained a widow for an additional fifty years and devoted herself to their children and preserving his memory. Loyal, sincere, and unselfish, she was the right helpmate for a man of genius.

The Betrayal of a New Nation

General Wilhelm von Knyphausen was given command of the British forces in New York, while Sir Henry Clinton sailed south with his troops to conquer Benjamin Lincoln's Continental forces in Charleston, South Carolina, during the winter of 1779-80. With his forces greatly diminished, Knyphausen was very careful to curtail his northern New York raids to only those necessary to feed his troops. However, southwest Connecticut and Westchester County, New York, especially along the coast, were still subjected to skirmishes with Tory and British parties, who plundered their property and took the local inhabitants prisoner throughout the winter and spring. The invaders were usually gone before the militiamen could assemble. In retaliation, these minutemen launched a few raids of their own, but lost more than they gained. The land owners were becoming discouraged and considered moving to safer places.

With an icy pathway across the Hudson River from Staten Island to the New Jersey coast, raids were conducted by both the British and the Americans. On 15 Jan 1780, American Major General Lord Stirling led three thousand men, mostly continentals, across the ice from the mainland to Staten Island. While his army sat in front of the British positions, New Jersey militiamen crossed over and plundered the local inhabitants. When the British failed to approach and do battle, Stirling decided he had lost his element of surprise and retreated off the island.

On the night of January 25-26, a Major Lumm of the British 44th Regiment led more than three hundred infantrymen from Staten to Newark, where he surprised the garrison, killing eight and capturing thirty-four without any British losses. Attacks such as these kept New Jersey in a constant state of alarm throughout the winter and into the spring—Hackensack and Bergen County each had a sizable raid.

As spring approached, Knyphausen studied his options. He had been told that Washington had sent detachments of his army to Chesapeake Bay, to Albany, and to Pennsylvania. The continental army, he believed, was scattered from Connecticut to New Jersey, with around 4,000 concentrated around Morristown. His spies had reported that the New Jersey militia were tired and wanted to stay home in peace. It was also reported to him that the New England continental brigades had mutinied and were close to deserting. Therefore, he decided to invade New Jersey in strength with 6,000 soldiers—all he could spare from his defenses, so he led his 6,000 men from Staten Island to Elizabethtown during the night of 5 June. His plan was to march quickly to the Short Hills between Springfield and Chatham on the first day, and then march quickly the next day against Washington at Morristown. He felt that Washington would either be forced to engage him or abandon many of his supplies and artillery.

Captain Ewald of the German jagers described it:

"General Knyphausen had hardly landed and marched off when he ran into enemy parties which made every step troublesome."

General Maxwell's continentals were on the alert in Elizabethtown. He led his eight hundred continentals in a slow withdrawal to Connecticut Farms, all the while sending out alarms to the militia units who assembled rapidly. They destroyed the bridges and used such impediments as they could to slow down the enemy. At Connecticut Farms, the Rebel forces numbered around 2,500 and they held the British for three hours before retreating.

Dr. Thacher, who was with the Americans, wrote:

"Our brigade, commanded by General Stark, soon joined Maxwell on the high ground near the village . . . . Colonel Angell's regiment of Rhode Island, with several small parties, were posted at a bridge over which the enemy were to pass, and their whole force of five or six thousand men was actually held in check by those brave soldiers for more than forty minutes, amidst the severest firing of cannon and musketry.

"The enemy, however, with their superior force, advanced into the village and wantonly set fire to the buildings. We had the mortification of beholding the church and twenty or thirty . . . houses and other buildings in a blaze . . . . Having thus completed their great enterprise and acquired to

themselves the honor of burning a village, they made a precipitate retreat
to Elizabeth Point, and the ensuing night crossed over to Staten Island."

Washington had ordered his generals to collect militia and move toward
Knyphausen's flanks, while he led his six brigades still encamped at Morristown
directly to the Short Hills. Washington arrived first. The enemy halted. A disappointed Knyphausen concluded,

"I found the disposition of the inhabitants by no means such as I expected;
on the contrary they were everywhere in arms."

On the night of 7 June, he withdrew his army back to Elizabethtown, after
burning Connecticut Farms. Word had arrived that Sir Henry Clinton was returning from the south and would be at Sandy Hook within a few days with a
large part of his army. With the fall of Charleston, Clinton divided his men and
left the command of the southern army to General Cornwallis. The British were
also aware that a French fleet was expected soon.

When Washington learned of Sir Henry's arrival in New York harbor and received word that six British ships-of-war had moved up the Hudson, he assigned
General GREENE to remain with a small force at Springfield and marched the
balance of his army slowly toward Pompton, sixteen miles northeast—within a
few good marches to the 200-foot-deep channel of the Hudson River that bends
around the fortifications at West Point. This first fort at the Point was modeled
after Ticonderoga, with high earth and log walls and four triangular ramparts
on a bluff at the river's bend, was named Fort Arnold. It had been built after
the Battle of Saratoga and it was armed with the heavy artillery that had been
captured with Burgoyne's surrender. On the east side of the narrowed and swift
waters of the Hudson was Constitutional Island, which was also fortified with
cannon. Between the east and west fortifications was a 1,097-foot chain with
links 12x18 inch in diameter and 2-inch-thick bar iron. Each link weighed over
one hundred pounds. This chain floated on log pontoons just below the river's
surface to block the passage of ships.

When the Marquis de Chastellux visited the stronghold that autumn, he
described West Point as a ring of forts perched on hills and cliffs in the shape
of an amphitheater, protecting each other. In addition there was a small city on
the outer plateau behind Fort Arnold with rows of wooden officer barracks, a

hospital, tents, a bakery, powder magazine, storehouses, and a jail.

On 6 July, still very fearful about his supplies and lack of enlistments, Washington wrote to his brother, Jack:

> "It is to be lamented, bitterly lamented, and in the anguish of soul I do lament, that our fatal and accursed policy should bring the [July] 6th upon us and not a single recruit to the Army." The army was "reduced almost to nothing by short enlistments," went "five or six days together without bread, then as many without meat, two or three times without either."

The early summer harvests were plentiful but army commissaries were redirecting them along with herds of cattle paid for by Congress (and destined for Washington's army) to the French in Rhode Island, who paid in gold, not depreciated continental paper money.

The French arrived in Newport, Rhode Island, on 10 July, and Washington sent Lafayette with an outline of his plans for operations against New York. General Heath had been sent earlier to greet them, but had somehow missed the timing. The troop commander was the handsome, fifty-five-year-old Comte de Rochambeau. He and his staff found "no one about in the streets; only a few sad and frightened faces in the windows."

They stayed at the local inn that night and were able to find "some principal citizens" the following morning. In their clean white uniforms, lapelled and collared in every hue of the rainbow, the young ladies of Rhode Island were entranced with the young French soldiers, and the Rhode Island assembly was quite charmed by the officer's speech and polite manners. The French reported that they were only the beginning and that more of their fleet was soon expected.

Aware of their approach, Sir Henry had removed his ships from the Hudson and pulled back his surrounding soldiers to more protective positions closer to New York City. Unfortunately for the Americans, three days after the French arrived; British Admiral Thomas Graves appeared off Sandy Hook with six-vessel reinforcement for the English fleet. When a large British fleet sailed into Long Island Sound toward Rhode Island, the smaller French fleet at Newport dared not meet the enemy and became blockaded at Newport. With this move of the enemy, Washington moved his army across the Hudson and marched towards King's Bridge that spans the East River into Manhattan Island. This threat quickly brought the British fleet back to New York harbor—about the end of

July, 1780. Washington then countered his orders and moved his army back into New Jersey, hoping for the arrival of the rest of the French fleet, with the possibility of bottling the British in New York. Without naval power, Washington felt powerless to do more. General Clinton refused to venture forth and only tightened his defenses. Once more it was the waiting game, Washington for the French fleet, which was being delayed at sea by the British, and Clinton for a more sinister event, still unknown to the Americans.

As Washington sat on his tall bay horse at King's Ferry, watching as his long columns of tired continentals trudged beside their horse-drawn cannon and groaning wagons full of wounded men, who were suffering under the hot summer sun from dysentery, cholera, and fever, on this last day of July, he was approached by Benedict Arnold. He had not been assigned to any specific duty since his trial, although Washington had decided to offer him command of his whole left wing.

Washington later recalled that Arnold

"asked me if I had thought of anything for him?"

The commander in chief was pleased to see Arnold back in the saddle and reporting back ready to fight.

"Yes, yes," he answered. Arnold was to have "a post of honor."

Arnold smiled, believing the post at West Point, where changes were being made, was to be his, but Washington went on: Arnold was to be a divisional commander, in command of the left wing.

"Upon this information," Washington continued, Arnold's "countenance changed and he appeared to be quite fallen, and, instead of thanking me or expressing any pleasure at the appointment, never opened his mouth."

Officers closer to Arnold said that his face had turned dark red, almost purple, as if he were angry. A perplexed Washington asked Arnold to ride on to his headquarters and wait for him.

As Washington rode back to his headquarters, he felt sad that the years of political haggling and inactivity seemed to have drained Arnold's fighting spirit so greatly that he would prefer an inferior command to the one he had offered, where he would be fighting by his side. Patiently, he argued with Arnold trying to prod him or embarrass him into accepting the command he had offered.

Arnold in turn with great determination reminded him of his injured leg and his need to have a less active assignment. At last, Washington consented to letting him "proceed to West Point and take command of that post and its dependencies." Because Arnold was a senior officer and more deserving, he expanded his duties to include not only all the Hudson River forts from West Point south to Dobbs Ferry on both sides of the river, but also, command of a corps of infantry and cavalry "advanced towards the enemy's lines."

Benedict Arnold was quick in selecting his headquarters—the confiscated mansion of Loyalist Colonel Beverley Robinson, commander of the King's American Regiment. It was a white, sprawling clapboard house that was set back a mile from the Hudson River on a bluff surrounded by dense trees, two miles south of the ferry crossing to West Point. The approaches to the house were not visible to the officers in the forts. This house was called Beverley.

On 12 August, Arnold began to systematically weaken the garrison by ordering 200 of the 1,500 soldiers up the river to cut firewood; another 200 were sent down the river to Haverstraw for outpost duty; he made no protest when Washington requisitioned four companies of artillery, and he found many reasons to distance others from the fort. On 16 August, he wrote to the newly appointed quartermaster general complaining about everything major or minor that he could find to harass and justify his own lack of initiative. Engineers had pointed out that the chain across the Hudson needed to be strengthened on each side of the river. He just ignored the advice. He sold food and supplies at the fort to the loyalist's ship's captain for gold or silver and put it in his own pocket, justifying his actions to his angry American officers by claiming that the money was owed to him by the government for past debts. His aide, Colonel Varick complained that if this became known to the farmers they would be unwilling to bring their produce to the fort, creating additional hunger and disease within the fort.

When a money-desperate congress was unwilling to give their generals a raise, he was livid and crude in his remarks, even suggesting that a committee of 1,000 to 1,500 of his soldiers march on congress. In late August, Arnold received a confirmation from British General Clinton that they would pay him 20,000 pounds for his defection and the surrender of West Point with 3,000 troops. He had weakened West Point's garrison by one-half in less than two months.

Washington wrote him,

"I shall be in Peekskill on Sunday evening, on my way to Hartford to meet the French admiral and general. You will be pleased to send down a guard of a captain and 50 at this time, and direct the quartermaster to have a night's forage for about 40 horses. You will keep this to yourself, as I want to make my journey a secret."

Realizing that Washington rarely went anywhere without his army, Arnold rushed a letter with his most trusted courier under an illegal flag of truce to Clinton to announce that General Washington would be coming. He suggested that if they received his message in time, their warships on the Hudson with a few hundred dragoons could capture Washington as he crossed on the ferry, or if that opportunity was missed, they could take him at Peekskill, where he would be spending the night, an easy ride for their nearest encampment of British dragoons.

Late in the afternoon of 18 Sep 1780, Arnold with his personally hand-picked guards arrived at King's Ferry. There they met General Washington, the Marquis de Lafayette, chief of artillery Henry Knox, aides Colonel ALEXANDER HAMILTON and Captain James McHenry, with a squad of nineteen of Washington's Life Guards. As they crossed on the ferry, the three-master-sloop-of-war *Vulture* could be seen with a spyglass floating silently in the distance. Evidently, Arnold's message had not arrived in time.

As Arnold rode on with Washington to Peekskill, he gave him his long letter that described the exact inventory, a detailed map of the fortification and the weaknesses he had found at the fort, which information had been requested by Washington. A duplicate copy of this had also been sent by Arnold to the British. Washington had been highly concerned about the fort and had de-scribed to him the additional defenses he was bringing in as support in case the British were to attack. He would meet with him at West Point upon his return from Hartford and lodge there on Monday, 25 September, to further discuss their plans of defense.

While Washington rode on to Hartford, Connecticut, to make his plans with the French Admiral and General, Arnold sent a coded message: If Clinton wanted to bag Washington as well as capture West Point, there would be no better time than 25 September. Washington was undoubtedly making plans with the French for the capture of New York. The British must act quickly. Arnold was to have an early breakfast with Washington that morning and then he would leisurely show him through the fort, delaying him on his departure as long as he could. To make their final plans, Arnold needed to converse immediately with their British spymaster John André, who had been his friend and contact throughout the whole conspiracy.

British Sir Henry Clinton wrote later of Arnold's defection:

"General Arnold surrendering himself, the forts and garrisons, at this instant, would have given every advantage which could have been desired. Mr. Washington must have instantly retired from Kingsbridge and the French troops upon Rhode Island would have been consequently left unsupported and probably would have fallen into our hands. The consequent advantage of so great an event I need not explain."

From his point of view, André's journey to meet with Arnold was to additionally insure that Arnold was not making a counterplot, and that

"the King's troops sent upon this expedition should be under no risk of surprise."

All along the vast land between the American and British armies was the area of no man's land. Those who dared journey between were subjected to the worst kind of rabble. The ones who claimed some allegiance to the Americans were called Skinners or of the upper party; those who made a claim to loyalist affiliation were the Cowboys or the lower party. Both were more interested in the plunder than in the politics. They would rob the travelers for their own gain, which was quite lawful under a recent New York act. The enemy ship *Vulture*, that had brought the British officer John André, had been forced to move down river by an enterprising American artilleryman that had bombarded her at Teller's point. The greedy Arnold and the handsome young patriot André designed their plans throughout the night, and when dawn approached, Arnold took Andre` to the home of his trusted friend Joshua T. Smith. Smith would later claim that he had been told that Mr. John Anderson, André's alias agreed upon by the two men, was a civilian who had only worn the redcoat to help him go through enemy lines and bring valuable information to Arnold.

John André (Anderson) was hidden until he could continue on by land at sunset with Joshua Smith to White Plains. Arnold left him with a horse, Mr. Smith as a guide, and a military pass that he felt would get them through the American lines. Andre' preferred to continue on in his military uniform, but Smith insisted that Mr. Anderson don a civilian coat and a beaver hat. He felt that in his redcoat he would not be able to go past the Americans regardless of whose pass he carried. Such was the lot of this spymaster, alias John Anderson, as he left Benedict Arnold to journey through no man's land on horseback.

About 9 o'clock that evening, the two horsemen were stopped about eight miles from Verplank by the American militia, who told them that night riding would be very dangerous below Croton River. It was decided that they should spend the night with a neighborhood farm family. The next morning, Saturday the 23rd, seven miles further on the road and after they had breakfast together, Smith left Anderson to travel the last 15 miles alone, because they were now entering the area considered to be the territory of the loyalists Cowboys.

Within the next hour, André was stopped by three bushmen. According to his story to Lieutenant Joshua King:

"He says to them, 'I hope, gentlemen, you belong to the lower party.' [British]

"'We do,' says one.

"'So do I,' says he, 'I am a British officer on business of importance and must not be detained.'

"One of them took his watch from him and ordered him to dismount. The moment this was done . . . he found he was mistaken and must shift his tone. He says, 'I am happy, gentlemen to find I am mistaken. You belong to the upper party, and so do I. A man must make use of any shift to get along, and to convince you of it, here is General Arnold's pass . . . and I am in his service.'

"'Damn Arnold's pass,' says they. 'You said you were a British officer. Where is your money?'

"'Gentlemen, I have none about me,' he replied.

"'You a British officer and no money,' says they. 'Let's search him.'

"They did so, but found none. Says one, 'He has got his money in his boots,' . . . and there they found his papers but no money. They then examined his saddle, but found none. He said he saw they had such a thirst for money, he could put them in a way to get it, if they would be directed by him . . . . [They replied,] 'If we deliver you at King's Bridge, we shall be sent to the Sugar House [prison] and you will save your money.'

"He says to them, 'If you will not trust my honor, two of you may stay with me, and one shall go with a letter which I shall write. Name your sum.'

"The sum was agreed upon . . . . They held a consultation a considerable time, and finally they told him, if he wrote, a party would be sent out and take them, and then they should all be prisoners. They said they had concluded to take him to the commanding officer on the lines."

Accordingly André was delivered to the American Lieutenant Colonel John Jameson, of the Second Continental Dragoons, in command of a detachment at North Castle. As a precaution, Arnold had ordered the officers at his advanced posts to look out for a John Anderson. If he came from New York, they were to send him to Arnold at his West Point headquarters. Following these orders, John Anderson was sent under guard to West Point. But Jameson decided that the papers "of a very dangerous tendency" should be sent directly to Washington, who he believed to be traveling somewhere between Danbury and Peekskill.

Later that Saturday, Major Benjamin Tallmadge, who served with the American secret service, returned from a scouting trip. He was highly concerned about the whole situation. He persuaded Jameson to bring John Anderson back to Lower Salem and hold him until they had further instructions from Washington. On Sunday, the prisoner was placed under the care of Lieutenant King, who wrote the following:

"He looked somewhat like a reduced gentleman. His small clothes were nankeen with handsome whitetop boots—in fact his undress military clothes. His coat, purple, with gold lace, worn, somewhat threadbare, with a small-brimmed, tarnished beaver on his head . . . . After breakfast, my barber came in to dress me, after which I requested him to undergo the same operation, which he did. When the ribbon was taken from his hair, I observed it full of powder. This circumstance, with others that occurred, induced me to believe I had no ordinary person in charge . . . . There was a spacious yard before the door, which he desired he might be permitted to walk in with me. I . . . disposed . . . my guard in such a manner as to prevent an escape. While walking together, he observed he must make a confident of somebody . . . as I had appeared to befriend a stranger in distress . . . . He told me who he was and gave me a short account of himself . . . . He requested a pen and ink and wrote immediately to General Washington, declaring who he was."

At Beverley, on 25 September, Washington sent some of his aides ahead with the message not to wait breakfast for him, as he would arrive later. [For security reasons, he had traveled a longer route and spent the night at Fishkill.] Peggy Arnold stayed in the large master bedroom with her baby. She would come down later, when Washington arrived. At the table was Benedict Arnold, his neighbor Dr. Eustis, ALEXANDER HAMILTON and James McHenry. They were eating when the muddy, rain dripping, Lieutenant Joshua Allen clamored into the house. He had an express message for General Arnold from Colonel Jameson.

An anxious Arnold read,

"Sir. I have sent Lieutenant Allen with a certain John Anderson taken going into New York. He had a pass signed with your name. He had a parcel of papers taken from under his stockings, which I think of a very dangerous tendency. The papers I have sent to General Washington."

After a quick reading, a very controlled Arnold, excused himself from the table, stating that he must go to West Point. They were to tell Washington on his arrival that he would be back in an hour.

After a quick visit upstairs with his wife, whom he informed of their failed venture and the capture of their mutual friend, Andre', he quickly left the house and galloped away. He was rushing to his barge to be rowed away to the British ship, the *Vulture*.

Within a couple of minutes, Washington arrived. He was met by Lieutenant Major Franks who with some confusion told him that Mrs. Arnold was still in her room; Lieutenant Colonel Richard Varick, Arnold's chief aide, was sick with fever and that General Arnold had been called to West Point, but would soon return. Yet unaware of any problem, Washington calmly told them that they would eat their breakfast and then join Arnold at West Point.

At West Point the commander in chief was disturbed at the condition of the fort, which he felt had been dangerously neglected. His agitation increased when he was told that Arnold had not been in the fort at anytime throughout the day. All this became quickly explained that afternoon when ALEXANDER

HAMILTON handed him a packet of papers—Jameson's dispatch, taken from André's boot. Inwardly, Washington was appalled at its contents as he shuffled through the pages; but his controlled composure never changed. It was now clear that Arnold had fled, probably down the river to the British vessel. Quietly, he ordered HAMILTON and McHenry to spur after him and then he sat down to dinner not mentioning it to anyone else.

After dinner General Washington asked Colonel Varick, who had dressed, accompanied him to West Point, and presided at the table that evening, to take a walk with him. During the privacy of their walk, he told Varick about Arnold. He further related that he had no suspicions about either he or Lieutenant Major Franks; but they must temporarily consider themselves under arrest. Varick had no qualms about telling the General all that he knew about Arnold's activities and the suspicions they had about Joshua Hett Smith. Varick sympathized with poor, unsuspecting Mrs. Arnold, whom he believed to be totally without knowledge of her husband's conspiracy until that morning when he told her he was leaving forever. He then described her frenzy of inexplicable grief. She had sobbed all day, convincing them of her innocence.

When the General and Varick returned from their walk, Peggy Arnold asked Washington to come to her room. Washington obliged her, accompanied by Colonel Varick, Lafayette and HAMILTON, who had only recently returned from his unsuccessful pursuit of Arnold. Here, she repeated her earlier insane act that had brought sympathy from Colonel Varick in the morning.

HAMILTON wrote to his fiancee, ELIZABETH SCHUYLER,

"She received us in bed with every circumstance that would interest our sympathy, and her sufferings were so eloquent that I wished myself her brother to have a right to become her defender . . . Could I forgive Arnold for sacrificing his honor, reputation and duty, I could not forgive him for acting a part that must have forfeited the esteem of so fine a woman."

General Washington was equally duped. He sent Peggy home to Philadelphia with Lieutenant Major Franks as her charmed escort. After a few months they would send her to New York to join her husband. It was several years before they discovered how greatly she was involved in the conspiracy.

The commander in chief, however, was not duped by the seriousness of the situation, nor was HAMILTON. After he had pursued the villain to the British ship and been given two letters from Arnold, one for Washington and one for Peggy, he had rode further west to inform General GREENE of the treachery. He suggested that a brigade be formed and marched immediately to King's Ferry, fearing that the enemy might attack that very evening. He then quickly rode to find Colonel Jonathan Meigs, whose corps was on the east side of the river, and hurry them north to strengthen West Point. As he crossed the Hudson he alerted the troops at Verplank to prepare. He hoped George Washington would approve his emergency measures.

On the morning of the 26th, General GREENE's shocking orders to his army read:

> "Treason of the blackest dye was yesterday discovered! General Arnold, who commanded at West Point, lost to every sentiment of honor, of public and private obligation, was about to deliver up that important post into the hands of the enemy. Such an event must have given the American cause a deadly wound, if not a fatal stab. Happily, the treason has been timely dis-covered to prevent the fatal misfortune. The providential train of circum-stances which led to it affords the most convincing proof that the liberties of America are the object of divine protection."

Washington quickly further shifted his regiments, and called forth his most trusted battle-seasoned units from New Jersey, Connecticut, and Massachusetts. He put West Point under General NATHANAEL GREENE's command. With Arnold personally now conspiring with the enemy, West Point must be preserved.

In a later year, an honest, angry John Lamb described the situation of Arnold's betrayal,

> "[Had André] exhibited a presence of mind worthy of his reputation for sagacity, the die had been cast which [would have] sealed the fate of the Highland passes, and of the army." West Point, "weakened as it was by the contrivances of Arnold, could not have made a successful resistance." The formidable British forces gathering for the kill were "sufficiently numerous to assault it on all sides at once."

André was immediately brought to Tappan for interrogation and a speedy court trial. Major Benjamin Tallmadge was with the escort and deliberately placed himself on the seat next to Andre' on the barge which took them down the river. He recalled later,

> "As we progressed on our way . . . Major André was very inquisitive
> to know my opinion . . . as to the light in which he would be viewed by
> General Washington and a military tribunal . . . . I endeavored to evade
> this question, unwilling to give him a true answer. When I could no longer
> evade . . . . I said to him that I had a much-loved classmate in Yale College
> by the name of Nathan Hale, who entered the Army with me in the year
> 1776. After the British troops had entered New York, General Washington
> wanted information respecting strength, position, and probable move-
> ments of the enemy. Captain Hale tendered his services, went into New
> York, and was taken just as he was passing the outposts of the enemy. Said
> I, with emphasis, 'Do you remember the sequel of this story?'
>
> "'Yes,' said André 'He was hanged as a spy, but you surely do not con-
> sider his case and mine alike.'
>
> "I replied, 'Precisely similar, and similar will be your fate.'
>
> "He endeavored to answer my remarks, but it was manifest he was
> more troubled than I had ever seen him before."

Efforts were first made to exchange André for Arnold, to which Sir Henry
Clinton scornfully answered that a deserter was never surrendered. André also
objected to

> "the impropriety of the measure."

HAMILTON was pleased with his answer and declared,

> "The moment he had been guilty of so much frailty, I should have ceased
> to esteem him."

There was much sympathy for André, whose handsome features and polite
manners melted even the hardest of hearts, including the tribunal of six major
generals and eight brigadiers. Washington, not wanting to condemn him on his
own authority, only quietly listened from the doorway. However, when the one
day trial ended and they concluded that he

> "ought to be considered as a spy . . . to suffer death." Washington with
> some misgivings gave his order, "The Commander-in-Chief directs the ex-
> ecution of the above sentence in the usual way this afternoon at 5 o'clock
> precisely."

Washington delayed the hanging until noon on 2 October, hoping for a last minute exchange of prisoners.

Benjamin Tallmadge, who had guarded the prisoner night and day with the help of another guard, had become quite endeared to the prisoner and sadly reported,

> "Major André . . . in truth . . . was a most elegant and accomplished gentleman. After he was informed of his sentence, he showed no signs of perturbed emotion, but wrote a most touching and finished letter to General Washington, requesting that the mode of his death might be adapted to the feelings of a man of honor. The universal usage of nations having affixed to the crime of a spy, death by the gibbet, his request could not be granted."

In a letter to his friend Colonel John Laurens on 11 October, HAMILTON wrote,

> "There was, in truth, no way of saving him. Arnold or he must have been the victim, and Arnold was out of our power."

Sir Henry Clinton, though grieving for his lost friend, promptly extended his hand in friendship to his newly commissioned general, Benedict Arnold. But Arnold's acceptance with the British army was observed to be tenuous:

> "General Arnold is a very unpopular character in the British army, nor can all the patronage he meets with from the commander-in-chief procure him respectability . . . . The subaltern officers have conceived such an aversion to him, that they unanimously refused to serve under his command."

From New York City, John Griffith wrote home to England about André:

> "He died a sacrifice to his country . . . . Loved and esteemed by those who knew him and admired by those that did not." When the account arrived at York, the soldiers shouted, "André! André!" and from the streets echoed, "Vengeance with the bayonet to the Sons of Rebellion!"

In the South, on 16 August, American General Horatio Gates had literally lost his army. With the surrender of Benjamin Lincoln's army at Charleston, British Commander Cornwallis had moved northwest and at Camden, South Carolina, about two-thirds the way to the North Carolina border, the enemies met, and the battle took place. As his militia and Continentals dispersed in all directions, Gates escaped the slaughter and rode quickly north to ancestral Hillsborough, North Carolina, where he hoped to collect his troops.

In Philadelphia, Congress was totally disillusioned with this general they had previously praised so warmly after his win at Saratoga. They now wanted Gates replaced in the South with NATHANAEL GREENE. Washington quickly approved their choice of generals and a disappointed GREENE left his post at West Point and a quieter winter there with his family. The Virginia continentals were to go south with GREENE. DANIEL MORGAN was also recruited from his Virginia home, where he had retired with his injured leg.

Cornwallis, however, was not sitting still in Camden. His army was on the move to Charlotte, North Carolina, then northward, while his infamous Tarleton raiders continued to bayonet and ravish North Carolina, as they had in South Carolina. It was on 7 Oct 1780, only five days after John André was hung, that the battle of King's Mountain occurred. It was really more of a civil war, with the highly organized army of southern loyalists battling the much smaller group of self-appointed angry mountain men of western North Carolina, eastern Tennessee and the southwestern tip of Virginia.

The victory of these southern American colonists was the definite turning point of the war in the South, and many have called it the turning point of the whole Revolution. It was totally unexpected by Cornwallis. He had not only lost much of his loyalist army, but had also found himself fighting against strong men that he had hoped would befriend him. Apprehension gnawed within the British general, as he moved his army northward toward Hillsborough—still expecting the strong support of the Regulators.

When Washington learned that Benedict Arnold had accepted a British general's commission and was recruiting a corps of loyalists from the refugee camp on Long Island, along with 212 deserters from the continental army, he decided that he must stop him. Secretly, he worked with Harry Lee, who had suggested an assassination. Together, they chose the twenty-three-year-old Sergeant Major John Champe of Lee's Virginia Light Horse—a Tidewater Virginian. Champe was a tall, powerfully-built man known for his "uncommon taciturnity and inflexible perseverance." He was extremely surprised when Lee called him into his tent and told him of his mission. He was to slip into New York, posing as a deserter, join Arnold's despicable army, and kidnap their leader. He was warned that Arnold was not to be killed. Washington wanted to make a public example of him and have him tried and hung for treason.

Champe accepted, although it hurt his pride to be considered by his friends and family as a deserter. On the moonless night of 20 Oct 1780, he galloped his horse past the continental army guard post at Totawa, New Jersey, and rode quickly toward Bergen, outdistancing an American patrol, which hurried back to report him as a deserter to Lee—the only one, besides Washington, who knew his true mission. If he had been caught, the punishment was instant death. Champe was to work with a secret agent, Baldwin, at Newark, who was paid "one hundred guineas, five hundred acres of land and three Negroes." Champe struggled through the heavy salt-marsh near Paulus Hook and plunged into the water. A British patrol boat fired on the pursuing American patrol while another boat crew picked up Champe.

Champe spent the weekend in the provost jail. Sir Henry Clinton personally interrogated him for two hours before he gave him the usual two guineas for desertion, and then released him onto the streets of Manhattan. While strolling the streets in his uniform, he caught the eye of Benedict Arnold, who soon confronted him. Champe praised Arnold and told him that it was his desertion that had inspired his own—true in a different way. Arnold bought him a drink and signed him up.

Over the next few weeks, Champe visited Arnold's home and found that he usually ended his day with a stroll in his garden and then visited an outhouse next to an alley leading down to the Hudson. Champe sent a message to Lee that he would capture Arnold on the evening of 11 December; everything was to be ready. Unfortunately, that very night, Arnold ordered his troops, including Champe, aboard transports to sail for Virginia. Champe had to go along or face charges of insubordination or desertion. For the next several months he marched through Virginia with Arnold, pillaging his neighbors and fighting his own troops. It was several months before he dared to desert again and return to his unit. Arnold's capture had failed.

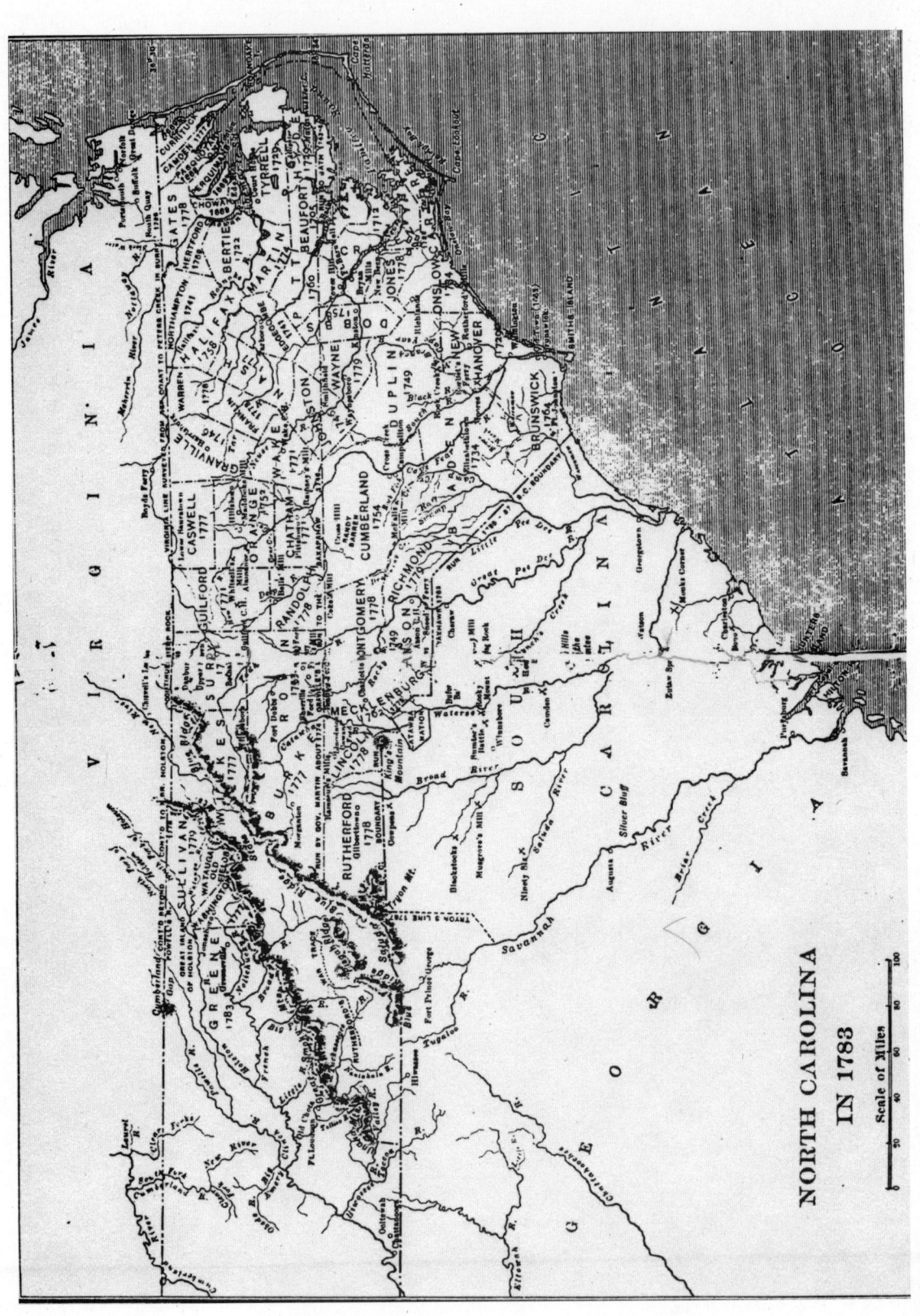

NORTH CAROLINA
IN 1783

Scale of Miles

93

NORTH CAROLINA—REVOLUTIONARY WAR—
ORANGE, GUILFORD COUNTIES

Governor Josiah Martin replaced Governor Tryon in North Carolina in 1771 when Tryon was made Governor of the New York colony. Edmund Fanning, Governor Tryon's friend, left North Carolina and went to New York also in that year. When the Revolution erupted, Fanning joined the British Army and advanced to the rank of general. He was wounded. His property was confiscated in 1779. He then went to Nova Scotia where he became lieutenant governor of Nova Scotia and later of Prince Edward Island.

Governor Martin was not popular with the friends of the former Governor Tryon, and when the Regulators had earlier asked him for pardon he listened to them. James Hunter, the Hamilton brothers, William BUTLER, Thomas WELBORN, Jeremiah FIELDS, and John Fruit were among those who petitioned for pardon. Governor Martin, although anxious to grant these pardons, felt compelled to wait for the approval of the crown.

[Note: Some descendants of the ALLREDs married WELBORNs and BUTLERs. MARY FIELDS of Granville County married HENRY IVIE II about 1750.]

When, in 1773, the British government advised an act of amnesty on the part of the Assembly—meeting in New Bern, the legislation was refused because it did not make enough exceptions. Their involvement with Assemblyman Fanning, Governor Tryon, and the War of the Regulators had created a desire for greater vengeance. Governor Martin made a tour of the "back country" of his province and was completely won over to the justice of the Regulator's cause.

In a letter to Lord Hillsborough he wrote,

"My progress through this Country My Lord hath opened my eyes exceedingly with respect to the commotions and discontents that lately prevailed in it. I now see most clearly that they have been provoked by insolence and cruel advantages taken of the peoples ignorance by mercenary tricking Attornies, Clerks and other little Officers who have practiced upon them every sort of rapine and extortion by which having brought themselves their just resentment they engaged Government in their defense by artful misrepresentations that the vengeance the wretched people in folly and madness aimed at their heads was directed against the constitution and by this stratagem they threw an odium upon the injured people that by degrees begat a prejudice which precluded a full redress of their grievances."

Having thus been convinced of their innocence, Governor Martin began action to secure pardons for them. They felt he was their friend.

In the early part of 1775 several letters from the various western counties expressing their loyalty to King George were received, much to the gratification of Governor Martin. The following was a letter from Guilford County, which included Randolph County at this time. It was signed by John FIELD and one hundred and sixteen men.

"His Majesty's most loyal subjects of the County of Guilford and Province of North Carolina beg leave to assure your excellency that we hold an open detestation to all illegal and unwarrantable proceedings against his Majesty's Crown and dignity, and as there is a general dispute between his Majesty and the Colonies of America, past our knowledge to determine what the event may be. We therefore hold a firm attachment to his Majesty King George the Third his crown and dignity. We therefore being an unhappy people, lying under the reflection of the late unhappy insurrection, we have therefore taken this opportunity to show forth our loyalty to his Majesty and his lawful commands and for further confirmation have hereto, subscribed our names as maintaining our rights under legal authority."

It has been estimated that between 50 to 70 percent of the North Carolina settlers were loyal to the crown in the early days of the Revolutionary War. When it began, the British gave full pardon to all the Regulators, except Herman Husband. A great majority of the loyalists were Scotch, who settled mainly in Cumberland and Bladen counties. Many of these had been defeated in the war between England and Scotland (1745). To come to this new country, they had sworn a solemn oath to become good and faithful subjects of George II of England. They were an extremely religious people (Presbyterian) and felt bound by this oath, as did many of the Regulators. The German Moravians and the English Quakers claimed neutrality, and were persecuted by whichever side occupied their territory. Episcopalians, in some cases, felt loyalty to both church and king.

A group on the east coast of North Carolina supported the British. These were the merchants who traded directly with England. Their survival depended upon British trade, and many had heavy debts owed to the English financiers. In New England, it was somewhat different, as their shipping came largely from the West Indies. With the onset of hostilities, some of these loyalists joined the British forces; but since the early fighting was in New England and lands north of Virginia, most detached themselves from the conflict until in November, 1778, when British General Clinton shipped 3500 men to take Savannah, Georgia, thus opening a second front in the southern colonies. To oppose them was Major General Robert Howe of North Carolina who was stationed nearby with about 700 continentals and 150 militia, the only American army in the South. Discovering their weakness, the British quickly surrounded them. The rebels fled through Savannah, leaving behind over 500 dead, wounded, and missing. Having secured Savannah, British General Prevost looked north towards Augusta, Georgia.

Anticipating a greater need in the South, Congress had requested the troops from Virginia and North Carolina to move south and help with the defense of South Carolina and Georgia. Ponderous and dependable General Benjamin Lincoln of New England was named commander and he arrived in Charleston, South Carolina, in December, 1778. CURTIS IVEY, of Sampson County, (formerly part of Bladen County, North Carolina,) was listed with his regiment, first as a lieutenant, later as a captain. REUBEN IVEY of North Carolina enlisted as a musician. After the war ended, CURTIS IVEY was active in the formation of the North Carolina Constitution and legislature, as a representative from Sampson County. General Lincoln with 1500 troops set out for Georgia and met Howe and his stragglers about 15 miles north of the Savannah River. Across the river were the British.

General Moultrie with the South Carolina troops wrote,

"We hear their drums beat every morn from our outposts; nay, hear their sentinels cough."

Joined by 3000 eager militia, General Lincoln sent three forces southward. One met disaster at Briar Creek on 3 Mar 1779, where 400 died and 600 scattered. Undaunted, Lincoln left Moultrie to defend the Savannah River and started north toward Augusta with his main army. British General Prevost quickly crossed the river and as Moultrie fell away before him and the local inhabitants scattered in panic, he rapidly changed his plans and went east toward Charleston. Had he driven straight to Charleston, he surely would have taken it, as it was practically defenseless; but he delayed, the army returned and defenses rapidly increased. However, Prevost had accomplished his original objective; General Lincoln was no longer in Georgia, and the British continued to fortify Savannah.

In the broiling heat of the humid southern summer, General Benjamin Lincoln lay ill in Charleston. The short term militia enlistments were wandering home. His army was about 800 continentals. On the sixth of September, word came that the wily French Admiral Estaing would come to Savannah with 4000 men for only two weeks, as he must be gone before the hurricane season. Arousing himself, his army, and the available militia, General Lincoln advanced toward Savannah—but not fast enough. Estaing arrived first and not waiting for the Americans or disembarking his men, demanded that Prevost surrender to the French. Prevost stalled until British reinforcements arrived. Negotiations ended. Rains drenched the continentals in their soggy barracks as attempts were made to prepare. On 4 October the artillery started. Prevost was ready. Lincoln wanted to start siege operations; with Estaing it was now or never. He wanted an assault on the British fortifications.

At dawn 9 Oct 1779, the French and American forces attempted to storm Provost's defenses. Within an hour the defender's ditch was filled with dead and the "plain was strewn with mangled bodies." It has been said that only at Bunker Hill had a single side sustained such casualties as the allied troops did on that foggy morning—800 killed or wounded to a British loss of 57 casualties. Estaing had enough. At sea his crews were dying with fever and scurvy, his ships were endangered and his troops a disaster. On 19 October, he boarded his troops and sailed away. Lincoln was left to face the enemy alone.

With the winter approaching in the north, Henry Clinton felt quite secure in New York and was delighted with his win in Georgia. With Estaing's forces scattered, he could go by sea. So he sailed south for the capture of Charleston with seventy-six hundred soldiers on 26 December. The wild winter winds off the North Carolina capes scattered fourteen escort vessels, sank a ship loaded with cannon, and necessitated the destruction of the cavalry horses. On 11 Feb 1780, the remaining fleet landed 30 miles from Charleston. For various reasons they delayed their attack for eight weeks, allowing General Lincoln with perhaps 2000 regulars and 2000 militia to prepare for them. Upon seeing their extensive fortifications with 80 cannon and mortars, Clinton called up 1500 more troops from Savannah and 2500 from New York, making a total of over 10,000 soldiers with a backup of about 5000 seamen. On the 29th and 30th of March, the British crossed the Ashley and marched unopposed until within 2 miles of the American lines. Seven hundred North Carolina regulars had arrived to help Lincoln and on 9 April seven hundred and fifty Virginians and some North Carolina militia arrived to give aid.

Lincoln made a stalwart stand; but on 11 May 1780, surrounded by enemies on sea and land with escape impossible, he capitulated. He was told by the British that there were those within who had reported daily to them of his activities. Five thousand continentals, militia and armed citizens with piles of weapons, horses, and ammunition were lost to the cause of liberty when they surrendered. The smug British officers gloated at their success and with new enthusiasm prepared for their "hoped for" rapid journey through the "back country" of the Carolinas, where they had been led to believe "they had many friends."

Clinton split his forces. One column marched westward to Ninety Six (a town in South Carolina near present day Greenwood); another was to take Augusta, Georgia, and the third, which he placed under the command of 42-year-old Charles, Lord Cornwallis, was to destroy a rebel force reported to be forming along the "Great Wagon Road" at Camden, South Carolina. He placed under the command of Cornwallis the brutal cavalry leader Tarleton.

While the main army was awaiting boats to cross the Cooper River, Tarleton took his legion swiftly into Georgetown, subdued them and collected signatures to an oath of allegiance and returned.

As they journeyed, Cornwallis discovered that the soldiers they had been seeking at Camden had left and were heading north to Salisbury. There were about 350 Virginians under the leadership of Colonel Abraham Buford. Realizing they were beyond the reach of his force, he ordered Tarleton to go after them. In fifty-four hours, Tarleton covered a hundred-and-five miles, and on 29 May 1780, they found their quarry.

Buford's first notice of their presence was a bugle sounding the attack on his rear guard as the cavalry rushed upon them with the horrid yells of infuriated demons. A flag for surrender was ignored as they shot and used their bayonets to butcher the bodies of both the living and their dead Virginian comrades—113 Virginians were killed on the field, 150 were so badly maimed that they were loaded into wagons and carried to the Church of the Waxhaws. Only 53 were sufficiently upright to be taken as prisoners. Of Tarleton's men, 5 were killed and 14 wounded. News of Tarleton's barbarous deed spread rapidly throughout the back country. This was not the act of a kindly conqueror. Was this the justice Governor Josiah Martin had promised them?

As Tarleton returned to the main army approaching Camden, a sleeping giant had been aroused. This was not the New England or New York smooth-talking nobility. This was their country! They grabbed their flintlock rifles, with which they were well acquainted, crossed the Blue Ridge Mountains, forded streams, and marched southeasterly toward South Carolina, increasing in number as they advanced slowly, determined, but not rash.

As Tarleton approached Camden, one of his lieutenants shot a peaceful Quaker boy playing in his front yard. The Cornwallis army continued their march; two other boys were accused of firing on them. One was hung immediately, the other taken into the army for punishment. Resistance in this busy little town of flour and lumber mills approached zero as the enemy paraded through the town. Proclamations and promises were made and the people flocked in to make their promises of submission and to remain peaceably at home. With South Carolina and Georgia cowed and fearful, a confident Clinton prepared to return to New York. Cornwallis was called back to Charleston to take over in these two southern colonies of South Carolina and Georgia.

Then one day before Clinton departed, he amended his previously generous proclamation of peace and safety and declared

"outlaw anyone who did not take an active part in settling and securing His Majesty's government."

He thought this a wonderful idea, as it gave his loyalist friends a chance to observe and drive out from among themselves their "dangerous neighbors." He left Cornwallis in what he thought to be the "face of tranquility and submission," and suggested he advance soon into North Carolina.

This "face of tranquility and submission" evidently didn't include the other parts of the body, for with his last amendment the people considered their oaths violated. Guerrilla bands were organized in the tangled swamps and forests to resist, under experienced leaders like Thomas Sumter, William Hill, Francis Marion, William Davie, and other officers who were not ready to cry defeat.

FRANCIS MARION.

After Charleston was captured by the siege of the British army, Thomas Sumter and Francis Marion led guerilla like militia groups to harass Cornwallis. Marion's Company consisted of twenty men and boys, white and black, half clad and poorly armed. But the number increased, and the "Ragged Regiment" soon became a terror. There was no telling when or where the sword of the fearless leader would fall. From the swamps at midnight, he and his men would suddenly dart upon the enemy encampments. During the summer and autumn of 1780, he swept around Cornwallis's positions, cutting his lines of communication, and making incessant onsets. [*Ridpath History of the World Volume VI*]

On 1 August, Sumter and company attacked the British post at Rocky Mount, and a few days later struck at Hanging Rock. Major Archibald McArthur had raised a Tory militia, which turned coat, seized their officers, and rushed off with about 100 sick into North Carolina. The whole country between the Peedee and Santee rivers "had flared into an absolute state of rebellion."

A continental army was on the march for South Carolina. General Horatio Gates was to be at the head. Congress had called him from retirement to command "this army without strength—a military chest without money, a department apparently deficient in public spirit and a climate that increases despondency."

Such was General Gates description in a letter home. Gates had found by the time he reached Hillsboro, North Carolina, his troops consisted only of the Maryland and Delaware divisions with Baron de Kalb as commander and 120 dragoons under the French Colonel Armand. They were without wagons and carried their baggage on their backs, foraging as they went, "often fasting for several days together and subsisting frequently upon green apples and peaches."

When Gates arrived at this hungry army's encampment at HOLLINGSWORTH's Farm at Deep River, on 25 Jul 1780, De Kalb gleefully greeted him with an eight gun salute and turned over his command with undisguised relief. MOSES ALLRED, brother of fourth-great-grandfather WILLIAM ALLRED, later married (about 1787) ELIZABETH HOLLINGSWORTH. If the soldiers were starving, the farmers were not doing much better. The crops had not ripened, and yet they had been stripped from their fields and their trees. Their animals, wagons and usable equipment were taken. Hillsboro, Sandy Creek, Deep River, Salisbury, Charlotte—this was the Great Road between north and south for the armies of the west.

Baron de Kalb handed General Gates a letter from General Thomas Sumter, the South Carolina Colonel now turned partisan general. He had been investigating the strength of the enemy in their various locations and suggested a plan for taking Camden, where he thought them to have only 700 men. With promises of a Garden of Eden within two weeks, Gates commanded his starving army to be ready to march on 27 July. From Deep River there are two roads to Camden, South Carolina. One went westward through Rowan and Mecklenburg counties, where the Scotch-Irish were predominately Whig and provisions were more plentiful. The other road was 50 miles shorter, but cut through a wilderness of pines with hundreds of little watercourses, a desolate and infertile region, and hostile Tory territory. Gates chose the shorter route.

The battle was a disaster. The untrained militia, under pressure, bolted and "ran like a Torrent and bore all before them." General Gates rode to the rear, but couldn't rally them. While Gates was lost in his efforts to pull his army together,

Lord Cornwallis continued his end of it with proficiency. As the American survivors ran from the field in wild disorder, they left several hundred dead and wounded on the ground. Among the dying was gallant old De Kalb, splattered with blood from eleven brutal wounds. He was plundered and stripped, even of his shirt. The Virginians, who knew nothing of the country, retraced their steps to Hillsboro. The North Carolina militia took the shortest routes to their own homes.

General Gates, quickly observing this fiasco, with some of his officers, determined that Hillsboro was the best place to reorganize an army, and with an excellent horse he traveled the 180 miles in three days. Here he devoted himself to reorganizing his army. The militia was gone. Only remnants of the Delawares and Marylands remained. In mid-September, Colonel Buford arrived with his mangled remnants and some new recruits. Fifty militia arrived and a body of Delawares retaken from their British captors by partisan Colonel Francis Marion, the "Swamp Fox," as Tarleton renamed him. In all, Gates put together a force of 1200.

To Cornwallis, his dream of conqueror of North Carolina, Virginia, Maryland, and Pennsylvania became more consuming. However, his army was sick. The heat! The swamps! Something was unhealthy. He decided to move his army to the Waxhaws where he hoped the higher, cooler country might be useful. Finally, around the 21st of September he began his northward march to North Carolina with a three-column thrust. He would go to Hillsboro by way of Charlotte and Salisbury; his right would secure Wilmington and the Cape Fear River as a supply route; his left, who were loyalists already in the "back country" of South Carolina under the leadership of Major Patrick Ferguson, would move northward in the shadow of the western mountains and join him at Charlotte.

Ferguson had moved northward as far as Gilbert Town when word came to him that

> "the hardy rebel homesteaders on the Watauga and Holston rivers beyond
> the craggy peaks of the Blue Ridge, which they called the 'overmountain
> men' were gathering rapidly, and were 3000 strong."

Ferguson had fought them briefly in the summer and then they had dispersed. He sent word to Cornwallis and asked for additional reinforcements. He dropped back to King's Mountain, where he decided to encamp and await these

> "back water men . . . a set of mongrels' as he had proclaimed them to the lo-
> cal people. King's Mountain was a rocky, wooded outlying spur of the Blue
> Ridge, rising some 60 feet above the plain around it. There was a plateau
> at its summit, about 600 yards long and about 70, to 120, feet wide. It was
> an excellent campsite for his 1,100 men. They inspected their weapons. To
> those who had no bayonet, he asked them to whittle down the handles of
> their hunting knives, so they could be fitted into the muzzles of their rifles.
> As they waited, Ferguson declared, "I am on King's Mountain, and I am
> king of this mountain and the Almighty God will not drive me from it!"

Ferguson's enemies began to gather at Sycamore Flats on the Watauga
the day Cornwallis started north. On 24 September, Colonel Isaac Shelby arrived with 240 men from Sullivan County, North Carolina; Colonel Charles
McDowell with 160 from Burke and Rutherford counties, North Carolina;
Colonel John Sevier with 240 from Washington County, North Carolina; and
Colonel William Campbell with 400 from Washington County, Virginia. The
next day they marched into the mountains, and tramping through snow "shoe
mouth deep" in the gap between Roan and Yellow mountains, made their way
to Quaker Meadows on the Catawba. Here Colonel Benjamin Cleveland joined
them with 350 men from Wilkes and Surry Counties. On a rainy Monday, 2 Oct
1780, they arrived within a days march of Gilbert Town, where they had heard
Ferguson was waiting for them. They were there without a commanding officer, so after deliberation they decided to send for General DANIEL MORGAN
or General William Davidson. Charles McDowell set out to find one of them.
Meanwhile they decided that they should confer daily and appointed Colonel
William Campbell as "Officer of the Day" to execute any plans adopted by the
regiments.

This group could not remain idle. They first proceeded toward Gilbert
Town, but finding that Ferguson was no longer there, they determined to pursue him with their best mounted, leaving the weaker horses and footmen to
follow as fast as they could. Sixteen-year-old James Collins wrote,

> "On Saturday morning, October 7th, 1780, the sky was overcast with
> clouds, and at times a light mist of rain falling."

Through this dismal country the overmountain men rode onward to King's

Mountain. After dismounting and securing their coats and blankets to their saddles, each leader made a short speech to his men, desiring all cowards to be off, immediately. Young Collins said he thought perhaps it might be good to leave; but the thoughts of being called a coward won out. He stayed and reported later:

> "We were soon in motion, every man throwing four or five balls in his mouth to prevent thirst, also to be in readiness to reload quick. The shot of the enemy soon began to pass over us like hail. The first shock was quickly over, and for my own part, I was soon in a profuse sweat. My lot happened to be in the center where the severest part of the battle was fought. We soon attempted to climb the hill, but were fiercely charged upon and forced to fall back to our first position. We tried a second time, but met the same fate. The fight then seemed to become more furious. Their leader, Ferguson, came in full view within rifle shot, as if to encourage his men, who by this time were falling very fast. He soon disappeared. We took to the hill a third time. The enemy gave way. When we had gotten near the top, some of our leaders roared out, 'Hurrah, my brave fellows! Advance! They are crying for quarter!'"

The Americans arrival at King's Mountain through the rain had caught this Tory militia totally unprepared. The height of the mountain gave the Tories an advantage; but the woods gave good cover for these rugged overmountain Americans.

Another sixteen-year-old, Private THOMAS YOUNG, had lost his shoes and was barefoot, but he carried his "large old musket" charged with two musket balls. He was on the north side of the mountain and would write:

> "The orders were, at the firing of the first gun, for every man to raise a whoop, rush forward, and fight his way as he best could. When our division came up to the . . . mountain, we dismounted and Colonel Roebuck drew us a little to the left and commenced the attack, I well remember how I behaved. BEN HOLLINGSWORTH and myself took right up the side of the mountain and fought from tree to tree . . . to the summit. I recollect I stood behind one tree and fired until the bark was nearly all knocked off and my eyes pretty well filled with it. One fellow shaved me pretty close, for his bullet took a piece out of my own gun stock. Before I was aware of it, I found myself apparently between my own regiment and the enemy, as I judged from seeing the paper which the Whigs wore in their hats and the pine knots the Tories wore in theirs, these being the badges of

distinction. On the top of the mountain, in the thickest of the fight, I saw Colonel Williams fall . . . I had seen him but once before that day. It was in the beginning of the action, as he charged by me at full speed around the mountain. Toward the summit, a ball struck his horse under the jaw, when he commenced stamping as if he were in a nest of yellow jackets. Colonel Williams threw his reins over the animal's neck, sprang to the ground and dashed onward. The moment I heard the cry that Colonel Williams was shot, I ran to his assistance, for I loved him like a father. He had ever been so kind to me and almost always carried a cake in his pocket for me and his little son, Joseph. They . . . sprinkled some water in his face. He revived, and his first words were, 'For _____ sake, boys, don't give up the hill!' . . . . I left him in the arms of his son, Daniel, and returned to the field to avenge his fate."

Patrick Ferguson, although waiting for the attack, had been surprised. One of his Tory scouts had just dismounted and proclaimed, "All clear!" when the enemy appeared below them in the dripping trees. With his shrill whistle and responsive horse, he directed his men with courage and alacrity. He wore a checkered hunting shirt over his uniform. The whistle, the shirt, his dress sword waving in his left hand, he was a fast moving, but a great target. Second-in-command, Captain Abraham DePeyster, saw his chief go down with several balls in his body. His foot was still in the stirrup. Ferguson's men lifted him down and propped him against a tree. There he died. At that moment, Colonel Shelby had just gained the eastern summit. Hope deserted DePeyster and he ordered a white flag to be flown.

Robert Henry heard the cry that Ferguson was dead and reported,

"I had a desire to see him, and went and found him . . . shot in the face and in the breast . . . Samuel Talbot turned him over and got his pocket pistol."

The battle was over. He was wrapped in a raw beef hide and buried on the field. These overmountain men had killed 157 Tories, wounded 163, and taken 698 prisoners. They had 28 of their men killed and 62 wounded. All of this took place in about an hour. There were no surgeons or water to help them as they buried the dead and gave such aid as they could to the wounded and dying.

As the autumn darkness enclosed them, both Tories and Whigs with troubled sleep stayed on the mountain until the first rays of the new morning sun displayed, as young Collins remembered, "the wives and children of the poor Tories, who came in great numbers. Their husbands, fathers, and brothers lay dead in heaps, while others lay wounded or dying . . . . We proceeded to bury the dead, but it was badly done. They were thrown into convenient piles and covered with old logs, the bark of old trees and rocks, yet not so as to secure them from becoming a prey to the beasts of the forest, or the vultures of the air; and the wolves became so plenty, that it was dangerous for anyone to be out at night for several miles around. Also the hogs in the neighborhood gathered into the place to devour the flesh of men, inasmuch as numbers chose to live on little meat rather than eat their hogs, though they were fat. Half of the dogs in the country were said to be mad and were put to death. I saw myself, in passing the place, a few weeks after, all parts of the human frame . . . scattered in every direction . . . . In the evening there was a distribution . . . of the plunder, and we were dismissed. My father and myself drew two fine horses, two guns, and some articles of clothing with a share of powder and lead. Every man repaired to his tent for home. It seemed like a calm after a heavy storm . . . and for a short time, every man could visit his home, or his neighbor without being afraid."

The disposal of the prisoners was a problem for these less organized patriots. They were taken first to Gilbert Town then north to Hillsboro, where they hoped General Gates would take charge of them. On the journey by foot, the prisoners were guarded by double lines of mounted Americans and obliged to carry two empty muskets, each weighing about fifteen pounds. They had been stripped of their shoes in many cases. Many of the victors were far from sympathetic to the prisoners and bullies beat the captives, slashed them with swords, and a committee of colonels established themselves as a jury to try some of the more obnoxious.

Thirty-six were found guilty of "breaking open houses, killing the men, turning the men and women out of doors, and burning the houses." Nine of these were hanged, but others were reprieved. Many prisoners escaped along the way. At Hillsboro, Gates appealed to Governor Thomas Jefferson of Virginia to tell him what to do with these burdensome problems, who needed to be fed and guarded. He was in great need of food and soldiers.

This "Battle of King's Mountain," on the border of North and South Carolina is considered by many to be the turning point of the Revolutionary War. Certainly, it was the turning point in the southern colonies. The effect of the victory over the Tories was instantaneous; a hopeless war of constant defeat had been given a new vision. The sleeping giant was now fully awake and the colonials began to unite in their new hope of freedom. This stalwart unyielding group of untrained "back country" North Carolinians and western Virginians (especially those who had pushed further west into what was later to become Tennessee, which had become an area of escape for many of the Regulators) had become the champions of all of the Americans.

It also had brought fear into the hearts of the British. Rumors had exaggerated the strength of these men, and Cornwallis, who had received Ferguson's appeal for assistance on the day of the battle, soon received word of Ferguson's death and the defeat of his army. The loyalists, on whom he had depended for support, remained silent in their homes. The strength of the British, so cocky and sure of themselves, was being questioned. On the fourteenth of October, one week after the battle, Cornwallis began his hurried retreat into South Carolina. The rainy season was upon them. The roads were deep with mud. Wagons and food vanished and the army was lacking in tents. The American militia was bolder and more daring in their harassment. Sickness increased within the ranks, and soon Cornwallis himself tossed in one of the hospital wagons. Fifteen days after leaving Charlotte, the army made camp at Winnsboro, between Camden and Ninety Six. All British plans for a winter campaign through North Carolina had disappeared.

[Note: ELIZABETH HOLLINGSWORTH, who married MOSES ALLRED, was the daughter of SAMUEL and RACHEL HOLLINGSWORTH of Randolph County, North Carolina. They probably owned the HOLLINGSWORTH farm referred to earlier. In the scant records that I have, a BENJAMIN HOLLINGSWORTH was not mentioned; but he was probably related in some way.

There was a THOMAS YOUNG of Iredell County, North Carolina, who might have been the father of young sixteen-year-old THOMAS YOUNG. The older THOMAS YOUNG was a brother of WILLIAM YOUNG who was the second-great-grandfather of the sisters MARY EVELINE YOUNG, MALINDA JANE YOUNG and SARAH EMILY YOUNG of Tennessee, who were the wives of RICHARD A. IVIE and WILLIAM F. IVIE, older brothers of great-grandfather JOHN LEHI IVIE.]

A history by the Rev. B. C. ALLRED tells us:

"When the Revolutionary war came close, my grandfather, JOHN ALLRED, shouldered his flintlock rifle and fought for the freedom of the American colonies to the end of the war. The fact of my grandfather's fighting against the British aroused the anger of Col. David Fannen, the leader of the Tories or British sympathizers, and he and his band of men went to my great-grandfather's in search of JOHN. My grandfather, who happened to be at home, saw them coming, snatched up his gun and secreted himself in the attic, and it so happened that they did not go up there to search for him. My great-grandfather also saw them approaching . . . . Fannen and his men . . . went out to his crib, later opened the crib door and let many barrels of corn run out, did the same at another log crib, then turned their horses loose in the lot to eat and trample the corn into the red mud. When they had eaten all they wanted them to have, they saddled them up and started on towards the western part of the county.

"My great-grandfather had a sprightly Negro by the name of Kiltyre whom Fannen took with him. The first night they spent at the widow Kindley's [or Lindley] near the river, who had a good many slaves. Kiltyre seemed so delighted with his new friends that Fannen told him to go down to the Negro cabins and spend the night, but Kiltyre never got to the cabins, and the next morning he was at home, where he remained until the old Master's death. In the division of the estate, Kiltyre fell to my grandfather where he spent the balance of his life."

The *Encyclopedia Americana* describes the David Fanning mentioned in the preceding history:

"FANNING, David, American freebooter: b. Wake County, N. C., about 1756; d. Digby, Nova Scotia, 1825. He was a carpenter by trade, but led a vagabond life. Late in the Revolutionary War he joined the Tories for the purpose of revenge; gathered a small band of desperados like himself, laid waste to whole settlements and committed fearful atrocities. For these services he received a lieutenant's commission from the British commander at Wilmington. At one time he surprised a court in session and captured and carried off judges, lawyers, clients, officers and citizens, and soon afterward seized Governor Burke and his suite. The name of Fanning became a terror to the country, and he was outlawed. At the close of the war he fled to New Brunswick, where he became a member of the legislature."

It didn't say he was related to Edmund Fanning, who had gone north with Governor Tryon and was made lieutenant governor of Nova Scotia; but they appear to be related in spirit, if not in fact.

[Note: The above JOHN ALLRED was probably the son of WILLIAM ALLRED, whose wife was ELIZABETH DIFFEE. They lived close to my direct ancestor WILLIAM ALLRED who married ELIZABETH THRASHER.]

On 5 Oct 1780, the Continental Congress in Philadelphia resolved that

George Washington order a court of inquiry into the conduct of General Gates and appoint a new officer to command the Southern Department until the court acted. He felt that GREENE was the most resourceful, accomplished officer he could recommend. He was to have Henry Lee's Legion and Baron von Steuben to assist him in training and regulating his army. General GREENE gave DANIEL MORGAN, who had quit the army in disgust after Gates' wild fiasco, the command of four regiments of infantry and a corps of riflemen. This part of his troops were to proceed west of the Catawba, while he proceeded east for Charlotte to an area he deemed more suitable for training, organizing and feeding his main army.

NATHANAEL GREENE

GENERAL DANIEL MORGAN
FROM THE ORIGINAL PICTURE IN THE ROTUNDA
OF THE CAPITOL, WASHINGTON

As MORGAN marched his men toward Ninety Six, he was joined by several small militia groups. From these groups, he found some excellent spies, who reported British and Tory movements. Cornwallis felt threatened by MORGAN's advance and gave Tarleton 750 men and two three-pounders to push MORGAN to either fight or flee. Tarleton soon found that Ninety Six was not threatened by MORGAN's position. Feeling confident, he rested his men and sent word to Cornwallis that he was going after them. He further suggested that Cornwallis move men to block their retreat. MORGAN watched the British movements closely. On 14 Jan 1781, he moved his troops to Thicketty Creek, as Tarleton advanced with a force of about 1100 to 1200 men. As they came closer, he moved further back until he reached a place called Hannah's Cowpens on the Broad River. Here he would make his stand. Tarleton was delighted. He felt the river and the mountain blocked their retreat. MORGAN, who realized the tendency of the less trained militia groups to run or retreat under fire, had deliberately allowed this 'no retreat' to insure that his men would stand firm.

When MORGAN told his men that here they would meet the enemy, THOMAS YOUNG received the news with great joy. YOUNG, our overmountain man from the Battle of King's Mountain, was a volunteer with William Washington's cavalry:

"We were very anxious for battle, and many a hearty curse had been vented against General MORGAN during that day's march for retreating as we thought, to avoid a fight. Night came upon us, yet much remained to be done. It was all important to strengthen the cavalry. General MORGAN well knew the power of Tarleton's Legion, and he was too wily an officer not to prepare himself as well as circumstances would admit. Two companies of volunteers were called for . . . . I attached myself to Major Jolly's company. We drew swords that night and were informed we had authority to press any horse not belonging to a dragoon or an officer into our service for the day. It was upon this occasion I was more perfectly convinced of General MORGAN's qualifications to command militia than I had ever before been. He went among the volunteers, helped them fix their swords, joked with them about their sweethearts, told them to keep in good spirits, and the day would be ours. And long after I laid down, he was going about among the soldiers encouraging them and telling them that the old wagoner [MORGAN] would crack his whip over Ben [Tarleton] in the morning, as sure as they lived. 'Just hold up your heads, boys, three fires,' he would say, 'and you are free, and then when you return to your homes, how the old folks will bless you, and the girls kiss you for your gallant conduct!' I don't believe he slept a wink that night."

The next morning, 17 Jan 1781, an hour before daylight, MORGAN's pickets were driven in, and Tarleton was within five miles, marching light and fast.

The troops were aroused with a thunderous shout from MORGAN,

"Boys, get up! Benny is coming!"

THOMAS YOUNG watched their approach:

"The morning of the 17th . . . was bitterly cold. We were formed in order of battle, and the men were slapping their hands together to keep warm—an exertion not long necessary . . . . About sunrise, the British line advanced at a sort of trot with a loud halloo. It was the most beautiful line I ever saw. When they shouted, I heard MORGAN say, 'They give us the British halloo, boys. Give them the Indian hallo, by G____!' and he galloped along the lines, cheering the men and telling them not to fire until we could see the whites of their eyes. Every officer was crying, 'Don't fire!' for it was hard matter to keep us from it. I should have said the British line advanced under cover of their artillery, for it opened so fiercely upon the center that Colonel Washington moved his cavalry from the center towards the right wing. The militia fired first. It was for a time, pop—pop—pop, and then a whole volley; but when the regulars fired, it seemed like one sheet of flame from right to left. Oh! It was beautiful."

The American line stood firm until the British charged them with the bayonet, when they retreated toward the reserve under Colonel Washington, a second-cousin of George Washington.

James Collins, the other young militia veteran of King's Mountain, reported:

"'Now,' thought I, 'my hide is in the loft.' Just as we got to our horses, they overtook us and began to take a few hacks at some, however, without doing much injury. They, in their haste, had pretty much scattered . . . But in a few moments, Colonel Washington's cavalry was among them like a whirlwind, and the poor fellows began to keel from their horses without being able to remount. The shock was sudden and violent; they could not stand it, and immediately betook themselves to flight. There was no time to rally, and they appeared to be as hard to stop as a drove of wild Choctaw steers going to a Pennsylvania market.

"In a few moments, the clashing of swords was out of hearing and quickly out of sight. By this time, both lines of the infantry were warmly engaged and we being relieved from the pursuit of the enemy began to rally and prepare to redeem our credit, when MORGAN rode up in front and waving his sword cried out, 'Form, form, my brave fellows! Give them one more fire, and the day is ours.' Old Morgan was never beaten."

The Encyclopedia Americana reads:

"Hannibal himself never wrought out a finer piece of tactics, or caught an enemy in a deadlier trap. Most of the British troops threw down their arms; the remnant fled with Tarleton, who barely escaped being cut down by Colonel Washington's sabre. Of the 1,100, 270 were killed and wounded, and 600 were taken prisoners, with two field-pieces and 1,000 small arms. The Americans lost 12 killed and 62 wounded. Nearly a third of Cornwallis' army including all his light troops were annihilated at a blow."

A grateful Congress voted MORGAN a gold metal. The Virginian House of Delegates voted to award him a horse "with furniture" and a sword, and a western Carolinian, John Miller, thanked the Lord in one of their meetings:

"Good Lord, our God that art in Heaven, we have great reason to thank thee for the many favors we have received at thy hands, the many battles we have won. There is the great and glorious battle of King's mountain, where we kilt the great Gineral Ferguson and took his whole army . . . . And the ever-memorable and glorious battle of the Coopens, where we made the proud Gineral Tarleton run doon the road helter-skelter, and, Good Lord, if ye had na suffered the cruel Tories to burn Billy Hill's Iron Works, we would na have asked any mair favors at thy hands. Amen."

While the country cheered, the tired, arthritic giant DANIEL MORGAN led his little army's retreat along the muddy roads of North Carolina to Sherrald's Ford beyond the Catawba.

When their victory report reached NATHANAEL GREENE, he was ecstatic and sent this praise with his orders to join him:

"I am much better pleased that you have plucked the laurels from the brow of the hitherto fortunate Tarleton than if he had fallen by the hands of Lucifer."

Since the enlistment of most of Stevens's Virginia militia was about to expire, GREENE's orders to MORGAN were to pull back and join forces near Salisbury. He sent orders to Salisbury and Hillsboro to take their prisoners and supplies into Virginia and wait. Cornwallis had joined Tarleton's unfortunate stragglers and was pursuing MORGAN's troops. The race was on. MORGAN traveled a hundred miles in less than five days, destroying river passages and guarding fords as he advanced up the Great Wagon Road. Cornwallis was anxious to catch him. Confident, he destroyed many of his cumbersome supply wagons, in order to move more swiftly. Always, MORGAN seemed to be just ahead of him—like a carrot held in front of the donkey's eyes. The British army wanted a battle before GREENE's army, joined with MORGAN's troops, reached the safety of Virginia across the Dan River. There were boats waiting to help the continentals across. On 14 Feb 1781, the continental army received their valentine. As the last of their disembarking army watched across the rapidly flowing Dan River on the Virginia side, they saw the frustrated advance troops of Cornwallis' army gathering on the other side—not able or desiring to cross into the highly fortified Virginia. The Americans would ask ex-governor Patrick Henry for more troops, organize, and would soon meet the British, when they were ready.

Cornwallis took his troops to Hillsboro; but the North Carolina Tories failed him. Food and equipment were scant. Another army had been there before them.

> "Our experience," he wrote Germain, "has shown that their numbers are not so great as had been represented and that their friendship was only passive."

When the British killed some of their draught oxen for food and went from house to house for provisions, the distress of the citizens increased considerably. Supporting an army without supplies was not fun and games. On 23 Feb 1781, word came to Cornwallis that GREENE was heavily reinforced by Virginians and had crossed the Dan River. He recalled Tarleton, and three days later marched from Hillsboro across the Haw River to a place near Alamance Creek, better to protect "the body of our friends . . . said to be assembling." This is the area of the ALLRED and ALDRIDGE properties on <u>Sandy Creek</u>, where the War of the Regulators was fought.

[Note: Living on a plantation on Hogan's Creek were JOHN THRASHER and his sons, JOHN, ISAAC and JOSEPH CLOUD THRASHER. ISAAC THRASHER was married to RUTH BARTON, and his brother JOHN THRASHER married her sister, SUSAN BARTON. The BARTON sister's father, DAVID BARTON had been killed by the Indians when he had explored frontier Kentucky with Daniel Boone. DAVID BARTON is believed to have come either from Pennsylvania or coastal Virginia, and was probably a descendant of THOMAS BARTON, who has not yet been tied in with our BARTON line. The THRASHERS and BARTONS also had land in Surry and Wilkes Counties, North Carolina, on the Yadkin River, which Brigadier-General MORGAN had crossed earlier with his troops as they rushed northward for the Dan River.

Shortly before these events, about 1780, our ancestor, WILLIAM ALLRED, son of THOMAS ALLRED of Sandy Creek, married ELIZABETH THRASHER, who was probably another child of JOHN THRASHER Sr.—if not a daughter, then a niece, as there were brothers of JOHN just across the Dan River in Pittsylvania County, Virginia. Third-great-grandmother SARAH ALLRED was born on 3 May 1781, in the midst of all this devastation and confusion. Randolph County had been divided off from Orange and Guilford Counties in 1779. Some of the THRASHERs later married WELBORNs, as did the ALLREDs.

Arriving in Hillsboro, North Carolina, from Ireland, around 1769 to 1775, were the FAUCETT families. Our ancestor, RICHARD FAUCETT (1769), was too young to be a soldier; however, he knew the problems associated with hungry armies surviving on his home land.

Fourth-great-grandfather ALEXANDER McKEE and family were in Orange County, when the 1790 census was taken. We do not have the date he enlisted in the colonial army as a private. For this service, he later received a land grant in Sumner County, Tennessee. He and his wife MARY had a large family. Their daughter MARY (1774) married RICHARD FAUCETT on the 28 Jan 1792 in Orange County. In some family histories, ALEXANDER McKEE's wife is shown as MARY BEAN, with no parents listed. There was an early British officer named WILLIAM BEAN who was stationed at Fort Loudon, across the Blue Ridge Mountains in what is now Tennessee, during French and Indian war times. When the British later closed this fort because of Indian troubles, he came east over the Blue Ridge mountains and lived in North Carolina for awhile. He later went back over the mountains into what became Watauga. It is said that his son, RUSSELL BEAN, was the first white child born in the Tennessee territory. Others soon joined him. From this group came many of the overmountain men.]

When GREENE decided to re-enter North Carolina, he sent Otho Williams with the light troops he had led in the retreat back across the Dan and stationed him near Hillsboro to discourage reinforcements from joining with the British. He was told to keep his troops between Cornwallis and GREENE's main army and to harass the British, if they started to remove toward Wilmington, North Carolina—their supply base.

Cornwallis started an offensive. He wanted to fight GREENE before his Virginia reinforcements arrived. On 6 Mar 1781, at 5:30 A. M., Cornwallis moved toward Williams troops across the Haw River. Williams moved his men toward the ford at Wetzell's Mill on Reedy Fork Creek, while GREENE began to march away with his main army. As they had done earlier on their retreat to the Dan, Williams would slow the enemy at a water course, then move quickly on. This game of cat and mouse continued for twelve miles. Williams found a place to make a stand and about twenty men were killed on each side. Williams retreated again, with Cornwallis following for about five miles—then Cornwallis gave up and went back to his original camp. It was a minor incident in the war; but it gave a strong message to the Tories. Many of them quietly went home, and the American militia poured into GREENE's camp. The message from the people seemed to be, "If you can win, we're on your side, otherwise—."

GREENE wrote Governor Thomas Jefferson of Virginia:

"The militia have flocked in from various quarters, but they come and go in such irregular bodies that I can make no calculations on the strength of my army or direct any future operations that can ensure me success. A force fluctuating in this manner can promise but slender hopes of success against an enemy regulated by discipline and made formidable by the superiority of their numbers. Hitherto I have been obliged to practice that by finesse, which I dare not attempt by force."

He wrote General George Washington that this tendency of the militia "to get tired out with difficulties and go and come," was a principal reason for making an attempt against Cornwallis while his army was large. He had 1,600 continentals, 2,600 militia and 160 cavalrymen of Lee's and William Washington's legions.

"The great advantage which would result from the action if we were victorious, and the little injury if we were otherwise, determined me to bring on an action as soon as possible."

GREENE knew that Cornwallis, who had been lured from his safe position on the coast was also anxious to engage the two forces. Time in this famine and guerilla infested region was against him. So GREENE turned up Troublesome Creek and crossed the country to Guilford Court House. He had felt this was a good location for a battle when he met DANIEL MORGAN's troops, as they raced to the Dan.

It was said that the Virginia troops were not impressed with the unproductive farm lands they traversed. However, the friendly Scotch-Irish and some fine grain fields impressed them. GREENE sent Henry Lee's legion with the militia under Kings Mountain's William Campbell to watch the enemy, while he and his other officers sat at council through most of the night.

Meanwhile, Cornwallis had moved his army and encamped near the Quaker meetinghouse at New Garden, in the forks of the Deep River. On 14 Mar 1781, it was reported to him that GREENE's army was at Guilford, some twelve miles northeast from his own camp. He was also told that the enemy's reinforcements had brought their strength to nine or ten thousand. At daybreak on the fifteenth, he broke camp. Around noon they were on the march to meet the enemy. Tarleton and his legion had preceded them. There was gunfire in the distance as the last troops went northward with disciplined precision. Henry Lee's troops met Tarleton's for a skirmish, then fell back to the courthouse.

The Guilford courthouse stood on the top of a hill in the midst of a wilderness. The Great Wagon Road from Salisbury to Hillsboro came from the southwest, through a deep depression, densely wooded on each side by forest. It passed through a rail fenced clearing and turned north of east up a half-mile slope into clearings on the right and an oak forest on the left. The courthouse was on the left in a right angle formed by the road to Reedy Fork. The main road continued on about a quarter of a mile where there was a wooded elevation, beyond which was another road going east of north.

DANIEL MORGAN, whose sciatica and hemorrhoids had required his return home to northern Virginia, had written to GREENE,

> "If the militia fights, you will beat Cornwallis; if not, he will beat you and perhaps cut your regulars to pieces .... A number of old soldiers are among the militia. Select them and put them in the ranks with regulars .... Fight the riflemen on the flanks. Put the militia in the center with some picked troops in their rear with orders to shoot down the first man that runs. If anything will succeed, a disposition of this kind will."

GREENE probably bore this in mind as he placed his troops. The North Carolina militia formed the first line. They were supported by the Virginia riflemen at an obtuse angle at each end. The right flank was supported by light infantry of Washington's legion and the left by Campbell's Rifles and Lee's Legion. They had centered two light fieldpieces on the road. The first line looked downhill over freshly planted corn—an excellent field of fire.

The second line, perhaps 300 yards behind the first was also militia, but with greater experience than the North Carolinians. They included Lawson's and Stevens' Virginians with a number of continental officers at their head. GREENE put his main force of regulars about five hundred and fifty yards behind the second line. The first two lines faced the road. This third line lay to the right, and formed a double line behind a small ravine, with two fieldpieces in the center. The Marylands and Delawares were on the left and Virginians on the right.

Having placed his men, GREENE rode to the first line and described the strength of their position.

"Three rounds, my boys," he shouted, "and then you may fall back."

He then left Henry Lee to encourage the nervous militia. He rode along the front telling them to stand firm, for he had whipped the enemy three times that morning and could do it again. It was about one-thirty when Cornwallis' troops marched into sight. British Colonel Webster rode to the front and yelled, "Charge!"

There was instant movement as they rushed forward with arms charged until they were within forty yards of the North Carolina militia who waited for them with their flintlocks leveled at them—the barrels rested on a rail fence.

"They were taking aim with the nicest precision . . . . At this awful period, a general pause took place. Both parties surveyed each other for the moment with the most anxious suspense . . . . Colonel Webster rode forward in the front of the Twenty-third Regiment and said, 'Come on, my brave fusiliers,'"

The British rushed forward into the enemy fire. Dreadful was the havoc on both sides. At last the Americans gave way and the brigade advanced to attack the second line.

Colonel Lee described it.

"To our infinite distress and mortification, the North Carolina militia took flight, a few only of Eaton's brigade excepted, who clung to the militia under Campbell which, with the Legion, manfully maintained their ground. Every effort was made by . . . the officers of every grade to stop this unaccountable panic, for not a man of the corps had been killed or even wounded . . . . All in vain; so thoroughly confounded were these unhappy men that, throwing away arms, knapsacks, and even canteens, they rushed like a torrent headlong through the woods."

Fortunately for the Americans, the 'old soldiers' and regulars stood firm, and the battle continued until GREENE felt he had crippled the enemy sufficiently to retreat west on Reedy Fork road to Troublesome Creek where they dug earthworks in the clay soil above the creek, while the rain pelted down. The battlefield had been won by Cornwallis; but he didn't want it. He left his wounded that were unable to travel to the care of the Americans and retreated back to his camp at New Garden. Eleven of his officers and 88 of his men were killed, 18 officers and 389 men were wounded, and 26 were missing. He had won the day, but his loss, especially of officers, was so great he felt paralyzed.

With food in short supply and an enemy rumored to be larger than reality, Cornwallis decided to pull back to the friendly Scotch settlement at Cross Creek and then all the way to his shipping at Wilmington, if necessary. Horace Walpole wrote:

> "Lord Cornwallis has conquered his troops out of shoes and provisions and himself out of troops."

As they marched through the country, the tattered Redcoats ignored the advice of their general and plundered as they went. A planter, William Dickson, wrote to his cousin in Ireland:

> "The whole country was struck with terror; almost every man quit his habitation and fled, leaving his family and property to the mercy of merciless enemies. Horses, cattle, and sheep, and every kind of stock were driven off from every plantation, corn and forage taken for the supply of the army and no compensation given, houses plundered and robbed, chests, trunks, etc., broke; women and children's clothes, etc., as well as men's wearing apparel and every kind of household furniture taken away. The outrages were committed mostly by a train of loyal refugees, as they termed themselves, whose business it was to follow the camps and under the protection of the army enrich themselves on the plunder they took from the distressed inhabitants who were not able to defend it.
>
> "We were also distressed by another swarm of beings (not better than harpies.) These were women who followed the army in the character of officers' and soldiers' wives. They generally mounted on the best horses and side saddles, dressed in the finest and best clothes that could be taken from the inhabitants as the army marched through the country."

GREENE thought his losses to be about 300 in the killed, wounded, and taken category—but a full thousand of his North Carolina militia had "gone home." He was cautioned by a friend to soften his own and his officers caustic remarks about them, or they would alienate the "bulk of the country." He wanted to confront the enemy again; but before he arrived at Ramsey's Mill on 29 Mar 1781, Cornwallis had crossed the Deep River and was on his way. GREENE gave up his pursuit, but determined to immediately carry the war into South Carolina. Cornwallis found Cross Creek barren and pushed on to Wilmington.

Refreshed in his comfortable headquarter at Wilmington, on 23 Apr 1781,

Cornwallis sent a letter to his superior Clinton in New York. He reasoned with him in the letter as to why he must go north to the Chesapeake and expressed his sorrow in not being able to wait for an answer. Knowing Clinton would not approve of his plan, he collected his much diminished army of 700 and started for Virginia. On the fourth of July, he ferried his soldiers across the wide James River and advanced toward Jamestown. The British Army had left North Carolina. The Virginia countryside would now feel the devastation of Tarleton's legions.

True to his word, General NATHANAEL GREENE took his continentals south into South Carolina, which the British had fortified with an army of oc- cupation of around 8000. GREENE enlisted the aide of the partisan generals, Marion and Pickins. Although his battle for Camden was chalked up as a British win, the team of Lee and Marion were snuffing out interior forts, and the British retreated to fortify Ninety Six, where Pickins had been sent, and who was soon joined by the other American forces. On 3 July, the British evacuated Ninety Six and fell back to Orangeburg. But the American soldiers needed rest, so GREENE pulled his troops from the humid, infested swamps back to the High Hills of the Santee to restore, drill and organize his mangled army during the dreadful heat of the southern summer.

On the night of 7 September, GREENE had brought his full strength army of twenty-two hundred, which now included the North and South Carolina militia, to within seven miles of the enemy camp at Eutaw Springs. So many of GREENE's men were deserters from the British, and so many of the British were deserters from the Americans, that GREENE has been quoted as saying,

"We fought the enemy with British soldiers and they fought us with those of America."

The British were completely surprised by the attack, and the Americans should have been victorious; but once more victory was taken from GREENE as some of his men became so engrossed in plundering the enemy camp that they forgot that the battle was still in progress. Both sides claimed victory—the British because GREENE's army had left the field,—the Americans because the redcoats dumped their supplies and marched off to join reinforcements coming from Charlestown. GREENE pursued a short way, then retired his men again to the High Hills of Santee to prepare for the siege of Charleston. This was the last major battle of the deep South, although guerilla warfare continued between the Whigs and the Tories for over a year. British forces were now only in Charlestown and Savannah.

[Note: Fourth-great-grandfather WILLIAM ALLRED, (son of THOMAS ALLRED) had a brother ELIAS ALLRED who evidently was charged with fighting with the British army: (FHL929.272 A157a Vol. I, p. I-100) "On the 13 Feb. 1782, ELIAS ALLRED, JOHN ALLRIDGE, and GEORGE JULIAN were charged with having joined the British and were bound to the court, but upon their appearing were discharged by Proclamation."

The proclamation offered amnesty, if they would enlist in the colonial army for a period of one year. This they did and they took an oath of loyalty to the continental cause. ELIAS is also listed in the DAR Patriot's Index. This index does not give the date of his enlistment, but states that he was a cavalry minuteman from North Carolina. It also says that he was born in Virginia the sixth of May, 1758, and died in Georgia in 1840. This could indicate that his father, THOMAS ALLRED, may have left his family in Virginia for awhile, as he appeared in the North Carolina land records before that date. There is a PATIENCE JULIAN who married WILLIAM ALLRED, probaby a brother of the JOHN ALLRED whose story of enlistment was told earlier. Her immediate family as shown in my records does not have a George, however. ELIAS is mentioned in his father's will and in the Nauvoo Temple records. He received some land benefits after the war and went to Georgia.

National Archives or British records do not list the loyalist troops from North Carolina, only the officers. The name MARTIN shows up as a given name in some ALLRED and IVIE families, perhaps in honor of the British Governor Martin? The British Lieutenant governor, with Governor Martin, was Frank Eppes. EPPES IVEY, born about 1781, was a son of PETER IVEY of Wake County, North Carolina, who was a brother of HUGH IVEY of Sussex County, Virigina. Thomas Jefferson also had close relations with the last name of EPPES.

Great-grandfather JOHN LEHI IVIE had a brother and an uncle MARTIN. He had a brother WILLIAM FRANKLIN IVIE. William Franklin, usually considered the number one loyalist in this country, was the oldest son of Benjamin Franklin, who despaired at his son's choice.

Among the ALLRED descendants there are marriages to the WELBORNs, the ELLIOTTs and the PUGHs (James Pugh was one of the six Regulators who were hanged, and Mary Pugh married Herman Husbands)—all strong regulators. HENRY IVEY III married JANE HOWELL of the Granville area. It was Rednap Howell who wrote the insulting poetry about Edmund Fanning that was distributed during the Regulator years.

As mentioned earlier, HENRY IVEY II married MARY FIELD, of this prominent North Carolina family who stood strong with the Regulators and with the British in the "Battle of Moore's Creek." Colonel William Field and his brothers Robert, Jeremiah and Joseph Field, were ordered to "raise the King's Standard at Cross Creek" and were taken prisoners. There is another interesting marriage, a great-grandson of one of these early North Carolina ALLREDs married a FANNEN, spelled as shown here.

Listed in *the DAR PATRIOT INDEX—Centennial Edition Part 1*—are five ALLRED names:

Elias: b 5-6-1758 VA d p 1846 GA m X Cav MM NC

John: b 7-8-1764 NC d 1-24-50 NC m Sarah Spencer Pvt NC

John Sr: b c 1736 d a 12- -1792 NC m Margaret Cheney PS NC

Jonathan: b 4-5-1758 NC d 4-5-1822 GA m Margaret Burt Sol GA

William: b c 1732 d a 5- -1833 NC m Elizabeth Diffee PS NC

Others, of course, are listed in other records; but this information is helpful in identification. The PS refers to Patriotic Service.

The oldest Association of the Baptist church in North Carolina was the "Sandy Creek Association," which was established in 1758, three years after Stearns and his company settled at Sandy Creek. It grew rapidly in this area, and then extended into other areas of North Carolina. The Quakers, of which Herman Husband was a member, were organized as the Cane Creek Meeting of Orange County in 1751. Herman Husbands is listed in their membership records, and it also gives his marriage date in 1762 to Mary Pugh. There is also an Amy Allen Husband and a William Husband in these records. No ALLREDs are listed. These were the two early churches of this area.

We find in the early Baptist records that there was an early Association called the "Big Ivey Association" in the southwest area of North Carolina, near the Georgia border. There was also a "Little Ivey Church," which is "now[?] the largest in this Association." The old record made this comment about the "Big Ivey Association": It "is an immediate offspring of the last one named; it was organized in 1821 and appears to have been the first colony which went off from this mother body, and not in the most agreeable manner. This has been called a "Free Will Baptist" institution . . . also "Liberty Association" as well as "Big Ivey Association." In reading this brief description, I was left to wonder if the "Ivey" name referred to some of our relations or to an ivy covered hill that the church house stood on.

We do know that third-great-grandmother SARAH (SALLY) ALLRED married ANDERSON IVIE about 1800, and they were among the early organizers of the Grove Level Baptist church in Franklin County, Georgia, "3rd Sat of May, 1802" with 62 members. MARY ALLRED, a younger sister of SARAH, married DAVID SANDERS, in 1802 at Franklin County, Georgia. DAVID SANDERS' father was Moses Sanders, who began the formation of this church in 1801. It is quite likely that the ALLREDs of Sandy Creek were members of the Sandy Creek Baptist Church, although I am unaware of any records that state this.

Fourth-great-grandparents WILLIAM and ELIZABETH THRASHER ALLRED left the Sandy Creek area within a few years after the Revolutionary War ended. ELIZABETH's brother (or cousin) ISAAC THRASHER went south about the same time. We find them both in the Pendleton, South Carolina, census record of 1790. (LOT and ANDERSON IVIE were also in Pendleton, South Carolina, at this time.) According to one researcher, WILLIAM and ELIZABETH ALLRED had moved on to Franklin County, Georgia, by 1795. Second-great-grandfather JAMES RUSSELL IVIE was born in Franklin County, Georgia, 30 Dec 1802.   We know from the above records that my ancestors were in the midst of the Revolutionary War in North Carolina. Whether they were Whigs or Tories might depend upon the person, time, and place of the different battles, as the militia seemed to switch sides quite often with the fortunes of war. At least some of the ALLREDs were involved in the War of the Regulators, although the extent is not totally known. Those involved probably took the Oath of Allegiance to King George III when it was offered by Governor Martin. An oath can be very important and binding to people of integrity, and the animosity of the colonial army who joined with former British Governor Tryon in the Battle of Alamance would be strong in their memories. Tarleton's brutal murders changed many loyalties.

That the ALLREDs lived in the county that instigated and collected a great amount of action is true. Their trust of the colonial government and the Sons of Liberty had been shattered. When Cornwallis moved his army south of Hillsboro, he went to their county, which would indicate that he probably thought he would be safer there. When the loyalists' lands were confiscated, after the war finally ended and a government was established, Randolph and Cumberland Counties had more lands taken from their counties than were taken from other western counties. That all the inhabitants of this area contributed to the sustenance of both armies, whether willingly or unwillingly, is obvious.

Some histories have claimed that the War of the Regulators was the first battle of the Revolutionary War. Most historians say, "No." Although they were fighting against the tyranny of the British government, they had no vision of the great general cause of the colonies; so, therefore, they call it an insurrection. As an outsider reading about it, with ancestors from the north, central, south, and west, I would observe that their desire for personal freedom from the despotism of a government regulated without representation was as strong, or stronger, than that of the Sons of Liberty. That the Sons of Liberty were mislead and betrayed them, when they could have given their support, seems obvious. British Governor Josiah Martin was wiser and gained their friendship. If the Sons of Liberty had been less steeped in the ideals and more in the rights of their countrymen, the British would probably have been driven out sooner, or never allowed a foothold in these southern states. The strength of North Carolina was in the west, not the east. It is possible that greater concern for these western counties might not have only shortened the Revolutionary War, but united the nation and prevented the Civil War—however, hindsight is always better than foresight.

JAMES RUSSELL IVIE's uncle and aunt, DAVID and MARY ALLRED SANDERS, had three children that were born in Franklin County, Georgia. Their oldest son was named MOSES MARTIN SANDERS, after his grandfather and perhaps Governor Martin? Their second son was named WILLIAM HAMILTON, and their daughter was SARAH. They were in Bedford County (now Marshall County), Tennessee, when NANCY was born in 1810, and DAVID JAMES in 1815. The tax list for Bedford County in 1812 includes DAVID SANDERS; JOHN CALVERT, JOSEPH CALVERT, ISAAC ALLRED, JAMES ALLRED, WILLIAM ALLRED Jun., ANDERSON IVIE and JOSEPH IVY—all close relations.

Uncle DAVID SANDERS died early in the year of 1815 from wounds he received during the Battle of New Orleans at the end of the War of 1812. His oldest son, MOSES MARTIN SANDERS (born about 8 months after second-great-grandfather JAMES RUSSELL IVIE), married a sister, AMANDA ARMSTRONG FAUSETT, of second-great-grandmother ELIZA McKEE FAUSETT IVIE. The two family histories of JAMES RUSSELL IVIE and MOSES MARTIN SANDERS paralleled one another in many ways for many years.]

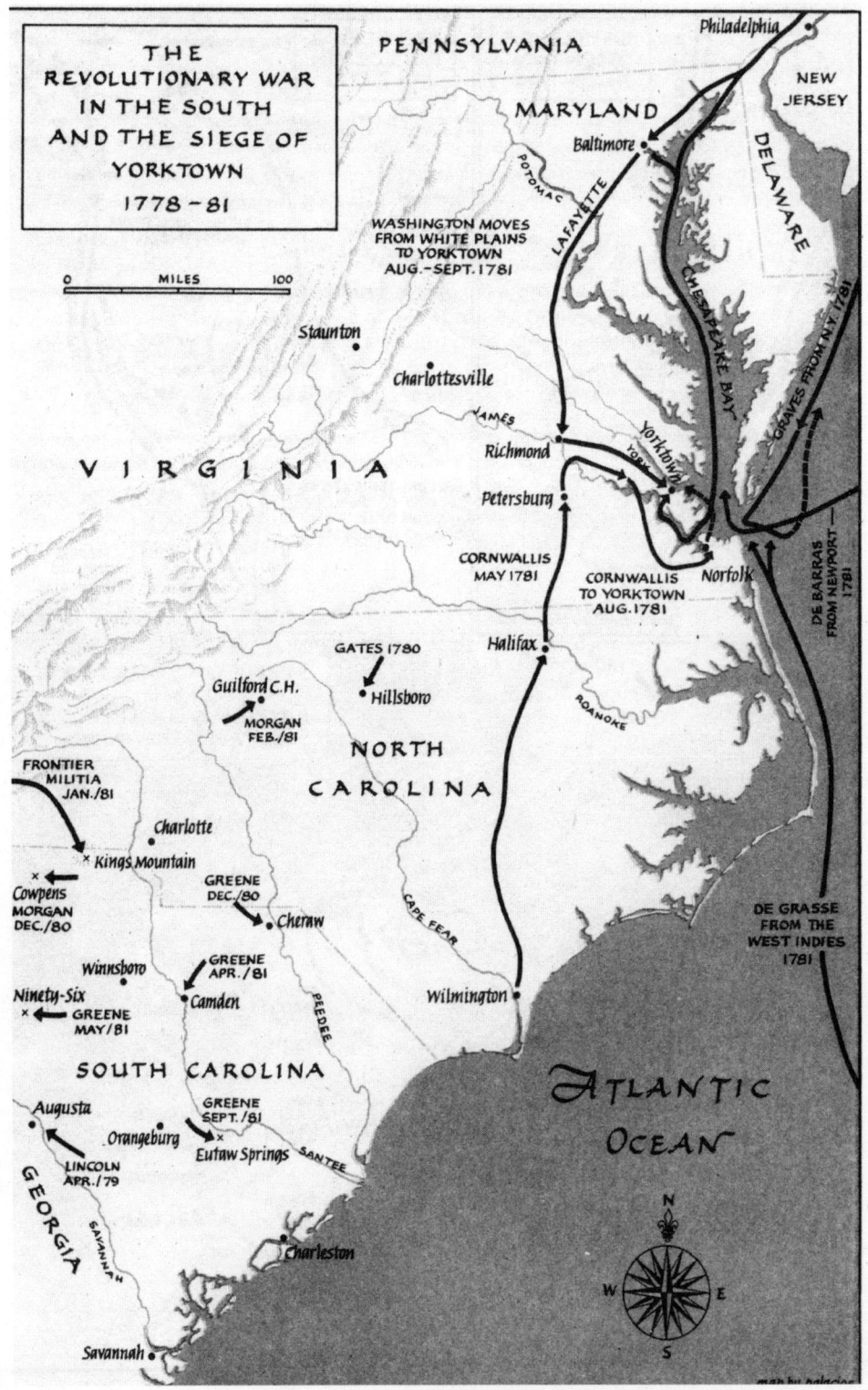

THE
REVOLUTIONARY WAR
IN THE SOUTH
AND THE SIEGE OF
YORKTOWN
1778-81

0   MILES   100

PENNSYLVANIA

Philadelphia

NEW
JERSEY

MARYLAND

DELAWARE

Baltimore

POTOMAC

LAFAYETTE

CHESAPEAKE BAY

GRAVES FROM N.Y. 1781

WASHINGTON MOVES
FROM WHITE PLAINS
TO YORKTOWN
AUG.-SEPT. 1781

Staunton

Charlottesville

JAMES

Richmond

YORK

Yorktown

VIRGINIA

Petersburg

CORNWALLIS
MAY 1781

CORNWALLIS
TO YORKTOWN
AUG. 1781

Norfolk

DE BARRAS
FROM NEWPORT
1781

Halifax

ROANOKE

GATES 1780

Guilford C.H.

Hillsboro

MORGAN
FEB./81

NORTH
CAROLINA

FRONTIER
MILITIA
JAN./81

Charlotte

× Kings Mountain

GREENE
DEC./80

×
Cowpens
MORGAN
DEC./80

Cheraw

CAPE FEAR

DE GRASSE
FROM THE
WEST INDIES
1781

GREENE
APR./81

Winnsboro

Ninety-Six
×   GREENE
MAY/81

Camden

PEEDEE

Wilmington

SOUTH CAROLINA

ATLANTIC
OCEAN

Augusta

Orangeburg

GREENE
SEPT./81
×
Eutaw Springs

SANTEE

LINCOLN
APR./79

GEORGIA

SAVANNAH

Charleston

N

W   E

S

Savannah

map by balacio

94

THE REVOLUTION IN VIRGINIA —
THOMAS JEFFERSON — THE IVEYS

Most of the original IVIE ancestors arrived and settled on the Norfolk Peninsula between 1613 and 1636. Our ancestor, GEORGE IVEY, and his three brothers were taken back to England in their youth after their mother and father died of a fever. The four sons returned in the 1660s when they were old enough to claim their inheritance. They married, and as the families expanded, the second sons purchased lands south of the James River in Suffolk County—westward from the Dismal Swamp and above the North Carolina border. This is the area where my third-great-grandfather ANDERSON IVIE was born in 1774—just before the Revolutionary War began—from his tombstone. It is believed by many that his father was JESSIE IVEY. It is difficult to determine which JESSIE IVEY, since two second cousins were born and christened in the same Albemarle Parish within a few years of each other. Only one is shown in the census records of 1792. One of them married SARAH ANDERSON; but that was several years after ANDERSON IVIE was born. So far, we haven't sufficient records to clear up this enigma. In one record, SARAH FOSTER is shown as his mother.

We do know that ANDERSON IVIE received sufficient schooling in his youth that he had beautiful penmanship. He was the one that chose to spell his last name as Ivie, because he had been told that this spelling was the most proper way. Several of his relations were burgesses in the British Williamsburg House of Burgesses, which included LANGLEYs and MASONs. A rather large number of his relations are found in the D. A. R. records, and they fought against the British as well as giving assistance in other ways. The city of Suffolk is about twenty miles southwest of Portsmouth, Virginia, and would have felt the impact of the British raiders.

The Norfolk Peninsula was first attacked by the British in 1775. This story is told in earlier chapters in which ship Captain WILLIAM IVEY, a cousin who lived on the peninsula, had two of his plantations and his shipbuilding business burned down by the British. Many slaves were taken when the British sailed away. Another attack was made by British General Matthews during the summer of 1779. Again Norfolk was destroyed, Portsmouth and Gosport were occupied, and 130 merchant vessels were burned or taken on the James and Elizabeth Rivers.

Except for these attacks, most of Virginia was left relatively unmolested by the enemy, although the British navy blockaded their shipping trade and used their waterways whenever they chose. The Virginians were quick to send DANIEL MORGAN and his crack riflemen to aid Washington in Massachusetts, Canada, Pennsylvania, and New Jersey. Thousands of other Virginia troops were sent north to New York, Pennsylvania, and then to the South as they were called for. Some troops, mostly from Kentucky, were sent with George Rogers Clark on his journey to capture the western lands of the Ohio River and then on to the Mississippi River. All the land west, including Kentucky, Ohio, and Illinois, was claimed by Virginia. It was the largest state of the thirteen original colonies—both in land and population. One record claims that at the end of the Revolutionary War, half of Virginia's population was beyond the western boundaries of present-day Virginia.

The state of Maryland, however, gave Virginia some trouble and wouldn't ratify the continental congress until Virginia gave a lot of this territory to the United States. It was January 1780 when Jefferson yielded and the second continental congress was totally ratified by all the states.

After the Declaration of Independence was signed, Patrick Henry became the governor of Virginia. Their constitution allowed for an election every year, but limited the number of terms to three. When Henry had served his three years, Thomas Jefferson was elected as governor—he took office on 1 Jun 1779. Jefferson had been in the Virginia Assembly and worked endless hours in forming and writing the laws of the state; however, his actual participation in the

No one spoke out stronger

for independence than Patrick Henry

of the Virginia House of Burgesses.

In the 5th grade we were taught the

last paragraph of his

strong oration that ended,

"Give Me Liberty or Give Me Death."

— PATRICK HENRY

---

military efforts of the Revolution was very limited. He was not a soldier, nor did he desire to command troops. He was quick to send men and supplies, if they were available. When the southern army called for more men, he countered by asking if they wanted his wounded and old men, as that was all he had left. His homeland militia was sparse and poorly trained. Virginia's terrain with many navigable rivers was difficult to defend against the British naval superiority.

When the Bostonians felt they could no longer feed the vast number of British prisoners (about 5,000) that were taken captive at Saratoga, the Americans marched them about 700 miles to Charlottesville, Virginia. The prisoners arrived in January 1779. It was the first time that the war intruded into the interior county of Albemarle, the blissful home of Thomas Jefferson. Jefferson arranged for Hessian Major General Baron von Riedesel and his family to rent Colle from Philip Mazzei, who was in Europe on a diplomatic errand. Mazzei's five-year experiment in wine culture was destroyed within a week by the Baron's grazing horses.

Jefferson welcomed and accepted the following British invitation:

"Major General Phillips sends his compliments to Mr. and Mrs. Jefferson, requests the favor of their company at dinner on Thursday next at two o'clock to meet General and Madame de Riedesel. Major General Phillips hopes Miss Jefferson will be permitted to be of the party to meet the young ladies from Colle" [the Baron's daughters].

Miss Patsy Jefferson became a close friend to the young ladies and the baroness. Monticello was opened to the Hessian musicians and scholars. The following, written by a German officer, appeared in a Hamburg newspaper:

> "My only occupation at present is to learn the English language. It is easier for me, as I have free access to a copious and well-chosen library of Colonel Jefferson's [who] possesses a noble spirit of building. He is now finishing an elegant building, projected according to his own fancy. In his parlor he is creating on the ceiling a compass of his own invention by which he can know the strength as well as direction of the winds. I have promised to paint the compass for it. He was much pleased with a fancy painting of mine. . . . As all Virginians are fond of music, he is particularly so. You will find in his house an elegant harpsichord, pianoforte and some violins. The later he performs well upon himself, the former his lady touches very skillfully and who is in all respects a very agreeable, sensible and accomplished lady."

Shortly after Jefferson had become governor of Virginia—still in the month of June, Sir Henry Hamilton, British Lieutenant Governor of Canada, was brought to him one evening in a very rough condition. He had been captured by George Rogers Clark in Vincennes, as reported in an earlier chapter. The young thirty-six-year-old Governor Jefferson, who had been so gracious to Phillips and Riedesel, treated Sir Henry Hamilton and his aide, Captain Guillaume La Mothe, with insolence. At his trial, Sir Henry Hamilton stated that they

> "were conducted to the Palace where we remained about half an hour in the street at the governor's door, in wet clothes, weary, hungry and thirsty, but had not even a cup of water offered to us."

Then Jefferson sent out orders that they were to be confined in the Williamsburg jail, and they were followed through the streets by a jeering, menacing crowd. At the jail, they were confined in a crowded cell with five common criminals and another of his aides.

> "The next day, we three were taken out about 11 o'clock and, before a number of people, our handcuffs taken off and fetters put on in exchange."

Sir Henry Hamilton further declared that he was

> "honored with the largest, which weighed eighteen pounds, eight ounces." They were "confined in the dungeon of the public jail, debarred the use of pen, ink and paper and excluded all converse except with their keeper."

Hamilton's imprisonment in the Virginia jail lasted 15 months. Jefferson finally sent him north. Prior to this, he wrote George Washington:

"You are not unapprised of the influence of this Officer with the Indians, his activity and embittered zeal against us . . . . You also perhaps know how precarious is our tenure of the Illinois country, and how critical is the situation of the new counties on the Ohio."

Although Jefferson's treatment of this important officer of the British was highly criticized by General Phillips and other British as well as some Americans, it is well to remember that in January 1778, the then Governor Patrick Henry had appointed the three secret "select men," Jefferson, GEORGE MASON, and Richard Henry Lee, to aide George Rogers Clark in his expedition against the British-aided Indians who were savagely raiding and scalping frontier Americans. Another major purpose of the "select men" was to expand the Virginia border to the Mississippi and eliminate both British and French claims to this area. Henry Hamilton, as the British officer in charge at Fort Detroit, had become known as "the Hair Buyer," because he had paid the Indians for the scalps of these early American settlers of Ohio, Kentucky and Illinois.

The British General William Phillips was traded several months after Jefferson's inauguration for American General Benjamin Lincoln [captured in the British siege of Charleston, South Carolina.] Shortly after, General Phillips was back directing the enemy in their marauding and burning of the state of Virginia.

It was May 1779, that the British made their devastating raid on Portsmouth, Virginia. It was a cruel reminder to the Virginians that the Revolution was still in progress and could be heading their way. Jefferson had introduced a bill in the Virginia legislature, shortly after the Declaration of Independence was signed, to move the capital of Virginia to Richmond. He had no love for the royal British capital at Williamsburg, either as a student or as a burgess. Change is difficult for those who prefer the status quo, and the legislative bill had not prospered. With the raid on Portsmouth, the bill was soon reintroduced with much better results. Virginia legislators began to fear for their lives and Richmond with its 1800 villagers became the capital of the state, and, as governor, Jefferson proceeded to design and build a city.

Sailing from New York City with one hundred ships, 13,700 regular soldiers, sailors and marines, on the day after Christmas, 1779, Sir Henry Clinton besieged Charleston, South Carolina. Benjamin Lincoln's forces were about one-third the size; but it took the British until 12 May 1780 to starve out the American army and the inhabitants and bring about the surrender of that city. Nearly the entire line of the Virginia continentals was killed or captured. Unaware, because of slow communication, Governor Jefferson did not find out that the city was in need of reinforcements until the day after they surrendered.

[Note: Then came the battle on the beautiful green field known as the Waxhaws, just south of the North Carolina border. The brutal Tarleton with his loyalist dragoons followed the retreating three hundred and fifty Virginia soldiers with their heavy wagons, under the command of Colonel Abraham Buford, and attacked them with sword and bayonet from the rear on the afternoon of 29 May. One hundred and thirteen Virginians were killed and another one hundred and fifty were so seriously wounded that Tarleton left them behind as he took the remaining fifty-three as prisoners of war. The wounded Americans were loaded in wagons and taken to a church where a good Irishwoman of the neighborhood dressed their wounds and comforted the dying. Five of Tarleton's men were killed and fourteen wounded.]

On the evening of 11 Dec 1780, Benedict Arnold marched his conglomerate army of loyalists, deserters, and some foreign troops into the British ships in New York harbor. They were being sent to the Chesapeake, perhaps to reinforce Cornwallis, or create a diversion in Virginia that would divide the southern army. But, unbeknown to most, Benedict Arnold's greatest desire was to capture one man—the man who had written and signed that heinous document of British treason—The Declaration of Independence. Arnold had tried, unsuccessfully, to give King George III the commander in chief, George Washington. Thomas Jefferson was number two on his list. He expected him to be at Richmond. As his ships moved into the Chesapeake to journey toward the James River, they were spotted by the Virginia militia.

On Sunday morning, 31 Dec 1780, Jefferson was warned by an aide to General Thomas Nelson of the state militia that two days earlier 27 ships had entered the Chesapeake—they might be British or they might be the long-awaited French. The governor immediately ordered General Nelson to the scene and to do whatever he deemed necessary. Jefferson then sent word to Baron von Steuben, the continental army commander for Virginia, who was at the nearby Chesterfield Courthouse. He then informed the Speaker of the House in the Virginia Assembly, Benjamin Harrison. After writing the militia officers in the coastal counties a warning, it was decided that a special Assembly would not be called or the militia called out until more information was obtained.

WESTOVER
CHARLES CITY COUNTY, VIRGINIA
BUILT ABOUT 1730 BY
WILLIAM BYRD II,
FOUNDER OF RICHMOND.

Our granddaughter
JENNIFER HAYNES
on the dock of
Westover
on the James River.
Traitor Benedict Arnold
left most of his troops
at Westover, when he
he took 900 of his
best to destroy Richmond.

Crossing the James River
on the Jamestown Ferry
toward Norfolk VA.
The State of Virginia
believes it is cheaper to
ferry the cars across, than
to build and maintain
bridges.
These three pictures
were taken by
HYRUM HAYNES
who grew up in
Colonial Heights, VA.

On 2 Jan 1781, another messenger arrived to tell Governor Jefferson that the vessels were British and they had been seen at Jamestown two days earlier. The highly concerned Jefferson tried to call an emergency Council meeting; but the necessary quorum of four could not be found. Jefferson wrote in his autobiography years later,

> "From a fatal inattention to the giving of due notice of the arrival of a hostile force, two days were completely lost in calling out the militia."

With considerable consternation, Governor Thomas Jefferson quickly called up the militia from six counties, then ordered the official records and military supplies carted seven miles above the falls to Westham. He still believed that Williamsburg was the destination of the enemy—but, perhaps, they were after the British prisoners near Charlottesville with transport ships to carry them away? He gave orders that the prisoners be removed as quickly as possible to Frederick, Maryland. Concerned that his family might be injured, he sent them with servants to stay with the Randolph relations at Tuckahoe. Still, he never even considered that he might be their target.

At 5 A.M. on 4 January, a servant was awakened by a banging on Jefferson's front door. It was another messenger. The ships had moved 70 miles up the James River and some had moved further up and landed at Westover, the Byrd estate, which was only twenty-five miles from Richmond. Then he was told the alarming news that the enemy invasion was led by the highly skilled and traitorous Benedict Arnold.

It was further reported that the enemy force at Westover on the north side of the bend was composed of over 1,500 soldiers that were marching rapidly toward Richmond. Jefferson quickly sent word to Baron von Steuben to take charge of the militia that he felt would be quickly arriving to defend Richmond; but at eleven A.M. on 5 January only 200 Virginians had arrived to defend the governor, council, and government offices.

Arnold's personal agenda was to instigate the scorched-earth policy, destroy the cannon factory at Richmond and the small arms depot at Westham, the warehouses stacked with vital supplies in both places, and bring the Americans, as well as Virginians, to their knees with his personal capture of their hero, Thomas Jefferson. Arnold in his usual flamboyant style was defying strict orders from his British leaders, who had carefully instructed him to take no unnecessary risks and quickly reinforce the British that were already at Portsmouth.

Leaving troops at Westover to protect his ships, Arnold marched his best 900 men, including mounted light infantry and field artillery, through the driving rain during the night. At first, the people of Richmond did not recognize Arnold as the enemy, for their uniforms were green instead of red. Arnold was able to get within range of Jefferson's house at Richmond before he open-fired his three-pounder and then sent a troop of his American legionnaires to find the governor.

They rounded up the servants and demanded to know the whereabouts of Mr. Jefferson. Unable to find him, they proceeded to ransack his home. Much of his library was mutilated, including three-fourths of his personal and state papers, which were carried off or burned. In his wine cellar, they drank his best Madeira until they were satisfied and destroyed the rest. They also marched off ten of his slaves to be sold for cash.

Arnold established his headquarters at City Tavern on Main Street. At first he offered to save the city, if the inhabitants would find Jefferson and have him sign a paper allowing the British to take all stored goods—especially the

"thirty to forty ships full of tobacco, West Indies goods, wine, sailcloth," that he found at the crowded wharves and in the warehouses along the James River. Arnold gave the merchants "until the next morning to obtain an answer from Mr. Jefferson, who was in the neighborhood."

Loyalist goods, ships and real estate were to be spared. But Mr. Jefferson was not to be found.

Arnold wrote General Clinton,

"As Mr. Jefferson was so inattentive to the preservation of private property, I found myself under the disagreeable necessity of ordering a large quantity of rum to be [staved in], several warehouses of salt to be destroyed, several public warehouses and [blacksmith and gunsmith] shops with their contents consumed by the flames."

These flames quickly spread in the wind to a sailcloth factory and to the powder magazines. Arnold reported that "a printing press and types were purified by the flames."

As the city burned, Mr. Arnold's legionnaires stripped the tobacco warehouses and rolled the bails down to his flotilla of ten captured American ships and thirty-four boats. Then the warehouses were burned—sparing only those belonging to any merchant willing to declare himself a loyalist. They were also given signed papers that would allow them to sail through British lines with their merchant ships. The Queen's Loyal Rangers were detached to march up the James River to Westham, where they were to destroy Jefferson's fledgling munitions plant and ammunition warehouses.

Jefferson had been a very busy man. When he had galloped the twenty miles to Westham to help with the evacuation of their valuable supplies, his horse stumbled and fell under him. Jefferson quickly yanked off his saddle, borrowed a horse from a nearby farmhouse and continued onward. All that day he worked tirelessly to preserve their supplies and ammunition and then rode on to communicate with militia leaders and civil leaders. When Arnold's paper eventually was delivered to him to sign, he refused. He felt quite certain that Arnold had no plans of staying in Richmond, and he believed that the militia would gather quickly enough that Richmond would be safe after his raid. Jefferson was an eternal optimist.

Of the fifteen tons of critical ammunition, only six tons was captured by the enemy. "They burnt and destroyed one of the finest foundries for cannon in America," reported Benedict Arnold to General Sir Henry Clinton. He further reported their destruction of "20 cannons, 310 barrels of gunpowder, several warehouses of oats." And he added that John Simcoe's Virginia-born rangers also burned the town of Chesterfield with its mills, clothing depot, and warehouses.

Then it was back to Westover for Arnold's army with their newly acquired American ships. On the following day, Arnold sailed back down the James River to follow his commander's orders to strengthen the British occupation of Portsmouth on Albemarle Sound—rather pleased in believing that he had created quite a diversion that could bring more Virginians back home and thus aid General Cornwallis in the south and Sir Henry Clinton in the north.

Washington responded and sent French General Lafayette with a feeble 900 man force of continentals, which kept increasing as Steuben continued to train new, raw recruits in Virginia.

But Jefferson had political enemies who started rumors that Jefferson was incompetent in not calling up the militia in time; negligent for not providing in his term in office for the state's defense; cowardly for running away from the enemy and not personally leading the militia in active resistance. Patrick Henry, a rival, spurred them on. Jefferson, who believed deeply in the rule of law, tried to reconvene the council in devastated Richmond. He unsuccessfully called a meeting every day from the sixth to the nineteenth of January—the date he was finally able to get together the required four members to make a quorum. He soon discovered that his friends were quite willing to let him take all the blame for the "disgrace" at Richmond.

Jefferson's wife had been ill with depression all the nine months of her pregnancy in 1779. On 15 April, when their five-month-old daughter, Lucy Elizabeth, died, he left the following message for the council,

> "The day is so very bad that I hardly expect a council, and there being nothing that I know of pressing, and Mrs. Jefferson in a situation in which I would not wish to leave her, I shall not attend today."

He then went off with his family to Monticello to bury his third child. To his young friend, James Madison, he wrote,

> "I think public service and private misery inseparably linked together."

Sometime soon after Richmond, he decided that he would not seek a third one-year term. He had no desire to command the troops.

Highly distressed with his circumstances, Jefferson offered a reward for the capture of Benedict Arnold. In one letter draft to General Muhlenberg he wrote,

> "You will readily suppose that it is above all things desirable to drag Arnold from those under whose wing he is now sheltered . . . . Having peculiar confidence in the men from the Western side of the mountains, I . . . ask you to pick from among them proper characters, in such number as you think best, to reveal to them our desire and engage them to seize and bring off this greatest of all traitors . . . . I will undertake, if they are successful in bringing him off alive, that they shall receive five thousand guineas among them and . . . . their names will be recorded with glory in history."

But Arnold remained safe under the British wing.

When under DANIEL MORGAN's command, the Americans scored another victory on 17 Jan 1781, at the battle of Cowpens against the hardened Tarleton, the Virginia House of delegates voted to award MORGAN a horse with "furniture and a sword." In England, Horace Walpole grumbled,

> "America is once more not quite ready to be conquered, although now and then we fancy it is. Tarleton is defeated, Cornwallis is checked, and Arnold not sure of having betrayed his friends to much purpose."

From his headquarters in Wilmington, Cornwallis wrote the following letter to London, addressed to the British Secretary of State of the Colonies, Lord George Germain. It was dated 23 April, 1781 and read,

"My Lord, I yesterday received an express . . . .informing me . . . that Major General Phillips had been detached into the Chesapeake with a considerable force with instructions to co-operate with this army and to put himself under my orders. This express likewise brought me the disagreeable accounts that the upper posts of South Carolina were in the most imminent danger from an alarming spirit of revolt among many of the people and a movement of General GREENE's army . . . . I have, therefore, under so many embarrassing circumstances (but looking upon Charleston as safe from any immediate attack from the rebels) resolved to take advantage of General GREENE's having left the back part of Virginia open and march immediately into that province to attempt a junction with General Phillips."

Cornwallis was aware that Phillips and Arnold had 5,500 men on the Chesapeake with very little opposition from the 1,200 Americans under the command of Lafayette. Two weeks prior to his letter to Germain, he had written General Phillips,

"I am quite tired of marching about the country in quest of adventures. If we mean an offensive war in America, we must abandon New York and bring our whole force into Virginia; we then have a stake to fight for and a successful battle may give us America. If our plan is defensive, mixed with desultory expeditions, let us quit the Carolinas (which cannot be held defensively while Virginia can be so easily armed against us.)"

Without waiting for an answer to another letter he had sent to Sir Henry Clinton, Cornwallis led his troops north to Virginia. Their number had increased to 1,435 men. About three weeks along the way, he received word that Phillips had died of a bilious fever and Arnold awaited him at Petersburg. On 20 May 1781, Cornwallis took command of the Royal forces on the Appomattox, his total strength was seventy-two hundred men.

[Note: Consider the plight of those early American settlers like the IVEYs who owned the surrounding land and had a hungry enemy army of 7,200 within less than a day's travel from their plantations, with such men as Tarleton and Arnold conducting raids for food and vengeance. The two JESSE IVEYs were around 30 years old. Young third-great-grandfather ANDERSON IVIE would have been seven years old. The book, "The Ivey Family in the United States" by GEORGE FRANKS IVEY, states that the father of DAVID ANDERSON IVEY was JESSIE, who died in 1834. He was the son of WILLIAM HUGH IVEY of

Sussex County, Virginia., who died in 1792. JESSIE married SARAH FOSTER and they had five children. DAVID ANDERSON IVEY's three sisters and brother are further mentioned (marriages and deaths), while he was not. If this information is correct, this JESSIE is the Virginia resident listed in the later census records.

One of the Virginia marriage records state that JESSIE IVEY married SARAH ANDERSON in Sussex County a few years after the Revolution ended. A son of ADAM IVEY named PEEBLES (who was a veteran of the Revolution and who had a brother JESSIE) was one of the witnesses of this marriage.

ANDERSON IVIE's birthday is given on his tombstone in Florida, Missouri.. Virginia is given as his place of birth in a Missouri census record. This, it would seem, was a marriage of cousin JESSIE, son of ADAM IVEY, since his brother attended as a witness. The alternative would be that it was a second marriage of ANDERSON's father, that SARAH ANDERSON became the young boy's step-mother and that his father's second cousin was a witness.

Our next record of ANDERSON IVIE was in Georgia, where he was a neighbor to his uncle, [NATHAN] LOT IVEY. He may have traveled southwest with him to Surry County, North Carolina, and then into Georgia for the land lotteries at the end of the century. ANDERSON IVIE married SARAH ALLRED of North Carolina, whose family also traveled south into Georgia. ANDERSON and his wife "SALLY" are listed as original members of the Baptist Church of Franklin County, Georgia. Second-great-grandfather JAMES RUSSELL IVIE was born there.

LOT IVEY won land in the lottery and moved south to Jasper County, Georgia, with his sons JOHN and BENJAMIN, who are mentioned in his Will. This "Will" also mentions "other children." One might have been THOMAS IVY, who is shown later as a member of the same Baptist Church of Franklin County. THOMAS IVY is the ancestor of Mrs. Coffee, whom my mother, LILLIE IVIE CONDIE corresponded with.

ANDERSON IVIE, with his wife and children, evidently didn't win any land in the many lotteries he entered, and they moved westward into Tennessee. His wife's parents, WILLIAM ALLRED and ELIZABETH THRASHER ALLRED, were also there, and later some of the ALLRED family bought land from ANDERSON IVIE in Tennessee. SARAH ALLRED IVIE's brothers JAMES, ISAAC, WILLIAM and JOHN ALLRED—with their families—joined their sister SARAH and her husband ANDERSON IVIE in Missouri in the early 1830's. In the 1840 census, SARAH's mother ELIZABETH THRASHER ALLRED, appears from the census to be living with SARAH and ANDERSON IVIE in Missouri.]

If British Field Commander Lord Cornwallis had acted quickly against the Americans, he might possibly have divided their forces in Virginia. Steuben and his trainees were near Charlottesville and Lafayette was defending Richmond. Both armies were too small to survive on their own. A rapid march between the two with his 7,200 men could possibly have taken Virginia. This would have divided the northern states from the southern and perhaps ended the seven-year struggle in favor of the king. But Cornwallis was a different temperament than Benedict Arnold. He feared being entrapped in the western country. His experiences in North Carolina had made him very cautious. In his mind, he needed a strong, fortified coastal base, more troops and solid directions from London. He again wrote to Sir Henry Clinton to abandon New York and join him in the Chesapeake.

Sir Henry had the opposite idea. He believed New York to be their strongest position and wanted Cornwallis to move his troops there by ship, as soon as possible. He expected Washington and the French fleet to be planning a combined attack against the city. So the debate went on. Both were determined in their own thinking. Letters went back and forth. They finally agreed that the area of Yorktown should be fortified, and Cornwallis hastened to move his forces through Williamsburg and then onward to this coastal village on the shoreline across from the point of the Gloucester peninsula, where the York River joins Chesapeake Bay.

Serving as a Virginia assemblyman until he was elected governor by this legislature with a six-vote margin in June of 1779, Jefferson had proposed many reform measures that would break up the privileges of the large landed aristocracy and the Anglican clergy in favor of the many farmers with small holdings or those working as tenets in those big, almost feudal estates. He had proposed tax-supported schools to give an education to both boys and girls for at least three years. He had tried to change the penal code so that only murder and treason were punishable by death. He wanted church and state to be totally separated. All of these bills had suffered defeat in the legislature. One of his reforms succeeded—a bill abolishing primogeniture in Virginia, which had required upon a man's death that the majority of his property must go to his oldest son. In 1778, Jefferson ran for the post of speaker. He was defeated by a margin of two to one. Patrick Henry had nominated him as governor; but he left him with an unmanageable, factional government in which Henry consistently tried to maintain personal control.

With British forces ever increasing, with little actual legal power left as a governor, with his fragile wife almost continually ill, Jefferson refused to be governor the third term. He pleaded with Washington to come to Virginia as a military and political commander to save Mount Vernon as well as the state. Washington, of course, would not do that. He believed that Cornwallis and his army would soon embark for New York. However, he did send his <u>Pennsylvania</u> Continental Line under Anthony Wayne to reinforce Lafayette at Richmond.

The mutinous activities of his continentals had increased since the mutiny at Morristown in the spring. Wayne's group had been particularly troublesome.

There was some concern about enlisting "for three years or the duration of the war." The mutineers decided it meant whichever came first. The military had the opposite view. Two mutineers were executed and the mutiny ended. Washington felt the discontent was a result of military inactivity, and he was delighted to send the Pennsylvanians southward. Washington then began to prepare for an offensive attack on the British in New York City. He brought the French troops from Rhode Island westward to combine their force with that of his own continentals.

With Lafayette's headquarter's at Richmond, the Virginia Assembly was moved inland again to Charlottesville, and Governor Thomas Jefferson moved his family back to Monticello, which was only a few miles to the south. Jefferson announced 2 Jul 1781, as his last day in the governorship. It was on 1 July that the prodigious American Captain Jack Jouett stopped at the Cuckcoo tavern around 11:00 o'clock at night and found Colonel Banastre Tarleton with 250 dragoons and mounted infantrymen relaxing a short while on their route to Charlottesville and Monticello, which was an additional forty miles inland. He quickly slipped away and, in Paul Revere style, took a wooded, less traveled, shorter route to warn His Excellency and the Assembly that the "the British are coming!" Just as the dawn was breaking, he prodded his exhausted horse up the hill to the mansion, and dismounting, wrapped his scarlet cloak around him and, with his face cut and bleeding from the bushes, banged on the door with the news.

Jefferson gave him a glass of Madeira and then sent him to warn the assemblymen in town. Several of them had spent the night at Monticello. The governor calmly hustled his family and his guests to a neighboring estate, then proceeded to discuss with his servants which articles within the household should be hidden. When a neighbor named Hudson breathlessly arrived to tell him the raiders were at the foot of the hill, he ordered his fastest horse, Caractacus, and started toward Carter's Mountain five miles away to join his family at Blenheim. As he began his ascent, he stopped and knelt to focus his telescope. In the process, he unknowingly dropped his short sword. Unable to locate any enemy troops, he decided to return to Monticello and rescue some of his papers. He was concerned that Monticello would be burned.

As he rode towards his home, he discovered that he had dropped his sword and changed direction again to fetch it. Fortunately, as he picked up his lost sword, he once more used his telescope. This time he saw that Charlottesville was swarming with the green-and-white uniforms of the loyalist light infantry. Then focusing to a closer range, he saw a troop of horsemen charging up Monticello after him. Jefferson quickly mounted and galloped into the woods toward Carter's Mountain and his family.

At Monticello, Jefferson's butler, Martin Hemings, had been handing the family silver to another slave, Caesar, who was under a loosened plank in the front porch floor. When the dragoons rushed up, he dropped the board over Caesar and the silver and stood firmly upon it. A British officer shoved the barrel of his pistol to Hemings' chest and threatened to fire unless Hemings told him where Jefferson was.

"Fire away, then," Hemings said.

Instead, the dragoons went inside to search. They remained for eighteen hours, drinking only a few bottles of wine. They had been warned by Tarleton that there was to be no looting. Jefferson, however, was not as fortunate at his Elkhill plantation, which he had inherited through marriage. Cornwallis made his headquarters there. They burned barns filled with corn and tobacco, carried off cattle and sheep and cut the throat of every horse too young to be ridden. They also convinced thirty of his slaves to come away with them. Most of them lost their chance for freedom when they died of smallpox in the British camp. In spite of his loss, Jefferson still owned two hundred slaves.

Patrick Henry was trying to escape with a group of assemblymen, including the assembly speaker, Benjamin Harrison, and John Tyler. They had taken to the hills, also. As they grew tired and hungry, they stopped at a cabin for food and shelter. The woman of the house demanded to know who they were. Patrick Henry explained that they were members of the legislature, and therefore compelled to leave Charlottesville when the enemy approached.

She was indignant and told them,

"Ride on, then, you cowardly knaves! Here my husband and sons have just gone to Charlottesville to fight for you, and you running away with all your might! Clear out! You shall have nothing here!"

Henry then explained the importance of the legislature and introduced her to Benjamin Harrison. Her reply was equally quick,

"I always thought a good deal of Mr. Harrison till now; but he'd no business to run from the enemy."

She started to shut the door.

Mr. Henry asked her to wait a moment and introduced her to the other members of the party. To which she responded,

"They here? Well, I never would have thought it."

For a moment she weakened, then continued,

"No matter. We love those gentlemen, and I didn't suppose they would ever run from the British, but since they have, they shall have nothing to eat in my house. You may ride along."

John Tyler retorted,

"What would you say, my good woman, if I were to tell you that Patrick Henry fled with the rest of us?"

"Patrick Henry! I would tell you there wasn't a word of truth in it. Patrick Henry would never do such a cowardly thing."

Tyler then pointed to him stating,

"But this is Mr. Henry."

The woman was astonished and considered this news.

"Well, then, if that is Patrick Henry, it must be all right."

With that she invited them inside and prepared a meal for them.

95

YORKTOWN

If the continental army had become somewhat mutinous from lack of inactivity as they waited and waited near New York City, consider the feelings of young ALEXANDER HAMILTON. He had been with George Washington as an aide since the Battle of Princeton, when he had distinguished himself as an officer proudly leading his artillery unit to glory there, as well as the early morning surprise attack on Trenton. He had refused other generals who had asked him to become their aide; but his admiration of George Washington, his desire for military promotion and his great love of his country combined in helping him set aside his command and retire from the spotlight. He now found, after these many years of being subservient to someone else—in spite of his greatness—that it was becoming more and more difficult for him to continually be the shadow behind the man. He had reached a point where their almost father, son relationship was becoming too binding. He wanted his own command. He wanted his own glory. He wanted his independence and free agency to achieve something wonderful as ALEXANDER HAMILTON.

Washington didn't want to lose him as an aide. He had become quite dependent on his many abilities: his fluent French; his creative writing; his active mind and continual advice and respect. When Colonel HAMILTON would ask for a command, somehow, the Commander in Chief could never find the right one to offer him. HAMILTON became discontent and allowed small differences to irritate him. His father-in-law, General SCHUYLER, who could understand the great service he was rendering his country, encouraged him to remain at his post. But he was another father figure. HAMILTON was young and ambitious. He jealously watched the careers of other close friends and aides that had pulled away. John Laurens was in France on a special mission for Congress. Scammell had his own command. His close friends, Lafayette and NATHANAEL GREENE offered to give him commands in the light horse; but Washington always needed him or felt that the men who had trained these troops should be given preference.

HAMILTON began watching for an opportunity to make the break. It came. After the General and his aide had worked until the midnight of 15 Feb 1781 getting out dispatches to the French allies at Newport, Rhode Island, they retired exhausted to their beds at New Windsor. Dawn brought another pressing order. HAMILTON was hurrying down the stairs when he passed Washington ascending, who directed him to join him in his room above. The young aide quickly delivered his papers to Tilghman then turned to ascend the stairway only to be stopped by Lafayette. After what he considered to be a quick exchange, he hurried up the stairs. An irritated George Washington was waiting at the top.

In HAMILTON's words,

"accosting me in a very angry tone. 'Col. HAMILTON (said he) you have kept me waiting . . . these ten minutes. I must tell you Sir you treat me with disrespect.' I replied without petulancy, but with decision 'I am not conscious of it Sir, but since you have thought it necessary to tell me so, we part.' 'Very well Sir (said he) if it is your choice' or something to this effect and we separated. I sincerely believe my absence which gave so much umbrage did not last two minutes."

HAMILTON continued: within the hour

"Tilghman came to me in the Generals name assuring me of his great confidence in my abilities, integrity, usefulness &c and in his desire in a candid conversation to heal a difference which could not have happened but in a moment of passion. I requested Mr. Tilghman to tell him, that I had taken my resolution in a manner not to be revoked."

HAMILTON further requested that Tilghman tell Washington that he did not want an interview at that time, but that he would remain in his position, as if nothing had happened, until his other aides returned, or he was replaced. Washington was glad that he was not totally deserting him, and the matter rested.

HAMILTON was with Washington and his party at Newport, Rhode Island, and was still collaborating and penning his documents and letters in early March 1781. Together, they watched as French Admiral Destouches sailed off for the Chesapeake with 1100 troops of General Rochambeau's soldiers. It was hoped that this larger force would be able to capture Benedict Arnold and not allow his forces to join with Cornwallis in their destruction of the southern states. Upon Washington's return to New Windsor, HAMILTON rode on to Albany to join Betsy at her father's home. Within a couple of weeks, he was back at headquarters helping with the discouraging work of writing letters for Washington, who was trying to find places for aspiring young officers. About the middle of April, BETSY joined him in their first independent home, the DePeyster house, just across the river on the east bank of the Hudson. Still, he worked for his general and for his country.

He prepared a letter for his friend John Laurens to take to France. It was decided that Washington should copy it in his own handwriting with his signature, to give it more importance. It bluntly stated that unless the French would give them fresh aid, all that they had done in the past would be forfeited. America needed a cash loan. Although their currency was presently weak, the letter reminded them of the vast land and opportunity that lay to the west, and the diligence and integrity of the American people, who would quickly repay their debts when the war had ended. He reminded them with his youthful vibrancy that Europe was old and in the process of depletion, while the United States was young with great untapped resources.

At this same time, HAMILTON sent a letter to the wealthy American, Robert Morris. In it he described how the great departments of government should no longer suffer from the fumbling of committees of Congress, but be entrusted to able individuals. He begged Morris to accept the office of public financier, to which he had been named. HAMILTON outlined the organization of a national bank which would

> "increase public and private credit. The former gives power to the state . . . and the latter . . . extends the operations of commerce among individuals. Industry is increased, commodities are multiplied, agriculture and manufactures flourish, and herein consists the true wealth and prosperity of the state."

The letter soon led to active cooperation between the two men.

Then he wrote a letter to George Washington, preferring that approach to a personal interview. He told him that his commission permitted him an assignment in the line, but since he belonged to no regiment he could command only in a specially formed light corps. He believed that, knowing his desire to serve his country, field officers would not oppose his appointment. Washington answered the same day, explaining that he could order as he chose, but

"it will not do to push that right too far . . . in a service like ours—and at a time so critical as the present."

A disappointed HAMILTON sent a letter in return telling why his case was different, and how field officers would not resent him like they had the previously unpopular appointments. Then, after escorting his wife, who was three months pregnant, to the home of her parents in Albany, he returned shortly to Washington's camp then at Dobb's Ferry, where the Americans were joining with the French from Rhode Island in what was believed would soon result in an attack on New York City and Staten Island. When nothing was said to HAMILTON about a command, he again wrote Washington. This time he enclosed his commission. The General quickly sent Tilghman to him, urging him not to resign and promising something close to his wishes would be offered. HAMILTON accepted and, by invitation, quartered with General Benjamin Lincoln at King's Bridge and was cordially received by his friends from both armies.

Three weeks later, general orders announced that Lieutenant Colonel HAMILTON would command the light companies of the first and second New York regiments; together with the two companies of York levies under Captains Sackett and Williams. Nicholas Fish would be major of the battalion, which when formed would join the advanced corps under the command of Colonel Scammell. This was everything that Hamilton had hoped for, and once more he began his meticulous preparations for his men. With great diplomacy, he was even able to convince Quartermaster Pickering that his militia needed shoes as well as his Continentals.

However, all the parading and skirmishing around New York was a front. Without stronger sea power, Washington and his armies did not feel strong enough to dislodge the British from the harbor, and Virginia had big problems. Around the end of May, a letter from Lafayette to his friend Colonel HAMILTON read:

> "I have . . . so many difficulties to Combat, so many Ennimies to deal with that I am just that much of a general as will make me an Historian of misfortunes and nail my name upon the ruins of what good folks are pleased to Call the army of Virginia . . . . We have 900 Continentals, their infantry is near five to one; their Cavalry ten to one our militia are not numerous, come without arms, and are not used to war . . . . The . . . great disproportion of forces gave the Ennemy such advantages that I durst not venture out ant listen to my fondness for enterprise."

If the militia in Virginia was weak, the militia who guarded the coastal regions of Rhode Island, Connecticut, and Westchester County, New York, all of which bordered Long Island Sound, had been toughened with six years of war, and they were truly minutemen. To this group, we must add the militia along both sides of the Hudson River through Orange County, New York, and the north and central parts of New Jersey. Their fair countryside had disintegrated into a "no man's land." Their duties were great and their love of freedom and dedication were strong. They tried to support their families and raise food that was taken from them by two armies and the constant raids of the loyalists. While the continentals were at times at rest, the duties of these militiamen never ended- - - day or night for twelve months of each year. Governor Clinton of New York suggested in one letter that they be given more time at home from their long work schedules or there would be no posterity to later inhabit the lands.

In January, 1781, when British Sir Henry Clinton received word through the efforts of his loyalists spies that the Pennsylvania continentals were in mutiny, he was afraid to launch a major offensive with the 4,000 troops he had sent to Staten Island, because he believed it would unite the Americans rather than divide them. He limited his involvement by smuggling two messengers through the highly guarded New Jersey militia line to the mutineers with a message that offered help from the British. But the Pennsylvanians indignantly spurned their offer, arrested the two men as spies and gave them to congress, who had them hung. Then the New Jersey continentals mutinied two weeks after. Washington quickly retaliated. He called upon Governor LIVINGSTON to call up all of his New Jersey militia to join with his loyal continentals and quell this latest insurrection. American Major General Robert Howe was to command the combined forces. With this threat hanging over them, the New Jersey regulars quickly submitted and returned to their duties.

French General Comte de Rochambeau, in Rhode Island, had submitted himself to be under Washington's command. When his army was moved westward toward New York and across the Hudson, he saw the destitution of the ragtag American army and the desolation of their countryside. After some skirmishes with the British, the French army returned eastward across the Hudson, and Rochambeau sent word to his French superiors of the Americans great need for naval support. Accordingly, he was able to report later to Washington at Hartford on 21 May 1781, that Admiral Comte de Grasse with the French fleet was on their way to the West Indies, and that they would be able to help the Americans for a short while before they went south to the islands that winter. Washington wanted the fleet to come to New York or Rhode Island; however, this older experienced warrior, Rochambeau, had a few ideas of his own. He had earlier witnessed the problem of attacking the British fleet in New York harbor, when their Admiral had decided that the entrance was too shallow for their larger ships. Of course, there was still Rhode Island; but he considered the Chesapeake to be more adapted for a sea battle against the British, and he took it upon himself to suggest this to the French Admiral de Grasse.

It was on 14 Aug 1781, that Rochambeau was able to send a message to Washington and inform him that French Admiral De Grasse was sailing for the Chesapeake with twenty-eight ships of war and three thousand crack French veterans. He would remain off Virginia until mid-October before sailing to the Caribbean, his real target for the winter.

With this great secret, Washington sprang into action. The British had often called him "the fox" and insultingly blown their hunting horns at times when they chased after him. This time, his cunning instincts desperately wanted Sir Henry Clinton to believe the fleet was going to New York, so secrecy was imperative—even his officers were not given their destination as he quickly ordered 2,500 continental troops to assemble and move southward.

"If we cannot deceive our own men," Washington explained to his inner circle of officers, "we can never deceive the enemy."

He tried to create the appearance that Staten Island was to be attacked. State militias were given quotas to immediately fill from Connecticut, Rhode Island, New York, New Jersey and Pennsylvania. His most urgent instruction to Lafayette was,

"Don't let Cornwallis escape!"

He feared that the British army might go south into North Carolina, if they knew. However, Cornwallis blissfully continued his fortifications at Yorktown and Gloucester. He had, by then, evacuated Williamsburg and collected his whole army to this area. Lafayette with his newly arrived Pennsylvanian continentals had quickly occupied Williamsburg, and moved his headquarters to that location.

'In New York, British General Clinton was completely fooled when it was reported to him that many American troops were collecting toward the south. He thought it was a diversion to trick him into sending more troops to Cornwallis thus weakening his army in New York. He considered Lord Cornwallis to be safely fortified at Yorktown and Gloucester in Virginia. He knew the French fleet was coming, and he sincerely believed that the battle for New York was eminent. He considered attacking and occupying again the weakened port at Newport, Rhode Island. Benedict Arnold, who had been brought back to New York, strongly suggested an assault on the American forces that had been left behind—forcing Washington to return to the north. But Clinton was hesitant. His housekeeper, a British captain's wife, was pregnant with his child. He had a problem with an older British General, James Robertson, who he accused of thievery and of roaming the countryside "smelling after every giddy girl." Twice he was temporarily blind. He hated personal confrontation and refused to leave his quarters to view the situation. He was a man of "letters"—both to command and argue. He drew elaborate plans; but he didn't act.

As the continentals with the total French army crossed the Hudson River again at King's Ferry, Clinton made no attempt to stop them. A French officer in amazement wrote,

"An enemy, a little bold and able, would have seized the moment of our crossing . . . for an attack. His indifference and lethargy at this moment is an enigma that cannot be solved by me."

On Saturday 25 August, the armies fanned out in three directions going south into New Jersey, and the march to Virginia was underway. In the Highlands of the Hudson, Washington left only General William Heath with a command of seventeen continental regiments, a regiment of continental cavalry, and a few independent units for a total of around three thousand men to stand guard. He trusted in the strong state regiments and militia. He felt that with the additions in the surrounding states, they could maintain their positions and discourage the enemy attacks.

From Colonel ALEXANDER HAMILTON's letters to his wife, we can trace his journey into Virginia. On the evening before the march, his command was increased by two companies from the Connecticut line. They crossed the Hudson at King's Ferry on 20 August and were at Haverstraw that evening. Five days later, they were on their way to Springfield, then on to Brunswick, Trenton, and the Delaware. They were encouraged to spread the word that the allied attack on New York was to be by way of Staten Island. Why else would they bring along thirty flatboats on carriages unless it was to cross the Kill van Kull? And why were large bake ovens constructed at Chatham, New Jersey, unless that place was to be a base for assailing Manhattan?

A few months earlier, an American spy had been found to be in the pay of the British, and he was allowed to see a map marked to suggest a naval and land attack on New York. The double agent, asked HAMILTON what the destination of the army was. Knowing the truth would be most misleading, he replied,

"We are going to Virginia."

Perhaps this helped to heighten Clinton's fears and confusion as he sat by and allowed the armies to go unchallenged into Philadelphia and beyond to the Head of Elk (Elkton) in northeastern Maryland—where they could launch their barges and sail south on Chesapeake Bay.

On 19 August, Washington had dinner with Rochambeau at Princeton before riding on to Trenton and then Philadelphia. He was anxious about the whereabouts of the French fleet. On the afternoon of 5 September, he was riding south from Chester, Pennsylvania, when a horseman came galloping down the road toward him. He handed him a sealed packet. Upon reading his dispatches, Washington ordered his advance party to turn and go back to Chester.

General Rochambeau was heading there by water. He had wanted to see the river fortifications that had been constructed on the Delaware River before the British had occupied Philadelphia. He was to land in Chester and Washington wanted to share his good news.

A very excited Washington was waiting, waving his hat with one hand and his handkerchief with the other, while Rochambeau's boat approached the dock. Washington embraced him and explained with great joy that, on 19 August, Admiral de Grasse with his twenty-eight warships had reached Chesapeake Bay and had brought with him 3,000 French troops to add to the 5,000 French soldiers already under Rochambeau's command. This colossal news left no excuses. Washington wrote Lafayette,

"We must take Cornwallis or be all dishonored."

It was two days later on 7 Sep 1781, that HAMILTON and his battalion of light horse embarked on the boats at Elkton to continue their journey south. The Americans had only sufficient boats to carry half of their troops. Since the light horse would be needed first in Virginia, HAMILTON's corps was given this preference. The other half marched southward to Baltimore, where they would continue by boat. The barges were crowded and slow. When they had been five days on the water, word came that the French fleet under Admiral de Grasse had left the Chesapeake to battle the British fleet and could no longer protect their flotilla of boats carrying the soldiers; therefore, HAMILTON and his men were ordered to seek safety at Annapolis. After a short stay, they once more embarked and continued southward on Chesapeake Bay, rounded into the mouth of the James River and landed at Williamsburg.

In New York, Sir Henry Clinton finalized his plans for an attack on Rhode Island and sent a naval expedition to Newport. To their dismay, they found that the French squadron of ships, under Admiral Comte de Barras, had been loaded with siege artillery and had sailed south to join Admiral Comte de Grasse at the Chesapeake. Frantically, Sir Henry tried to assemble a strong force to relieve Cornwallis, but his ships were limited. As a diversion, Benedict Arnold belatedly raided and burned New London and Groton.

As Cornwallis hastened to complete his fortifications around Yorktown, Virginia, he was unable to see the entrance of the Bay from his fort. He was told of the arrival of the French fleet by a British naval lieutenant who described the event to him and reported that the 104-gun Ville-de-Paris, which was in the lead, displayed the flag of Admiral Comte de Grasse. Cornwallis immediately sent a message to Sir Henry Clinton.

> "There are between thirty and forty sail within the capes, mostly ships of war and some of them very large."

Before this message reached New York, the British fleet under Admiral Thomas Graves had sailed from Sandy Hook heading for the Chesapeake. Graves knew only that de Grasse was somewhere on the seas and that French Admiral Louis de Barras might have taken his ships away from Newport. But Graves, like Clinton had believed the Americans were preparing to attack Staten Island, and he expected no opposition to his fleet at Chesapeake Bay. He proceeded leisurely toward his destination. On 5 September at 9:30 A.M., a lookout on the British admiral's frigate sighted what he believed to be the masts of ships anchored in Chesapeake Bay ten miles away. An older naval captain assured the lookout that they couldn't be ships but might be the charred trunks of pines, which the Virginians often burned for their tar and left them standing.

French Admiral de Grasse was at first equally complacent. He thought the British fleet was French Admiral de Barras's ships arriving from Rhode Island. When they drew nearer and his vision cleared, he realized a sea battle was eminent for which he was unprepared. He had just sent two thousand of his sailors ashore to gather firewood and water. He had twenty-four warships moored within the bay without easy maneuverability. The gunships of both navies were designed to carry only their cannon. Basically, they were platforms with masts and canvas sails that rose one- hundred- to two-hundred feet. They were very difficult to turn in the confines of a harbor. In battle, their crews were shut up with the cannon in small cells, where they shot off a thousand pounds of metal ball with each broadside. The gunners were dangerously exposed to enemy shells. Sand was scattered on the decks to keep the men from slipping on the blood that they knew would soon be flowing.

The six-foot-two Admiral de Grasse moved his ships into a defense position at the mouth of the bay as rapidly as possible with his fastest ships in the lead. The British had the advantage, as they were coming with the wind in compact formation.

When de Grasse saw a gap in the center of his formation and was struggling to take care of it, British Admiral Graves suddenly dropped the sails on his flagship, much to the chagrin of his own officers. It seems that the British fleet had a damaged ship, the *Terrible*. It was part of Admiral Hood's fleet that had come from the Carribean and had joined forces with Graves. Five pumps were barely keeping her afloat and she had lagged behind Graves's fighting line.

It was 4:00 P.M. before both admirals decided it was time to fight. Then British Admiral Graves mixed up his signal flags. A pennant went up that told the fleet to bear down and engage; but the previous pennant remained in place, also. Admiral Hood at the rear was puzzled and slow in bringing up his ships. The aim from both sides was mutually ruinous. Each crew suffered more than two hundred casualties. The British ships were the most damaged. After ninety minutes of cannon fire, three of their ships, in addition to the *Terrible*, had large holes in their hulls. As the darkness of night enclosed them, the two fleets floated on the waves across from each other, while their crews patched up both sailors and ships.

The next morning, British Admirals Graves and Hood angrily debated the mixup of the signals. Then for forty-eight hours the fleets drifted further out to sea, neither side willing to be the first to engage. Graves was unaware of the difficult situation that Lord Cornwallis and his British army were in, with the American and French armies quickly surrounding them. He only saw his enemy at sea, and if de Grasse had no desire to fight, neither did he.

About 100 miles from the bay on 9 September, the French Admiral made the first move to return to the Chesapeake and take control. British Admiral Hood watched with alarm as he saw the enemy's ships in full sail. His temper raged even higher when he learned that Admiral Graves didn't know where the French were going. Graves tried to salvage the *Terrible* until 11 September, before removing her crew, burning her, and then going to Chesapeake Bay.

They found the French in total control. Admiral de Barras had arrived with his fleet from Rhode Island. The combination of the two French fleets, prepared for the defense of their position, was impenetrable. Admiral Graves sent a message to Rear Admiral Hood seeking advice. He simply answered,

"Sir Samuel [Hood] would be very glad to send an opinion, but he really knows not what to say in the truly lamentable state we have brought ourselves."

With that, Graves decided to sail back to New York and repair his ships. Cornwallis, who he had made no effort to contact, would just have to defend himself until they could return next month.

Meanwhile, George Washington had left his army and generals behind and quickly trotted southward the sixty miles to Mount Vernon. It was six years since he had seen his home and plantation, and he found they had been badly neglected. He called in the Fairfax militia to quickly help him prepare for the American and French officers that were to be his guests on the 10th of September. His "remarkably spoiled" stepson, Jack Custis greeted him. He was now twenty-eight and the father of four children. The overweight Jack insisted on going south by carriage. He wanted to at least see this "last" battle. Since he was Martha's last male child, she had insisted that he be exempt from military duty. Unfortunately, while observing the battle from the distance, he contracted a camp virus, probably malaria, and died soon after.

With great concern for the outcome of the sea battle, Washington hastened south from Mount Vernon the following day and arrived at Williamsburg on a beautiful sunny day, 14 September. He was accompanied by Rochambeau, Adjutant General Edward Hand, and members of his staff, which now included Colonel John Laurens, who had recently returned from France. Washington with courtesy dismounted at the French camp for any reception they may have planned. Soon an excited Lafayette, who had been aroused from his sickbed, with Virginia Governor Thomas Nelson and General Claude St. Simon (head of the French troops that had arrived with Admiral Comte de Grasse) galloped into the camp to greet the commander in chief. St. George Tucker of the American army, describing the scene in a letter to his wife, said Lafayette

> "caught the General round his body, hugged him as close as it was possible, and absolutely kissed him from ear to ear once or twice . . . . the whole army, and all the town were presently in motion . . . men, women, and children seemed to vie with each other in demonstrations of joy and eagerness to see their beloved countryman."

Young twenty-year-old Lieutenant Ebenezer Denny of the parading Pennsylvania brigade wrote in his journal the following day,

"Officers all pay their respects to the Commander-in Chief. Go in a body. Those who are not personally known, their names given by General Hand and General Wayne. He stands in the door, takes every man by the hand. The officers all pass in, receiving his salute and shake. This is the first time I had seen the General. The presence of so many general officers and the arrival of new corps seem to give additional life to everything. Discipline the order of the day. In all directions, troops seen exercising and maneuvering. Baron Steuben, our great military oracle. The guards attend the grand parade at an early hour, where the Baron is always found, waiting with one or two aides on horseback. These men are exercised and put through various evolutions and military experiments for two hours. Many officers and spectators present. Excellent school, this."

Washington's headquarters was now at the picturesque red brick British Governor's Palace with its trim lawns, hedges, mazes, and separate kitchen, where the whistling boys would carry the hot food from the kitchen to the cooler large dining room within the palace. They were required to whistle, as they hastened along, to insure that they were not eating the dinner before it arrived. The news of the results of the naval encounter had not yet arrived.

It was early in the morning on the 15th of September that a letter arrived from de Grasse announcing that he was once more in possession of Chesapeake Bay. Two days later a cutter arrived to convey Washington and Rochambeau to the French flagship. One of Washington's aides reported that Admiral de Grasse had pulled himself up to his full height, kissed Washington on both cheeks and cried, "My dear little General!" The French soldiers crowded the deck to get a glimpse of the most famous man in America. Near sunset, as Washington left the Ville-de-Paris with a full-gun salute from the French, he was very pleased to have been given the Admiral's promise that he would lengthen his stay till at least the end of October. His plans for a siege on Yorktown would proceed as they had planned, unless the British forced a battle. Lord Cornwallis, however, calmly continued his fortifications. Sir Henry would soon be there, as promised, to aid in their defense, or evacuate them to safety. But included with his fortifications was an underground sanctuary for his own protection.

At five o'clock, in the darkness of the morning of 28 September, the American drums beat the "march," and the advance rifle corps and cavalry guard moved off toward the right. The light infantry of Peter Muhlenberg were next, followed by a fieldpiece, then the rest of Muhlenberg's Brigade. Next came the rusty and frayed brown-and-red clothed Canadians of Moses Hazen (with the MONTEEs and perhaps fourth-great-grandfather JOSEPH POYER,) followed by two more fieldpieces. Wayne's Pennsylvanians with fourth-great-grandfather Captain ELISHA BARTON were next. Then another fieldpiece, followed by the Marylanders and other Americans. The vast army of the French followed with their artillery mixed within their column.

A French officer wrote,

"The two armies left Williamsburg in a single column and marched . . . five miles to a fork . . . . Here the Americans took the road to the right (south), and we arrived in the evening in two columns in sight of York. The place was immediately invested. Some English dragoons came up to see what was going on, but two companies of Grenadiers and Chasseurs were advanced with two pieces of four, which sent them back immediately."

In the British camp at Yorktown, Captain Samuel Graham of the Seventy-sixth Regiment of Foot reported,

"On the twenty-eighth September, information was given by a picket . . . that the enemy were advancing in force by the Williamsburg road. The army immediately took post in the outward position. The French and Americans came on in the most cautious and regular order. Some shots were fired from our fieldpieces. The French also felt the redoubt on our right flank . . . but did not persist. The two armies remained some time in this position observing each other. In ours there was but one wish, that they would advance . . . . we overheard a soliloquy of an old Highland gentleman, a lieutenant, who drawing his sword, said to himself, 'Come on Maister Washington, I'm unco glad to see you. I've been offered money for my commission, but I could na think of gangin' hame without a sight of you! Come on!'"

American St. George Tucker's diary reveals his feelings,

"[This campaign] will probably be more important than any other since the commencement of the American war.

"Sat. 29. This morning about eight o'clock, the enemy fired a few shot from their advanced redoubts, our right wing having now passed over Munford's Bridge. About nine or ten, the riflemen and jagers exchanged a few shot across Moore's Mill Pond, at the dam of which the British had a redoubt. A few shot were fired at different times in the day and about sunset from the enemies redoubts. We had five or six men wounded, one mortally and two others by the same ball.

"Sunday, 30th. This morning, it being discovered that the enemy had abandoned all their advanced redoubts on the south and east ends of the town, a party of French troops, between seven and eight o'clock, took possession of two redoubts on Penny's Hill or Pigeon Quarter, an eminence which it is said commands the whole town . . . It is now conjectured by many that it is Lord Cornwallis' intention to attempt a retreat up York River by West Point, there being no ships yet above the town to prevent such a measure."

As the Americans began converting these former British outer redoubts for their own use by changing the direction of the cannon, and so forth, four men of Captain James Duncan's regiment [under Colonel ALEXANDER HAMILTON] were killed by a single cannon ball on the night of 2 October, James Duncan [the relationship, if any, to my husband's JAMES DUNCAN ancestor, who didn't come from Scotland to America until 1848, is unknown] wrote in his diary that evening,

"A militia man this day, possessed of more bravery than prudence, stood constantly on the parapet and d—d his soul if he would dodge for the buggers. He had escaped longer than could have been expected, and growing foolhardy, brandished his spade at every ball that was fired till, unfortunately, a ball came and put an end to his capers."

Across the mile-wide mouth of the York River, the British cannon blasts were a constant boom. Gloucester Point was fortified with a line of entrenchments, four redoubts and three batteries, mounting nineteen guns. The allies, French and American, made no attempt to take these batteries; instead, they kept heavy detachments in the country to prevent British foraging and repel the enemy, if they should attempt to use the peninsula as an escape route. On 3 October there was a brief skirmish with the British cavalry when they moved in closer to the British works to close off the point completely, surrounding Cornwallis and his British army.

The next day two deserters from the British managed to escape from Yorktown to the allied lines. They reported that Cornwallis' army was

"very sickly to the amount of two thousand men in the hospital and that the troops had scarce ground to live upon, their shipping in a very naked state, and their cavalry very scarce of forage."

This, of course, was not new information to their foes, which were close enough to observe their encampment. It was time to proceed with their next operation, the opening of the first parallel in front of the British main defenses with the placement of their American and French artillery batteries.

Lieutenant Denny, of the Pennsylvania brigade, observed,

"Generals and engineers in viewing and surveying the ground are always fired upon and sometimes pursued. Escorts and covering parties stationed at convenient distances under cover of woods, rising ground, etc., afford support. This business reminds me of a play among the boys, called Prison-Base."

The dark of night was usually preferred for the digging; but the moon was full and usually visible, until the heavy rains started.

On the night 5 October, Sergeant Joseph Martin later recalled,

"One-third part of all the troops were put in requisition to be employed in opening the trenches. A third part of our sappers and miners were ordered out this night to assist the engineers in laying out the works. It was a very dark and rainy night. However, we repaired to the place and began by following the engineers and laying laths of pine wood end to end upon the line marked out by the officers for the trenches. We had not proceeded far . . . before the engineers ordered us to desist and remain where we were and be sure not to straggle a foot from the spot while they were absent from us. In a few minutes after their departure, there came a man alone to us, having on a surtout, [long overcoat] as we conjectured (it being exceedingly dark), and inquired for the engineers. We now began to be a little jealous of our safety, being alone and without arms and within forty rods of the British trenches. The stranger, inquired what troops we were, talked familiarly with us a few minutes, when, being informed which way the officers had gone, he went off in the same direction, after strictly charging us, in case we should be taken prisoners, not to discover to the enemy what troops we were. We were obliged to him for his kind advice, but . . . we knew as well as he that sappers and miners were allowed no quarters, at least are entitled to none, by the laws of warfare and, of course, should take care if taken. . . not to betray our own secret.

"In a short time, the engineers returned and the aforementioned stranger with them. They discoursed together some time, when by the officers often calling him, 'Your Excellency,' we discovered that it was General Washington. Had we dared, we might have cautioned him for exposing himself so carelessly to danger at such a time, and doubtlessly he would have taken it in good part if we had . . . It coming on to rain hard, we were ordered back to our tents and nothing more was done that night. The next night . . . the sixth of October, the same men were ordered to the lines that had been there the night before. We . . . completed laying out the works. The troops of the line were there ready with entrenching tools and began to entrench, after General Washington had struck a few blows with a pickaxe, a mere ceremony, that it might be said, 'General Washington with his own hands first broke ground at the siege of Yorktown.' The ground was sandy and soft, and the men employed that night ate no 'idle bread' . . . so that by daylight they had covered themselves from danger from the enemy's shot."

While the Americans dug the trenches, the French troops on the extreme left under St. Simon's diverted the enemy by quickly building a battery to challenge the British artillery across Yorktown Creek and to cut off enemy communications between Gloucester Point and Yorktown.

The following morning, the trench was enlarged and smoothed out. Platforms were built for the heavy artillery. Tradition demanded a special ceremony for the opening of a siege, which began at noon when the Americans of Benjamin Lincoln's division marched from their camp with drums beating, colors flying—carrying their muskets. They entered the parallel entrenchment and marched to their posts, where they implanted their flags upon the parapet.

Fifteen hundred troops then relieved Lincoln's division, who had done the work and officially opened the parallel. Captain James Duncan, included in this number, was part of Colonel ALEXANDER HAMILTON's battalion, and he wrote,

"this honor was conferred on our division of light infantry. And now I must confess, although I was fond of the honor, I had some fear, as I had no notion of a covered way and more especially as I was posted in the center with the colors. We, however, did not lose a man in relieving, although the enemy fired much. The covered way was of infinite service. Immediately upon our arrival the colors were planted on the parapet with this motto: *MANUS HAEC INIMICA TYRANNIS.*

"Our next maneuver was rather extraordinary. We were ordered to mount the bank, front the enemy, and there by word of command go through all the ceremony of soldiery, ordering and grounding our arms . . . . Although the enemy had been firing a little before, they did not now fire us a single shot. I suppose their astonishment at our conduct must have prevented them, for I can assign no other reason. Colonel HAMILTON gave these orders, and although I esteem him one of the first officers in the American army must beg leave in this instance to think he wantonly exposed the lives of his men."

From the diary of American Lieutenant William Feltman:

"This morning, nine o'clock A.M., a deserter from the enemy's artillery came to us . . . . He informed us that Cornwallis had given . . . orders . . . not to be afraid of the Americans, that they had not any heavy pieces of ordinance, except a few pieces of field artillery. He also informed the soldiery and inhabitants that the French fleet was inferior to him and were afraid to attack him that they came to this place to procure a quantity of tobacco, and . . . would set sail in eight or ten days . . . and leave the continent . . . but [the soldiery] have more sense than to believe his weak expressions."

Serving in the British lines was a young twenty-two-year-old German soldier, Stephen Popp. On 1 August he wrote in his diary,

"there are reports that we are in a very bad situation."

On the pleasant sunny day of 9 October, it read,

"still no firing by the enemy, although we kept discharging our guns at them."

He was probably unaware that in a traditional siege, the enemy did not fire until they had completed all their preparations and then the initiating ceremony would begin in unison.

At three o'clock on that afternoon, the continental flag was raised over the American battery on the right and the white flag of France rose above their batteries. George Washington was given the honor of touching a match to fire the first shot—from the French cannon. Colonel Philip van Cortlandt, of the Second New York Regiment, remembered,

"the first gun which was fired I could distinctly hear pass through the town . . . . I could hear the ball strike from house to house, and I was afterwards informed that it went through the one where many of the officers were at dinner, and over the tables, discomposing the dishes, and either killed or wounded the one at the head of the table."

An American officer exclaimed "Forty-one mouths of fire were suddenly unmasked, Happy day! We return the hostile fire. American and French flags twisted on our batteries."

Early on 10 October, the French Grand Battery opened with ten eighteen and twenty four-pounders and four more mortars, and the Americans added four more eighteen-pounders.

Within the British lines, the young German Stephen Popp, with much more concern, would remember,

"The heavy fire forced us to throw our tents in the ditches. The enemy threw bombs, one hundred, one hundred fifty, two hundred pounders; their guns were eighteen, twenty-four and forty-eight pounders. We could feel no refuge in or out of the town. The people fled to the waterside and hid in the hastily contrived shelters on the banks, but many of them were killed by the bursting bombs. More than eighty were thus lost, besides many wounded, and their houses utterly destroyed. Our ships suffered, too, under the heavy guns and batteries. Soldiers and sailors deserted in great numbers. The Hessian Regiment von Bose lost heavily, although it was in our rear in the second line, but in full range of the enemy's fire. Our two regiments lost very heavily too. The Light Infantry posted at an angle had the worst position and the heaviest loss. Sailors and marines all served in defending our lines on shore."

Near the shoreline, south of Yorktown, there were two British redoubts with moats and a tangle of abatis that were very challenging to the allied American and French forces as they proceeded to extend their zigzag entrenchment toward Yorktown, in an effort to open a second parallel one-half the distance to Yorktown (about 300 yards.) They were called number 9 and number 10. Lafayette was placed in charge of the destruction of number 10 and Rochambeau of number 9. When Lafayette assigned his Virginian Campaign Lieutenant Colonel Gimat to lead the light infantry charge, Colonel ALEXANDER HAMILTON bristled. He immediately sought a conference with Lafayette. He was senior in rank to Gimat. He wanted this opportunity to actually command. The decision was finally taken to Washington, and an ecstatic HAMILTON emerged from the conference shouting to his troops, "We have it! We have it!"

Throughout the day of 14 October, the Americans had fired on the two redoubts, breaking down the outer barricade of spiked trees, and then onward. In the darkness of night, on a signal of six cannon shot in rapid succession, both storming parties sprang from the nearest trenches and advanced. HAMILTON had commanded his troops to advance with unloaded muskets. The redoubt was to be taken with the bayonet. HAMILTON was the first over the parapet and into the fort. Lt. Colonel Laurens had circled and came in from the rear, Fish from the left side. Lt. Col. FRANCIS BARBER led the supporting column. HAMILTON reported,

> "The redoubt was in the same moment enveloped and carried in every part."

Sergeant Martin, part of the sappers and miners led by New York Captain James Gilliland, wrote of his experience in the event,

> "The sappers and miners were furnished with axes and were to proceed in front and cut a passage for the troops through the abates . . . . At dark the detachment . . . advanced beyond the trenches and lay down on the ground to await the signal for . . . the attack, which was to be three shells from a certain battery . . . . All the batteries in our line were silent, and we lay anxiously waiting for the signal . . . . Our watchword was, 'Rochambeau.' Being pronounced, 'Ro-sham-bow,' it sounded when pronounced quick like, 'Rush on boys.' We had not lain here long before the . . . signal was given for us and the French . . . the three shells with their fiery trains mounting the air in quick succession. The word, 'up up' was then reiterated through the detachment. We . . . moved toward the redoubt we were to attack with unloaded muskets. Just as we arrived at the abatis, the enemy discovered us and . . . opened a sharp fire upon us. We were now at a place where many of our large shell had burst in the ground, making holes sufficient to bury an ox in. The men, having their eyes fixed upon what was transacting before them, were every now and then falling into these holes. I thought the British were killing us off at a great rate. At length, one of the holes happening to pick me up, I found out the mystery of the huge slaughter. As soon as the firing began, our people began to cry, 'The fort's our own!' . . . The sappers and miners soon cleared a passage for the infantry who entered it rapidly. Our miners were ordered not to enter the fort, but there was no stopping them . . . . I could not pass at the entrance we had made, it was so crowded. I, therefore, forced a passage at a place where I saw our shot had cut away some of the abatis. Several others entered at the same place. While passing, a man at my side received a ball in his head and fell under

my feet, crying out bitterly. While crossing the trench, the enemy threw hand grenades . . . into it. They were so thick that I at first thought them cartridge papers on fire, but was soon undeceived by their cracking. As I mounted the breastwork, I met an old associate hitching himself down into the trench. I knew him by the light of the enemy's musketry, it was so vivid. The fort was taken and all quiet in a very short time."

Lieutenant Colonel Count Guiliaume de Deux-Ponts, who led the French attack on the 9th redoubt, wrote,

"The six shells were fired at last, and I advanced in the greatest silence. At a hundred and twenty or thirty paces, we were discovered, and the Hessian soldier . . . on the parapet cried out, 'Werda?' to which we did not reply but hastened our steps. The enemy opened fire the instant after the 'Werda.' We lost not a moment in reaching the abatis, which . . . at about twenty-five paces from the redoubt, cost us many men and stopped us for some minutes, but was cleared away with brave determination. We threw ourselves into the ditch at once, and each one sought to break through the fraises and to mount the parapet. We reached there at first in small numbers, and gave the order to fire. The enemy kept up a sharp fire and charged us at the point of bayonet, but no one was driven back . . . . Our fire was increasing and making terrible havoc among the enemy who had placed themselves behind a kind of entrenchment of barrels, where they were all massed and where all of our shots told. We succeeded at the moment when I wished to give the order to leap into the redoubt and charge upon the enemy with the bayonet; then they laid down their arms and we leaped with more tranquility and less risk. I shouted . . . . 'Vive le Roi!' which was repeated by all the grenadiers and chasseurs who were in good condition, by all the troops in the trenches, and to which the enemy replied by a general discharge of artillery and musketry.

"I never saw a sight more beautiful or more majestic. I did not stop to look at it. I had to give attention to the wounded and directions to be observed towards the prisoners. At the same time, the Baron de Viomenil came to give me orders to be prepared for a vigorous defense, as it would be important for the enemy to retake this work. An active enemy would not have failed, and the Baron . . . judged the English general by himself."

But the redoubts, with guns turned, became part of the Allied second parallel.

HAMILTON regretted that nine of his men were killed and thirty-one wounded, including a number of officers. The enemy casualties were much less. Twenty were captured. The French, with a larger force, had proportionately similar losses.

Washington proclaimed,

"Few cases have exhibited stronger proofs of Intrepidity, coolness and firmness than were shown upon this occasion."

The following morning 15 October, a gloomy British General Cornwallis observed the disaster of the preceding night. Upon retiring to his quarters, he wrote the following to Sir Henry Clinton,

"My situation now becomes very critical. We dare not show a gun to their old batteries, and I expect that their new ones will open tomorrow morning. Experience has shown that our fresh earthen works do not resist their powerful artillery, so that we shall soon be exposed to an assault in ruined works, in a bad position, and with weakened numbers. The safety of the place is, therefore, so precarious that I cannot recommend that the fleet and army should run great risk in endeavoring to save us."

However, Cornwallis had not given up. Throughout that day and the next, skirmishes continued between the two armies. In the dark of the night of the 16th, in desperation, he contacted Banastre Tarleton, commanding at Gloucester Point, and told him to assemble his troops on the peninsula. He was planning a breakout and march to the north with their able troops. He wrote a letter to Washington that was to be left behind asking for clemency for the wounded and ill. Tarleton remembered,

"A number of sailors and soldiers were dispatched with boats from Gloucester to assist the troops in passing the river. Earl Cornwallis sent off the first embarkation before eleven o'clock that night . . . and purposed himself to pass with the second, when he had finished his letter to General Washington . . . Much of the small craft had been damaged during the siege, yet it was computed that three trips would be sufficient to convey all the troops that were necessary for the expedition. The whole of the first division arrived before midnight, and part of the second had embarked when a squall, attended with rain, scattered the boats and impeded their return to Gloucester. About two o'clock in the morning the weather began to moderate, when orders were brought to the commanding officers of the corps that had passed to recross the water. As the boats were all on the York side . . . in order to bring over the troops it required some time to row them to Gloucester, to carry back the infantry of the first embarkation. But soon after daybreak they returned under the fire of the enemy's batteries to . . . Yorktown."

The squall blew itself out before dawn; but it took with it the will of Cornwallis to continue the siege. Hessian Johann Dohla of the British front lines recalled,

"Early at the break of day the bombardment began again from the enemy side even more horribly than before. They fired from all redoubts without stopping. Our detachment . . . could scarcely avoid the enemy's bombs, howitzer shot, and cannon balls any more. One saw nothing but bombs and balls raining on our whole line. Early this morning, the English light infantry returned from Gloucester and mounted their post . . . . They said it would be impossible to break through there . . . nothing at all can pass in and out any more. Also, this morning right after reveille, General Cornwallis came . . . and observed the enemy and his works. As soon as he had gone back to his quarters, he immediately sent a flag of truce with a white standard over to the enemy. The light infantry began to cut their new tents . . . to pieces . . . so one expected an early surrender."

On the American side, about ten o'clock, Ebenezer Denny later wrote,

"I had the pleasure of seeing a drummer mount the enemy's parapet and beat a parley, and immediately an officer, holding up a white handkerchief, made his appearance outside their works. The drummer accompanied him, beating. Our batteries ceased. An officer from our lines ran and met the other and tied the handkerchief over his eyes. The drummer [was] sent back, and the British officer conducted to a house in rear of our lines. Firing ceased totally . . . . I never heard a drum equal to it—the most delightful music to us all."

American St. George Tucker concurred in his diary, 17 Oct 1781,

"A solemn stillness prevailed. The night was remarkably clear, and the sky decorated with ten thousand stars. Numberless meteors gleaming through the atmosphere afforded a pleasing resemblance to the bombs which had exhibited a noble firework the night before, but happily divested of all their horror. At dawn of day [the eighteenth] the British gave us a serenade with the bagpipe, I believe, and were answered by the French with the band of the Regiment of Deux-Ponts. As soon as the sun rose, one of the most

striking pictures of war was displayed . . . . From the Point of Rock battery on one side our lines completely manned and our works crowded
with soldiers were exhibited to view. Opposite these at the distance of two
hundred yards, you were presented with a sight of the British works, their
parapets crowded with officers looking at those who were assembled at the
top of our works. The Secretary's [Thomas Nelson's] house with one of the
corners broke off and many large holes through the roof and walls, part of
which seemed tottering . . . afforded a striking instance of the destruction
occasioned by war. Many other houses in the vicinity contributed to accomplish the scene."

And while the soldiers contrasted the long-awaited beauties of peace with
the horrors of the many preceding days and years, two generals tried to manipulate to their advantage the terms of surrender. The British General Cornwallis
tried to achieve the terms that Burgoyne had won at Saratoga. Washington had
never approved of Gates' generosity. He wanted the harsher terms that the
British had demanded of his second in command General Benjamin Lincoln
after the siege of Charleston, South Carolina.

After many letters through the lines, negotiations were finally set up in
a front room of Moore's small white frame house. Cornwallis' aide, Major
Alexander Ross, and Colonel Thomas Dundas were the British peace commissioners. Washington chose his aide, Colonel John Laurens, as his commissioner
and Rochambeau's choice was Viscount de Noailles, Lafayette's brother-in-law.
Negotiations dragged on through the night until early in the morning of 19
Oct 1781. An American officer wrote a short description of the highly debated
terms of surrender.

"[Major Ross] observed, 'This is a harsh article.'
"'Which article?' said Colonel Laurens.
"'The troops shall march out with colors cased and drums beating a
British or a German march.'
"'Yes, sir,' replied Colonel Laurens, 'it is a harsh article.'
"'Then, Colonel Laurens, if that is your opinion, why is it here?'
"'Your question, Major Ross, compels an observation which I would
have gladly suppressed. You seem to forget, sir, that I was a capitulant at
Charleston, where General Lincoln after a brave defense of six weeks [in]
open trenches by a very inconsiderable garrison against the British army
and fleet . . . and when your lines of approach were within pistol shot of

our field works, was refused any other terms for his gallant garrison than marching out with colors cased and drums <u>not</u> beating a German or a British march.'

"'But,' rejoined Major Ross, 'My Lord Cornwallis did not command at Charleston.'

"'There, sir,' said Colonel Laurens, 'you extort another declaration. It is not the individual that is here considered. It is the nation. This remains an article, or I cease to be a commissioner.'"

Washington reviewed the terms later that morning. He approved most of them and denied a few. In his journal he wrote,

"I had the papers copied . . . [sent word to Cornwallis] that I expected to have them signed at eleven o'clock and that the garrison would march out at two o'clock."

Shortly before noon, the senior British naval officer arrived at captured Redoubt #9 with the articles subscribed to by Cornwallis. General Washington had a line added:

"Done in the trenches before Yorktown, in Virginia, October 19, 1781," and then he signed, "G. Washington."

Rochambeau and Barras then added their signatures, and it was done— Admiral de Grasse was ill on board his vessel.

At noon, Ebenezer Denny recorded in his diary,

"All is quiet. Articles of capitulation signed. Detachments of French and Americans take possession of British forts. Major [James] Hamilton commanded a battalion which took possession of a fort immediately opposite our right and on the bank of York River. I carried the standard of our regiment . . . . On entering the fort, Baron Steuben, who accompanied us, took the standard from me and planted it himself."

At 2:00 o'clock, Cornwallis pled illness and sent his representative, the Irishman Brigadier General Charles O'Hara of the Guards, who first tried to present his sword to Rochambeau, who quickly referred him to the American commander, George Washington. Washington refused to accept the sword "of so good a hand" and sent him to his second in command, General Benjamin Lincoln, who accepted the sword. As the British marched forward to dispose of their guns in the designated way, an officer of the New Jersey Line recorded:

"The British officers in general behaved like boys who had been whipped at school. Some bit their lips, some pouted, others cried. Their round, broad-brimmed hats were well adapted to the occasion, hiding those faces they were ashamed to show. The foreign regiments [German] made a more military appearance, and the conduct of their officers was far more becoming men of fortitude."

In contrast, in the American camp a colonel recalled,

"I noticed that the officers and soldiers could scarcely talk for laughing, and could scarcely walk for jumping and dancing and singing as they went about."

On 22 October, The Marquis de Lafayette wrote a friend,

"The play, sir, is over. Washington has given a dinner for British General O'Hara. So, also, has Rochambeau, and a French officer present has been amazed at the 'sang froid and gaity even' of O'Hara and fellow English officers at dinner. The British troops and their mercenaries, except most of the officers who have been granted paroles, have started filing off for Winchester and Fort Frederick, the places assigned for their American captivity. Lieutenant Reuben Sanderson of the Fifth Connecticut, serving with the late Colonel Scammell's corps, has spent two days in Yorktown, the first 'Collecting Tents,' the second, 'Collecting N_____s till 5 o'clock.'"

These were the slaves that had been promised their freedom by the British, but were not included in the surrender terms. Loyalists and American army deserters were not given any special consideration, either.

That winter, Rochambeau remained in Virginia. NATHANAEL GREENE was aided in South Carolina with the Pennsylvania, Maryland, and Virginia forces under General Arthur St. Clair. The rest of the continentals sailed northward up Chesapeake Bay to Head of Elk and then marched on to Jersey and the Hudson.

In Monticello, an embarrassed and former governor, Thomas Jefferson struggled to write the proper letter of congratulation to his friend, Commander in Chief George Washington. Jefferson's honor had been questioned by many Virginians, because of his flight from Benedict Arnold, his refusal to accept his third term as governor, and his escape to Carter Mountain. His frail wife was pregnant again for the sixth time in eight years, and this time something was very wrong. She had gained a great deal of weight and was unable to attend to

YORKTOWN BATTLEFIELD
When Cornwallis surrendered and ended the siege at Yorktown, the British still occupied New York City, Savannah and Charleston.

Washington sent part of his army south, but most of them went with him north to confront Sir Henry Clinton. The French fleet moved eastward into the Atlantic—they would continue their war with the British there. The short cannon on the right was from France.

Alexander Hamilton knew the war was basically over, gave his command papers back to General Washington, and hurried home to New York—he needed to become a lawyer to fulfill his dreams and support his family.

Sir Henry Clinton, the King, and British parliment knew they were defeated also—but delayed the final surrender to claim all the advantages they could.

The victory monument was authorized 29 Oct 1781 by the Continental Congress, but it would not be constructed for 100 years—after the Civil War had ended—it was completed in 1884.

YORKTOWN VICTORY MONUMENT
This monument was authorized by Continental Congress, October 29, 1781, just after the news of surrender reached Philadelphia. Actual construction began 100 years later and was completed in 1884. The original figure of Liberty atop the Victory shaft was severely damaged by lightning. A new work replaced it in 1956. The shaft of Maine granite is 84 feet in height to which Liberty adds another 14 feet.

her duties as a hostess or to her household affairs. He remained at her side, writing his history of Virginia until after the little girl was born at one o'clock in the morning of 8 May 1782, although his countrymen had forgiven him and tried to enlist him in further service to his country.

Thomas Jefferson's daughter Patsy, who was almost ten years old, wrote later about the following days with her father and dying mother:

"He nursed my poor mother in turn with Aunt Carr and her own sister—sitting up with her and administering her medicines and drink to the last. For four months that she lingered, he was never out of calling. When not at her bedside, he was writing in a small room which opened immediately at the head of her bed."

In her last hours, Patty Jefferson asked her husband not to marry again. She had been raised by a stepmother, and she did not want that for her little girls. Jefferson agreed; but he could not stand the truth of the situation. He fainted and had to be carried from the room. He was unconscious for an hour. Patty died at age thirty-three on 6 Sep 1782. Three weeks later, Jefferson emerged from his library; but all he could do was ride hour after hour, day after day, over the wooded area that surrounded his home, with his daughter Patsy at his side.

Fifty years later, she wrote,

"The violence of his emotion to this day I dare not describe to myself."

To his French friend Chastellux, who had visited him shortly before the birth of his baby daughter, Jefferson wrote,

"A single event wiped away all my plans and left me a blank which I had not the spirits to fill up."

But life goes on for all of us. When a smallpox epidemic raged once again in Virginia, Jefferson took his children to be inoculated near Richmond. The mansion had become a hospital with Jefferson serving as the chief nurse when he received a letter on 25 November from ROBERT R. LIVINGSTON, the president of the Continental Congress, appointing him by a unanimous decision to go to France to negotiate the peace with Great Britain.

The following day, he wrote congress:

"I will employ in this arduous charge, with diligence and integrity, the best of my poor talents, which I am conscious are far short of what it requires."

So, as soon as it was safe for the children to travel after their inoculations, he arranged to have the baby and Maria taken to his sister-in-law's at Eppington, and sent his sister Martha and the Carr children back to Monticello. His business affairs were turned over to two trusted friends, his brother-in-law, Francis Eppes, and his neighbor Nicholas Eppes. Ten-year-old Patsy accompanied him on his journey—first to Philadelphia and then on to France. They left Monticello on 19 Dec 1782, for Philadelphia. It is of interest that fourth-great-grandfather WILLIAM ALLRED, across the border in North Carolina, had a brother named EPPES ALLRED. He was a young participant in the continental army.

~ 96 ~

ONE NATION, UNDER GOD!

After the Yorktown victory, Washington returned to Philadelphia. He still had to deal with Congress about clothing and feeding the army through another winter. New York City, Savannah and Charleston were still occupied by the British. He had asked French Admiral de Grasse for aid in South Carolina, only to be refused. De Grasse had his own war to fight with the English, and, after being trounced by British Admiral Sir George Rodney late in 1781, he limped home to France with his fleet. Washington could not predict what the British would do next, partly because London would not even know about the surrender until around noon on the twenty-fifth of November, when a messenger informed Germain. He quickly drove to Downing Street to inform the prime minister personally.

Washington began planning his spring and summer campaign. He believed that the British had around 13,000 troops in New York City and his available army was slightly short of 10,000. He had about 10,000 British prisoners to feed. The loyalist and British raids in Westchester County, New York; Monmouth County, New Jersey, and along the coastal region of New York Sound continued. Money was almost nonexistent. At the Yorktown surrender, the Americans discovered Cornwallis' treasure chest with 1,500 pounds. The French suggested that the British should be allowed to keep such an insignificant amount; but the Americans were desperate and refused—wishing it was more. The army needed to be paid.

While the Americans struggled and dug in for more of the same everlasting war, the British parliament and general population had no doubt about the magnitude of the Yorktown victory. King George the Third was inconsolable and even wrote a letter, which was not sent, declaring his abdication of the throne. Germain resigned his post when the embittered Sir Guy Carleton, governor of Canada, refused to replace Sir Henry Clinton in New York as long as Germain remained in authority. The British in general blamed Clinton for their brave General Cornwallis' defeat. Parliament was able, with a close vote, to replace the Prime Minister with a man considered more willing to end the war and accept the United States as a nation. But Lord Rockingham died, and a less favorable prime minister was appointed.

When word reached Washington, he lamented,

> "The death of the Marquis of Rockingham has given a shock to the new administration and disordered its whole system . . . . That the King will push the war as long as the nation will find men or money admits not of a doubt in my mind."

Benedict Arnold had arrived in London. He felt that the British could still win and urged the king to allow him to help plan their defeat; but the tide of that nation had turned. They were at war with their old enemies, the French. Spain was helping the Americans. John Adams had convinced the Dutch at Amsterdam, the financial capital of Europe, to loan the United States five million pounds, and they had declared war on England, too. Adams was now negotiating with the Russians. The British debts were escalating. The people were tired, bored, and ashamed of any defeat. The thoughts of peace and a lucrative trade with the Americans before their ports were closed to them in favor of other nations seemed more and more worthwhile. Controlling those rebels on such a distant and vast continent seemed more difficult. Orders were given to General Sir Guy Carleton to cease initiating any further battles and to prepare the troops in New York City, Savannah and Charleston for evacuation. Washington did not know this, and when rumors were reported to him that this was the case, he refused to believe them—feeling it was a trick to catch him off his guard. Sir Guy did not arrive in New York to relieve Sir Henry Clinton until May 1782.

It was in March 1782 that an incident occurred that involved some of our loyalist third-cousins from the LIPPINCOTT ancestral line. It seems that at the time the British commissioners arrived at Elizabethtown, New Jersey, for the first exchange of prisoners of war, a schooner commissioned by William Franklin's Board of Associated Loyalists stood off Long Branch, thirty miles away, to pick up two of their Loyalist Associators. Ashore, a brief fight ensued, and the rebels captured loyalist PHILIP WHITE, one of the cousins. He was never seen alive again. Rumors reported that WHITE was cut down by sabers and his arms and legs hacked off. The loyalists were very anxious about their fate. Cornwallis had deserted them in the Yorktown surrender terms, and they were to be treated as traitors.

On 8 Apr 1782, while the prisoner talks continued at Elizabethtown, the Board of Associated Loyalists in New York City gave its permission to remove an American prisoner from the provost jail. Captain Joshua Huddy had been captured in a raid on New Jersey four days before PHILIP WHITE disappeared. Huddy had admitted that he had pulled the rope that strangled loyalist STEPHEN EDWARDS, another cousin—three years earlier. Huddy was taken out of the jail by loyalist Captain RICHARD LIPPINCOTT, another third cousin, who bore the name of our early American common ancestor. The removal papers were signed by William Franklin, president of the Board of the Associated Loyalists, and countersigned by General Sir Henry Clinton. LIPPINCOTT was to exchange Huddy and two other prisoners for three rebels. Instead, with twenty-two other loyalists, he took Huddy ashore and ordered him hanged. A sign was pinned to his chest: it ended with the words,

"Up goes Huddy for PHILIP WHITE."

An outraged Washington demanded that Clinton send him the man responsible for the execution. Clinton ordered LIPPINCOTT arrested, and he was given to the Americans for trial. His four-month trial ended in an acquittal. To Washington, LIPPINCOTT's guilt was only part of William Franklin's complicity, which had been unjustly covered up. He ordered the hanging of a British prisoner of war of equal rank to Captain Huddy, unless Clinton turned over William Franklin, the man he felt was really responsible.

Washington chose ten officers that had been taken prisoner at Yorktown and told them to draw lots. They refused to do this and made an appeal to Sir Henry Clinton. Washington ordered lots to be drawn for them, and the lot fell on Captain Asgill of the Grenadier Guards. Washington ordered him brought from Virginia to his headquarters at Morristown, New Jersey, where he was placed in solitary confinement.

A huge gallows was erected outside his cell window. Congress studied the LIPPINCOTT court-martial papers Washington had given them and decided that William Franklin was the guilty party. While Washington prepared to go forward with his threat, the British prisoner's mother, a wife of a member of the British parliament, wrote a personal letter to the French Queen, Marie Antoinette, pleading for her intervention as a mother to save the life of her son. The French king and queen immediately complied, sending a letter to Washington that was "enough to move the heart of a savage" and asked the French minister to intercede with Congress. Benjamin Franklin, in Paris, felt mortified by his son's involvement. Washington was embarrassed that he had been made to appear the brute for ordering the execution of an innocent officer and a gentleman. He bowed reluctantly to the pressure of Congress, and Asgill was freed from his solitary confinement. But all remained convinced that William Franklin had given the verbal orders. William Franklin was soon taken safely to England on a ship that was heavily guarded by a British convoy. Accompanying him on this journey to London was Captain RICHARD LIPPINCOTT of New Jersey.

It was not until 12 Mar 1783 that news arrived from France that on 30 Nov 1782 a treaty of peace had been signed in Paris that granted the Americans their independence. This treaty, however, was not effective until Great Britain and France had finalized the peace treaty between their two nations. The first two weeks of April became important as letters amongst British General Carleton, Washington, and Congress bounced back and forth. It was on 16 April that Washington received official orders from Congress to terminate all hostilities and he quickly announced to his army that

"all fighting was to end immediately."

Carleton was equally quick to let him know that sufficient ships were not quickly available for the evacuation of New York City. In fact, it was not until 25 Nov 1783 that the British garrison completed its withdrawal and Washington immediately sent his trusted artillery commander, General Henry Knox, with his cheering troops into the city to establish order. Washington and New York Governor Clinton rode into the city a little later in the day. They were escorted by a militia unit, the Westchester Light Dragoons. The newly arrived Americans found that half the houses had been burned or destroyed, leaving at least half of the remaining inhabitants destitute. The city was filthy with its roads partially torn up; but the flag of the United States of America once more gloriously flew over the city. It had been eight-and-one-half years since the old lead statue of King George III had been torn down in the city to make bullets. But many of New York City's inhabitants, the loyalists, were not cheering as they watched the tall masts depart toward the Atlantic.

The Long Island and Staten Island garrisons completed the British evacuation on 3 December. Savannah had been evacuated in July; but it was December before NATHANAEL GREENE and his toughened troops replaced the British in Charleston.

King George III is quoted as saying that if Washington could give up power, he would indeed be the greatest man of the eighteenth century. It was not difficult for Washington. He was more than ready to give the military command back to Congress. Martha had joined him in New York City, she was not feeling her best; but not all of New York City was a drudge. The British left behind business markets that were well supplied with foreign goods—something that was not readily available in this war torn country. She and her commander in chief went shopping for their grandchildren who had so recently lost their father, Jack Custis. They avoided goods that were made in England. Wherever they went, they were surrounded by all ages. Everyone wanted to see their hero. Invitations to dinners with delicacies they had not seen in years were profuse. There was a "most splendid" display of fireworks on Broadway, near the Bowling Green. However, as soon as the port was emptied of those ships he had so long detested and plotted against, Washington was anxious to return to Mount Vernon with his wife.

Brevet Lieutenant Colonel Benjamin Tallmadge, the young handsome dragoon officer who had managed Washington's secret service, kept a journal of the events. He wrote,

> "On Tuesday, the fourth of December, it was made known to the officers then in New York that General Washington intended to commence his journey on that day. At twelve o'clock the officers repaired to Fraunes Tavern in Pearl Street, where General Washington had appointed to meet them and to take his final leave of them. We had been assembled but a few moments when His Excellency entered the room. His emotion, too strong

to be concealed, seemed to be reciprocated by every officer present.

"After partaking of a slight refreshment, in almost breathless silence, the General filled his glass with wine, and turning to his officers, he said, 'With a heart full of love and gratitude, I now take leave of you. I most devoutly wish that your latter days may be as prosperous and happy as your former ones have been glorious and honorable' . . . Such a scene of sorrow and weeping I had never before witnessed, and hope I may never be called upon to witness again . . . . The simple thought that we were then about to part from the man who had conducted us through a long and bloody war, and under whose conduct the glory and independence of our country had been achieved . . . seemed to me utterly insupportable. But the time of separation had come, and waving his hand to his grieving children around him, he left the room, and passing through a corps of light infantry who were paraded to receive him, he walked silently on to Whitehall, where a barge was in waiting. We followed in mournful silence to the wharf, where a prodigious crowd had assembled to witness the departure of the man who, under God, had been the great agent in establishing the glory and independence of these United States. As soon as he was seated, the barge put off into the river, and when out in the stream, our great and beloved General waved his hat and bid us a silent adieu."

The General then proceeded on horseback through Brunswick, Trenton, Philadelphia, Wilmington, and on to Annapolis, always surrounded by crowds of joyful and excited people. At Annapolis, where congress was then convening, he presented to them his official retirement papers, which included his expense account, the only money he would be paid for his eight-and-a-half years of service. He concluded his remarks to them by stating,

"I consider it an indispensable duty to close this last solemn act of my official life by commending the interests of our dearest country to the protection of Almighty God and those who have the superintendence of them to his holy keeping."

He was home at Mount Vernon with Martha and the grandchildren on Christmas Day, 1783.

ALEXANDER HAMILTON

After the Yorktown victory 18 Oct 1781, Colonel ALEXANDER HAMILTON waited only for the final surrender before he relinquished his commission and returned home to his wife. His first child was expected soon. Philip was born in January 1782. There would be seven more children. He felt, rightly, that the last major battle of the Revolutionary War had been won and recognized that a different sort of battle was needed, if the thirteen colonies were to be united into a strong, liberty loving nation. All the years he had spent with Washington had taught him the weaknesses of the Continental Congress and the present problems of the Confederation Congress. He sorely knew the problems that arise from lack of finances. He knew of the selfishness and intrigue that had involved the military, the thirteen states, and congress. He was still in his idealistic later twenties, and he visualized a great nation that could stand against the powers of the world, if great leaders led the way. He felt he was one of these great men and was willing to devote his indefatigable energy toward this end. He was also determined to be independent of all others—financially, socially, and morally.

To accomplish these purposes, he chose the law. There were no law schools in that day. A young man prepared himself by "reading law" in the office of an established attorney while serving as his clerk, copyist, and general flunky—and paid for this privilege of apprenticeship for at least three years. In January of 1782, the State Supreme Court of New York had suspended the three-year-requirement

> "in favor of such young Gentlemen who had directed their Studies to the profession of the Law, but upon the breaking out of the present war had entered into the Army in defence of their country—provided that such gentlemen pass a rigorous bar examination by the end of the court's April term. HAMILTON convinced them that he qualified as one of these young gentlemen and begged for an extension until October to prepare for the exam, which they granted to him. After intense study and a grueling oral examination, he was admitted in July as an attorney qualified to practice before the Supreme Court (cases and documents), and on 26 Oct 1782, he was admitted to practice as counsel before the Supreme Court (argue cases).

He had access to the large private law library of one of his wife's relatives, JAMES DUANE, to aid him in accomplishing this amazing feat in the nine-month period. As an attorney, he was meticulous in his briefs and presentations and rose quickly to the top ranks among the two or three dozen lawyers in New York City. Judge Ambrose Spencer, who heard two generations of America's greatest lawyers, said,

> "In power of reasoning, HAMILTON was the equal of Webster, and more than this can be said of no man. In creative power HAMILTON was infinitely Webster's superior."

Chancellor Kent, in 1832, who had practiced during HAMILTON's lifetime, ranked HAMILTON first and attributed his greatness to "his profound penetration, his power of analysis, the comprehensive grasp and strength of his understanding," and his firmness and frankness of character. He put in endless hours of "hard grinding work;" but, like Cicero of old Rome, his presentations appeared effortless, easy and without flaw.

Robert Morris, whom HAMILTON had helped convince to take on the nation's financial problems and then had continued to aid him in his early endeavors, wanted HAMILTON to accept the duty of collecting the national revenues within the area of New York state. HAMILTON agreed to do this on a part time basis, if he could employ the help he needed and be paid appropriately for his services. His independent nature would not permit him to be dependent on others, or controlled by them. He had neither Mount Vernon nor Monticello to return to, nor would his pride allow him to accept subsistence from his father-in-law. He would be his own man, although my very-distant-cousin-in-law PHILIP SCHUYLER was very supportive and proud of his young son-in-law.

As the young lawyer examined the requirements of this new position, he questioned how he could earn his salary, and wrote Morris,

> "The whole system (if it may be so called) of taxation in this state is radically vicious, burthensome to the people and unproductive to government. As the matter now stands there seems to be little for a Continental Receiver to do. The whole business appears to be thrown into the hands of the County treasurers, nor do I find that there is any appropriation made of any part of the taxes collected to Continental purposes, or any provision to authorize payment to the officer you appoint."

However, he felt he could work with the legislature to rouse a response to Morris's applications. On 13 Jul 1782, he received his commission from financier Robert Morris to attend (as a lobbyist) the New York special legislative meeting at Poughkeepsie that had been called to provide congress with war revenue. It was like squeezing blood from a turnip. To extract even a little, "mountains of prejudice . . . are to be levelled." For adequate results, the tax system of the state would have to be renovated.

HAMILTON proposed taxes on lands, houses, and luxury possessions; excises on salt and tobacco; polls of servants; stamps for legal documents; and import duties. With the exception of imports, he sought to classify and graduate the taxes to correspond with ability to pay. He recommended an excise tax on distilled liquors which was strongly protested, but allowed tavern licenses. Special interests and concern against any tax intervened when the proposal reached committee; but they allowed a valuation of land tax.

HAMILTON was disappointed with what he had accomplished in regards to the New York taxes; but he did have one positive action to report to Robert Morris. In collaboration with Senator SCHUYLER, they had prepared joint resolutions that had passed both houses on 20 Jul 1782, in which it was proposed

> "to Congress to recommend, and to each State to adopt the Measure of assembling a general Convention of the States, specially authorized to revise and amend the Confederation, reserving a Right to the respective legislatures, to ratify their Determination."

It was the first call of a public body for a constitutional convention. The resolutions further described the perilous posture of the country from continued British hostilities and from the need to bolster public credit. HAMILTON's question was,

> "What avails it for one State to make [reforms or exertions] without the concert of the others?"

Two months later HAMILTON and SCHUYLER collaborated again for a convention of the public creditors of New York, and they hoped all the states would act similarly. The meeting was held in Albany on 24 Sep 1782. After much discussion of the real financial problems of the state, a new meeting was decided on—in Poughkeepsie on 19 Nov 1782. There is no record of this happening. Perhaps it was because their main instigator, ALEXANDER HAMILTON, had been elected a delegate to the Confederation congress for a term of one year, beginning the first Monday in November. HAMILTON was the only new delegate. He would serve with the reelected New York team—JAMES DUANE, William Floyd, John Morin Scott, and Ezra L'Hommedieu. When HAMILTON had been nominated by the house, SCHUYLER had withdrawn his nomination in the Senate to give favor to his up-and-coming young son-in-law.

The Revolution, of course, was still in process, and HAMILTON's very close friend John Laurens with his troops had been sent to help NATHANAEL GREENE in South Carolina. When he received the news of HAMILTON's election, Laurens sent him a congratulatory letter expressing his great delight that he was serving in public life. He added his opinion that his friend

> "should fill only the first offices of the Republic," perhaps being sent to Paris as a peace commissioner. Laurens himself found military service languid. He begged HAMILTON for the continued "consolation of your letters."

HAMILTON expressed his deepest feelings in his reply:

> "Peace made, My Dear Friend, a new scene opens. The object then will be to make our independence a blessing. To do this we must secure our union on solid foundations; an herculean task and to effect which mountains of prejudice must be levelled! It requires all the virtue and all the abilities of the Country. Quit your sword my friend, put on the toga, come to Congress. We know each others sentiments, our views are the same; we have fought side by side to make America free, let us hand in hand struggle to make her happy."

It is believed that Laurens never received this letter, because two weeks later he was killed in what NATHANAEL GREENE called "a paltry little skirmish" with an enemy foraging party on the Combahee River. HAMILTON felt the "deepest affliction" at the personal loss of his friend and grieved that America could not have the services of a patriot of "so many excellent qualities." One could speculate that many of the factional problems that arose in the next few decades—and beyond—might have been avoided, if the two young companions had been able to bring the northern and southern states into a union with as much camaraderie as this northerner and southerner had developed for each other as aides to the commander in chief.

HAMILTON found it difficult to exert his influence in the confederation congress. The majority of the members of the New York delegation were controlled by what was known as the Clintonians—the political forces that kept

Governor George Clinton in office for so many years. They represented, in New York, "the mountain of political force and prejudice" that ALEXANDER HAMILTON would have liked to see leveled. They were large landholders in the state, and although sympathetic with the rebel cause to which they had greatly contributed, they were anxious to retain all the privileges and control that they had enjoyed in the past, such as permanent seats in the legislature. When all his efforts became frustrated by his own state's delegation, he applied to Governor Clinton to send a replacement.

> "Having no further view in public life, I owe it to myself to enter upon the care of my private concerns without delay."

Upon being relieved, he returned to New York City and his practice of law.

In 1783, HAMILTON had been asked by his brother-in-law, JOHN BAKER CHURCH, and CHURCH's partner, Jeremiah Wadsworth, to organize a bank in New York, since they were both in Europe at that time. They wanted to be the dominant stockholders. Other pressures had taken precedence until February 1784, when it became known to him that Chancellor LIVINGSTON with a number of others had petitioned the legislature for an exclusive charter for a "land bank." He wrote ANGELICA's husband, J. B. CHURCH, explaining,

> "I thought it necessary not only with a view to your project, but for the sake of the commercial interests of the state to start an opposition to this scheme; and took the occasion to point out its absurdity . . . .to some of the most intelligent Merchants, who presently saw the matter in a proper light and began to take measures to defeat the plan."

The "proper light" was to recognize that, if incorporated, it would (1) have a monopoly on banking in the whole of New York state, and (2) two-thirds of its capital was to be subscribed in land security, with only one-third in cash—both grievous errors to the merchants and common people of the state.

> "Some of the Merchants . . . set on foot a subscription for a money-bank and called upon me to subscribe."

HAMILTON agreed, feeling he could later sell the greater part of his subscription to CHURCH and Wadsworth. The fifty-percent subscription sold immediately, accepting only gold or silver coin or bank notes, and the money bank was organized with Alexander McDougall as president and ALEXANDER HAMILTON, who probably wrote its constitution, as a director of this newly formed Bank of New York.

HAMILTON petitioned the legislature for the charter, which conferred limited liability on its stockholders and prohibited the bank from engaging in trade. William Seton was to be the manager and was sent to Philadelphia to learn the daily bank activities in the only other existing bank in America, the Bank of North America. Seton was a Scotch merchant with enough loyalist leanings to remain in the city during the British occupation. Upon returning from Europe, Wadsworth and CHURCH bought their shares and HAMILTON kept only one. Jeremiah Wadsworth became the second president, while HAMILTON remained a director, until he was made Secretary of the Treasury—adding first-hand knowledge of banking to his vast educational preparation. He was constantly concerned about the welfare of the wage earners and the small merchants who needed credit to grow.

Another group that had his compassion was the slaves. He had observed and disliked slavery as a young child growing up on an island in the West Indies. Unlike many prominent leaders of his day, he never owned a slave. He was a founding member of the "New York Society for Promoting the Manumission (freeing) of Slaves and Protecting Such of Them as Have Been or May Be Liberated." In 1785, the second meeting of the society named him chairman of a committee, with his friends Robert Troup and White Matlack, to recommend procedures. John Jay was the first president. Shortly before HAMILTON was elected for the second time to the New York Assembly, he joined with a number of other petitioners to beg the legislature to end the slave trade, which they described as

> "a commerce ... repugnant to humanity, and ... inconsistent with the liberality and justice which should distinguish a free and enlightened people."

During the Revolution, HAMILTON had joined with John Laurens in a proposal to grant freedom to slaves who would enlist in the continental army. The proposal was rejected. In 1785, as a member of the Manumission Society, he exchanged letters with southerner Henry Laurens, also sympathetic and attempting to help. Henry Laurens wrote back that his efforts to abolish the importation of slaves offended many:

> "a whole Country is opposed to me . . . the Number of wretched Slaves, precarious Riches, is our greatest Weakness—but alas! these Southern States are not at this moment in a disposition to be persuaded tho' one should rise from the dead . . . God forbid our conversion be too long a Delay, shall be the Effect of a direful Struggle."

HAMILTON's determination and vision of his new nation would not allow him to really quit public service. He could retreat momentarily while he struggled for his personal financial independence; but his battle for freedom would not end. He had three main goals. First, a constitutional convention to create an executive and a judiciary branch. He strongly believed that Congress needed to be controlled. His second goal was to see that George Washington was made president, as he felt he was the only man who had the love of all the colonies and would be able to pull the union together. His third goal was to become, personally, the nation's minister (or secretary) of finance with sufficient power to save the nation financially from anarchy, secession of the states, or from aggressive foreign powers. This would include sufficient money to pay for a standing army and navy that could ensure the continuance of the United States of America.

A New Constitution is Formed

HAMILTON had found a close friend in James Madison while he was in Congress and the two of them wrote endless pamphlets and tirelessly worked to bring about the constitutional convention. HAMILTON's work in New York was more in the area of making the convention actually happen through converting all the people, rich or poor, to the fact that a stronger central government was needed. James Madison's efforts in Virginia led the way in the actual wording and preparation of the document. It took four years to make it happen. Nobody worked harder than HAMILTON to bring it about.

Under the confederation government, HAMILTON continually complained that congress had no power over commerce. They had no power to make trade treaties that could stop the bickering and back-biting between the states, or with foreign countries. Vegetables from Connecticut or firewood from New Jersey could not enter Manhattan Island without paying a tariff. Tobacco was restricted from crossing the Potomac and Chesapeake Bay without duties.

Smuggling was becoming rampant. The state taxes had diverted the fur trade to Montreal, Canada. In Massachusetts, the patriotic militiamen were now debt-ridden farmers, and the western counties rebelled against foreclosures on their lands. Under the leadership of Daniel Shays, a brave captain of the Revolution, they formed an army and attacked the government arsenal at Springfield. James Madison, in Virginia, is quoted as saying,

> "the present anarchy of our commerces," and "most of our political evils may be traced up to our commercial ones."

In 1784, a proposal in the Virginia legislature for a federal convention failed because Patrick Henry wielded sufficient power to oppose a closer union. Madison tried another direction—a special meeting at Alexandria to discuss trade across the Potomac and Chesapeake, which was helped when the hospitality of George Washington brought them to Mount Vernon. This meeting included Virginian commissioners Mason and Henderson and Marylanders Chase and Jeifer. This group was to be expanded in further meetings to include Delaware and Pennsylvania,

> "who will then naturally pay the same compliment to their neighbors."

In March 1786, Governor Clinton submitted to the New York legislature the invitation of the Virginians to send commissioners to a meeting of the states

> "for the purpose of framing such regulations of trade as may be judged necessary to promote the general interest."

The New York legislature was slow to act; but finally appointed at the end of their session the following delegates: ROBERT R. LIVINGSTON, Leonard Gansevoort, ROBERT C. LIVINGSTON, ALEXANDER HAMILTON, JAMES DUANE, and Egbert Benson. Annapolis, Maryland, was chosen as the meeting place, avoiding Congress and the commercial towns,

> "in order to disarm adversaries of insinuations of influence from either of these quarters."

Maryland, whose capital was the host town, sent no delegates in an attempt at neutrality.

The meeting was to begin on the first Monday, September 1786; but the commissioners were very slow in arriving. After a decent interval of impatient waiting, only five states had arrived: New York, Virginia, Pennsylvania, Delaware, and New Jersey. The states of New Hampshire, North Carolina, Massachusetts, and Rhode Island had appointed delegates, but none of them arrived in time. Connecticut, South Carolina, and Georgia had not even appointed delegates. Then there was the additional problem, New York and Pennsylvania were not officially represented, since there were only two delegates from New York, HAMILTON and Benson, and one from the Quaker State. Each state needed three to be official.

Their non-authoritative discussions were held for three days in regards to commerce. Then Abraham Clark of Newark, New Jersey, called their attention to the wide option New Jersey had given them. It allowed their delegation to consider —

> "and other important matters, might be necessary to the common interests and permanent harmony of the several states."

This new opportunity was quickly seized. They would recommend to the states and to Congress the calling of a convention to revise the Articles of Confederation. HAMILTON either volunteered or was deputized to write the fatal defects of the existing plan of union. His first finalized statement was objected to by the governor of Virginia, Edmund Randolph, as

> "too strong; whereupon Madison said to Hamilton: 'You had better yield to this man, for otherwise all Virginia will be against you.'"

So Hamilton's plea

> "was toned down . . . to suit tender stomachs, and in this . . . milder shape was adopted." Unable to proceed with their commercial assignment, those present "were unanimously of the opinion that some more radical reform was necessary," and "they, with one voice, earnestly recommended" the Philadelphia meeting "with power to revise the confederation at large."

It was solicited that

> "Commissioners . . . meet at Philadelphia on the second Monday in May next, to take into consideration the situation of the United States, to devise such further provisions as shall appear to them necessary to render the constitution of the Foederal [sic] Government adequate to the exigencies of the Union."

The act for that purpose would then be reported to congress, and when agreed to, be confirmed by the legislature of every state.

The convention of the five middle states had unanimously succeeded in agreement of purpose, time, and place for a new or amended constitution. It was a strong beginning; but only that. These delegates still had a great challenge, individually, to persuade their own states, as well as non-attendant neighboring states of the imperative need for stronger union. Probably the greatest challenge fell on HAMILTON of New York.

HAMILTON was an elected member of the New York Assembly that met from January to April in 1787. SCHUYLER was still a member of the New York Senate. HAMILTON was still concerned that his state was still obstructing payments of revenue to congress. He assailed the complaint of Clinton's supporters that congress was attempting to dictate to the state legislature. The assembly voted against HAMILTON and praised Clinton for his negative stand. HAMILTON complained that New York was not adhering to the Treaty of Peace and tried to repeal their legislation that penalized loyalists. He pointed out that, from a selfish view, New York should not give the British any excuse for holding the western military posts . . . diverting the valuable fur trade—thus finally succeeding in repealing a restrictive part of the Trespass Act.

One of his strongest stands was on behalf of the Green Mountain Boys, who were threatening to secede from the nation and join with Canada. Neither New York, nor New Hampshire legislation, appealed to them. They had become their own rather independent democratic territory. HAMILTON forged the way to help them become the fourteenth state in the nation, and Vermont gained her statehood on 14 Mar 1791.

[Note: About fifteen years later, 23 Dec 1805, a baby boy, Joseph Smith Jr., was born in this state at the small town of Sharon. His struggling parents, Joseph Smith Sr. and Lucy Mack Smith, were living in Lebanon, New Hampshire, in the early 1800s.]

HAMILTON insisted on a large and independent electorate in New York. The will of the people was the very basis of a freedom loving nation, although at least one-third of their people were illiterate. He would not have them, as proposed, be guided by the inspectors of elections. Rather, let them be solicited by all parties and reach their own conclusion as best they could.

He succeeded in obliterating from a bill a requirement that would have made a woman with a stillborn child appear before a magistrate with a witness to prove that she had not murdered her child. He felt the poor woman was punished enough by the loss of her child, and should not be obliged to suffer doubly by being

"compelled . . . to publish her shame to the world."

HAMILTON, temporarily, was not able to overturn a feature in the New York divorce bill, which stated that a marriage partner convicted of adultery would not be allowed to remarry. This was a measure very close to his heart, for his mother, under the Danish law of the island, had not been allowed to marry his father, JAMES HAMILTON, when she was divorced by Lavien, thus making his own birth illegitimate.

It was February 1787, that HAMILTON made the motion in the assembly that five delegates be appointed to meet in Philadelphia for the Constitutional Convention. The assembly accepted, but then consented to the motion in the senate for only three delegates. This limit was a deliberate movement by the Clinton forces, after SCHUYLER had introduced five participants in the Senate. The cut was on a motion by John Haring, a faithful follower of Governor Clinton. It carried by a vote of eleven to seven. In the actual choosing of the delegates in the assembly, every member (52) voted for Robert Yates; HAMILTON had the nomination of all but himself; his own nominees, DUANE and R. R. LIVINGSTON, came fourth and fifth. The senate named Yates, HAMILTON and Lansing as their three. Yates and Lansing, as Clinton stalwarts, would create a majority, thus insuring that the New York vote would be against any change that would weaken the New York Constitution in favor of any national control of their state. In April, a disappointed HAMILTON tried again to increase the number to five and recommended Chancellor LIVINGSTON, John Jay, JAMES DUANE and Egbert Benson as desirable choices. He mentioned John Jay's experience in domestic and foreign affairs. The assembly passed his motion; but the senate again rejected it.

At the convention in May, which only came about after George Washington had agreed to be the chairman, a quorum was in place and ready to commence on 25 May 1787. The delegates agreed to keep their proceedings secret. It was feared that many premature ideas and thoughts would not be presented, if these remarks were made public and allowed to be spun by the press and interested parties in their home states. They wanted to be able to present their finished product to the people without the prejudice and malice that might arise from venomous factions. Many took notes for their own use, and James Madison's were quite complete. After all the others had died, he wrote a complete history of the event. Notes of others are available.

ALEXANDER HAMILTON nominated Major William Jackson for secretary. HAMILTON was given a place on the rules committee. Then, with the rules adopted, he sat with little to say for the next four weeks. He took a few notes and added a few of his own thoughts on his memorandum, while his friend James Madison, with the support of his Virginia delegation, presented the Virginia plan, which reduced the autonomy of the states. The New Jersey plan, which basically left the authority of the states intact, was then presented. Finally, on 18 June, HAMILTON broke his silence and created uproar in the convention with a five-hour speech. He explained he was not offering a plan for adoption, or even for debate. He was giving his own ideas, which later he would apply as amendments to the proposals of others. He told why the Virginia plan was insufficient reform and that the New Jersey plan deserved only dismissal.

Rufus King recorded in his notes on the speech,

"You must make the national Sovereignty transcendent & entire."

HAMILTON's stunned colleague Robert Yates wrote in his notes, "all federal governments are weak and distracted . . . we must establish a general and national government, completely sovereign, and annihilate the state distinctions; and unless we do this, no good purpose can be answered."

James Madison's notes contained the following:

"In his private opinion . . . the British Govt. was the best in the world; and . . . he doubted . . . whether anything short of it would do in America." The new Constitution should approach as closely to monarchy as "republican preference would allow." The chief executive should serve for life, be an elective king. He referred to Shays's insurrection in Massachusetts, and the state's inability to protect life and property even within its own confines. He mentioned how offending executives could be impeached and even convicted. HAMILTON was quoted as exclaiming, "What if all the

Charters & Constitutions of the States were thrown into the fire, and all their demagogues into the ocean. What would it be to the happiness of America."

Probably HAMILTON gave these extreme views to wake up the convention to reach higher than they were doing, for much of his talk explained and even contradicted these statements, as his later actions most assuredly did. One week later Yates recorded that he said,

"Real liberty is neither found in despotism or the extremes of democracy, but in moderate governments . . . . if we incline too much to democracy, we shall soon shoot into a monarchy."

HAMILTON was also quoted as saying,

"as States are a collection of individual men which ought we to respect most, the rights of the people composing them, or of the artificial beings resulting from the composition [?]" and another wrote it this way, "is it our interest . . . to sacrifice individual rights to the preservation of the rights of an artificial being, called states?"

His long speech was a buffer that allowed others to express themselves without the fear of retaliation, for HAMILTON had expanded the height of the debate to a higher nationalist level, which made their remarks less threatening. Whatever his reasoning, he gave ammunition to his future foes, which they would long remember, and although this speech was supposedly confidential, political enemies have long memories and with his own aspirations for the greatness of this nation, he was to find out that he had many of these enemies.

After finding that everything he was working for was being negated by his own two state delegates, he began to feel that his efforts were useless and he returned to New York on some pressing legal business—but not inactivity. He published a rebuke to Governor Clinton, who was blatantly knocking the whole idea of the convention. In Connecticut, he attempted to quiet a rumor that the convention was trying to install the British Duke of York as king in the United States. In New York, he persuaded two friends against a duel.

Back in Philadelphia, the convention was not going well. Chairman George Washington wrote him a letter.

"I am sorry you went away. I wish you were back. The crisis is equally important and alarming, and no opposition . . . should discourage exertions till the signature is fixed."

HAMILTON returned briefly in mid-August to find that New York's Yates and Lansing had walked out. Realizing their differences in opinion, he refused to vote for the state of New York and left again. He returned in early September and participated actively until the conclusion. He wanted, but never got, a larger number of members in the House of Representatives, which he felt would then better represent the people. In contrast to his speech, he gave James Madison his own draft of the Constitution, as he would like to see it. It was very close to the one that was finally accepted. HAMILTON was able to help them with some changes in the Electoral College. Some members did not want to give their completed document to Congress for its approval. HAMILTON spoke out boldly and insisted that courtesy compelled the risk, if risk there was. Three members of the convention were refusing to sign the document—Edward Randolph and George Mason of Virginia, and Elbridge Gerry of Massachusetts. HAMILTON asked them the question,

> "Is it possible to deliberate between anarchy and Convulsion on one side, and the chance of good to be expected from the plan on the other?"

They would not yield. HAMILTON immediately went to the desk and wrote in the names of the states, ready to receive the signatures of their delegates. He signed his own signature to the document as an individual. He did not believe that he could sign for New York.

His friend Gouverneur Morris, who had not planned to sign until HAMILTON had convinced him that it was the nation's only hope, summed up many of their feelings when he said,

> "The moment this plan goes forth all other considerations will be laid aside—and the great question will be, shall there be a national Government or not?"

Benjamin Franklin, the oldest member present, in his address to the Convention, stated:

> "Sir, I agree to this Constitution, with all its faults, if they are such; because I think a general government necessary for us, and there is no form of government but what may be a blessing to the people if well administered; and I believe farther that this is likely to be well administered for a course

of years, and can only end in despotism as other forms have done before it, when the people shall become so corrupted as to need despotic govrnemnt, being incapable of any other."

Hamilton's most remembered contribution to the Constitution now began. He conceived the idea of essays published in the newspaper four times a week that would explain the need for the new Constitution to the people of New York State under the title of The Federalist. He wanted Gouverneur Morris, John Jay, James Madison and himself to do them. Morris refused. John Jay did five and then became ill and unable to do more, so it was left to Madison and HAMILTON. The first one, the introduction, was written by HAMILTON. Numbers 2 through 14 were to address the importance of union to the "political prosperity" of America; John Jay handled national defense. HAMILTON's topics were maintenance of order at home and on the economic advantages of union, and Madison tackled the demolition of Montesquieu's widely accepted theory that republics could govern effectively only in small territories. Numbers 15 through 22 pointed out the inadequacies of their present Confederation, or anything similar, for the purpose of union. Madison took the poor history of confederations, while HAMILTON spoke of their inability to legislate for individuals, its ineffectiveness in getting cooperation with the various states, its lack of revenues, its inability to regulate commerce, its lack of authority in the courts of law, and the problem of equal representation of the states, regardless of land size and population. Essays 23 through 36 were written by HAMILTON and treated on "the necessity of a Constitution, at least equally energetic with the one proposed." Numbers 37 through 51 were written by James Madison, and were designed to show the conformity of the Constitution to "true republican principles."

These Federalist Papers, written for the people of New York State, were distributed individually and in a bound edition throughout all the colonies and contributed greatly to the understanding and importance of a new Constitution and its final ratification by all the states.

Rhode Island was the last state to ratify the Constitution. It feared that it would be swallowed up by the larger states that surrounded it. It waited until 29 May 1790 to join the union. During the Revolutionary War, they had furnished almost 12,000 enlisted men, and under the confederation government, they had the same vote as any of the larger states. They saw the Constitution as a dilution of their rights as individuals. With the adoption of the Bill of Rights, which guaranteed religious freedom among other guarantees, and with the strong promises of President George Washington regarding the manufacturing of goods, when he toured their state, they united their strength with the other states.

With a new Constitution, HAMILTON's first goal for this new nation was achieved. George Washington was elected president with the unanimous vote of the Electoral College. When Governor George Clinton of New York was gaining rapidly in electoral votes for vice-president, George Washington stated that he felt John Adams was better suited. The vice-presidential vote for Adams was not unanimous; but he won. HAMILTON's second goal had happened without contention.

97

FUNDING A NATION

HAMILTON's third goal was to become Secretary of the Treasury. When the new president, George Washington, asked financier Robert Morris what to do about the public debt, Morris was quick to reply,

"There is but one man in the United States who can tell you; that is, ALEXANDER HAMILTON."

Washington spoke with HAMILTON soon after and HAMILTON arranged for Robert Troup to prepare to take over his law offices. On 27 May 1789, less than four weeks after Washington's inauguration, Madison wrote Jefferson that HAMILTON would probably be appointed as soon as the office was created. But in late July, the young lawyer was still in New York and had accepted John Adam's son as an apprentice in his law office. He hesitated to accept Washington's nomination, because he felt, that in order to succeed, he needed three conditions to be in place. The first one he felt he already had— it was the support of his friend James Madison, the most able and powerful man in the House of Representatives.

He was less confident about his second condition, believing it necessary that the finances must be under the control of one man, rather than the three man treasury board of the past Confederation. His most important and third condition was that the treasury office must have some independence from the executive and be allowed to deal directly with congress. Although he loved Washington and trusted him implicitly in the areas of state and war, he was concerned that the former general knew almost nothing about fiscal management, taxation, commerce, and other responsibilities of a treasurer. And in addition, he realized that just the everyday administration of treasury affairs would be so complex and exacting that full compliance with Washington's proceedings (as he had found them during the war) would be paralytic.

If ALEXANDER HAMILTON accepted this office as secretary of the treasury, he knew he had his greatest challenge still facing him. It was probably a job no one else wanted. The finances of the nation were beyond the scope of almost everyone. The country owed huge debts to foreign nations who now wanted to be paid. The government owed their continental army veterans a great deal of cash they didn't have, and these men were close to universal mutiny—even before the war ended. Robert Morris had given his personal notes to help the country survive until his vast wealth was nearly gone. Poverty was everywhere throughout the nation among the less fortunate. They had given their services (and many lives of their loved ones) for what they considered a great cause, only to find they were basically bankrupt, while a few powerful men had exploited the situation and gained even greater power. But HAMILTON had been preparing himself, and he felt that, if he could obtain these three conditions, he could succeed. Moreover, he would welcome this opportunity to solve this burdensome problem. He visualized a free and happy nation with opportunity for everyone.

There was nothing in the Constitution that stated how the executive branch should be run. A secretary of state was common in other nations. Washington wanted Thomas Jefferson appointed to that office; but he was still in France. The president would wait for him. He needed a secretary of war. General Henry Knox was his man. He appointed the six members to the Supreme Court of the nation. These men were to hold office for the rest of their lives. John Jay was appointed as chief justice. The decision of how the department of the treasury was to run, however, was not up to George Washington, but belonged to Congress, who debated and wrangled as the months went by.

HAMILTON's old friend, Elias Boudinot from New Jersey, had opened the subject on 19 May. He proposed that "an officer be established for the management of the finances of the United States." He further suggested that his duties be specified along lines entirely acceptable to HAMILTON: in addition to superintending the national treasury and finances, he would "examine the public debts and engagements, inspect the collection and expenditure of the revenue, and form and digest plans" that would be submitted directly to the

House. James Madison quickly stated that the executive department had three departments: state, war, and the treasury. Since the state and war departments had only one man appointed to head them, so it should be with the treasury. All should have only a single secretary in charge. Then the debates and committee meetings went on with checks and balances for the protection of the nation by allowing auditors, defining which house was to nominate, which to confirm the presidential appointments, and so forth. The bill finally passed the house in late June. It was now the senate's turn to make their additions and subtractions. Differences were reconciled. The bill reached the president on 2 September and he signed it into law.

Nine days after he signed the bill, Washington sent HAMILTON's nomination as secretary of the treasury to the senate for confirmation, along with nominations for comptroller, Nicholas Eveleigh; for treasurer, Samuel Meredith; for auditor, Oliver Wolcott Jr., and for register, Joseph Nourse. The senate confirmed them the same day, on Friday, 11 Sep 1789. A very happy HAMILTON accepted and was at work the beginning of the next week.

The challenge was awesome. To establish the credibility of the new nation, he must persuade the investors, present and prospective, that the United States had both the determination to honor its obligations and the wherewithal for doing so. The ability of the nation to borrow money after the revolution was very near zero on the international as well as the national level. No one trusted them. Then, secondly, he must convince the people or their representatives that the wolf was at the door and the time had come to pay their way. It would also be very nice if he could do this and keep everybody happy and content—no insurrections, or mutinies, just a union of hardworking, diligent people, who honored their debts. It was not an easy task.

Once more, HAMILTON had three objectives. The first was to establish a sinking fund. This was to be the cash that he would use to pay the interest and later the principal on the debt, as well as meet the current needs of the country. To an individual, this could be likened to cash in the bank. As the debt was paid it would become smaller, sinking slowly as the need became less and the debt was lowered. Of course, revenues from taxes and duties would be placed in it. Currently, these were not sufficient to keep it from sinking out of sight. He would need to fund it through congress and then raise the needed revenues to sustain it, keeping the expenditures of the nation at a bare minimum.

His second objective was to capitalize the national debt. The nation had war debts of over $10 million in loans from the French, Dutch, and Spanish. At the end of 1789, the United States was $1.6 million in arrears for interest payments and nearly $1.4 million behind on their scheduled repayments of principal with an additional $464,000 falling due each year. To establish the credit of the United States, congress must act quickly and decisively. He pointed out that public credit was normally earned "by good faith, by a punctual performance of contracts. States, like individuals, who observe their engagements, are respected and trusted: while the reverse is the fate of those, who pursue an opposite conduct." Ordinarily this type of credit took years to establish. HAMILTON, with the help of congress, planned to have it immediately.

The domestic debt was another thing. It was over $40 million. In the past, congress had raised funds in several ways. It had issued unsecured paper money, by issuing bonds called loan office certificates, and by issuing promissary notes for paying and sustaining the army. The paper money had a face value of more than $200 million; but it bore no interest and had depreciated to practically nothing. The official devaluation was 40 to 1. Of the army-related debt, about $16 million was outstanding in 1789, with another $13 million in interest due. In setting up his national accounting method and double entry books, HAMILTON realized that for every liability (debt), there must be a second entry or asset—the higher the debt, the greater the asset. They certainly had the debts; but what were the offsetting assets of the nation? The United States had land, which they had fought for and won—real estate. They had people who would work and produce and pay off this debt—income. Furthermore, they had ALEXANDER HAMILTON, who with all his honor and organizational genius, would see that they did it. These items were not cash, but an intangible faith in the future income of our nation. By capitalizing the paper at its face value, HAMILTON gained assets in addition to those that were still owed to the people, for much of the paper had been previously paid for. This created a nation with a positive net worth, which established a good credit rating.

Congress was quick to act on these two objectives and the international financiers bought it. He was able, then, to refinance the foreign loans by borrowing from the Dutch with lower interest and longer repayment terms and then using this borrowed money to pay off the French debt. Afterwards, he would borrow from the French and pay off the Spanish, negotiate a new loan with the Spanish to pay off the old higher interest Dutch loans, and so it went. It was not necessarily in this order. The foreign debt was his first priority and their terms were met with implicit punctuality.

However, in the capitalization of the domestic debt with the advantage it gave to the national credit, there was a domestic problem that was difficult to reconcile. HAMILTON's reorganization required that these fiscal instruments would, at first, not be redeemable for cash, but that interest only would be paid on them until the nation had sufficient cash to redeem them at full value. He had wanted the interest at 6 percent on all of them, but Congress designated various types at 3, 5, and 6 percent. The individual servicemen or suppliers to whom these original papers or notes were issued had commonly sold them to someone else for less (in some cases only a small fraction) of their face value, which was the amount the United States was now recognizing and paying the interest on. Those who held these papers and notes were delighted for they had considered them before as practically worthless; but the poorer people who had sold them for less in order to just survive, felt cheated out of the difference that was gained by the new purchasers, who obviously were wealthy enough to pay them the price they had already received.

It might be added, that when HAMILTON was made secretary of the treasury, (and even in anticipation, although he had been very closed mouthed about what he planned to do,) many of those who were able tried to buy up these papers from the less informed, especially in the frontier locations, where their value was far from obvious or even understood.

HAMILTON, although regretting that the profits could not go to the original holders, stood firm in his position that to indulge in any entitlement scheme would destroy the international credit, as well as indulge in the everlasting and entangled problem of subsidizing and trying to balance or interfere in the lives of the individual citizens by taxing one group to give to another. Government could be too controlling in a free nation. But as the nation prospered in those early days, resentments and jealousies abounded. These feelings would be played upon by HAMILTON's enemies, who were increasing, and who already knew how to exploit even unavoidable situations to enhance their own personal glorification and power structure in the eyes of the people by the use of the press and hearsay.

One way that Congress was able to help the veterans and less fortunate individuals was with land grants and/or a chance to purchase western lands at a very reasonable price—the Homestead Act for example, which would not be enacted until later.

HAMILTON's third objective was the national assumption of the debts of the various states. He planned to capitalize these, just like he had the national debt, thus increasing the net worth of the nation to an even higher figure. Some states had been very penny-wise and had paid most, if not all, of their debts. Other states had not worried very much about them; this included most of the larger states. The "assumption" action by the U. S. Congress required the consent of each state after their final approval. The frugal states resented the spendthrift states, which could get rid of their debts so easily, and the spendthrift states hesitated to give their debts to the federal government because they felt that in assuming their debts, the state was losing control of something. What it was, many were not sure; but if HAMILTON wanted the debt that was probably reason enough to oppose the bill.

In the end, they all consented, but Virginia and their nearby states held out until they were able to amend the bill by placing the future site of the national capitol buildings on the banks of the Potomac River. It would be a separate district, bordering both Maryland and Virginia. At that time it was located in New York City, which they felt already had too much power. Pennsylvania insisted that it be moved, as soon as possible, to Philadelphia, where it remained for the next ten years. During this time, the isolated uninhabited swamp and forest area of Washington, D.C., was built into a community large enough to house a national government.

As it turned out, President Thomas Jefferson was the first to occupy the partially finished White House in 1800. At that time, the Capitol building was still lacking its dome and the rotunda beneath. There were no sidewalks, lots of muddy roads and very little housing for the elected, the appointed, and all their staffs. They left their more pleasant homes and communities for the not so great housing of the Capital to participate in the difficult but tantalizing and powerful activity of government. Their wives and children either stayed in their comfortable homes in the various states or tried with difficulty to find proper housing, schools, markets, and entertainment. The ambassadors from the various countries were not impressed with their accommodations, either—especially the British Ambassador and his wife, who were deliberately shunned and mortified by President Jefferson.

ALEXANDER AND ELIZABETH SCHUYLER HAMILTON
SCULPTOR BY GAETANO FEDERICI 1880 -1964

These busts were made sometime between 1930-36 along with a tall full-sized statue of ALEXANDER HAMILTON which stands on a high pedestal overlooking the Passaic Falls and the first mill in our nation to be established for manufacturing to begin in our new nation. HAMILTON brought George Washington with him and together they choose this first location. Those who worked in this manufacturing mill established the city of Paterson, New Jersey. Among other cloth, they brought the first silk manufacturing into America, which was quite successful. This Historical Site is missed by most tourists. The Hamilton Club Building to preserve his heritage is located near the statue.

THE GREAT FALLS OF THE PASSAIC RIVER

[Note: Higher, and a few miles north of this location is the city of Hawthorne, New Jersey, where one of my sons and his family presently live.]

98

DIVISION, FACTIONS AND WORD DUELS

When Thomas Jefferson had left Monticello, planning to go to Paris, France, as a commissioner to help with the peace treaty in December, 1782, the journey was first delayed and later totally aborted. The high seas had become dangerous with national piracy, and a previously sent agent had been captured and placed in the Tower of London. It would not be until the middle of 1784, after the treaty had been signed, that Jefferson would join Benjamin Franklin and John Adams in France. He would remain in France five years. Prior to his French appointment, he served as a member of the Virginia delegation to the continental congress, which had soon changed their location from Princeton, New Jersey, to Annapolis, Maryland. Jefferson was appointed as chairman of the committee on ratification of the peace treaty, and was in congress when George Washington arrived and gave congress his resignation and expense account as commander in chief of the United States army, after the British had evacuated New York City, in December 1783.

As Jefferson revised his book, *Notes on Virginia*, he warned,

"It can never be too often repeated that the time for fixing every essential right on a legal basis is while our rulers are honest and ourselves united. From the conclusion of this war, we shall be going downhill."

Congress was almost as fatiguing for Jefferson as being the governor of Virginia had been. The delegates were slow to arrive, and the lack of quorums was often frustrating. Although a lawyer himself, he wrote, that congressional time-wasting was inevitable so long as people sent lawyers,

"whose trade it is to question everything, yield nothing and talk by the hour."

As the year 1784 opened, the peace treaty still needed to be ratified, and there were only two months left for its lawful ratification. It was 14 January before the necessary representation from two additional states arrived to make a quorum of nine states, which was the number needed to ratify the treaty. This, they promptly did.

In these two final years as a lawmaker, Jefferson became head of the key committees and wrote 31 major reports and documents that strengthened and stabilized the American confederation. He proposed the world's first decimal system based on the dollar to make money exchange easier and established the coinage of pennies, dimes, dollars, ten dollars, and so forth. The system was adopted by congress in 1785. He worked hard on plans to expand the government to include the western territory, and proposed the future orderly formation of fourteen new western states——this was highly debated then, as well as later, for it created votes in congress that would dilute the power of the original thirteen states.

He wrote and attempted to pass the Ordinance of 1784, which was hotly debated. It read,

> "That after the year 1800 of the Christian era, there shall be neither slavery nor involuntary servitude."

The north was with him. He needed seven votes to pass it. On 19 Apr 1784, the vote was taken. Unfortunately, John Beatty of New Jersey had a cold, and was not present. All his southern state friends deserted him, leaving only six favorable votes. Jefferson was disgusted, and later wrote:

> "South Carolina, Maryland, and! Virginia! voted against it."

To the French historian, he penned:

> "The voice of a single individual would have prevented this abominable crime from spreading itself over the new country. Thus we see the fate of millions unborn hanging on the tongue of one man, and Heaven was silent in that awful moment!"

Two weeks later, word arrived that John Jay was resigning as one of the American ministers in France, so Jefferson, who was disgusted with congress, claimed the post. On 7 May 1784, congress appointed him to join Franklin and Adams to negotiate treaties of amity and commerce with sixteen European states as well as the Barbary powers to carry out a policy formulated by Jefferson himself. Four days later, he left congress and hurried back to Monticello to pack. He took his oldest daughter, Patsy, and his favorite servant, James Hemings, with him.

Then he headed north. He wanted to embark from Boston, saying,

"I mean to go through the Eastern states in hopes of deriving some knowledge of them from actual inspection and inquiry."

Virginia and congress had always been his home. He had never been in two-thirds of the thirteen states. A year later, he described the differences he found in the northern and southern people:

"In the North they are cool, sober, laborious, persevering, independent, jealous of their own liberties, and just to those of others, interested, chicaning, superstitious and hypocritical in their religion.

"In the South they are fiery, voluptuary, indolent, unsteady, independent, zealous for their own liberties, but trample others, generous, candid, without attachment or pretentions to any religion but that of the heart."

He was to say that Pennsylvania, because of its temperate climate, had formed

"a people free from the extremes both of vice and virtue."

This tall, redheaded American and his young daughter traveled from Le Havre to Paris in his best Monticello-made phaeton. They were admired by the French, while they, in turn, were overwhelmed with the beauties of the countryside as well as the ancient and more modern castles and palaces of this nation, where civilization was reaching its peak of opulence and poverty. During the next five years, Jefferson would come to know the caprices of Queen Marie Antoinette at her gaming table and the French nobility, who were very interested in this new writer and musician from America.

After the toast of Paris, Benjamin Franklin, was called back to America about a year later (where he helped with the formation of the constitution), and John Adams was sent to represent the Americans in London, Jefferson remained the only American minister in Europe. He grew to love France and its people and gave much advice to Lafayette as he strove to make it into a republic. Jefferson was to work on trade treaties and loans with most the nations of

Europe, including Sweden, Denmark, Portugal, and Austria. He came in contact with agents that were planning a revolution in Brazil against Portugal. He secretly wrote John Jay, encouraging U. S. support—a forerunner of the Monroe Doctrine. He was able to gain a naval confederation against the Barbary pirates with Russia and Portugal.

In March 1786, John Adams urgently sent for Jefferson to come to London, where they were secretly to negotiate commercial terms with Tripoli. Later, Jefferson journeyed throughout France and even went secretly into Italy, where he illegally obtained some of their top quality rice plants. He hoped to start the variety in Virginia. He became fascinated with the olive tree. On his journey, he was greatly interested in the French grapes and wine production.

On 10 Jun 1787, he drove into Paris after an absence of 104 days, reporting that he had "never passed three and a half months more delightfully."

When news came to Jefferson of Shays's Rebellion and their forced surrender in Massachusetts, he wrote to Abigail Adams that he hoped the Massachusett's government would pardon them:

> "The spirit of resistance to government is so valuable on certain occasions that I wish it to be always kept alive. It will often be exercised when wrong; but better so than not to be exercised at all. I like a little rebellion now and then. It is like a storm in the atmosphere."

When John Adams sent him a copy of the new Constitution that was to be ratified in the United States, he wrote back that there were

> "things in it which stagger all my dispositions to subscribe" to it. Then he continued, that "all the good" of the new frame of government "might have been couched in three or four new articles" added to the Articles of Confederation, a "good, old and venerable fabric."

To Washington, he wrote about his concern that he feared a trend away from civil liberties in America toward despotism could result from the unlimited number of presidential terms, and compared the president to a king. He further stated,

> "I was much an enemy to monarchy before I came to Europe. I am ten thousand times more so since I have seen what they are. There is scarcely an evil known in these countries which may not be traced to their king as its source, nor a good which is not derived from the small fibers of

republicanism among them."

In April 1788, his young, nine-year-old daughter Polly had finally arrived from Virginia, after Jefferson had struggled for three years to get her to Paris. Polly had stayed with her Aunt Eppes after her mother died, when she was only four years old. She didn't know her father, and was not desirous to go to France. Finally, upon the insistence of her father, she was smuggled aboard a ship, accompanied by the young thirteen-year-old servant, Sally Hemings, who played with her until she fell asleep and the ship was on its way. Sally (who was the daughter of his chef) was only a frightened child herself; but the ship's captain was kind to them and the two young girls arrived safely in London into the arms of Abigail Adams. Jefferson had pled that he was too busy to come and had sent his servant Petit to bring the unwilling child to Paris. Jefferson then placed her in the French convent school of Panthemont where his older daughter Patsy had been placed for her education. With her sister, she adjusted quickly, and the two daughters would spend their weekends with their father, bringing with them their classmate, KITTY CHURCH, the daughter of ANGELICA SCHUYLER CHURCH—the sister of ELIZABETH SCHUYLER HAMILTON.

In London, as the wife of an Englishman, ANGELICA had become a close friend of the lovely Maria Cosway, the wife of the English artist Richard Cosway, who was about twice her age and had been commissioned to do some artwork in Paris. Maria had been the close companion of the lonely Jefferson since mid-1786. She had returned to England when her husband's work in Paris was completed. Jefferson and Maria quietly exchanged letters. She renewed their acquaintance by personally returning to Paris, after he had returned from his European tour. Jefferson had kept the love letters, which were found by his children and grandchildren after his death.

As his older daughter Patsy matured, she began to think of joining the Catholic Church and becoming a nun. This was an awakening to Jefferson. He had always wanted Patsy to marry a Virginian. He quickly decided it was time for the family to return to Monticello, and requested six months' home leave; but events in Paris were rapidly changing. He would need to remain somewhat longer. This was in November of 1788.

STORMING OF THE BASTILE — DRAWN BY F. LIX

Secretly, he helped Lafayette prepare and establish the new French constitution, while maintaining American neutrality publicly. In July, when the French prison, the Bastille, was stormed by Lafayette's troops, Jefferson reported to John Jay, who had replaced John Adams in London when Adams was recalled to become vice president of the United States,

> "The people rushed forward and almost in an instant were in possession of a fortification of infinite strength. They took all the arms and discharged the prisoners, [they found only seven sick or insane inmates], and such of the garrison as were not killed in the first moment of fury, carried the governor and lieutenant governor to the Place de Greve (the place of public execution), cut off their heads and sent them through the city to the Palais Royal."

On 17 July, Jefferson stood on his balcony at the Hotel de Laneac on the Champ-Elysees as Lafayette rode out to Versailles at the head of his militia and then rode back, with his triumphant armed guards accompanying the royal carriage of Louis XVI

"through the streets of his capital" as a crowd of "about 60,000 citizens of all forms and conditions armed with the muskets of the Bastille and the Invalides [and] pistols, swords, pikes, pruning hooks, scythes, etc., lined the streets . . . . People in the streets, doors and windows saluted them everywhere with cries of 'vive la nation.'"

On the night of 4 Aug 1789, Jefferson, who was still maintaining his neutrality, reported to John Jay that the National Assembly "mowed down a whole legion of abuses—abolished all titles of rank, all abusive privileges of feudalism": titles, provincial privileges, "the feudal regimen generally."

On 26 August, Jefferson somewhat compromised his neutrality by giving in to the pleadings of Lafayette and eight other factional revolutionaries and hosted a dinner conference, when Lafayette claimed it

"as being the only means to prevent a total dissolution and a civil war . . . . These gentlemen wish to consult you and me . . . . I depend on you to receive us."

Jefferson wrote,

"The discussions began at the hour of four and continued till ten . . . . I was a silent witness to the coolness and candor of arguments . . . . The result was [the] concordats [which] decided the fate of the constitution." The next day, Jefferson hurried out to Versailles to explain "how it had happened that my house had been made the scene of conferences of such a character."

But Montmorin already knew everything that had happened. A worried Jefferson remained in bed the next six days with a very severe migraine headache, which he seemed to develop quite often when he was under great stress.

Jefferson and his family left Paris for England on 26 Sep 1789. While his ship waited on the English coast in mid-October to take him to America, he wrote to a friend in France, after reading the London paper, that the situation in France was "much worse than when I left you . . . . Heaven preserve your country and countrymen, whom I love with all my soul." He still expected to return to France, not knowing that on 13 October George Washington had written him from New York, asking him to become the first Secretary of State. The appointment awaited him in Virginia when he stepped off the ship.

Jefferson had been the strongest member of the confederation congress and had left America with disgust for the lack of support he had felt when his southern friends in congress refused to accept his bill that would have put an end to slavery and indentured servitude after the year 1800. America was then a nation where the rights of the states stood strongly against the interference of federal law, and the federal and state debts were almost insurmountable. It was a nation that could have easily fallen apart into separate states or factions. Five years later he returned to a totally different federal government with a new constitution, regulated debts and sufficient power to collect their revenues and control rebellions. He found a president who was loved and supported by the people. He found ALEXANDER HAMILTON as the strong leader of the Federalists, who dominated the congressional seats. If Mr. HAMILTON was not greatly loved, he was greatly respected and admired by the people as the nation gained the unity of the state's commerce and the United States became a recognized international power with a strong credit-rating. Federal judges were being appointed throughout the nation—diluting state control of the judiciary.

He watched as the hospitable Washington enjoyed the social events and delighted in the attention he received from countrymen and foreign representatives. He resented HAMILTON, who was able to work with the Federalist congress and pass the bill that gave the nation a new United States National Bank in Philadelphia, and then he saw it spread into many states, giving financial credit to many who would not otherwise be able to grow through their own efforts. Manufacturing was beginning, especially in New England, where it was recognized that this was a way to survive as a state in a small territory. He watched the activities of the seaports in New York City and Philadelphia. They were busy. Merchants were growing in wealth, as was the United States with its numerous revenue agents and customs collectors.

As Secretary of State, which he felt should be the number two seat in the nation, he had around six people that reported to him; HAMILTON had over five hundred in his busy treasury department. Jefferson found it very difficult to work under George Washington, who was meticulous in his demand for constant reports and carefully read and criticized every one of them, as he pleased, not giving Jefferson the respect and admiration he had come to expect from his past accomplishments and much greater travel. Jefferson was jealous of HAMILTON who had known about Washington's procedures and had been able to avert most of this problem by insisting on a more definite description of his office operations before he accepted his appointment—legally working with congress and bypassing the president.

Jefferson had never been convinced that a federal government was right for America. He still longed and clung to his vision of his olden days in Virginia and the importance of state rights. He equated these rights with the rights of the people who were 95 percent agricultural and depended on the land. Jefferson felt that Washington and HAMILTON were becoming too powerful, too fast, and would soon push the nation into a monarchy. The nation still had a standing army, and money was being spent for a navy that could protect the merchant ships. Jefferson believed that his own knowledge as a statesman, in contrast to that of the two military men, who had constantly risked their lives for the nation for eight years, to be superior and more dedicated to the rights of men. He needed to turn the nation to his more pacifist's thinking.

HAMILTON became the major victim of his attack. Jefferson wanted to stop the National Banks. He wanted to stop any judiciary control in the states. He started rumors that HAMILTON had talked too incessantly and passed fiscal laws that Congress did not really understand. He resented the fact that HAMILTON was trying to convince the nation that trade agreements with Great Britain were more important to United States commerce than those agreements with the past French government, [which had disintegrated into anarchy—the reign of terror.] HAMILTON also wanted the nation to adhere to its signed peace agreement with the British and recognize the rights of the loyalists, hoping that in return the Britons would recognize their need to honor the treaty and evacuate the British forts along the Great Lakes, which they were still occupying and where they were still continuing to stir up the Indians into hostility against the settlers that were rapidly moving into the extended territory in the northwest (Ohio, Indiana, and Illinois, at that time).

His first move was to convince HAMILTON's friend, James Madison, that HAMILTON was a dangerous person with his eyes set on becoming a royal monarch. Madison had been Jefferson's student as a younger man and dearly loved him. In the choice between HAMILTON and Jefferson, he quickly stood by Jefferson, remembering the little things that HAMILTON had said at the

Constitutional Convention and HAMILTON's evident belief that the English people could now be trusted more than the riotous French republic. Madison thrilled to the story of the French Republic and Lafayette's part in trying to establish it. He trusted Jefferson's assessment of that most-favored nation and his mentor's belief in its eventual triumph. With Madison on his side, Jefferson located two or three other loyal friends in the legislature who would stand by him with their speeches, votes, and silent acceptance of his seditious leadership. James Monroe, another of his former students, was especially vituperative. Jefferson called his group the Republicans.

Washington was often the final vote in his regular cabinet meetings. Henry Knox, the Secretary of Defense, stood solidly behind HAMILTON. Jefferson opposed HAMILTON almost invariably whatever the issue. Jefferson usually got the support of his close relative, Attorney General Edmund Randolph. Washington, although always conciliatory, usually accepted HAMILTON's position. He had fought literally the vindictiveness of congress and their incompetence to properly fund his army (with HAMILTON at his side), and he was not willing to see his nation destroyed, or retrograded into debt and anarchy.

HAMILTON at times could rightfully be accused of being high-handed, but he never stooped to underhanded methods. When Jefferson was absent from his desk for two months taking a trip into New England with James Madison—[This junket is believed to be a political attempt to extend the Republican Party into the northern states.]—HAMILTON was drawn into diplomatic conversations with Major George Beckwith, a confidential agent to the Governor of Canada, Lord Dorchester, whom in turn would report to the British cabinet in London. HAMILTON repeatedly claimed that the conversations were informal and totally noncommittal, that they had come about only because of Jefferson's absence from his desk, and that his informal talks were basically related to trade relations with England, which HAMILTON had favored for many years. It was not until 1795 that the Jay Treaty was passed. No harm had been done in anyway to either country. However, by speaking with Beckwith, Jefferson felt that HAMILTON had stepped into his state department territory. Jefferson's absence and unwillingness to work in what HAMILTON considered a sensible way with the British had brought the agent to HAMILTON's door. But Jefferson made the most of it and extended his character assassination of HAMILTON to include conversing with a British spy.

One of HAMILTON's problems in combating Jefferson was the time factor. His duties in the Treasury, with all the extensions that he was working on, were so immense that he didn't have time to dwell on the destructive forces that were building up against him. In contrast, Jefferson had the time, ideology, and determination. HAMILTON was not a theorist. He believed in an ever changing daily world of practical work and survival with its many challenges.

HAMILTON's old enemies in New York were ever active. General PHILIP SCHUYLER had been elected to the U. S. Senate in 1789, along with Rufus King in New York. There was a long term and a short term. They drew for the two positions. SCHUYLER drew the short term. This one ended 17 Mar 1791. Robert Troup wrote HAMILTON from Albany after the next disappointing election.

> "About an hour ago the election of Senator was brought on in the Assembly. Burr suceeded by a decided majority. He has a decided Majority also in the Senate. The thing therefore may be considered as settled. The twistings, combinations, and maneuvers to accomplish this object are incredible .... The Chancellor [ROBERT R. LIVINGSTON] is singularly happy. We are going headlong into the bitterest opposition to the Genl Government."

A few hours later William Duer supplied additional information:

> "Mr. Burr was this day elected by both houses, to succeed General SCHUYLER, by a large majority in the Senate, and of five in the House of Representatives [Assembly]. This is the fruit of the Chancellor's Coalition with the Governor [George Clinton] . . . . Our Political Situation, my Friend has a most Gloomy Aspect."

Another friend wrote,

> "Strange unions have been brought about by our artful perservering Chieftain [Gov. Clinton] . . . . Many who were Federalists sucked into his Excellencys Vortex, & the Chancellor's family become one of the principal satellites of this Noxious planet. Hence it is that a blessed accession of strength will be added to the Senate of the U States in the person of Col. A. Burr . . . . He is avowed your enemy, & stands pledged to his party, for a reign of vindictive declamation against your measures. The Chancellor hates, & would destroy you."

This change in the senate was the result of at least two things. <u>First</u>, George Washington and the Federalists had ignored Chancellor LIVINGSTON in assigning their patronage positions. John Jay had been made Chief Justice; Rufus King, Senator; and Gouverneur Morris, diplomat in London. <u>Second,</u> Aaron Burr was quick to see the opportunity and persuaded Governor Clinton to name LIVINGSTON's brother-in-law, MORGAN LEWIS as the Attorney General of New York, which brought the LIVINGSTON power to the anti-Federalist camp. Some believe that Burr's hatred and animosity to HAMILTON's programs in the Senate added to the antagonism of Jefferson and Madison. But maybe it was the other way. Maybe they were the original plotters with Burr and LIVINGSTON on their junket tour into New England and had secretly brought about SCHUYLER's defeat, ending his strong support of HAMILTON in the Senate.

Burr, it is said, had more talent than principles. His selfish ambition was manipulative. He gave allegiance to no one but himself and his mature daughter, Theodosia, whom he adored. In his letters to her, he constantly gave her advice and added loving descriptions of his many female conquests as a bachelor when he traveled to the various cities. Burr came from affluent parentage and had been a classmate of HAMILTON's at King's College [Columbia], when they were young men. He had accompanied Benedict Arnold on his journey to conquer Quebec, and had advanced to the office of Colonel in the Revolutionary War, leading his men valiantly at the Battle of Monmouth Court House in New Jersey. He became a lawyer in New York City after the war, and sometimes joined HAMILTON in legal cases. On the surface they were friends, often attending in apparent congeniality the same social functions. This challenge in the Senate was his first overt act against HAMILTON, although the jealousy or hatred may have begun earlier. Something had happened to bring about the statement,

"He is avowed your enemy."

In 1791, Jefferson and Madison set up their propaganda machine. Most of the newspapers in the country favored the administration. Madison sought out his old college friend Philip Freneau, who had been working as a journalist the past few years. He was quite notorious for his venomous writings. Madison played on his hatred of the British and their king. He described how the monarchists were secretly trying to take over the federal government. Jefferson and Madison arranged financial backing for the newspaper and pledged that they would find subscribers. In addition to these private arrangements, Freneau would be hired as a translator in the State Department, a job that would require very little time and still furnish him with a modest income. It would also give him a contact with Jefferson, who wanted to remain anonymous.

Secondly, they would support a measure in the post office department to allow a cheap rate for newspapers—very necessary for wide distribution throughout the country. (The act they got through congress established a rate of 1 cent for a distance up to 100 miles and 1 ½ cents for further distances. It had been 6 cents for letters up to 30 miles and 12 ½ to 30 cents for longer distances.) He was to praise the administration moderately and be fair-minded in his reporting for the first three months of operation to build the confidence of the people; but he could attack the American judiciary for cases involving suits between British and American debtors, and other similar cases that would be popular with the people. Madison gave him a series of unsigned political editorials of a rather neutral nature to get him started. The *National Gazette* began operation in October 1791. The unsigned editorials of the *Virginians* soon changed their color.

And abruptly everything changed. Jefferson was the "Illustrious Patriot" and "Colossus of Liberty" who stood almost alone in defending America against HAMILTON's cabal. Freneau's paper would repeat and build upon the theme that HAMILTON aspired to establish a monarchy, aristocracy, plutocracy, and corruption in America. He had built a system that had put the public wealth in the hands of the rich "foreign and domestic speculators." The paper was having an effect. Madison's personal bills passed the legislature 3/4s of the time, and although the Republicans still lacked the power to pass their major issues, the Federalist's power was being carefully eaten away.

HAMILTON, at first, refused to accept the warnings of his friends that Jefferson and Madison were his enemies, until their actions between March and May of 1792 made it impossible to deny. It is beyond the scope of this book to give the details; but his friend William Duer, who had been the assistant secretary of the treasury for the first six months, had become seriously indebted to every possible friend or entity that would loan him speculative money in an effort to establish what was called the Million Bank with some subsidiaries. He had as his associate and relation-by-marriage WALTER LIVINGSTON, who belonged to the manor PHILIP LIVINGSTON side of the family nearer to Albany. This side of the LIVINGSTON family had split from the ROBERT R. side of the family when the chancellor had appropriated some of their land and placed a watermill on it. The fierce enmity between them had not improved with ROBERT R.'s switch to the Clintonians.

Apparently JOHN R. BROCKHOLST and EDWARD LIVINGSTON were short sellers contracted to deliver most of the New York bank stock that the Duer syndicate had contracted to buy, and they attempted to weaken the bank and dry up Duer's credit, draining the bank of as much of its specie reserves as possible. HAMILTON gave his support and advice to the New York bank and other banks that were indirectly involved, and thus they were in good condition when Duer's syndicate collapsed.

Duer wanted HAMILTON's help, which was sympathetically refused. Duer was a ruined man, besieged by angry mobs of creditors. With his credit gone, he couldn't negotiate new terms, and on 23 March he was imprisoned for his debts. WALTER LIVINGSTON fled the city, after transferring all his tangible property to his brothers as protection against foreclosure on the $160,000 in notes he had endorsed for Duer. A few of Duer's associates absconded with funds; but most stayed and were ruined.

HAMILTON was deliberate and methodical in his effort to protect public credit and the banking system. He made no effort to protect the speculators. He said,

"Tis time there should be a line of separation between honest Men & knaves."

He employed all parts of his authorized authority to stabilize the whole. Then he was confronted with a dangerous obstacle. Jefferson had watched with delight the whole affair, and had irresponsibly told everything, with an extra spin, to his cohort Freneau, who exaggerated the story additionally in his newspaper. It was quite widely known that the panic in New York would climax on 15 April, the day that Alexander Macomb, another partner in the Million Bank, had a half-million dollars in security purchases falling due, which most everyone felt he could not pay. HAMILTON felt it was imperative to prepare the sinking fund to be ready to stabilize the bank. Jefferson, however, maliciously connived with Attorney General Edmund Randolph to tie up the sinking fund with a legal technicality. HAMILTON had John Adams on his side—the swing vote was John Jay's, who was absent, but had left a letter expressing his authorization to use the fund. Jefferson strongly objected to the letter; but Randolph broke under the pressure and the funds were released barely in time. Macomb soon joined Duer in debtor's prison, and the sinking fund was carefully used to control the crisis.

When it was over, HAMILTON sold his last 1 ½ shares of Bank of New York stock at the lower price and added to it the dividends it had accumulated; he gave the proceeds to his friend of the revolution, Baron von Steuben, to pay an old court judgment against him (unrelated to the Duer or Macomb problems.) HAMILTON told manager Seton he did not want to be involved in an institution he had aided in the public interest.

Earlier, in 1792, while all of this was happening, on 8 March, Madison with his other Republican congressmen attempted to force HAMILTON to resign by opposing his normal request for additional supplies for the year. HAMILTON's "overthrow was anticipated as certain and Mr. Madison, laying aside his wonted caution, boldly led his troops as he imagined to a certain victory." The vote was a hard blow to Madison. HAMILTON's friends had rallied. The vindictive Madison lost his victory by a four-vote margin.

Madisonians continued their attack on HAMILTON whenever and however they could. As the session ended in May and many of HAMILTON's friends had gone home, Madison moved that in the future all sinking fund purchases be made at the lowest possible market price, thus insinuating that HAMILTON had been padding the pockets of his friends in his purchases, giving them ammunition for their next session. With the legislature closed and an election approaching, the Republicans marked their objectives. Increased representation in congress was probably top on their list of objectives; close behind this objective, they wanted to replace Vice-President John Adams with George Clinton. George Washington had not yet consented to seek a second term. If he were to refuse, Clinton would then be in line for president.

When Madison's attempt to force the resignation of HAMILTON in congress failed, Jefferson took on the task of turning President Washington against him. It was late in May. He had allowed three months of adulterated slander and sedition from Freneau's newspaper to take its effect. The bank crisis was near its peak. Jefferson wrote a long letter to Washington. His first charge was fraudulent bookkeeping to pad the public debt. The interest rate was too high; creating an enormous tax burden, which "will produce evasion and war on our citizens to collect it."

HAMILTON had made the debt attractive to foreigners, which would drain the nation of hard money for the payment of interest. He complained about the banks, which

> "nourishes in our citizens habits of vice and idleness, instead of industry and morality." Most importantly, they provided means for corrupting the legislature . . . "to prepare the way for a change from the present republican form of government to that of a monarchy."

He then accused HAMILTON of this sinister conspiracy. But, there was one hope, with the Republicans controlling congress, the

> "worst of the evils could be undone." That failing, the result would be the secession of the South, for "the division of sentiment and interest happens unfortunately to be so geographical." HAMILTON's monarchists and paper men being concentrated in the North, pure republicans in the South.

Horror of horrors! Six weeks later Washington had not destroyed HAMILTON. Jefferson decided it was time for a personal verbal confrontation, while Washington was in Philadelphia. He then repeated his charges, adding some fantastic embellishments. Washington was not impressed. The charges of a monarchy he thought to be nonsense and dangerous, and he chided those who repeated them. He had seen the financial distress of the nation and had marveled at HAMILTON's ability to turn it around. If anybody was encouraging monarchy, he told Jefferson, it was such irresponsible newspapermen as Freneau who

> "seemed to have in view the exciting opposition to the government," and actually fomented resistance to the excise law in Pennsylvania. He declared that the irresponsible charges of Freneau and his ilk (unaware of Jefferson's

and Madison's connection) "tended to produce a separation of the Union
. . . and that whatever tended to produce anarchy, tended, of course, to produce a resort to monarchical government." He added that "he considered
those papers as attacking him directly," for "in condemning the administration of the government, they condemned him." Washington disagreed
with his thoughts on the north and south. He declared that "the people in
the eastern States were as steadily for republicanism as in the southern."
Having "seen and spoken with many people in Maryland and Virginia" on
his recent tour, "he found the people contented and happy."

When Washington returned to Mount Vernon, he wrote HAMILTON
about the various charges, not revealing their source; but stated that they came
from people who were unfriendly to the national government, such as "my neighbour, & quondom friend," the militant anti-federalist George Mason. He listed
the charges under 21 headings, each of them taken verbatim from Jefferson's letter of 23 May. Clearly, he was asking for more ammunition to quiet these rebel
accusations, when he encountered them. He signed his letter "with affectionate
regard"—a sentiment that was absent from his correspondence with Jefferson.

HAMILTON's reply was a document of 14,000 words. He began by apologizing for the "severity" of expression that appears "here and there." He had not
"fortitude enough always to hear with calmness, calumnies, which necessarily
include me, as a principal Agent in the measures censured."

But the letter was restrained and business like. Here are a few short quotes.

"It is a strange perversion of ideas, and as novel as it is extraordinary, that
men should be deemed corrupt & criminal for becoming proprietors in
the funds of their Country . . . . The only path to a subversion of the republican system of the Country, is, by flattering the prejudices of the people,
and exciting their jealousies and apprehensions, to throw affairs into confusion, and bring on civil commotion. Tired at length of anarchy, or want
of government, they may take shelter in the arms of monarchy for repose
and security. Those then, who resist a confirmation of public order, are the
true Artificers of monarchy . . . . No popular Government was ever without
its Catalines & its Caesars. These are its true enemies."

When HAMILTON finally realized that Jefferson and his formerly trusted
friend Madison were the real source of his character defamation, he wrote letters
to the newspapers under different pseudonyms to counter the vicious attacks

on his character (and the government). One of his chosen names was Amicus, who claimed he could speak about the secretary of treasury "from a long, intimate, and confidential acquaintance with him, added to some other means of information."

He wrote four chapters about Jefferson's recent past that cast doubts upon his loyalty to the national government. He revealed how Jefferson, as a minister in France, had proposed that the debt due that kingdom from the United States should be sold to individuals in Holland, so that when the confederation went bankrupt—as it then appeared on the verge of doing—the loss would fall upon private investors and no discredit would be suffered at the French court. (Congress had rebuked Jefferson for suggesting it.) He described Jefferson's dislike of the constitution and the methods he had used to stop its ratification. He told how Jefferson had obstructed all administration measures for restoring public credit and, in fact, nearly all measures that had not originated with himself. HAMILTON explained that it was in violation of public faith to attack them once they became national policy and contracts and commitments had been made on the basis of them. He revealed that Jefferson had been instrumental in the establishment of Freneau's newspaper as a party instrument, using government funds to vilify government itself and "to disturb the public peace, and corrupt the morals of the people." On the Reign of Terror, which was almost into its full flower in France, Jefferson was quoted as saying,

> "Rather than it should have failed, I would have seen half the earth desolated; were there but an Adam and Eve left in every country, and left free, it would be better than as it now is."

In one last attempt to convert George Washington to his own philosophies, on 1 October, after first meeting with Washington's now belligerent neighbor, George Mason, Jefferson paid a visit to the president at Mount Vernon. When Washington rejected every charge he made about HAMILTON's wickedness, a sulking Jefferson departed. He later claimed that Washington had grown senile. Shortly after, Freneau became more bold and implicated Washington in his smears, at times, as well as HAMILTON. The evening of 1 October, Jefferson wrote a letter to Madison complaining that the United States Bank, which was being proposed in Richmond, Virginia, was an "act of treason against the state, and whosoever shall do any act under co-lour of the authority of a foreign legislature [He considered the United States Congress a foreign legislature]—whether by signing notes, issuing or passing them, acting as director, cashier or in any other office relating to it shall be adjudged guilty of high treason & suffer death accordingly."

The animosity of the two secretaries grew harsher as the days went by. Peace between the two seemed futile. HAMILTON told the president that he would try to be cooperative, but unless the attacks on his person ended, Washington would have to choose between them. Jefferson made the choice for him when the president received his letter filled with self-justification and ending with his intention to resign at the end of Washington's first term. (But Jefferson stayed nine months into his second term.) Washington wanted harmony; but if that was impossible, he felt much more secure in running the department of state than he did the treasury department. He accepted Jefferson's resignation; but requested HAMILTON to remain, at least to the end of his term. He was very reluctant at that time to seek a second term.

In the fall elections of 1792, HAMILTON was greatly concerned about the vice presidency, especially when it appeared that the Republicans might support Aaron Burr, whom he considered very dangerous. When that threat subsided and George Clinton became their man, he wrote a few letters urging his friends to support John Adams, and then left the campaigning to others. Jefferson, at least in appearances, did the same. His followers, however, were very active and very organized. Washington was again elected president, unanimously, with John Adams as vice president, not unanimously; however, the next congress would have a Republican majority.

Knowing this, the Republicans became determined to do nothing in the lame-duck session but to harass HAMILTON and prevent any additional legislation that might benefit his department. Jefferson's destructive agenda (including splitting the treasury into two departments, abolishing the bank, repealing the excise tax, requiring the treasury to pay and accept only specie, and excluding "paper holders" from service in congress) was not passed either.

99

WASHINGTON'S SECOND TERM;
THE "WHISKEY BOYS"

In May of 1792, HAMILTON wrote a letter to Edward Carrington of Virginia in which he described why he believed Jefferson disagreed so strongly with him. He wrote that in France, Jefferson

> "saw government only on the side of its abuses. He drank deeply of the French Philosophy, in Religion, in Science, in politics. He came from France in the moment of a fermentation which he had had a share in exciting & in the passions . . . of which he shared both from temperament and situation." He came to America "electrified plus with attachment to France and with the project of knitting together the two Countries in the closest political bands." It made him suspicious of all governments that were not the most democratic and local. Jefferson and Madison "have been found among those who were disposed to narrow the Federal authority . . . subversive of the principles of good government and dangerous to the union peace and happiness of the Country."

As the vitriolic newspaper disputations settled down a little after the reelection of George Washington in the fall of 1792, Congress took up the gauntlet against HAMILTON. Jefferson and Madison devised resolutions, which were introduced into the House by Giles of Virginia, which required the investigation of HAMILTON's conduct in the Treasury. The intent was to drive him from office, as his foes believed that he could not possibly clear the charges in the time available—the resolutions were passed on 23 Jan 1793, and congress was to adjourn on 3 March.

They underestimated HAMILTON's abilities. By February 19th, he had submitted the last of seven reports, totaling some 60,000 words and a large mass of figures, which amounted to a financial history of the entire national government. While he prepared his extensive report, a special committee of fifteen with Giles as chairman investigated the treasury department and all their officials—including HAMILTON's personal finances. They had hoped to find some kind of dirt to exploit against him. HAMILTON had been meticulous in his record keeping. The disappointed committee found nothing.

The overconfident Jefferson had already drafted a series of resolutions condemning HAMILTON for many of the same things that he, through the *National Gazette*, had already publicly charged him with. After reading HAMILTON's reports and with his own investigation, Giles dropped several of the more extreme resolutions; but the remaining nine were submitted to the House on 28 February and 1 March. The votes were taken in a special evening session of the House on 1 March. Every resolution was rejected by a large margin, which included many Virginians who deserted the Republican cause. Only five members of the House, including Giles and James Madison, voted for every resolution.

Congratulations flowed into HAMILTON's office from New England, New York, New Jersey, and even the lower southern states. The Republican congressmen who had deserted Jefferson's cause, however, found that they were subjected to vicious campaigns when they returned home. Forgive and forget was not the agenda of the Republican Party—it was bent on the destruction of the banks, federal judges, and tax revenues, which they felt threatened the rights of the states, especially Virginia. They saw ALEXANDER HAMILTON as the only man strong enough to stop them—just as financier Robert Morris had told Washington that HAMILTON was the only man who could save the nation from financial destruction. HAMILTON himself had written his friend John Laurens that "mountains of prejudice must be leveled."

Washington, the great arbitrator, had suffered enough through his eight years of physical battle for the new nation and as chairman of the Constitutional Convention that he was relieved when Jefferson finally resigned as secretary of state and went home at the end of 1793. But Jefferson's beliefs ran deeper. Without official duties, he had more time to devote to his party of Republicans.

The term Democrat was used by their opponents first as a slur. Years later, it became the Democrat/Republican Party. It was the beginning of the Democrat

Party, and it forced the Federalists to recognize themselves as a party. The two-party system had begun, which Washington and many others had hoped would never come about. In general, the northern states stood behind the established Federalist Party, and the Republican Party, backed and usually controlled by Jefferson and Madison, was preferred by the southern states and their extended western states. In many ways, they were the precursors of the South's fight for "States Rights" in the impending Civil War.

The exception in the northern states was New York where the Livingston-Clintonians had joined with the Republicans to defeat PHILIP SCHUYLER in the Senate with Aaron Burr as their replacement. Robert Troup had written HAMILTON that Burr

> "is avowed your enemy, & stands pledged to his [Republican] party, for
> a reign of vindictive declamation against your measures. The Chancellor
> [ROBERT R. LIVINGSTON] hates, and would destroy you."

HAMILTON had wanted to retire from public service, also, and had trained his replacement; but foreign affairs were changing rapidly. On 20 Sep 1792, at the village of Valmy, a ragged army of 18,000 Frenchmen went up against the powerful Prussian army and forced them to retreat. The French held, and the next day their national convention proclaimed France a republic. In the following weeks this citizen's army pushed onward over the Austrian Netherlands. On 19 November the national convention issued a manifesto urging all the world's peoples to overthrow their rulers and promised their support. When Washington received the news, he was enthusiastic and stated

> "there was no nation on whom we could rely, at all times, but France; and
> that, if we did not prepare in time some support, in the event of rupture
> with Spain and England, we might be charged with a criminal negligence."

A delighted secretary of state, Thomas Jefferson, responded to Washington by stating that

> "was the very doctrine which had been my polar star, and I did not need
> the successes of the republican arms in France . . . to bring me to these
> sentiments."

HAMILTON saw it differently and felt it was a time to maintain a firm neutral position. He believed the new French Republic to be in a very unstable situation.

On 21 Jan 1793, the Republic of France beheaded their king, Louis XVI, and declared war additionally on England, Russia, and Holland. It was two months before Washington became aware of it in April 1793. Washington was highly concerned. He then saw the wisdom of HAMILTON's bid for neutrality. Jefferson, however, was not convinced. With some debate, Washington's cabinet decided to remain neutral and made a formal declaration of that nature, realizing that every year of peace would strengthen the new nation. They were not anxious to

DEATH OF LOUIS XVI IN THE PLACE DE LA CONCORDE
— DRAWN BY VIERGE

be engaged in another fighting war or in turning the Dutch or Spanish against them, who still had unpaid loans. The French were asking advances on the payment of their debt to help in their war effort. This brought up the question: if the Americans paid this debt by borrowing from the Dutch and if the French Republic lost the war and the monarchy was restored on the throne, would the French king refuse to recognize the payment that had been used against him by the French rebels and require a second repayment? Then there was the Spanish. What was Spain going to do? Spain and Britain had been close to war over their still remaining American possessions. Fearing the French, Spain soon joined with England. As HAMILTON had predicted, the French Republic had overstretched its reach. Disagreement among their ranks divided them as the revolution became more and more barbarous. Twenty thousand Frenchmen would be beheaded before the Reign of Terror ran its course.

Neutrality was declared by the cabinet, against the objections of Jefferson; but the Republican house challenged the right of the executive to declare it. HAMILTON upheld the executive position by reminding them that congress could act by declaring war; but the executive was under oath to maintain peace.

Still, when the new French minister Genet arrived from Europe, he landed at Charleston, South Carolina, and refused to recognize George Washington's administration and his neutral position. Genet set about converting southern merchant ships into privateers and arming them with cannon and ammunition. He personally commissioned the captains of these vessels and gave them the right to attack British merchant ships and claim the cargo for themselves. To claim neutrality, Washington needed to stop this, which he did—but only after several British ships had been plundered. American merchant ships were plundered in return, when England questioned the neutrality of the United States.

The unhappy secretary of state Jefferson secretly helped Genet, first by showing his own disrespect for President Washington's administration and the neutrality order, and then by covertly helping him with the funds to aid a French military mission into Spanish New Orleans. Genet was interested in claiming these Spanish lands for France. Part of Genet's mission involved stirring up the frontiersmen against the United States government by revolting against the whiskey taxes, claiming that the federal government was taxing them without any reciprocal benefits to themselves. Democrat/Republican groups were springing up as he moved along. Talk of secession with the help of the British was rumored in Kentucky—Spain as an alternative. The Indians were becoming more and more warlike as new settlers arrived. Violence and harassment of revenue agents seemed to follow Genet as he moved northward through the frontier.

To better realize how the French and Jeffersonians viewed these westerners east of the Mississippi, whom we often think of as solid hard-working pioneers, the Frenchman Crevecoeur described them at that time as "no better than carnivorous animals of a superior rank." Law was a stranger among them; clan and kin were all. They rarely worked, hard or otherwise; rather, like their Scotch-Irish ancestors, they provided for their necessities by maintaining herds of swine and cattle, which roamed wild in the woods and were rounded up and driven to eastern markets once a year. Far from being oppressed by government, they ignored it; they rarely paid taxes or paid for the land they inhabited; any official who attempted to enforce the law among them did so at his mortal peril. They distilled little if any whiskey as a "cash crop" to be sold in the east. Rather, they distilled it in prodigious quantities and drank almost all of it themselves.

[see *Alexander Hamilton, A Biography* by Forrest McDonald p. 297] This view, of course, was not the whole story; the majority were paying their taxes and upholding the law. However, this type of insurgency was in America as well as in France, and when it was aroused by cunning leaders, mobs formed and dirty deeds were done—not only to the revenue agents, but to those who diligently paid their taxes.

As events progressed in Europe, on 3 Aug 1793, the cabinet was able to agree that they should ask France to recall Genet as a French minister. HAMILTON wanted to demand it and suspend him; but Jefferson feared that France would be offended and Genet was allowed to continue his mischief while an anemic request was sent to Europe. To counter this, HAMILTON took up his pen once more in order to discredit Genet. The first of his nine essays, signed "No Jacobin," was published on 31 July, and it stunned the public when he announced that Genet had "threatened to appeal . . . to the People." In his following essays his readers became aware more and more of Genet's insulting attitude, his flouting of presidential authority and his overall subversive behavior.

But HAMILTON was not the only one who recognized the danger. Prior to his first essay, a group had met in Boston to support the neutrality of the nation with Stephen Higginson, a friend of HAMILTON, leading the gathering. This was followed with twenty more meetings throughout New England during the month of August. All of them adopted resolutions that supported neutrality and urged the vigorous punishment of violators. In New York, inspired by John Jay and Rufus King, a large public meeting and the chamber of commerce took a stand not only supporting neutrality but also condemning foreign diplomats' efforts to deal with the people of the nation rather than with the executive branch. Following New York's lead, meetings were held in New Jersey, Maryland, and Delaware.

In Richmond, Virginia, on 17 August, John Marshall organized a public meeting that caught the Republican leaders, Madison and Monroe, off-guard. They were visiting at Monroe's plantation when they heard the news, and immediately set about improvising a resolution that treated Genet's mischievous actions as minor indiscretions, and to denounce the anti-Genet resolutions as "active zeal displayed by persons . . . of known Monarchial principles." A last minute letter arrived from Jefferson warning them of the seriousness of Genet's activities. This cooled their ardor, and the Republicans lost the war of resolutions.

Rufus King wrote HAMILTON that

"It was never expected that the executive should sit with folded Arms, and that the Government should be carried on by Town Meetings, and those irregular measures, which disorganize the Society, destroy the . . . influence of regular Government, and render the [executive] . . . a mere pageant."

However, these town meetings did demonstrate the support of the people for the administration and their stand against a foreign threat. Genet was later recalled by the French; but remained quietly in America and with his smooth, polite European manners was accepted by many in American society. He didn't want to return to France—his French party had lost its power. He married a daughter of Governor George Clinton.

Toward the end of August, a new fever developed. This time it was physical and it hit Philadelphia with a vengeance. The yellow jack, or yellow fever, raged through Philadelphia killing over 5,000 inhabitants.

The first week of September, HAMILTON contracted it, and BETSY succumbed three days later. The HAMILTONs were very fortunate. His old boyhood friend, Dr. Edward Stevens, was in town and treated them. His method of treatment differed from that of the famous Dr. Benjamin Rush, who was considered to be the greatest physician of his time by most of the city's inhabitants. Rush felt that yellow fever could best be cured by a very minimal diet, purging the digestive system with harsh laxatives to prevent further infection and draining the infected blood with leaches. Most of his patients obviously died. HAMILTON's Doctor Stevens took a radical approach for that day. He believed the body needed food and water for survival, and he was opposed to draining the blood. His treatment was a full diet, cold baths, laudanum (opium), and cinchona bark (quinine). While they were surrounded by death, the HAMILTONs were cured in five days and were removed to the SCHUYLER home in Albany for recuperation. It was November before the secretary of treasury was able to resume his duties with his full strength.

While he had been gone, several changes occurred. Genet's recall had arrived from France; Freneau's *National Gazette* had closed its doors for lack of funding, and a disheartened Jefferson had decided that his effectiveness as secretary of state had ended and had again sent in his formal resignation to George Washington—effective on 31 Dec 1793. His nine-month overstay from his last resignation was to end. However, Jefferson left with a majority of his Democrat/Republicans in congress, who were still trying to destroy trade with Great Britain in favor of their glorious French. A war with the English was threatening and a new thorough investigation of HAMILTON was proposed by this body. A tired and impatient HAMILTON could not retire as he had planned. George Washington was also tired of the office of president and the rivalry he had found in the cabinet. He appointed the usually neutral Edmund Randolph to replace Jefferson, and increasingly relied on his advice—perhaps angry at HAMILTON's desire to retire.

In the crucial months to follow, the British war threat took precedence. On 13 Jan 1794, William Loughton Smith gave a powerful speech in congress proving that trade with Britain was far more advantageous than anything the French could offer, and that the Republican policy of commercial restrictions against them would severely damage the United States. Then news arrived that the British were making a truce with Portugal that allowed the Barbary Pirates to prey upon American merchant ships in the Atlantic and Caribbean. A special caucus was held with three senators, four representatives, HAMILTON and Knox. They believed that this was a ploy by the British to bring the Americans in line. More than 300 American vessels had been seized in the West Indies shipping in late December 1793.

The caucus proposed that six 44-gun frigates should be built and the resolutions were submitted to Congress. Madison protested, claiming it would be cheaper to bribe the pirates than to build a navy. Congressional members of the caucus championed HAMILTON's view that "in times of peril the nation must negotiate for peace but prepare for war."

HAMILTON tried to get Washington to declare his support; but Washington appeared to be more interested in Mount Vernon than the pirates or the British through the next few weeks. HAMILTON took the lead; he could not sit by in a national crisis. On 10 March, the House passed the bill authorizing the establishment of the six frigate navy—one of them was the U.S.S. Constitution that now sits in Boston harbor as an historical site. On 12 March, Connecticut's Oliver Ellsworth, a member of his caucus, met with Washington and suggested he appoint an envoy extraordinary to go to Great Britain to work out a peaceful solution to the problems between the two nations, suggesting ALEXANDER HAMILTON as the best appointee. Washington replied only that he doubted HAMILTON's suitability for he "did not possess the general confidence of the Country." Washington offered no alternative. Congress was paranoid of any action that could result in war and stood still on the issue.

Then, towards the end of March, news arrived at the capital that Lord Dorchester, the governor of Canada, after hearing of Genet's agents working among his French Canadians, had informed the Six Nation Indians that an Anglo-American war was imminent, and was inciting the Indians to join with them against their common enemy, the United States of America. Congress reacted by resolving to raise an army of 50,000 men and to place an embargo upon shipping—normally this was done just before a declaration of war.

The inflammatory defamation of HAMILTON was continuing in congress by its special investigation, and he was required at many daytime and evening committee meetings to defend his position nationally and personally. As difficult as the overall situation was, he could not afford to 'lose his cool.' War with Britain would destroy the Union, and undoubtedly dissolve the revenue system he had worked so hard to create and maintain. The Republicans in congress were in favor of measures that would bring on the war, while constantly opposing measures that promoted the defense of the nation. States were taking sides—mostly along Federalist and Republican Party lines, which meant northern states against Jefferson's southern and western states, with George Washington unwilling to commit either way. Controlling his personal feelings, HAMILTON sat down and wrote one of the most important letters of his lifetime.

The letter was to George Washington. It was long, detailed, and pleading. He hoped to arouse him to recognize the seriousness of his inactivity. The president must send an envoy to London, and HAMILTON withdrew himself as a possible candidate—urging that John Jay be appointed as the minister.

On 15 April, Jay was offered the position. He conferred with HAMILTON and taking the treaty HAMILTON had prepared for negotiations, accepted the mission. An international incident ground to a stop and the Jay Treaty, very similar to the one HAMILTON had sent with Jay, was signed in 1795 by both nations. His letter to the president had also cemented HAMILTON's relationship with George Washington, who was closer and more reciprocal than ever before. Washington usually took strong Federalist stands throughout the rest of his administration and relied heavily on HAMILTON's advice. After HAMILTON resigned at the end of 1794, Washington still sought his advice—some say even more.

In May 1794, HAMILTON was completely exonerated by the investigative committee in congress. The Virginian William Heth observed,

> "The more you probe, examine, & investigate HAMILTON's conduct; rely upon it, the greater he will appear."

Five days after the committee issued its report, HAMILTON withdrew his resignation, although he claimed he was "opposed by the strongest personal & family reasons." He could not leave until he could clear up the Indian and revenue situation that had developed on the frontier.

That spring in the Creek Indian lands of west Georgia, frontiersmen and speculators were encroaching upon Indian rights and talking of secession with the Spanish. Similarly in Kentucky, they felt that the United States needed to give them more protection from the hostile Indians, and they alternated in their choice of their secession between seeking protection either from the Spanish or the British. On HAMILTON's suggestion, the Georgia governor employed the state militia at the expense of the federal government to stop the secessionists. In Kentucky a presidential proclamation was given that forbade assembling for military expeditions unless it was authorized by law; then they organized a military enlistment for 2000 Kentucky volunteers to join with General Anthony Wayne in a campaign against the Indians in Ohio.

But the southwestern Pennsylvanians were a harder lot. Drastic action might have been averted if a group of office-hungry demagogues seeking election to the Pennsylvania legislature hadn't stirred up the voters, suggesting defiance against the whiskey excise tax in the areas where three new societies of the violent, militant left-wing Democrat/Republicans had just been organized. There were about three dozen of these societies in the nation that honestly believed

HAMILTON was the head of a monarchical and plutocratic conspiracy; that the purpose of his financial system was to crush the poor with taxes and give it to the rich, and that the excise tax was the tax of tyrants who would crush the people under military despotism—literally swallowing the rantings of Philip Freneau's newspaper and his successor, Benjamin Franklin Bache.

The fuse was lit in mid-July when the excise inspector, General John Neville, with federal Marshall David Lenox set out toward Mingo Creek, west of Pittsburgh—the location of the most violent of the Democratic/Republican societies—to serve notice on the settler's delinquencies. On 16 July, as the sun was beginning to show its face across the horizon, a mob of approximately forty men, many armed, made a quick attack on Neville's home. They were repulsed and one was killed. They brought in 500 additional men, while Neville brought in 17 soldiers to defend his house. There was an exchange of gunfire and one of the leaders of the insurgents was killed, while some of the soldiers were wounded. Vastly outnumbered, the soldiers surrendered. The rebels destroyed the house. Neville and Lenox fled the area.

Violent acts followed, with threats to oust all federal authority. A call went out to form a rebel army of 6,000 men to attack the government fort at Pittsburgh. About 6,000 men gathered and began their drills, while planning their march on the town. Armed mobs beat, tarred and feathered excise officers, forcing them to resign. They destroyed the distilleries and property of neighbors who insisted on paying their excise taxes. On 26 July they robbed the post rider of the mails. Unfortunately, the state and county officials, if they acted at all, supported the rebels.

Washington acted quickly. Under the militia act of 1792, the president was authorized to call out the militia only if a federal judge certified that laws of the United States were being opposed "by combinations too powerful to be suppressed by the ordinary course of judicial proceedings." The documented evidence was placed in the hands of Associate Justice James Wilson, who gave his certification on 4 August. Meanwhile, Washington had convened a cabinet meeting with top officers from Pennsylvania, who feared to act forcibly against their people.

Washington then asked his cabinet for alternate suggestions. His new

Attorney General, William Bradford, insisted upon armed intervention on the ground that "insurgency was high treason, a capital crime punishable by death." Secretary of State Randolph feared that such force would alienate the affections of the people at large, and recommended that further judicial proceedings be attempted first. HAMILTON perceived the situation as a threat to national security. He reminded them that the United States mail had been robbed and they also needed to get funds to General Wayne to pay their soldiers. He admonished them further to remember that if Jay's treaty failed, the nation could find itself at war with the British, which would also eliminate their import duties. He felt it was a dangerous precedent to allow internal resistance to lawful taxation. But there was a deeper matter at issue. HAMILTON asked the question,

> "Shall the majority govern or be governed? Shall the nation rule, or be ruled? Shall the general will prevail, or the will of factions?" He further stated that there were two forms of government, one of force and the other of laws. "The first is the definition of despotism—the last, of liberty. . . . Those, therefore who preach doctrines, or set examples, which undermine or subvert the authority of the laws, lead us from freedom to slavery; they incapacitate us for a GOVERNMENT of LAWS, and consequently prepare the way for one of force, for mankind MUST HAVE GOVERNMENT OF ONE SORT OR ANOTHER."

HAMILTON then proposed an action that he felt would preserve the laws: a display of force so powerful as to make the actual employment of force unnecessary. For this mobilization he wanted 12,000 militiamen—6,000 from Pennsylvania, and 2,000 each from New Jersey, Maryland, and Virginia. They would rendezvous six weeks hence, on 10 September. In the meantime, according to law, the president should issue a proclamation

> "commanding the Insurgents to disperse and return peaceably to their respective abodes within a limited time." Whether force would be employed would "depend on circumstances as they shall arise," but HAMILTON hoped and believed that the show of such imposing power would "deter from opposition, save the effusion of the blood of citizens, and secure the object to be accomplished."

Washington followed HAMILTON's suggestions, with one exception—he issued his proclamation on 7 August. Defense Secretary Knox followed the president's instructions and sent the proper letters to the four states to collect a militia of 12,950 men, after which he requested a leave of absence to attend to some land speculations in Maine. His request was granted, on the stipulation that HAMILTON would become the acting Secretary of War and make provisions for supplying the troops while he was gone.

This army would include our young, great-uncles of Hunterdon County, New Jersey: PHILIP COOLEY; JAMES LIPPINCOTT; and JOHN and ENOCH BARTON, who were part of the 2,000 New Jersey militia, as well as many distant cousins. Major General DANIEL MORGAN, of Virginia commanded the Virginia troops, leaving Wayne in his fight with the Ohio Indians as second in command. HAMILTON accompanied MORGAN's Virginians on the trek. He was needed to insure that all troops were paid for their services; to provide for the necessary equipment and supplies, and to be sure that his revenue agents were protected and given proper instructions. President George Washington personally took his place as commander in chief for three weeks, until he felt everything was in order. He then turned his command over to 38-year-old Governor Henry Lee of Virginia and went back to Philadelphia.

[Note: Governor Henry Lee is referred to usually throughout the Revolution as Light-Horse Henry Lee. He was born in Westmoreland County, Virginia, 29 Jan 1756. He graduated from the College of New Jersey in 1774; he became a captain in Colonel THEODORIC BLAND's legion of Virginia cavalry in 1775, and in 1777 joined with Washington's army in Pennsylvania. Many of his military accomplishments have been mentioned previously in the northern and southern battles of the war. He had four children by his first wife, Matilda Lee, who died in 1790. His second wife was Ann Hill Carter. They had six children, the last of whom was the Civil War general, Robert Edward Lee, born in Stratford, Westmoreland, Virginia on 19 Jan 1807. Robert E. Lee married Mary Anna Randolph Custis, who was the granddaughter of John Parke Custis, the adopted son of President George Washington.]

DANIEL MORGAN was promoted to Major General in December, 1793. He was particularly interested in this military campaign, because his daughter was the wife of Colonel Presley Neville, the son of the General Neville whose house had been attacked and burned. He had been erroneously informed that his daughter and their children "had fallen a sacrifice to the fury of the insurgents." Making his own plans for her rescue, he was relieved when a letter arrived from his son-in-law. Colonel Neville wrote,

"But to relieve your anxiety, I come immediately to the point, and inform you that Nancy and the children are well; that she behaved with resolution and dignity during the business; and indeed, evinced a fortitude and strength of nerves that I did not expect, especially as she had not been

very well .... She is safe at Pittsburg, respected by the people, and if necessary, will be protected by the military." Still, showing the great concern of
his fellow Pennsylvanians, the letter went on, "I yesterday received a letter from a gentleman in that country. He writes me that they have heard
you are to command the Virginians. It had also been mentioned that you
intended to go out and look after my family. He begged me, in the most
earnest terms, to prevent your going, as they would most assuredly insult
and even destroy you, and that it might put my family, who are now safe, in
a dangerous situation."

The enlistments throughout the four states were rapidly filled, even in
Pennsylvania. Some delay occurred when the guns and ammunition were slow
in arriving from New London, Connecticut. By late October the army was on its
way. Fifteen hundred more soldiers had been added—to be more convincing.
The rains poured down, as they tramped through the mountains. HAMILTON
opened all of Washington's letters, giving Governor Henry Lee any that per-
tained to the insurgence. The others were forwarded on to Washington along
with Hamilton's daily report of the journey.

Arriving near Pittsburgh, the New Jersey and Pennsylvania troops, composing the right wing of the army, were directed to take position with their left towards Budd's ferry and their right towards Greensburg. The Marylanders and
Virginians formed the left wing between the Monongahela and Youghiogany
rivers, with their left towards the Monongahela. This took a few days, and then
MORGAN with the light troops and cavalry advanced into Washington County,
accompanied by HAMILTON, the federal judges, and some who had been
forced to flee by the insurgents—including General Neville, Colonel Presley
Neville, and Major Kirkpatrick. The fearful people of Pittsburgh received them
with joy and were quick to point out and give assistance in arresting their neighbors who had made "themselves conspicuous in the recent outrageous proceedings." Twenty were arrested immediately and turned over to the judiciary. When
HAMILTON arrived two days later there were 150 prisoners; but many of the
leaders had escaped into the lands of the Mississippi River.

HAMILTON advised the judges to be lenient, forgiving taxes over a year old,
and gave them a generous amount for the whiskey he purchased for the troops.
Cash was very scarce on the frontier. Whiskey was about their only marketable

product. The Mississippi River, still controlled by the Spanish, imposed foreign duties that took the profits from most anything that could be shipped by water. Overland shipping was slow, expensive, and dangerous. Pittsburgh would become the coal, iron and steel center of the nation; but in 1794 they grew the corn and wheat and then distilled it into packages small enough to handle. The sale of whiskey gave them some cash, even after the revenue agents took their share. HAMILTON increased the federal agents in the area to at least one in every western county and auditors came more regularly.

The army size had squashed the rebellion without a battle, as hoped. HAMILTON's popularity increased throughout the nation along with Washington's. It was time for him to retire with honor. He sent in his resignation to be effective 31 Jan 1795. The confident president accepted it, as long as he would help the administration when it was needed, which he most assuredly did. He was constantly called upon by the new secretary of treasury. Defense Secretary Knox would call on him for advice. George Washington sought his counsel on most issues of importance, as did HAMILTON's friends in the Supreme Court and attorney general's office.

At the end of his second term, Washington asked HAMILTON to write his farewell speech, which HAMILTON did—knowing Washington's desires probably better than any other man. Of course, Washington read and corrected it, until it was to his liking; but the bulk of the wording of this famous document is HAMILTON's. When Washington had first planned to retire after only one term, he had asked James Madison to write his farewell speech. Washington had given that one to HAMILTON to revise; but HAMILTON used little, if any of it.

Washington's unwillingness to serve a third term was a surprise to those who had accused him of wanting to be a king. It was welcomed by those who wanted to replace him. John Adams, the vice president was considered the likely choice; but Thomas Jefferson, Aaron Burr and Thomas Pinckney had their own agendas, and a new political battle began.

[Note: The year 1790 is a bonanza for genealogists. This was the year of the first United States census, which listed by name the various heads-of-households throughout the nation. Unfortunately, the names of wives and children were not included and were mere numbers, as were slaves. But it still offers help in the location of families. From these records and the additional taxpayer and New Jersey militia records, we find that our fourth-great-grandfathers ELISHA BARTON and JOHN COOLEY were residents of Hunterdon County, New Jersey. The BARTONs were in the Amwell township and the COOLEYs were in the Alexandria township at that time. There were double weddings between the two families in the next two years. My third-great-grandparents JOHN BARTON and MARY COOLEY were married on 25 Sep 1791, and MARY's older brother PHILIP COOLEY, child number one, married MARGARET, the ninth child of the BARTONs on 7 Oct 1792.

PHILIP COOLEY is listed in the Hunterdon County militia of 1792. JAMES LIPPINCOTT is also listed as a member. He was probably a first cousin, as PHILIP's mother was ABIGAIL LIPPINCOTT (COOLEY). In the BARTON family, NOAH's two younger brothers, JOHN and ENOCH, were members of the militia and marched westward to stop the Whiskey Rebellion. Third-great-grandfather NOAH is listed as exempt—but no reason is given. His father, fourth-great-grandfather ELISHA BARTON was a Captain with the Pennsylvanians of the continental army when the Revolutionary War ended. According to area histories, he built a large colonial style house in the Amwell township of Hunterdon County, New Jersey. In the New Jersey taxpayer's lists, he is named in 1780, 1784, and 1786 as a taxpayer. In the 1789 list, he is shown as ELISHA BARTON & SON. His oldest son and first child HENRY BARTON died in June, 1786—the reason is still unknown to us. Third-great-grandfather NOAH BARTON was their sixth child, but second son. NOAH is listed in 1786 as a taxpayer and he was probably the "son" part of ELISHA BARTON & SON in the 1789 listing. Perhaps his usefulness in this capacity gave him an exemption from the militia in 1792. ELISHA and his Long Island Dutch-descendant wife, JEMINA VAN KIRK BARTON, remained in Hunterdon County and were buried there.

NOAH and his wife MARY COOLEY BARTON later moved with their children to Northumberland County, Pennsylvania, where they lived at Sunbury—a small town located at the junction of the western and northern branches of the Susquehanna River. The grandparents of John D. Rockefeller also moved to this valley. Many of JOHN COOLEY's family moved westward into the southwest counties of Pennsylvania, and expanded from there into the Ohio River valleys. These western settlers [and relations] spelled their name with a double L—COOLLEY. JOHN & ABIGAIL COOLEY had 12 children. ELISHA and JEMINA BARTON had 14 children. Many were daughters, which broadens the number of related surnames.

Many of the 1790 census records are missing, especially in the south. In North Carolina we can find ALEXANDER McKEE as a resident of Orange County, North Carolina. The IVEYs of Sussex County, Virginia, are in the census records, including JESSE, ADAM, HUGH and others; but many of the Virginia county records are nonexistent—perhaps burned or destroyed in some way during the wars. While searching the Salt Lake Genealogical and History Library, I discovered a small book with early Orange County, North Carolina deeds. A much larger Orange County then included Randolph and other counties. It had recently been divided from Granville County. An explanatory preface stated that these land records were buried before the British occupation of Hillsbourgh, Orange, North Carolina, with the hope of preserving them from destruction. Unfortunately, they had molded in the ground and only part of it was readable.]

100

SAMUEL MASON,
THE CAVE IN THE ROCK ROBBERS

Sometime after the Revolution and before the Louisiana Purchase, a bank was established in frontier southwestern Pennsylvania. Arriving from Virginia as one member of the bank management team was SAMUEL MASON. He was married and had six children when this story begins. MASON had been a Captain in the Revolutionary War, serving with the other Virginians. His father was THOMAS MASON of Norfolk, Virginia, and his grandfather was Captain GEORGE MASON of Norfolk, a legislative burgess at Williamsburg in 1705-6. The term captain in early Norfolk usually meant a sea captain. GEORGE was the eleventh child of LEMUEL MASON, (born about 1628), a gentleman of Lower Norfolk, whose father was my common ancestor FRANCIS MASON, who came to America on the ship *John and Francis* in 1613 from London, England, as a young man.

[Note: GEORGE MASON was not closely related to George Washington's neighbor George Mason, although both of their ancestors had arrived in Virginia in the early 1600s. My relationship to this family was a daughter of FRANCIS MASON named ELIZABETH, (born about 1630), whose granddaughter, ELIZABETH LANGLEY, married GEORGE IVEY. GEORGE IVEY inherited a second plantation on the Norfolk peninsula from his wife's grandmother upon her death, according to her will. FRANCIS MASON is a tenth-great-grandfather (13th generation).]

Well, SAMUEL MASON, the grandson of the captain and burgess, GEORGE MASON, was caught by one of HAMILTON's national auditors embezzling funds from the bank in Pennsylvania. He was tried by the judge and sentenced to be hung. Somehow he was able to escape and fled westward to the Ohio River. Finding a suitable cave and other companions of depraved character, he organized the group known first as the Cave in the Rock robbers on the Ohio River. They would lure boatmen to their supposed general store, and perhaps kill them, claiming all the booty as well as the boat, which they took down the Mississippi to Natchez and New Orleans to sell. The gang made travel along the Ohio River very dangerous. They evaded the law quite successfully— long enough to become a legend and every robbery or murder was blamed on them. If the buzzards collected above, the settlers believed it to be another murder by SAMUEL MASON. There was a legend of a great hidden treasure, which was never found.

When the Mississippi became open to more commerce and the Ohio became more settled and lawful, they became pirates on the Mississippi River and then further extended their activities to the Trace Trail in 1801. The Trace Trail exists today; but it is a beautifully paved highway through the old wilderness that connects Nashville, Tennessee, to Natchez and the great Mississippi River. In the early 1800s, it was a tangled, densely foliated, overgrown trail that was so narrow, dark and overhung in places that, almost like a cave, the traveler's vision was obscured from his surroundings. (Back in the cave on the Ohio, other robbers replaced them.)

It is believed that MASON's gang included his brother JOHN, his sons THOMAS and MANGO, an Irishman named Thomas Setton, the brutal Wiley 'Little' Harpe, and perhaps a dozen others—enough to keep their men posted in Natchez, Bayou Pierre, and as far north as New Madrid. There were a number of women and at least three children in their community, which was located near Walnut Hills. They found robbery along the Trace Trail safer, easier and more profitable than pirating, as they could take cash instead of selling the cargo. They retained enough of a conscience that they never robbed the religious missionaries, ministers, or priests of any religion.

MASON and his men would hide in the cane brakes or dark spots along the Trace and wait for a traveler to approach. Suddenly they would leap out in front of them, with their rifles or pistols leveled at their victims and relieve them of their purses. Although blamed for many deaths, only two killings and a possible third can be definitely linked to them.

William C. C. Claiborne had been sent in 1801 by President Jefferson to try to settle disputes between the various American, Spanish, French, British and Indian settlers who were all claiming deeded ownership to various lands.

Claiborne was furious at MASON's depredations, as well as those attributed to these robbers, and spoke out strongly.

> "While these Sons of Rapine and Murder are permitted to Rove at large, we may expect daily to hear of outrages upon the Lives & properties of our fellow Citizens."

He told Colonel Daniel Burnet that "these men must be arrested," and offered a reward of $2,000 for SAMUEL MASON. Militia were sent time and again to stop them; but always returned empty-handed.

Trace post rider John Swaney encountered MASON quite often as he rode the road with his mail sacks. He claimed that MASON would greet him amiably, and even inquire about what was being said of him in Natchez and Nashville. Swaney recalled,

> "He often told me not to be afraid of him, as he was after money and not letters, and that he did not wish to hurt anyone, but money he must have."

The northbound merchants were at greater risk, for they had the cash to bring back from the sale of their merchandise. They would try sewing it into their clothing or placing it in rawhide bundles with the hope of concealing it. But MASON's lookouts were quite adept at spotting it, and sent word ahead. Jefferson tried posting troops along the trail, and offered $400 for the capture of any bandit, as MASON and his gang were not exclusive in the robbery profession. Jefferson also suggested that travelers go in caravans for their protection.

In August 1803, a Major Brashear of Kentucky started north from Natchez with $2,000 in gold in his saddlebags. As he moved north, he chose a bad companion named Tranium. A few days later Brashear's body was found at Kegg Spring, near Duck Creek. His horse, his money, and companion had moved on. A few weeks later the Natchez newspapers reported a sad story of a flatboat "robbed and sunk" near Walnut Hills. It was coming down the Tennessee River from Maysville, Kentucky, carrying flour, whiskey, bacon, two oarsmen, two slaves, and cash from recent sales—all were missing and MASON's gang was blamed for the two incidents.

[Note: Duck Creek is given in many of our records as the birthplace of several of the younger children of third-great-grandparents ANDERSON and SARAH ALLRED IVIE over a decade later—further to the east in Bedford County. They were still in Franklin County, Georgia, at this time.]

A vigilante group known as the Natchez Lynchers decided to take matters into their own hands and started up the trail to an area they believed the robbers were hiding out. At the Pearl River they found some evidence that the villains might be in the area. Tired, they decided to rest their horses and refresh themselves. Two of them chose to bathe in the river and swam to the other side, where MASON and his men stealthy waited for them behind the trees. The swimmers were snatched up by the robbers and held hostage. Their friends across the river were ordered by MASON to lay down their cash, arms and ammunition, or he would kill the hostages. Complying with the demand, the Lynchers piled up their weapons and watched helplessly while the hunted became the victors, crossed the river and collected their booty. MASON set the hostages free and then disappeared into the wilderness with his men.

In January 1803 the robbers rented a house at Little Prairie, Missouri, not far from New Madrid. The Spanish authorities, who were still governing that area, captured MASON and his gang and put them in the New Madrid jail, collecting $7,163 in banknotes. The gang was put on trial, where it was decided that they should be sent down the river to New Orleans for sentencing. At New Orleans, the commander felt he should turn them over to Claiborne, since most of their crimes were in the Mississippi Territory. As the sloop carried the prisoners up the river, a bad storm came up. One of the gang managed to get a gun and shot the captain. All of them escaped in the process. A distraught Claiborne was additionally unhappy when the gang arrived in Natchez, where SAMUEL's brother, JOHN MASON, was jailed and the gang arrogantly broke him out.

MASON became aware that Claiborne had offered $2,000 for his capture when he found a "WANTED" poster in the possession of one of his victims. MASON laughed and was quite impressed with his notoriety. He jovially showed it to his men. Unfortunately for MASON, some of his men, unhappy with some harsh words he had recently directed against them, viewed the reward in a sinister way. John Sutton and James May were alone with MASON one evening, and one of them buried a tomahawk in his skull, probably while he was sleeping. They then cut off his head, placed it in a sack and took it to Greenville on the Trace, to present it to a judge of the circuit court and claim the reward. Many people of the town and surrounding country came to view the mutilated, grizzly head of the criminal and personally identify him. Satisfied that the head really was SAMUEL MASON's, the judge handed the betrayers the $2,000 reward.

Unfortunately for the killers, they were also identified. As they attempted to leave town, the two were arrested and the $2,000 was reclaimed by the sheriff. They were tried, convicted and hanged, not for MASON's murder, but for another victim that had been waylaid on the Trace two months before. After this, robberies along the Trace were much less common

~ 101 ~

John Adams elected President

When HAMILTON's cabinet office ended 31 Jan 1795, he had no large plantation to return to. His assets included a bank account of about $1,800, and some property in upstate New York of 5,450 acres—barely worth more than the amount he had paid. He owed debts of over $17,000. His expenses as secretary of the treasury were about twice his salary. As the country had grown wealthy from his abilities, he had done nothing to increase his own wealth—unwilling to allow even a small implication of inside knowledge mar his moral character or that of his country. He turned down an offer of his friend Troup that was legal and would have made him wealthy,

> "because there must be some public fools who sacrifice private to public interest" and "because my vanity whispers I ought to be one of those fools and ought to keep myself in a situation the best calculated to render service ... [the stakes] may be for nothing less than true liberty, property, order, religion .... it has been the rule of my life to do nothing for my own emolument under cover—what I would not promulge I would avoid. This may be too great refinement. I know it is pride. But this pride makes it part of my plan to appear truly what I am."

He carried this "pride" into his law practice, charging fees much smaller than what many of his colleagues collected. In one judgment of about $120,000, he would take only a fee of $1,500—although he was offered much more. Aaron Burr, who participated as co-counsel for part of the litigation, demanded a fee several times larger. HAMILTON's services were in great demand by every major merchant and financier in New York City. He was counsel for the Holland Land Company, which was making large land purchases on behalf of Dutch investors; for the United States Insurance Company, which was greatly involved in the international wars; for the city of Albany, and the state of New York. He did not limit his law practice to the affluent, but took on the masses of smaller businessmen, land dealers and craftsmen. Through his dedicated hard work, his income grew rapidly, first doubling his income as the secretary of treasury and then increasing it to three or four times that amount.

[Note: In checking for the wills of my relations along the Hudson and in New York City, I found his signature as a lawyer on many wills in my search.]

But money was only a by-product of HAMILTON's efforts. In his quiet deliberate way he was transforming American law and American society. Through his efforts, the laws that had favored the status quo of a wealthy, inherited, feudal European cast system of lords and masters with indentured servants and slaves was slowly giving way to the common-law rights of these less fortunate individuals. His work insured that the legal course of America's economic development was firmly planted—through franchises to private developers and through the market rather than through government subsidies and regulation. His efforts in the insurance laws aided shipping and other business developments by stabilizing rates with risks.

A group of Virginia Republicans challenged the federal tax on carriages which had been passed with HAMILTON's recommendation in 1794. Attorney General William Bradford asked HAMILTON to plead the case as special counsel for the government. His three-hour argument, before a full house, was so powerful that even many of those "in the habit of reviling him" were swept away by "his eloquence, candour and law knowledge." Many years later Justice Joseph Story reminisced,

> "I have heard Samuel Dexter, John Marshall, and Chancellor LIVINGSTON say that HAMILTON's reach of thought was so far beyond theirs that by his side they were schoolboys—rush tapers before the sun at noon day."

In London, John Jay was able to negotiate the treaty that avoided a new war with the British, and it was sent back to America for ratification shortly after Congress had adjourned in March of 1795. Washington called the Senate to meet in a special session in June and kept the terms of the treaty secret until that time, hoping to avoid the propaganda of the republicans who favored the French; however, they were sufficiently aware that John Jay had taken

HAMILTON's suggested treaty with him, and the war of words began again. The Senate struck out one objectionable article in the treaty and then ratified the rest with a twenty-to-ten vote. Washington, concerned about the evident negative public opinion, hesitated to sign the document. No one in the cabinet alleviated his fears, so once more he turned to HAMILTON.

HAMILTON sent back his careful analysis of each article, suggesting in the end that the treaty should be signed because it avoided war and fairly settled most points of dispute. He complimented Jay on his handling of a difficult situation. He then took up his pen again and defended it publically in a series of essays, signing them as "Camillus."

Jefferson wrote Madison,

"HAMILTON is really a colossus to the anti-republican party. Without numbers, he is an host within himself. They have got themselves into a defile, where they might be finished; but too much security on the republican part will give time to his talents and indefatigableness to extricate them."

The Republicans were obviously not anxious to give the English any advantage as "most favored nation" over their beloved France.

It was believed that Secretary of State Randolph had convinced Washington to be slow in signing the treaty, although his delay was related more to British seizure of American ships and how to best handle the situation. Englishman George Hammond gave Oliver Wolcott Jr. (HAMILTON's replacement as secretary of treasury) an intercepted dispatch in which the French minister, Fauchet, reported to his superiors that Randolph had sought a bribe from Fauchet to influence American policy. Wolcott hastily summoned President Washington back to Philadelphia and showed him the translation of the dispatch, whereupon an angry Washington signed the Jay Treaty unconditionally, and Randolph resigned in disgrace.

Six years earlier Washington had an endless number of talented men to choose from for his secretary of state; but with the ruthless attacks that had been made on his previous cabinet members, no decent man wanted any part of it. Washington had asked four different men—each one had turned him down. In desperation he wrote HAMILTON who after careful consideration replied that if no first-rate person was attainable,

"A second rate must be taken with good dispositions and barely decent qualifications . . . . T'is a sad omen for the Government."

Timothy Pickering took over the office duties temporarily. Three months later in November he was made the secretary of state with full-time duties. In the meantime, HAMILTON had been Washington's constant consultant in matters of state. Pickering's appointment changed little, because of his lack of experience. The greater problems were taken to HAMILTON by both Pickering and Washington. They would basically ask him what to do and then do it.

As Washington relied more and more on HAMILTON's advice in the great deluge of problems that were evolving so rapidly, HAMILTON was consistently losing his influence with congress. He had never wanted a political party. What he wanted was friends that supported a federal government with sufficient power to unify the states; but the anti-Republicans increasingly felt that they needed more strength and unity against the sorry tactics that were being used against them. HAMILTON's loyal country first attitude and his strong support of George Washington were not always to their liking. As the Federalists developed into the Federalist Party using tactics similar to those of the Republicans during the winter of 1795-6, HAMILTON found himself often distanced from their leadership—he was incapable of subordinating his own judgment to that of a faction or party.

Those who say that HAMILTON started the Federalist Party are incorrect. He had led the way by writing the Federalist Papers to bring about a constitutional convention; by supporting the constitutional federal government with all his ability; by developing the nation's financial system, and by defending his nation in word and deed. Because of his strength and abilities, others had followed him and his opponents saw him as the force that needed to be destroyed. This is quite different from deliberately forming an organized party that works for a specific power agenda with the destruction of their opponents in mind.

The presidential election of 1796 added another enemy to HAMILTON's list. In those days the votes in the Electoral College were cast and the candidate that received the most votes became president; the one that came second would be the vice-president. HAMILTON expected John Adams to win the presidency by a large majority, but he was worried about the vice president—the #2 spot. John Jay was considered to be a strong candidate until the public debate about the Jay Treaty with England became so intense. The strong republican leader Thomas Jefferson appeared to be next in line, and even the French had decided to work for his election.

The French had recalled Fauchet as their minister in America and replaced him with Pierre Adet. James Monroe was the American minister in France. Rumors abounded about French attacks on American vessels and the need for the United States to end their neutrality and choose one side or the other. At the end of May, Wolcott informed the president that Adet, with the support of Albert Gallatin, had sent three French agents into the frontier states to canvass and encourage them to look to France, in the event of a war and support Jefferson in the election.

Then Wolcott and Pickering somehow procured a letter Monroe had written to Dr. George Logan of Philadelphia that indicated that Monroe, a close friend of Jefferson and Madison, had been sending confidential information to editor Bache for use in attacking the administration's foreign policy. The cabinet recommended to Washington that Monroe be replaced with someone who supports the administration. Washington and HAMILTON had already decided this needed to be done, and Charles Cotesworth Pinckney of South Carolina was sent as a replacement. HAMILTON had recommended him as a

> "faithful organ near the French Government to explain their real views and ascertain those of the French . . . at the same time a friend to the Government & understood to be not unfriendly to the French Revolution."

For awhile the French withheld their electioneering, concerned that Washington might seek a third term, if he felt his efforts of the past eight years were to be undermined by the pro-French electorate. The timing for action was left to their minister Adet. Adet asked HAMILTON for letters of introduction that he could use to tour the northern states and view the country. That was his outward reason. His real reason was to talk to the Republicans in New York and New England and better understand their political sentiments. His conclusion was that only a fear of war could shake the people of New York, New England, and Philadelphia from their unswerving support of John Adams. Then Adet waited until very near the election, after Washington had announced his retirement and published his Farewell Address.

On 31 October Adet published in Bache's *Aurora* his first of four "campaign documents." It announced that the French navy would

> "treat the flag of neutrals in the same manner as they shall suffer it to be treated by the English" No genuine neutral could have cause to complain, for a nation was in fact acting as a belligerent "if through weakness, partiality, or other motives, they should suffer the English to sport with their neutrality, and turn it to their advantage."

Washington was alarmed and wrote HAMILTON, who quickly prepared a detailed letter warning him against a harsh rebuttal; but to be polite and confident in his manner. He must try to avoid a rupture with France, and if that failed, he must be sure that the People knew that he had done all that he could to avoid war. The letter was too late. Pickering, with Washington's approval, had already published a rather caustic reply. HAMILTON sent a second letter of advice, but on that same day the voters of Pennsylvania went to the polls and chose a slate of fourteen electors, all pledged to Thomas Jefferson.

Adet then published his other three campaign documents. One was to the French citizens in America ordering them to wear the tricolor cockade of the Revolution. A rumor was circulated that the French fleet was on its way to New York. The second was an announcement that diplomatic relations were being suspended. The third was a review of past friendships with the United States and praise for Jefferson's adherence to pure republican principles.

HAMILTON was appalled. He had planned to give his full support to John Adams for president and Thomas Pinckney (a brother of Charles Coteworth Pinckney) for vice president, which seemed to be the choice of most of the New Englanders; but with this latest subversion, which he attributed to Jefferson, he feared that the New Englanders might waste their second vote—not vote for Pinckney—believing that the southerners would waste their second vote—not vote for Adams—thus, putting Pinckney in first place. HAMILTON's concern that Jefferson would become vice president put him on the campaign trail to New England, asking them to vote for Adams <u>and Pinckney</u>. John Adams took personal offence and nothing could be said that would change his mind. His dislike of HAMILTON was carried to his grave.

HAMILTON's political advice was ignored in New England and in the

south. Thirty-nine of the New England electoral votes were given to other candidates and South Carolina voted equally for Pinckney and Jefferson. Adams
became president by a margin of three votes and Jefferson became vice president. When the new president took office in March 1797, HAMILTON was
totally ignored by Adams and his wife Abigail. However, Adams did keep the
old cabinet members, and they were not hesitant to seek his help.

JOHN ADAMS

THOMAS JEFFERSON

In Europe, the French refused to accept a new diplomatic American minister
to replace Monroe. A new star was rising; Citizen General Napoleon Bonaparte
with his Army of Italy was fighting the Austrians.

HAMILTON attempted to influence Congress in avoiding war with the
French similarly to the method they had used with the British through the Jay
Treaty. He further suggested that since they would not recognize Pinckney as an
American minister, that they should send a group of three commissioners and
include one pro-French such as Madison. He found only a deaf ear in Congress,
including those of the Federalist Party, who had truly ignored him. He soon
ceased to send them his advice. President Adams was quite self-sufficient. In
the cabinet, McHenry took notice and presented HAMILTON's solutions to
foreign policy to the president as his own recommendations. Adams ended up
with a very similar approach and HAMILTON wrote the following,

"I like very well the course of Executive Conduct." Of the house he stated that they were long on "hard words" and short on proper action. "Real firmness is good for every thing—Strut is good for nothing."

But HAMILTON had a very personal problem. In his early years as secretary of treasury, the seductive Maria Reynolds had come to his office for help. She told him she had been deserted by her husband and left totally helpless in the city. A beautiful woman in distress was difficult to turn away unaided. He took her address and personally took her some money. It was evidently a trap to compromise him. She succeeded. After an affair of some length, HAMILTON was approached by her husband who demanded payment or public exposure. HAMILTON gave him $1,000 in hush money and ended the liaison. Maria, however, wept and proclaimed her undying love for him and he continued to see her. Her husband went to the scurrilous republican newsman Clingman with a story of HAMILTON's corruption in the personal use of public funds for his own speculation (the one thousand dollars). Clingman took the evidence to the republican leaders, who appointed a three-man-committee to approach HAMILTON with the information. It was December, 1792.

HAMILTON had kept very good records, including all his receipts. He explained that the funds were all his own and disclosed that Maria was his mistress; but the government funds had never been touched in any way. The committee was embarrassed and satisfied that there was no fraud and gave him a signed statement to that effect, apologizing for their intrusion into his private life and promised their secrecy. A weeping Maria returned to her husband and HAMILTON became wiser in his actions. However, James Monroe, of the committee of three, kept copies of the documentation of HAMILTON's indiscretion for possible future use.

Feeling that HAMILTON had been responsible for his recall from the French ministry, Monroe evidently felt no qualms against giving the story that HAMILTON had used James Reynolds as an agent in private speculations to the notoriously abusive journalist James T. Callender who published the old charge of misuse of public funds. Maria wasn't mentioned.

HAMILTON requested each of the members of the former three-man-committee to give him a signed statement that they had been "perfectly satisfied" and had found "nothing in the transaction which ought to affect my character as a public Officer or lessen the public Confidence in my Integrity." Two of the three immediately sent back their signed statements; but Monroe refused to do so. HAMILTON's pride would not allow him to leave even the smallest blemish on his reputation regarding his administering of the treasury funds with absolute propriety, and he could see no way to defend himself except by publishing a full disclosure of the affair with all the supporting documents. He was aware of the great pain that such a disclosure would have on BETSY and his children; but could not come up with any alternative.

> "The charge against me," he explained in what became known as the *Reynold's Pamphlet*, "is a connection with one James Reynolds for purposes of improper pecuniary speculation. My real crime is an amorous connection with his wife."

A lurid description and documentation of the whole affair followed. HAMILTON's caprice was laughed at throughout the country; but his honor and thoroughness as a public servant remained intact. His wife quickly forgave him, but she never forgave James Monroe. In their later years, he approached her and asked her to let their past differences be forgiven and forgotten. BETSY replied,

> "Mr. Monroe, if you have come to tell me that you repent, that you are sorry, very sorry, for the misrepresentations and the slanders, and the stories you circulated against my dear husband, if you have come to say this, I understand it. But, otherwise, no lapse of time, no nearness to the grave, makes any difference."

After the three commissioners left for the European continent, it was months before any news arrived in America about relations with France. Congress met in November without any serious legislation. On 24 Jan 1798, President John Adams decided that no news must mean bad news and called his cabinet together to ask what they should do, assuming the mission had failed. He was basically asking whether he should recommend that the United States declare war on France and/or seek an alliance with the British. Adams was personally inclined toward war, but not the alliance. Pickering felt that both would be appropriate. Wolcott considered his treasury budget and doubted whether they could afford either of them. McHenry delayed his answer and privately went to his friend HAMILTON for advice.

HAMILTON, after consideration, said he opposed both. War left little room for negotiations and as to an alliance with England? "Twill be best not to be entangled." But since France was already engaging in a maritime war—claiming the booty of captured American merchant ships, he recommended that the United States should fight back on the seas. He would permit the arming of merchant vessels; complete as rapidly as possible the building of the last three frigates that had been authorized (three of them were already completed) and they should authorize the rapid building of twenty sloops of war. They should attack any French privateers they find hovering around the coastline, but not unarmed French merchant vessels—and no embargo should be declared on them. HAMILTON further suggested that land forces of 20,000 troops should be organized with 2,000 cavalry, and a provision that an additional 30,000 could be called up in case of war. If war with Spain were to come also, they should immediately seize Spanish Florida and Louisiana, which he felt were the obvious sites the French would use to invade the United States. Then as a final matter of "the most precious importance" the president should proclaim a day of "fasting humiliation & prayer."

Three weeks after HAMILTON's letter reached McHenry, word came from Europe that the three commissioners would not be received by the French minister Talleyrand, unless the United States paid them a bribe of $250,000 for the privilege of being officially received. It was also clear that if they were received, the French would want an additional $6 million in tribute in case the depredations on the seas continued. The French also declared that they had authorized the seizure of any neutral vessels that carried any English-made products whatever—which meant any American vessel, as nearly every ship had some equipment that was made in England.

Adams immediately made a declaration of war, but hesitated to send it. The American public was outraged when the French demands became known. The war fever mounted. French agents and sympathizers were repressed. President Adams found himself to be a greater and greater hero with every war statement he uttered.

HAMILTON was later accused of fanning the frenzy; but the opposite was true. His voice was one of moderation; but no one heard it. He wrote a few articles calling for resistance to France but not going beyond what he had already written. He turned down a senate seat that was offered him when one New York seat became vacated, and said "No" when it was suggested he might be called to the war department. He was not asked for further advice, nor did he give any, except to suggest that an American frigate be dispatched to South Carolina to attack a British man-of-war that was harassing American shipping, and then wrote to Wolcott that a sedition bill pending before the Senate be dropped as it was

> "highly exceptionable & such as more than any thing else may endanger civil war.... Let us not establish a tyranny. Energy is a very different thing from violence. If we make no false step we shall be essentially united; but if we push things to an extreme we shall then give to faction body & solidarity."

HAMILTON has also been accused of conspiring to take control of the impending army. This was not the case. George Washington felt he would be called to command and asked HAMILTON for assistance. HAMILTON stated that he would serve "only if I am invited to a station in which the service I may render may be proportioned to the sacrifice I am to make"—meaning his great loss of income. He further told him that "the place in which I should hope to be most useful is that of Inspector General with a command in the line." The inspector general had the administrative responsibility for the actual organization of the army.

By mid-July Washington had accepted Adams appointment as commander in chief; but only on two conditions: that the chief officers "shall be such as I can place confidence in," and that he would not be called into the field until the "urgency of circumstances" made that indispensable. Reluctant to take on the duty at all unless he could rely on HAMILTON "as a Coadjutor, and assistant in the turmoils I have consented to encounter." He then asked that HAMILTON be assigned as inspector general, with the rank of major general and be placed above the other major generals that he had selected, Charles C. Pinckney and Henry Knox. Fearing that Washington might change his mind, Adams immediately submitted the names to the Senate, who promptly confirmed them.

McHenry and Pickering had both urged Washington to place HAMILTON above the other two generals; but Washington had hesitated, realizing that

HAMILTON's field experience was not as great, and he questioned that Pinckney would accept the commission, if he were outranked by HAMILTON. HAMILTON told Washington,

> "If the Gentlemen concerned are dissatisfied & the service likely to suffer by the preference given to me—I stand ready to submit our relative pretensions to an impartial decision and to wave the preference. It shall never be said, with any color of truth, that my ambition or interest has stood in the way of the public good."

When Henry Knox refused to serve unless he was the ranking officer, Adams reversed his position, feeling he had the right to do so as president and deliberately placed HAMILTON beneath both of the generals. The bickering never ended until George Washington became aware of it and flatly stated that he would not serve, unless the order was placed as he had originally requested— giving HAMILTON the ranking position. HAMILTON would be the only officer called immediately into active duty to organize the army with troops, uniforms, supplies, etc. and be ready when the definite need arose. Adams with great reluctance agreed. He realized he must satisfy Washington.

But lacking the support in Congress as well as that of President Adams, HAMILTON's efforts to organize the army were constantly thwarted. It reached a climax when the overly jealous Adams returned in early October from his home in Braintree, Massachusetts, to Trenton, New Jersey—the temporary capital to avoid the yellow fever, which was again rampant in Philadelphia. Adams usually resided at his home unless Congress was in session. By chance, General HAMILTON was also in Trenton. He was meeting with Secretary of War McHenry and General JAMES WILKINSON to work out the deployment of WILKINSON's old army on the frontier. An irate Adams saw it differently, probably as an attempt by HAMILTON to replace him somehow in the next election, or as a military power play.

The old Federalist nineteenth-century historian Cooke described Adam's feelings this way,

> "Again had HAMILTON risen up like a spectre in his path. To meet him, the intriguer, there, with his coadjutors, Pickering, Wolcott, and McHenry .... had roused the lurking demon of suspicion in his breast, and from that moment he was ungovernable. He had nearly been the victim of a plot, but

the chief actor had too soon discovered himself."

In anger, Adams ordered Pickering to deliver his instructions for "peace at any price with the French" to the envoys and have them set sail for France within two weeks. HAMILTON pleaded in vain with Adams to stop the mission, feeling that the French Directory was about to topple and that the British would resume their attacks on the American ships. Adams enjoyed his superiority of position and refused to budge. Within the month, the French Directory fell in a coup d'etat that gave their power in France to Napoleon, and within a few more months the British inflicted terrible damage on American commerce.

The mission resulted in a brilliant triumph for France. It had removed an antagonist and resumed their shipping privileges with a cost to the American people of $12 million. All that the United States gained from the mission was a cessation of a failing nation's hostilities. In a separate agreement, signed the same day but dated the next, France obtained Florida and Louisiana from Spain with the stipulation that this land was not to be sold to the Americans. Then, when it suited their purposes, France resumed their pirating of American vessels. They had gained control of the Caribbean and the Mississippi River commerce, and the American frontier was further squeezed into a corner with no outlet for production. HAMILTON had been right; but to no avail, Adams was the president.

The mission was believed by the public to have stopped the current need for the army, and during the next session of Congress it was abolished. The republican forces with the self-sufficient Federalists that were proclaiming HAMILTON as an American Napoleon left him to dismantle the army alone without even a fight to preserve the American rights against the rapid territorial expansion of the insatiable tyrant that was enveloping the European continent so explosively. Adams was quite pleased with his subjugation of HAMILTON, ignoring his own national subjugation to the French. After all, the American public would praise him for peace; the long effect would not come until later. HAMILTON went back to rebuild his law practice; but he insisted on being called General HAMILTON thereafter. That was all he got.

~ 102 ~

THE DEATH OF GEORGE WASHINGTON,
JEFFERSON ERA BEGINS

On the morning of 13 Dec 1799, George Washington wrote in his diary, "snowing and almost three inches deep . . . wind at northeast and mercury at 30."

He had what he considered a cold; but he set out anyway riding his usual rounds on his plantation of about 8,000 acres on the Potomac River. Later he wrote,

> "Continuing snowing till one o'clock and about four it became perfectly clear: Wind in the same place but not hard. Mercury at 28 at night."

Arriving back at the mansion house, his great coat was soaked through and his clothes damp; his neck was wet and snow was hanging from his hair. Dinner was waiting, so he ate without changing his damp clothes. His secretary Lear wrote in a letter to his own mother that Washington was

> "very cheerful" and read parts of the newspaper "aloud as much as his hoarseness would permit."

Lear urged him to take some medicine before he went to bed. Washington declined.

> "You know I never take anything for a cold. Let it go as it came."

About 3:00 A.M. he awakened Martha from her sleep, complaining that he had a very sore throat and was not feeling well. His voice was a whisper and his breathing difficult. [It is believed that he had strep throat.] Martha wanted to call a servant; but her husband feared that Martha might catch cold in the process. She suffered from malaria, and would get chills and fever several times a year. At dawn when the maid came to light the fire, Washington sent her to fetch Rawlins—the overseer who usually cared for the sick slaves. He also asked her to get his secretary Lear. Dr. Craik was summoned; but on Washington's insistence, Rawlins bled him before the doctor arrived. Martha begged him not to bleed him too much; but Washington ordered, "More!" When Dr. Craik arrived he applied Spanish fly to Washington's throat to draw a blister, and then he bled him again.

[Note: Spanish flies is cantharidin, a product obtained from certain dried beetles and a few varieties of caterpillars. It was an old counterirritant dating back to Hippocrates. Internally, 30 mg. is considered to be fatal. Currently, it is advised that it never be used on a sore directly or on the mucous membrane, as it causes burning in the mouth, thirst, difficulty in swallowing, swelling, and blistering of the tongue. This doesn't sound like a very appropriate or enjoyable procedure for strep throat.]

When Washington tried to gargle with sage tea and vinegar he nearly choked. Craik quickly recognized that he couldn't swallow and sent for another doctor. Then he bled Washington again.

Doctors Gustavus Brown of Port Tobacco and Elisha Cullen Dick of Alexandria arrived between three and four in the afternoon. Craik and Brown conferred and agreed that it was quinsy (acute tonsilitis) and felt that his treatment should be more bleeding and blisters followed by purges with laxatives. The younger thirty-seven-year-old Dr. Dick, a graduate of Edinburgh School of Medicine, disagreed. He felt that Washington was suffering from

"a violent inflammation of the membranes of the throat, which it had almost closed, and which, if not immediately arrested, would result in death."

He felt they should use a new procedure he had learned in Scotland, a tracheotomy below the infection to allow him to breathe. He pleaded with them to not bleed him again.

"He needs all his strength—bleeding will diminish it."

Craik and Brown ignored his advice and asked Washington's consent to bleed him the fourth time. This time "the blood ran very slowly." Around four o'clock Washington had rallied a little and was able to swallow. Craig took advantage of this to give him calomel (mild mercurous chloride) and other laxatives.

At about four-thirty Washington asked Lear "to ask Mrs. Washington to come to his bedside." He then asked her to go down to his office and get his two wills, and then insisted that she burn the old one. Martha threw it into the fire and preserved the other one in her closet. As the evening approached, he whispered to Lear,

"I find I am going. My breath cannot continue long."

He then asked Lear to arrange all his military papers and accounts, to which Lear agreed. With a smile he stated that death "is the debt which we must all pay," and that he "looked on the event with perfect resignation." Later, when his old French and Indian War companion, Dr. Craik came in, Washington whispered to him,

"Doctor, I die hard, but I am not afraid to go. My breath cannot last long."

The other doctors came in wanting him to sit up, but Washington without complaint asked to "be permitted to die without further interruptions." His last request was to Lear.

"I am just going. Have me decently buried and do not let my body be put into the vault in less than three days after I am dead." Only a tearful nod was given. "Do you understand?"
"Yes sir."
Washington whispered his last words, "Tis well."

He died at ten o'clock, five hours later with Martha by his side, on the night of 14 Dec 1799.

While the nation mourned the passing of their hero, a new century slipped quietly into its place in time on the American continent. Washington had actively led them prayerfully and steadily through eight years of a difficult war; he had been the convention chairman of their unequaled constitution, and he had served as their president through those eight demanding formative years. For over twenty-five years, he had been the central figure in American life. Now a new century had arrived with a new leader. It would not be a century of peace and harmony, for the seeds of division, power, and greed had already been planted.

John Adams later recalled his last meeting with Washington over two years before when Washington had congratulated him as the new president—just before leaving Philadelphia to go to Mount Vernon. Adams wrote,

"He seemed to enjoy a triumph over me. Methought I heard him say, 'Ay! I am fairly out and you fairly in! See which of us will be happier!'"

But in the quiet of Mount Vernon, Washington at that time had many less-agreeable comments. One of them was his belief after the Whiskey Rebellion that the

"Self-created" Democratic/Republican Societies "have been laboring to sow the seeds of distrust, jealousy and of course discontent" and still could trigger "some resolutions in the government."

At Philadelphia, he had written his friend Benjamin Walker in Virginia,

"If you read the 'Aurora' in this city, you cannot but have perceived with what malignant industry and persevering falsehoods I am assailed." The editor Bache "intended to weaken if not destroy the confidence of the public" in his presidency.

Washington wrote of these opposition journalists as

"discontented characters" motivated by an "opinion that the measures of the general government are impure."

Bache had blasted the Washington administration as

"enemies of democracy." Washington was not the father of his country but "weak" and "inept."

Freneau had printed,

"He holds levees like a king, makes treaties like a king, answers petitions like a king and employs old enemies like a king .... Swallows adulation like a king and vomits offensive truths in your face."

Washington had said,

"It is well known that, when one side only of a story is heard and often repeated, the human mind becomes impressed with it insensibly."

To Henry Lee he wrote,

"no man was ever more tired of public life."

He had described his dilemma to John Adams as his "disinclination to be longer buffeted in the public prints by a set of infamous scribblers."

He had felt emotionally wounded by the long years of infighting and character assassination by the press. He had taken no salary during the war and sustained private losses during his administration. He had never sought an office, and yet he was attacked as ambitious and greedy. He was to say,

"It might be expected at the parting scene of my public life that I should take some notice of such virulent abuse. But, as heretofore, I shall pass them over in utter silence."

He never complained in the newspapers; but then, he had ALEXANDER HAMILTON to champion him; but HAMILTON's destruction was progressing rapidly and nearly to its end. Washington's death had left him without office and nearly without influence beyond his daily law practice, as the election of 1800 would prove.

This view of Mount Vernon from the West is the carriage entrance. On the opposite side is the front entrance from the Potomac River. The house is made of carved logs that are painted white with a mixture of paint and sand— to give it an appearance of stone. Located left beyond the covered walk way were rooms reserved for the servants of visiting guests.

Beyond the covered area on the right is the kitchen, carriage houses, stables, slave quarters, blacksmith shop gardens, and the tomb of both George and Martha Washington with some of their family members.

GEORGE WASHINGTON

By 1800, the public vote for president was quite minimal. The partisan leaders in most of the states had become quite adept at manipulating the state governments to their own advantage. By that time, DeWitt Clinton, a nephew of Governor George Clinton, had been appointed mayor of New York City. It paid much more than what he made as a senator in Congress. The spoil system was in effect and every officer in the city from street cleaner to policeman got their job by being willing to take orders from the higher powers and sharing any commissions with their superiors. Family relation or close alliance was becoming essential for any individual political growth or appointment in the city. The New York individual vote was legislated to only include those who had a sufficient amount of property that, they hoped, would share the views of their leaders. The state legislature was being similarly controlled by the more elite political leaders. Five other states had made their legislatures less democratic and two-thirds of the presidential electors would be chosen by state legislatures. The election of 1800 would reflect the will of the politicians, not the will or the vote of the people.

In New York, Aaron Burr planned his power play. In 1799, the Federalists had gained control of the city with only a marginal lead, so Burr waited until they announced their slate of candidates for the legislature—most were practically unknown. Then he convinced a more renowned group of candidates to oppose them in name only, as it was an office they considered a lowly position. These candidates included ex-Governor George Clinton, Judge Brokholst Livingston and General Horatio Gates. Burr's slate easily won and the Republicans would control the state legislature, which would appoint republican electors to choose the new United States president.

HAMILTON was quick to come up with a solution. He felt that Burr had stolen the election with a trick and suggested a special session of the old legislature. They could change the election law and provide for popular elections of the electors by district. This would give the Federalists control of at least half of the electors—enough to win the presidency. Unfortunately for the Federalists, New York's current governor, John Jay, refused to do this and the New York electors would all vote for the republican candidates, which meant Jefferson and Burr in the fall of 1800. Two years later, HAMILTON proposed a U.S. constitutional amendment, that never materialized, that would elect the president by a popular vote for the state electors in each district of each state, thus allowing a split electoral vote in the states.

President John Adams, still fiercely angry at HAMILTON, didn't help his situation. He blamed HAMILTON for the New York election results. To get even, he demanded the resignation of the "traitors" in his cabinet, whom he believed to be McHenry and Pickering. Strangely, he left Wolcott in the cabinet, which was probably the closest to HAMILTON. He so completely lost his self-control when he dismissed McHenry that those who might have favored Adams lost their respect for his managerial abilities. When HAMILTON read McHenry's account of the interview, he commented on Adams,

"The man is more mad than I ever thought him and I shall soon be led to say as wicked as he is mad."

But HAMILTON did not show any belligerence towards Adams. Instead, he decided to strongly support the Federalist candidates much in the same way as in the last election. He would do his best to urge the New Englanders to vote for Adams and his own choice, Charles Cotesworth Pinckney from South Carolina.

HAMILTON attempted to get the New Englanders to vote for both Adams and Pinckney, but wrote what he hoped would be a secret letter to the Federalist leaders, explaining carefully the shortcomings of Adams; but he still urged their support of both Adams and Pinckney. One of the leaders published the letter— to the delight of the Republicans and consternation of Adams. However, it did increase the New England support for Pinckney—all but one of the electors supported both men. Down in South Carolina, General Pinckney insisted that the electors vote for both Federalists or for none at all. Whether it was for that reason, or just a solid south support for Jefferson, South Carolina gave all their votes equally to Jefferson and Burr, thus giving the election to the Republicans. Jefferson and Burr tied for the presidency with equal votes.

With a tie, the election would then go to the House of Representatives. The Federalists were in the majority at that time; but the Constitution stipulated that each state was to have only one vote from all their representatives. On this basis, the Federalists had six votes, the Republicans had eight and two states had a split vote. The Federalists had caucused and decided to support Burr, hoping that by supporting him he would help them in the future.

HAMILTON did not sit still and wait. He would choose Jefferson. For all his flaws, HAMILTON wrote that Jefferson had a

> "temporizing rather than a violent character," and thus was unlikely to go to extremes in undoing Federalist measures. HAMILTON would "add to this that there is no fair reason to suppose him capable of being corrupted."

By contrast, Burr was driven by his lust for power.

> "He is sanguine enough to hope everything—daring enough to attempt everything—wicked enough to scruple nothing."

HAMILTON further claimed that his reasons were not personal.

> "If there be a man in the world I ought to hate, it is Jefferson. With Burr I have always been personally well. But the public good must be paramount to every private consideration."

The Federalists, however, no longer looked to HAMILTON for advice. The vote was deadlocked for thirty-five successive times. Finally, on the thirty-sixth ballot, with HAMILTON's constant urging, James Bayard, the only delegate from Delaware, broke with his party and changed his vote. Thomas Jefferson became the next president and Burr would be the vice president.

HAMILTON helped his uncle-in-law, STEPHEN VAN RENSSELAER campaign for Governor of New York State in April. His friend Robert Troup described the public reaction:

> "At one of the polls General HAMILTON, with impunity by the populace, was repeatedly called a thief; and at another poll with the same impunity he was called a rascal, villain, and every thing else that is infamous in society! What a commentary is this on republican virtue! He assures me that nothing short of a general convulsion will again call him into public life."

When George Washington died in December 1799, he was 67 years old. John Adams was 64 years old at the beginning of the century. Thomas Jefferson was 56 years old, at that time. James Madison was 48 years old. Patrick Henry was 63 years old when he died in June of 1799. Washington's neighbor, George Mason, who is considered the father of Virginia's Bill of Rights, died in 1792 when he was 67 years old. Samuel Adams was 77 years old at the turn of the century. Benjamin Franklin died at age 84 in 1790. STEPHEN HOPKINS was 78 years old when he died in 1785. ALEXANDER HAMILTON was the youngest of this group. He was 44 years old with a large and relatively young family when the new century arrived. Washington had a long-term nearly father and son relationship with HAMILTON. He appreciated and utilized his great talents. Jefferson and Adams saw him as a personal threat to their well-earned political positions as well as their social beliefs—reflected in their older Virginia and New England traditions. They looked for his faults, not his talents, and if the faults were not there, they were willing to exaggerate and create them. It is usually easier for younger men to overlook the weaknesses of older men, whom they consider to be on their way out, than it is for an older man to not feel threatened by a determined, energetic younger generation that disagrees with their sage leadership and is quite capable of replacing them. HAMILTON seemed willing to appreciate them, but not to the point of sacrificing his own thoughts and ideas—nor to any other person, group, or faction. Adams and Jefferson would later become close friends, corresponding by letter until they both died on the fiftieth anniversary of the Declaration of Independence; but neither of them changed his opinion of HAMILTON, whom they described in regards to his birth and actions in very unflattering terms.

~ 103 ~

DUEL—JEFFERSON, HAMILTON AND BURR

As the new century began, the Federalist Party described themselves as the party that upheld the United States Constitution, before, during, and after its ratification. They thought of themselves as the "wise and the good," men of virtues, talents, and property—best suited by birth and/or achievement to run the country. Their proof was the prosperity of the country. The Constitution with its central government and HAMILTON's fiscal management had allowed the United States to become a strong international nation that allowed all men equal opportunity to work and produce their own economic stability, whether they were agricultural, manufacturer, or service oriented. They saw the original states as secondary in nature giving strength internationally in this subjective unity. They favored the English, the French, or Spanish only to the extent as to which would be the most beneficial to the current needs of the country. They were generally opposed to slavery and its increasing proliferation into the frontier Indian lands of Georgia, Alabama, Mississippi, Kentucky, and Tennessee. They favored a navy and army that were strong enough to defend their interests. They wanted a vibrant commerce between states and other nations, incorporating international and state laws.

The Democrat/Republicans, under the leadership of Jefferson and Madison, were the opposition party—but not a loyal opposition party—as the English liked to call theirs. Jefferson had felt that the Articles of Confederation were quite adequate, with a few minor changes. He feared the new strength of the nation; it was moving too fast to international greatness. With his love of the French and the republic he had helped them organize, they could do no wrong in his eyes. He gave far too much credit to the French for their help in winning the Revolutionary War and ignored far too greatly the efforts of the United States army and its citizens, including Washington and HAMILTON. While the deadly drums had beat and the cannons had fired their destruction, he had sat comparatively quiet at Monticello with his books and theories, considering laws that would free mankind of tyranny and bring about a utopia of goodwill and harmony, with educated men, like him, as their leaders.

Jefferson had tried to stop the fast advance of slavery throughout the South and into the Indian Territory before he went to France; but the animosity his resolution had brought about was more than he wanted to deal with. He needed his own slaves to care for his inherited lands. He had over 200 of them. He probably loved his black servant, James Hemings, but he never placed his needs as equal to his own, in spite of the slave's architectural and management abilities in the creation of Monticello and its surrounding lands. Jefferson tolerated the island in the West Indies that gave the blacks their freedom, but he would not allow blacks or Indians the right to their own states, with representation in Congress. His equality of all men allowed for the leadership of an educated few, who would condescend enough to work for the good of the less fortunate with theories, if not in practice. His own equality was reserved for his educated friends of quality. In Monticello, there is a beautiful guest room on the first floor that is still called the James and Dolly Madison room.

The Democrat/Republicans were not interested in a strong army or navy—call up the militia, if needed. They did not like banks and fought against them—considering them to be tools of an aristocracy. They did not want federal government laws or judges that could interfere with their state authority and personal style of living—state rights must take precedence. It was not just a matter of slavery that divided them from these high-minded Federalists—if the blacks and Indians were allowed an equal vote in some states they would out-number those of white descent. This was far more equality than the southern "men of quality" wanted—the northerners had relatively no slaves and had driven-out most of their Indians during the Revolution, and had already claimed the Ohio/Illinois territory for their westward expansion.

New York City was the commercial capital of the new nation with a population of around 65,000 in 1804. In the early 1790s, Jefferson and Madison had seen the means of dividing this city and had not wasted time in doing it; but it required the destruction of ALEXANDER HAMILTON, politically. Governor George Clinton and his stronghold feared the free-thinking, efficient HAMILTON who threatened their own power. HAMILTON had personally signed the Constitution, while their delegates had trotted back to their fortress. HAMILTON's animosity toward the Livingston-Clintonians and their tight control of the city and state, had given the republicans a strong entry into New York politics. Burr had recognized this as an open door for him to be the agent that united them under the Republican banner. His quick rise to power by playing both ends of the stick had given him many wins over HAMILTON's personal positions. It had culminated in Burr's tie with Thomas Jefferson for president of the United States. But HAMILTON did not quietly go away. HAMILTON, although not one of his political opponents, had managed to break the tie in favor of Jefferson, and somehow, HAMILTON kept coming back into Aaron Burr's life one way or another.

Burr had some strong ideology of his own. He was against slavery, wanted a strong army and navy, and even suggested that the women be given the right to vote—something both Federalists and Republicans had considered to be even more revolting than the vote of the blacks and Indians. This was certainly not the position of either end of the republican stick, nor did it come in the middle. Burr was actually his own man; but with cunning, he had allowed both sides to believe they could use him and manipulate him according to their wishes. HAMILTON, from long association, knew differently and considered him very dangerous to the country. He felt that if there was to be a Napoleon in America, it would be the sly Aaron Burr.

In 1804, 83 percent of the nation was farmers. Jefferson flattered them with such statements as,

"Those who labor in the earth are the chosen people of God," the only sure guardians of American liberty.

In the minds of these farmers, Jefferson was the man who had written the Declaration of Independence—a trusted and valiant leader of their personal rights. They knew little else about him, such as his desire to weaken the Constitution and undermine the administration of George Washington and the economic growth and defense of the nation, or of his strong affinity for the French nation. They believed him when he said the Federalist Party was a party of elite, money-grabbing merchants and lawyers who looked down on honest farmers and cheated them at every opportunity—"that filched . . . immense sums . . . from the poor and ignorant."

The majority of these farmers in 1804 deified Jefferson and believed him when he told them that HAMILTON was trying to turn America into a mirror image of England, a country where financial speculation, political corruption, and mobs of disenfranchised factory workers required an army to keep the aristocrats in power.

They did not understand the reality of the situation. Jefferson was really urging a status quo: a government very similar to the old colonial English states, before the Revolution, in which slavery, indentured servitude, and the legal control of the commerce by governors and legislatures of the states allowed very little opportunity for the small farmer to rise above the level he was born into. Jefferson was praised for his purchase of the Louisiana Territory from the French. It would bring new land for the small tenant farmers. Nothing was said of the huge 100,000-plus-acre land sales of the most fertile lands to the republican political leaders in the South and New York Republicans such as ROBERT R. LIVINGSTON, who had cash or banking credit to purchase the land at a price, as Jefferson had written, "we can buy an acre of new land cheaper than we can manure an old one," after it had been ruined with the over production of tobacco, corn, and the new king—cotton. Great numbers of slaves were required on these western plantations, which allowed the southern plantation owners to sell their own personal slave production, which had multiplied greatly beyond their needs. Jefferson put on a show of frugal economy in the new White House at Washington D.C., but Monticello was far from mediocre.

High on a wall of Monticello in the greatest location of his grandest room, Jefferson placed paintings of the three men he considered to be "the three greatest men the world had ever produced": the English mathematician and natural philosopher Isaac Newton (1641-1727); the English philosopher John Locke (1632-1704), and the English statesman Francis Bacon (1561-1626).

Newton as a young man left his family farm under the protest of his elders

MONTICELLO, HOME OF THOMAS JEFFERSON, AND HIS GARDENS, 2004

[PHOTOS BY HYRUM HAYNES]

to favor the library and the laboratory. Perhaps, the cartoon picture of him sitting under an apple tree, as opposed to plowing the surrounding fields when the apple fell on his head might be more literal than legend. Locke's philosophy included the superior qualities of working the land over all professions—except, of course, his own choice—not to be a farmer. Bacon had preceded the other two as a combination statesman, scientist, and agricultural observer. He had watched some plantations in Ireland and had sagely only observed,

> "Take it from me that the bane of a plantation is when the undertakers or planters make such haste to a little presentable present profit as disturbeth the whole frame and nobleness of the work for times to come."

Such was the plight of Virginia in 1800.

In early Virginia, tobacco had been the cash crop. It was a tedious process that required a large amount of human labor. It was a crop that depleted the soil, and to be profitable in supporting the economic needs of a large plantation, it required cheap labor. To the Southerner, that meant many slaves.

The cotton gin was invented in 1793 by the Yale graduate Eli Whitney of New Haven, Connecticut, who had gone south to teach school in Georgia. His invention had been stolen before he was able to get his patent, and others profited from his mechanical genius. He was unable to get proper funding in the south, so he returned to Connecticut to manufacture the cotton gins; but lawsuits to protect his rights took all his profits and his original fund of $50,000, which had been given him by the state of South Carolina. In 1798, he was able to get a government contract to make firearms for the anticipated war with France. Once more he became ingenious in the construction of his machinery at Whitneyville, Connecticut—this time it was patented and very profitable. He was the first to divide labor and build machinery that allowed for the manufacture and assembly of separate parts. The age of New England manufacturing was beginning, as HAMILTON and many of the New Englanders had hoped.

In the South, with Whitney's invention of the cotton gin, "King Cotton" had replaced tobacco as the most important cash crop, and England with their many factories was becoming the south's most favored nation to purchase their product. Unfortunately, the cotton also depleted the soil, and the southern planters looked west for new lands where they could profitably use their surplus slaves in the great fertile, level lowlands of Georgia, Alabama, and Mississippi.

It was probably also unfortunate for the South that Jefferson and his republican following had been successful in stopping a bank from going into Richmond to help the manufacturing, other businesses, and the "real farmers", as George Washington liked to call those who cultivated, fertilized, and planted their own lands, without the help of slaves. Without the credit a bank could give them, the South became more and more vulnerable to outside forces—foreign and the northern states.

Great Britain was the largest winner. They had all the benefits of their old American colonies, without any obligation to help them in any way. They set the price of cotton and kept it as low as possible, limiting profits, and forcing more and more exploitation of the land, the slaves, and the less fortunate whites, while

England sold their finished products back to the cotton growers with greater and greater profits for themselves. The British needed their money. They were at war with France, and Napoleon was looking hungrily in their direction.

COUNTRY OF THE CHEROKEE AND THE CREEK INDIANS

Map showing the Headright area of Georgia
Prepared by staff, Georgia Surveyor
General Department, Atlanta, Georgia

THE CIRCLED COUNTIES HAD IVEYs LISTED IN THEIR CENSUS RECORDS

OF THE FIRST HALF OF THE 19TH CENTURY.

The nation's first census had been taken in 1790. Careful maps were drawn of all the states, which extended the states of Virginia, North Carolina, and Georgia to the banks of the Mississippi River. Their maps showed most of present day Georgia, West Virginia, Tennessee, Alabama, Mississippi, and the old Northwest, as Indian Territory, probably designated to the Indians by earlier treaties. Florida, which extended all along the coastal region to Louisiana, still belonged to Spain, as well as the vast lands west of the Mississippi River that extended westward to the Pacific Ocean. As the new century began, Spain had given their claim to the Louisiana land to the French by treaty in exchange for their own safety from the tyrannical momentum that Napoleon was gaining in Europe. France promised by treaty not to sell it to the United States. Spain kept Florida and the coastal land between. Economically, they didn't want the Americans to have free access to the Caribbean Sea and all their sugar islands.

After Napoleon usurped Europe, England and Russia became his barrier to further expansion. His first march was toward England; but he needed money for flatboats to take his army across the channel. ROBERT R. LIVINGSTON was the American minister in France. As negotiations began with the Americans— breaking the treaty Napoleon had with the weakened Spanish—President Jefferson sent James Monroe to help with the Louisiana Purchase. Jefferson wanted to be sure his administration got the credit, instead of LIVINGSTON. $15,000,000 was a lot of cash to come up with in the new nation. Many in the northern states were objecting to it. They felt that as soon as Napoleon had conquered England he would ignore his purchase agreement, as he had with Spain, attack the United States and claim the whole continent.

The United States was not prepared for war. When Congress had voted to eliminate the army of Washington and HAMILTON a few years previously, they had left only a small frontier army of less than 1,000 soldiers under Brigadier General JAMES WILKINSON.

[Note: Past chapters tell how WILKINSON got his promotion from colonel to brigadier general after Burgoyne's surrender at Saratoga. As an aide to General Gates, he was chosen to carry the message of the American victory on horseback to Congress—who was safely in York, Pennsylvania. He, under Gates' order, had deliberately ignored informing General Washington and his army, who were also in Pennsylvania. While drinking one evening on his journey, he started the rumor that resulted in the exposure of the Conway Cabal against the commander in chief. Washington had not approved WILKINSON's promotion. He had many colonels ready and more capable for advancement; but Congress gave it to WILKINSON, anyway. Delivering a message seemed quite inconsequential and unfair. DANIEL MORGAN was still only a colonel at that time.

Any close relation to my WILKINSON ancestors has not been established. He came from Maryland, which was settled to a great extent by the Catholics. My WILKINSON ancestors seem to have strong Quaker leanings and lived in Rhode Island, New Jersey and Pennsylvania.]

President Jefferson funded the Louisiana Purchase by selling these south-ern lands that were shown on the maps as Indian Territory in huge grants to his anxious southern planter friends and northern republican speculators. They, in turn, borrowed the money from the supposedly corrupt Dutch and New York banks (as the Jeffersonian Democrat/Republican's called them). The $15,000,000 was raised and French minister ROBERT R. LIVINGSTON be-came one of the largest deeded absentee land owners in the southern states. Slaves were needed to profitably grow the cotton, creating a market for Virginia's and the other southern original colonies surplus slaves.

[Note: Eighty-five percent of the eight hundred-fifty thousand slaves sent westward between 1790 and 1860 came from Virginia, Maryland, and the Carolinas. Three times as many were sold during the last half as were sold during the first half. See Roger G. Kennedy, *Mr. Jefferson's Lost Cause* p. 108.]

As for the Indians that inhabited these lands, they had no deeds. The United States had fought Great Britain and was given the right to these lands by the Europeans. The Indians had helped the British; therefore, they lost. As for the "real farmers", let them have the mountainous regions where slaves could not be easily controlled and where land was not as fertile, or saleable.

As for the actual purchase, LIVINGSTON had slyly convinced Napoleon that it was quite worthless to France. Napoleon needed the money to cross the English Channel with over 180,000 troops, and he believed that by "giving" the Louisiana land to the Americans, they would aid him in his destruction of the English. Quite the opposite occurred over time. The small islands of Great Britain depended greatly upon their navy and their factories for survival. The large cotton plantations in the south proliferated. WILKINSON with about half of his small army was sent to the French port of New Orleans to control the city and open the Mississippi River for American commerce. Waiting in the harbor for the bales of cotton were the English ships to carry them to England and its factories. The planters of the South became increasingly dependent on English cash. Jefferson, however, was still treating the British minister and his wife very shabbily. His stark republican ideas refused to acknowledge any protocol, unless it was with the French.

In England, William Pitt had been replaced by the pacifist Henry Addington, who had cut the size of his army. Addington quickly called for volunteers and 300,000 responded. Unfortunately, he was short of arms and could only supply them to about one-third of that number. They also lacked discipline and coordination of authority. As Napoleon's factories spit out more and more artillery, arms, and ammunition, Napoleon waited only for the right weather. He needed a heavy storm, which was usually followed by a calm, in which the strong British navy would not have enough wind in their sails to blow up his French flotilla of flatboats carrying his army across the channel—generally believed to result in the end of the British nation and their inadequate army.

The fearful Addington devised his plan. He would send spies and assassins to the continent. Their object would be to kill Napoleon and replace him with a descendent of the Bourbons, Prince LOUIS-ANTOINE, DUC d'ENGHIEN, now living in Baden—a descendent of the Huguenot PRINCE of CONDÉ, a first cousin of Henry IV of France. Napoleon became aware of the secret plan of the English, and sent a small army to capture the prince, whom he sent before his firing squad (or strangled) on 21 Mar 1804. [See the Conclusion of Part II: STANDING FIRM] The plot, however, disturbed Napoleon and his followers sufficiently that they decided they should make Napoleon an emperor, thus creating a new line of descent to his throne that would eliminate all kings and church power. This idea became more important to Napoleon than conquering England. He needed to convince his nation of French republicans and European remnants of the Holy Roman Empire that it was best for them to be rid of the old French and European dynasties and replace them with his own.

The Spanish, highly concerned about their American possessions, sent their ambassador to the United States, the Marques de Casa Yrujo, to threaten the United States with war over their supposed purchase of Louisiana and their ever encroaching settlements within what they believed to be the boundaries of east and west Florida. Yrojo stormed into Secretary of State James Madison's office screaming curses and insults directly in his face. His anger seemed to center around a customs district in Mobile [Alabama] that had been created by Congress and signed by Jefferson. The president retreated. He was not prepared for war; but he began negotiations to try to purchase the Florida lands by sending

James Monroe to Spain, who was then in England. ROBERT R. LIVINGSTON was to ask Napoleon to help persuade the Spanish to sell; but matters became worse. American merchant ships were being attacked and their cargo claimed by both the French and Spanish ships in the Caribbean. The small U.S. navy including the U.S.S. Constitution was in the Mediterranean Sea fighting the Barbary pirates at Tripoli. While he was in London, Monroe had complained that he was totally ignored by the queen, and if he was invited to any event, he was always on the bottom of the list. This was in retaliation for the crude and smug way that Jefferson had treated their British minister in the United States.

In New Orleans, neither the French, nor the Spanish, were leaving. The inexperienced governor of the territory, Claiborne, who spoke only English, bombarded Jefferson with letters, and he wrung his hands in despair. WILKINSON's love of food, drink, and glory did not inspire much confidence; neither did the size of his army. In February 1804, Vicente Folch, the Spanish governor of West Florida, visited New Orleans. WILKINSON wanted to meet with him. He had decided to renew his lapsed relationship with Spain as their secret Agent 13. He wanted to increase his stipend to $4,000 a year and be paid the $20,000 they already owed him. In return, he promised that they would not need to worry about the Americans going further into Spanish lands. Folch had no money; but he suggested the Marques de Casa Calvo; he had been allotted $100,000 for "expenses"—a word that in 1804 frequently included bribes. WILKINSON considered his relationship with Jefferson to be excellent. He was constantly charming the president by sending him gifts of Indian relics and unusual plants, as well as many letters of obsequious praise and favorable descriptions of the new frontier.

WILKINSON was paid $12,000 by the Spanish for 22 pages of his reflections that gave advice and observations on how to keep the Americans in line. His advice included: do not sell Florida; bring Napoleon into their game, and as for the expedition that was being planned for Meriwether Lewis and William Clark by President Jefferson, arrest them when they cross the Mississippi River. So, early in the year of 1804, both the leaders of Spain and France knew that the American army general was for sale and that the United States was less prepared to defend itself than the British were prepared to defend England.

[Note: Our ancestors in Virginia and north-central North Carolina would probably be classed under Washington's definition as belonging to the "real farmer" class, as they possessed few, if any, slaves. They had suffered from the British occupation and destruction of the South during the war, as well as the deterioration of their lands caused by its overuse in crop production, especially in eastern Virginia. Their children of the Revolutionary War had grown up, and this younger generation sought the new lands to the west. When the Georgia land lottery began around the turn of the century in Franklin County, Georgia, third-great-grandfather ANDERSON IVIE, now over 25 years of age, was there from the tidewater area of Virginia. It appears that he left home as a young man to travel west with his uncle, LOT IVEY, and his family in search of new lands and was in Surry County, North Carolina, when the 1790 census was taken. Here, they had trouble with land that had been double deeded. From there, they went south into Pendleton, South Carolina, a county in the western part of the state—bordering North Carolina and Georgia. WILLIAM and ELIZABETH THRASHER ALLRED were there from Randolph County, North Carolina, with their family and many other close relations, including many from ELIZABETH THRASHER's family as well as several of WILLIAM ALLRED's brothers.

In Franklin County, Georgia, ANDERSON IVIE was married to WILLIAM and ELIZABETH ALLRED's oldest daughter SARAH. They had a small lot of land on which they paid Georgia taxes. It bordered the small lot of his uncle. LOT IVEY won his land in Randolph County, Georgia (later Jasper County) —near Atlanta. He moved westward to that county with his two sons, JOHN and BENJAMIN. Third-great-grandfather ANDERSON IVIE entered the lottery every year; but he evidently never won any land. His winnings were his wife, SARAH ALLRED, and their children who were born in the early 1800s and included my second-great-grandfather JAMES RUSSELL IVIE, born in 1802 in Georgia. ANDERSON and SALLY [Sarah Allred] IVIE are listed among the charter members of the Baptist Church in Franklin County, where he served as their clerk. Unfortunate in the yearly land lotteries he entered, ANDERSON and his wife and children moved further west into Tennessee and by 1829, they were in Missouri. Many of the SARAH'S brothers with their families came, too.]

The elusive land deals and double-deeded controversies over land ownership had moved the IVIEs further and further west—clearing lands, splitting rails, and dealing with Indians who felt betrayed and angry. It might be said that they were being used similarly to the plan Jefferson had proposed to Washington in regards to Florida, which duplicity Washington had refused to be a part of. Jefferson had written,

> "[Florida] is meant for our people . . . [If we send colonists in, as they invited us to do] . . . . It will be a means of delivering to us peaceably, what may otherwise cost us a war. In the meantime we may complain of this seduction of our inhabitants just enough to make [the Spanish] believe we think it very wise policy for them, and confirm them in it. This is my idea of it."

It was my ancestors with other "real farmers" that were the pawns of "this seduction," protecting the fringes, while the absentee Livingston/Clintonians and the more daring planters spoiled the land and reaped the harvests with their slaves.

But these men with hundreds or thousands of acres were really not as free as the less fortunate independent small planters, for they had great debts. Their quantity of land and slaves created its own responsibility to a system subject to the demands of government, foreign trade, and the consumption of many mouths. Jefferson, himself, never able to clear his debts, remained at his home in Monticello until his death in 1826 only because of the generosity of his creditors.

Jefferson wrote to one of his overseers,

"I consider a woman who brings a child every two years as more profitable than the best man of the farm, what she produces is an addition to capital, while his labors disappear in mere consumption."

In 1819 there was a cotton recession. Jefferson wrote,

"beyond the mountains we have good slaves selling for one hundred dollars, good horses for five dollars and the sheriffs [in bankruptcy sales] generally the purchaser."

In 1804, Jefferson had problems in the east, also. He had tried to unite the nation after his inauguration by proclaiming,

"We are all Republicans. We are all Federalists."

But he had done his job too well in the previous decade. John Randolph, the leader of the Old Republicans, wrote,

"In our Virginia quarter, we think the great work is only begun; and that without substantial reform, we shall have little reason to congratulate ourselves on a mere change of men." They had rallied under this banner during the election and called the electoral victory "the revolution of 1800."

The Old Republicans would not be content until there was a complete overhaul of the Constitution and the American Government. This brought about what was at first a quiet division in the Republican Party—the Old Republicans and a more moderate variety. The short, thin James Madison loved the Constitution he had been so instrumental in forming. Always the diplomat, he tried to moderate both sides and protect his friend, President Jefferson, from extremism.

The new vice president, Aaron Burr, was looked on suspiciously by the party. They had needed him to win their election; but they found his position as the deciding vote in the Senate uncomfortable. Too often, the federalist senators would balance their republican votes and the decision would be left to

Burr to vote "Aye" or "Nay." They were never quite sure which way it would be for they knew he loved a good battle and a strong central government almost as much as their hated enemy, ALEXANDER HAMILTON. They also knew he hated slavery, and this was definitely not the old Virginia view. At first he seemed to vote and support President Jefferson; then, when Jefferson started to show favoritism to the New York mayor, DeWitt Clinton, whom Burr disliked immensely, the Federalists edged in and invited Burr to one of their finer parties on Washington's birthday celebration in 1802. Burr accepted the invitation. When it became his turn to offer the impromptu toast from the head table, the suave vice president raised his glass with the words, "To the union of all honest men" and charmed some important federalists into believing that a third-party of moderates standing in honest union between Jefferson and HAMILTON with Burr as their candidate might be the politics of the future.

Aaron Burr liked politics. He once said it was a life that provided "fun, profit and honor." For him, the life of a lawyer was drudgery. At that time, politics was his only source of income. He was in debt. His beautiful New York estate, "Richmond Hill", with beautiful furnishings and twenty-six acres, was designed for his pleasure and ambition. He even liked the jovial General JAMES WILKINSON and corresponded with him about Kentucky and the west. If he intended to keep up his life of "fun, profit and honor," he must be concerned about his political future.

Jefferson became fearful as he watched Burr's popularity with the British diplomats, who preferred the vice president's epicurean parties to the stoic entertainment of his Republicans. Burr's willingness to flaunt convention and court the ladies, even to the extent of suggesting that they could vote, was not popular with the Old Republicans. Editor James Cheetham of the *American Citizen* newspaper began a scurrilous attack on the vice president, and delivered a copy of his paper secretly to President Jefferson, who would contribute his ideas from time to time. When the rumor started that George Clinton was going to run for two offices—governor of New York State and the United State's vice president in 1804—many were concerned, especially Burr. Rumor also stated that if George Clinton won both offices, ROBERT R. LIVINGSTON would be appointed to replace him as the governor of New York.

Burr felt the slight completely. He had depended on Clinton's support in his past election. He sought an audience with President Jefferson. Jefferson met with him; but the president was so cool and unreceptive to Burr's plea to be appointed as either the English or French minister that Burr left the president's office with the certain knowledge that in Jefferson's eyes he was expendable. The Republican Party had moved upward and squeezed him out.

Burr considered the Federalists and his invitation to their celebration of George Washington's birthday. Burr's toast "To the union of all honest men" had gained him some momentum. There was quiet talk among some of the Federalists in favor of a secession of the northern states from the southern states, because of Jefferson's attack on the Constitution. Burr knew that HAMILTON would unequivocally oppose such an action, and although Burr had not said "Yes" to those who had approached him to lead this faction, he had not discouraged them. He decided to test the water by running for governor of New York in the coming April election; but, always the careful politician, waited to see what George Clinton would do. When it was announced that George would seek the vice presidency and supported Lansing for governor— Burr threw his hat into the ring as a candidate for the office of governor of New York State.

Lansing, however, had not yet agreed to run for the office. After visiting with George Clinton and his nephew, Lansing realized that their support depended upon his obeisance. Lansing would not be bought, and withdrew his name from consideration. ALEXANDER HAMILTON was quite willing to support Lansing; but when he withdrew from the race, HAMILTON tried to get Rufus King to run. He refused, not wanting to indulge in any smear campaign or any pandering, realizing that the legislature and the City of New York were controlled by the Clintons. The republicans gave their support to New York's attorney general, MORGAN LEWIS, the son of GERTRUDE LIVINGSTON LEWIS—sister of ROBERT R. LIVINGSTON. With Aaron Burr and MORGAN LEWIS, to choose between, ALEXANDER HAMILTON refused to support either one and announced his neutrality—a no-win game for him.

It was a vicious campaign. Newspaper editorials and printed handouts were rampant. Money flowed from supporting bank executives. The *Morning Chronicle* editor supported Aaron Burr and pictured him as standing stalwart against the Livingston/Clintonian regime. William Coleman in the *New-York Evening Post,* a friend to HAMILTON, tried to be neutral, but still reported negatively from time to time on both candidates. James Cheetham's *American Citizen* increased their unyielding smear of Aaron Burr and attempted to involve ALEXANDER HAMILTON by quoting his past 1800 turn of the century statements in opposition to Burr; but HAMILTON repeated his neutrality and tried to stay out of the fray.

A handbill of Aaron Burr's entitled *PLAIN TRUTH* was directed to "the independent electors of the state." In it was a list of the names of LIVINGSTONs and Clintons and their relatives and in-laws employed by the state, with each of their exact salaries. If MORGAN LEWIS were elected, the voters would be electing

> "an order of NOBILITY in the country." To New York's northern farming counties, Burr pled, "Many of you have fought and bled by my side. Old Soldiers, will you forsake your comrade?"

Cheetham replied to this by publishing a letter of JAMES MORGAN's— probably a second or third cousin to my BARTON ancestors who served in the Revolution. This letter appeared in the 7 April issue of the *American Citizen.* MORGAN, a former member of the Westchester militia, claimed that in 1780 or 1781 he had loaned the army a horse to carry a letter to West Point. The next day, when he went to collect his horse, Colonel Burr told him the steed had not yet returned. MORGAN stayed overnight in a nearby house and asked again for his horse the following morning. Burr sent him to a nearby farmhouse to collect it, accompanied by a corporal. When they got there, the corporal opened sealed orders from Colonel Burr.

The orders told the corporal to flog MORGAN, who stated,

> "I was stripped naked, then tied to a tree, and the corporal who carried the orders was expressly charged to be the executor of his malicious purpose. I then received THIRTY NINE LASHES ON MY NAKED BACK!!" MORGAN further claimed that "acts of a similar nature were frequent with Colonel Burr to gratify his capricious temper." Cheetham added a postscript to MORGAN's letter saying, "in consequence of the INHUMAN treatment mentioned by Mr. MORGAN, Gen. Washington superseded Mr. Burr and appointed Gen. Hull of Massachusetts to the command."

Burr's editor of the *Morning Chronicle* quickly lashed back, stating that MORGAN had been flogged after repeated warnings not to cross the lines. Letters from Westchesterites portrayed MORGAN as a suspected spy who was lucky to get off with the lashing. They also included a letter from MORGAN's brother, who claimed the order for the flogging was not from Colonel Burr, who resigned from the army in 1779. This was followed by a rebuttal from Cheetham—a handbill replete with affidavits from MORGAN and several of his Westchester friends confirming the contents of MORGAN's original letter. The Clintons saw that it was circulated throughout the state and the term "Poor MORGAN" was added to Cheetham's already bulging arsenal, while voters commiserated with the mistreated loyal militiaman.

Cheetham reminded the voters as the election drew near that their heroic, departed father of their country, George Washington, had warned them to

"*BEWARE OF AMBITION;*" further, referring to Burr's change of parties, "*THAT A DESERTER SHOULD NEVER BE TRUSTED*" and that it was imperative to choose, "*THE CANDIDATE SELECTED WITH THE APPROBATION OF YOUR POLITICAL REPRESENTATIVES*" instead of an individual whom "*NO HONEST MAN CAN IN CONSCIENCE CONSENT TO SUPPORT.*"

Thus he tried to counter Aaron Burr's slogan "A union of honest men." by trying to bring the departed General Washington to the aid of MORGAN LEWIS.

This brought William Coleman's response in his supposedly neutral *Evening Post*. He wondered how the Clintonians of all people could claim a fellowship with George Washington, who loved and honored the Constitution, while George Clinton had spent most of his life subverting it. He stated further that he believed Washington's remarks were directed toward DeWitt Clinton.

"The solemn bombast, the profound hypocrisy, the mixture of rage and terror could come from no one else. Pride, power, revenge and ten thousand a year [the mayor's take home pay] all unite to instigate him."

He then followed these remarks with a report of *smashing* Federalist victories in the gubernatorial races in New Hampshire and Massachusetts.

Cheetham kept the political dirt flowing with endless accusations describing Burr in various ways: a secret spy for the British; a notorious lover with a list of his companions of "ill fame" and another list of those he had tried to seduce; various lawsuits he had never finished; his seduction of a tradesman's daughter; a man who would buy the vote of the free Negroes with special entertainment, and whatever lies, slanted truth, or partial truths they could find.

From Albany came a report that Chief Justice MORGAN LEWIS was appalled at the depths to which DeWitt Clinton had sunk to stop Burr. The *Commercial Advertiser* quoted MORGAN LEWIS as saying

> "he would rather have seen the government in h____, than he would have been a candidate, had he known how the election would have been conducted."

Aaron Burr wrote his daughter in South Carolina on 25 April,

> "I too write in a storm; an election storm. The thing began yesterday and will terminate tomorrow.... Both parties claim majorities, and there never was, in my opinion, an election of the result of which so little judgment could be formed. A.B. will have a small majority in this city if tomorrow should be a fair day, and not else."

Unfortunately for HAMILTON, on that same day, the *Evening Post* published an editorial titled "Electioneering Arts" and included an "extract from a handbill from Albany" It was written by Dr. Charles D. Cooper to Andrew Brown, Esq of the City of Bern in the same county and dated "12th April 1804." It read:

> "Dear Sir:
>
> "You will receive some election papers and some of them also in the German language. I presume you will make use of them in the best advantage. Have them dispersed and scattered as much as possible—the friends of Col. Burr are extremely active and will require all our exertion to put them down—it is believed that most of the reflecting Federalists will vote [for] LEWIS. Genl. HAMILTON, the Patroon's brother-in-law it is said has come out decidedly against Burr, indeed when he was here he spoke of him as a dangerous man and ought not to be trusted. Judge Kent also expressed the same sentiment—the Patroon was quite indifferent about it when he went to New York—it is thought that when he sees Genl. HAMILTON and his brother-in-law Mr. CHURCH (who Burr some time ago fought a duel with, and who, of course, must bear Burr much hatred)-—I say many feel persuaded that Mr. RENSSELAER will be decidedly opposed to Mr.

Burr—if you think any of us can aid you in the election in your town, let us know and we will give you what assistance in our power—can you send me word what you think will be the result of the election in your town?

"Yours Sincerely,

"Charles D. Cooper   [Addressed to A. Brown, Esq.]

"Postscript: Perhaps it [would] be of use to shew part of this letter that relates to the Patroon, HAMILTON and CHURCH to some of the patroon's tenants—I leave it to your discretion."

Editor Coleman of the *Post* added his negative comments on the letter, in which he claimed that General HAMILTON had "repeatedly declared" he would not oppose Colonel Burr in favor of MORGAN LEWIS "or any other candidate nominated by the prevailing tyrannical faction, after they drove the Honorable Chancellor Lansing to decline." He gave as his source "a highly respected Federal character and near connection of General HAMILTON."—referring to General PHILIP SCHUYLER.

Coleman further maintained that Judge Kent was determined to vote for Colonel Burr and that STEPHEN VAN RENSSELAER had

"determined on giving a firm and decided support to the election of Colonel Burr. Judge Tayler himself had reported hearing the Patroon say this a few days before he departed for New York." Coleman continued further, "The falsehood and malice of the above letter [Dr. Cooper's] will be seen by all who shall read the following."

He then printed a letter from General SCHUYLER that stated that HAMILTON had favored Lansing but after LEWIS's nomination had said he would not interfere in the election. SCHUYLER also confirmed that Judge Kent had told him personally that Burr was getting his vote.

Dr. Charles D. Cooper was a son-in-law of Judge Tayler, who had invited ALEXANDER HAMILTON to dinner in Albany in February, when HAMILTON was presenting his famous lawsuit before the New York Supreme Court in which he established the right to use the truth as a defense against slanderous accusations—perhaps HAMILTON's greatest performance as a defense attorney. He certainly had impressed Judge Kent and the very large audience that had gathered to hear him from all around. Cooper was present at the dinner party at Judge Tayler's home and was equally awed by General HAMILTON's legal abilities and he took his casual assessment of Aaron Burr at the dinner table very seriously.

The above handbill and General SCHUYLER's letter had both been printed separately in the *Albany Register* previous to Coleman's printing on 25 April. Dr. Cooper took offence to General SCHUYLER's letter, feeling he was being called a liar, and had retaliated with another of his own in which he declared as a final statement,

> "For really sir, I could detail to you a still more despicable opinion which Gen. HAMILTON has expressed of Mr. Burr."

These words were ignored by most people in the midst of the slurs that were being flung by both sides in this tight election; but they would surface in a deadly fashion within a few months and reverberate across the country.

On the following day 26 April, Coleman could not retain his semblance of neutrality any longer, and his *Evening Post's* lead story blasted the republican's with such lines as the following: Chief Justice MORGAN LEWIS had post election plans to humiliate the Federalists in every possible way; Ambrose Spencer had declared that after the election a Federalist would know "what it was to be scourged in reality," and DeWitt Clinton had declared he had his foot on the Federalist's necks and would never let them up. Coleman threw out the question,

> "Is there a Federalist in this city having the spirit of a man in him whose indignation does not instantly kindle at the sight of this? —To the polls then—to the Polls!! And down with this insolent, malevolent, villainous faction."

On 27 April, the votes were counted and totaled on Manhattan Island and Burr was ahead by 100 votes. It would be another five days before the results of northern New York were gathered and totaled—it was 500 miles to the distant farm lands. But the Burrites were confident of victory. Cheetham had noted in his paper that

> "Gen. HAMILTON, Colonel Troup, JOHN B. CHURCH" and several others had not voted for either candidate, and further stated that "their conduct had been honorable and manly."

This was probably not any consolation to HAMILTON. If Aaron Burr won,

Burr would be the undisputed leader of the Federalist Party; Burr would be in position to challenge the Jefferson/Clinton ticket in the fall and would, with his son-in-law Alstom's money and support, probably have the South Carolina vote additionally to pull him to the top. If Burr failed in the national election, he would be in position to lead the Federalists in their threatened secession from the nation, if they so opted. HAMILTON could not have been happy about this prospect. But the Federalists in general were quite delighted. They were tired of George Clinton's greed for public office and his nephew's arrogance as the mayor of New York.

Then on 30 April, the votes arrived from the other counties, and it became apparent that Burr had lost the election by 7,000 to 8,000 votes. Cheetham's newspaper proclaimed that Jefferson had never been neutral on the election and gave Jefferson credit for his secret victory. On 1 May, Burr wrote his daughter in his usual way and ended with a rather cheerful remark,

"The election is lost by a great majority: tant mieus." (It is just as well.)

Of the fifteen New York seats in the United States Congress, the two representatives that had supported Burr during the election lost their seats. After praising himself for leading out in the opposition to the election of Burr, Cheetham gloated as he wrote,

"So much for the union of all honest men."

Burr was quite heavily in debt. During the campaign the Livingston/Clintonian legislature had threatened the Merchants Bank by refusing to grant it a charter. Burr was heavily involved in this bank and his estate *Richmond Hill* was mortgaged with them. ALEXANDER HAMILTON was approached by the Merchants Bank directors to help them in their wording of the early draft of their bill to fight against the New York legislature. HAMILTON never hesitated to assist them, stating that the original bill was "dangerous to the Mercantile interest."

All indications are that HAMILTON did not want political activity; rather, he avoided political involvement. In 1801, his oldest son, PHILIP, had been killed in a duel—defending the honor of his father. HAMILTON had stayed with him the night before and advised him to throw away his first shot. Unfortunately, his opponent did not. HAMILTON's oldest daughter was so distraught and depressed so deeply on losing her brother that she never really recovered.

Judge Kent visited the HAMILTONs for a weekend at their recently completed Harlem Heights home on the Hudson—*The Grange*. In a letter to his wife, he remarked that HAMILTON's deranged daughter ANGELICA, now nineteen, "has a very uncommon simplicity and modesty of deportment." His stay with the HAMILTONs convinced him that politics and fame were not for him. He told his wife that he was resolved to pursue his ruling passion:

"literary and elegant retirement and a glowing and vehement attachment to my wife and children." He was "assuredly" not interested in "ambition or glory."

In May 1804, Burr received three interesting letters. The first was from his Scotch friend Charles Williamson, who had bought millions of acres of land in upstate New York for speculation, with the intent of selling parcels of land to investors in England. He had married an American girl. He was in Bath, near Albany, and wanted advice on how to divorce his angry wife, Abigail, who had developed (because of his infidelity) "the temper of a devil." He was in the process of transferring his land deal to Robert Troup, and planned to go to England later that year. As for politics, he would say nothing until they met in "one month's time." Meanwhile he wanted vice president Burr to know that

"no circumstance can lessen the most respectful and sincere regard and esteem of your affectionate friend."

The second letter was from General JAMES WILKINSON. It read:

"To save time of which I need much and have little, I propose to take a bed with you this night, if it may be done without observation or intrusion— Answer me and if in the affirmative I will be with [you] at 30 after the 8th hour."

This was on 23 May. The private meeting was held, and the next day, WILKINSON sent another letter as he resumed his journey to Washington D.C. It read,

"You are deceived, my friend, with respect to the size of the rum barrel of Louisiana the answer being 450 lbs,"—probably veiling the size of his army. He further added that he was on his way "with prayers and wishes for your prosperity and happiness" and "with warm prospect . . . your affetiate [affectionate] and faithful friend."

This was followed within a few hours by a post script, inviting Burr to visit the general before he left New York, "to see my maps," referring to his military maps of Texas and the Spanish southwest.

It was a joyful Burr that wrote his daughter within the next few days, beginning by assuring her he would "never again be so long without writing you," and following with this positive fatherly advice, in much the same tone as he had done in the past. It seemed as if the failures of the recent past had ended and the future was alive with opportunity.

A few weeks previous to the above letters, General HAMILTON had received a letter from General JAMES WILKINSON. HAMILTON was a retired major general and WILKINSON was presently an active brigadier general. He had been under HAMILTON's command through the possible threatening war with France in 1797. WILKINSON told his former chief that New Orleans was attracting

> "men of all nations, ages, professions, Characters & Complexions, and women too." He added that he would give a "Spanish province for an interview with you." He further added that the "infernal design of France" was "obvious to me," suggesting that he believed Napoleon planned to take back Louisiana as soon as possible. Then, as for the "destinies of Spain," they were in "the hands of the U.S."

Here he referred to the Floridas, Texas and the Mexican Territory beyond. There is no indication that HAMILTON ever met with him; but the letter gives us an indication of General WILKINSON's ideas at that time.

On 18 May 1804, Napoleon accepted the title of Emperor, which was to be "hereditary in the family of the present chief magistrate." He accepted this title in accordance with the will of the French people, as expressed in resolutions and petitions from his followers across France. It would be another six weeks before this stunning news would reach America—so much for the Republic of France and Thomas Jefferson's adoration and help with their republican constitution. But the majority of the American people would fail to make the connection— they had the Louisiana Purchase!

When British Charles Williamson arrived at *Richmond Hills*, he found Burr in a rather ill state. Bandages covered much of his head. He was suffering from a debilitating sinus infection coupled with a painful migraine headache that seemed to attack him during times of great stress. Undoubtedly Williamson received help on his divorce procedures and on his estate transfer to Robert Troup. In addition, political events and future speculations occupied a great deal of time, also. Minutes of their meeting, of course, were never taken. We are left with our own imaginations to determine what might have been said. Indications are that Williamson left Burr with the understanding that Williamson planned to recruit an army of recent immigrants to America and that they would support Burr in his attack on the Spanish possessions in the New World. He also left him with Coleman's newspaper editorial in his hand [regarding General ALEXANDER HAMILTON's supposed comment about a "still more despicable opinion" of Burr].

At 11:00 A.M. on June 18th, Burr's very close friend, William P. Van Ness, appeared at General HAMILTON's law office with the following letter.

"N York 18 June 1804

Sir,

I send for your perusal a letter signed Ch. D. Cooper which though apparently published some time ago, has but very recently come to my knowledge. Mr. Van Ness who does me the favor to deliver this, will point out to you that Clause of the letter to which I particularly request your attention.

You might perceive, Sir, the necessity of a prompt and unqualified acknowledgment or denial of the use of any expressions which could warrant the assertions of Dr. Cooper.

I have the honor to be

Your Obdt s'

A. Burr"

A very busy HAMILTON looked up from his desk and responded that "despicable" was too "general and undefined" to warrant a "specific answer." He then asked Van Ness to return to Burr and ask him to identify "particular expressions" and he would be glad to "recognize or disavow them." Van Ness doubted the Colonel was inclined to do this. The two men debated for a few minutes with Hamilton finally agreeing to give his answer later in the day.

At one-thirty in the afternoon, HAMILTON visited Van Ness at his house saying,

> "a variety of engagements" would prevent him from giving the matter his full attention until Wednesday, when HAMILTON hoped he could give Van Ness an answer that was "suitable" and "compatible with his feelings." HAMILTON then stated he was sorry that Mr. Burr had adopted this course. It required HAMILTON to give the subject "some deliberation."

Van Ness agreed with the delay, and HAMILTON spent Tuesday evening at a party his wife was giving and Wednesday morning in court—Van Ness also was present. HAMILTON told him he'd have his answer in the afternoon. Van Ness waited at his home throughout the afternoon—there was no reply. Going out to dinner, upon his return, he found HAMILTON's answer waiting for him.

HAMILTON's hasty answer was basically a rewording of his earlier contention, that "despicable" and "more despicable" were not "worth the pains of a distinction." He also reminded Mr. Burr that Dr. Cooper, not he, had used the word under contention. He continued,

> "I will add, that I deem it inadmissable, on principle, to consent to be interrogated as to the justice of the inferences, which may be drawn by others, from whatever I may have said of a political opponent in the course of fifteen years competition." To accept such an interrogation would expose him to, "injurious imputations" from every person to whom he may have talked or written during this decade and a half. HAMILTON ended by hoping that Mr. Burr would see it the same way. If not, "I can only regret the circumstances, and must abide the consequences." HAMILTON then added, "The publication by Dr. Cooper was never seen by me till after the receipt of your letter."

[Note: The language of insult between gentlemen usually required a specific term, unmistakably from the lips of the insulter, such as rascal, coward, liar, scoundrel, to (honorably?) bring about a duel with gunfire.]

The contentions between the two men continued with letters exchanged between their two seconds, Van Ness and Pendleton, until on 27 June it became evident to both seconds that reconciliation between the two duelists was impossible, and the "interview" [duel] was inevitable. To HAMILTON, it was impossible to apologize without a specific word, time, and place. He had said too much throughout the years. To submit would label him a coward, for it was well known among his countrymen how he felt about Burr. Colonel Burr was implacable. He had deliberately started the fray and he would not budge to any of General HAMILTON's maneuvers to avoid the interview. It was as though HAMILTON's blood or his political kill by cowardly submission were the only solutions Burr would agree upon.

Why would Burr turn on HAMILTON with such viciousness? As a lawyer, he was quite aware that his premise was based on hearsay, which would have been thrown out of any legal court. Both the Livingston/Clintonians and President Jefferson in their newspapers had been far more severe and direct on Burr, in their accusations than HAMILTON had been. Burr was not an impulsive man; he was a calculating and manipulative man. Considering the secret meetings he had with General JAMES WILKINSON, and his British friend Williamson, is it possible that Burr's future plans included the overthrow of the United States, and that his part in the plot was to begin by getting rid of HAMILTON? Did he feel that HAMILTON was the only man that would stand in the way of the aggressive military coup he had in mind? If so, then if Cooper's letters had not come to his attention, he would have found an equally insulting statement to accuse HAMILTON with—months after the fact. He was too wise and unfeeling as a politician to allow this basically unnoticed news article to bring about this incident unless he planned to profit by it. He saw it as a win, win situation. If HAMILTON refused, the General's military and political career would end. As a coward, HAMILTON would not be accepted by the military to raise an army and save the nation, and HAMILTON was, in Burr's opinion, as well as others, the only man that could get the support of the militia and his countrymen at that time.

In the military, HAMILTON outranked WILKINSON. He could find the money to supply the army, if the need became apparent. HAMILTON would fight against the secession of the New Englanders. He would fight against tyranny in the west, as he had done in the Whiskey Rebellion. He would never quit defending the Constitution and the preservation of the nation, if he were called upon to do so. Burr also knew from the past duels that HAMILTON had fought, as well as the advice he had given his son, that he would probably play the gentleman and throw away his first pistol shot. Burr had no intention of doing so. As Robert Troup had warned HAMILTON years ago,

"Burr will destroy you, if he can."

Why, then, later on, did WILKINSON turn against Burr? Maybe other events changed his outlook. He looked at the British, the Spanish, Burr's small army, and Jefferson's favors and chose the United States. One thing that Burr had not counted on was the unifying of the Americans against him in labeling the incident as a deliberate "MURDER!" The country, in general, had winked at the duels of the past; but they saw this one differently. With HAMILTON's death, all fear of the accusations circulated by the Republicans against HAMILTON regarding his ambitions evaporated. He was no longer a threat. Most of the country was quick to see HAMILTON as the hero and Burr as the dirty little villain who killed him.

Duels had been outlawed in New York State at that time—that is why the place for the duel would be across the Hudson on the New Jersey shore at Weehawken. After HAMILTON died, New York charged Aaron Burr with "Murder!" Burr's lawyer claimed that the duel took place in New Jersey. In New Jersey there was a quick reaction to make duels retroactively illegal in their state, and to also charge him with murder. Throughout the nation, after HAMILTON's death, legal dueling ended, and the majority of the people mourned and praised their hero.

Allowing sufficient time for the updating of wills and final preparations, the duel took place on 11 Jul 1804. The duelists needed to row across the three miles of water that separated New York City from the dueling place at 5:00 A.M.; Nathaniel Pendleton had written the rules. The distance was to be 10 paces, or about 30 feet. Both sides had agreed on HAMILTON's physician, David Hosack. Van Ness and Burr reached the dueling ground first and began clearing away the underbrush and tree limbs to get a relatively clear space two paces wide and ten paces long. It was an isolated beach that could only be reached from Weehawken at low tide. The steepness of the cliffs behind guaranteed that they would not be interrupted. HAMILTON, Pendleton and Dr. Hosack came from another dock in what is now known as Greenwich Village. The doctor remained with the boatman, while HAMILTON and his second climbed the trail to find Burr and his second. The coin was tossed by the seconds. Pendleton won both throws. He would have his choice of the pistols and position. They had previously agreed to use the pistols of JOHN B. CHURCH. Pendleton chose to position HAMILTON with his back to the cliff, facing the light, perhaps feeling that Burr's silhouette outlined against the glistening river would make the best target. HAMILTON told him he had decided to throw away his first shot; he was not sure about his second round. Burr said he needed only one shot.

The two seconds loaded the pistols with powder and a "smooth ball," as required by the rules. The duelists took their positions. The seconds approached them, their pistols loaded. As Pendleton gave General HAMILTON his weapon, he asked,

"Do you want the hair spring set?"

"Not this time," replied HAMILTON.

According to Burr and Van Ness, HAMILTON raised his pistol "as if to try the light," and asked them to pardon him. He said the "direction of the light" made it hard for him to adjust his eyes. With his left hand, he drew spectacles from his pocket and put them on.

Pendleton asked if they were ready. Both replied, "Yes."

"Present!" Pendleton proclaimed, allowing them to shoot whenever they chose.

Both men had assumed the duelist's stance, the right foot about twenty-six inches in front of the left foot, the face positioned over the right shoulder, the stomach sucked in, the right thigh and leg covering the left leg. The pistol was held somewhat to the left, where it could deflect a bullet. Both men leveled their pistols and the two shots rang out within seconds of each other. Van Ness thought HAMILTON had shot first and spun his head to see if Burr had been hit at the instance Burr's shot boomed out. Van Ness saw his body jerk and thought he had been hit, but later discovered he had a rock under his foot that slipped under his weight as the shot was fired.

Pendleton thought Burr fired first. His eyes had remained on HAMILTON and he saw HAMILTON's arm jerk upward as he pulled the trigger. To his horror he realized that HAMILTON had been hit. Gunsmoke enclosed the duelists for a brief moment; then still holding his pistol, General HAMILTON fell forward on his face. The large lead ball had penetrated HAMILTON's right side a little above the hip, gone through his liver and diaphragm, and lodged in his vertebrae.

Pendleton shouted, "Dr. Hosack!"

Van Ness rushed forward and led Burr down the path toward the water, and according to one account, shielded him with an open umbrella, to stop the testimony of the boatman and Dr. Hosack as to his presence at the scene.

At their boat, Burr hesitated. "I must go and speak to him," he was reported as saying; but Van Ness persuaded him against it and forced him bodily into the boat, and they were soon crossing the Hudson River.

Dr. Hosack found HAMILTON half sitting on the ground in the arms of Pendleton. HAMILTON gasped,

"This is a mortal wound, Doctor."

He lost consciousness shortly after. The doctor raised his bloody shirt to examine the wound, feeling that the duelist was probably right, since he could find no pulse or heartbeat and his breathing had stopped. The two men felt they must get him to the water, if there was any possibility for his survival. Pendleton was quick to tell the Doctor that HAMILTON had refused to fire at Burr. They carried him to the edge, where the land dropped sharply to the water's edge. With the help of the oarsman, they placed him in the boat and were soon crossing the Hudson. Dr. Hosack was rubbing HAMILTON's face with spirits of hartshorne. He applied it to his neck and chest, then his wrists and hands, hoping to invigorate the body. Fifty yards from the shore, HAMILTON suddenly gave a deep sigh and started breathing again. The hartshorne, the cooler river air, or (more likely) his own soul's determination to live and protect his honor had brought back his life—at least, temporarily. As he gazed about him, he whispered:

"my vision is indistinct."

Slowly his pulse returned to normal and his breathing became regular; but his wound was too painful to touch.

As his vision cleared, HAMILTON saw his brother-in-law's pistol case open in the bottom of the boat with the gun lying outside it.

"Take care of that pistol," he said. "It is undischarged and still cocked—it may go off and do harm." Then he added, looking at Pendleton, "Pendleton knows I did not intend to fire at him."

"Yes," replied Pendleton, "I have already told Dr. Hosack that."

For a few moments there were only the sounds of the oars as they dipped into the water and the heavy breathing of the oarsman as he pulled the boat forward across the river. Then Dr. Hosack began his questions. HAMILTON reported that he had lost all feeling in his body from the waist down. He could not move his legs. When the New York coastline was quite near, HAMILTON asked them to send for his wife, but break the news to her gradually.

"Give her hope," he urged.

Waiting at the Greenwich Village dock, was HAMILTON's good friend William Bayard. A servant had seen the two men leave earlier and informed Bayard, who suspected a duel and had rushed to the dock. The merchant broke into almost uncontrollable tears when he saw the helpless HAMILTON lying in the bottom of the boat. The Doctor asked him to prepare a bed for his friend, and the inhabitants of Bayard's home joined in his weeping. The Doctor's report noted that HAMILTON appeared to be the only one keeping his composure.

HAMILTON then requested Bayard to send a servant for Benjamin Moore, the Episcopal bishop of New York and the president of Columbia College. The bishop arrived as requested; but he was not happy that the injury was the result of a duel, or that HAMILTON was asking for communion, although he had never joined his church. Leaving his message, he departed to give the dying man "time for reflection."

HAMILTON then asked them to send for John M. Mason, pastor of the Scotch Presbyterian Church. This was the church he had belonged to in his youth on the island of St. Croix. Mason rushed to his side, but sadly informed him that it was against church policy to give the communion privately. He then tried to assure him that communion was only a "pledge of forgiveness of sin" that Jesus had purchased by his death on the cross. The same forgiveness was available to HAMILTON by faith. The dying man wanted more assurance and asked that they plead with Bishop Benjamin Moore to come as soon as possible.

Around noon his wife, ELIZABETH SCHUYLER HAMILTON arrived. Obediently, no one had told her the truth of his condition. She was quick to assess the situation and became quite frantic with grief. Her husband declared in his strong firm voice:

"Remember, Eliza, you are a Christian."

Bishop Moore returned, and after getting HAMILTON's pledge that, if he recovered, he would never fight a duel again, he asked him if he could "live in love and charity with all men?" HAMILTON replied that he had "no ill will" toward Colonel Burr. He had met him with a "fixed resolution" not to do him any harm. He forgave him for "all that happened"—the challenge and the duel. The bishop then gave HAMILTON the communion he had requested, and reported that he received it "with great devotion" and "his heart afterwards appeared perfectly at rest."

Dr. Hosack gave a different account of his patient's condition. He claimed that HAMILTON was in a great deal of agony and kept muttering, "My beloved wife and children." He remarked that he slept quite peacefully that night after he gave him a large dose of laudanum [tincture of opium].

Meanwhile, a half-mile away from Bayard's house at *Richmond Hill*, Aaron Burr was starting to get secondhand stories about his own participation in the duel and the happenings at the Bayard home. William Van Ness received the following note from the vice president,

"There is in circulation a report which is ascribed to Mr. Pendleton & which he must forthwith contradict." If Van Ness could not come to Richmond Hill, Burr would visit him in the city, even though the latter "would you know, not be very pleasant."

There was a desperate tone to the letter. It would seem that Mr. Burr was beginning to get the idea that his "interview" of that day had not accomplished the result he had anticipated. Later, Nathaniel Pendleton would receive a letter inquiring kindly about the health of Mr. HAMILTON from William P. Van Ness. It ended with what was probably the real purpose of the letter when he concluded by hoping that Pendleton would not publish anything in the newspapers until they conferred on a statement that was acceptable to both sides.

The following day a letter arrived to Dr. Hosack.:

"Mr. Burr's respectful Compliments. He requests Dr. Hosack to inform him of the present state of Genl. H. and of the hopes which are entertained of his recovery.

"Mr. Burr begs to know at what hours of the [day] the Dr. may most probably be found at home, that he may repeat his inquiries. He would take it very kind if the Dr. would take the trouble of calling on him as he returns from Mr. Bayard's."

About the same time, Nathaniel Pendleton was writing a letter to Rufus King, who had left for Massachusetts a few days before the duel. It read in part,

"Before you read this, our dear and excellent friend HAMILTON will be no more . . . . Burr's first shot was fatal . . . . I have just left him and the doctors say he cannot outlive the day." He added that the news had already "occasioned a strong public sensation which will be much increased when he is dead."

When Gouverneur Morris learned the sad news, he hastened to HAMILTON's bedside and arrived on the morning of 12 July. He found his friend

"speechless"—comatose and obviously dying. "The scene is too powerful for me, I am obliged to walk in the garden to take breath."

Shortly after, he returned to the bedside where several of HAMILTON's friends had gathered. General HAMILTON died at two o'clock in the afternoon. Bishop Moore was to say, he expired "without a struggle, and almost without a groan." With tears streaming down his face, one of HAMILTON's friends turned to Morris and said,

"If we were truly brave we would not accept a challenge. But we are all cowards."

To this Morris observed that the friend was one of the bravest men alive, but he doubted if he would "so far brave public opinion as to refuse a challenge."

Hosack then quoted in Latin the words of the Roman poet Horace, which referred to another general in another age. The translation was:

"When will incorruptible Faith and naked Truth Find another his equal? He has died wept by many."

On 12 July, William Coleman in his *New-York Evening Post* published a letter written by Bishop Moore. The letter denounced dueling, advertised his church, and explained the need HAMILTON felt for communion. It sympathized with HAMILTON's "afflicted" family and the nation's loss of a "great statesman and real patriot." It brought tears to the eyes of its readers, exonerated HAMILTON and implicated Burr.

New York's Common Council met to discuss the funeral. The public would pay for it. Bells that had been forbidden during funerals would be muted, but rung periodically during the services. All flags on the ships in the harbor would be flown at half-mast. The stock market and all businesses would close their doors. They requested that everyone wear black crepe on their left arm for thirty days in respect for "the Integrity, Virtues, Talents and Patriotism of General ALEXANDER HAMILTON." The lawyers passed a resolution declaring their "universal confidence and veneration" for him, and called him "the brightest ornament of their profession." The Tammany Society, whose Democrat/ Republican members had previously regarded him as the incarnation of evil, found beautiful phrases to honor him with.

On Friday, 13 July, James Cheetham's usually caustic newspaper *American Citizen* proclaimed to its readers that:

> "Death has sealed the eloquent lips of GENERAL HAMILTON! . . . As soon as our feelings will permit, we shall notice this deplorable event, this national loss."

On that same day, there was a meeting of the two seconds, William P. Van Ness and Nathaniel Pendleton, at the home of Doctor Hosack to discuss what details were to be released to the press. They found they could not agree on certain items such as why Van Ness had refused to accept HAMILTON's last letter and which of the two duelists had shot first. Both seconds insisted on maintaining their personal views of the matter. An extremely worried Van Ness insisted that Burr and he had a right to prevent the publication of any article that appeared to make the vice president appear guilty. They did agree to consult their notes and reach an agreement at their next meeting. Pendleton and a friend returned to Weehawken to track the course of HAMILTON's bullet. They found where it had passed through the limb of a cedar tree, twelve-and-a-half feet from the ground and four feet toward the cliff from the mark on which Aaron Burr had stood. To Pendleton it verified his belief that HAMILTON had shot wild, squeezing the trigger when Burr's shot hit him and his arm flew upward.

At home at Richmond Hill, Burr wrote a letter to Van Ness:

"The most abominable falsehoods are current and have issued from the house where H now lies." In their letter exchanges, Van Ness had sent him a draft of the proposed press release. Burr was especially anxious about "the falsehood that H fired only when falling and without aim." That "has given rise to very improper suggestions—the fact does appear to me to be important."

Burr was also concerned about money. He needed $1,000 in cash as soon as possible, and he begged Van Ness to make up his "deficiency" of $780.

HAMILTON's body was moved to JOHN B. CHURCH's home on 25 Robinson Street. The funeral procession would start there and the Sixth Regiment of New York's militia assembled in front of the house with their guns reversed, muzzles down, as a sign of mourning. At noon the front doors opened and the mahogany coffin with eight pallbearers, including William Bayard and Oliver Wolcott Jr., emerged into the street. The artillery with their six cannon led, followed by the soldiers. The military band, with muffled drums, played a march. The sixth regiment was followed by the members of the Society of the Cincinnati [officers of the Revolution], which were followed by numerous clergymen. Then came the coffin escorted by the pallbearers, followed by HAMILTON's gray horse, carrying his boots and spurs reversed. Two black servants dressed in white, wearing turbans trimmed in black, led the horse. HAMILTON's family followed; then Gouverneur Morris, who was to give the funeral oration, came next in his carriage. (He had a wooden leg that prevented him from walking.) Members of the bar and other dignitaries followed by the faculty of Columbia College and students in their mourning gowns were next followed by the Tammany Society, Mechanic Society, and "citizens in General."

The procession marched along Beckman, Pearl, and Whitehall Streets and then up Broadway to the Trinity Church. William Coleman reported in his *Evening Post*,

"the streets were lined with people; doors and windows were filled, principally with weeping females, and even the house tops were covered with spectators."

The battery and the men-of-war in the harbor fired their cannon in a steady salute. Noticeably absent were ex-governor George Clinton and his nephew, Mayor DeWitt Clinton.

Gouverneur Morris's oratory in the fresh air differed from the Marcus Anthony oration in Rome centuries before. Whereas Anthony tried to stir up the crowd, Morris recorded in his diary that he did not want to excite emotions "too strong for your better judgement." He asked the people to avoid any act that might "again offend the insulted majesty of the law . . . . Let me entreat you to respect yourselves." The coffin was carried into the Trinity Churchyard where Bishop Moore read the service of the dead. Volleys resounded, while the cannon fired in the harbor, and William Coleman wrote that the scene "was enough to melt a monument of marble." Morris wrote in his diary,

> "How easy it would have been to make them for a Moment absolutely Mad!"

The coroner's jury met with what seemed to be an obvious attempt to indict Burr with murder. Nathaniel Pendleton gave his testimony, ignoring previously printed statements. He would tell the whole truth. He believed Van Ness to be sincere; but he disagreed on certain points and elaborated on HAMILTON's statements about the pistol on their homeward journey. The *Evening Post* printed the details.

On 18 July, Burr wrote Alston that he was about to be driven into a

> "sort of exile," and the uproar might end in "an actual and permanent ostracism." Burr continued, "our most unprincipled Jacobins [Clintonians] are loudest in their lamentation for General HAMILTON after describing him for years as 'the most detestable . . . of men.'"

Cheetham [editor of the *American Citizen*] was reporting that three of the vice president's followers had supposedly spent weeks combing newspapers for something that would entitle Burr to issue a challenge. Another rumor reported that the Burrites had met and decided that Burr should fight one of a list of four or five people who were slandering him, and Burr had chosen HAMILTON as his preference.

There was talk of burning Burr's New York townhouse and another mob that would burn *Richmond Hill*. The Federalist newspapers throughout the nation denounced Burr and pictured the American eagle in mourning, while HAMILTON and George Washington met around the celestial throne. Burr was right in his letter. The Clintonians, in praising their former opponent

HAMILTON, showed no sympathy for this man that had helped them and President Jefferson in their past elections. They depended on the short-sightedness of the public. Vice President Burr must be eliminated and destroyed politically. This was their opportunity.

Realizing that the forces against him could possibly result in a murder charge in New York and highly aware that such a charge would result in imprisonment without bail, Burr slipped into a boat in New York harbor around 10:00 P.M., Saturday, 21 July. He was accompanied by John Swartout and his black valet. Through the dark of the night, they rowed out of the harbor, past Staten Island to Perth Amboy. Here they sent the servant ashore to the home of Thomas Truxtun to ask for shelter.

The commodore was amazed that Burr was still in the boat, and rushed to the landing to welcome him. As they walked to the house, Burr explained the long hours they had been on the water and asked for a cup of coffee. Truxtun insisted on their partaking of a full breakfast, after which Swartout and his valet rowed back to New York. Burr asked where he could get a horse to ride to Philadelphia. Truxtun reminded him that it was Sunday, and he would need to wait until Monday. Truxtun was to write later that:

"Little was said of the duel." He observed that Burr "appeared to feel more sorrow and regret" than he had seen in other men on similar occasions.

At one point he told the vice president how much he admired General Hamilton; Burr became quite agitated, and he quickly added that he felt an equal esteem for Burr.

Monday he drove Burr in his carriage to Cranberry, New Jersey, where Burr found horses to complete his journey. Truxtun soon discovered that his neighbors and friends in more distant locations objected to the hospitality he had shown Burr. Comments reached such a height that he wrote an article that was placed in the *Evening Post*, in which he blamed Dr. Charles Cooper for revealing things a gentleman may have said but never intended to be made public.

Burr was not welcomed in Philadelphia, either, and even his daughter was upset about the duel and the feelings it had invoked throughout the nation against her father. Burr wrote to ask her not to force him to think "you are dissatisfied with me a moment. I can't just now endure it." But Burr had a reason to go to Philadelphia. It was a reason that would not become known until British records were shared with the Americans.

On 6 Aug 1804, British Ambassador Merry, who much preferred Vice President Burr's parties to those of President Jefferson, sent the following letter to England, addressed to the British foreign secretary, Dudley Ryder, Lord Harrowby, and beginning with the words,

> "Most Secret—My Lord, I have just received an offer from Mr. Burr the actual vice president of the United States (which Situation he is about to resign) to lend his assistance to His Majesty's Government in any Manner in which they may think fit to employ him, particularly in endeavouring to effect a Separation of the Western Part of the United States from that which lies between the Adantick [sic] and the Mountains, in it's whole Extent— His Proposition on this and other Subjects will be fully detailed to your Lordship by Col. Williamson who has been the Bearer of them to me, and who will embark for England in a few Days.—It is therefore only necessary for me to add that if, after what is generally known of the Profligacy of Mr. Burr's Character, His Majesty's Ministers should think proper to listen to his offer, his present Situation in this Country where he is now cast off as much by the democratic as by the Federal Party, and where he still preserves Connections with some People of Influence, added to his great Ambition and Spirit of Revenge against the present Administration, may possibly induce him to exert the Talents and Activity which he possesses with Fidelity to his Employers—"

On 11 August, Burr wrote to his daughter, Theodosia, that he would embark on a voyage to Saint Simon's Island, which was the home of his South Carolina friend and Republican senator, Pierce Butler. On 1 September, he wrote Charles Biddle that he had arrived and was safe and comfortable. He also reported that there was little or no public censure of him for killing General HAMILTON in a duel. On the contrary, he was

> "overwhelmed with all sorts of attention and Kindness—Presents are daily sent . . . . I live most luxuriously."

Historian Thomas Fleming in his book *Duel* stated,

> "This local reaction was typical of the way most southerners felt about Burr's deed."

While he was there, Burr spent much time exploring Spanish East and West

Florida, as requested by WILKINSON, who had let him view his military maps.

Burr returned through Savannah, Georgia, and on 19 October he started north and arrived soon in Petersburg, Virginia. The local Republicans made him the guest of honor at an "elegant supper." That evening he learned that the New Jersey grand jury, under the guidance of an angry Federalist judge, had indicted him for murder. An editorial in the Trenton Federalist had printed that

> "the honor of New Jersey demands that its shores should no longer be made places of butchery for the inhabitants of New York and Pennsylvania."

In New York, the coroner's jury indicted him, William P. Van Ness, and Nathaniel Pendleton for participating in a duel. He also discovered that his creditors in New York had moved on his New York assets. Richmond Hill had sold for $25,000—less than one-fifth of what he had considered selling it for in 1802. John Jacob Astor had bought the land at a bargain price, and would later subdivide it into 400 small house lots and make a fortune. Under the circumstances, Burr soon believed it would be wiser for him to stay safe and remain in Washington D.C., where he was immune from subpoenas. Here he was still vice president for several months, and he would be able to preside in the Senate during the coming session, 5 November.

With the Twelfth Amendment to the Constitution in place, the presidential election of 1804 was changed to elect the president and vice president as a ticket, instead of a single competition with the vice president coming in second. The Jefferson/Clinton ticket won by a landslide. The Electoral College vote was 162 to 14. The Federalist's ticket of Charles Cotesworth Pinckney/Rufus King had only won in Connecticut and Delaware. All talk of a secession of the northern and New England states ended. It was a disaster for the Federalists. Burr was quick to see that his future had to be in Florida and/or the western territories.

As president of the Senate, Burr felt no need whatever to placate President Jefferson, whom he detested almost as much, if not more, than he had HAMILTON. The Federalists in this lame duck session were very anxious to preserve their judges, whom Jefferson was almost frantic to get rid of. The previous session had retired one judge, who was getting older and somewhat senile, by impeachment and removal, as it is allowed in the Constitution. Jefferson and his Democrat/Republicans were planning to impeach all the Federalist

Supreme Court justices and replace them with those of their own party. The impeachment of Samuel Chase by the Jeffersonian controlled House was not difficult; but the following judgment to remove him from office is reserved for the Senate. Burr's untimely arrival in the Senate might compromise the Republican plans.

Senator William Branch Giles of Virginia immediately wrote a letter to the governor of New Jersey asking him to quash the murder indictment of Burr without sending it to the legislature. Secretary of State James Madison and Secretary of the Treasury Albert Gallatin befriended Aaron Burr, and even President Jefferson invited him to dinner at the palace several times. Burr's stepson Bartow Prevost was made judge of the superior court of the district called the Orleans Territory, and his brother-in-law, Dr. Joseph Browne, was made secretary of the Louisiana Territory. Even more significant to Burr, Brigadier General JAMES WILKINSON was appointed governor of the Louisiana Territory—while continuing to still keep his assignment, rank and salary as commander in chief of the U. S. army.

Burr was not taken in by their apparent friendship. He had certainly dealt with the Republicans and Jefferson previously. This obvious friendship from his previous enemies only alerted him more keenly to the knowledge that they wanted something—desperately—the impeachment of Samuel Chase. He accepted their favors and waited for his time.

He wrote his daughter that

"Wilkinson and Brown Will serve most admirably as eaters and laughers .
. . . And I believe in other particulars."

Whether from hatred of Jefferson, or Burr's sincere wish to preserve the checks and balances that were evident in the Constitution, Burr orchestrated a magnificent production that brought the public into the court scene by building additional galleries in the Senate, all decorated with patriotism, while he displayed a calm command of the Senate and insisted on the dignity of the Senators to be in keeping with their high offices. The Chase trial began on 4 Feb1805, with Aaron Burr in charge of the senate.

Chase's defenders were Joseph Hopkinson of Philadelphia, Charles Lee of Virginia (former U. S. Attorney General), and Robert Goodloe Harper, Philip

Barton Key, and Luther Martin, all from Maryland. The Republicans had called as one of the witnesses Chief Justice John Marshall, and they were able to lead him into several damaging statements against Chase. After many days, Luther Martin summed up for the defense and flatly accused the Jeffersonians of trying to destroy the Supreme Court. He said he was not only defending Justice Chase, a friend of thirty years, but he was also defending his fellow citizens against a pernicious scheme to demolish a bulwark of liberty.

At noon on 1 March, the vice president announced to the senators,

"You have heard the evidence and arguments adduced on the trial of Samuel Chase, impeached for high crimes and misdemeanors: You will now proceed to pronounce distinctly your judgment of each article."

Burr ordered the secretary of the senate to poll the senators on the eight charges, asking each man whether he considered each particular charge a high crime or misdemeanor. The chamber was filled to capacity, with both galleries occupied and about four hundred standing in the rear. This procedure of facing the people and answering each charge individually required each senator to look carefully into his own conscience before giving his answer. Each one would be accountable for his answers. Did he really consider each of the eight individual charges a high crime or misdemeanor? He must answer with a strong voice—eight times—"guilty" or "not guilty." The vote count was totaled and given to Burr, who stood quietly for a long moment before announcing,

"Samuel Chase Esquire, stands acquitted of all the articles exhibited by the House of Representatives against him."

The Republican/Democrats had failed to get the two-thirds vote that was needed, not even coming close on many of the charges.

With Judge Chase's acquittal; the Senate reached a new pinnacle of respect; the judiciary third branch of the Constitution was held intact, and Burr earned a place in history that softened the feelings of the Federalists. Federalist Senator Plumer wrote in his journal that Burr had

"done himself, the Senate and the nation honor." One newspaper declared that Burr had presided "with the dignity and impartiality of an angel, but with the rigour of a devil."

However, Burr had increased the hatred of Jefferson and Clinton against him to an even fiercer height. He had challenged them directly and had demonstrated his ability to lead fearlessly under great odds. Jefferson would not forget this. If Burr hadn't sold his services to another set of employers, the name of Aaron Burr might have overcome the infamy of the duel. But on second thought, there would probably not have been a duel, if Burr and the British agent Williamson hadn't believed that HAMILTON was a threat to their plan.

Jefferson would not give up. He took the battle to the House of Representatives where he called for a Constitutional Amendment to allow any federal judge to be removed by a simple majority vote of the House and Senate. He also tried to add another amendment, permitting a state legislature to recall a sitting senator by majority vote, anytime it so pleased. The proposals were not approved; but it shows the extent to which the Democrat/Republicans, with Jefferson at the helm, were willing to go in their efforts to destroy the Constitution, and that HAMILTON's fears for this document were warranted. It is an irony that Aaron Burr had killed HAMILTON, but had in turn with great skill saved the document that held the nation together.

Among HAMILTON's papers that he had prepared before the duel was a letter he left for his wife, ELIZABETH SCHUYLER HAMILTON. It read,

"The Scruples of a Christian have determined me to expose my own life to any extent rather than subject myself to the guilt of taking the life of another. This must increase my hazards & redoubles my pangs for you. But you had rather I should die innocent than live guilty. Heaven can preserve me and I humbly hope will, but in the contrary event, I charge you to remember that you are a Christian. God's Will be done! The will of a merciful God must be good.

Once more Adieu My Darling darling Wife AH"

General ALEXANDER HAMILTON was heavily in debt when he died. Some of his friends asked for donations to keep his family out of the poorhouse; but by 1 October, they had only raised $19,000. Some felt that her father, General PHILIP SCHUYLER should be able to support his daughter and her children better than they could. On 18 Nov 1804, General SCHUYLER died. He had mourned for his son-in-law for the past four months—feeling guilty for the small part he played in Dr. Cooper's second letter that included the deadly phrase, a "more despicable opinion" of Burr. In his will he left his daughter some land in various parts of New York but little or no cash. He had his debts, too.

Wolcott, Gouverneur Morris, and a few friends formed the ALEXANDER HAMILTON Association later in November and began selling shares in it, paying the subscribers with the upstate New York lands that HAMILTON had bought for speculation. Nine months later the funds were still short of the $100,000 they needed. Their fund contained only $40,000. The estate would need to be sold. Fortunately for BETSY and their two daughters and five sons, when the estate was auctioned, a group of wealthy supporters bought *The Grange* for $30,000 and sold it back to the widow for $15,000.

Wolcott continued soliciting donors for the family's relief for the next four years, until he had over $80,000—cash enough that she could live with dignity, if not with wealth, to the end of her life, which would be fifty years later in 1854. With the help of her children and friends, the ever faithful and stalwart ELIZABETH stood solid and was able to collect letters and documents that have preserved her husband's accomplishments and memory through the years. With the exception of John Adams and his family, most of the Federalists gave him great credit, second only in their regard for President Washington, in the birth and survival of the United States of America and its ability to become the power and light of the world for the common man.

~ 104 ~

THE BURR CONSPIRACY

C hanges were happening rapidly in Europe. On 18 May 1804, the day
Napoleon declared himself to be the emperor in Paris, England's Prime
Minister Henry Addington's government collapsed and William Pitt returned
again as the leader of Great Britain. Pitt was far more concerned about Napoleon
than he was about Burr's desire to conquer Texas and Mexico for them. His
efforts were directed to Europe and he sent agents into Russia, Austria, and
Prussia with fat pockets of cash and ideas to create distension against the newly
endowed Napoleon. In one way he was successful; but only in delayed action.
The ploy diverted an angry Napoleon into internal Europe, where with his brutal forces he destroyed and conquered in total the Austrian and Russian armies.
Only the English Channel separated him again from the small British Islands.
Napoleon would no longer wait for the weather. He combined his naval forces
with those of the Spanish fleet and headed for England.

On 21 Oct 1805, the British Admiral Horatio Nelson intercepted the combined armada and in a tremendous naval battle destroyed it off the southwest
coast of Spain at Cape Trafalgar. Admiral Nelson lost his life in the fray. Napoleon
quickly changed his invasion plans to building a stronger European Empire and
starving the English into submission. All alone in their struggle for survival, the
English vigorously armed themselves, no longer interested in America. About
10 years later, at dawn on 18 Jun 1815, Wellington would meet Napoleon on
the Waterloo battlefield in Belgium. France left 25,000 dead on the battlefield
and a total of 64,602 during the whole Belgium campaign. A similar amount
of casualties was reported by the English. In America, the news always came
several months later.

[Note: My next-door neighbor in Provo, whom I was helping with her genealogy, wrote to her husband's distant relatives in the Southern states and was informed by them that his middle name Nelson was given to him, because he was a direct descendent of Admiral Horatio Nelson. How fun!]

On 2 Mar 1805, Burr took his seat in the U.S. senate, as usual. Judge Samuel Chase had been acquitted the previous day. It was Saturday. There would be no session on Sunday. On Monday, 4 March, Jefferson would be inaugurated, for his second term, and George Clinton would become vice president. About 1:00 P.M., Burr surprised the Senators by announcing calmly that he had a "slight indisposition" [sore throat] and that it might be the best time to withdraw. He then proceeded to give his farewell address. He first apologized to the senators that he had been hard-handed on the previous day, defending his position by claiming to have been sincerely interested in the dignity of the senate. He had tried to rise above party and friends and hoped he had succeeded. He hoped they would continue in this fashion. He reminded them that he had spent ten years as a senator or vice president. He considered it a

> "sanctuary and a citadel of law, of order, of liberty." Whenever Americans struggled to resist "the storms of popular phrenzy and the silent arts of corruption" the final battle would take place here. If a demagogue or a usurper ever succeeded in destroying the Constitution, a calamity he hoped God would avert, the "expiring agonies will be witnessed on this floor."

He expressed his personal interest in them as well as his friendship for each of them, and ended by stating,

> "I have now, Gentleman, only to tender you my best wishes for your personal welfare and happiness."

With that, he walked out of the Senate chambers. There were tears of regret throughout the Senate. Senator Mitchill wrote to his wife,

> "There was a solemn and silent weeping for perhaps five minutes . . . . He is a most uncommon man, and I regret more deeply than ever the sad series of events which removed him from public usefulness and confidence . . . . Where he is going or how he is to get through with his difficulties I know not."

Burr wrote his son-in-law,

> "In New York I am to be disfranchised, in New Jersey hanged. Having substantial objections to both, I shall not, for the present, hazard either,

but shall seek another country." He then added that he had not "become passive, or disposed to submit tamely to the machinations of a banditti." He expected to triumph over Jefferson "and his clan affect to deplore, but secretly rejoice at and stimulate the villainies of all sorts which are practiced against me. Their alarm and anxiety, however, are palpable to a degree perfectly ridiculous. Their awkward attempts to propitiate me reminds one of the Indian worship of the evil spirit."

With his intense bitterness, Burr failed to see the turning of the political tide. With Jefferson's vicious attack on the judges, which extended into Pennsylvania's Supreme Court, the Republican's were splitting into factions. In New York, the Livingston/Clinton alliance was breaking apart. Governor MORGAN LEWIS had no enthusiasm for DeWitt Clinton's orders, and the general public was beginning to believe that they had sold out their Empire State to Virginia. In Congress, John Randolph was unhappy with Jefferson's support of the planters and slave expansion in the south. Spain had no intention of selling East or West Florida to Jefferson—negotiations were at a standstill.

Congressman Matthew Lyon visited Burr at the suggestion of General WILKINSON, who was spending the winter of 1804-5 in Washington, claiming that the General was anxious to help him make the transition from vice president to an office worthy of his talents. He urged Burr "to mount his horse the fourth of March, and ride through Virginia to Tennessee," telling everyone along the way that he was going to settle in Nashville and practice law. By next July he would have numerous friends, attracted by his celebrity and suavity, which would be eager to send him to Congress. Once there, Lyon was certain he would become speaker of the house, which he considered to be the third-ranking office in the government.

Burr's cool response was that he was having a houseboat built in Pittsburgh. He planned to explore the western waters—perhaps as far as New Orleans. Lyon warned him that he would lose his chance in Tennessee. Burr's answer was only, so be it. It seems he was more interested in three other visitors that had been sent by WILKINSON, who claimed to be disenfranchised citizens of Louisiana. They carried with them a "remonstrance" from EDWARD LIVINGSTON— Burr's friend, who shared his hatred of Jefferson. The document asked the question,

"Do political axioms on the Atlantic become problems when translated to the shores of the Mississippi?"

They were demanding the right to vote and an independent state, rather than an old colonial style governor. They also wanted the right to import as many slaves as they needed. As a final threat, they said they would go to France—Napoleon himself. Burr assured them of his sympathy and support. They continued to distribute their papers throughout Washington D.C.

On a second meeting with Matthew Lyon, Burr asked him if he would talk to Jefferson about sending him as an ambassador to England or France. Lyon was later to claim that "I told him very bluntly, I would not." He was highly aware of Jefferson's dislike of Burr.

Before Burr left the capital, he made a visit to the British embassy and had a meeting with their Ambassador Anthony Merry. Merry wrote a letter to London, addressed again to Foreign Secretary Lord Harrowby, on 29 Mar 1805. It was put on board a mail packet ship. Unfortunately for Burr, the packet ship was captured by the French and never reached London. The fact was not discovered until six months later, at which time a copy was sent with an explanatory cover letter. (The Americans did not know of this letter at Burr's trial.)

The long letter outlined Burr's plan to detach Louisiana and the western states from the Union and how the three agents, who claimed to represent the majority of the people in New Orleans, had expressed their strong desire to support Burr in doing so. From the British, Burr would need some naval support—a squadron of perhaps two or three frigates and some smaller vessels to scatter any attempt by Jefferson's administration to blockade New Orleans. (The small U. S. navy was still in the Mediterranean Sea at Tripoli.) In addition Burr wanted 100,000 pounds to finance the enterprise. Merry added that it was a small price to pay for these almost "exclusive" customers of English products. He believed that they would be too small to compete with England on the high seas, because they had only "one bad port," New Orleans, from which to ship and would probably never have merchant marines. Merry gave his strong approval.

Burr's ambition did not stop with a separate country of Louisiana. He envisioned the conquest of Texas and Mexico with its silver and gold, and he even hoped New England and the western states would join him. Louisiana and the

British were only his starting plan, hoping for the control of the Caribbean Sea and its islands to be his in the long term. On 10 Apr 1805, he wrote his daughter Theodosia:

"As the objects of this journey, not mere curiosity . . . may lead me to Orleans, and perhaps farther, I contemplate the tour with gayety and cheerfulness."

As rumors and suspicions of his activities in the west filtered back to the east from loyal Americans, or perhaps from Spanish or French sources, the following questions were printed in the *Gazette of the United States*, Philadelphia's Federalist newspaper.

"Is it a fact that Colonel Burr has formed a plan to engage the adventurous and enterprising young men from the Atlantic states to come into Louisiana?

"Is it one of the inducements that an immediate convention will be called from the states bordering on the Ohio and Mississippi to form a separate government?

"Is it another that all the public lands are to be seized and partitioned among those states, except what is reserved for the warlike friends and followers of Burr in the revolution?

"How soon will all the forts and magazines in all the military ports at New Orleans and on the Mississippi be in the hands of Col. Burr's revolution party?

"How soon will Col. Burr engage in the reduction of Mexico, by granting liberty to its inhabitants, and seizing on its treasures, aided by British ships and forces?"

The questions as stated were reprinted in newspapers across the nation. General WILKINSON became cooler and more distant from Colonel Burr, who with determination went forward with his plan. Why should the General risk his friendship and position with President Jefferson for a lost cause? He may also have realized that Burr's ambitions were different than he had planned. What about the Spanish and his promises to them? To be on the losing side was not in WILKINSON's future plans.

Having not yet received his 100,000 pounds from the British, Burr returned to Washington and Ambassador Merry's office, with the news that he had made a firm commitment to his friends in the West to "commence operations" in March of 1806. The ambassador replied that he would be glad to send his message; but he didn't know if anyone in London would listen. He explained that their friend Charles Williamson had lost his chief patron. Lord Melville had been accused of massive corruption and forced to resign. He was facing impeachment charges.

Burr learned further in Washington that the British were capturing the American merchant ships to prevent them from trading with France. Burr wrote WILKINSON,

> "We are to have no Spanish war except in ink and words. Great Britain is just
> now making alarming and systematic encroachments on our commerce."

Evidently, Burr and WILKINSON had hoped that Jefferson would declare war on Spain and create an army to take Florida by force. The two of them then intended to take over the U. S. army and divert it for their own purposes. Several weeks later Burr learned that the British Prime Minister William Pitt was dead. This would further diminish the possibility of any help from the English.

Still unwilling to give up, Burr sought a political appointment again and made a visit to President Jefferson. This time, if we can believe Jefferson's account of his visit, Burr threatened him with "much harm," if he refused. It is possible Burr wanted the appointment to personally gain foreign support for his conquest.

Jefferson wrote that he had stated in his reply "that Burr had lost the confidence of the people." . . . that "not a single voice" had been raised to renominate him for vice president. He further explained that he had no worries about him doing him further harm. About a month later, Burr wrote to WILKINSON that "the execution of our project is postponed till December." Burr had seen a different Washington upon his return. Jefferson's control of Congress was weakening with John Randolph's lack of support. The public was viewing Jefferson as a weak president in allowing the British capture of American ships, and the skirmishes on the borders of the Spanish Floridas were a constant reminder to the people that Jefferson was not the strong leader that George Washington had been.

In Burr's megalomanic mind, he considered invading Washington D. C., with 500 men and chasing Jefferson back to Monticello. He told several people that "men of property energy and talents" would welcome such a revolution—and he had no doubt that Congress would accept him. Did he consider himself the American Bonaparte? If so, he had difficulty financing and gaining the support of the necessary people. Anyway this plot never materialized.

Without the 100,000 pounds of British sterling, Burr took his plan to Philadelphia. His former good friend Charles Biddle wanted nothing to do with his plans. In New Jersey, Commodore Truxtun was offered the position of commander of the navy Burr was planning for the conquest of Mexico. Truxtun turned him away. Ex-Senator Jonathan Dayton of New Jersey, however, believed in him. He had recently purchased 25,000 acres of land in Ohio. By this time, several people had warned President Thomas Jefferson of Burr's plans. With all his other problems, it appeared that Jefferson had ignored the situation, and Burr canvassed northern New York, western Pennsylvania and Ohio to recruit an army and raise funds for his enterprise. He gathered a force of about 1,000 men and headed down the Ohio River towards New Orleans, expecting the co-operation of General JAMES WILKINSON for his December conquest.

Jefferson's silent, mostly passive action suddenly changed in November. He had abandoned all thoughts of a war with Spain, since Napoleon claimed he would join with Spain, if the Americans attacked them. Jefferson had known about Burr's activities from his postal employees in the west and was also concerned about General WILKINSON. Gideon Granger was Jefferson's Postmaster General in his Cabinet. Between the two of them, they had set up a very effective spoils system within the department that, in some texts, Granger is given the credit for originating the fine tuning of the idea—at least, during Jefferson's administration. With their carefully chosen agents throughout the country, who were quite adept at the censoring of the mail, news in distant states came as rapidly and safely as the mail itself.

[Note: Granger was a Yale graduate who was elected from Connecticut to the House of Representatives. His ever-strong support of Jefferson and the Republican Party in New England had given him his office as Postmaster General, which he kept throughout Jefferson's and the first years of James Madison's presidency. Desiring to be appointed to the Supreme Court to the point of blackmail, Madison appointed another and displaced him in 1814, ignoring his threats. At that time Granger moved to northwestern New York and was elected as one of New York's Senators in 1819. He gave 1,000 acres of land to help in the construction of the Erie Canal.]

Minutes of the Cabinet meeting on 22 Oct 1806, recorded in President Jefferson's hand, referred to some information brought them by Granger that originated with General WILLIAM EATON:

> "General WILKINSON being expressly declared by Burr to EATON to be engaged in this design as his lieutenant, or first in command, and suspicion of infidelity in WILKINSON being now become very general, a question is proposed what is proper to be done with him on this account as well as for his disobedience of orders received by him June 11 at St. Louis to descend with all practical dispatch to New Orleans ... and then repair to take command at Natchitoches, on which business he did not leave St. Louis till September."

In the minutes of 25 October, a discussion of the activities of Aaron Burr was included. When General EATON was called as a chief witness at the trial for Aaron Burr in Richmond, Virginia, he would not mention General JAMES WILKINSON in his testimony. Shortly after his testimony, Congress suddenly authorized a check made out to EATON for $10,000 for a claim they had previously denied and held in committee.

Years later, 1810, in a letter to former President Jefferson, Granger claimed the gratitude of Jefferson for intelligence operations in 1805-6. His letter stated:

> "You, Sir, know that I gave you authentic information of Burr's conspiracy and how I got that information. You also know, sir that it was by your advice .... I allowed the Federalist to assume a free intercourse with me. It was to aid my country and you ... on the advice of General Dearborn [Sec. of War] ... when I sacrificed my own character and feelings to preserve the feelings and character of others, who were dear to you and to me. My conduct was equally correct and honorable in 1808."

Another informant was GEORGE MORGAN, an old Princeton classmate of Aaron Burr's. Sometime in September of 1806, Burr paid him a visit at Morganza—his estate near Pittsburgh. After Burr departed, MORGAN wrote a long letter to Thomas Jefferson. The President later claimed that this was his "first" concrete news of Burr's conspiracy. Miraculously, MORGAN's land claims in Indiana were reopened and approved, and MORGAN would be another witness for the prosecution.

[Note: MORGAN, relationship unknown, was the Indian agent that brought the letter from Chief Cornstalk to congress in the early days of the Revolution. MORGAN had remained loyal to the United States government during the war, serving without distinction. He left the service in 1779 complaining of being insufficiently appreciated. In 1789, he was able to get a land grant from the Spanish government on the understanding that he would garrison it with American officers and troops; however, they required him to take an oath of allegiance to Spain, as one of the conditions. His settlement on the Mississippi River was called New Madrid. When the king of Spain proved less generous than he anticipated, GEORGE MORGAN turned to Jefferson to help him clear some land titles in Indiana and renew his American citizenship.]

General JAMES WILKINSON was quick to assess the situation. On 26 Nov 1806, his special messenger, Thomas Adam Smith, arrived at the President's office with papers damaging to Burr concealed in a special compartment in his boot. Some of the documents, WILKINSON later confessed at the trial, were forgeries; but this was unknown or at least overlooked by Jefferson at that time.

Jefferson issued a proclamation alleging an "illegal combination of private individuals against the peace and safety of the Union." On 22 Dec 1806, Congressman John Randolph obtained an inquiry to the President from the House of Representatives as to the meaning of this rather vague proclamation. Jefferson boldly responded with the name of Aaron Burr. Most politically involved individuals began to rid themselves of any connection they may have had with Burr; but former president John Adams did not like the proclamation or Jefferson's willingness to add Burr's name to it. He wrote to Benjamin Rush that

> "the lying spirit" of Virginians was at work concerning Burr and that if Burr's guilt were "as clear as the noonday sun ... the first magistrate ought not to have pronounced it before a jury had tried him."

The governing power in Louisiana was invested in Jefferson's appointed governor, William C. C. Claiborne, and in his appointed council and was governed much like the old thirteen original British colonies. Adams saw no Bill of Rights to inhibit Jefferson from taking Burr into custody.

During a secret session, Jefferson's Republican whip in Congress, William Branch Giles, proposed that in dealing with Burr, the right of habeas corpus be suspended, supporting his case with some rather mysterious documents and letters that were somehow soon conveniently lost. WILKINSON soon received his orders from Jefferson:

> "It is my wish to have them [Burr and his chief of staff] arrested and carried off ... If you fail, your expenses shall be paid. If you succeed I pledge the government to you for five thousand dollars."

About this time, another possible relation enters the scene. JOHN McKEE was the Indian agent to the Choctaw tribe. This tribe claimed the territory south and east of the lower Trace Trail which extended south into the Spanish West Florida lands. On the north and west side of the Trace were the Chickasaws, a more violent and aggressive Indian tribe that had fought the Choctaws almost relentlessly prior to the Revolutionary War and then fearlessly stood with the British throughout that war. JOHN McKEE was an American, born in Rockbridge County, Virginia. He was sent to the Choctaws after the Revolution had ended, and in general had succeeded in establishing a relatively peaceful condition between the Americans, the Choctaws and the Spanish. At the time of Burr's so called conspiracy, McKEE had been replaced by Silas Dinsmoor; but he still resided in the area and was a close friend of Dinsmoor, who was born in New Hampshire.

[Note: This Colonel JOHN McKEE (born in 1767, married Mary (Polly) Patton in 1797—Rockbridge) was a descendant of the eleven McKEE brothers that came to Lancaster County, Pennsylvania, in 1738. Two of these, "Jon. McKee and Rot. McKee left Lancaster Co. and went to Kerr Crk. in what is now Rockbridge Co. Va., settling on part of Borden's grant. Some of the bros. settled near Wheeling, W. Va. and Pittsburg, Pa., while the others remained in Lancaster Co. Pa." (Geo. Wilson McKee: 1890). JOHN (b.1767) is the grandson of JOHN, son of ROBERT (1692-1774). Col McKEE's grandfather JOHN McKEE married Esther Houston, which makes him a cousin of Samuel Houston (Texas), also of Rockbridge County, Virginia. His father was WILLIAM McKEE, who married MIRIAM, whose maiden name was also McKEE.

My fourth-great-grandfather ALEXANDER McKEE, named his oldest child JOHN, (born in 1771 in Orange County, North Carolina.) My third-great-grandmother is MARY McKEE, who married RICHARD FAUSETT. They named a son WILLIAM. They are probably descendants of one of these eleven brothers, and therefore all are related someway. Both Rockbridge and Orange Counties are on the Great Wagon Road that goes south from Pennsylvania. Residents along this trail usually came from Pennsylvania, especially the Scotch and Irish. One of Pennsylvania's early Indian agents, THOMAS McKEE (b.1695 in Ireland - d.1773 in Lancaster County, Pennsylvania) could have been one of these eleven brothers. He married a Shawnee Indian girl and was the father of ALEXANDER McKEE (b. 1723), who was the loyalist colonel who led the Indians in the Ohio valley during the Revolutionary War. THOMAS and his Shawnee wife, had at least five other children. Records in the AF, SLC, UT, show THOMAS McKEE's father was ALEXANDER McKEE, (b. 1665, Antrim, Ireland, d. 1740, Lancaster, Pennsylvania; md. ELIZABETH GORDON). Are they the parents of the eleven brothers?]

In an earlier letter to his daughter, Theodosia, Burr described his journey to Dinsmoor's residence on the Trace Trail, which passed Dinsmoor's door. The

"road . . . you will see laid down . . . on the map . . . as having been cut by the order of the minister of war . . . is imaginary, there is no such road."

[Note: The Trace Trail was told about previously as the area of the robber SAMUEL MASON, who was captured in New Madrid in the latter part of 1803, escaped, and was later killed by his men on the Trace for the $2,000 reward offered by Claiborne.]

Burr further described the region between Washington, Mississippi, and the Choctaw Indians as

"a vile country, destitute of springs or of running water—think of drinking
the nasty puddle water, covered with green scum, and full of animaculae—
bah!... [H]ow glad I was to get [into the high country,] all fine, transpar-
ent, lively streams, and itself [the Tennessee] a clear, beautiful magnificent
river."

On 23 Jul 1805, Dinsmoor gave a ball that was attended by both Aaron Burr
and JOHN McKEE at the Chickasaw Agency House, which was near the village
now known as Houlka, Chickasaw County, Mississippi.

McKEE reported of Burr,

"He speaks so much of the disadvantage that results to the western country from their not making themselfes heard on the floor of Congress that
I cannot help thinking western popularity and power may be his pursuit
at present—what he means to do with it let those who know him guess."

During the 1790s, when George Washington and General ALEXANDER
HAMILTON prepared the nation to fight the French, JOHN McKEE was com-
missioned a colonel and prepared the Choctaw Indians to take West Florida from
Spain and stop the French, if they tried to land on the coast of the Caribbean.
The war never materialized because of an angry president, JOHN ADAMS; but
Colonel JOHN McKEE kept his title.

Dinsmoor was in Natchez on 7 Jan 1807. In a letter to JOHN McKEE of
that date, he wrote,

"We are all in a flurry here hourly expecting Colonel Burr and all Kentucky
and half of Tennessee at his back to punish General WILKINSON, set the
Negroes free, rob the banks and take Mexico. Come and help me laugh at
the fun."

Burr arrived by water on 11 January. He had asked Lieutenant Jacob
Jackson, at Chickasaw Bluffs, how many warriors McKEE "could raise." McKEE
came down to Natchez to meet Dinsmoor; where he introduced Burr to some
friends—from the West Florida border. He shared a room with Dinsmoor until
Burr surrendered to the authorities of the Mississippi territory.

On 25 January, McKEE wrote General WILKINSON,

"I have little doubt that ere this you will have set me down as a Burrite, and
as little that you will believe me when I assure you that as yet I am not; and

I must know the object and the means better than I do before I can be."

On 5 February, news arrived that the former vice president had escaped and was believed to be in Choctaw territory. On 8 February, WILKINSON wrote McKEE,

"If you want to distinguish yourself, and tax the government beyond denial, go alone and seize Burr."

McKEE responded that

"I never was a Burrite, nor can I ever give myself up to schemes of lawless plunder . . . . I might have engaged in any honorable enterprise, however hazardous, but the late one, such as it has been represented is such as I hope no friend of mine will ever suspect me of favoring . . . . May your purse keep pace with your heart, and may you live a thousand years."

When Aaron Burr, accompanied by his friend Robert Ashley, escaped General JAMES WILKINSON and his troops in Natchez, they traveled along the Trace Trail past the village of Washington, Mississippi. From there, they went east into Choctaw territory. Burr was disguised "in an old white hat, a pair of Virginia cloth pantaloons and old Virginia leggings, and an old Virginia cloth coat." This was from President Jefferson's description.

The editors of the *Burr Papers* described the journey,

"Contemporary investigators found willing witnesses to almost every aspect, real or imagined, of his activities before the second week of February, but no one could be located who was willing to give evidence on AB's travels through 200 miles of wilderness to Wakefield, in present-day Washington Co., Ala. where he appeared on 18 Feb. He could not have made the journey without friends willing to give him lodging and fresh mounts; but the Mississippians who aided him in that desperate flight proved more loyal and discreet than the followers he had chosen elsewhere."

According to Albert James Pickett's *"History of Alabama, and incidentally of Georgia and Mississippi"*, a young lawyer Nicholas Perkins and his muscular clerk, Thomas Malone, were playing backgammon in their cabin in the hamlet of Wakefield, when two mounted travelers came to their door and asked the road to Colonel Hinson's house. Burr was dressed in the costume described by President Jefferson: the tobacco stained wide-brimmed hat, homespun trousers, a long frontiersman's jacket with a hunting knife slung over his shoulder, and a tin cup hanging from his belt. Burr's appearance did not fool Malone. He later stated that he knew the man was a gentleman by the way he sat upon his horse.

Perkins was quick to remember the bounty money and slipped away to gain the help of the local sheriff, Theodore Brightwell, who lived in a nearby cabin. Brightwell agreed to accompany Perkins to Colonel Hinson's home and left Perkins outside in the cold, while he joined the two men inside at dinner. After waiting two hours, Perkins gave up and rode off to Fort Stoddard and Edmund Gaines—the lieutenant in charge.

The following morning, while Burr and his new companion, Sheriff Brightwell, were descending the bank of the Tombigbee River, Perkins and Gaines with a squad of soldiers surrounded them. The sheriff claimed he had no idea that his friend was the notorious ex-vice president. Burr protested that they had no right to arrest him; but, with their pistols drawn, he was reminded that they were only doing their duty. Their orders were from Mr. Jefferson and their governor. Burr nodded his head, conceding defeat. Burr spent a week imprisoned at Fort Stoddard, while Gaines sought instructions from WILKINSON and a promotion—he got both. If they could deliver the slippery ex-vice president to Richmond, Virginia, Perkins and Gaines would share the bounty money of $2,000. Richmond was 1,500 rugged miles away—through Indian Territory.

When Burr's companion, Ashley, was picked up by the Gaines soldiers and questioned, he claimed that

> "he had met Col. Burr by accident, found him a pleasant traveling companion and had come with him to that place."

Ashley was popular in the area and was turned loose. Gaines reported to WILKINSON that

> "Ashley has made a wonderful effect on many of them—the plans of Burr are now spoken of in terms of approbation, and Burr in terms of sympathy and regard. I am convinced that if Burr had remained here a week longer the consequences would have been of the most serious nature."

It is well to remember that this area of the nation at that time was still under treaty with the United States as an Indian territory. With the Louisiana Purchase, the Mississippi River was opened for commerce; but Spain still owned the southern coastal area and made trade with the West Indies very difficult for this inland area. There had been several attempts earlier to form Free states in this territory that would stop the expansion of slavery. Most of the prominent McIntosh family had been anti-slavery for generations, and Lachlin McIntosh had welcomed Burr as family in 1804. The family remembered Burr as the daring young officer that had risked his life to carry the mortally wounded body of General Robert Montgomery away from the fray, during the Revolutionary War Battle for Quebec. The heroic Montgomery was the husband of JANET, a sister of New York's Chancellor ROBERT LIVINGSTON. The early original Livingston was a Scotchman, although he had come from Holland, and he and his family had intermarried with the New York Dutch lines, including the RENSSELAER line; but they were still proud of their Scottish heritage.

When the early Scotch came to America, many of them settled in North and South Carolina, and then migrated westward as their families grew. They were less concerned about intermarrying with the Indians than other immigrants; in fact, the very early British Indian agents were encouraged to marry the Indian maidens as a way of promoting peace between the races. In general, the Scotch remained more loyal to England and the Indians than other colonists. With President Jefferson's willingness to sell these Indian lands to the slave holders of the south and displace the current inhabitants, it is understandable why former Vice President Burr with his anti-slavery platform—that included making free states and giving Indians and women the vote as well as the free black people—would gain him a great deal of support in this part of the South. Colonel JOHN McKEE was at least willing to listen to Burr and not totally condemn him. With almost 200 years having passed since John Smith's colony landed at Jamestown, Virginia, intermarriage between the races, or their descendants, was not uncommon.

Leaving Fort Stoddard and the Tombigbee watershed at a widening called Lake Tensaw, Gaines, Perkins and their carefully picked men took Burr at gun point and continued along the trail called the "Three Chopped Way" to Fort Wilkinson, in Georgia, on the Oconee River. Gaines had built this single-file horse route through the forest to carry the mail between the two settlements. It followed an old Indian path, and they had blazed three trees to guide them. It took them past the abandoned French Fort Toulouse, and the ruins of the trading posts of the McIntoshes and MacGillivrays, to the Creek agency, with Benjamin Hawkins—the chief Indian commissioner among the Muskogee. There were no bridges or ferries. At times they found canoes and their horses swam the cold rivers beside them. Other times, both men and horses would swim the rivers. It was February, and even in this southern forest, it was cold.

According to the *American History Magazine*, April 1897,

"Hundreds of Indians . . . thronged the trail, and the party might have been killed in one moment . . . In the journey through Alabama the guard always slept in the woods, near swamps of reed, upon which the belled and hobbled horses fed during the night. After breakfast, it was their custom again to mount their horses and march on, with a silence which was sometimes broken by a remark about the weather, the creeks, or the Indians . . . . Though drenched for hours with cold . . . rain, and at night extended upon a thin pallet, on the bare ground, yet, in the whole distance to Richmond, this remarkable man [Burr] was never heard to complain that he was sick, or even fatigued."

Gaines, Perkins and their men never complained, either. Gaines became a general in the War of 1812 and fought the Creeks and Seminoles in Alabama and Florida and the Sacs and Foxes in Wisconsin. In 1819-20, he was Andrew Jackson's deputy in the seizure of Florida.

West of the Oconee River, the group passed over an area of land that had been purchased from the Creek Indians in 1805 called the Forbes "Purchase." Earlier, in 1799, the Tory William Augustus Bowles had attempted to establish an independent free nation for a combination of whites, blacks, Seminoles and Creek Indians. This attempt failed when he was kidnaped at McIntoch Bluffs only five years before Burr's capture, and he was taken into custody—where he slowly and conveniently died unobtrusively.

Their travels then brought them to the overgrown charred remains of the little forts and villages that had been the Oconee Republic in 1794—established by Elijah Clarke. The government complained and Clarke gave up his idea and returned to the nation he had fought for in the Revolutionary War. He received a pension for the rest of his life.

Shortly after, they arrived at Fort Wilkinson on the Oconee River that had for years separated the Indian Territory from the settlements of the white people. Cherokee country was further north, extending into Tennessee. Fort Wilkinson was in the country of the Creek Indians, and with the 1805 purchase, the Georgia land lottery was still in process.

[Note: Residing at this time, 1807, near the northwestern South Carolina border in Franklin County, Georgia, were my third-great-grandparents —ANDERSON and SARAH ALLRED IVIE and their older children. Second-great-grandfather JAMES RUSSELL IVIE was nearly five years old. ANDERSON IVIE was not successful in obtaining land through the lottery; but his uncle LOT IVEY with his two sons, JOHN and BENJAMIN, had won land and were living near the Oconee River in Baldwin County—later divided to form Jasper County. Many IVEY cousins were also successful in the lotteries, and they were scattered throughout the state of Georgia. SARAH ALLRED IVIE's mother was ELIZABETH THRASHER, before she was married to WILLIAM ALLRED. WILLIAM and ELIZABETH and their children and some of ELIZABETH's brothers and sisters with their THRASHER families were in Franklin County, too. Today, there is a small town of around 1,000 inhabitants called IVEY about 15 miles below the larger city of Milledgeville. This larger city now surrounds the old location of Fort Wilkinson, in Baldwin County. Milledgeville claims a vineyard outside Fort Wilkinson created along the Oconee River with vines that had been sent to their commander Colonel Boot by Lafayette.]

At the fort, Perkins and Gaines risked staying at a tavern with their prisoner. Their host began asking questions about the prisoner. Burr's biographer, James Parton, wrote,

"Burr, who was sitting in the corner near the fire, raised his head, and, fixing his blazing eyes upon the unsuspecting landlord, said, 'I am Aaron Burr—what is it you want with me?' The poor landlord, amazed at the information, and struck with the majestic manner of the man, stood aghast, and without a syllable of reply, glided about the house, offering the party the most obsequious attentions."

Concerned by this incident and the power that Burr seemed to command, the captors redoubled their precautions. Their next objective was Augusta, Georgia, and two days later they were in South Carolina, where "Burr from old had been a popular favorite." They would not chance the main route to Richmond, but took a backwoods route to the village of Chester, South Carolina. A stone monument on their main street tells this story:

"Perkins . . . changed the order of their march, placing two men in front of the prisoner, two more behind, and one on each side of him. In this manner they . . . passed near a tavern, before which a considerable number of persons were standing, while music and dancing were heard from within. Here, Burr threw himself from his horse, and exclaiming in a loud voice, 'I am Aaron Burr, under military arrest, and claim the protection of the civil authorities.' Perkins snatched his pistols from his holster, sprang to the ground, and in an instant was at the side of his prisoner. With a pistol in

each hand, he sternly ordered him to remount. 'I will not!' shouted Burr . . .
. Perkins, unwilling to shed blood, but resolute to execute the commission
intrusted to him, threw his pistols upon the ground, caught the prisoner
around the waist . . . and threw him into the saddle. One of the guard seizing the bridle of Burr's horse led him rapidly away, and the whole party
swept through the village in a mass, and disappeared."

Malone later reported that the party paused to regroup a few miles out of
town. He found Burr weeping in anger and frustration, and other members of
the party, including Malone, were weeping in sympathy.

"Perkins watched his prisoner more closely than ever, for in this State lived
Colonel Joseph Alston—a man of talents and influence, afterwards governor—who had married the only daughter, and, indeed, the only child of
Burr. Afraid that the prisoner would be rescued at some point in this State,
he exhorted his men to renewed vigilance."

Alston and Theodosia's home was between Camden and Stateburg—
eastward.

Then Perkins sneaked back into Chester, where he purchased a closed carriage. With Burr sequestered safely inside, the carriage rolled onward through
the back roads of South Carolina and along the Great Wagon Road of western
North Carolina, where many of my relations still resided. When they were safely
into western Virginia, Burr was allowed to mount his own horse. On 25 Mar
1807, the journey took them past the plantation of John Randolph at Roanoke,
who wrote Joseph Hopper Nicholson of Maryland,

"Col. Burr (quantum mutatus ab illo!) passed by my door the day before
yesterday under a strong guard."

Representative John Randolph, a cousin of Jefferson's, would later be the
foreman of the grand jury that would hear the Burr Conspiracy indictment, before Burr came to trial with the Supreme Court Chief Justice John Marshall, another of Jefferson's relations, at the helm. Another cousin, Edmund Randolph,
formerly attorney general of the United States, would be one of Burr's attorneys.

When Burr arrived at Richmond, Chief Justice Marshall was quick to arrive and take control. President Jefferson was equally quick to announce publicly that Burr was guilty of treason—"beyond question." Marshall was not going to let Jefferson hang the man that had rescued the Supreme Court from the

Jeffersonian Republicans in the Justice Chase case without ensuring that Burr was given every opportunity for a fair trial. Marshall held a hearing in the state of Virginia's House of Delegates. It was the only room large enough to hold the crowd that was rapidly arriving to see this bit of history. The question was to determine if he should be placed in jail, or allowed to be free on bond, and whether his indictment required a grand jury investigation.

CHIEF JUSTICE JOHN MARSHALL

Burr's chief defense attorney, John Wickham, advanced the idea that, even if Burr had been planning to assault the Spanish Empire, it was "meritorious," because President Jefferson himself, at the opening session of Congress, had denounced Spanish "provocations" along the vaguely defined border and said war between the two nations was imminent. Former Attorney General Edmund Randolph spoke for the defense. He ridiculed the idea that someone could commit this crime by "supposed intention" when the Constitution clearly stated an overt act was required.

Jefferson's present attorney general, Caesar A. Rodney, expressed for the prosecution his regret that a man, he had once considered his friend, had formed a "chain of circumstances" that showed beyond doubt the former vice president was guilty of a "most heinous crime." He also insisted the government was not persecuting Mr. Burr, and he would receive a fair trial. He then made a quick exit back to Washington and left the federal attorney for Virginia, George Hay, to conduct the prosecution in Richmond.

George Hay was a son-in-law of James Monroe and very devoted to President Jefferson. On an earlier occasion he had battered the head of newspaperman James Callender with a club for revealing Jefferson's supposed liaison with his slave Sally Hemings. Most of the Jefferson historians claim that Jefferson was innocent of this charge—that she was only thirteen when she accompanied his daughter to Paris, and Jefferson had other interests for his attentions than this child of his chief servant. They claim the culprit was a cousin of the president's, who was not the most reputable member of the extended family.

The next day, John Marshall ruled on the government's motion. The Chief Justice announced that he could only find probable cause for trial on the misdemeanor of waging war against Spain; and on the charge of treason, he found the government's evidence of probable cause—the cipher letter purportedly written by Burr to General WILKINSON, detailing the revolutionary plans of the conspirators—too weak to commit Burr to prison. Quoting from Blackstone, John Marshall stunned the prosecution by stating that he could not allow "the hand of malignity" to seize an individual and deprive him of his liberty. He then carefully added that he was not suggesting any particular malignity in the case before him, although the gasps throughout the audience suggested they knew whom he referred to. Marshall then set the bail at $10,000 and adjourned the court until 22 May, the opening of the summer term. Burr's friends quickly raised the necessary $10,000 to free him.

President Jefferson was not happy with this ruling, which arrived as rapidly as the fastest horse could carry the news. In his angry letters to his fellow Republicans, he predicted that Marshall's tactics would spur the constitutional amendment Jefferson's followers had recommended after the Chase trial, which permitted Congress to remove any judge who failed their standard of good behavior. Jefferson was throwing down the gauntlet: If Burr was acquitted; John Marshall would find himself on trial.

Marshall strongly held his ground. He would adhere to the Constitution. He declared that treason was a charge that was

> "most capable of being employed as the instrument of those malignant and vindictive passions which may rage in the bosoms of contending parties struggling for power."

In a furious attempt to build Jefferson's case for treason, federal marshals crossed the Allegheny Mountains into the frontier states and, after endless interviews over the next seven weeks, brought back to Richmond 140 potential witnesses. The population of Richmond went from 5,000 to 10,000 people. Aaron Burr was equally active. He gave exquisite dinners for his friends, supporters, and other socialites that were tempted to attend. He added four more lawyers for the defense, including his strong supporter in the Chase trial, Luther Martin. Andrew Jackson came from his home in Nashville, Tennessee, to proclaim from tree stumps and the steps of the state capitol building that Burr was innocent, Jefferson was a tyrant, and General WILKINSON was an abominable liar in the pay of the Spanish. It was an interesting crowd with elegant New Yorkers and other sophisticated easterners mingling with the muddy boots and frontier styles of the westerners.

By 22 May, the government had assembled their grand jury—"twenty democrats and four federalist," according to the letter Burr wrote to his daughter, Theodosia. Among the jury was Jefferson's strong supporter from the senate, William Branch Giles. Giles had already declared Burr guilty on the floor of the senate. Again, Chief Justice Marshall came to Burr's aid by allowing him to challenge the jury. Upon being questioned by Burr, both Giles and another close friend of Jefferson, ex-Senator Wilson Cary Nicholas of Virginia, quickly withdrew. Congressman John Randolph was one of only a few who admitted his mind might be changed by fresh facts and arguments. Marshall appointed him the foreman.

To his embarrassment, Prosecutor George Hay reported that General WILKINSON had not yet arrived from New Orleans. He was the only witness that could testify to the authenticity of the cipher letter that had given the evidence that resulted in Aaron Burr's arrest. To this, Burr took the offensive and asked the chief justice to issue a subpoena to President Jefferson, ordering him to hasten to Richmond with the full text of the letter as well as copies of his response to WILKINSON and of his orders for Burr's arrest. Federal Attorney Hay declared it was out of the question; but the defense countered (especially Luther Martin) to assail Jefferson's role in this "peculiar case." Marshall stated his disapproval of what was said "in the heat of debate," but did not stop it; then, he again stunned the prosecution by issuing the subpoena.

In explaining his ruling, Marshall maintained that the president, unlike a king, was no more immune to a subpoena than any other citizen. His only exemption would be if his duties as chief magistrate demanded his "whole time." He then added that it was apparent that the government "wished" to convict Burr and it was the duty of the court to give him every means to exonerate himself. The prosecution objected to the word "wished." Marshall substituted the word "expected," which they also objected to; but Marshall left it at that.

Jefferson responded that he was perfectly willing to surrender the Wilkinson letter but only he, as president, could decide what other papers might properly be sent. He further stated in a letter to Hay, which was read in open court, the "paramount duties" of the nation made his personal attendance in Richmond impossible. The defense accepted this as fulfilling the subpoena, and since the witness for the prosecution, General JAMES WILKINSON, had then arrived in his full gold-braided military uniform, the prosecution continued their case before the grand jury. Jefferson and Hay had put a lot of trust in WILKINSON and after interviewing him for several hours, Hay told Jefferson he was utterly convinced of the general's "unsullied integrity"; but the foreman of the grand jury, Randolph, did not share this trust. John Randolph had already described him as "the most finished scoundrel that ever lived."

In the witness chair, WILKINSON was forced to acknowledge that he had erased certain portions of the cipher letter— (which revealed a previous correspondence with Burr.) When he was asked if he had a fore-knowledge of the plot, he declined to answer on the grounds that he might incriminate himself. Marshall allowed him the right to the 5th Amendment; but the grand jury tried to indict him for "misprision of treason." This was the crime of knowing that treason was going on, but doing nothing about it. The motion was made and defeated by a vote of 9 to 7. John Randolph asked Burr to produce the prior letter, showing WILKINSON's complicity; but Burr refused, saying he could never reveal a private letter unless he was forced to it by "the extremity of circumstances." The answers of both men seemed to indicate that they were probably both guilty in the plot, which, of course, was the truth—but the evidence was not produced for a court decision.

The government then produced around fifty witnesses to prove that Burr had accumulated an army with guns on an island in the Ohio River— Blennerhasset Island, a day's journey north from Frankfort, Kentucky, where

Burr was at that time—for the purpose of seizing New Orleans, revolutionizing the west, and attacking Mexico. The prosecution felt this was their best proof of overt action by Burr. On 24 June, the grand jury indicted Burr for treason and misdemeanor. They also charged Harman Blennerhasset, the owner of the island, who had given Burr $25,000, and five other conspirators, including ex-Senator John Dayton.

Burr was placed in their disgusting county jail, where his attorneys complained of the difficulty of conferring with him. Luther Martin wrote to Burr's son-in-law, Joseph Alston, "did any government thirst more for the blood of a victim?" Burr urged both Alston and his daughter to attend his trial, saying it would be less agonizing than hearing about it by letter and newspaper.

The actual trial began on 10 Aug 1807. The jury selection required several days. After he had interviewed around ninety prospective jurors, Aaron Burr gave up and let the prosecution make the selection. It had become obvious to him that if he escaped being hung, it would be because of Chief Justice John Marshall and not because of the decision of twelve honest and good men.

The trial centered on Blennerhasset Island and Burr's connection to this collection of 1,000 armed men. One of their first witnesses was Commodore Thomas Truxton of New Jersey; however, Burr had only outlined his plans to him, which he had rejected totally. He was not connected in anyway to the island, or any overt act, nor was any of their early witnesses.

The prosecution then tried to prove that treason had been committed on Blennerhasset Island. A hired-laborer of Harman Blennerhasset was their star witness—a man named Jacob Allbright. He described the events of 10 Dec 1806. It seems that the local Ohio militia under the leadership of General Edward Tupper had raided the island and tried to seize Harman Blennerhasset. Several of the men on the island raised their muskets and General Tupper and his men made a hasty exit. No shots were fired.

Aaron Burr did his own cross-examination of Allbright. He asked him if he knew General Tupper. Allbright said he did and proceeded to show Burr where he was seated in the audience. Burr had no more questions; but for all who were present, there was a big question. Why was General Tupper in the audience and not in the witness chair? The answer was not given at the trial, but was contained in a deposition that Tupper had previously made, in which he had stated that he never had a warrant for anyone's arrest and that no guns had been leveled at him on the night of 10 December. He claimed he had spent a pleasant evening chatting with Blennerhasset for a half hour and then withdrew.

The prosecution then called several more men who told the court that the men were making bullets and talked of conquests. Burr's attorneys flocked to the bench. Was Judge Marshall going to let the prosecution bring all 140 witnesses to the stand only to corroborate Allbright's testimony? Why was Tupper sitting silently in the audience?

Once more, alarmed George Hay listened as Judge Marshall agreed with the defense and ruled that it was time to hear arguments on whether further collateral evidence was admissible. The prosecution faltered, unable to come up with proof of an overt act.

Luther Martin summed up for the defense. He spoke for three full days— 118 pages of court records. He told of the public clamor against Burr and wondered if American justice had become "mere idle form and ceremony to transfer innocence from the goal to the gibbet." He ended by hoping that God would illuminate the court's "understandings."

Chief Justice Marshall spent the weekend writing his decision—one of the longest opinions of his career. It included citing additional authorities. He argued that a man who conspired to assemble an army to commit treason can only be convicted if the government proves both the conspiracy and an overt act. In Burr's case the government had proved neither. Therefore all the collateral evidence in the mouths of the government's witnesses was inadmissible. He closed his decision by noting that the government's attorneys had hinted several times he was risking impeachment if he ruled for Burr.

"That this court dares not usurp power is most true. That this court dares not shrink from its duty is no less true."

If Jefferson had thrown down the gauntlet, Marshall had picked it up.

The next day, 1 September, Hay informed the jury he had nothing to add in response to the ruling. Assistant Prosecuting Attorney William Wirt was quick to comment to a friend,

"Marshall has stepped in between Burr and death."

The jury retired for less than an hour and returned with the verdict:

"We of the jury say that Aaron Burr is not proved to be guilty under this indictment by any evidence submitted to us."

The defense objected to the wording; but Marshall let it stand. There was still the trial for the misdemeanor of waging war against Spain, and an attempt by Hay to transfer Burr to Ohio for another treason trial. With Marshall's continued help, Burr made it through the legal court, as did the others who had been indicted. But the reputation of Burr was sullied beyond repair through the newspapers and public opinion. He was shunned by even his old second—Van Ness.

British agent Williamson talked him into going to London, which he did for a few years—without results. When the British drove him from their country, he tried to approach Napoleon, who refused to even give him audience. A poverty-stricken Burr finally returned to America on borrowed money, in 1811, and was able to develop a law practice on Staten Island—large enough to sustain his needs.

His ten-year-old grandson, Aaron Burr Alston, died. His daughter Theodosia had health and marriage problems. Her husband, Joseph Alston, could not forgive her father for drawing him into the plot. The bankrupt Harman Blennerhasset had blackmailed him for $10,000—threatening to reveal his part in the conspiracy. Theodosia's symptoms were thought to be cancer and she boarded the schooner Patriot in Charleston to seek medical help and visit her father. The ship never arrived in New York. Many believed it had been captured by pirates and the passengers and crew had been murdered. John Alston wrote Burr,

"Oh my friend, If there be such a thing as the sublime of misery, it is for us that it has been reserved." Burr responded that he felt "severed from the human race."

But life goes on. Alston became the governor of South Carolina for a few years, then, soon after, became extremely depressed, and, in 1815, he died. Burr lived until 1836—outliving Jefferson and Adams by ten years. One day in New York City, Judge James Kent, then chancellor of the state, saw Burr on the other side of the street. An angry Kent pushed through the traffic to shout in Burr's face,

"You are a scoundrel! Sir! A scoundrel!"

A younger Burr would have challenged him; but an older, wiser Burr simply raised his hat, bowed, and said,

"The opinions of the learned chancellor are always entitled to the highest consideration."

On another occasion Burr is quoted as saying,

"I should have known that the world was wide enough for HAMILTON and me."

But he was not always that complacent. A friend talked him into revisiting the Weehawken dueling grounds again when he was an old man. The friend said that Burr described HAMILTON as malevolent and cowardly. It was not true, Burr raged, that HAMILTON did not fire at him. He had heard the bullet whistle in the branches above his head. As for HAMILTON's remarks . . . they read "like the confessions of a penitent monk."

General JAMES WILKINSON fell short in the estimation of those who attended Burr's trial in Richmond. George Hay told Jefferson he had lost his trust in him. However, the stubborn Jefferson continued to defend and support him, in spite of the numerous lies and contradictions that Burr's defense lawyers were able to extract from him. But then, JEFFERSON never attended the trial, and he probably realized additionally that WILKINSON could do him and his party a great deal of harm, if he felt trapped. Congressman John Randolph had the dubious honor of being singled out by WILKINSON with a challenge to a duel for calling WILKINSON a "finished scoundrel." Randolph simply replied:

"I refuse to sink to your level."

This angered the general to the point that he "posted" Randolph in various parts of Washington D.C. as a "prevaricating, base, calumniating scoundrel, poltroon, and coward."

Randolph just ignored the postings and was accepted without equivocation among all of Congress and his other associates.

President Jefferson called for a new trial in Ohio, which never happened. He tried to impeach Chief Justice John Marshall and sent his recommendation and the trial records to Congress. Congress sat on the proposals, doing nothing. John Marshall's ruling in Burr's behalf banned further attempts of "constructive treason"—the conspiracy without the overt act—from American jurisprudence, affirming, as most history students agree, the intent of the Constitution and the founding fathers. It was a ruling that even ALEXANDER HAMILTON would have been happy with, as it strengthened the judiciary as the first line of defense against a runaway legislature and uncontrolled presidents.

A NATION IN TROUBLE—
JEFFERSON, MADISON, AND MONROE

When Jefferson took office in 1800, he tried to undo all the things he had criticized ALEXANDER HAMILTON and George Washington for doing. Jefferson was against their friendship and trade with the British; their establishment of the Bank of the United States and subsidiaries; the sinking fund; a strong federal judiciary throughout the states; a large standing continental army; the further construction of naval ships to defend our coast lines and protect our American merchant ships. Jefferson wanted territorial expansion, but not by military acquisition. He was a strong advocate of the rights of the states and dreamed of a nation that was self sustaining, without a need for foreign commerce, much like he had built on his estate at Monticello.

Through his love of France, he was able to purchase the Louisiana territory by borrowing money from individuals, who, in turn, purchased from the federal government large tracts of the southern lands still under treaty with the Indians—compromising the agreements of previous authorities in the government and allowing the expansion of slavery into all the southern states, new and old. It appears he had lost his vision of freeing the slaves—believing that they were not yet able to sustain themselves. He also seemed to have lost his trust in the less fortunate white immigrants—after watching the terror that came from the French revolution and the rise of the emperor Napoleon Bonaparte.

When the Burr trial was completed in 1807, Jefferson's second term as president was falling apart. Spain would not even consider a peaceful purchase of East or West Florida and felt the Louisiana territory was an illegal international sale. It had only been sold to France on the condition that they couldn't sell it to the United States. The British would stop many U.S. vessels explaining that they were looking for deserting British sailors. They would then take as their property any American sailor who could not prove his citizenship with papers in his possession and force him into the service of their royal navy—never allowing him ashore.

[Note: The impressments of sailors were really another form of slavery. I knew an older former German man in Pioche, Nevada, in 1957, who was shanghaied in his youth for three years, only reaching the American shore by swimming a considerable distance during the night.]

Sometimes the British claimed the cargo and destroyed the ship. With the British and French at war and food in demand, Napoleon decided to treat all neutral vessels as enemy ships and claimed his share of the sailors and the bounty. The quantity of American seamen captured through this process is estimated by some historians to be over 10,000.

Jefferson's answer to the shipping problem was to place an embargo on all U. S. shipping—this approach was ratified by Congress. It was Jefferson's belief that American cotton, lumber, rum, and tobacco would be in such demand in Europe that he could bring these nations to their knees, allowing the Americans to negotiate kinder treaties. Unfortunately, the British had stockpiled their cotton, and England was quite willing to close their doors to American trade, giving them a greater market for their own goods.

When he was in France, Burr would tell Napoleon, in his efforts to further destroy our country, that there were "40,000 unemployed angry seamen in the United States—ready to engage in any undertaking whatsoever, provided that it offers a remote prospect of honor and rewards." Burr is further quoted as saying,

> "All classes of people are today discontented with the actions of the government. Even the friends of the administration share this dissatisfaction, but they uphold and justify, as best they can, the timid policy that is being followed."

New Englanders, who were much more dependant on ships and commerce, once more began to talk of secession and smuggled their goods into Canada. William Coleman, who was still editing the *New-York Evening Post*, gave the embargo his prime attention. He pointed out that the Embargo Act was costing the United States $50,000,000 a year—more than enough to build a larger navy to protect our vessels.

To squash the rampant smuggling along the Canadian border, the distraught Jefferson had to order his small U. S. army to move north and protect his Embargo Act. Nathaniel Macon of North Carolina supported this military action. New York's William Coleman editorialized, accusing Jefferson and Macon of being indifferent to the starving laborers and bankrupt merchants of the North. He further asked the question "Why should they worry?" They each had over one hundred slaves working for them. They would have food on their tables.

In the closing weeks of Jefferson's second term, congress repealed the embargo; (but it would be modified and tried again during Madison's administration.) It had failed, and with it much of Jefferson's already faltering prestige. James Madison followed him with two terms as president—not because of his popularity, but because the Federalist Party had no strong organizational leader to oppose him. Madison was elected "unanimously"—but around 30 percent of the congressmen boycotted the caucus that nominated him. James Madison was followed by two presidential terms for James Monroe, another strong Jefferson Democrat/Republican from Virginia. He was followed by the son of John Adams—John Quincy Adams, who called himself a Republican. Through all this, there was not any strong presidential leadership, nor strong support from the people—nor did any strong opposition arise to challenge them, although there was a great deal of discontent throughout the northern and frontier states and territories. Jefferson was to lament in December of 1808, "I am now . . . chiefly an unmeddling listener to what others say." In this way, he had unwillingly achieved one of his goals—to reduce the power of the executive branch of the United States government.

In the Northwest Territory of the Ohio River, new Indian leadership was coming forward. The Shawnees, Tecumseh, and his brother—known as the Prophet, began rallying all the tribes to fight against the further infiltration of the Big Knives into what they considered to be Indian Territory. It was their belief that the land deals between the whites and small individual tribes should not be honored as legitimate sales, as the territory belonged to all the Indians. They contended that these hunting grounds had no definite tribal borders, and, therefore, no tribe could claim the rights of ownership to any of these lands. The two brothers had been born in the Shawnee Scioto valley in or near Chillicothe, Ohio. Their parents had come there from the Alabama Territory of the Creeks shortly after they were married. Their father was a Shawnee with parentage that may have included some mestizo blood (in this case a mixture of Indian and white.) Their mother was from a different Shawnee clan and may have had some Creek ancestry. The handsome Tecumseh's skin was lighter than most of his companions. He stood about five feet ten inches with an athletic, straight-backed, well-proportioned frame that included broad square shoulders and finely formed muscular limbs.

The Shawnee tribe had been driven west during the Revolution. When it became known that great numbers of Indians, some from great distances, were congregating to listen to the Shawnee Indian prophet at a Shawnee Indian village recently established at Greenville, Ohio, near the Indiana border, Governor Kirker of the recently formed State of Ohio called a meeting with the Indians at what was then the capital of the state, Chillicothe, on 19 Sep 1807. Tecumseh arrived at the conference dressed in a suit of neatly trimmed deerskin, and was admired by those who were present. He was described by various people as "one of the finest-looking men I ever saw," as "very prepossessing . . . noble looking . . . one of the most finished forms I have ever met." One listener recalled that he spoke fluently in the Shawnee tongue, adding weight to his emphatic and sonorous words with elegant gestures. Another marveled at his "impetuous and commanding" speech and said he was reminded of the eloquence of Aaron Burr.

William Wells was the United States Indian agent at Fort Wayne. A translation of Tecumseh's speech was written as follows:

> "Congress has a great many good men. Let them take away Wells and put
> one of them there. We hate him. If they will not remove him, we will!
> When the Indians are coming in to hear the Prophet, he sets doors to stop
> them. He asks them, 'Why go ye to hear the Prophet? He is one possessed
> of a devil, I would as soon go to see a dog with the mange.' When we want
> to talk friendly with him, he will not listen to us, and from beginning to
> end his talk is blackguard. He treats us like dogs."

Tecumseh was questioned as to his meaning, when he said they would remove Wells. He softened his tone and explained that the Indians would simply ignore him. He further stated that the Indians would be leaving Greenville, soon, and he asked for their help with their new establishment. They would need a store where the Indians could trade and purchase goods and an agent that was reliable. He explained that Stephen Ruddell would be the perfect appointment.

[Note: Stephen Ruddell was the older of two brothers who were captured by the Indians when they were twelve and six years old. Their Kentucky parents were Isaac and Elizabeth Ruddell. They had been raised by the Indians and had fought with them until the wars were ended by the treaty of Greenville in 1795. Stephen had gone to Missouri with his foster mother, but returned to Kentucky in 1798, where he became a Baptist preacher. He would visit the Shawnee village and proselyte for the Kentucky Baptist Church. His younger brother, Abe, had more difficulty with white people and kept many of his wilder Indian ways.]

John McDonald, who was present, wrote:

"When Tecumseh rose to speak, as he cast his gaze over the vast multitude which the interesting occasion collected together, he appeared one of the most dignified men I ever beheld. While this orator of nature was speaking the vast crowd preserved the most profound silence. From the confident manner he spoke of the intention of the Indians to adhere to the treaty and live in peace and friendship with their white brethren, he dispelled as if by magic the apprehension of the whites. The settlers immediately returned to their farms, and the active hum of business was resumed in every direction."

Governor Kirker was also impressed. He dismissed the militia he had been collecting and wrote to President Jefferson on 8 Oct 1807,

"I sincerely believe these people are injured . . . for there does not appear on strict examination anything against them. On the contrary, their lives are peaceable and the doctrines they profess . . . are such as will do them honor."

He passed on Tecumseh's objections to Wells and his requests for further support.

President Jefferson would later tell John Adams that the Prophet

"was a visionary, enveloped in their antiquities, and vainly endeavoring to lead his brethren to the fancied beatitudes of their golden age. I thought there was little danger of his making many proselytes from the habits and comforts they had learned from the whites to the hardships and privations of savagism, and no great harm if he did. We let him go on, therefore, unmolested."

Tecumseh was quite honest in expressing his desire for peace at that time. The two brothers moved west into Indiana and formed their new village on the junction of the Wabash River and Tippecanoe Creek early in 1808. The whites called their new settlement Prophetstown. From here they hoped to extend the prophets influence over the Wisconsin and Illinois tribes.

The governor of Indiana was the rugged frontiersman William Henry Harrison—future president of the United States of America. Harrison was not impressed with his new colony, as he had tried earlier to warn other Indian tribes against this professed prophet. He had written to the Delawares:

> "If he is really a prophet, ask him to cause the sun to stand still, the moon to alter its course, the rivers to cease to flow."

Unfortunately for Harrison, the Prophet had been told by the whites that there would be a total eclipse of the sun on 16 Jun 1806. By forecasting this event his reputation as a prophet was accepted as law by the Indians, and more and more tribes began aligning themselves in earnest behind Tecumseh and his prophet brother.

During his first summer in Prophetstown, upon an invitation from the British General William Claus in Upper Canada, Tecumseh with five companions made a trip to Detroit and crossed the Detroit River to the Canadian side, arriving at British Fort Malden (Amherstburg). Tecumseh was greeted with great joy by the over-70-year-old Indian superintendent Matthew Elliott, who had recently replaced THOMAS McKEE—both spoke fluent Shawnee.

[Note: McKEE was the son of ALEXANDER McKEE, the British Indian agent during the revolution who had remained loyal to the crown and the Indians. Colonel ALEXANDER McKEE had been captured by the Americans in their western battles with the British. McKEE, the prisoner, had been exchanged by the British for some American prisoners, and he with his family had been given land in Nova Scotia. THOMAS McKEE, whose mother and grandmother McKEE were both Indians, had grown up in Ohio and knew Tecumseh in his childhood.

At first, with their long Canadian border to protect and their war with France, England had continued to give presents to the Indians, hoping for Indian support—if needed. Then, London did not want to be accused of inciting the Indians against the Americans—they were not prepared for war. So, in the previous three years, they had discouraged the Indian confederacy and discontinued their gifts to the Indians. Through this time, THOMAS McKEE was their Indian agent at Fort Malden, their most important western post. Unfortunately for the British, McKEE was drunken and incompetent. It was reported that the fort was "going to ruin as fast as possible." Part of McKEE's problem was lonely depression—no instructions for months at a time and no presents. This garrison of fifty men had basically been forgotten by the rest of the world.

On 22 Jun 1807, the British ship *Leopard* had fired upon an American frigate, the *Chesapeake*, while searching for deserters. Three Americans had been killed, causing great indignation against the British throughout the United States. Eleven days before, McKEE had written the British, "The discontent of the Indians arises principally from the unfair purchases of their lands; but the Americans ascribe their dissatisfaction to the machinations of our [British] government." McKEE had warned the Prophet "the Indians must never be the first to attack."]

After the *Leopard-Chesapeake* incident, and after the appropriate delay that communication across the Atlantic entailed, London became more concerned with their distant fort on the Detroit River, realizing that it was very vulnerable to any attack by the United States. British General Claus sent for the Prophet; but Tecumseh answered the call, leaving the Prophet at home to run the village and counsel his many believers. It was on 13 June that Tecumseh sat down with William Claus and Matthew Elliott, who desperately wanted the Indians on their side again, if the Americans were to attack. They expressed their willingness to supply guns and ammunition, as well as much food and wampum as presents from the British. But Tecumseh showed no desire to take the king by the hand. He admitted he was building a multitribal settlement on the Wabash to defend their land and said he would strike the Americans, if necessary; but "at present" he wished to stay out of the quarrels of the whites. He was deeply distrustful of the redcoats. Tecumseh believed that several chiefs had been killed, when they were shut out of the British fort in 1794.

The British continued to court him and brought in additional chiefs from other tribes, as well as Lieutenant Governor Gore of Canada. Gifts and entertainment followed. Tecumseh remained firm in his position; but he also knew where he could find help, if he ever needed it. Through the next few years, the importance of the Prophet diminished, and, increasingly, the tribes looked to Tecumseh for their strength and the leadership of the Indian confederation. Governor Harrison blissfully continued his land grab, showing no concern for the needs, or the dignity of the Indians. Slowly, through the demands and skirmishes of the various warrior chiefs and his increasing distrust of Harrison and other American leaders, a peace seeking Tecumseh realized that if Indian lands were to be preserved, it would require a major confederated tribal war. He also knew he was the only one that could lead this vast Indian rebellion. He took the message of unity of the Indian nations into his ancestral south—to the Chickasaws and the Creeks. The Cherokees and Choctaws were of a more peaceful nature and were fearful of the Creek and Chickasaw tribes and chose not to join.

With his face painted the black color of war, Tecumseh addressed 5,000

Creeks, later known as the Red Sticks, on the banks of the Tallapoosa River.

"Burn their dwellings," he shouted. "Destroy their stock. The red people own the country . . . . War now. War forever. War upon the living. War upon the Dead; dig up their corpses from the grave; our country must give no rest to a white man's bones." [*Westward Expansion*, Ray Allen Billington / Martin Ridge]

This was quite a different speech than the one Tecumseh delivered in Ohio about four years before. According to Canadian John Sugden's book, *Tecumseh, A Life,* which is very well documented, there are no actual records of this speech to the Creeks—his appearance seems to be agreed upon. Probably these authors were quoting secondhand reports from Red Sticks, who wanted the stronger, more immediate message. According to Sugden, Tecumseh left the Creeks, and journeyed into the lands of the Osage, Fox and Wisconsin tribes with a message of confederation and peace for the present—at least, until he was ready and could direct the coordinated Indian campaign. Tecumseh only planned to fight, if a peaceful solution was impossible, and then as a united Indian nation—with a coordinated army of all the tribes. Although he was accused of the heightened Indian massacres, this was not his vision, and he spoke strongly against these uncontrolled acts of the various tribes.

But while Tecumseh delivered his unity speeches in the south and west, Governor Harrison, who was at Vincennes, quickly recognized the opportunity that Tecumseh's absence afforded him to attack the warrior's home at Prophetstown. With a thousand troops from Virginia and Kentucky, he started northward along the Wabash on 26 Sep 1811. They stopped along the way and built two strong fortifications: Fort Harrison at the site of Terra Haute, and a log blockhouse at the mouth of the Vermillion River. The army reached Prophetstown on 6 November and camped within a mile from the Indian town on a ten-acre triangle of land, which was bordered by a thick marsh, a creek, and heavy woods. That night the troops sleep on their arms, while the Indian Prophet performed magic rites to render the enemy impotent and his warriors invincible.

Just before the sun peaked over the horizon, the Indians moved forward through a cold, slow-falling rain and surrounded the sleeping Americans. One of Harrison's guards detected a movement in the bushes and fired. Quickly the

Indians rushed into the camp, sweeping past the enemy outposts and into the northwest corner of the American camp, where Captain ROBERT BARTON's regulars held the rear line and Captain Frederick Geiger's Kentucky riflemen protected the left flank. The American line buckled; but within a few minutes, these seasoned soldiers formed their solid lines and began pouring a murderous fire into the ranks of the attackers. The surprised Indians at first fell back, then broke completely when Harrison's cavalry charged upon them from two directions. Concerned about a second attack, Harrison and his men built additional breastworks until 8 November, when his scouts discovered Prophetstown was deserted. The American army destroyed the vacated Indian town and returned to Vincennes.

This Battle of Tippecanoe was not a strong victory for Harrison. His men had outnumbered the Indians by about 300; the whites had held their ground; but both sides counted 38 dead and 150 wounded. When Tecumseh returned, he was very angry with his brother, and the warriors who were retaliating against the frontier settlements with fire and the tomahawk. He wanted unity and negotiations, not uncoordinated mayhem. By the spring of 1812, the settlers were fleeing from their outlying cabins; and fear swept into the hearts of even the more populated regions of Ohio and Kentucky. They placed the blame on the British.

Harrison wrote:

"The whole of the Indians on this frontier have been completely armed
and equipped from the British King's stores at Malden."

The solution seemed quite simple. The United States must conquer Canada, destroy Fort Malden and end this alliance of the British with the Indians. Congressman Henry Clay from Kentucky was named the speaker of the house, when the election of 1810 sent sixty-one representatives to congress who favored war with Britain [known as war hawks] to represent the voice of the people. The seven northwest congressmen were probably the noisiest and most persistent in their demands. There were ten war hawks from New England, fifteen from the middle states, and twenty-nine from the south. Congress debated and squabbled over the issues. In general, they cared little about the Indians, Canada, or the distressed unemployed; most were much more concerned about the national honor and their hatred of Great Britain, or more importantly, winning their own elections and keeping their president in power.

Madison, with the recommendation of the retired President Jefferson, had asked for a decision for war. On 18 June 1812, Congress said, "Yes," and the United States officially began the armed conflict. Jefferson, sounding more like HAMILTON or Burr than the sage of Monticello, predicted the end of the war within six months with very little blood shed, and he urged Madison to use "hemp and confiscation" to deal with antiwar protestors in New England. Ever critical of General HAMILTON, and even George Washington, Jefferson and Madison placed great confidence in the state militia.

As it turned out, the bloodshed was anything but minimal, and the Canadian invasion became a series of disasters for the Americans. Their tiny regular army, strengthened by hosts of untrained militia, was not prepared, nor many of their commanding officers seasoned in actual military warfare. What little money the nation had was soon gone—and United States credit with it. The Bank of the United States had been eliminated in 1811, when Vice President George Clinton [still the office-seeking hangover from Jefferson's presidency] was the swing vote in the senate for its destruction. By 1814, the United States government was totally bankrupt with nothing to even pay the salaries of their clerks in Washington D.C. Desperately, President Madison tried to borrow from the New York bankers. William Coleman denounced the offer of 6 percent interest as being too low, and the bankers invested in British treasury notes instead.

Later in the year of 1812, DeWitt Clinton ran for president on an anti-war platform. He was backed by the Federalists who had denounced the war with England. His support included many of HAMILTON's old friends: Gouverneur Morris, Rufus King, John Jay, and others. DeWitt Clinton lost in the electoral college—he got 89 votes to 128 for Madison. He won in New York, New Jersey, and all the New England states, except Vermont. The vote demonstrates the opposition this part of the country had for a war against the British.

[Note: When the Americans declared war on the British, on 18 Jun 1812, it is well to remember a few dates surrounding the problems that the British faced, regarding their war with France. Between June and September of 1812, Napoleon was marching to Moscow. By October, his starving army started their long journey through the cold winter back to France, arriving broken and disheartened in January, 1813. The combined European anti-Napoleon forces, including the English, destroyed his power and forced his abdication from his throne on 12 and 13 Apr 1814. He was exiled to the island of Elba, off the shore of Italy, on 4 May. Louis the XVIII was placed on the throne of France with a republican assembly to control his actions.

At the beginning of March 1815, the restless and bored Napoleon executed his carefully made plans, escaped the island and returned to France. By 16 March, he had collected an army of at least twenty thousand soldiers, and began his march to Paris. The King's army was outnumbered, and Louis XVIII fled to Ghent before Napoleon entered Paris and claimed the city. By 25 Mar 1815, the Allies—Britain, Austria, Prussia, and Russia—had signed the Treaty of Vienna, pledging their armies until Bonaparte "be put absolutely beyond the possibility of exciting troubles." 16-18 Jun 1815 was the Battle of Waterloo.

France left 25,000 dead and wounded and 220 cannon on the silent battlefield of Waterloo and a total of 64,603 casualties during the entire Belgium campaign, compared to the Allies 62,818. A little after six o'clock the morning of Saturday, 15 Jul 1815, Napoleon was placed aboard the ship Bellerophon, with full honors and escorted to the captain's own cabins. As they put to sea, Napoleon watched the shores of his empire fade from sight. His brother Joseph, in another ship, accompanied his vessel as they sailed for the United States. Napoleon arrived in Plymouth, Massachusetts on 7 Aug 1815. Ten weeks later, he stepped ashore on an isolated island owned by the East India Company called St. Helena. On the island, he was slowly poisoned by his supposed friends in 1821. His wine was laced with arsenic until he was greatly weakened. In April, calomel, a mercury poison, was given him by his doctors—supposedly in an effort to save his life. On 3 May, he was given a massive dose of mercuric cyanide. "Shortly thereafter he became unconscious and completely paralyzed." Napoleon died on Saturday, 5 May 1821, at 5:49 P.M.

With their war with France taking a priority in London, the American War of 1812 was basically an unwanted additional nuisance for the English. France and Spain were not interested in an all-out war with the United States, either. The unrest extended into Spanish Mexico. In 1810, a Mexican priest Miguel Hidalgo y Costilla led a revolt against Spanish rule. The uprising was put down; but it started Mexico's struggle for independence. On 21 Sep 1821, Mexico finally won their independence from Spain.]

In the Old Northwest Territory, Tecumseh was well advanced in collecting his western Indian warriors. There were about 800 warriors in the immediate vicinity of Prophetstown, where the Shawnees had rebuilt 40 cabins on the original site that had been destroyed by the Americans. The 800 included the surrounding area with 160 Kickapoo houses sheltering over 100 warriors, and the Winnebagos had built 40 longhouses on Ponce Passu Creek. There were extensive cornfields that had still not ripened. On the Illinois River, there were 650 warriors living principally on corn and fish, mostly Potawatomis with some Kickapoos, Miamis and a few Ottawas and Ojebwas. Across the Mississippi, it was believed that the Dakota Sioux had around 1,200 warriors on the Minnesota River. Then there were the Fox, Sac, Wyandot, and the Delaware; it was believed that in these combined allied tribes, Tecumseh had a total of at least 4,000 warriors, although they were thinly scattered. Food was scarce until harvest time arrived.

Tecumseh sent 30 Shawnees, Kickapoos, and Winnebegoes to Fort Harrison, begging for corn. They were unsuccessful; the fearful Americans had been scouting their actions. Taking ten of his best warriors, Tecumseh decided to visit the British at Fort Malden. He wanted to talk with the Wyandots, as well. On 17 June, they arrived at U. S. Fort Wayne. They stayed several days, talking with the new agent, Benjamin Stickney—a young man in his upper thirties. At Fort Wayne, a proclamation arrived from Governor William Hull of the Michigan Territory. It was a warning to the Indians that, if they did not stay neutral through the coming war between the Americans and the British, they would be defeated and dispossessed of all their lands. He further told them that he was bringing a large army to reinforce the garrison at Fort Detroit.

Tecumseh, at first, tried to gloss over his trip to British Fort Malden and a recent Indian raid—which he blamed on the Potawatomis. Stickney was not deceived and further warned him that he would probably encounter Hull's army, if he continued his journey. When Tecumseh left Fort Wayne to continue his northward journey on 21 June, the two principals did not even shake hands. A smiling Tecumseh hastened onward. He believed he had a wonderful advantage. Just as he was planning to launch his war, a bigger conflict was about to begin between the Big Knives and the British. This vision of a combined British and Indian war against the Americans would fit nicely with his own plans. The spirit was with him.

When Tecumseh arrived at Fort Malden near the end of June, his smiles probably departed. The frustrated British, almost deplete of supplies and ammunition, were frantically trying to organize their dilapidated Fort Malden into a useable fortification. Elliott had sent the red tomahawk to all the tribes, as a cry for help; but many Indian villages preferred to sit quietly, not wanting to be on the losing side. The superintendent at Amherstburg, Matthew Elliott, was considered brave, but too old for active participation—especially with his lumbago. THOMAS McKEE, who he replaced, was considered imprudent and frequently drunk. The storekeeper George Ironside, Elliott, and McKEE, were related by blood or marriage to the Shawnees. They all spoke the Shawnee language fluently and were frequently called upon as interpreters.

British Major General Isaac Brock, who was given the command of all of the extensive territory of Upper Canada, had been given only 1,600 regulars and 11,000 militia to defend this fourth of the Canadian provinces, whose white inhabitants numbered around 77,000. [Compare this to the white population of 677,311 living in Kentucky, Ohio, and the territories of Illinois, Indiana, and Michigan.] Fort Malden's share of soldiers amounted to 300 regulars of the 41st Regiment of Foot, under an experienced, middle-aged Scot, Captain Adam Muir—a detachment of Royal Artillery headed by Lieutenant Felix Troughton, and around 600 Canadian militia, mostly without uniforms. The Indian warriors, who had arrived, would sit, eat, drink, smoke, and converse on the beach, and would come and go with their families as they saw fit—usually there were 200 or more of them just sitting and waiting. Tecumseh was not impressed with his allies.

Approaching this conglomerate of British, Canadians, and Indians was Brigadier General William Hull. Accompanying him were the Tippecanoe veterans, the 4th Regiment of the United States Infantry under Lieutenant Colonel James Miller, and 1,200 Ohio militia commanded by Duncan McArthur, Lewis Cass, and James Findlay. They were struggling through the standing water and timber of the Maumee swampland, assailed by blackflies, mosquitos, and heavy rain. They skirted the head of Lake Erie to the path that led north to Detroit. Tecumseh and the British, of course, expected them, and were kept well-informed of their progress by their scouts and part of the local inhabitants. Tecumseh wanted to attack them, but was persuaded to wait by his allies. Hull's force reached Detroit on 6 July; his army included around 2,000 soldiers, counting the militia and the garrison at Detroit, with one medium-sized field piece of artillery.

On 12 July, the American's ferried across the Detroit River into Canada and occupied, without resistance, the town of Sandwich. Most of the villagers had fled their homes, and the troops that had been garrisoned there had pulled out the previous day, when they saw the first activities of the Americans. The American flag, for the first time, was hoisted on Canadian soil. Hull threatened the Canadians, and many of their militia began to desert. At Fort Malden, the number of militia dropped from 600 to 400 and it was reported that the four hundred were "in such a state as to be totally inefficient in the field." In Amherstburg, Elliott claimed, "The people here are much dejected and have removed all their effects out of the place." Tecumseh still had his ardor for battle and with great leadership was able to keep his small band of 300 Indian warriors together, although many surrounding chiefs requested the protection of the Americans.

On 16 July, 280 Americans caught the redcoats relaxing at Aux Canard. The British had not even destroyed the bridge, and Colonel Lewis Cass soon controlled the bridge—the only defensible position above Fort Malden. Fifty Indians had rushed to support the British. The Americans believed that they were led by Tecumseh and THOMAS McKEE. In the skirmish, a British sentry was killed and two were wounded. That night the Indians, expecting a major battle the next day, performed their war dance, and in the morning, with nearly nude bodies painted black with stripes, they rushed northward to meet the Big Knives. They were amazed when they found that the Americans had abandoned the bridge, after tearing it apart. The British built a new battery with a small breastwork on the south bank and brought the *Queen Charlotte* up the Detroit River to cover the mouth of the Aux Canard with its guns. The battle never happened.

The Indians returned triumphant. McKEE, painted and naked like his Indian companions, led fifty exhilarated warriors into Amherstburg. One was waving a fresh scalp high on a pole. Unknown to those watching, it was the hair of the dead British sentry that was desecrated.

But the British and Indians were not the only ones to be amazed that the American troops had left the bridge. Major James Denny of the Ohio volunteers wrote home to his wife,

> "Our general is losing all the confidence he had in the army. He holds a council of war every day, and nothing can be done—and councils again. The result is still the same."

It was a pattern that would not change. Hull's inaction and fear demoralized his men. In contrast, Tecumseh's steady attacks and persuasive orations increased his authority and respect. The neutral Indians began to change their allegiance and follow their war leader. In a few weeks, Tecumseh had 600 warriors willing to fight with him. Hull became more cautious and worried about his communications line, which the Indians were attacking. He brought his 250 troops back across the Detroit River to his fort. His officers had prepared a siege on Fort Malden; but he would not consent to initiating it.

On 13 August, just before midnight, a splutter of musketry at Fort Malden welcomed their British commander, General Isaac Brock. Convinced that Niagara was temporarily safe from attack, he had brought 50 of the 41st British regulars and 250 of the Canadian militia with him—personally taking command. The first leader he asked to see was Tecumseh. He explained to the Indian leader that ammunition was short; but he had a plan. Recognizing the personal fear of the Indians that apparently possessed the American general, William Hull, Brock hoped to bluff him into surrendering by attacking Detroit. If that failed, he hoped he could at least draw him out to battle. The jubilant Indians were quick to agree, and the night of 15 August, hundreds of canoes with 530 Indian warriors quietly crossed the river to land near the River Rouge below Detroit. They were led by Tecumseh, Roundhead, Matthew Elliott, THOMAS McKEE, Walk-in-the-Water, Main Poc, and Splitlog. The red men filed quietly into the woods a mile and a half inland, ready to assault the flank and rear of any force that contended in anyway to stop Brock's landing of his 800 troops and artillery.

The morning of the 16th, the tall figure of British General Brock could be seen riding at the front of his advance guard; the artillery, regulars, and uniformed militia followed, and the rest of the militia brought up the rear. Tecumseh's men slipped north through the forest, collecting horses and sheep, looting empty houses and gathering up prisoners as they went—spreading fear throughout the countryside.

British shells from across the river at Sandwich and from the British gunships screamed as they arched and landed within the 2 to 3 acre fort that had the commanding position on a hill overlooking the river. Sitting on a small rise before the fort were two twenty-four-pounders and a six-pounder, loaded with grape and canister shot—trained upon the head of the British column. Then the British commander received word that there were American reinforcements only a short distance away. Brock continued his steady march, but changed his plan for drawing the enemy from the fort. He would storm the fort immediately, before the additional soldiers arrived.

A Canadian militia captain, who was not actually present until afterwards, reported that

"Tecumseh extended his men, and marched them three times through an opening [in the woods] in view of the garrison, which induced them to believe there were at least two or three thousand Indians."

This may or may not have been true; but Hull admitted at his court-martial that he had been influenced by the news that the Indians were breaching the outskirts of the town.

It was about 10 A.M. when the American batteries fell silent and a white flag appeared over the walls of the fort. Hull was ready to surrender his fort, the town, and the whole of his army of 2,188 soldiers. Brock's bluff had worked; but, even he had difficulty understanding Hull's disgraceful reasoning. The American flag had flown over the fort for seventeen years. As the Union Jack was raised, voluminous cheers resounded from the Indians and their British allies, while the countenance of the American soldiers showed amazement and disgust with tears exuding from their eyes as they laid their 3,000 rifles into an ever-increasing pile.

Some historians take a broad view to the defeat, recognizing that Hull had long tried to get the nation to gain naval control of the Great Lakes. The over-confident president and congress had not listened. Others blame the lack of a military leadership and troop training that had been ignored by presidential and congressional leaders for so many years. Still others blamed the slow American attack on Niagara that allowed General Brock the time, resources and men to lead the attack. But William Hull was, of course, still responsible, and he was the one that received the court-martial and was condemned to death. Then they pardoned him, because of his former services; but the public never forgot. Historians often forget the importance of this victory to the elated Tecumseh, who believed once more that the spirit was indeed with him and with his greater dream of a united Indian nation. In his mind, the British were helping him to conquer the Americans, not the other way about. Hull's greater fear was the organized, uncivilized Indians, not the king.

The pillaging of the territory by the Indians and the attacks on other American forts continued rapidly and successfully—with the aid of the British, of course. More and more Indians arrived to support their leader. The Big Knives were humbled. In a brief six weeks every American post on the upper Great Lakes west of Cleveland had been eliminated. This included Fort Dearborn at the southern tip of Lake Michigan, where Chicago now sprawls over its countryside. British General Isaac Brock left this part to some of his junior officers and the fearless leadership of Tecumseh, whom Canadians still honor and give great credit for saving their country. General Brock needed to get back to Fort Niagara—American troops were coming.

NIAGARA. HORSESHOE AND AMERICAN FALLS.

NIAGARA FALLS

The upper photo/postcard was a souvenir my father brought home as a serviceman in World War I in 1918-19. The lower photo was taken by Hyrum Haynes in August 2004. Goat Island on the American side (left) separates the two falls. These photographs were taken from or near the bridge that connects Canada to the United States. It is obvious that the Canadian view on the right is much more attractive to visiting tourists, but the river and falls have changed very little.

It was on 13 Oct 1812, that the battle for Queenston occurred. Leading this fray for the Americans was the New York militia commander, Major General STEPHEN VAN RENSSELAER of Albany. He felt that he outranked Brigadier General Alexander Smith, who was to help with the campaign; but Smith was regular army and believed that a part-time militia general should support, not command, the standing army. Smith refused to submit to his command. RENSSELAER created further resentment when he commissioned his less experienced nephew, militia Colonel SOLOMON VAN RENSSELAER, to lead the initial attack on Queenston. Included in this attack were three very capable lieutenant colonels of the regular army: Winfield Scott; John R. Fenwick, and John Chrystie.

The campaign had a rather awkward beginning. On 11 October, they were to cross the Niagara River, but all their oars had been placed in one boat, and somehow it disappeared. This created a wearisome two-day delay, and increased the awareness of the enemy. Colonel SOLOMON VAN RENSSELAER finally crossed the river two days later, with 300 militia volunteers from New York and 300 members of the 6th and 13th Infantry Regiments, under Lieutenant Colonel Chrystie. Other forces were left in the rear to provide reinforcement when it was needed.

British General Isaac Brock had reinforced Queenston and the heights outside of town, which overlooked the river, with two thousand highly trained and experienced soldiers. These included the grenadier and light infantry companies of the 49th Regiment. Brock had also positioned four cannon in the area. Soon after the Americans landed on the Canadian side of the river, the British grenadiers open fired from the heights. Colonel VAN RENSSELAER was severely wounded. Captain John Wool of the 13th Regiment led the American forces to a safe place at the base of the hill. The wounded VAN RENSSELAER ordered Captain Wool to attack the heights. When a volunteer remembered a little-used fishing path up the side of the hill, Wool secretly led the bulk of his troops safely up the heights to a position above the British soldiers and the town of Queenston. General Isaac Brock, again at the head of his British troops as they charged up the hill, was mortally wounded, and his aide-de-camp, Lieutenant Colonel John MacDonald was killed leading a third push.

The Americans established a firm position; but reinforcements for the red-coats would arrive soon. Captain Wool had also been injured, and Winfield Scott assumed command of their preparations. Major General STEPHEN VAN RENSSELAER ordered the wounded to be sent back with the boats that were to pick up the American reinforcement to aid Colonel Scott.

The British reinforcements were led by Major General Roger H. Sheaffe along with several hundred Mohawk Indians, led by the famous Indian war leader of the Revolutionary War, Joseph Brandt. They surrounded and attacked the American position.

The American boats arrived on the opposite shore carrying the wounded, mutilated soldiers in full view of RENSSELAER's reinforcement of inexperienced militiamen. When these young soldiers witnessed this horror and heard that the feared Mohawks were attacking in force, they refused to leave the American soil and join Scott and his troops. General VAN RENSSELAER entreated them; but the majority ran away, and the general had to tell Scott that no further reinforcements could be expected.

The Mohawks led the British up the hill to the American position. Brigadier General William Wadsworth of the New York militia quickly agreed that the best hope for their outnumbered army was a rapid retreat to the American side of the river. The retreat became a panic with some men jumping from the heights into the river. Scott was forced to surrender.

The British took 958 prisoners, including stragglers and deserters. The Americans had 90 killed and 150 wounded. The British army and Canadian militia had 14 killed (including their general, Isaac Brock) and 77 wounded. The Indians reported 5 killed and 9 wounded. A very discouraged Major General STEPHEN VAN RENSSELAER resigned three days later. General JAMES WILKINSON was brought to help.

[Note: STEPHEN VAN RENSSELAER was the brother-in-law of ALEXANDER HAMILTON—their SCHUYLER wives were sisters, whose mother was also a VAN RENSSELAER. STEPHEN was the heir to the extensive lands that had originally included Albany, and he still bore the Dutch title of Patroon. His wealthy Dutch ancestor, KILLIAN VAN RENSSELAER, had originally purchased these large tracts of lands from the Mohawk and other Indian tribes. Unwilling to come to America himself, KILLIAN first sent his nephews to establish Fort Orange, where Albany is now located, and Fort Good Hope, where Hartford, Connecticut, is located. His third nephew, JAN CORNELISSON COELE, remained on Long Island and was later killed in the Indian War of 1643. According to some genealogists, I am supposed to be descended from the nephew that went to Connecticut. When the British claimed Hartford, ancestor

PETER COLET returned to New York. He married JAN's widow, AEITJE COELY. They had one son, ancestor WILHELM PIETERSON COLET. As Fort Orange became safer and more settled, KILLIAN sent his own son to occupy the position of Patroon over the village that would later be called Albany, but was then called Rensselaerwyck. His nephew ARENDT VAN CORLEAR established Schenectady, New York, and was loved by the Mohawk Indians, as well as the Dutch settlers. CORLEAR drowned in Lake Champlain in 1667. He had no children. When the British, under King Charles II, took New York from the Dutch, KILLIAN was able to retain his lands, because he had provided a grand home of refuge for the young Charles II, when he was swiftly secreted to Holland, after his father, Charles I, was beheaded and Cromwell with his parliament controlled England.]

Further to the north, by Lake Champlain, American General Henry Dearborn drilled 5,000 troops until mid-November, and then marched northward toward Montreal. At the Canadian border, the militia refused to go on. They insisted they were only to fight in their own state. Dearborn was old and weak. He marched his troops back to winter quarters at Plattsburg. He saved his army by keeping them away from the enemy.

With the winter of 1812 fast approaching, northern activities came to a halt. Most of Canada, the Great Lakes and the St. Lawrence River were frozen. Military activities were limited to preparations for the campaigns of 1813. General William Henry Harrison, governor of the Indiana territory and intrepid in his desire to triumph over Tecumseh, was given the command of the unfortunate General William Hull.

On the southern shore of Lake Erie where the small northwest tip of Pennsylvania has a small shoreline is an island called Presque Isle [Erie, Pennsylvania]. It was at this location that the determined, daring young Commodore Oliver Hazard Perry began a massive shipbuilding program. His idea for an American naval squadron of many light and maneuverable ships was finally approved and in the production process. Its purpose was to block the British naval communication line between Forts Niagara and Detroit. He had the support for his supplies and manpower from three states: Ohio; Pennsylvania, and New York. The final purpose was American naval control of Lake Erie—something that General William Hull had previously requested many times before and had never been able to get any congressional support.

Probably, the humiliation the Americans had suffered from their land attacks on Canada prompted the American government to act quickly; but the naval success the Americans had experienced in the Atlantic was exhilarating and very encouraging, especially to New England.

Eight hundred miles northeast of Boston, the frigate *Constitution* under the command of Captain Isaac Hull, met and captured the British frigate *Guerriere* on 19 Aug 1812, after a fight of thirty minutes. Hull reduced the enemy vessel to a complete wreck, killed or wounded one-third of their crew and made prisoners of the rest of them. On 18 October, the American sloop, *Wasp*, met the British sloop, *Frolic,* and completely demolished her. On the 25th, the 44 gun frigate, *United States*, fought the 38 gun British frigate, *Macedonia,* and gained another victory. These victories surprised the world. The British forbade their vessels to fight the Americans, unless they had superior or at least equal tonnage. The American privateers flooded the Atlantic and were very successful in capturing 500 vessels during the fall and winter of 1812-13. The Marine Insurance for the Irish Sea rose to 13 percent.

[Note: In the southern United States, another battle was in process. My ancestors, ALEXANDER McKEE and MARY BEAN McKEE, had moved from Orange County, North Carolina, to Sumner County, Tennessee, toward the end of the 18th century, when this area was opened for American settlers. Accompanying them was their third child [my third-great-grandparents] MARY McKEE and her husband RICHARD FAUSETT and their five young children. They had been married in Orange County, North Carolina, on 28 Jan 1792. ALEXANDER and MARY McKEE's fourteenth and last child, SAMUEL, was born in 1801, at Gallatin, Sumner County, Tennessee. RICHARD and MARY McKEE FAUSETT would have 14 children, also. Both of these families moved further south to Maury County, Tennessee—near Columbia, about 1809. Maury County borders the Trace Trail on the east side. The Duck River, which was the southern border of the original territory of Nashville, cuts through the middle of this county. Columbia is very near its southern bank, around 45 miles south of Nashville. My second-great-grandmother, and their 8th child, ELIZA McKEE FAUSETT was their baby as they journeyed to this newly acquired land from the Indians, where six more children would be born.

Further east in Tennessee, but still just south of the Duck River, ANDERSON and SARAH ALLRED IVIE recorded their first land purchase in Bedford County, Tennessee, in 1813. The land was a farm a little south of Duck Creek, near Shelbyville. Evidently, this river that collected the western waters of the higher mountains of eastern Tennessee and carried them to the far western Tennessee River was smaller at Shelbyville than it was further on, as all our IVIE records say Duck Creek. My second-great-grandfather JAMES RUSSELL IVIE, their oldest son, was ten years old—too young to carry the heavy musket of a soldier in this War of 1812. Even further south and a little east near the Alabama border was the town of Bean's Creek. Located in this Franklin County village of Tennessee was the young 25-year-old Davy Crockett and his family.

It is quite possible that Beans Creek was named after the early Tennessee settler Captain WILLIAM BEAN, who came to Tennessee in 1769 with his family. He built a cabin at the mouth of Boon's Creek, and, according to the *Americana Encyclopedia,* it is believed he was the father of the first white child born in Tennessee—RUSSELL BEAN. His relationship to my fourth-great-grandmother MARY BEAN is uncertain; but at least two of MARY BEAN McKEE's great-grandchildren on my FAUSETT line married members of the BEAN family of Tennessee. My very close girl friend at Twin Falls High School, CAROL BEAN, is a fourth-cousin, although neither of us knew it at the time.]

~ 106 ~

DAVY CROCKETT, THE WAR OF 1812

In the book *David Crockett Scout,* by Charles Fletcher Allen, J.B.Lippincott Company, Philadelphia & London, 1911, there is an excellent description of Crockett's participation in the War of 1812, which should give us an idea of the area and a view of the war as experienced by the young soldiers from Georgia and Tennessee that participated. The following are a few excerpts from this book:

"The danger of an Indian uprising became imminent during 1812, and after the United States had formally declared war against Great Britain, on Jun 18th, every pioneer looked to his rifle and supply of ammunition. While Tecumseh's messengers were distributing the calendars of red sticks to the Creek chieftains, the British warship *'Guerriere'* was taking New England sailors from the decks of American vessels in sight of New York City. England was landing supplies and agents at Pensacola, for use among the restless Indians, the Spanish acting as go-betweens. Uncle Sam was surrounded by the growling dogs of war, without a friend in the world.

"While thus the clash of arms drew near, Davy still hunted and farmed and trapped on Bean's Creek, adding to his fame as a rifleman, and, as he said when he had become known in Congress, 'laying the foundation of all his future greatness.' Every day the two parties among the Alabama Indians became more truculent, and frequent encounters ended in bloodshed. In the spring of 1813, the prophet Francis (ordained by Tecumseh), Peter McQueen, and High-Head Jim began a predatory warfare upon the peaceful Indians and half-breeds, who had good houses and farms. With more than three hundred followers, the hostile leaders set out for Pensacola with their plunder . . . a force of two hundred American volunteers overtook the Indians at Burnt Corn, sent them flying, and proceeded to divide the plunder left by the enemy. Before they had finished this, the Indians attacked

769

them in turn, having rallied when no longer pursued, and the volunteers were driven back and dispersed. As they are not known to have lost more than two of their number, they do not seem to have been very desperate fighters.

"When Hurrican Ned . . . brought the news of this to Franklin County, he predicted an attack by the Creek war party, who were being urged by British agents to paint themselves for battle. Red Eagle would have temporized with his chieftains, but they seized his children and his negro slaves as hostages while he was away from home, so he prepared, perforce, to strike a decisive blow at the progress of civilization . . . the tom-toms were beating, the frenzied braves smeared themselves with vermilion till their naked bodies were like flames of fire. The white settlers and the friendly Indians flocked to the various forts, hastily built of logs. In Fort Mims three or four hundred men, women and children, with about two hundred volunteers sent as a garrison by General Claiborne, came together in the middle of August.

"About the 27th of the month, a badly scared negro returned to Fort Mims from a hunt for stray cows. He had seen the woods full of Indians, apparently covered with blood . . . . [When] the scouts failed to find . . . the thousand braves . . . the negro had a close escape from being flogged for lying. Two days later two other negroes claimed to have seen the Indians, and were whipped. Red Eagle and his savages crept from their hiding-places, and were within a hundred feet of the gates before they were discovered. Then it was found that the gates were blocked by drifted sand and could not be closed. For some hours the battle raged, and before sunset all but twenty or thirty of the people in the fort had been killed and scalped. A few had escaped through the stockade, and some had been spared as slaves . . . Red Eagle rode away from the scene of butchery, and when he returned, on his fine black horse, more than five hundred lay dead and mutilated within the fort. No half-way position was now possible, and until the end of the war he was active and aggressive."

The whole western slope of the mountains now awoke to the danger.

"Calls for men were answered by North and South Carolina and Georgia, and Tennessee . . . . All . . . agreed that Andrew Jackson should be the one to lead the volunteers into Alabama, but he was in bed, suffering from a wound in his left shoulder, caused by two slugs from the pistol of Thomas H. Benton, in a free-for-all fight. The two men were afterwards reconciled and became friends . . . .

[Note: This is the same Senator Benton that is spoken of many times in later Chapters of this book. The altercation took place on 4 Sep 1813 over a misunderstanding over a duel of his brother's,, in which the brother was stabbed, Jackson shot and Benton was thrown downstairs. They were bitter towards each other for many years, but became very supportive of each other later in their political lives. Benton's daughter Jesse eloped and married J. C. Fremont in 1841—the western explorer who later ran for president of the United States against Buchannan. Sentor Benton endorsed Buchannan.]

While Jackson is generally spoken of as a great Indian fighter, he was not at this time entitled to such a reputation. A few years before, he had been chosen Major-General of Volunteers, but most of his actual fighting had been with his personal and political foes. He killed Charles Dickinson in a duel for slurs upon Mrs. Jackson, and had ridden full tilt at Governor Sevier with the intention of running over him."

Crockett enlisted as a volunteer at Winchester. He described his wife's reaction:

"my wife, who had heard me say I meant to go to the war, began to beg me not to turn out. She said she was a stranger in the parts where we lived, had no connections living near her, and she and our little children would be left in a lonesome and unhappy situation . . . . It was mighty hard to go, against arguments like these; but my countrymen had been murdered, and I knew that the next thing the Indians would be scalping the women and children all about there, if we didn't put a stop to it . . . . Seeing that I was bent on it, all she did was to cry a little, and turn about to her work. The truth is, my dander was up, and nothing but war could bring it right again."

The volunteers mounted and went south to Huntsville, Alabama, forty miles south. They were joined by 1,300 mounted men.

"Davy's company was one that stuck together, under the same leader, Captain Jones, until they returned to Tennessee. Jones was later sent to Congress."

Major Gibson, who was about to go into the Coosa country to get information about the Indians, asked Captain Jones to let him have two men who could be relied upon as woodsmen and riflemen. The Captain called Davy, who was

"strong and healthy, with a full beard. Davy expressed his willingness . . . if he might choose his own mate . . . . he picked out a friend named George Russell. When Gibson saw Russell he said he hadn't beard enough to suit him; he wanted men, not boys. At this Davy's dander was up, and he told the Major that by this rule a goat would have the call over a man; that he knew what sort a man Russell was, and that he was not likely to be left behind on a march . . . . the Major relented and sent them both.

"The first day they reached and crossed the Tennessee at Ditto's Landing, and camped seven miles south, guided by an Indian trader. The next day the Major took seven of the men, giving Davy charge of those remaining, with orders to meet him at night fifteen miles beyond the house of a Cherokee named Brown . . . . They traveled through a rather barren country, sometimes across prairie-like land where wild flowers were abundant and beautiful. In the low places were cane-brakes, often fifteen to twenty feet high. The scouts avoided the open spaces, fearing both Indians and snakes, which sometimes crippled or killed a horse.

"Night came on without the Major appearing, and Crockett's squad camped among the trees. The hoot of an owl came floating through the silence of the evening, and was at once answered by Davy. It was the signal of the half-breed, who soon afterward came into the gleam of their fire. The morning broke, and there was still no news of the other party of scouts. As usual, Davy decided to go ahead, and passed through a Cherokee village, twenty miles farther south, reaching the house of a squaw-man, named Radcliff, in time for dinner. This man they found badly scared. He told them that ten painted Creeks had left the place during the forenoon; if they learned that he had fed the scouts, they would kill his whole family and burn the house . . . . a few of his men wanted to turn back . . . . But Davy knew that some of the men would stand by him, and he determined to go ahead. When he started on, the whole party went along, for the few who wished to go back were afraid to do so alone. Soon after dark they reached a camp of some friendly Creeks . . . . The moon was at its full . . . . They tied their horses ready to mount at a second's notice, and lay with their guns by their sides.

"They had scarcely dozed when a cry like that of an angry panther rang through the night . . . . Then an Indian appeared in the bright moonlight, with the news that the war party had been crossing the Coosa all day at the Ten Islands, on their way to fight Jackson's army, then gathering at Fayetteville, in Tennessee. In a few minutes every Indian in the camp had fled, while Davy and his men 'put out in a long lope' on the back trail, to give notice to the force they had left at the landing, sixty-five miles away . . . . Having crossed the Tennessee, they reached the volunteers' camp, and reported to Colonel Coffee. To Davy's disgust, the Colonel seemed to place little confidence in the story he had to tell, so far as the imminence of danger was involved. The little band of scouts had ridden their tired horses sixty-five miles in eleven hours by moonlight, and forded the river, and they were disgusted by their reception. Davy said that he was burning inside like a tar-kiln, and wondered that the smoke was not pouring out of him as he withdrew.

"The next day the Major came into camp with a similar report, which set Colonel Coffee into what Davy called 'a fidget.' He at once threw up breastworks twelve hundred feet long, and dispatched a messenger to hurry up Jackson's army. It always rankled in Davy's memory that the word of a common soldier and scout could be so lightly held, while the Major's report was never doubted for a moment. Davy had much to learn in a world where so many unjustly receive pay and praise for work that is done by obscure toilers.

"Still suffering and weak from his wound, Jackson arrived at Huntsville with his command the next day, October 11, 1813."

Huntsville is located on the Tennessee River, where it winds its way through northern Alabama, then north to the Mississippi River. Jackson now had at least 2,000 men; but no supplies. Major Reid, of his staff wrote:

"At this place, we remain a day to establish a depot for provisions; but where these provisions are to come from, God Almighty only knows. I speak seriously when I declare that we may soon have to eat our horses; which may be the best use we can put a great many of them to."

The army moved south, scouting parties searching for food, as well as Indians. Colonel Coffee was promoted to General Coffee, along with the promotions of other men. Part of the force was made up of friendly Cherokees, under their chief Dick Brown. When they reached a point called Ten Islands, on the Coosa River, they heard of a gathering of Red Sticks at a town ten miles away. Jackson sent nine hundred men, under General Coffee, to attack them, which included Davy Crockett and the friendly Cherokees, who wore white feathers and deer tails on their heads to distinguish them from their Creek enemies.

"At daybreak, Colonel Allcorn, with the cavalry, in which Davy served, went to the right of the line of march, while Coffee and Colonel Cannon kept to the left, soon enclosing the town completely with a cordon of horse and foot. The Indians discovered their approach, and manifested their defiance with yells and frantic beating of their drums. As they refused to come out, Captain Hammond and two companies of rangers advanced to bring on the action. The Indians seem to have believed this small force to be all with whom they had to deal, for, as Davy says, they soon came at them 'like so many red devils.' As the rangers fell back, the main army line was reached, and the fight was on. The Creeks fired a volley and ran back to their huts. Slowly the cordon of soldiers closed upon them, and one of the most desperate Indians fights of history took place. The Red Sticks asked no quarter, firing from the shelter of their cabins until they were shot dead by the soldiers who came to their doors, or charging with shrill war-cries between the impassable walls of gleaming rifles that surrounded them. Refusing quarter even from the Cherokees, whom they had known as friends before, they fought till they could no longer lift their guns or draw their knives in a last effort . . . . the squaws rushed through the hail of bullets to ask for mercy . . . . Every brave was killed, and eighty-four women and children were taken prisoners. General Coffee counted one hundred and eight-six dead Indians, while of his own force but five were killed and forty wounded. Though they had gained a decisive victory, the soldiers were in terrible straits for food, and when everything in sight had been eaten, they learned that 'Hunger is sharper than the Sword.'"

In November 1813, Jackson and his men built a fort at Ten Islands, on the north shore of the Coosa River, and many refugees clustered into the stockade. It was named Fort Strother, after the owner of the land. It was on the 7th that a friendly Indian runner arrived with the news that in their town of Talladega 150 friendly Creeks were besieged by more than a thousand Red Sticks and their allies. With only a short supply of food and water to survive on, the warriors gave them three days to surrender—wanting them to change their allegiance and fight against Jackson and his army. The village had scorned them. The runner claimed he had only escaped by disguising himself as a wild pig.

General Jackson was impressed with their loyalty and immediately crossed the river with two thousand men, including eight hundred cavalry. It was sun-up on the 8th when the army saw Talladega,

"and deployed to right and left, for the purpose of surrounding the hostile Creeks," who had carefully prepared an ambush. Major Russell and Captain Evans were saved when the friendly Creeks, after trying in vain to call them to a halt, "two of them leaped from the walls, ran to [Russell's] horse's head, and pointed out the danger. At once the hidden warriors fired on them."

Crockett said,

"They came forth like a cloud of Egyptian locusts, screaming as if all the young devils had been turned loose, with the old devil of all at their head. They were all painted scarlet, and were as naked as when they were born."

Russell and his volunteers left their horses and ran to the fort. The surrounding soldiers fired on the Red Sticks, who "fell in heaps." Four hundred painted warriors fell before their survivors were able to break through Jackson's lines and escape. When Davy returned about a year later,

"he saw the bleaching skulls scattered about like gourds upon a winter field."

After returning to Fort Strother, the volunteers, whose enlistment for sixty days had expired long before, decided it was time to go home for fresh horses, clothing, and, of course, food. Jackson would not give his permission, feeling he needed every man. There was a bridge they needed to cross, before they could leave camp. The men were determined; but so was the General. He aimed a cannon at the bridge and flanked it with his remaining soldiers, armed with rifles. One story says that

"their general gave the malcontents a few seconds in which to go back, with the promise of shot and shell if they refused; and then, the mutineers gave in and asked for terms."

Davy Crockett's story was different. He claimed,

"The discontented volunteers, with flints picked and guns primed, marched across the bridge, amid the clicking of the gunlocks of the militia, some of whom had run at the battle of Talladega."

Whatever, Davy and his men returned to Tennessee, where many re-enlisted later, including Crockett. After, Davy Crockett and Andrew Jackson were no longer friends.

When Crockett returned to the Creek country, Jackson had less than 1,000 whites, with about 250 Cherokees and friendly Creeks. One of the companies had only officers whose men had gone home. Major Russell was in command of a body of scouts, of whom Davy was one. It is strange that such a small force could not be supplied with provisions—evidently not backed by the government. A war with the Alabama nations was not important on the Atlantic coast. It was from the ranks of the ill-fed volunteers of Kentucky and Tennessee that victory came.

"In January, 1814, Jackson's little army pushed on to the Horseshoe Bend of the Tallapoosa River, and camped in a hollow square, with every prospect of being attacked by hostiles, who were in great numbers in the vicinity. Two hours before dawn, the pickets were heard firing. Throwing brush on the camp-fires, the volunteers waited for the attack, expecting to see the Indians by the glare of the flames; but the Creeks kept out of sight, and were themselves aided in aiming by the light in the camp. Four whites were killed and a number wounded, and although several charges were made, Jackson found it necessary to retreat . . . back to the Enotachopeo Creek. The savages fell on the rear guard, which Colonel Carroll was commanding."

The commander, Colonel Perkins, was on the right flank, with Colonel Stump on the left, both of whom fled—followed by their men.

"As Stump rode frantically past Jackson, the general tried to cut down the coward with his sword, but missed him. Colonel Carroll was left with 25 men, and was in danger of being cut to pieces by the yelling and triumphant warriors.

"Then the scouts under Russell, with the aid of the artillerymen, who had only one six-pound cannon, sprang to the aid of the rear guard . . . . While the artillerymen were dragging the piece up the bank of the creek and loading it with grape, Davy's company, led by old Major Russell, rushed across the stream and attacked the left flank of the Indians, who outnumbered the whites ten to one . . . . The cannoneers, at last swept the ranks of the savages, huddled in the narrow descent to the creek, with a hail of grape. Then the scouts fell on the demoralized enemy, who took to the woods, and Jackson's army was saved."

They counted 189 dead Indians, and 20 volunteers were killed with 75 wounded.

With iron tenacity Old Hickory, in the face of such disastrous losses, practically without an army, and with no supplies for the friendly Creeks, renewed his appeals to the people of Tennessee and Kentucky, and hopefully awaited their response. Every day of delay made the danger greater, for the Creeks were constantly securing firearms, powder and lead from the British agents at Pensacola. The volunteers, returning home, stirred the hearts of their neighbors with the story of Jackson's bravery and self-sacrifice, and the indifference of the people turned to enthusiasm. Before February ended, Coffee returned to Alabama with two hundred of his old brigade, soon followed by 2,000 men from western Tennessee, and 2,000 more from the mountains of eastern Tennessee. Every man was a rifleman. The Choctaws also offered the stubborn general all their warriors to fight the Creeks.

After the battle of Tohopeka, in March, 1814, in which Jackson completely routed the hostile Creeks, the victorious general planned his attack on Pensacola. He made terms with the Indians on 7 Nov 1814, and occupied Pensacola. He then marched his army toward New Orleans, where the British army (instead of the Indians) fought the Americans.

TECUMSEH, FORT DETROIT—THOMAS McKEE

In the Northwest Territory, extending from the Mississippi River eastward, past Lake Michigan, to Fort Detroit (occupied by the British in August 1812,) the victorious Indians tried to extend their occupied territory with a siege on Forts Wayne and Madison, where many of the scattered white settlers had fled in terror. The British were not anxious to support Tecumseh in this further adventure, and stalled—hoping to negotiate a peace with the Americans. The Napoleonic affair in Europe was all the war they cared to have. The Indians lacked the cannon, ammunition, and food to sustain a long siege; but their numbers had continued to swell.

By 12 Sep 1812, Tecumseh was able to collect an expedition of 600 warriors from Amherstburg, led by Roundhead, Elliott, and himself. Following close behind was Muir with 150 British regulars, 100 militia, a six-pounder, and a howitzer. THOMAS McKEE set out on the 15th with 200 Ottawas and Ojibwas who had just arrived from Michilimackinac. The allied confidence was high, and they boasted that they would conquer with a clean sweep to Vincennes and Fort Massac; but somewhere along the way, they discovered they were too late. The siege of Fort Wayne had broken. American militia Major General William Henry Harrison, having abandoned his office as governor, had arrived on the 12th with fresh supplies and 2,000 men from Piqua. The attackers dispersed. Only four Americans were killed in this allied attempt against the two forts; however, savagery continued creating great concern throughout the countryside.

Winter had arrived and the Detroit River was frozen over with thick ice. It was January 1813. General Harrison hoped to collect 4,000 men, meet at the Maumee rapids, then cross as a unit the ice-covered river and capture Canadian

Fort Malden. One wing of his force, Winchester's column of 1,300, had established itself at the rendezvous by the middle of the month. Without waiting for Harrison, Winchester advanced part of his force to Frenchtown, the small settlement on the north bank of the River Raisin, and had driven out a rather small party of British militia and Indians, while he was still bringing up reinforcements.

British Colonel Proctor, who was in command at Sandwich, was awakened at two o'clock in the morning of 19 January with the urgent message that the Americans were at the River Raisin only thirty miles south of Detroit. Not knowing the strength of the enemy, Proctor crossed the ice and quickly assembled all his available troops, Indians and equipment at Brownstown, then rapidly moved through the heavy snow toward the Raisin to meet the enemy—hoping to catch them off their guard. He had 597 British regulars and militia, six pieces of artillery, and 700 Indians under Roundhead.

At daybreak of 22 January Proctor and Roundhead found the American troops on the north shore of the Raisin, unprepared and very vulnerable. Winchester, still in his nightshirt had not expected them. No sentries had been posted and their reserve supplies were still across the river. Soon the men of Winchester's right were running for their lives through the deep snow, throwing down their guns as they attempted to reach the south bank across the river. The mounted Indians outflanked them and shot them down like deer, or butchered the exhausted survivors with their tomahawks. Only a little over 30 escaped of the approximately 900 hundred men who were either captured or left to stiffen in the bloodstained snow. Winchester was captured, stripped of his nightshirt, and brought to Roundhead.

British Colonel Proctor promised to protect the captives, but he left around 80 sick and wounded American prisoners behind in unguarded houses at Frenchtown as he hastily fled back to a more fortified position—fearing Harrison's arrival with additional troops. The next day, 50 inebriated Indians attacked Frenchtown. They hauled the injured men from the houses—beating, shooting, and axing them. Others were burned to death, while their dwelling went up in flames. Some of their broken bodies were thrown into the street to be torn by foraging hogs. The battle was another disaster for the United States. A Kentucky historian estimated the total loss at 290 killed and 592 captured.

When the details of the massacre of their wounded sons became known, the Kentuckians had a new call to battle—"Remember the Raisin!"

The British loss was 24 killed and 161 wounded. The Americans made no further plans for a winter attack; but the exuberant Indians flocked into Amhurstburg, reassured that with the help of the British they could defeat the Big Knives. When the snow melted and after Tecumseh returned, Proctor wrote his superiors,

> "I shall risk an attack on him [Harrison] in a few days, especially as Tecumseth is at hand."

On 23 April he embarked his troops, destined for Fort Meigs at the mouth of the Maumee River.

General Harrison had quickly occupied Fort Meigs when the terms of enlistment of the Pennsylvania and Virginia troops expired and they returned to their homes. He had with him Captain Ebenezer Wood, an early graduate from West Point. Wood was an engineer with great skill and energy. Harrison had been ordered to remain on the defensive until the United States could build a naval squadron large enough to take control of Lake Erie. He was determined to keep it with his 1,200 man garrison, half of them regulars and volunteers, half militia from Ohio and Kentucky, and expecting more from Kentucky under Brigadier General Green Clay.

Meigs was a formidable fortress. It had a tall timber picket, with seven two-story blockhouses, five raised batteries, and towers at each of several gateways, enclosing nine acres of land. It was four hundred yards long and half as wide, and to repel anyone who dared attempt the pickets, it was skirted by ditches and in parts an abatis, or breastwork of stakes. It had four eighteen-pounders, five twelve-pounders, four six-pounders, and five howitzers, the ammunition for these was securely lodged in two subterranean magazines.

Wood had created a work of uncommon resilience. As soon as he had ascertained the position of the enemy guns over the river, Wood had the garrison working in shifts. Masked from the eyes of their enemies by a line of tents, they threw up an enormous mound of earth that ran like a gigantic worm the length of the interior. They called it a traverse, and it was twenty feet wide and twelve feet high. On 1 May, Wood wrote:

"orders were directly given for all the tents in front [of the mound] to be instantly struck and carried into the rear of the traverse. This was done in almost a moment, and that beautiful prospect of beating up our quarter, which but an instant before presented itself to the view of the eager and skilful [British] artillerists, had now entirely fled, and in its place suddenly appeared an immense shield of earth, obscuring from his sight every tent, every horse . . . and every creature belonging to the camp . . . Those canvas houses [tents] . . . were now with their inhabitants in them entirely protected in their turn."

Once the traverse had been completed the men dug recesses into the reverse side of it, away from the British batteries, and sheltered there during bombardments. It was muddy and squalid, but it protected them against the cannonballs and shrapnel that were propelled from the enemy artillery.

The disgusted Tecumseh compared the Big Knives to groundhogs flitting in and out of their burrows; but the extended dirt groundwork gave the Americans the protection they had hoped for. One American boasted to his family,

"There is not a stronger place of defense in the states than this is at this time."

One American, who kept a diary, counted 1,649 enemy discharges from the morning of the first through the fifth of May, 1813.

Then on the morning of the fifth, eighteen flatboats swept down the rapids of the Maumee River carrying fourteen hundred Kentucky troops under Brigadier General Green Clay. This tipped the balance; there were more troops defending the fort than besieging it. Harrison decided to take advantage of it and destroy the British batteries on the north side of the fort. The first twelve boats, containing over eight hundred troops with Colonel William Dudley in command, were to land opposite Fort Meigs and spike the British guns before they joined their companions in the fort. Harrison also launched an attack below the fort in which Colonel John Miller and 350 regulars, volunteers, and militia slipped from the fort and passed along a small ravine to surprise the British guns. They captured 41 redcoats, drove others away with their Indians and militia and spiked their artillery. Tecumseh counterattacked with a party of Indians, recovering the guns and almost outflanked one of the American militia companies. Miller's regulars made a rapid charge to save the endangered militia, and they were able to return to the fort, but 30 men were dead and 90 were wounded.

Harrison had hoped that the two events would take place at the same time; but Dudley and his men had not completed their attack and returned to the fort as directed. A small group of Indians had lured them into an ambush in the forest, where Tecumseh and his men had quickly assembled and surrounded the unsuspecting Colonel with his command. Pandemonium ensued. Dudley was among those who were killed in the fray. Many of the American soldiers attempted to return to the British battery they had just taken; but the English had counterattacked and awaited them. The Americans, of course, preferred surrendering to the British for the Indians would rarely take a prisoner. Considering them useless baggage, they would kill them and collect their scalp, rather than feed or exchange them. Tecumseh, however, attempted to stop this carnage and worked with the British. There are many stories and legends of his clemency.

The British sent their prisoners to the crumbling old Fort Miami—a short distance away. It was more like a pen than a fort as the remaining walls were only about four feet high. Once the prisoners were all in the enclosure, some of the Indian warriors pushed the guards away and rushed into the enclosure while others clambered over the fallen walls. Some of the British guards cried out to stop them, but the Indians were in an angry mood. When one aged British regular tried to protect the Americans, an Indian shot him dead.

A fearsome figure, painted black, mounted the wall, pointed his musket at a prisoner and killed him. The warrior then calmly reloaded his piece and shot two more before he laid his gun aside, jumped down with his tomahawk in hand and killed a fourth victim. He then scalped them in front of the other horrified prisoners, who crawled over each other in an attempt to escape. The Indians raised a chilling war whoop and readied their weapons. One of Dudley's soldiers, Leslie Combs, who managed to escape, wrote later:

> "He who has never realized cannot imagine. A description is impossible. Without any means of defense or possibility of escape, death in all the horror of savage cruelty seemed to stare us in the face."

Two men rode into the garrison, one an Indian [Tecumseh] in fringed deerskin and with an elegant sword, the other an aging white man [Elliott] whose severe features were set beneath gray hair. Tecumseh dismounted quickly, appalled by the scene before him. Combs, who expected the worst, saw the "noble looking chief" stride "hastily into the midst of the savages." He sprang lightly upon "the high point of the wall," where he could be seen by the whole throng, and "made a brief and emphatic address. I could not understand his language, but his gestures and manner's satisfied me that he was on the side of mercy." Matthew Elliott added his authority to the proceedings, and waved his sword. It was believed that most of the angry Indians were Ojibwas and Potawatomis, who may not have understood Tecumseh's words, either; but they knew the graceful figure before them, and could not mistake his anger. Slowly the Indians dispersed. The captive Americans were escorted back to the fort by the British and exchanged around 14 May. Prisoners were difficult to care for on the frontier.

This battle of 5 May ended the action at Fort Meigs. Most of the Indians rushed home to celebrate their victory in their own fashions. Less than twenty Indians remained. Tecumseh and Proctor had no choice but to abandon their siege. The British reported their casualties as 14 killed, 41 taken prisoner, and 47 wounded. The Indians never made any reports. Their casualties were probably higher. Harrison reported 135 Americans killed, over 630 taken as prisoners, and 188 others wounded. Soldier Daniel Cushing wrote home from Fort Meigs,

> "The sight of dead men has become no more terrifying than the sight of dead flies on a summer day."

In the months that followed Tecumseh was at the peak of his reputation. His scouts had quoted him as saying,

> "It was eight years since he was working to fix this war, and that he had every thing accomplished, and that all the nations from the north were standing at his word."

The Indians believed him truly blessed by the spirits and believed he had exceptional supernatural power. Among the British soldiers fighting drearily to hold the Niagara frontier that summer, Charles Askin wrote,

> "I wish we had Tecumseh here to help us out of our difficulties."

But the land battles with the British mostly stood still that summer in the old northwest and Upper Canada, until the naval battle for the control of Lake Erie ended.

"On 23 August, an Indian council was held at Brownstown when some pro-American Wyandots from Tarhe arrived to warn their fellow tribesmen that General Harrison was coming in great force. They admonished them to 'Stand aside now, before you are destroyed!'"

Walk-in-the-Water proposed that they should desert the British when Harrison advanced; but Roundhead disagreed.

"We are happy to learn your Father [Harrison] is coming out of his hole," he said, "as he has been like a ground hog under the ground, and [his coming] will save us much trouble in walking to meet him!"

The Indians had not been told about the perilous situation that Proctor and his Right Division were in. At Amherstburg, soldiers, food, and ammunition were very scarce. They had given 250 troops, and most of their cannon with ammunition and supplies, to aid the acting naval commodore, Robert Heriot Barclay, who had arrived at Amherstburg in June to command the British naval squadron. Proctor evidently was concerned that the Indians would desert in great numbers, if the truth were told. On 24 August, when American Commodore Perry and his fleet came within sight and the British ships remained in port, Tecumseh became suspicious and questioned the courage of the redcoats. Proctor simply answered that they weren't ready.

The Indians watched as the British fleet of six vessels weighed anchor and worked their way down the Detroit River toward Lake Erie on 9 September to meet the enemy. They carried on their decks much of the artillery that had been used to defend Fort Malden and lay siege to Fort Meigs. With a spyglass, British second-in-command Lieutenant Colonel Warburton watched the cannonading that filled the air with great clouds of smoke that proclaimed the intensity of a desperate sea battle about thirty miles to the south near the Bass Islands. He reported that the British had won, but the gunsmoke was so dense and the distance so far that it could not be verified.

The three-hour battle ended, but no ships returned to the harbor to report, though the wind was fair. Days passed. On 14 September some agitated Indians arrived from Fort Malden to report to Tecumseh that their allies, the British, were dismantling and destroying Fort Malden. Contrary to their promises to the Indians, the British were in the process of retreating.

The Indians were quick with their denunciations, and some threatened violence. Tecumseh demanded that

PERRY ON LAKE ERIE

Elliott bring Procter to a council. The general, who had been staying at the town of Sandwich, finally faced the Indians in a council house at Fort Malden on 18 September. Young John Richardson described Tecumseh,

> "the brilliancy of his black and piercing eye, gave a singularly wild and terrific expression to his features. It was evident that he could be terrible."

With Samuel Saunders interpreting, Tecumseh was quoted as saying

> "listen! Our fleet has gone out. We know they have fought. We have heard the great guns, but know nothing of what has happened .... Our ships have gone one way, and we are much astonished to see our Father [Procter] tying up everything and preparing to run the other, without letting his red children know what his intentions are .... You always told us you would never draw your foot off British ground. But now, Father, we see you are drawing back, and we are sorry to see our Father doing so without seeing the enemy. We must compare our Father's conduct to a fat animal that carries its tail upon its back, but when affrighted, it drops it between its legs and runs off."

Tecumseh wanted to fight the Americans. There were still 2,500 redcoats and warriors, plus their Canadian militia, a fort and some large cannon.

> "The Americans have not yet defeated us by land; neither are we sure they have done so by water. We, therefore, desire to stay here, and fight our enemy should they make an appearance. If they defeat us, we will then retreat

with our Father [Great Britain] . . . . Father! You have got the arms and ammunition which our Great Father [the king] sent for his red children. If you have an idea of going away, give them to us, and you may go and welcome for us. Our lives are in the hands of the Great Spirit. We are determined to defend our lands, and if it is his will, we wish to leave our bones upon them."

The humiliated Proctor then admitted that he had known for a week that Barclay's squadron had been entirely vanquished and that the Americans reigned supreme on Lake Erie. This gave the Americans control over the main source of their supply and communication with Great Britain. Their second source was by land along the Thames River to the north. If the Americans, however, sent their ships northward up the Detroit River to Lake St. Clair and the mouth of the Thames, they could cut off all contact with eastern Canada—starvation or surrender would be the result. The British and Indians were consuming fourteen head of cattle and seven thousand pounds of flour a day, more than their location would be able to supply under siege. It was finally agreed that the two allies would retreat north and make a stand at the forks of the Thames. About twelve hundred warriors joined the retreat.

On the morning of 27 September, the British scouts on duty below Amherstburg spotted the American ships in the distance. Harrison and his army were on their way to invade Canada. Fort Malden and their public buildings had been burned—the families evacuated. Tecumseh with Colonel Matthew Elliott and THOMAS McKEE watched from the distance as five thousand American soldiers marched triumphantly into Amherstburg about 4 o'clock in the afternoon. With sadness, they turned their horses northward to join the British at the forks of the Thames—bringing up the rear, helping the families and stragglers as they proceeded; but carefully watching the enemy. When they reached Sandwich, they found it deserted. The British moved faster than the Indians could with their families.

Procter had difficulty finding a suitable place to make a stand. He was not decisive, partly because he preferred to leave the Indians and save his men. Tecumseh and his Indians had expected upon arrival at the forks to find the British busy with fortifications. Instead, there were only three or four dismounted guns lying helpless in the grass with a hut containing a few small arms nearby, but no sign of Procter or his troops.

That night Tecumseh conferred with his chiefs and warriors at their camp near John McGregor's mill. Their decision was to retreat to Moraviantown, where Tecumseh would try again to make Procter fight. Tecumseh sent their resolution to Warburton the next morning. In the meantime, Tecumseh conducted a rearguard action to delay Harrison's pursuit. At first they tried to burn the bridge—the wood was too damp, so they pulled up the planking. There was then a two-hour skirmish. Harrison had brought more than 3,000 men up the Thames, and he turned Johnson's regiment of 1,000 mounted Kentucky volunteers and two six-pounders upon the Indians. Three Americans were killed or fatally wounded, as were a few Indians. Tecumseh was struck in the arm by a ball. Unable to do more that day, the chief withdrew his warriors after setting fire to the small arsenal the British had established at the forks.

Some of his chiefs started to waiver. Walk-in-the-Water quietly slipped away with his warriors. A few Shawnees and Delawares left, also. Others were scattered. When Tecumseh formed his battle lines the next day, only five hundred warriors got into position. A fatalistic despondency was enveloping the retreating forces. Roundhead was no longer with him. He had died of natural causes during the time of the sea battle for Lake Erie. Tecumseh missed the strong support of this Indian chief. Ammunition and supplies were short; it was disheartening to see them squandered by the British, who in their haste had destroyed or left much along their path for the Americans to claim. Tecumseh spent the night at Christopher Arnold's mill, partly to protect it from Indian warriors who might have set it on fire.

The next morning, on 5 Oct 1813, Tecumseh rose early and was chatting with Arnold's neighbor, who spoke several Indian languages, when he was spotted by sixteen-year-old Abraham Holmes, who had silently traveled two miles up the river—just to behold the Indian chief. He claimed that Tecumseh appeared grave in countenance and earnest in conversation, but of an altogether superior presence. Scampering back to his home, the young boy found that the Americans had already arrived there. Their horses were grazing outside his house. When the American cavalry approached Arnold's, Tecumseh mounted his horse and sped upriver. It was his practice to actually see the enemy before riding on. This was his way of protecting his people from danger and fulfilling his role as chief. Tecumseh forded the Thames to the north bank and the new defensive position that Proctor was preparing with fortifications for the inevitable battle that he could no longer postpone. Only a few miles behind, the American army forded the river above Arnold's. Both sides intended to fight.

Tecumseh found the hungry and shabbily faded redcoats of the 41st Regiment of Foot standing in lines with no protection. They were perfect targets. No Indian would fight like that. They had killed a beef to feed the men, but found that they had sent all their cooking utensils to Moraviantown. They would have food waiting for them—after the battle. Much of their ammunition had been lost. They carried single-shot smoothbore muskets, but had only the cartridges in their pouches. Their number had dwindled to around 450 soldiers.

The Indians occupied the thicker woods to the right of the British line, between the small swamp and a much larger one that ran along the foot of a low ridge about 650 yards from the river. Tecumseh had agreed with Procter that the Indians would turn the American's left while the British contained their right. By squatting behind the trees and brush between the two swamps, the Indians could rip the attackers' front and left simultaneously with gunfire. The ground was marshy and thickly forested. It would bog down the American horsemen, provide cover for the Indians, and furnish a means of escape if the battle went against them. Tecumseh's numbers had dwindled to only a third of what he had a few weeks ago.

British Captain William Caldwell, who was stationed near the Indians, remembered later in his life that before the firing began he had been seated on a log with Tecumseh, THOMAS McKEE, and a young Shawnee. Suddenly, Tecumseh started as if shot. Caldwell asked him what was wrong. Tecumseh answered that he "could not tell, but it is an evil spirit which betokens no good." Disturbed, Caldwell suggested that the chief should not fight that day, but Tecumseh would not hear of it and shook the foreboding off.

William Henry Harrison arrived between 3 and 4 o'clock. He had only 120 regulars; but they were backed by R. M. Johnson's regiment of 1,000 Kentucky mounted volunteers—armed with long rifles, tomahawks, and knives. These riders were garbed in leather hunting smocks, and were drilled in maneuvers of every description. They were mobile, skillful, and afraid of nothing. Many thirsted to revenge the losses of the River Raisin and Fort Meigs. Behind Johnson's regiment were five brigades of Kentucky militia, which were personally commanded by Isaac Shelby, the sixty-three-year-old plucky governor of the state. In addition, Harrison had the strong support of 260 Shawnees, Delawares, Wyandots, and Senecas, which he had recruited in Ohio. He had brought two six-pounders with him. They out-numbered the enemy three to one.

The Battle of the Thames, or the Battle of Moraviantown as it is sometimes called, lasted only one half-hour. It began with a ferocious attack by the American's First Regiment against the British, rather than the Indians. The charge was led by Lieutenant Colonel James Johnson—a brother of Colonel Richard Mentor Johnson of the Kentucky mounted volunteers. From Tecumseh's position, the Indians heard the sound of the American bugle and then the rapid fire from the rifles of the thundering mounted Kentuckians. Then there were two volleys of musketry from the British lines. Tecumseh must have known within a very few minutes that his British support on the left had been quickly surrounded and captured. There had been no cannon fire; it had been captured quickly by Harrison's regulars. Procter made a weak attempt to rally his men and then galloped away with his aide, Captain Hall, losing 43 of his men—18 dead or seriously wounded. Shortly, he was in Moraviantown, where he had posted some of his army to protect the settlement. From horseback, he gulped down a quick drink, and ordered his artillery chief to rearrange their guns. That was his last attempt at leadership. When the Americans arrived, there was little resistance, and Procter had escaped to the east. Matthew Elliott described his conduct as "shameful in the highest degree."

Following close behind his first battalion who had attacked the British, American Colonel R. M. Johnson led his second battalion toward Tecumseh's position across the small swamp. At the front, Jacob Stucker's company formed a line of skirmishers on foot that advanced toward the woods. Tecumseh ignored the skirmishers. With limited ammunition, his guns waited for the two—four hundred yards apart—columns of horsemen that followed behind. In an effort to draw out the Indians from their covered position, Colonel Richard Mentor Johnson led twenty of his sharpest riflemen—who had all volunteered—to move rapidly forward on their horses in front of the skirmishers. The Indians rose from their cover and sent a crashing volley into the oncoming riders, filling the air with acrid, thick powder smoke. The ground was strewn with dead and wounded men and thrashing horses. Colonel Johnson had been hit four times, but remained in this saddle. His injured horse had become entangled in some dead tree branches.

Then as the supporting columns rushed in, they were greeted with another sharp round of bullets. Colonel James Davidson, who rode at the head of the left column, received wounds in his chest, stomach, and thigh. The swampy ground was creating problems for the horses and many dismounted and fought face to face with their wildly painted foes.

Both parties charged, only to be repulsed. Tecumseh, painted red and black, could be seen from time to time by his fellow Indians leading and encouraging their efforts. They recognized him in the fray by his bandaged wounded arm, which he continued to use very effectively, and the large British medallion he wore dangling from his neck.

The Colonel freed his entangled horse from the dead branches. His peripheral vision sighted an Indian rushing toward him with a raised tomahawk. He rapidly raised his gun, loaded with a ball and several buckshot, and trained it upon the left side of the oncoming chief's chest and fired. Tecumseh fell to the ground. One American recalled that the Indians

"gave the loudest yells I ever heard from human beings and that ended the fight."

In the farther right, gunshots continued briefly until the word of their chief's death reached them, and then it stopped. Silently, the Indians withdrew past the cloud of gunsmoke and into the swamp, away from the Big Knives.

American Major Thomas Rowland wrote a friend,

"Tecumseh is certainly killed. I saw him with my own eyes. It was the first time I had seen this celebrated chief. Their was something so majestic, so dignified, and yet so mild in his countenance, as he lay stretched on his back on the ground where a few minutes before he had rallied his men to the fight, that while gazing on him with admiration and pity, I forgot he was a savage. He had received a wound in the arm and had it bound up before he received the mortal wound. He had such a countenance as I shall never forget. He did not appear to me so large a man as he was represented—I did not suppose his height exceeded five feet ten or eleven inches, but exceedingly well proportioned. The British say he compelled them to fight."

It was a decisive American victory. Harrison had fifteen men slain or mortally wounded; the Indians had similar losses, but the British lost 634 men killed or captured before, during, or immediately after the battle of the Thames and Moraviantown. Some of the British admitted that their greatest loss was the alliance they had with the Indians and the loss of Tecumseh, who lay dead on the battlefield. Richard Mentor Johnson is quite universally credited as being the officer who shot Tecumseh. He claimed that he shot an Indian in the chest, but he was not sure that it was Tecumseh. An Indian Potawatomi friend of Tecumseh, Shabeni, who had retired in Illinois, gave the following story during an interview in the United States Hotel, Chicago, in 1839.

"Tecumseh was a very brave but cautious man. He had, however, been wounded in the neck and became desperate. He thought his wound was mortal, and told his warriors that, as he must die, there could be no risk in rushing forward to kill Col. Johnson. He did so, and Shaw-ben-eh saw him when he fell. His object was to strike the colonel with his tomahawk before he saw him, and a moment more of inattention and the colonel's head would have been sundered. He was shot just as his arm reached the full height to strike the fatal blow."

Shabeni described the colonel's horse as large and white, with occasionally a jet black spot. He was asked where and how they buried Tecumseh. Shabeni stood up, and with eloquence declared,

"None but brave warriors die on the battlefield. Such, afraid of nothing when alive, don't care for dogs, wolves or eagles and crows, when dead. They want the prairie, the whole prairie, to lie upon. So Tecumseh, the bravest man that ever was, whom the Great Spirit would not let be killed by the common soldier, but sent to Col. Johnson to be killed, wanted no grave nor honors. He let every animal come and eat of his flesh, as he made every red man love, and every white man fear him."

Not long after the engagement was over, Tecumseh's body was discovered on the field. It was identified by Anthony Shane, who was with Harrison's Indians and some of the captured British officers. They observed that the chief had been hit several times because his body bore numerous injuries: a bullet hole, too small to admit a man's little finger, near the heart; one or two wounds caused by buckshot; and a cut on the head. Trophy-seeking soldiers scalped and stripped the corpse. The next day, some latecomers tore pieces of skin from the back and thigh to make into razor strops. Shane condemned this outrage and when Harrison, accompanied by Commodore Perry, viewed the body on 6 October, the general confessed that he was "greatly vexed and mortified" by the sight. It was rumored that the body was given to the Canadians who took it back to the town of Sandwich; but no burial spot has been conclusively identified. Other stories have been told, and some historians have squabbled over the details amid the many reports, stories and legends that have come forward; but the above is probably the most accepted version of this brief battle. Evidently THOMAS McKEE survived the battle, but not for much longer. The Ancestral File records his death as 1814.

The Ottawa chief Naiwash, who had been the second chief in the battle, is quoted as saying in October 1814,

> "We Indians . . . from the westward, perhaps the Master of Life would give us more luck if we would stick together as we formerly did . . . and we probably might go back and tread again upon our own lands. Chiefs and warriors, since our great chief Tecumtha has been killed, we do not listen to one another. We do not rise together. We hurt ourselves by it. It is our own fault . . . . We do not, when we go to war, rise together, but we go one or two, and the rest say they will go tomorrow."

CANADA, GENERAL JAMES WILKINSON, FORT MCHENRY

Across Lake Erie at its eastern end, the American senior major general Henry Dearborn made some early attempts in 1813 to acquire the Canadian land that extended between Lake Ontario and Lake Huron for the United States. On 27 Apr 1813, he launched an attack on the town of York [now Toronto, Canada]. A sharp battle ensued and the Americans victoriously gained possession of the town and burned the British government buildings.

A month later American naval Commodore Chauncey compelled the English to evacuate Fort George on the Niagara, while the English made an unsuccessful attack on Sackett's Harbor, where Chauncey had built his ships—near the northeastern end of Lake Ontario and a short distance across the lake from Kingston, Canada. At first the American militia fled; but their regulars held their positions. Winds prevented the English ships from cannonading the Americans, and as the scattered militiamen were reorganized, the English evacuated. British General Prevost lost 48 men killed and 211 wounded or missing, while among the British seamen only 1 was killed and 4 wounded. The Americans had 23 killed and 111 wounded. Unfortunately for the Americans, Lieutenant Chauncey, a younger brother of the Commodore, had been instructed not to let the British capture the ammunition stored in the harbor. Believing that their fort had been conquered by the British, he set the naval warehouses afire. Fortunately for the Americans, their largest ship under construction in the harbor, the *General Pike*, was only slightly damaged and almost repaired when the commodore returned from Fort George.

Major General Henry Dearborn, who had been given the overall command of the campaigns in western and northern New York on 27 Jan 1812, was born in Hampton, New Hampshire, in March 1751. When he was practicing medicine at Portsmouth, the news arrived of the Battle of Lexington, 20 Apr 1775. He joined with the 60 volunteers from his home area, and marching sixty miles to Cambridge, they arrived the next day. He was a captain at Bunker Hill and went with Benedict Arnold on his failed expedition to conquer Quebec. He was a major when Burgoyne surrendered at Saratoga and distinguished himself at the Battle of Monmouth courthouse in 1778. He was with Sullivan's expedition against the Indians in 1780, and at Yorktown in 1781. In 1782, he was given garrison duty at Saratoga. Dearborn was twice a member of congress and President Jefferson appointed him to be his Secretary of War, where he served eight years. Under Madison, he was first made collector of Boston. His war campaigns of 1812 had not been successful, but his background was superb. When his army had moved northward to take Montreal, he was unable to gain the strength he wanted from his New York militia, who believed that their enlistments did not require them to cross the St. Lawrence River, as it took them beyond the border of their state.

Armstrong had become Secretary of War under President Madison, and commanded Major General JAMES WILKINSON to cut off British supplies at Kingston and then march along the St Lawrence River and join Major General Wade Hampton, who commanded the troops on Lake Champlain. Hampton was to march up the Chateau River from his headquarters at Four Corners (now Chateaugay), New York, toward the St. Lawrence. They would join forces and continue toward Montreal. The two generals were not happy with their orders, partly because they had hated each other since the Revolutionary War; but they reluctantly agreed to Armstrong's plan.

On 21 Oct 1813, Hampton's army began their journey. At the Canadian border, Hampton had the same trouble Dearborn had experienced the previous year. The New York militia refused to leave their state. Hampton had 4,000 regulars, so he continued on without the New Yorkers. On 25 October the march halted. A combined force of French/Canadian volunteers, various militia units, and Indian warriors, all under the command of Napoleonic War veteran Lt. Colonel Charles de Salaberry, had blocked the road with log abatis and built fortifications alongside.

Hampton sent Colonel Robert Purdy with a detachment of soldiers across the river to attack the enemy from behind. Unfortunately Purdy's troops got lost in the forest overnight and in the morning faced Canadians on both sides of the river. Purdy skirmished with the enemy for two days—unable to find Hampton or get a message to him.

While Purdy was losing his way in the forest, Hampton got a message from Armstrong that convinced him he would not get any additional troops. He wanted to retreat back to Four Corners; but he would not abandon Purdy. Around 2:00 P.M. the following day, he made a formation in front of the abatis. According to the Canadians, their redcoats let out a great yell that convinced Hampton he faced a greater force than he had anticipated. Firing went on for two hours; but Hampton refused to order a charge. He eventually retreated. When Purdy found his way back, the two commanders agreed to withdraw and return back to their headquarters. The Americans lost 50 men. The Canadians reported 2 killed, 13 wounded, and 3 captured.

Major General JAMES WILKINSON with his army of 8,000 troops moved up the St. Lawrence River toward Kingston, Canada. The journey was difficult and many men and boats were lost in the broad waters of the river. WILKINSON almost called off the attack, and many reported he appeared gradually to lose his mind as they advanced. The British detachments followed him on the river and bank, with Lt. Colonel Joseph Morrison commanding the British regulars on the north shore, knowing there were eight miles of rapids at Long Sault. WILKINSON sent Brigadier General Jacob Brown with a party ahead to clear opposition forces around the rapids. The successful Americans were able to secure food by plundering the farms.

By the time WILKINSON encamped at Chrysler's farm on 11 November, he was incapacitated, and he placed Brigadier General John P. Boyd in command of 2,500 soldiers to stop the British Commander Joseph Morrison. There was much confusion and eventually the Americans moved back across the river and the battle ended, although no officer remembered calling a retreat. The American casualties were 102 killed, 237 wounded, and around 100 taken prisoner. The British losses were smaller: 23 killed, 148 wounded, and 9 missing.

Immediately following the battle, WILKINSON received word that Hampton had been defeated. This convinced WILKINSON to go into winter quarters. He blamed Hampton for his retreat, but he was relieved of his command and faced a court-martial in early 1814. WILKINSON was acquitted, but his reputation for incompetence ended his military career.

The year of 1814 brought Napoleon's overthrow and consequently peace in Europe. The British troops that had fought in Europe were sent to Canada and to the southern United States border on the Caribbean Sea. The British navy, the unquestioned mistress of the seas, created an unsurpassable barrier all along the Atlantic coastline of the United States. With England at peace with France and their own former allies in other European countries, they had no need to worry about Europe—at least, for a little while. They had three objectives: reclaim Lake Erie and invade New York through Albany by controlling Lake Champlain; create a diversion by attacking Washington D. C. and burning the government buildings like the Americans had done at York (Toronto), and their third objective was an attack on New Orleans and Pensacola to control the Caribbean coastal area, the Mississippi River, and the vast western lands— much like Aaron Burr had proposed to them when he was in England.

By this time, the United States government was bankrupt and the nations of Europe were not willing to make loans. The Bank of the United States, which ALEXANDER HAMILTON had struggled so hard to build and maintain, had been closed in 1811, after Vice President George Clinton gave the swing vote in the senate against renewing its charter. The New England states were still unhappy with the national leadership from Virginia and were considering secession. Their militia had not participated in the war, since their states were not yet under attack; however, the British *H.M.S. Sharron* had challenged the *U.S.S. Chesapeake* in a sea battle near Boston on 1 Jun 1813. The more experienced British seamen were able to board the American ship. American Captain James Lawrence was killed and uttered his famous last words, "Don't give up the ship." The fight on the deck lasted only fifteen minutes with 60 Americans killed and 85 wounded. British Captain Broke was wounded, with 49 of his countrymen and 33 of his crew killed. Broke survived his wounds and was hailed for his victory as a national hero in London. In the south, Jackson was still fighting the

Creeks and their allies.

But on the plus side, the Indians were no longer a great threat in the old northwest and Tecumseh was dead. The Americans had successfully fought the Indians and their British allies and controlled Lake Erie. They had also experienced freedom from England since 1776. The population had multiplied considerably. This young, new generation, thirty-eight years later, was not as experienced in war as their parents were; but they were learning. Loyalty to England was no longer a consideration, nor did they look to France or Spain. A new spirit of liberty and freedom was uniting the white people who had come from Europe to rid themselves of its tyranny and aggrandizement of the elite. They would not call the English "our Father," or be dependent like Tecumseh and the Canadians were. The old Jeffersonian love of the Articles of Confederation with its state rights and boundaries was being buried in favor of national unity and an independence from foreign colonialism with its serfdom. The year of 1814 was really the true beginning of the United States of America.

When the frozen St. Lawrence River thawed and the ice tumbled out into the Atlantic Ocean, British ships arrived in mass into Canada. Reports say that the British soon had 17,000 men near Montreal building ships and preparing for their summer campaign into New York via Plattsburg and Lake Champlain. In addition, they had reinforced the troops at Niagara, Kingston, York and other forts.

The American summer campaign of 1814 began when Brigadier General Jacob Brown invaded Canada on 3 July in a bid to extend the American control of the Niagara frontier. Brown had 5,000 regular troops backed by 4,000 New York militia. Canadian Fort Erie on the northeast tip of Lake Erie across from Buffalo, where the Niagara River begins its flow through Niagara Falls and into Lake Ontario, was quickly occupied by the Americans and they moved northward without difficulty until they approached the Chippewa River, about two miles south of Goat Island—but on the Canadian side.

British Major General Riall had collected 2,000 troops to stop the Americans, whose advance force was Brigadier General Winfield Scott's First Brigade of regulars. Riall dispatched Lt. Colonel Thomas Pearson and his men to halt Scott's advance and destroy a major bridge. There were several skirmishes on 4 July; but Scott made good use of his field artillery and continued onward. Finally, the Chippewa River stopped the American advance. Riall fortified its northern bank with his regulars, militia forces, and Mohawk Indian allies. Scott encamped one mile to the south at Street's Creek.

On the morning of 5 July, Scott sent a detachment of his 3rd Brigade commanded by Colonel Peter B. Porter to advance and attempt to cross the river west of the British fortifications, where the Canadian militia and Indian troops were waiting. When Porter's troops entered the forest on the west and confronted the enemy, the advance soon ended, and the untrained militia turned and fled back toward the creek. With this, the British regulars crossed the river with bayonets fixed. General Scott re-formed his men, and sent his artillery forward to meet the enemy. There was a heavy exchange of artillery fire. While the British continued to move forward, Scott enclosed them on three sides with a U-shaped formation. When the two sides were close enough to exchange musket fire, the British were caught in crossfire. The American artillery was able to explode a British caisson, basically stopping their artillery fire. Scott ordered a charge and Riall's British regulars retreated at the advance of the American bayonets. Riall surrendered. The British loss was 148 regulars killed and around 100 militia and Indians killed or captured. The American casualties totaled around 44 killed and 98 wounded.

The victory for the American generals, Brown and Scott, was significant. It was the first time in the War of 1812 that a group of American regulars had faced British regulars in open battle and won. Public praise for the U. S. army for years to come was based on the victory at Chippawa. Unfortunately for Brown, the victory was short-lived. Riall was reinforced by British General Drummond and in the Battle of Lundy's Lane, a few miles further north above Niagara Falls, on the 25 July, two large armies faced one another again. The armies advanced and then retreated throughout the day. At 9:00 P.M. the Americans controlled the hill, after fresh reinforcements arrived. At 12:00 P.M., Drummond tried three times in vain to push the Americans off the hill. Both Winfield Scott and Jacob Brown were injured during these encounters. With water and ammunition running low, his army dwindling in numbers, and nearly all his officers injured, Brown decided to withdraw his forces. With his army of around 700 men,

Brown retreated south toward Fort Erie. Drummond did not follow. New reinforcements arrived and were successfully positioned to withstand a rather weak try by the Americans the next day.

The British soldiers lost 81 killed and 562 injured. The American casualties were 171 killed and 573 wounded. So many British and American corpses littered the hill that many were gathered together and burned on the field. The British veterans of the European wars who were present claimed that the fight was every bit as fierce. It was the bloodiest battle of the War of 1812, and although it was considered a loss, it proved once again that the American regulars could stand well against the British regulars, even if the cost of life was high. Winfield Scott, so prominent in his leadership, had to retire from the war—his wounds were too severe. The Americans held their ground until autumn and then withdrew their forces to Niagara.

Controlling the Atlantic coast with their ships, British Vice Admiral Cochrane took command of their naval operations in Chesapeake Bay. As a diversion, he landed 4,000 marines and regulars under Major General Robert Ross, fresh from the Napoleonic Wars. The main British force started up the Pawtuxet River on 19 August. They made a feint toward Baltimore. Secretary of War William Armstrong had appointed Brigadier General William Winder, a political ally of President James Madison, to command the newly created Tenth Military District. Winder was incompetent as a commander and his militia was slow in arriving. It was generally believed that the British would not attack Washington, so very little effort was made to fortify the capital. Finally as the enemy approached Bladensburg, about six miles east of Washington on 24 August, it became very clear that the British had no desire to spare this central site of the United States government. They were advancing directly towards it.

At Bladensburg, the American commanders placed their 6,000 troops in defensive positions; but they lacked tactical prowess. Militia brigadier general Tobias Stansbury at first deployed troops in three lines facing east toward the Potomac River, but Secretary of State James Monroe, who held no formal military command, rearranged two of the lines. Because of Monroe's meddling, the three American lines were too far apart to support one another, and when the battle began, no solid position could be maintained.

Just before the fighting commenced, President Madison and several cabinet members, who had ridden out to urge on the troops, started to cross the Potomac directly into the advancing British front line. They were warned off by a scout at the last moment; but the American troops, who had meant to destroy the bridge the presidential party had been about to use, were consequently unable to do so, leaving the American position open to a British attack.

Around 1:00 P.M. British Major General Ross led his troops across the bridge over the Potomac and quickly flanked the first American line. As the militia troops fled, the first line fell back. Ross's men then charged the second American line, and Brigadier General Winder ordered his men to retreat toward Georgetown, where he hoped they could re-form. The retreat quickly turned into a chaotic rout that was later referred to as the "Bladensburg races." The British fired on the exposed American lines from covered positions. Additionally, the British fired Congreve rockets, which flared over the field in noisy, erratic patterns, frightening the Americans, most had never fought nor seen a battle.

Only one section of the American force held. Joshua Barney, a hero of the Revolution, had no military rank. He commanded an American flotilla on the Pawtuxet as a sailing master commandant. Arriving with a force of seamen and marines, he attached his company to the American third line. Barney's men held their position, firing on the British with heavy naval guns dragged from their ships. Their ammunition was very low when the cover from the American militia collapsed. Barney was wounded and captured; but most of his force escaped.

The battle lasted three hours. It was a crushing defeat for the Americans. They had killed 64 British and wounded 185, while the American losses were less—26 killed and 51 wounded; however, the American loss of the battle opened the way for the enemy to invade Washington D. C., where the British burned and destroyed much of the nation's capital. The president, his cabinet and other officials escaped into Virginia.

Leaving the deserted city behind, General Ross turned his attention to Baltimore, Maryland. Here he met better resistance and Ross was killed in the fray. Vice Admiral Cockrane's attack on Fort McHenry on 12-14 September was unsuccessful. On 15 September, the British gave up their campaign against Baltimore and withdrew from the Chesapeake. This American victory is still celebrated by the poem "Defence of Fort M'Henry," written by Francis Scott Key, an American diplomat detained onboard a British ship. The poem, set to music as *The Star-Spangled Banner*, became the official national anthem of the United States in 1931.

Meanwhile in Canada, while the Chesapeake was being attacked, Major General Sir George Prevost had collected his 17,000 well-trained British soldiers to invade the United States at the confluence of the Richelieu River and Lake Champlain. Their shipbuilding was completed. They would move south by land and by water. Unfortunately for the Americans, their Secretary of War William Armstrong had decided that no northern invasion would occur, and on the last day of August, he ordered Major General George Izard, the commander of the American forces at Plattsburg, to leave their well-constructed defenses between the Saranac River and Lake Champlain and take most of his forces to Sacket's Harbor.

Brigadier General Alexander Macomb was left in charge of the 2,500 soldiers who remained to defend the nation at Plattsburg. When word arrived that the British were coming in force, he quickly pressed thirty-three hundred Vermont and New York volunteer into service. Greatly outnumbered, they were able to slow the solid British advance by frequent raiding parties and by destroying all the bridges leading to Plattsburg; but the British advanced steadily southward to Plattsburg.

On 6 September, Prevost was unable to find a ford across the Saranac River, so he decided to wait for his naval support. Three days later they arrived with their 37-gun *Confidence* supported by the 16-gun *Linnet*; the 11-gun *Chubb*; the 11-gun *Finch*, and twelve small gunboats. British Captain George Downie was in command.

Awaiting their arrival on the American side was Lieutenant Thomas Macdonough. He had the newly completed American fleet with their 26-gun *Saratoga*, supported by the 20-gun *Eagle*; the 17-gun *Ticonderoga*; the 7-gun *Preble*, and ten gunboats. Macdonough realized that his guns were inferior to those on the British vessels, which could fire from a longer range than his guns were capable of doing. He anchored his ships to draw the British into closer range, believing his guns to be superior for short-range encounters.

When the naval battle began on the morning of 11 Sep 1814, the Americans took some heavy blows from the enemy's long-range guns. The *Confidence* gave a broadside to the American *Saratoga*, but was unable to close in. Captain Downie was killed when the *Saratoga* was able to counterattack. As the *H.M.S. Finch* attempted to engage the *U.S.S. Ticonderoga*, the smaller *U.S.S. Preble* was able to send it onto the shoals of Crab Island, where the gunboats pounded it apart. The *Preble* was in turn disabled by the

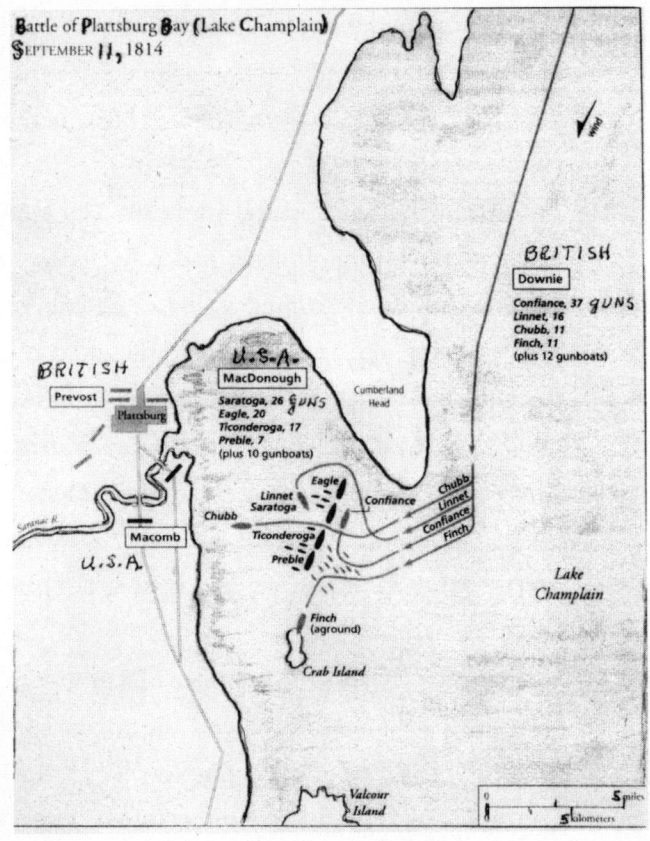

British gunboats. The *U.S.S. Eagle* was knocked out of action by the *H.M.S. Confidence*, while the *H.M.S. Linnet* silenced the starboard guns of the *U.S.S. Saratoga*.

It looked ill for the Americans, but Macdonough weighed anchor and was still able to maneuver his ship to fire on the *Confidence* with his portside weapons. Lieutenant James Robertson, who was now commanding the *H.M.S. Confidence*, tried to counter-maneuver but his large bulky ship was unable to respond as quickly, and he failed. Under very heavy fire from the *Saratoga*, the crew of the *Confidence* began to waver, and at 10:30 A.M., the British ship surrendered.

During this naval battle, Major General Prevost had ordered a land attack. Some of his forces had pushed across the river and engaged the front lines of the American militia. As the British paused for reinforcements, Prevost learned about their naval defeat. Realizing that even if he were successful, his supplies could be cut off by the American's control of Lake Champlain, with little delay, he ordered his men to retreat. Casualties were light, considering the severity of the encounters. The British reported 92 killed, 119 wounded, and over 300 captured or deserted. The American casualties included 89 killed and 120 wounded.

This American victory in Canada, which was soon followed by the American victory at Baltimore and Fort McHenry, raised the American morale from the depths of despair to a new high. These two successful American battles, when word reached Europe across the Atlantic to Ghent, Belgium, hastened the negotiations between the two countries to end the war.

In the closing weeks of 1814, the British landed 7,500 veterans near New Orleans in an apparent move to take over the city and give them control of the economy of the western states—hoping to persuade the westerners to secede from their silk stocking easterners. But Major General Andrew Jackson's army of frontiersmen turned out to be much tougher opponents than President Madison's eastern militia. Jackson arrived on 1 December to find New Orleans unprepared for the expected British attack, and promptly called on his own volunteers to change the laxity in their defenses.

The British fleet arrived two weeks later, and the action began with skirmishes and indecisive battles continued in varying degrees of success and failure for each side. The immediate prelude to the main battle began on January 1, when British artillery began to bombard the American lines. Most of the British guns overshot their targets and many were wiped out when the American artillery answered their fire. The exchange continued for two hours. It took another week for the British to prepare for their final attack, which would include almost 6,000 highly trained regulars, against Jackson's motley force of 5,300. As a diversion, the British sent 600 men under the command of British Colonel William Thornton to take over the American guns that were protected by General DAVID MORGAN's Louisiana and Kentucky militia. They were supposed to attack during the night of 7 January, but Thornton's men could not get across the river until early on 8 January.

Meanwhile the main attack began on the American line by the canal. It was actually Jackson's strongest point and the British were destroyed by heavy artillery fire before they could make a dent. There was a heavy fog and the British commander Pakenham hoped it would mask his advance against the eastern bank; but as his men marched toward the American line, the fog suddenly lifted, exposing them directly to the deadly hail of American fire. Wave after wave of steady British advance was cut down by a steady cannon, rifle, and musket fire. The American fire was so accurate that the British troops barely made it to within one hundred yards of their enemy's line. As the bodies piled up before the American line, Pakenham was killed. Major General John Lambert, who was second in command, surveyed their casualties and called a halt to the entire action, including Thornton and his men, who were somewhat more successful. The British loss was 300 killed, 1,262 wounded, and 484 taken prisoner. Only six Americans in Jackson's line were killed and seven wounded. One of these casualties was great-uncle DAVID SANDERS, who died from his wounds. During the entire month of action before the New Orleans battle, the British suffered 2,450 casualties, compared to an American total of only 350.

[Note: DAVID SANDERS, first cousin and close friend of second great grandfather JAMES RUSSELL IVIE, was severely wounded and died shortly after the Battle of New Orleans. This war of volunteers from Tennessee and Kentucky included many cousins, close and distant, who were undoubtedly part of Jackson's volunteers, including the surnames of: FAUCETT; IVIE; IVEY; ALLRED; McKEE; BRADEN; McKNIGHT; WATTS; WILES; FREELAND; STONE; CRIPPIN; PARKS; BROOKS; PAUL; PARK; HAMILTON; BEAN; PURSELL; BALDRIDGE; SMITH; BUTCHER; SANDERS; HOLLAND; TURNER; MILLIGAN; MITCHELL; STEELE; YOUNG; BILLINGSLAY; BILLINGTON; ROBINSON; LONG; MOORE; BRADEN—the surnames of the married daughters of McKEE, IVIE, and FAUSETT spouses of Tennessee and Georgia.]

After this British attempt to conquer New Orleans on 8 Jan 1815, Jackson's sharpshooters, with the help of the pirate Jean Lafitte, had routed the British regulars with such a decisive victory that the New Englanders, who had met at Hartford, Connecticut, to discuss their long simmering scheme of regional secession, swept their concerns against remaining U. S. citizens under the table once and for all.

While the defeated British fleet limped back to England, word arrived from London that the Treaty of Ghent had been signed on 24 Dec 1814, and the war had ended. The boundaries were fixed very close to the original lines that existed before the Americans started the war; but the events had changed the political and economic outlook for the westerners. No longer would the Indians be a great threat in the old northwest. In the south, the Creek warriors had made a treaty and western Florida was occupied by Jackson and his troops. Thousands of wagons pushed into the newly acquired territories. The Americans had new heroes. Both Andrew Jackson and William Henry Harrison would in due time become presidents of the United States of America—a united country that believed they could hold their own on the land and on the sea.

As Madison's second presidential term drew to a close, he designated (with a nod from the sage of Monticello) his Secretary of State James Monroe as his heir apparent. The cynical Aaron Burr, who was residing in New York, wrote about this nomination in a letter to his son-in-law Joseph Alston, who had been the governor of South Carolina from 1812 to 1814. Burr denounced "congressional nominations" as "hostile to all freedom and independence of suffrage." More galling was the way "a certain junto of actual and factitious Virginians" had run the federal government for twenty-four years and now thought of it as "their property." The Jeffersonians had stayed in power, Burr maintained, by "promoting state dissentions" which made it impossible for a strong leader to emerge elsewhere.

As for the candidate Monroe, Burr described him as

"naturally dull and stupid—extremely illiterate—indecisive to a degree that would be incredible to one who did not know him—pusillanimous and of course hypocritical—has no opinion on any subject and will always be under the govt. of the worst men." This, Burr wrote, "is a character exactly suited to the views of the Virginia junto."

Burr urged Alston to rouse himself and South Carolina to action. The time was

"extremely suspicious for breaking down this degrading system." There was a man on the political horizon—born in South Carolina—who could do it. He was a leader of firmness and decision and real standing with the public. His name was Andrew Jackson. Burr urged Alston to organize "a respectable nomination" before the congressional caucus named Monroe. The Tennessee general's success would be "inevitable."

But Alston lacked the energy and desire that Burr had hoped for. In his return letter, he said he agreed with him; but

"the spirit, the energy, the health necessary to give practical effect to sentiment, are all gone." He added that he felt "too entirely unconnected with the world, to take much interest in any thing."

A few months later, Alston joined his wife and child in death. Aaron Burr, who was ostracized by other leaders and most of the citizens, left the historians no further records of attempts to influence American politics. He died without much attention in 1836. Jackson led his army against the eastern Indians to claim East Florida, became governor of Tennessee and, in 1828, became the president of the United States of America.

In 1821, another notable in Tennessee was beginning his political rise to fame. The following account is taken from *Davy Crockett Scout* by Charles Fletcher Allen:

"Davy was now becoming a man of weight in the county, and even beyond its borders. Politics then was the same keen game as it is to-day, a little cruder, perhaps, but not more scrupulous. The leaders were looking for men who could get votes, and in Davy they saw great promise. He was asked to run for the Legislature [state], and in February, 1821, he agreed to. As the election was not until some months later, he took a drove of horses to North Carolina, and was gone three months. As soon as he returned he began an active campaign, in those days called 'electioneering.' He says that he found the people expected him to tell them about things of which he knew nothing. His ideas of government and constitutions were scarcely nebulous, and it behooved him to listen to the words of wisdom that fell upon his ears. Like many wise men and judges, he knew enough to 'reserve his opinion,' and to follow the example of the Tar Baby, who 'kept on sayin' nothing.' The Assembly district comprised two or three counties, and it required much travelling to cover the field. The most trying event in Davy's history was undoubtedly his coming before the Duck River people at the time of the big squirrel hunt and barbecue—[where our IVIE and FAUSETT ancestors lived at that time].

"From all parts of the district the squirrel-hunters came, with the best rifles the world had ever seen. When Davy was chosen by one of the two sides he received the best possible advertisement. The hunt lasted two days, and only the scalps were needed in the count, the squirrels being eaten by the hunters. The nuts were yet unripe, but the corn had suffered from the little animals' greed, and they were fat and saucy. Black squirrels, grey squirrels, foxies, red squirrels, all helped to swell the count. Davy killed a large number in the way by which he had made a reputation: he 'barked' them by shooting between the squirrel and the limb on which it sat, generally killing it without a scar. When the scalps were counted it was found that Davy's side had won, and their opponents furnished the materials for the barbecue, and provided music for the dancing that followed.

"All day great fires had been kept going in long pits dug in the ground, hard, dry beech and maple being used for fuel. On the next morning, the last day of the hunt, half of a fatted ox or deer was placed over the coals of each pit on an iron rod or a green sapling, and slowly roasted, being carefully watched, seasoned, and basted with fat. When everything was ready, the meat was cut from the bones by skillful carvers, and the hungry crowd was served. There is no sauce like hunger, and no meat like that roasted over a bed of hardwood coals. After the feast, came the dancing. But between the barbecue and the time for the 'Virginny Reel' and 'Money Musk,' with the hoedowns, pigeon-wings, and other rural embellishments, the people had to be amused, and Davy was called on for a speech.

"What he thought and did in this crisis is best told in his own words: 'A public document I had never seen, nor did I know there were such things; and how to begin I couldn't tell. I made many apologies, and tried to get off, for I know'd I had to run against a man who could speak prime, and I know'd, too, that I wasn't able to shuffle and cut with him. He was there, and, knowing my ignorance as well as I did myself, he also urged me to make a speech. The truth is, he thought my being a candidate was a mere matter of sport, and didn't think for a moment that he was in any danger from an ignorant backwoods bear-hunter. I found I couldn't get off, and so I determined just to go ahead, and leave it to chance what I should say. I got up and told the people I reckoned they knowed what I had come for, but if not, I could tell them. I had come for their votes, and if they didn't watch mighty close I'd get them too. Then I tried to speak about something else (about government), until I choked up as bad as if my mouth had been jammed and crammed chock full of dry mush. There the people stood, listening all the while, with their eyes, mouths, and ears open, to catch every word I would speak.

"'At last I told them I was like a fellow I heard of not long before; he was beating on the head of an empty barrel near the road-side, when a traveller, passing along, asked him what he was doing that for? The fellow replied that there had been some cider in that barrel a few days before, and he was trying to see if there was any then; he said if there was, he couldn't get it out. I told them there had been a little bit of a speech in me a while before, but I believed I couldn't get it out.'

"Having in this way set the crowd to roaring with laughter, Davy told them a few stories, then took the first chance to say that he was as dry as a powder-horn. A great cheer rose as he led the way to the stand where rum, apple and peach brandies, cider, and buttermilk were to be had.

"Then came the country dances, the name being a popular rendering of the French term 'contredanse' and the figures the same as might have been seen—before the Revolution—in the gay court of Louis the Fourteenth; as Davy, thoroughly at home, took his part in the extravagant features of the frolicsome reels and riotous quadrilles, he made votes by the hundred, and when the day of the election came about he had two-thirds of all those cast."

Davy was elected to the Tennessee State Legislature in 1821 and 1823. He studied hard and even learned to read and write. He had a shrewd common sense, a homey wit, independent in his thinking, willing to stand against Governor Andrew Jackson, if he felt he should. He was elected to the United States Congress in 1826 and 1828. He was defeated in 1830, because he refused to support President Andrew Jackson on his Indian bill—however, he was re-elected in 1832. He joined Texas in their battle against Mexico and was killed by Santa Anna at the Battle of the Alamo in 1836.

It was probably quite difficult for President Madison, former President Jefferson, and future President Monroe to finally change their long-standing position against HAMILTON's Bank of the United States and give it a charter, after closing it down before the War of 1812. However, with the economic devastation that the nation was suffering, they quietly changed their tone and the bank's doors opened in 1816 with as little fanfare as possible. A more humble administration had been forced to recognize what ALEXANDER HAMILTON had known when the Revolutionary War came to a close—America needed money, an army and a navy to survive and develop industry and become an independent international nation.

It is also an irony that Jefferson's fear and accusations that George Washington and ALEXANDER HAMILTON would create a monarchy were totally groundless, whereas his own power control lasted throughout twenty-four years and set the stage for the division of the nation into a devastating Civil War. It should be recognized, however, that Jefferson had attempted to stop the expansion of slavery; but the opposition he experienced was too great. His own personal debt obligations kept him from giving his own slaves their freedom. He was controlled economically, as well as by the people. Although he and his friends had the greater power as a group, there was a constitution that checked that power. The greater power rested with the people, who were becoming more and more concerned and demanding of their liberties.

When Jefferson died on 4 Jul 1826, the same day John Adams died, and exactly fifty years after the Declaration of Independence was adopted, Jefferson wanted three memories recorded on his tall tombstone at Monticello. His epitaph reads:

> *"Author of the Declaration of American Independence,*
> *Of the statute of Virginia for religious freedom,*
> *and Father of the University of Virginia."*

He chose well. Not even Aaron Burr would disagree that he should be given great credit for these accomplishments, for which we are all most grateful. HAMILTON had been right to use his own limited influence in the House of Representatives to break the tie in favor of Jefferson for president, rather than his opponent Aaron Burr, in spite of their animosity toward him personally. He trusted in Jefferson's love of his country and the liberties of the common man.

Some historians have stated that Jefferson was an atheist. This is not true. They are ignoring part of his writings in which he stated that although he had not joined with the religions of the day, he believed that Christ would restore his church to the earth in its purity. The original British Virginia colony did not separate their religion from their government. The Church of England was the established religion in that colony. Our Virginia ancestors' christenings and marriages were recorded in these early church records. Jefferson wanted freedom from this controlling state religion of Great Britain, which still encroached upon the freedom of choice for his countrymen. The bordering states of Pennsylvania, Maryland, and North Carolina had already given this right of choice to their citizens; all religions were welcomed into their borders. Virginian James Madison is not only remembered for his strong leading support in the establishment of our United States Constitution; but he is also given great credit for his unending insistence on the addition of the Bill of Rights to the United States Constitution before Virginia would ratify it. The Bill of Rights guaranteed, of course, the religious freedom of choice for the citizens of the whole nation.

Jefferson was always interested in education. He had attended The College of William and Mary at Williamsburg as a youth. He had written the *History of Virginia*. He loved books, and when he founded the University of Virginia located in Charlottesville near Monticello, he donated his vast library to it. He believed that the real greatness of our country lay with the proper education of our youth, and he did his best to give them this opportunity. He realized, as many others have, that our liberties can be lost in only one generation.

[Note: Both Jefferson and Madison were with George Washington, HAMILTON, STEPHEN HOPKINS, and the other founding fathers who signed the Declaration of Independence and established the basic freedoms of our country, when this group appeared in spirit to Temple President Wilford Woodruff on two consecutive days in the St. George Temple in Utah. These men of spirit asked to have their temple ordinance work for the dead done shortly after the temple was dedicated in 1877—in the first L.D.S. temple completed in Utah.

MOSES MARTIN SANDERS was privileged to participate in this temple work, acting in one instance as the proxy for Benjamin Franklin. Also present on this occasion was James C. Bleak, a counselor in the temple presidency and an ancestor of our good friends, Nelson Bleak and his children of Lincoln County, Nevada. MOSES MARTIN SAUNDERS or SANDERS, born 17 Aug 1803, in Grove Level, Franklin County, Georgia, was the son of DAVID SAUNDERS, who died from his wounds ishortly after the "Battle of New Orleans", and his wife, MARY ALLRED. He was their oldest son and a first cousin of second-great-grandfather JAMES RUSSELL IVIE, who was born 30 Dec 1802, also, in Franklin County, Georgia. They married sisters, ELIZA and AMANDA ARMSTRONG FAUSETT, making their children double cousins.]

~ 109 ~

YOUNG ABRAHAM LINCOLN

When the War of 1812 ended and new lands were obtained by treaties, or purchased from the Indians, wagons by the thousands moved westward into the newly obtained territories. The population of New England alone had increased to over eight million. The families of two young boys destined to have a great influence on our nation and its people joined in this westward movement for new land. One of these young boys was ABRAHAM LINCOLN. In 1816, THOMAS and NANCY HANKS LINCOLN with their two children SARAH and ABRAHAM left their log cabin at Knob Creek near Elizabethtown, Kentucky, and crossed the Ohio River into Indiana. ABRAHAM was seven years old at that time.

According to Carl Sandburg in his book *Abraham Lincoln, The Prairie Years*:

"Poor white men were having a harder time to get along. Hardin County had been filling up with negroes, slave black men, bought and sold among the rich and well-to-do. The Hodgens, La Rues, and other first families usually had one or two, or six or a dozen, Negroes. More than half the population of Hardin County was colored. And it seemed that as more slave black men were brought in, a poor white man didn't count for so much; he had a harder time to get along.

"While these changes were coming in Kentucky, the territory of Indiana came into the Union as a state whose law declared 'all men are born equally free and independent' and 'holding any part of the human creation in slavery, or involuntary servitude, can only originate in usurpation and tyranny.' In crossing the Ohio River's two shores, a traveler touched two soils, one where the buying and selling of black slaves went on, the other where the negro was held to be 'part of human creation' and was not property for buying and selling. But both soils were part of the Union of states."

Young Abe had been given his grandfather's name. Grandfather ABRAHAM LINCOLN was living in Rockingham County, Virginia, when the Declaration of Independence was signed and delivered to King George. He was a farmer with a 210-acre farm that had been deeded to him by his father, JOHN LINCOLN. ABRAHAM was a captain in the Virginia militia that had fought against the Cherokee tribe who had trouble understanding the squaring-off and fencing of property and the accompanying deeds. In Massachusetts, a kinsman, AMOS LINCOLN, had dressed as an Indian and boarded a British ship with some of his countrymen and dumped their tea cargo into the bay. AMOS would become a captain of artillery in the colonial army.

Grandfather ABRAHAM's first cousin, HANANIAH LINCOLN, was a captain in the 12th Pennsylvania Regiment under General Washington at the Battle of Brandywine. JACOB LINCOLN, ABRAHAM's brother, was a captain at the Battle of Yorktown. These LINCOLNs in Virginia had come from Berks County, Pennsylvania, down the Great Wagon Road. ABRAHAM married BATHSHEBA HERRING, and they had three sons while residing in the Shenandoah Valley. Their boys were named MORDECAI, JOSIAH, and THOMAS.

Young ABE's father THOMAS was still in the arms of his mother when she signed her name beneath that of her husband on the land sale deed on 24 Sep 1781, declaring that "she freely and voluntarily relinquished the same without the Force threats or compulsion of her husband." Both wrote their own names: Abrm Lincoln and Batsab Linclon. Then they packed their rifle, ax, and plow, with other personal belongings and joined a party which was heading down the Wilderness Trail through the Cumberland Gap and then north and west into Kentucky. Arriving safely in Kentucky, grandfather ABRAHAM filed claims for more than 2,000 acres of land located on the Green River. Three or four years later, as he was working in a field, he was killed by the rifle shot of an Indian. His children and his grandchildren would scatter throughout Kentucky, Tennessee, Indiana, and Illinois.

The young child THOMAS was passed among his kinsmen until he reached maturity. As a young teenager he liked Sarah Bush. Unfortunately for the young man's desires, she preferred Daniel Johnson, who also wanted her. THOMAS must look again. This time it was at the young brunette NANCY HANKS, who returned his ardor. She was also called Nancy Sparrow because she was living as the adopted daughter of Thomas and Elizabeth Sparrow.

NANCY was born in Virginia in 1784. Her mother, LUCY HANKS, was nineteen when she left NANCY's father in Virginia and traveled the Wilderness Trail with her tiny daughter and other members of her family through the Cumberland Gap into Kentucky. In Kentucky, LUCY married Henry Sparrow and her sister ELIZABETH married his brother Thomas Sparrow. LUCY and HENRY had nine children, and their mother taught them all to read and write.

TOM LINCOLN had observed that NANCY HANKS was shrewd, dark, and lonesome. He had seen her at the church camp meetings; he had seen her preaching in cabins against the firelight of the burning logs. She believed in God, in the Bible, and in mankind. She liked people, babies, animals, flowers, and eternities outside of time. She was a believer in God and his creations. Every day there was scrubbing, washing, patching, fixing. There was little time to think or sing about the glory she believed in; but it was yonder.

In June 1806, it was recorded by the county clerk that the Reverend Jesse Head had "joined together in the Holy Estate of Matrimony agreeable to the rules of the Methodist Episcopal Church" THOMAS LINCOLN and NANCY HANKS.

It was the fall of 1816 when the small family arrived at TOM LINCOLN's claim of a quarter section of the black soil by Little Pigeon Creek, across the Ohio in the southwest corner of Indiana. The claim was recorded in the government building at Vincennes. Their material possessions were few. They were without a horse, a cow, or a house, but they had land in a state that believed in freedom and in God, and they had the ability to learn and work hard. There were still Indian problems, but this was not new. They were out of the slave territory of Kentucky, and they rejoiced in the fertility of this new state. Here, NANCY would die of milk fever, and TOM would return to Kentucky and marry another wife, the widow of Daniel Johnson and his former love, SARAH BUSH (Johnson). She would continue to insist that young ABE should be educated in school and from the Bible. The tall lanky ABRAHAM LINCOLN grew in the shrewd wisdom of his second mother and the wit and story-telling ability of his father towards his future destiny. As a young man, he would join with the militia in the Indian war that became known as the Blackhawk Indian War. (Not to be confused with the Black Hawk Indian War that occurred in Utah, towards the end of the Civil War and beyond, in which, Utah militia colonel JOHN LEHI IVIE, my great-grandfather, participated.)

The following quote is LINCOLN's own description of his childhood memories, which was taken from a book by J. N. Larned, *A Study of Greatness in Men, 1911.*

> "I remember how, when a mere child, I used to get irritated when anybody talked to me in a way I could not understand. I do not think I ever got angry at anything else in my life; but that always disturbed my temper, and has ever since . . . . I can remember going to my little bedroom, after hearing the neighbors talk of an evening with my father, and spending no small part of the night walking up and down, trying to make out what was the exact meaning of some of their, to me, dark sayings. I could not sleep, although I tried to, when I got on such a hunt for an idea, until I had caught it; and when I thought I had got it I was not satisfied until I had repeated it over and over; until I had put it in language plain enough as I thought, for any boy to comprehend. This was a kind of passion with me, and it has stuck by me; for I am never easy now, when I am handling a thought, till I have bounded it north and bounded it south, and bounded it east and bounded it west."

Larned further quotes one of his boyhood friends as saying:

> "When he appeared in company the boys would gather and cluster around him to hear him talk . . . . He argued much from analogy, and explained things hard for us to understand by stories, maxims, tales and figures. He would almost always point his lesson or idea by some story that was plain and near to us, that we instantly see the force and bearing of what he said."

ABRAHAM LINCOLN seemed to have an insatiable thirst for making the confusions of his day simple and understandable to the public mind, not for his own glorification, but for an inate feeling within him that he could be useful to others. His hatred of slavery was immense, as it was to his parents, who had moved from Kentucky to avoid it; but he did not condemn the people of the South. He was ever calling for the unification of the nation under its constitution. His efforts to make things better were deeply ingrained in his actions. His political career was not based on personal power or aggrandizement, but was based on his strong belief that he could help preserve his country. He prepared in the best way that his circumstances would permit. If he appeared lazy to some neighbors, it was probably from his ability to relax and enjoy his surroundings of people and things, for his mind and heart seemed to always be indefatigable with continuous activity and demands. His simplicity required great thinking and effort—and an audience.

According to Larned, his early accomplishments politically include: at the age of 18, searching for more reading material, he found a volume of the *Revised Statutes of Indiana*, the *Declaration of Independence, the ordinance of 1787*, and the *Constitution of the United States*—all of which he studied diligently. To these important studies, he added the knowledge he craved in talking directly with men of various stations in life, in small or large groups. He would shuffle all sorts into public gatherings, and join many groups—on the street, at the country post-office and store—in and around the court-house. When he reached the age of twenty-three, he announced himself a candidate for the general assembly of Illinois. In the little town of New Salem, where he had lived one year, he received 277 votes out of the 300 that were cast. It was a strong Democratic district and he had filed as a Whig. He lost this election, but the people who knew him well strongly supported him. Two years later, he successfully tried again and would represent his people in the Illinois legislature from 1834 to 1842.

Since legislatures only met for short periods of time and were not a lucrative occupation, he supported himself mostly by manual labor—farming, rail-splitting, flat-boating to and from New Orleans, and some clerking in a country store. His first undertaking at skilled labor was in the office of deputy county surveyor, for which he qualified himself by six weeks of intense study, day and night. Once this means of support was acquired, he seriously began his study of law, continuing his surveying until he had won his admission to the bar. At which time, he left New Salem and moved to the larger town of Springfield, Illinois, which with his influence in the state legislature, had become the capital of the state. Quoting from *A Study of Greatness in Men* by J. N. Larned:

> "His mind was never stirred very deeply by party contenions over national banks, tariffs, and internal improvements, on which he sided with Henry Clay; but a righteous indignation, which represented everything

of bitterness that his reasonable nature could feel, was wakened quickly when the champions of slavery made claims and aggressions beyond its constitutional rights. He hated the institution, as his father and mother had hated it; but he respected the obligations of the national contract of Union too profoundly to lend countenance to any attack on slavery within its legalized domain. . . . When the Illinois assembly, in 1837, adopted resolutions disapproving of those doctrines [of the abolitionists], he was one of two members who protested against the resolutions, because they did not, at the same time, condemn slavery as an institution, and because they denied the constitutional power of congress to abolish it in the District of Columbia. "

[Note: These time periods are quite interesting from an L.D.S. Church point of view. It was in 1838 that the serious persecution of their members in Caldwell County, Missouri, began in earnest, which forced them to leave Missouri and move into the state of Illinois, where they built Nauvoo and were granted a City Charter that included the right to form their own military militia. LINCOLN's political career was quite dormant through these years where the animosity was built up against them, the martyrdom of the Prophet Joseph Smith in Carthage, Illinois, and their forced evacuation of Illinos in 1846. (See the early chapters of *Part I: DRIVEN)*]

ABRAHAM LINCOLN served in the United States Congress for a single term—1847–49. Larned states:

"The time was that of the Mexican War, and Lincoln's skill in exposition was brought to use in illuminating the iniquitous claim and false pretenses that brought the war about. At the same time he gave his vote for supplying the means that were needful for the prosecution of the war. He branded the iniquity of the government which had dragged the country into an unrighteous attack on a weak neighbor, but he would not help to cripple the army which obeyed, as it must, that government's command. [In this 1909 book, Larned claimed further:]

"It was the morally patriotic course, which every conscientious American of our time who studies the circumstances of the Mexican War has to approve. In its day, however, it was an unpopular course in many parts of the country."

LINCOLN quit Washington D.C. in the spring of 1849, and devoted himself to his practice of law for the next five years. He would speak at the funeral of Senator Henry Clay in 1852.

The Kansas-Nebraska Bill was introduced in 1854 by Senator Stephen L. Douglas of Illinois—its author. It stated:

"All questions pertaining to slavery in the Territories, and the new States to be formed therefrom, are to be left to the people residing therein."

With these words it not only repealed the Missouri Compromise of 1820, but opened possible slavery to large areas of our country in which it had previously been barred—thus bringing great controversy into every new state on a highly controversial issue.

This awakened in ABRAHAM LINCOLN a deep conviction that this law would tear the country apart. State would be against state. The people within the states would divide against each other in a great controversy that would destroy the very heart of the liberty that had been fought for less than 80 years before.

"He could not keep himself out of the thickest of the political battle which opened then, or be anywhere in it save far forward in the front; for no other man entered it with such powers as his, so wrought to their utmost pitch." [Larned, 1909]

This Bill, the Kansas-Nebraska Bill of 1854, resulted in "Bleeding Kansas" as predicted by LINCOLN. Larend continues:

"There was six years of fiery agitation and [Stephen L.] Douglas was driven to uphold his doctrine of sovereignty by rebellion in his own party. The old political organizations dissolved. Anti-slavery Whigs and Democrats came together and formed the (new) Republican Party. LINCOLN, from the first, was the recognized leader . . . in Illinois, and it came near to seating him at once in the Senate of the United States. In 1856, at the national Republican convention, he was proposed for Vice-President, on the ticket with Fremont, and received the second highest number of votes. [James Buchanan of Scotch-Irish decent from the Lancaster area of south-eastern Pennsylvania was elected president of the United States that year.] In 1858, when Douglas came to Illinois for reelection to the Senate, LINCOLN was the candidate chosen to oppose him.

"Douglas was now the conspicuous man in America; his fight for the retention of his seat in the Senate was the exciting event of the day, and the joint debates to which Lincoln challenged him had the nation for their audience. Reports of the speeches of the antagonists were published far and wide at the time, and subsequently in a volume, of which 30,000 copies were sold in a few months. "

These printed *Lincoln-Douglas Debates* show LINCOLN as

"something more than beyond the common, —that they were masterpieces of argumentative oratory."

One of the early ones, given in Peoria, in October 1854 was well reported. Throughout all the debates, LINCOLN always felt kindly and sympathetic towards the South, but always stood strong for the constitution of our nation and its right to unify this nation. The following are quotations from that speech.

"I think," LINCOLN said quietly, "I have no prejudice against the Southern people. They are just what we would be in their situation. If slavery did not now exist among them they would not introduce it. If it did now exist among us we should not instantly give it up. This I believe of the masses North and South. . . . When they remind us of their constitutional rights, I acknowledge them, not grudgingly, but fully and fairly; . . . But all this, to my judgment, furnishes no more excuse for permitting slavery to go into our own free territory than it would for reviving the African slave trade by law. . . .

"Slavery is founded in the selfishness of man's nature, —opposition to it in his love of justice. These principles are in eternal antagonism, and when brought into collision, so fiercely as slavery extension brings them, shocks and throes and convulsions must ceaselessly follow. Repeal the Missouri Compromise, repeal all compromises, repeal the Declaration of Independence, repeal all past history, you still cannot repeal human nature. It still will be the abundance of man's heart that slavery extension is wrong, and out of the abundance of his heart his mouth will speak. . . .

"Much as I hate slavery, I would consent to the extension of it rather than see the Union dissolved, just as I would consent to any great evil to avoid a greater one . . . . "

These few small quotes are only small pieces of his multitude of words in his debates with Stephen L. Douglas that were read throughout the nation in his attempt to stop the carnage that was swiftly approaching—just as he had predicted it would when the Kansas-Nebraska Bill was passed into law.

LINCOLN would lose this contest for the U. S. Senate; but he would win his next election for president of the United States—against this same opponent. He had challenged Douglas by his shrewd questioning of him on his "Freeport doctrine," (that the inhabitants of a territory, in the exercise of their "popular sovereignty" might keep slavery from entering it by police regulation and "unfriendly legislation." Douglas was compelled to maintain his stand after the Dred Scott decision of the Supreme Court had been given a few months before. LINCOLN's friends had warned him that this was an unwise approach, since many of the citizens of Illinois would take Douglas' side. To them, LINCOLN answered:

> "Gentlemen, I am killing larger game; if Douglas answers, he can never be President; and the battle of 1860 is worth a hundred of this."

Larned made this observation:

> "The Democratic party was broken into sectional factions by that 'Freeport doctrine,' which LINCOLN's unselfish acuteness had drawn into dispute, and the triumph of the Republican party in 1860 was practically assured."

It is of interest to me that Joseph Smith Jr. knew Stephen L. Douglas, who was a lawyer in Springfield when he obtained his charter for the city of Nauvoo around 1840. He had told Douglas that he would aspire sometime in the future to the office of President of the United States; but if he ever lifted his hand against the *Mormon* people, he would lose that election. After the martyrdoms of Joseph and his brother Hyrum Smith (1844), Douglas accompanied Governor Ford of Illinois, as his legal council. Ford brought his army to drive these *Mormon* people from the state of Illinois shortly after, and Douglas legalized his actions.

[Note: On December 25, 1832, Joseph Smith Jr. with "some of the brethren were reflecting and reasoning upon African slavery on the American continent and the slavery of the children of men throughout the world. " The following is a part of the answer they received from their prayers. [see D&C Section 87]

> *"Verily, thus saith the Lord concerning the wars that*
> *will shortly come to pass,*
> *beginning at the rebellion of South Carolina,*
> *which will eventually terminate in the death and misery of many souls; And*
> *the time will come*
> *that war will be poured out upon all nations,*
> *beginning at that place.*
> *For behold, the Southern States will call on other nations,*
> *even the nation of Great Britain, as it is called . . . ."*]

~ 110 ~

YOUNG JOSEPH SMITH

The second young man (about twelve years old), who moved westward with his family after the War of 1812 had ended, left the Green Mountains of Vermont behind and journeyed across the Hudson River, through eastern New York, past Utica, above the Finger Lakes and into the land east of Niagara Falls, which had been made much safer from Indians and foreign powers. The God-fearing and visionary Smith family arrived at the small town of Palmyra, New York, quite destitute of cash, but full of hope. They were there shortly before the Erie Canal was constructed through this territory. A rather smooth, small hill, now called the Hill Cumorah, was within walking distance. Young Joseph Smith, born 23 Dec 1805, would impact the lives of all my ancestors living at that time, as well as their generations to come, more than any single individual in the history of America.

Joseph's mother, Lucy Mack Smith, recorded her own history, after the death of her husband, and after her two sons, Hyrum and Joseph, had been murdered by a mob in Carthage, Illinois, in 1844.

Her Mack ancestors came to America and lived in several towns surrounding New London, Connecticut. Her father, Solomon Mack, was born in that area on 26 Sep 1735. He had participated, as a young man in the French and Indian War, marching with his British regiment to Fort Edwards in 1755, and then on to Lake George in 1758, where Lord Howe "fell at the onset of the battle." In the spring of 1759, the army marched to Crown Point, where

"they were discharged." Solomon returned to Connecticut, where he married Lucy's mother, Lydia Gates, a schoolteacher. In 1776, Solomon "enlisted in the service of [his] country and was for a considerable length of time in the land forces, after which [he] went with [his] sons, Jason and

Stephen, on a privateering expedition, commanded by Captain Havens
.... When hostilities ceased and peace and tranquility were again restored,
[they] freighted a vessel for Liverpool. Selling both ship and cargo in this
place, [They] embarked on board Captain Foster's vessel, which [Solomon]
afterwards purchased; but, in consequence of storms and wrecks, [he] was
compelled to sell her, and was left completely destitute ... struggled a little
longer to obtain property .... After an absence of four years, about penni-
less, [he] determined to follow phantoms no longer, but devote the rest of
life to the service of God and family."

The Mack family moved to New Hampshire and Vermont, where the youth
Joseph Smith Sr. and his family resided at that time, having come from Topsfield,
Massachucetts. Lucy Mack was the youngest of eight children: four older brothers; twin sisters, Lovisa and Lovina; then Lydia; followed by Lucy. Her oldest
brother, Jason, became a preacher when he was 20 years old. He belonged to a
group called the Seekers. He was engaged to be married when his father insisted
that he accompany him on his trip to Liverpool. When they returned, he found
that his bride-to-be had married another, four months before. It seems that his
sweetheart's new husband had deceived her. Working in the post office, he had
destroyed Jason's letters and had even forged another, which told of his death.
The young woman was heartbroken when she saw Jason. She died within two
years. Jason continued his preaching.

Lovisa Mack was married, and two years later became very ill with consumption (tuberculosis.) She sent for her twin sister Lovina to take care of her.
Near death, Lovisa was miraculously healed by her faith for a few years; however, Lovina had contracted the disease. As it became debilitating, Lovina sent
for her youngest sister Lucy to care for her. Lucy had married Joseph Smith Sr.
at that time. Lucy compassionately stayed and nursed her until she died. She
was buried near her sister Lovisa, who had died shortly before. In caring for her
sister, Lucy became ill with tuberculosis, also.

One evening when the doctor had given up all hope that she could survive
the night, she later recorded:

"My mind was much agitated during the whole night. Sometimes I contemplated heaven and heavenly things; then my thought would turn upon
those of earth—my babes and my companion .... I made a solemn cov-
enant with God, that, if he would let me live, I would endeavor to serve

him according to the best of my abilities. Shortly after this, I heard a voice say to me, 'Seek, and ye shall find; knock, and it shall be opened unto you. Let your heart be comforted; ye believe in God, believe also in me.' In a few moments my mother came in, and looking upon me she said, 'Lucy, you are better.'"

Lucy searched diligently among the Christian churches of the day to find one that she could embrace with all her heart. Finally, she reached a conviction that it was not on the earth and used the Bible as her guide. She found a minister that baptized her without trying to force her into his own thinking.

Joseph Smith Sr. and his wife Lucy worked hard, but financial security seemed to elude them, usually because of the dishonesty of others. Then after three seasons of crop failures in Vermont and the War of 1812 had opened up this new territory, they moved westward to Palmyra, New York, where it was said that the wheat grew bounteously. Joseph Sr. went first and then sent his wagon and team with a driver to bring Lucy and the family of eight children. Along the way, the driver attempted to desert them and leave them stranded, but Lucy was quick to boldly confront him in front of other people. He was fired and the family soon arrived on their own abilities in Palmyra. Once more, they worked hard, read the Bible, and sought God.

INTERIOR OF JOSEPH AND LUCY SMITH'S FIRST HOME IN PALMYRA, NEW YORK.
IT SHOWS THE FIREPLACE WITH ITS COOKING AND EATING FACILITIES. THE SLEEPING
QUARTERS FOR THE CHILDREN WERE ABOVE, WITH THE RAFTERS SHOWING.

In 1820, young fourteen-year-old Joseph Smith Jr., like his mother, was also confused about the many Christian churches. Revival meetings were common, with each church seeking to increase their membership and professing their own beliefs as the "the truth, the way, and the life" that would gain for them the entrance into heaven and eternal life. While reading in the Book of James (1:5, 6) in the Bible, the boy discovered the passage that read,

"If any of you lack wisdom, let him ask of God,
that giveth to all men liberally,
and upbraideth not;
and it shall be given him.
But let him ask in faith, nothing wavering."

With those words burning in his bosom, he realized that he, indeed, lacked wisdom as to which church was true, and, if God would not criticize him, he would approach Him through prayer.

The Sacred Grove is still there, north of Joseph Smith Sr. and Lucy's first home in Palmyra. It was here that God the Father and his son, Jesus Christ, appeared to the young boy in answer to his prayer, and the new dispensation of the "Fullness of Time" began. Joseph found out that they were two separate, glorious beings of flesh and bone that communicated directly to him in his own language and told him to join none of the churches. He was amazed at their light, power, and love; but he had also, prior to their appearance, experienced the darkness and power of an adversary that, were it possible, would have destroyed him.

The young boy quickly found, after telling his story, that he was soon despised and persecuted by professors of religion, and that these sáme feelings spread rapidly throughout the area. Nevertheless, in his history, he stated,

"I had seen a vision; I knew it, and I knew that God knew it,
and I could not deny it, neither dared I do it;
at least I knew that by so doing I would offend God,
and come under condemnation."
[Joseph Smith—History 1:25]

He continued to work in the fields by Palmyra with his father and brothers; then on the 21 Sep 1823, he prayed to our Heavenly Father before retiring, asking new questions. He was astonished by the appearance of the Angel Moroni, who gave him additional instructions, including the actual location in the Hill Cumorah of the buried golden records of Moroni's once righteous people, the Nephites, who, after a thousand years, became the wicked civilization that had been destroyed by their brethren, the Lamanites, fourteen hundred years previously. Joseph Smith Jr., who had little schooling, after waiting four years, as directed by the angel, would translate these ancient records, with the help of God. The *Book of Mormon, another Testament of Jesus Christ* would be published in 1829, prior to the establishment of The Church of Jesus Christ of Latter-day Saints in 1830.

[Note: The early history of the L.D.S. Church and my family's involvement is told in more detail in Part One: DRIVEN.]

THE PROPHET MORONI BURYING THE GOLDEN PLATES IN THE HILL CUMORAH
400 AD — HE APPEARED TO JOSEPH SMITH JR. AS AN ANGEL 21 SEP 1823.

[This photo is of a woodburned copy of the Arnold Freiburg painting done by a Colombian artist in South America. I don't know his name.]

After these records were translated and printed in 1829, The Church of Jesus Christ of Latter-day Saints was organized 6 Apr 1830. Persecution drove the saints into Kirtland, Ohio—near the bottom of Lake Erie. Here they built a temple and extended their missionary work into Michigan, Illinois, Kentucky, Tennessee, and Missouri—where a second settlement in Jackson County was established, and where sometime in the future, according to revelation from God, the New Jerusalem would be located. In the winter of 1833, persecution drove these southern saints back across the Missouri River into Clay County. Joseph Smith Jr. organized Zion's Camp with 205 men in 1834 (see Part I: DRIVEN) to help his people be restored to their legal rights, if possible. They were not successful, but Joseph with a few companions were able to cross the Missouri into Independence so he could set his feet "once more on the goodly land." From the *Tenth Article of Faith, Pearl of Great Price:*

> *"We believe in the literal gathering of Israel*
> *and in the restoration of the Ten Tribes;*
> *that Zion (the New Jerusalem) will be built upon*
> *the American Continent;*
> *that Christ will reign personally upon the earth;*
> *that the earth will be renewed*
> *and receive its paradisiacal glory."*

The prophet Joseph Smith would be taken into Jackson County again by his captors in the fall of 1838 when, according to the *Autobiography of Parley P. Pratt,* who was with him at this time, the leader, General Wilson of Jackson County described the reason for the persecution of the *Mormon* people:

"We Jackson County boys know how it is; and, therefore, have not the extremes of hatred and prejudice which characterize the rest of the troops. We know perfectly that from the beginning the Mormons have not been the aggressors at all. As it began in '33 in Jackson County, so it has been ever since. You Mormons were crowded to the last extreme and compelled to self-defence; and this has been construed into treason, murder and plunder. We mob you without law; the authorities refuse to protect you according to law; you then are compelled to protect yourselves, and we act upon the prejudices of the public, who join our forces, and the whole is legalized, for your destruction and our gain. Is not this a shrewd cunning policy? When we drove you from Jackson County, we burned two hundred and three of your houses; plundered your goods, destroyed your press, type, paper, books, office and all—tarred and feathered old Bishop Partridge, as exemplary an old man as you can find anywhere. We shot down some of your men, and, if any of you returned the fire, we imprisoned you . . . And let a set of men serve me as your communities have been served, and I'll be d—d if I would not fight till I died. It has been repeatedly insinuated, by the other officers and troops that we should hang you prisoners on the first tree we came to on the way to Independence. But I'll be d—d if anybody shall hurt you. We just intend to exhibit you in Independence, let the people look at you, and see what a d—d set of fine fellows you are. And, more particularly, to keep you from the G-d d—d old bigot of a Gen. Clark and his troops, from down country, who are so stuffed with lies and prejudice that they would shoot you down in a moment."

Joseph Smith Jr. was allowed to speak to the people on the street of downtown Independence—for his last time in that county. At least one women was brought to tears and she cried after them as they were taken back across the Missouri River toward their jails, first into Richmond and then into Liberty,

"God bless you!"

~ 111 ~

THE POLITICIANS DIVIDE THE PIE

The city of Twin Falls, Idaho, where I attended junior high school and graduated from high school, is quite unique in its basic design. The central city was built on the diagonal, surrounded by major highways extending north, south, east, and west—with 5 points of highways at each corner. Beyond the diagonals on the north side, a new housing complex, with FHA loans available, was built estending in strait compass directions shortly before World War II began—called the president's streets. They start at the 5 points on the west with Washington Street and continue eastward with the name of each president through Lincoln Street. We moved to the first block of Tyler Street in April 1942— 4 months after the Japanesse bombed Pearl Harbor.

Tyler (1841-1845) was the tenth president of the United States one hundred years prior to my new adventure— (1941-1946). The sixth street is Quincy Street—to distinguish President John Quincy Adams (1825-1829) from his father, President John Adams (1797-1801). Jackson Street (1829-1837) was next to Quincy, followed by Van Buren (1837-1841), with Harrison Street (1841-1841) preceding Tyler Street (1841-1845). With this arrangement, we became quite familiar with the order of the first sixteen presidents, and it additionally piqued our interest in these early, less celebrated, leaders.

President John Tyler, for whom our street was named, grew up on a beautiful plantation on the James River by Charles City, Virginia, and was elected vice president with William Henry Harrison, the Indiana Territorial governor and general in the old northwest during the War of 1812. Their campaign slogan was "Tippecanoe and Tyler too." William Henry Harrison, the ninth president, died from an illness after serving only one month in the office of president. Vice president John Tyler brought back the presidency once more to the Virginians for the rest of that four-year term. Harrison was the first president to die in office. Tyler did not seek reelection and was followed by Polk (1845-1849). The second president to die in office. President Zachary Taylor (1849-1850), "Old Rough and Ready—Forty years a Soldier" was a Kentucky homesteader, who had distinguished himself during the Texas and Mexican Wars. His daughter, Sarah, was the first wife of Jefferson Davis, the president of the Confederacy during the Civil War. His vice president that replaced him was Millard Fillmore (1850-1853) of Buffalo, New York. President Fillmore was noted for being studious and temperate with extreme integrity. Both Taylor and Fillmore were Whigs.

Before continuing on with these presidents, I would like to diverge and include a little history of three great statesmen of this period of time. All three would have liked to be the president of this nation and were very influential senators—none became the president.

The people of the United States of America from colonial times had split opinions on several issues that had divided their loyalties within this nation. During Washington's administration, it began quickly with the splits already explained between Secretary of State, Thomas Jefferson and Secretay of the Treasury, ALEXANDER HAMILTON. Their life styles and visions of a truly great nation were quite different. HAMILTON wanted basically opportunity for all people and was quite willing to struggle physically to get it, even to abolishing slavery. He was George Washington's clerk and his confident throughout most of the war and during his administration. Jefferson placed his vision on theory and law, and had not been at the battle front phycially like HAMILTON. He knew only by observation the deep feelings of those who struggled only for opportunity and their very lives—the slow "silk stocking" approach to governing a country as the Articles of Confederation had allowed, with the various states looking out for their own interests, suited Jefferson. The Constitution, which had come about while he was assigned as the minister in France, was really not necessary in his thinking—a few changes to the old Confederacy was his basic belief.

Jefferson, returning from his assignment to France, immediately became the Secretary of State and had soon pulled Madison into similar beliefs and together they had struggled to minimize the Supreme Court, eliminate the national banking system, lessen national taxation, decrease the tariffs to sell their cotton to foreign countries, decrease considerably the size of the army and navy, and in general, place the country in a more vulnerabe position worldwide—less able to compete or contend as a group of states with foreign countries and ever subject to the disagreements between the various small and the more powerful state governments. Without money, manufacturing, or credit in these northern smaller states, life was very difficult—their opportunity for growth was being squashed.

The Federalist Party, who took their name from the Federalist Papers organized by ALEXANDER HAMILTON before the constitution was adopted by the states, had disowned HAMILTON as their party leader in favor of John Adams, before, during and somewhat after his administration—when it became necessary to defend their needs for a stronger federal government against the supposed Republican/Democrat faction of strong state confederation ideas that Jefferson and Madison had promoted and organized.

The North saw Virginia and the southern states with their slaves and large plantations as an extention of the nobles of Europe—almost like the old feudal system, with all powerful masters in total control of his wife, children, and slaves. Only the head of the household could vote, and his vote became more powerful as his slave numbers increased. His voice was supreme in his household—his wife, children, and others on his property were subject to the whip as well as the slaves, if he so desired.

In return, the Southerners claimed that the Northerners were just as bad as they were with their control of their employees in their factories. There were no child labor laws, or wage controls placed on these factory owners either. The division within the country was growing stronger by the difference of their views regarding the military, banks, courts, tariffs, and slavery.

When presidents Jefferson, Madison, and Monroe, all from the state of Virginia, followed each other without interruption, the Federalists spoke of secession from this nation that seemed to be forgetting them—leaving their needs behind. The northerners wanted banks that gave credit, manufacturing, protective higher tariffs—that was their economy.

The champion of this Federalist position in these northern states following John Adams was **Senator Daniel Webster** (born 1782 in Massachusetts). His extraordinary oratory ability and keen legal knowledge had won him the hearts of all New Englanders and extended into New York, Pennsylvania, New Jersey, and Delaware, where manufacturing, shipping, and trade agreements became very important to their livelihoods.

As the country had moved westward, the peace treaties of the government with the American Indians became a problem. Immigrants kept coming from the tyranny of Europe; the Revolutionary War and later the War of 1812 veterans needed to be paid for their services with new land grants since, without money, an under-funded central government had only land with which to pay much of their debts. The Indians had mostly joined with the British during the wars—so—their land treaties became void and the victors moved westward.

Tobacco and cotton grew better in the unused flat southern lands of the Carolinas, Georgia, Alabama, and Mississippi. This much hotter land was better suited for hard work by a darker-skinned people. More slavery, larger plantations, and harsher methods of control ensued. The new South stood behind Andrew Jackson of Tennessee to fight for their expansion through this region, securing the coastal areas along the Gulf of Mexico, and the most important trading port with the British for their cotton at New Orleans. Jackson's military expansions of land and legislative victories created the "Trail of Tears" that sent the southern Indians west of the Mississippi River.

In the northwest of that day, it was left to Governor William Henry Harrison of Indiana Territory to face the British of Canada at Fort Detroit, who "were helping their loyal Indians" to fight the Americans—according to the view of Tecumseh. In this part of the United States of America, it was **Senator Henry Clay** of Kentucky (born 1777 in Virginia) that claimed the support and power that furthered these expansions into Ohio, Indiana, Michigan, and Illinois. It was his strong voice that pushed the pacifist President James Madison into declaring war on England in 1812, when the British were so greatly involved in their war against Napoleon's France. He had hoped with his "Hawks" to annex Canada. In 1820, Senator Clay had shown great statesmanship in passing his

"Missouri Compromise" into law. This temporarily stopped slavery extending farther than Missouri and defined the new Free states—without slavery.

The third Senator to note was **Senator John Caldwell Calhoun** of South Carolina., born in 1782. He graduated from Yale in 1804; passed the South Carolina bar in 1807; served two terms in his state legislature before being elected to Congress in 1811, where he joined with the "Hawks" of Henry Clay. As a member of the Committee of Foreign Relations, he reported a bill for declaring war, which passed in June 1812. In 1817, he became the Secretary of War in President James Monroe's cabinet and retained this office through seven years—bringing order into an area of government that had been in great confusion and neglect. In 1824 he became vice-president under President John Quincy Adams, and then again under President Andrew Jackson. In 1828, a protective tariff law was passed that hurt agriculture in the South, where it was called "The Tariff of Abominations". Calhoun prepared a paper in which he stated:

> "The United States is not a union of the people, but a league or compact between soveriegn states, any of which has the right to judge when the contract is broken and pronounce any law to be null and void which violates its conditions."

This paper was issued by the state of South Carolina and was known as "The South Carolina Exposition." It was not a new thought, but expressed the feelings of many previous statesmen, particularly those that followed Jefferson and Madison and their thoughts on the early Articles of Confederation, but even New England Federalists subscribed at times to this same idea of secession. It was in 1828 that friendly relations between John Calhoun and Andrew Jackson were broken off—for several reasons—and when he couldn't nullify this protective tariff law, Calhoun resigned as vice-president and returned as the United States senator from South Carolina. As a senator, he was able to bring about a compromise on the tariff issue in 1832.

He tried to avoid the slavery issue whenever he could—fearing for the Union of the states. He opposed Jackson's removal of Federal funds from the National Bank and also spoke strongly against his "spoil system." He supported the election of Van Buren (of the mid-Hudson River area of New York State.)

Seeing the great division that was rapidly approaching between the North and the South, he thought it might be good to have two presidents—this would prevent the passage of any bill that was offensive to either side.

[Note: John C. Calhoun died in March of 1850. Daniel Webster described him in his eulogy as an attractive personality of irreproachable character.]

The "spoil system," mentioned above, was first developed strongly in the the city of New York by DeWitt Clinton during his many terms as mayor of that city. It has been mentioned earlier in previous chapters. His office as mayor brought him greater riches than any public office of that day. A description of this system is given in Noah *Webster's Third New International Dictionary* as,

> "a practice of regarding public offices and their emoluments as so much plunder to be taken from the defeated party and distributed to members of the victorious party — opposed to *merit system*."

ALEXANDER HAMILTON was opposed to this "unfair" practice in the city and state of New York and his opposition created strong enemies against him. Mayor Clinton controlled the appointments of all city positions, including police officers, local courts, postal workers, street cleaners, fireman, city planners, parks, hospitals, schools, local revenue agents and anyone else he could control. These "appointees" were bound to give their loyal support to him or they would lose their employment at any time he desired. Any breach of loyalty by word or vote, regardless of the fairness or legality of the situation resulted in the loss of their employment and the good will of Clinton's office. If you worked for the city, you did what you were told to do. With so many dependent on him, he insured his continuous re-election.

This practice of the *spoil system* spread into the politics of New York state government. The following are quotes from *The Encyclopedia Americana (1945 first edition)* under the heading **Van Buren, Martin**:

> "Eighth President of the United States: b. Kinderhook, N. Y. 5 Dec 1782; d. there 24 July 1862. His father, Abraham Van Buren, was of Dutch descent, a farmer and a tavern-keeper. . . . In 1796, when 14 years of age, entered the law office of Francis Sylvester, where he read law and other subjects. In 1802 he entered the law office of William P. Van Ness of New York, an influenential man and close friend and defender of Aaron Burr. The later paid considerable attention to young Van Buren. . . ."

Martin Van Buren advanced through the *spoil system* as surrogate of Columbia County; in the State senate 1812 to 1820; in February 1815-1819 attorney-general; United States senator in 1821 and re-elected in 1827, but resigned his seat in 1828 on his election to the governorship of New York.

"His father was a Jeffersonian-Republican, and Van Buren followed him politically. The Senate politics of New York were factional and complex in this period. It was out of this situation that the principles involved in the spoils system were developed. It was a thoroughly established system when Van Buren was made a member of the "Albany Regency," and he had in his own person experienced its operation, both to his advantage and disadvantage. The "Albany Regency" was a group of men organized to control the politics of New York and was sponsor for the spoils system in local, State and national affairs. . . . . In general he was a strict constructionist, a States Rights man, and against the United States Bank. He was closely associated with Senator Benton of Missouri and Andrew Jackson, and thus laid the foundations of a life-long intimacy with these men. . . . He resigned the office (Governor of New York state) in March 1829 in order to become the Secretary of State in Jackson's cabinet. . . . Van Buren was responsible, more than any other man, for the political creed of Jackson's administration. He resigned in 1831, because he felt that the public measures of the administration would be attributed to his intrigue, and thus made to injure the President. Van Buren has been accused of being primarily and chiefly responsible for the "Spoils system" which flourished under Jackson . . . . In June 1831 Van Buren was appointed Minister to England and spent some months abroad. In January 1832, however, the Senate rejected his appointment. Before his return to New York 5 July 1832 he had been nominated for the vice-presidency, and elected in November. While he held this office he was the chief adviser of the President. . . . The Democratic-Republican Convention which met at Baltimore 20 May 1835 was anxious to find a man to preserve the unity of the party and one who would carry on the principles of Jackson's administration. Van Buren received the unanimous vote of the convention. His platform declared that Congress did not have the power to distribute the surplus revenue without a constitutional amendment. He was **opposed** . . . to internal improvements at national expense; to a recharter of the United States Bank and to the abolition of slavery in the District of Columbia. He was elected to the presidency by a combination of the Middle States and New England against the West, which voted for Harrison, with the South divided. . . ."

The Panic of 1837

To really understand the panic of 1837 we need to be sure we understand some basic financial principles. Just like it takes two people to create a family; it takes two people to make a trade. To get something you want from someone else, you need something you have produced that the other party wants—and a trade is made. Hopefully it is fair to both parties, or it is morally wrong—perhaps even stealing that which really belongs to someone else. If your neighbor has an apple tree that produces apples and you have chickens that produce eggs, a trade could be made, if you want to—an apple for an egg. That is called *barter.*

But since apples and eggs are not easy to carry around to exchange, something smaller needed to be agreed upon by all parties concerned in the exchange of goods—*a medium of exchange.* The precious metals, especially gold and silver, were agreed upon, and the values of various products or services were set to make it fair to all people in any exchange. This type of exchange was called *specie.* The governments created their coin mints and guaranteed their value by standardized weights and balances —even extending into international trades.

These coins worked for small exchanges, but safely carrying around larger quanties was not only very heavy, but very dangerous. Governments put their gold and silver in huge storage vaults and placed security guards around them for protection; then they printed their I. O. U. treasury certificates that could be traded at any time by any person who had one for the actual gold or silver in their vaults—whatever was stated on the certificate. In my earlier lifetime, there were lots of *silver certificates* circulating as currency thoughout our nation—backed by the silver in Fort Knox.

But back in 1829, the persistent attacks upon the United States Bank that resulted in its downfall as a Federal institution began when President Andrew Jackson questioned the constitutionality of the bank and doubted its ability to establish a sound currency. He wanted to place it under the management of the Treasury Department with the right to receive both private and public deposits but to make no loans. Both branches of congress ignored his suggestion. In 1831, Senator Benton of Missouri took up the fight, stating the evils against all kinds of bank notes, and especially a type of bank draft.

Congress wanted to renew the bank's charter, and it passed both branches, but was vetoed by President Jackson—afraid of the evil of a money monopoly. He wanted to remove all federal funds from the bank, and believed the people were with him when he was re-elected in 1832. The Secretary of the Treasury, W. J. Duane, obstinately refused to do this, and he was replaced by Taney, who on 26 September issued an order directing the deposit of public moneys in certain local banks, known as the Jackson "pets". Every effort of law and human protection was made to secure these public funds in these banks.

In 1835 the public debt had been paid off; custom receipts had steadily increased; and beginning in 1830 there was an enormous expansion in revenue from the sale of public lands to people moving into the new territories—much of it on credit with interest charged by various land banks. These banks were not really under government control, but issued their notes (or checks) to the government to pay for the federal land purchased in a middle man agreement.

The challenge to the federal government seemed to be "what to do with the surplus." Henry Clay wanted it to be distributed among the states, but the original states believed it should go only to them, since the public land had been ceded to pay off their Revolutionary War debts—others wanted large internal improvements, fortifications, or education. It became impossible to pass a distribution law, but on 23 Jun 1836 an Act was created that would send $37,000,000 to the states—distributed in four quarterly payments in 1837 according to the number of representatives each state had in the House of Representatives. In all of their bickering and bargaining no one suggested that maybe they were collecting more revenue than they needed to collect, or selling the land at too great a price, or that the actual producers of the revenue should have a right to reclaim some of the excess. With the *spoil system* intact, they only saw it as a way to increase their own control over what they believed to be their own federal power right of decision, or the right of their own state's government.

On 1 Jul 1836 the Treasury Department issued an order known as the *Specie Circular.*, which is described in the *Americana Encyclopedia*:

"a treasury circular drafted by Senator Benton [of Missouri] and issued at President Jackson's orders 11 July 1836, which directed that nothing but gold and silver should be received in payment for the public lands. The next Congress passed a bill to rescind this specie circular, but President Jackson killed it by his veto. It was claimed by President Jackson's opponents that the circular contributed greatly to bring about the ruinous financial crisis of 1837." [underline added]

In actuality the central executive government had taken it upon themselves to change the whole <u>medium of exchange</u> that had developed by their neglect or lack of protection throughout the nation. They did it without any regard for the people who had bought the land or the private banks that had been the agents. The less-fortunate became even more unfortunate, and many blamed those closest to them—their local banks, neighbors, and friends—who with the scarcity of gold and silver at all levels could no longer fulfill their promises.

The federal government started minting more coins to help the situation, but still refused to receive checks, notes, or currency—only *specie*, feeling [or pretending] they were protecting the people's money. Somehow Jackson's "Pets" survived, as any very strong *spoil system* should allow, as they were the banks where the federal *specie* money had been placed, but the other banks, who could not collect *specie* from their many mortgages to people who hadn't any gold or silver, or any way to get it, were forced into bankruptcy. Their mortgages were called in and much land once more became federal land, usually auctioned to the highest bidder—often the sheriff, lawyers, or prominent men of wealth who had gold or silver—and usually at a much reduced price.

As these people saw their hard work and means of support taken away, they blamed others. Their fierce anger increased collectively and mobs formed—not really knowing who to blame, they trusted no one. It became a PANIC, and it was across the whole nation. New York City was hit very hard.

Joseph Smith Jr. was living in Kirtland, Ohio, at this time. To meet the needs of the people who were continually arriving they had chartered a bank—not one of Jackson's "Pet's." The need for credit in their new land purchasing was very great. Smith also had an interest in a general store to support his family, while he continued his inspired revision of the *New Testament*. He was very generous by nature and probably allowed too much extended credit in his general store to the new and less established arrivals that were coming to Kirtland.

When this *Panic of 1837* arrived in Kirtland, all of the above occurred, and in addition many of the members of the Church blamed their prophet—he should have warned them, taken care of them, or something. Bitterness became rampant. Their beautiful Kirtland Temple, where Elijah and Moses had appeared to usher in the "Last Dispensation of Time" as prophesied in the last two verses of the *Old Testament* was taken over by a mob of the discontented and they defended their right to it with guns. Joseph Smith's store was forced into bankruptcy. Some of his Twelve Apostles were deserting him, calling him a "fallen prophet." Even the ever loyal Parley P. Pratt was discouraged and after spending an evening in prayer, he came to him the following day a much humbler man to apologize for his thoughts—and with even a stronger testimony of Christ. He remained Joseph Smith Jr.'s devoted friend.

In Clay County, Missouri, where the refugees from Jackson County and other members had gathered, a Stake Presidency had been established by Joseph Smith in 1834. Financial problems had occurred, the members objected and the whole Stake Presidency apostizied from the Church in the spring of 1838, which included two of the three witnesses to the *Book of Mormon*. The third witness who lived in Kirtland also left the Church—but none of them denied their testimony of the *Book of Mormon* as long as they lived. Two of them would later be re-baptized. Some of my close relations in Missouri left the Church at this time. An early chapter in *Part I: DRIVEN* gives more details. Of course, The Church of Jesus Christ of Latter-day Saints survived and still kept growing very rapidly.

It was the fall of 1838 that Joseph Smith Jr. and companions were taken prisoners. While in Liberty jail, as he heard of the deep suffering of his people as they were driven from Missouri, he cried out to God. In answer to his prayer, *Section 121 of the Doctrine and Coventants* was given to him. The following are some quotes from this section that refer to the power or *Priesthood* of God and God's answer to the adversity the saints were suffering at this terrible time.

"O God, where art thou?
And where is the pavilion that covereth thy hiding place?
How long shall thy hand be stayed, and thine eye . . .
Behold from the eternal heavens the wrongs of thy people . . . ?

. . .

My son, peace be unto thy soul; thine adversity
and thine afflictions shall be but a small moment;
And then, if thou endure it well,

God shall exalt thee on high;
Thou shalt triumph over all thy foes. . . .
Behold, mine eyes see and know all their works, and I have in
reserve a swift judgment in the season thereof, for them all; . . .
What power shall stay the heavens?
As well might man stretch forth his puny arm to stop the Missouri
river in its decreed course . . . as to hinder the Almighty from
pouring down knowledge from heaven
upon the heads of the Latter-day Saints.
The rights of the priesthood are inseparably connected
with the powers of heaven, and cannot be controlled nor handled
only upon the principles of righteousness.
That they may be conferred upon us, it is true;
But when we undertake to cover our sins, or to gratify our pride,
our vain ambition, or to exercise control or dominion
or compulsion upon the souls of the children of men,
in any degree of unrighteousness, behold, the heavens withdraw
themselves; the Spirit of the Lord is grieved;
and when it is withdrawn,
Amen to the priesthood or the authority of that man. . . .
We have learned by sad experience that it is the nature
and disposition of almost all men, as soon as they get
a little authority, as they suppose, they will immediately begin to
exercise unrighteous dominion. . . .
No power or influence can or ought to be maintained
by the virtue of the Priesthood,
only by persuasion, by long-suffering, by gentleness
and meekness, and by love unfeigned;
By kindness, and pure knowledge,
which shall greatly enlarge the soul without hypocrisy,
and without guile—
Reproving betimes with sharpness,
when moved upon by the Holy Ghost; and then
showing forth afterwards an increase of love towards him
whom thou hast reproved lest he esteem thee to be his enemy.

. . . be full of charity towards all men,
. . . let virtue garnish thy thoughts unceasingly; . . ."

THIS AERIAL WINTER PHOTO WAS TAKEN OF THE OLD LOG RANCH HOUSE AT CONDIE HOT SPRINGS
RANCH NEAR CAREY, IDAHO, AROUND 1960. THE SNOW HAD MELTED AROUND THE SOUTH YARDS,
BECAUSE THE HOT SPRING IS IN VERY CLOSE PROXIMATY. THE HIGHER MOUNTAINS TO THE NORTH
DO NOT APPEAR, BECAUSE OF THE LOW-LAYING SNOW CLOUDS.

Only by persuasion and love unfeigned

I, BROOKIE CONDIE, was three years old, living in our two-story log
ranch house in Carey, Idaho, in 1932. My older sister by 20 months shared a full
sized bed with me on the second floor above the kitchen. I don't remember the
upstairs' events that resulted in my sister and I being moved from upstairs, but I
do remember being put in our parent's bedroom on the first floor, north of our
larger kitchen, and being told kindly to be quiet and go to sleep. My sister began
to tease or tickle me again, as she must have been doing upstairs. I tried to be
quiet, but she wouldn't stop. In desperation, I pulled up both of my legs and
placed my feet in the middle of her body, and with all the force I was capable of,
I pushed her out of the bed, and she fell to the floor.

She immediately screamed and cried out very loud,

"Daddy! Mother! BROOKIE kicked me out of bed!"

She jumped up and ran into my mother's arms in the kitchen to be examined for any injuries.

My very tall father came into the room, enclosed me in his arms, and returned to the kitchen, which was lighted by a beautiful large gas lamp with two mantles sitting in the center of our round kitchen table. He held me carefully in front of him and looked deeply into my eyes. Without anger, he searchingly asked,

"Did you do it accidentally or on purpose?"

I didn't know what to say, for I didn't know the meaning of either word. I thought that purpose sounds like purple, and purple was a pretty color so I said,

"On purpose," —probably shedding a few tears, for I was quite fearful.

He pulled me close to him with his strong arms and hands, comforted me, and sincerely thanked me for telling the truth.

I remember first thinking *"Oh, oh, wrong word."* But as he drew me close the fear left, and I decided it was the right word after all, for I knew then that he really loved me.

Our parents tucked the two of us back in their bed, and our father admonished us to be kind to one another, and thanked me again for telling the truth. As they left the room, I looked at my older sister and she gave a smug look that seemed to say, *"Be careful, I'm still bigger than you."* Then she turned over and we both went to sleep to wake-up in the morning in our own bed upstairs.

I remember my thoughts as I went to sleep that night.

"I had learned the meaning of two new words. I had found out my legs were stronger than I realized, and that my sister had stopped her teasing. I had found that telling the truth had taken away my fear of punishment—even if it was not intended. But most important, from that point on I never doubted that my very tall, strong, handsome father really did love me as much as any of his children. He was not my enemy, but he loved the truth and wanted me to be kind to others—just like he expected them to be kind to me."

I have never forgotten the incident, and my sister and I, who shared our bed until she left for college, became very close friends. I have no memories of her ever teasing me that way again, or of my pushing her out of bed. I do remember her drawing an imaginary line down the middle of our bed upstairs and telling me which side was hers, and which side was mine—shortly after the above incident took place.

The 1933 Change in the "Medium of Exchange"

In the fall of 1932, demoncrat Franklin Delano Roosevelt of New York state was elected president. His father was a noteable banker in New York City. As soon as possible after he took his oath of office and became president in 1933, this new president called in all the gold coins across the nation—they would no longer be recognized as *specie*. The banks throughout the nation were to pay the people around 21 dollars for each troy ounce of gold coin, and then after a limited time offer, it would be illegal for anyone to own any gold coins—gold rings or jewelery were fine. The collected gold coins went into Fort Knox—until he established an international price for gold at 35 dollars a troy ounce.

This fiasco of power, in a sense, stole from each previous owner of any gold coins across the nation—individual, corporation, or bank—approximately 40% of the true value of their gold holdings, which their government had forcefully taken for its own use.

The president then closed every bank in the nation and made his own rules for establishing new charters. This forced the smaller banks to call in their loans, regardless of previous agreements with their customers, and liquidate enough of their secured properties to pay off any indebtedness the bank might have. The mortgages that were nearly paid were the first to go, because they offered the best chance for the bank to take this property and sell it at a profit, unless, of course, the debtor could come up with the balance in cash or currency for the rest of his loan, which would also help liquidate the bank. Cash poor because they needed their loan, with no banks open to borrow from, many lost their mortgaged-secured property—even if it was nearly paid for.

This *exchange* history is told in more detail in *Part II: STANDING FIRM*, as well as some of the others things FDR did after he took his oath of office.

In 1932, under President Hoover, the stock market had been starting its recovery from the Panic of 1929-1931, but these actions started a new dip in the American economy, because the government of the nation, in changing its *medium of exchange* was not being fair to its entire people and FDR lost the trust of the losers. Additionally, the *spoil system* was even more imbedded throughout the nation, and special favors and privileges were magnified to an extent great enough to allow President FDR four terms—until his death in office —the very thing that (republican/democrat) Thomas Jefferson and his friends had tried to blame their opponents of trying to do in those early years of our nation.

He and his cohorts also blamed the longer depression recovery onto former President Hoover who died in the later part of 1933 in his home in California.

Harrison, Tyler, Polk, Taylor, Fillmore, Pierce, Buchannan

It is said by some that President Martin Van Buren (1837-1841) was not the cause of the panic, and took measures to help the people. If so, he was a very close friend of those who caused it during those last years of Andrew Jackson's presidency. Van Buren was a one-term president. William Henry Harrison of Indiana, a hero of the War of 1812, with John Tyler of Virginia for vice president won in 1840. Harrison chose his cabinet, took his oath of office, and lived only one month longer—when an infection fatally struck him.

John Tyler then became president. He had changed his former Democratic Party affiliation to the Whig Party before this election, but his true loyalty was to his old friends—Jefferson, Madison, and Monroe, all from Virginia. Jefferson had died in 1826; Monroe died in 1831, Madison in 1836. His presidency was not in the plan of Senator Henry Clay when his Whig Party [hawks and abolitionists] had agreed to include Tyler to get the Virginia/Southern vote.

Tyler was very independent minded and had been taught well by his previous Virginia presidents and friends—his father had been the governor of Virginia from 1808-1811 and United States district judge 1812-1813. His mother was Mary Armistead, the heiress and only daughter of Robert Armistead. President Tyler was born 29 Mar 1790. In1811, young Tyler was elected to the Virginia state legislature and became a firm supporter of President James Madison's war policy.

The following quotes are those of R. C. McGrane, *Professor of History, University of Cincinnati,* as recorded in the *Americana Encyclopedia 1945 edition:*

Tyler "condemned, as arbitrary and insubordinate, the conduct of General Jackson in Florida, and delivered an elaborate speech against the national bank. [As a U. S. congressman] he opposed the Missouri Compromise on the ground that Congress had no power to legislate for or against slavery in any Territory. In 1821 he declined re-election and retired to private life; but in 1823 he was again elected to the Virginia legislature. From 1825 to 1827 he served as governor of the State, when in the latter year he was elected United States senator to succeed John Randolph. . . . [In the election of 1832, he supported Jackson] as the least objectional candidate; comdemning South Carolina's nullification doctrines, while objecting to Jackson's proclamation of 10 Dec. 1832. . . . on the 'Force Bill,' allowing the President extraordinary powers for the collection of duties, he was the only senator to vote in the negative.

"With the opening of Jackson's war on the United States Bank, Tyler broke with the administration and began to associate more closely with the opposition soon to be designated as the 'Whigs.' Tyler saw in the unbridled democracy of Jackson a tendency toward despotism, 'under the leadership of a headstrong and popular chief' and to him the 'only safeguard for constitutional government lay in strict construction.'"

A constructionist of the United States Constitution would view its "literal powers" as opposed to viewing it as to its "implied powers." Tyler did not approve of Senator Benton's Act that Jackson had incorporated to accept only *specie* in the payment of the sale of United States land, shifting his position more strongly toward the Whig Party.

"The Whig Convention of 1839 nominated General Harrison [for President] in order to secure the votes of the anti-Masons and National Republicans, whom Clay had alienated, and Tyler was chosen as his running mate in order to obtain the votes of those Democrats who were dissatisfied with the administration [Van Buren]. . . . [After President Harrison's death and Tyler's replacement, Tyler] immediately . . . found himself in a conflict with Congress over their attempt to re-establish a national bank. Tyler had always held that Congress could not create a corporation within the State without the consent of the State. Therefore, Tyler vetoed the two bills presented to him as not incorporating his ideas, and after the second veto all the Cabinet members [appointed by Harrison] resigned, except [Secretary of State Daniel] Webster, who was then negotiating the Webster-Ashburton Treaty [U.S./British]. Thenceforth throughout his administration Tyler was a President without a party and in constant strife with Congress. . . . In August 1844, after having been nominated at an irregular Democratic convention at Baltimore in May, Tyler withdrew from the race. "

Tyler held no furher office until South Carolina adopted its ordinance of secession and he became the president of the Peace Convention, which met in Washington 4 Feb 1861. When congress rejected the Virginia ideas, he

> "advocated the immediate secession of Virginia. In May 1861 he was elected a member of the provisional Congress of the Confederate States, and the following autumn was elected to the permanent Confederate Congress, but died before taking his seat." [R. C. McGrane]

He died 18 Jan 1862. President John Tyler, of the street where I lived in Twin Falls, Idaho, thus became the

> "only President who renounced his citizenship of the Republic which honored him with its highest office." [*Know Your Presidents*]

Past president Martin Van Buren (Democrat), felt cheated out of his second term as president and was quick to proclaim his desire to be a candidate in 1844. Henry Clay (Whig), who had so many plans for President William Henry Harrison, who had died in office, thought it was time for him to be president. Senator Daniel Webster of Massachusetts, whose oratory and efforts was always in strong favor of a stronger federal government and unity of the states, had broke with Van Buren and Jackson on their destructive measures of the banks and decided to favor Henry Clay (Whig), although he had in effect defied him by remaining on Tyler's cabinet as Secretary of State. He hated the *spoils system.*

Van Buren had made a terrible mistake for his nomination by declaring quite vocally in April that he was opposed to the annexation of Texas as a state. Henry Clay had also stated his desire to stop it that same day, when he was in Raleigh, North Carolina. This was a very sensitive question for the Southern states—Texas would undoubtedly be admitted as a slave state, if it was annexed. The excitement all over the south was intense. They wanted Texas added to the nation.

It was 1844 and, at the Democratic convention in May, the Southern Delegation with Calhoun of South Carolina in control refused to nominate Van Buren and on a quick vote, all his desires for a second term presidency were washed away in defeat. There was no quickly available candidate to turn to, so they stood behind President John Tyler (a Whig), who they felt would strongly support the annexation of Texas. It took Tyler until August to withdraw from the race. His presidency had not been a happy one. After some maneuvering, Polk, a strong pro-Texan of Nashville, Tennessee, was chosen as the Democratic candidate. Calhoun, who was then, as always, a powerful leader in the South, supported Polk with enthusiasm and he was elected president—to the great disappointment of both Van Buren of New York and Henry Clay of Kentucky.

Who was James Knox Polk? It was a question that they would soon find out. His quick bold caption in my *Know Your Presidents* book reads:

> "From camp cook-boy in back woods of Tennessee he fought ill health and poverty to an education and to the White House."

Polk was born 2 Nov 1795 and died 15 Jun 1849, shortly after his term as president ended that same year. He was buried in Nashville about 12 miles from the gravesite of Andrew Jackson. I have not researched his ancestory but one history states it was Scotch-Irish.

As I've read his brief life histories, I have been amazed at what he accomplished during his four years as a president of this country. It even appears to be a miracle that he was in the white house. Texas was annexed, like the southern states wanted, but with it the nation added the whole southwestern border of our current United States, its southeastern coast line, and its northern border with Canada. It was a great expansion of our borders—with the approval, of course, of Henry Clay and Daniel Webster, who had worked with the British in establishing these boundry lines (although they had tried to draw them further north).

The Oregon Trail became a thoroughfare across the wilderness. Gold was discovered in California. All this was accomplished, not to conquer a people, drive them out, or enslave them, but to bring them a new birth of freedom and the protection of a constitution of government that was inspired by God. California would be a free state, as President Polk had wanted, as would Nevada, as Lincoln had wanted—along with all the other states—Iowa, Michigan, Wisconsin, Oregon, Arizona, —the list goes on. The 13 original states would become the 48 states, each with a star of their own and the protection of that great document created by the committee with George Washington as their leader. Two more territories would be added to these states, Alaska and Hawaii—again extending our freedom, not our slavery, to others. Calhoun, of South Carolina, had loved the Constitution of the United States, and at the right time, he gave us James Knox Polk as president to open new doors into the west.

Another noteable leader was making his name known through this period of time—General Zachary Taylor with no party affiliation. The Whig party claimed him for his popularity as the top general during the Mexican War (where Polk had also been an officer) and because he had served with William Henry Harrison during the War of 1812. His daughter Sarah was the wife of Jefferson Davis, the future President of the Southern Confederacy, whose son would serve as one of their Southern officers.

The Zachary Taylor's home was in Louisville, Kentucky. "Old Rough and Ready" was a soldier for forty years. He had many slaves. He was the second president to die in office, at the age of 66 on 9 Jul 1850, after being president for a little more than a year. My *Know Your Presidents'* book gives him these

"Personal Characteristics: Typical soldier, noted for rugged honesty and loyalty. Last words: 'I have endeavored to do my duty: I am ready to die.'"

[Note: My direct ancestors and their close relations were part of this great expansion into the west where freedom of religion; the right to bear arms; to assemble; speak freely, and all the rest of these guaranteed rights were extended. They came from the south and the north, and I love them all. Their story of this time period is told in volume one of *Broad are the Branches. They participated in the Mexican War and were with the Batallion that claimed California for the United States.*]

Vice President Millard Fillmore became, after Taylor's death, the thirteenth president of the United States of America from 1850 until 1853. His whole "Twig" cabinet immediately resigned—but President Fillmore still had powerful friends in congress. Taylor's inexperience had gathered many strong leaders to try to direct his policies. As Taylor's plans for the nation moved more and more toward the southern position, vice president Fillmore, in charge of the senate, moved more toward Daniel Webster and Henry Clay's position of strength—so things were done in those next three years. According to William E. Dodd, professor, University of Chicago, *Americana Encyclopedia:*

Millard Fillmore was born 7 Feb 1800 in Summer Hill, Cayuga County, New York. His parents were from New England and had obtained their early frontier farm land at least fourteen years before the end of the war of 1812—14. There were many Indians throughout this area. Life was hard. He studied law at Buffalo by Niagara Falls. He became well-known in the area and served two years in the New York State legislature and

> "identified himself with the repeal of the harsh law of the State for the imprisonment of debtors. In 1832 he was sent to the national House of Representatives as a follower of Henry Clay. During the next decade he alternated between membership in the House and the work of his profession, building . . . a reputation as a political leader. "

He had a political win with the "landslide "of 1840, and became the chairman of the House Ways and Means and as such drew the (abominable) tariff bill of 1842, becoming thus a representative of the industrial and financial interests of the North against the South, who formed an alliance with the West to combat it. He ran for governor of New York, but was defeated by Silas Wright, the Democratic candidate.

> "Three years later he was elected comptroller of the State of New York, and three years later [1848] nominated on the Whig ticket as vice president to Zachary Taylor."

Both Daniel Webster and Henry Clay unitedly opposed Taylor's nomination, and refused to support it. Taylor was a slave-holder, and their views for a strong union of states were disturbed by the prospect—Taylor won anyway. During Taylor's year in office, Daniel Webster gave a great oration that favored the need for unity in the country, but Taylor held out to a point that many feared there would be war. After his unanticipated death, and the resignation of his cabinet, Webster and Clay welcomed the new President Fillmore with open arms. Webster became his

> "Secretary of State and served the ideals of the country well, . . . Clay, Webster, Fillmore, and the Southern Whigs, aided by the Northern Democrats, arranged for the admission of California, the organization of New Mexico, the payment of the Texan claims, the prohibition of the slave trade in the District of Columbia, and the return of fugitive slaves."

Some of these compromising positions irritated the northern Whigs. Henry Clay had died in 1852 and was not affected. ABRAHAM LINCOLN gave the oration at his funeral—but the party would not nominate either Fillmore or Webster for president that year. Fillmore returned to Buffalo, travelled in Europe, married again, and died 8 Mar 1874.

In Utah, during his administration, a new county was established in the center of the state. They called it Millard County and built a new fort, naming it Fort Fillmore. Because of its central location, Brigham Young thought it would be a good location for their state capital and the first legislative building of Utah was built there. Only a few sessions were held in it, and Salt Lake City claimed the honor. My husband's early British ancestors on his mother's side, were numbered with these settlers in Fort Fillmore—DUNCANs from Scotland and STOTTs and NIELDs from Yorkshire and Lancashire, England.

It was during Millard Fillmore's administration that Japan was opened to Western Civilization by Admiral Perry, and in the state of Maine—1852—their legislature passed the First Prohibition Law. That same year in Missouri, my third-great-grandfather ANDERSON IVIE died and was buried in the tiny village called Florida, while in 1852 my great-grandparents JOHN LEHI IVIE and MARY CATHERINE BARTON were married in the President's office in Salt Lake City, Utah.

The Democratic convention of 1 Jun 1852 was quite interesting. There were three strong candidates: Lewis Cass, James Buchanan, and Stephen L. Douglas. Lewis Cass was born in Exeter, New Hampshire, 1782, but in 1800 he removed to Marietta, Ohio, where he studied law. In December 1802, he was admitted to the bar, and was elected to the Ohio legislature in 1806. He served in the military during the first year of the war of 1812; then in 1813, he was appointed governor of the Michigan territory—which then included Wisconsin. He held this office until July 1831. There was no territorial legislature, so with his federal judges his office was quite powerful and included all Indian affairs.

There were about 40,000 Indians in this territory with about 9,000 warriors. As the nation kept taking more and more land for the white pioneers, keeping peace and their tolerance and love was difficult, but he was quite successful at it. Up to the time of his resignation in 1831, he had concluded 22 treaties with the Indians, by which cessions had been acquired in Ohio, Indiana, Illinois, Michigan and Wisconsin, to an amount equal to one-fourth the entire territory of these states. In August, 1831, President Jackson appointed him to his cabinet as the Secretary of War, and in 1836 he was appointed as minister to France, where he was on excellent terms with Louis Philippe. Near the end of his ministry, France was able to suppress the slave trade. He returned from France and was a senator 1845-48, when he was nominated by the democrats for president of the United States, which he lost to Zachary Taylor, a Whig.

The three democrats, Cass, Buchanan, and Douglas, each wanted the nomination at Baltimore, 1 Jun 1852, and had shown bitter personal rivalry to obtain it. It was on the 35th ballot that Virginia broke from their candidate and gave their votes to the relatively unknown lawyer Franklin Pierce. On the 49th ballot, Pierce received 282 votes to the 6 votes for all the other candidates, and the "dark horse" was on his way to the presidency.

Franklin Pierce was the fourteenth president, and the youngest (49 years old) up to his time. The handsome young man had enlisted as a private in the Mexican War and had quickly risen through the ranks until he became a brigadier general when General Scott advanced his troops on Mexico City. Pierce was born in New Hampshire. He had been highly educated, a member of the bar; a democrat; a member of the House of Representatives, and then a senator, before his election as president. President Jackson had liked him and had helped him at times in his career. Pierce was not opposed to slavery, and believed it was guaranteed in the constitution—for which he was a strict constructionist. The South believed him to be a "safe man", and in the November election he received 1,601,474 popular votes to the 1,386,580 votes for General Winifred Scott, the Whig candidate. In 1853, he would appoint Jefferson Davis of Mississippi, the future president of the Southern Confederacy, as his Secretary of War. It was believed by many that Davis influenced him a great deal throughout his term as president.

Pierce stated in his inaugural address:

> "The policy of my administration will not be controlled by any timid forebodings of evil from expansion. . . . Our position on the globe renders the acquisition of certain possessions not within our jusisdiction eminently important for our protection."

In these remarks, he was considering the annexation of Cuba and other areas of Central and South America as slave states. After failing to make Nicaragua a slave state, he was able to purchase a strip of territory on the southern border of New Mexico—about 50,000 square miles for $10,000,000 from Mexico. It was known as the Gadsen purchase, because James Gadsen was his agent. This strip of land was needed to continue his plans for a southern railroad line into California, which expansion, he hoped, would procure slavery throughout these new territories of the South.

Democrat Senator Stephen L. Douglas of Illinois wanted to build railroads into the newly extended northwest of the Oregon Territory. He prepared and passed the Kansas-Nebraska bill in 1854, which nullified the earlier 1820 Missouri Compromise, which had prohibited the extension of slavery beyond its borders. It further gave the right of decision to the citizens of each new state to be a free or slave state.

This Kansas-Nebraska bill woke up a rather quiet ABRAHAM LINCOLN, who had left politics and was practicing law at that time. He spoke out boldly against this bill—predicting it would create extreme problems in the new states. It would turn families, friends, communities, and cities against each other and further divide the states of the nation. He helped to organize the new Republican Party and threw his hat into the ring for Illinois senator against Stephen L. Douglas at the following election—as told in a following chapter of this book. Quoting from the *Americana Encyclopedia*, Marcus W. Jernegan of the University of Chicago states:

> "This action of Pierce wrecked his administration. He immediately organized Kansas and Nebraska as territories, and supported the pro-slavery party in Kansas during the remainder of his term of office, in an effort to prevent the admission of Kansas as a free State. Thus he helped make the Democratic party of the North subservient to that of the South, and supported the slave power in its extreme demands for more slave territory. He believed that this would satisfy the South and thus disunion and civil war would be avoided. He was under the influence of Jefferson Davis, his Secretary of War, and this accounts, in part, for his attitude on several important public questions. . . . He was opposed to the methods of the Abolitionists, but supported the North when war broke out."

The fifteenth president was James Buchanan (1857-1861), the last democrat to be president for twenty-four years. He was from Wheatland, near Lancaster, Pennsylvania. Unmarried, a lawyer, he spent his life in public office, as a congressman, senator, a minister to Russia and to England before his term as president of the United States. He desired to preserve the union of the North and South through compromises that delayed the actual war, and when South Carolina seceded, 20 Dec 1860, his strict interpretation of the law, recognized that *States Rights* gave credibility to the secession; but he would not recognize them as a separate country. Democrat Stephen L. Douglas of Illinois split from his views. With other parts of the Democratic Party following his lead, Douglas opened the way for the election of Republican ABRAHAM LINCOLN, who had become well-known through his anti-slavery debates with Senator Douglas when the two of them opposed each other in their race for senator of Illinois.

During Buchanan's administration, General Albert Sidney Johnston was sent west with 2,500 soldiers to subdue the *Mormons* in Utah and replace their territorial government with an *anti-Mormon* federal governor administration and federal judges—all appointed by the president of the United States. They traveled west in 1857, south of the Platt River. North of the Platt was a large company of *Mormons,* crossing the plains for more peaceful reasons. The two companies would observe each other as they journeyed on the way. With this group of *Mormons,* was young great-grandmother HELEN SWANN and her parents, my second-great-grandparents, EPHRIUM and FANNY JONES SWANN, from Herefordshire, England, who were on their way to to join with the saints in the Salt Lake valley. Great-grandmother HELEN SWANN (Condie) would latter tell the family that there was much loud cursing and swearing among the marching army, but she really felt sorry for them when their advance supply wagons were burned by the very small *Mormon* army that had been sent to stop them—but not to kill anyone. Among these young militia soldiers were my mother's grandfather—JOHN LEHI IVIE and his brother JIM.

This was a very expensive journey for the United States military, and it is claimed by some that Buchanan sent Johnston's Army to help bankrupt the nation before the South seceded and the Civil War began. This may have been the desire of some, but Buchanan seems too much of a pacifier to have been the instigator for that reason—but maybe. When Buchanan was elected, Davis returned to the senate, where he strongly continued to attempt to pull Kansas in as a slave state—heating up an already flaming tinder-box. Jefferson Davis had graduated from West Point in the same class as Generals Robert E. Lee and A. S.

Johnston, among other generals of the Civil War—including U. S. Grant.

General Albert Sidney Johnston was born in Mason County, Kentucky, on 3 Feb 1803. With his southern beliefs, and with the early contention preceding the Civil War between the Kansas jayhawks and the Missouri bushwhackers, he was anxious to leave Utah. In the fall of 1860, he took his army back to New Orleans. He led over 39,000 Confederate soldiers at the Battle of Shiloh (Tennessee) on 6 Apr 1862. He was so skilled and able that some speculate that had he not been shot in the leg and bled to death within 15 minutes, just prior to his final push to victory over northerner General Ulysses S. Grant, the South would have been the victors at Shiloh. Beauregard, unfamiliar with his plan, was slow to take advantage of their strong position. The ammunition was low. He grew fearful and withdrew his troops. It is further speculated that had the South been successful at that time, along with General Robert E. Lee's victories in Virginia, the whole outcome of the Civil War might have been different. Perhaps this was one of those little moments "that form the destiny of men."

Our sixteenth president, ABRAHAM LINCOLN, is familiar to all of us. His journey from the log cabin to the White House is legend. At 19, he served as a hired man on a flat boat to New Orleans. At 22, he was a village store clerk. The next year, he was a captain in the 2nd Blackhawk Indian War at age 23; after which, he ran for the Illinois legislature. At 27, he was famous as a state orator, but was earning only a meager living as a surveyor—so poor he walked the 100 miles to the legislature. That year, he was admitted to the bar. When he was 33 years old, he married the ambitious Mary Todd. He was 38 years old when he was elected to congress. At 47, he helped organize the present Republican Party and nearly became their first candidate for vice president of the nation—defeated. At the age of 49, he ran for the senate and was again defeated. He became president of the United States when he was 52 years old, in 1861. Serving in this office throughout the Civil War, he was assassinated in 1865, at age 56, becoming our first martyred president. He was buried in a tomb in Springfield, Illinois.

By the mid-term elections of 1862, LINCOLN's administration was not the most popular party in Washington D.C. The war was not going well. With Bull Run and Antietam behind them, the Army of the Potomac had little to show for the lives and money spent. After Antietam, just two weeks before the elections that fall, Lincoln announced his preliminary draft of the Emancipation Proclamation. Many northerners thought he had turned the Civil War into a fight to free the slaves instead of their original purpose of reuniting the nation. The Democrats wanted "the Constitution as it is and the Union as it was," with slavery unimpaired. Furthermore, in waging war, many northerners accused LINCOLN of usurping the individual rights of citizens and pictured LINCOLN as a tyrant and dictator. It was an election of political disaster for the Republicans. Next there was the defeat of the Union at Fredericksburg in mid-December. In March, 1863, R. I. Dana, a popular writer and lawyer, sent a letter to Charles F. Adams, LINCOLN's ambassador in London. It read,

> "As to the politics of Washington, the most striking thing is the absence of personal loyalty to the President. It does not exist. He has no admirers, no enthusiastic supporters, none to bet on his head. If a Republican convention were to be held to-morrow, he would not get the vote of a State."

The Democrats wanted peace at any price and felt that they had the mandate of the past election to support them against this stubborn Republican president. A war of virulent words began. Newspaperman Horace Greeley took up his pen in defense of the administration. The Copperheads (anti-war Democrats), continued their harsh words. But the tide was turning in the Southern waters. The Northern armies were more organized and proficient. In the South, there was the specter of starvation looming. Ammunition and other necessities were running low. They asked the British for help. The Northern ships blocked their harbors. Confederate President Jefferson Davis was beginning to feel the bitter heat, much like ABRAHAM LINCOLN. He had his southern anti-war Copperheads, too. Varina, Davis' wife, had left her children at play on the second story balcony of their Southern White House at Richmond, Virginia, to take a basket lunch to her tired husband in his office. While uncovering and serving the lunch, a servant ran to them. Their son, Little Joe, had climbed over the connecting angle of the bannister and fallen twenty feet to the brick pavement below. His young brother Jeff was by his side, crying,

> "I have said all the prayers I know how, but God will not wake Joe."

The Southern White House

(Photo by Hyrum Haynes)

~ 112 ~

CLARA BARTON AND THE CIVIL WAR

I have the Franklin Mint's pewter rendition of the National Historical Society's CIVIL WAR CHESS SET. The two pewter kings of this chess set are Generals Ulysses S. Grant for the North and Robert E. Lee for the South. Honored as the North's queen in this set is my many times removed cousin CLARA BARTON. CLARA was born in 1821 to a New England farm wife. Her father was STEPHEN BARTON Sr., who was a veteran of the War of 1812's British/Indian Michigan battles against our country in 1811-14. She was descended from the same early New England BARTONs as I am—the sea captain EDWARD BARTON of the early 1600s.

Prior to James Buchanan's presidency (1857-1861), the highly competent CLARA BARTON was able to obtain a job as a copyist in the U.S. Patent Office in the City of Washington. An unmarried, highly independent woman, she was the only woman to work in that department who was paid directly for her services. Of course, she was paid less than her male co-workers. When Democrat James Buchanan took office, she was fired shortly after. She had made an error, in their opinion, of boldly telling her fellow workers that she favored retaining a union of the states—the woman must go! She returned to her family home in New England for a few years until Republican ABRAHAM LINCOLN took his oath of office in March 1862. She was then able to get her old job back, at less pay, and returned to the nation's capital.

South Carolina had warned the nation prior to the election in November 1861 that they would secede from the Union if LINCOLN was elected president, so they had done just that and proceeded to take over the U. S. forts, arsenals, and other property belonging to the United States government within their state. Peace negotiations had continued, but President Buchannan's heart was more with the South than the North. Georgia, Alabama, and Mississsippi had rapidly followed South Carolina, and they had all withdrawn their represen- titives from congress. By the time of LINCOLN's inauguration in March seven states had withdrawn from the union—others were threatening to follow. The city of Baltimore, Maryland, had a nest of insurgents, who had planned to kill LINCOLN when his special B&O Railroad train arrived, where he had planned to make a speech on his journey to his first inauguration at Washington D.C. The plot had been discovered, the train never stopped, thus thwarting the inci- dent; but the animosity within that neighboring city still remained. There were many more northerners who were not pleased with his election. Even the abol- ishioners believed him too weak against slavery, but LINCOLN knew that if he came out against slavery, he would lose all the Border States and even some in the North.

When he took his heroic oath of office on that day in March to "preserve, protect and defend" a broken Constitution, and was commissioned to restore authority and character to a government which treason had betrayed and feeble- ness had abased, he knew exactly that slavery, as much as he disliked it, could not be the purpose, or the Constitution, his office, and the very nation would be dissolved.

Unwilling to give up U. S. property, but too small to retaliate against the whole South Carolina militia, Major Anderson and the U. S. garrison troops had kept the Stars and Stripes flying above Fort Sumter in the Charleston harbor— waiting for the orders from their commanding officers. The Southern militia then placed them under siege—hoping for their surrender without bloodshed.

Many in the North wanted to send in ships and begin military activity, but LINCOLN would not allow them to do so. He still hoped he could reason with these Southern gentlemen—but his soldiers in the fort were in need of food and water. He had the following note delivered to the Southern militia:

> "I am directed by the President of the United States to notify you to expect
> an attempt will be made to supply Fort Sumter with provisions, only; and
> that, if such attempt be not resisted, no effort to throw in men, arms or
> ammunition will be made without further notice, or in case of an attack
> on the fort."

So when the food supplies arrived and the Southern army fired on the 73 man U.S. garrison at Fort Sumter, in Charleston harbor, South Carolina, on 12 Apr 1861, (five weeks after LINCOLN's inauguration), President LINCOLN called it an insurrection and asked for an army of 75,000 volunteers to put down the rebellion.

When the Sixth Massachusetts Regiment marched through Baltimore en route to protect Washington City from the rebels of neighboring Virginia, the soldiers were attacked and a riot ensued on 19 April—the anniversary of the Battle of Lexington and the "shot heard around the world." When the riot was over, twelve civilians and four soldiers—the first casualties of the Civil War—were dead.

The Sixth Massachusetts included many of CLARA BARTON's old school friends from her home town. She wrote,

> "I look out upon the same beautiful landscape—the same clear blue sky, the same floating clouds—the face of nature is unchanged—nothing there indicates that the darkest page in our country's history is being written in lines of blood! . . . some dark impending war . . . an omen of evil import to those who have dared to raise the hand of rebellion against the common country."

With no barracks to house these soldiers in Washington D. C., the Sixth Massachusetts took up residence in the Senate Chamber. Their beds were on the carpeted floors. Across the Potomac, in Alexandria, a large flag of the Confederacy was flying visibly above the taller buildings. By 21 April, all rail and telegraph lines had been cut. The capital of the nation was isolated. On the streets, it was common

> "to see little spruce clerks and even boys strutting about the streets, and as-serting that 'We had no Government,—it merely amounted to a compact but had no strength. Our constitution was a mere pretense, and govern-ment a myth.'"

In her cries for help, CLARA wrote further,

> "If it must be, let it come; and when there is no longer a soldier's arm to raise the Stars and Stripes above our Capitol may God give strength to mine."

That same day, the Seventh New York regiment marched into the city and onward to the White House. Early the next morning the Eighth Massachusetts arrived; they were followed by the First Rhode Island Regiment, who found their quarters in CLARA's Patent Office among the odd exhibits. Additional soldiers arrived, filling the Treasury Department, the Center Market, behind City Hall, in the Navy Yard on Franklin Square, in warehouses. CLARA then wrote,

> "We are an armed city. Thirty thousand soldiers armed to the teeth, marching and counter marching drilling in squads, companies and battalions, the roll of the drums bursting upon your ears at almost every moment, the long lines of dark, dusty men, as some new Regiment files up the Avenue, with their canteens and haversacks, and thousand bristling bayonets glimmering in the sun."

CLARA might have tried to join with Dorothea Dix, who was recruiting women volunteers to organize military hospitals and appoint female nurses to help relieve the suffering soldiers. Dix had issued a press release,

> "No woman under thirty need apply to serve in government hospitals. All nurses are required to be plain looking women. Their dresses must be brown or black, with no bows, no curls, no jewelry, and no hoops."

Although CLARA was over thirty, her independent free spirit and femininity would not do well under these dictatorial conditions.

Appalled by the stories of suffering that reached her from the battlefields, where wounded soldiers had sometimes lain for days without help, she advertised for provisions to help the wounded, donating most of her own salary. The supplies were quite easily obtained, but less easily distributed in the field. So, CLARA BARTON prevailed upon the surgeon general and finally received his permission to travel unhampered on the battlefields to minister to the needs of the wounded. Heedless of the great personal dangers she faced and always upholding with dignity her femininity, she became known as the "Angel of the Battlefield." She was at Fredericksburg, the Wilderness Campaign, Charleston, and countless other perilous battles. At the war's end, she superintended a four-year search for missing soldiers. In 1869, while visiting abroad for her health, CLARA BARTON became affiliated with the International Red Cross, which she later introduced into the United States.

A distant cousin and friend of CLARA BARTON who helped her at times in her Red Cross activities was poetess, mother, and pianist JULIA WARD

HOWE. JULIA's great-grandfather was Samuel Ward of the First Rhode Island Regiment that accompanied Benedict Arnold on his command up the Kennebec River in his attempt to take Quebec from the British. She was a first cousin of NATHANAEL GREENE's son, and a descendant of Roger Williams. Her ancestors had been among the many yearly elected Rhode Island governors. In the autumn of 1861, JULIA accompanied the

"Governor and Mrs. Andrew, Mr. Clarke and the Doctor, who was one of the pioneers of the Sanitary Commission, carrying his restless energy and indomitable will from camp to hospital, from battlefield to bureau. She longed to help in some way, but felt that there was nothing she could do—except make lint, which we were all doing.

"I could not leave my nursery to follow the march of our armies, neither had I the practical deftness which the preparing and packing of sanitary stores demanded. Something seemed to say to me, 'You would be glad to serve, but you cannot help anyone: you have nothing to give, and there is nothing for you to do.' Yet, because of my sincere desire, a word was given me to say, which did strengthen the hearts of those who fought in the field and of those who languished in the prison."

As the group returned from a review of the troops near Washington, their carriage was surrounded by marching regiments. With the delay the group started to sing the war songs of the day. In the course of this they sang,

"John Brown's body lies a-mouldering in the grave.
His soul is marching on!

"The soldiers liked this, cried, 'Good for you!' and took up the chorus with its rhythmic swing.

"Mrs. Howe," said Mr. Clarke, "why do you not write some good words for that stirring tune?"

"I have often wished to do so!" she replied.

"Waking in the gray of the next morning, as she lay waiting for the dawn, the word came to her.

"Mine eyes have seen the glory of the coming of the Lord —

"She lay perfectly still. Line by line, stanza by stanza, the words came sweeping on with the rhythm of marching feet, pauseless, restless. She saw the long lines swinging into place before her eyes, heard the voice of the nation speaking through her lips. She waited till the voice was silent, till the last line was ended; then sprang from bed, and groping for pen and paper, scrawled in the gray twilight the *Battle Hymn of the Republic.*"

She crept back to bed and fell asleep. In the morning, she had forgotten the words. The poem was published in the *Atlantic Monthly.* It was

"sung, chanted, recited, and used in exhortation and prayer on the eve of battle. It was printed in newspapers, in army hymn-books, on broad-sides; it was the word of the hour, and the Union armies marched to its swing.

"Among the singers of the "Battle Hymn" was Chaplain McCabe, the fighting chaplain of the 122d Ohio Volunteer Infantry. He read the poem in the "Atlantic" and was so struck with it that he committed it to memory before rising from his chair. He took it whither he was sent after being captured at Winchester. Here, in the great bare room where hundreds of Northern soldiers were herded together, came one night a rumor of disaster to the Union army. A great battle, their jailers told them; a great Confederate victory. Sadly the Northern men gathered together in groups, sitting or lying on the floor, talking in low tones, wondering how, where, why. Suddenly, one of the negroes who brought food for the prisoners stooped in passing and whispered to one of the sorrowful groups. The news was false: there had, indeed, been a great battle, but the Union army had won, the Confederates were defeated and scattered. Like a flame the word flashed through the prison. Men leaped to their feet, shouted, embraced one another in a frenzy of joy and triumph; and Chaplain McCabe, standing in the middle of room, lifted up his great voice and sang aloud, —

"Mine eyes have seen the glory of the coming of the Lord!"

"Every voice took up the chorus, and Libby Prison rang with the shout of 'Glory, glory, hallelujah!'

"The victory was that of Gettyburg. When sometime after, McCabe was released from prison, he told in Washington . . . . [about] that night in Libby Prison, he sang the 'Battle Hymn' once more. The effect was magical: people shouted, wept, and sang, all together; and when the song was ended, above the tumult of applause was heard the voice of ABRAHAM LINCOLN, exclaiming, while the tears rolled down his cheeks, —

"'Sing it again!'"

[Note: These quotes are taken from the book *Julia Ward Howe* by two of her daughters: Laura E. Richards and Maud Howe Elliott. They added the following in parenthesis: "Our mother met Lincoln in 1861, and was presented to him by Governor Andrew. After greeting the party, the President 'seated himself so near the famous portrait of Washington by Gilbert Stuart as naturally to suggest some comparison between the two figures. On the canvas we saw the calm presence, the serene assurance of the man who had successfully accomplished a great undertaking, a vision of health and of peace. In the chair beside it sat a tall, bony figure devoid of grace, a countenance almost redeemed from plainness by two kindly blue eyes, but over-shadowd by the dark problems of the moment. . . .

"When we had left the presence, one of our number exclaimed. 'Helpless Honesty! As if Honesty could ever be helpless.'"]

When I was a teenager, every student was required to memorize Lincoln's Gettysburg Address. He gave it at the dedication of the Gettysburg National Cemetery, 19 Nov 1863, and it describes to all of us the sacrifice of those in our nation who have valued freedom, God, and Country so dearly. Please read it again, thoughtfully. Equality is mentioned, national survival—imperitive.

"Fourscore and seven years ago
our fathers brought forth on this continent a new nation, conceived
in liberty, and dedicated to the proposition
that all men are created equal.
"Now we are engaged in a great civil war, testing whether that
nation, or any nation so conceived and so dedicated, can long
endure. We are met on a great battlefield of that war. We have come
to dedicate a portion of that field as a final resting-place
for those who here gave their lives that that nation might live.
It is altogether fitting and proper that we should do this.
"But, in a larger sense, we can not dedicate—
we can not consecrate—
we can not hallow—this ground.
The brave men, living and dead, who struggled here,
have consecrated it far above our poor power to add or detract. The
world will little note nor long remember what we say here, but it
can never forget what they did here.
It is for us, the living, rather, to be dedicated here
to the unfinished work
which they who fought here have thus far nobly advanced.
It is rather for us to be here dedicated to the great task
remaining before us—that from these honored dead we take
increased devotion to that cause for which
they gave the last full measure of devotion;
that we here highly resolve that
these dead shall not have died in vain;

that this nation, under God, shall have a new birth of freedom;
and that government of the people, by the people, for the people,
shall not perish from the earth."

The *Battle Hymn of the Republic* is included in the current hymn book of my church—stanzas 2 and 3 have been removed, probably because they refer more to the camps and soldiers of Civil War days, and also to make it shorter. They also changed "die" to "live". The following includes all five original verses: The music in one book is attributed to William Steppe—others say unknown.

THE BATTLE HYMN OF THE REPUBLIC

1. Mine —eyes have seen the glory of the coming of the Lord;
He is trampling out the vintage where the grapes of wrath are stored;
He hath loosed the fateful lightning of His terrible swift sword;
His truth is marching on.

2. I have seen Him in the watchfires of a hundred circling camps;
They have builded Him an alter in the evening dews and damps;
I can read His righteous sentence by the dim and flaring lamps;
His day is marching on.

3. I have read a fiery gospel writ in burnished rows of steel;
As ye deal with My contemners, do with you My grace shall deal!
Let the Hero born of woman crush the serpent with His heel,
Since God is marching on.

4. He has sounded forth the trumpet that shall never call retreat;
He is sifting out the hearts of men before His judgment seat.
Oh, be swift, my soul, to answer Him! Be jubilant, my feet;
Our God is marching on.

5. In the beauty of the lilies Christ was born across the sea,
With a glory in his bosom that transfigures you and me;
As He died to make men holy let us die [live] to make men free,
While God is marching on.

CHORUS: *Glory, glory, hallelujah! Glory, glory, hallelujah!*
Glory, glory hallelujah! His truth is marching on."

[JULIA WARD HOWE, 1819-1910]

On 4 May 1864, at Wilderness, Virginia, Southern General Robert E. Lee attacked from the undergrowth, having waited silently until Grant's Union Army under General Meade had crossed the Rapidan River. They dented the Federal lines, but were forced to retreat and erect new defenses near Lee's headquarters. While this desperate struggle was continuing in the east, in Nevada, the small town of Panaca was born—the second oldest town in Nevada. Brigham Young, with Jacob Hamblin's suggestion, had sent a colony to settle the area of Meadow Valley, which the settlers then thought was part of the Utah Territory. Genoa (an 1849 *Mormon* trading post near Carson City) outdates Panaca as number one. (Some maps show Carson City and Virginia City as part of California in the original Nevada Territory.) Among these early L.D.S. settlers of Panaca was the Lee family, whose descendants claim a close relationship to General Robert E. Lee. These Lees were the grandparents of Harold B. Lee, the eleventh president of the L.D.S. Church of Jesus Christ (1972). Their old home still stands in the block south of our home. It has been remodeled, but the original structure is still there.

In 1860, the Comstock Lode, the richest deposit of precious metals ever found in the world, had been discovered and the miners flooded into Virginia City from California and came in wagon trains from the East on the Overland Trail. Other mining discoveries followed nearby. Washoe County became the center of treasure hunters from all over the world. When the Civil War broke out, the scant citizens of Nevada sent loyal troops to the front lines of the North. In September of 1863, an election was held for delegates to form a state constitution. The adoption of the 13th and 14th Amendments to the United States Constitution, which eliminated slavery and involuntary servitude, needed one additional vote by a loyal state. President Lincoln chose Nevada to be that new state, and on 31 Oct 1864, Nevada was given statehood, which swung the vote to the positive for these two amendments.

[Note: Amendment XIII (Adopted 1865) abolishes slavery; Amendment XIV (Adopted 1868) creates their citizenship, representation, loss of political privilege for acts of insurrection or rebellion, and gives Congress their right to enforce these actions. Interesting to me, it limits these privileges to only male citizens over 21 years of age—women and children are not included.]

Though their population was small, by the close of the Civil War, Nevada had produced $43,000,000 in gold and silver, which was of material assistance to the North. The State line was drawn; Panaca was included, along with Treasure Hill, 11 miles to the north, where silver deposits were said to be by the Indians. Pan-nuk-ker appears in Powell's vocabulary of the Ute of the White and Uintah Rivers, also a subdivision of the Southern Numa—its meaning is "metal, money, wealth."

Sharing the Meadow Valley Wash with Panaca a mile or two to the north was Bullionville—now a ghost town site. It was here that the miners built their mills. The area grew rapidly. The city of Pioche was built on Treasure Hill and grew to over 10,000 people by the early 1870s. It is said by some to have been the most violent city in the west with 240 claims bringing in gunmen to fight for their ownership. Seventy-three men were killed and occupied boot hill before anyone died a natural death. Over half of the Latter-day Saints who settled in the small town of Panaca wanted nothing to do with Nevada, and they moved back into the Utah Territory. The more populous Territory of Utah would not be granted statehood until 1894, thirty years later. Pioche soon became the county seat of Lincoln County, named after the president who gave them their state. The county then extended south to include the southern border of Nevada, along the Colorado River. It also included a small Mormon settlement called Las Vegas.

When the Republicans held their convention in June of 1864, there was still a question about who would be their candidate for president. Ulysses S. Grant was considered by some to be a better choice than President ABRAHAM LINCOLN. Grant was quite indignant when he was approached and stated,

> "Nothing would induce me to think of being a presidential candidate, particularly so long as there is a possibility of having Mr. LINCOLN reelected."

The war was going better for the North. LINCOLN was given the Republican nomination with Andrew Johnson as vice-president. Johnson had been appointed by LINCOLN as the military governor of the State of Tennessee.

The Republican dissenters, the Cleveland 400, broke with the party and nominated John C. Fremont for president. They called their new party "Radical Democracy." Fremont was the popular western explorer, who had written about his adventures in the west, including his personally spun version of the Mexican War in California. As a northern general in the Civil War, fighting against the southern general Stonewall Jackson, LINCOLN had found him incompetent and fired him. It was believed that the purpose of the "400" and his candidacy was to defeat LINCOLN by splitting the party—anyone but LINCOLN. As the North continued to win their battles and his campaign appeared to be fruitless, Fremont withdrew from the race and supported LINCOLN.

[Note: As a young man Fremont had eloped and married Senator Benton's daughter from Missouri.]

The democrats were still anchoring their platform in anti-war "Peace at any Price." They nominated another unhappy "fired" general for president, George Brinton McClellan. They still wanted "Union as it was." Slavery was acceptable. Needless to say, the South hoped McClellan would win. McClellan had been an exceptional general in organizing and training his troops; but his performance was usually too late or ineffective. McClellan felt that he would have the support of his soldiers; but the military stood strongly behind LINCOLN who got 116,887 votes, with only 33,748 for McClellan. The platform of the democrats appeared cowardly to them. The lives of their lost comrades should mean something of greater worth than capitulation.

When all the votes were counted, LINCOLN, who so many had thought could not be elected, won. He received a popular vote of 2,213,665 to 1,802,237 for McClellan. In the electoral vote he won 212 to 21. McClellan carried only three states, New Jersey, Kentucky, and Delaware. Additionally, there only remained one democrat governor in the North—Joel Parker in New Jersey. George McClellan resigned his commission in the army, and wrote his mother,

"The smoke has cleared away, and we are beaten!"

On 10 November, U. S. Grant sent a telegram to Washington, reading,

"The election having passed off quietly, no bloodshed or rioit [sic] throughout the land, is a victory worth more to the country than a battle won."

When the news reached the picket line, the sentinels in Grant's army fired their muskets to share the news with the Confederates across the Petersburg, Virginia, trenches.

It was a hot day in July 2004 that we visited the Petersburg battlefield. GROVER had left his hat back in the home of some of HYRUM's relatives in nearby Colonial Heights, Virginia. Not wanting him to get sunburned, we stopped by their gift shop to buy a hat. All they had were the soldier's hats of the two armies. GROVER chose the deep blue hat of the Union army. As he

started for the cash register to pay for it, HYRUM, who had grown up in this area, stopped him. Very seriously he told him,

"Wait a minute ! You're in the South. I think you better get the grey hat."

Not willing to give up his blue hat, he purchased one of each. On the first stop (depicted in the above picture) he wore the blue hat, leaving the grey one in the mini-van. The looks on the faces of many who were also touring the area were so negative that he changed his hat to grey on the next excursion to the Big Crater.

The big crater had been blasted out by the cannon shots from the north in an unsuccessful attempt to kill the southern soldiers who had dug their trenches and were successfully defending themselves.

That night, the miners of the Union troops filled sacks with dirt while they mined a passageway for a surprise attack on the enemy from behind their fortifications. Sadly, for the north, the Confederacy discovered the plan and a great number of the Union troops were massacred as they exited from the tunnel into the huge crater on the other side, which was increasingly filled-up with the bodies of blue-capped soldiers.

As we left the Big Crater area where a large group had gathered to hear the tour guide, a younger man caught up with us and referring to GROVER's grey cap he smilingly commented:

"Well, we can see where your ancestors came from. "

THE HAYNES FAMILY IN FRONT OF THE NORTHERN ENTRANCE INTO THEIR MINE.

We quickly countered, "We have relations from both sides," and changed the conversation to other things.

In our home in Nevada, we have placed the two army hats on each side of our pewter Civil War chess set. The opponents can wear the colors as they plot their actions.

On 4 Mar 1865, ABRAHAM LINCOLN was inaugurated as president for the second time. The following is taken from his Inaugural Address:

"On the occasion corresponding to this four years ago, all thoughts were anxiously directed to an impending civil war. All dreaded it—all sought to avert it. While the inaugural address was being delivered from this place, devoted altogether to saving the Union without war, insurgent agents were in the city seeking to destroy it without war—seeking to dissolve the Union, and divide effects, by negotiation. Both parties [sic] deprecated war; but one of them would make war rather than let the nation survive; and the other would accept war rather than let it perish. And the war came.

"One-eighth of the whole population was colored slaves, not distributed generally over the Union, but localized in the southern part of it. These slaves constituted a peculiar and powerful interest. All knew that this interest was, somehow, the cause of the war . . . . Neither party expected for the war the magnitude or the duration which it has already attained. . . . Each looked for an easier triumph and a result less fundamental and astounding. Both read the same Bible, and pray to the same God; and each invokes His aid against the other. It may seem strange that any men should dare to ask a just God's assistance in wringing their bread from the sweat of other men's faces; but let us judge not, that we be not judged. The prayers of both could not be answered—that of neither has been answered fully . . . . With malice toward none; with charity for all; with firmness in the right, as God gives us to see the right, let us strive on to finish the work we are in; to bind up the nation's wounds; to care for him who shall have borne the battle, and for his widow, and his orphan—to do all which may achieve and cherish a just and a lasting peace among ourselves, and with all nations."

One month later on 5 April, LINCOLN, with his son, Tad, holding his hand, walked into the Confederate White House in Richmond, Virginia, amid the cheers of the Union army and the former slaves that came out to greet him. He sat in the chair that had been occupied by Jefferson Davis only shortly before, and the Union troops broke into a loud hurrah. Four days later, on April 9th, General Robert E. Lee signed the papers of unconditional surrender, ending the long "War Between the States."

Six days later, 15 Apr 1865, ABRAHAM LINCOLN was attending a play at Ford's theater in Washington D.C. when the actor and assassin, John Wilkes Booth, started a new struggle for unity in American history by shooting the president, and shouting "Sic semper tyrannis!" ("Thus always to tyrants!").

THE HEADQUARTERS OF GENERAL ROBERT E. LEE IN RICHMOND, VIRGINIA.

He jumped from LINCOLN's booth down onto the stage and escaped. Booth was captured; refused to surrender, and was killed on 29 Apr 1865.

~ 113 ~

EPILOG

It was 7 May 1945—V-E Day. Hitler was dead; the Germans had surrendered. There was great excitement in our U.S. History class in Twin Falls High School as we waited for our delinquent teacher, Miss Rees. It was very unusual for her to be late. We felt almost like the whole World War II had ended—confident that V-J Day would not be very far away and our 16 million young American soldiers would return home. The class buzzed with the many changes that we anticipated in our daily lives:

No more rationing of gasoline and tires for our cars; older boys to date; no more food rationing; an end to the luxury tax; we could again buy bananas, real butter, photographic film, and nylon stockings. We would no longer need our red and blue food stamp ration books or tokens. Pennies would be made of copper again. There would be new post-war automobiles, refrigerators, and other new appliances; the blue and gold star flags would be removed from most of our windows. We remembered our dead friends and relations.

We would learn later that over 50 million people world-wide were killed in World War II.

My best friend, CAROL BEAN (also an unknown fourth-cousin), sat next to me. We had arrived very early, the previous September, to join the line to register for Miss Rees' only American History class. Miss Rees was probably in her early 60s, but very popular with the students as an exceptional drama teacher. She also taught a world history class, which we took our junior year. Miss Rees was able to make history live in our lives by constantly asking us,

"What does that event mean to you?"

"What can you learn from that event that will help you?"

"Why do we study history?"

"Will knowing this make you a better or wiser person?"

Current events were mandatory. One raised hand was never enough to be called on to answer a question. She liked to see hands from at least half the class and usually called on one of the more reluctant students to answer the question. She threatened an "F" if we ever said on a test that the Civil War was fought because of slavery instead of "state rights in opposition to our national constitution."

As Miss Rees finally entered the classroom, she held in her hand a hymn book she had just retrieved from a Protestant chapel. With tears streaming from her eyes and collecting on the lower part of her glasses, in her solid dramatic voice she read without further comment on the subject:

> *"God of our fathers, known of old,*
> *Lord of our far-flung battle line,*
> *Beneath whose awful hand we hold*
> *Dominion over palm and pine;*
> *Lord God of Hosts, be with us yet,*
> *Lest we forget,*
> *Lest we forget.*
>
> *The tumult and the shouting dies;*
> *The captains and the kings depart.*
> *Still stands thine ancient sacrifice,*
> *An humble and a contrite heart.*
> *Lord God of Hosts, be with us yet,*
> *Lest we forget,*
> *Lest we forget.*
>
> *Far-called, our navies melt away;*
> *On dune and headland sinks the fire.*
> *Lo, all our pomp of yesterday*
> *Is one of Nineveh and Tyre!*
> *Judge of the nations, spare us yet,*
> *Lest we forget,*
> *Lest we forget."*

[RUDYARD KIPLING, 1865-1936]

As I make my final cuts and additions to these pages, the computer tells me it is 22 Dec 2011—66 years since that day in May 1945, and an additional 80 years since ABRAHAM LINCOLN was assassinated because of his fortitude to preserve the nation and give new meaning to the Constitution, for both the North and the South, and the equality of mankind under its laws. I ask myself:

How are WE doing as a nation now?

Do we appreciate our Constitution inspired by God?

Is our nation the light of freedom to the world?

Do we defend the truth as we understand it with charity for all?

Do we remember our parents, friends, and neighbors that have sacrificed so much to give us this precious freedom from slavery, serfdom, and world tyranny?

Each one of us adds or detracts from these questions by our own individual response to these questions. Are we part of the givers or the takers each day?

The *Old Testament of the Holy Bible* ends with these two verses,

MALACHI 4:5, 6:

"Behold, I will send you Elijah the prophet before the coming of the
great and dreadful day of the Lord:
And he shall turn the heart of the fathers to the children,
and the heart of the children to their fathers,
lest I come and smite the earth with a curse."

To a few leaders of The Church of Jesus Christ of Latter-day Saints, Elijah the prophet appeared in the Kirtland Temple and started the fulfillment of this prophecy in 1836 by restoring the key that binds and seals the hearts and righteous souls of people throughout the nations of the world together—both the living and the dead. If you check the civil records of the nations of the earth, many of these birth and death records began in 1837, and the interest in genealogical research has been increasing world-wide ever since. Church records of births and baptisms go further back—most of their recordings extend back into the 1600s. The brotherhood (including the sisterhood) of all righteous people is important to God, our Father. We are all his sons and daughters.

During mid-September 2011, I joined with my sister ADELIA in Riverside, California, when her companion had an accident and was unable to to go on a *Gadabout Vacations'* tour to Branson, Missouri. We had a great time. I had been through Upper Missouri quite a few times, but this was my first time into the Ozarks of Lower Missouri. We were shuttled into LAX and then onto Southwest airlines. With a quick stop at Denver, Colorado, we landed at Kansas City, Missouri, airport, where we were bussed to the Westin Crown Center Hotel in downtown Kansas City, Missouri, for the evening—all of this in less than twelve hours.

As we flew over this 2000 mile expanse of the nation, I remembered the Mormon Battalion that had walked every step of the way carrying their backpacks, heavy guns, and ammunition, while building new roads, 100-foot-deep wells, crossing mountain ranges, wide rivers, at times without food or water, in 1846-7 in order to secure this territory as part of our American nation.

They had come from the Territory of Council Bluffs, Iowa, marched down the eastern side of the Missouri River and crossed it at Fort Leavenworth; marched to Santa Fe, (now New Mexico); down the Grand River until it turned eastward (forming the present boundry of Texas); continued west through winds, rains, and snow to the Mexican town of Tucson (Arizona); marched onward and with heavy wagons pulled by oxen that carried their supplies, passed by friendly Indian settlements—crossed the Colorado River, the Sierra Nevada Mountains. They killed some buffalo, some wild horned cattle for food, but never fired a shot at any man, woman, or child. They shouted for joy and saluted with their cannon when they first saw the Pacific Ocean in the distance, and then continued on to the Mexican communities of San Diego and Los Angeles. It doesn't seem so very long ago when you are 80 plus years old, but my air flight was a huge change from those days of my great-great-grandparents.

The next morning on our journey to Branson we went by motorcoach to the Truman Presidential Museum & Library, and my thoughts returned to the spunky short "I'm from Missouri and have to be shown" president with his small round eye glasses who without hesitation stated,

"The buck stops here!"

I recalled those last months of World War II. It was not as easy as we thought it would be back in May on V-E Day. The Japanese were fierce enemies. Here was a president, like LINCOLN, who had to choose the lesser of two evils. I remembered my husband's older brother, CHAD. He was stationed on Tinian, an island near Guam, and was part of the maintenance crew for the *Enola Gay* (named after the pilot's mother). CHAD had helped load the heavy atom-bomb on this bomber. Only the pilot knew of the potential power of this unusually large single bomb. The detonator was carried on separately by the pilot. Two armed bombers flew nearby until the shores of Japan came into view, but their plane had no armour to protect them from enemy fire; it would rely on the extra speed it would gain without armour to get back to the base at Tinian. They had been given four possible destinations, depending on weather conditions. Hiroshima was the only one without rain or cloud cover. It would be the target. Within minutes of their destination, with enemy guns from the mainland exploding continuously slightly lower—but bouncing the *Enola Gay* with their turbulence—the pilot called his crew together and explained to them the terrible cargo they were carrying and gave them their instructions to put the detonator carefully into the bomb. It was mandatory they wear the very dark glasses that were provided after the bomb was dropped; definitely not look at the explosion, and buckle up tightly for the aftershock—and then get out of there! Within seconds, the world would know the results of their mission—but Japan still refused to surrender. Several days latter another bomb was dropped on Nagasaki and Japan surrendered.

I watched the *History Channel* a few years ago when they explained that the Japanese were within two weeks of having sufficient numbers of a very secret, newly developed, and much faster JET fighters from plans given to them by Germany—a great threat to our whole propeller air force and navy planes (none of which could go faster than the speed of sound)—thus their delay in surrendering. Russia did not declared war on Japan until after the atom-bomb was dropped.

As we motored south through the Missouri/Kansas border counties, the Missouri bushwhackers and Kansas jayhawkers came to mind. I looked for the craggy rocks and dense foliaged forests the bushwhackers had hidden in, as well as picturing in my mind the ugly consequence when Union border commander Thomas Ewing signed into law General Orders, No. 11. Roughly 20,000 people were given 15 days to evacuate these four border counties before the Union soldiers fired their homes, crops, forests, fences, creating a blazing inferno, until all that was left was the tall brick or rock chimneys standing as sentinels in the midst of their smoldering lands in 1863—with cattle and pigs tearing through the countryside. The old men, and women with crying babies tramped eastward to try to find some kind of food and lodging.

[Note: The following descriptive quotes of Missouri in those days of 1861-5 are taken from *Missouri's Scarlet of Blood and Crime*, by Rev. W. M. Leftwich, D. D. —see CHC volume I pp. 546-553 by B. H. Roberts.]

"The extremists, north and south, whether religious or political, found the heartiest supporters in Missouri: . . . 'Here houses were divided, two against three and three against two,' a man was set at variance with his father and the daughter against her mother, and the daughter-in-law against her mother-in-law, and 'a man's foes were they of his own household. . . . the children shall rise up against their parents and cause them to be put to death:' and the spirit of contention was too rife to confine itself to the hostile armies, or even the lawless bands of armed men, who, in the name of one party or the other, satiated their diabolical hatred and inordinate cupidity by robbery, plunder, pillage, and depopulation with fire and sword. . . . This state furnished the bravest men for the armies and the most dastardly cowards for 'home protection.' . . . While their brave sons fell upon the fields of honor . . . the warfare at home presented scenes of outrage and horror unsurpassed by anything in the annals of civilized warfare, if, indeed, there can be such a thing as civilized warfare . . . The offices of law and the courts were alike powerless to punish crime and protect innocence: 'and because iniquity did abound the love of many waxed cold,' . . . more than one . . . were called from their beds at midnight to be shot down like dogs, or butchered like hogs in the very presence of their families, without warning, without any known provocation, and without knowing their murderers. . . .

"Many a well stocked farm was stripped of everything that could be carried off and the dwelling burnt to the ground, because it was said the family had southern sympathies; . . . Ministers of the gospel suffered in common with others. . . . They fled to the army for protection, or the brush, and banded together for revenge. . . . Property and life were thus put at the mercy of unprincipled detectives and spies, selected often from the lowest and most unscrupulous classes of men and women. . . . Men and famlies broke up, and taking what they could with convenience and safety fled for life and protection, some north, some south, some to Canada, some to California, some to the army, some to the large cities, and some to the brush. . . .

"The moral forces of society were paralyzed, powerless, the old standards of virtue, integrity, honest and right principle were broken down and swept away, and men became reckless of the laws of God and man. In the fury and fire of partisan strife, and amid the familiar scenes of blood and death, men trampled upon right, crucified truth, murdered innocence, loved vengeance, despised virtue, abandoned principle, forgot their loves, left their dead unburied and their buried uncoffined, and hung upon the bloody war path like avenging furies.

"Missouri lived to see their system of slave labor abolished by the setting free of some one hundred and fifteen thousand slaves, valued at $40,000,000, eight thousand of whom were 'martialed and disciplined for war' in the federal armies, and many of them marched to war against their former masters. ... In other states the war lasted at most but four years; but counting her western border warfare in the struggle for Kansas, the war was waged in western Missouri from 1855 to 1865, ten years; and for many years after the close of the Civil War, a guerrilla warfare was intermittently carried on by bands of outlaws harbored in western Missouri—especially in Jackson, Ray, Caldwell and Clay counties—that terrorized the community and shocked the world by the daring and atrocity of their crimes—including bank robberies in open day, express train wrecking and robberies, and murders. Not until 1881 was this effectually stopped...."

[Note: As told in more detail in *Part I: DRIVEN*, my second-great-grandfather's brother TOM returned from Utah to Missouri where his mother, my third-great-grandmother SARAH ALLRED IVIE, was still living in 1859. After he was released from jail by General Albert Sidney Johnston at Camp Floyd, Utah, he was killed by bushwhackers, it is believed, in 1862. One of the bushwhackers might have been his brother-in-law, who also was probably killed in 1864—when his will was probated. It had been predicted by Brigham Young, according to my ALLRED cousins, that TOM would be "killed in a cornfield and the vultures would pick his bones." My elderly eighty-one-year-old Missouri third-great-grandmother's will was probated in Missouri April 1862. We have not yet discovered where she was buried. Was she a good woman? I believe so. Her daughter SARAH IVIE LONG's will was probated around the 1870s. She left an inheritance to her five children and her two brothers, THOMAS C. IVIE and my second-great-grandfather JAMES RUSSELL IVIE. She evidently didn't know that both of them had been killed—TOM by the bushwhackers and JAMES by Black Hawk and his warriors in Utah. Later the Monroe County, Missouri, clerk advertised that they had not yet claimed their inheritance.]

Back to our tour to Branson with director Bob Alsup, we were given a rest stop at Hard Work U. This is a university that requires their students to work their way through to their loan-free bachelor's degrees—if they qualify as needy, able, and willing students. With the supervision of the faculty, the students build and care for their beautiful buildings, campus, church, patios, fields, vegetable gardens, milk cows, cattle, pigs, advertise and sell their produce, art work, sewing, books, technology, buss and wait tables, cook their own dining hall meals—along with the meals for the faculty and paying guests. Their graduates do not have any problems finding jobs for they have learned to work, produce, sell, study, expand their talents, and feel the satisfaction of enjoying the results.

At Branson, during our four day stay, we attended six highly professional theater shows in different theaters, visited the largest and very interesting Titanic Museum, shopped in the Old Town Branson businesses of yester-years, and had dinner on board the Showboat Branson Belle, while being entertained by great musicians and comics, as we cruised around the large lake. All of this was done without crude jokes or actions and with great courtesy and care for children and older people. All the programs included patriotic, country, operatic arias, Hollywood, and religious music—performed by professionals. It was fun with great entertainment and excellent restaurants. The greatest part of the audiences was senior citizens and military people. They arrived by bus loads. Many families arrived on the weekend.

ADELIA AND BROOKIE BY THE SHOW BOAT.

When our *Gadabout* troop collected in the motorcoach to return to Kansas City, our director Bob asked the group which was our favorite show. Mostly we agreed that although we loved all of them, the *Brett Family Show* came in first. Their 26-year-old talented *Mormon* returned missionary Master of Ceremonies had won the honor of best MC by the local Branson judges. He pulled his family, and the audience, into a fast-paced production of singing, dancing, and a good-feeling variety comedy that will be long remembered. He even included dribbling a basketball with such control of the ball that university offers have been profuse, but the family chooses to stay together. The Three Texas Tenors appeared to be our second choice. They had come in second place in TV's *America has Talent.*

On our way back to Kansas City, the sixth day, I noticed a junction sign pointing to Johnson County, on the right. This reminded me of my grandfather GIBSON A CONDIE. On his 1887 Southern States church mission, age 19 to 21, he spent many months in Johnson County, [see *Part II: STANDING FIRM,*] where he baptized the Henry James family—among others.

I remembered the last time I saw my grandfather alive. He was 95 years old and my former Chief of Police uncle JAMES IRA and aunt MARY LLOYD CONDIE, with my cousins MARY LOUISE and BOB BUNKER, and their son BOB, were driving him from Alhambra, California, to Stevensville, Montana, where my uncle JAMES A. and aunt ADA CONDIE BAIRD were living at that time. Aunt ADA was a nurse, and grandfather's health was in need of more attention by this very willing daughter.

On their journey north, they stopped over-night with us in Pioche, Nevada. We took the group to Mrs. Wah's for one of her amazing steak dinners at Caselton's Combined Metal's (closed down) mining operation. Mrs. Wah and her husband were of Chinese descent and cooked for the remaining maintenance miners in one of their larger metal buildings. In the evenings, if we made reservations, they would serve the local groups either a very large T-bone steak or a Chinese dinner. The shrimp cocktail was the first course (large prawns shipped in fresh from San Francisco) in a special ketchup/horseradish sauce. The second course was a light Chinese soup with hot rolls and butter with a side-dish of fruit (usually a half peach or pear in light syrup). Next—the large inch-thick very tender steak with a perfectly baked fresh Idaho potato and a side-dish vegetable. The last course was a homemade and fresh strawberry pie topped with real whipped cream. The strawberries were raised in her own garden. It was more food than grandfather wanted, and most of his dinner was passed on to the male cousins, who took very good care that it was not wasted. They were quick to tell us it was as good as any in Los Angeles.

The group stayed that night at a local motel, but grandfather wanted to stay with us. He tried out our living room couch and said it would do very well, if we could furnish him a pillow and blanket. He then proceeded to tell us about his mission to the Southern States. Once in awhile we could say "Yes" or nod our heads, but mostly we listened, for even 95-year-old men enjoy an audience— and he was fun. His eyes would sparkle and he would chuckle with delight with his stories. It was 3:00 A.M. before we went to bed that night. We loved him, and he obviously had loved his mission and an opportunity to tell us about it.

It began in Rutherford County, North Carolina, where he could view from a distance at times *King's Mountain* of Revolutionary War fame. Then he took the *Turkey Tail Railroad* back to Chattanooga, Tennessee, where he viewed the cemetery where 25,000 Union troops were buried and climbed the mountain to view the Civil War battlefield. He took the train to Kansas City, Missouri, where he saw trolleys that were not horse-drawn for the first time. Then it was on to Johnson County. He would end his mission in the Kansas countryside across the Missouri River. All of this was done without purse or script—except the *Bible* and the *Book of Mormon*. He preached, taught, prayed, healed and comforted the sick, and was seldom hungry or without lodging in the midst of these good Christian people, whom he loved.

Back in Kansas City from our trip to Branson, our motorcoach drove past the huge Union Pacific railroad depot; then making a few additional turns we parked in the Hallmark Visitors Center parking lot for another adventure. We were greeted by their very gracious receptionist who explained to us the magnificent huge mural *The Four Seasons* designed by retired Hallmark artist Don Dubowski and crafted by 100 company artisans and technicians—done in various metals and covering a 25 by 8 foot portion of the wall in their reception room.

In many ways, it reminded me of my home landscape. We have the apple blossoms and iris in the spring; followed by water lilies in our ponds with occasional coveys of quail. We do not have the swans, but large groups of Canadian geese fly overhead and honking, land in the swamp lands west of our home— going north in the spring and south in the fall. During the season, the hunter's shotguns can be heard from time to time. The barn swallows make their nests on the storm drains by our kitchen window, where we watch them feed their little ones the flying insects over our ponds through the spring and summer. They fly south with their broods near the end of August. The long-legged sandhill cranes come at times in the early mornings mostly and try to spear our many varieties of frogs and fish, but will not go into the deeper water. They fly away awkwardly if we make any noise. The tufted blue and white kingfishers will watch from our oak tree or a nearby post—they live up to their name when the fish appear. The cattails form in the summer and fall, and freeze when winter approaches. One winter, with snow on the banks of our ponds, nine tufted, multicolored wood ducks arrived and stayed a few days. They seemed to enjoy our warm pond, and would slow their rapid descent into the water by placing their spread webbed feet in front of them as brakes to slow down their fast landings, quacking happily to their companions as they smoothly spun around in the available water. The mule deer can be seen around our town throughout the year. I saw eleven in our neighbor's yard yesterday. We fenced them out of our yard, because they eat and destroy most plants and gardens. A group of about twelve sleep during the day in a large grove of Russian olive a short distance behind my daughter's home. One time after a long hot summer, the reservoirs were nearly dried up and while my husband was working in our yard, a large bald eagle swooped down at a great speed into our larger pond—going deeply into the water. He shortly surfaced with one of our foot long gold fish in his claws, and then landed on a nearby power pole to greedily eat it, while we watched. I read about the bald eagles in our *Birds of North America* book. I hadn't known before that bald eagles eat fish and golden eagles eat rodents. They can spot fish from a great distance and dive into the water going as fast as 200 miles per hour.

We had been told by our tour guide before we went into the Hallmark Center that we needed to tour their restrooms —whether we needed to use their vacilities or not, for they were magnificent. We were not disappointed.

Afterwards we were guided to their theater for a video about founder, J. C. Hall. Young Mr. Hall grew up during the great depression of the 1930s, like I did. His family was very poor. As a child, he tried to help his family by selling post cards from a shoe box to the passengers that arrived in Kansas City on the Union Pacific Railroad. From this humble beginning, with his American ingenuity, he was able to expand his tiny business to what it is today—world-wide Hallmark greeting cards, sold in Hallmark stores, and the *Hallmark Channel* television production. They claim—

"Hallmark! When you Care enough to send the very Best!"

One of their stores was our neighbor-next-door for 20 years, when we owned Swallows Drugs in the University Mall in Orem, Utah. They were our competitors, as we sold American Greeting Cards, but their personnel were our friendly customers for many of the other things that we sold.

I was impressed with a painting in the Hallmark Fine Art Collection that was commissioned by Hallmark Card founder J. C. Hall to commemorate the rebuilding of Kansas City after the 1951 flood—*The Kansas City Spirit*, created by artists Norman Rockwell and John Atherton. I like the portrayal of the huge manly architect rolling up his shirt sleeves and getting to work when trouble came. I like his size—a giant in the earth that goes forward to meet any challenge this world might give him. I like the action—building, not sitting still; airplanes flying; trains moving; crops harvested. I even like the contented look on the face of the corn-fed Hereford steer in the stock yard, chewing his cud and getting fat before giving his all to the restaurants and homes across America. To me the picture not only shows the *brotherhood* required in the building of Kansas City, but also the *brotherhood* and the Spirit of the American People, as written in that beloved song we still sing about our country—*America the Beautiful*:

> *Oh, beautiful for spacious skies, For amber waves of grain,*
> *For purple mountain majesties Above the fruited plain! . . .*
> *Oh, beautiful for pilgrim feet, Whose stern, impassioned stress*
> *A thoroughfare of freedom beat Across the wilderness!*
> *America! America! God mend thine ev'ry flaw,*
> *Confirm thy soul in self-control, Thy liberty in law.*
>
> *Oh, beautiful for heroes proved In liberating strife,*
> *Who more than self their country loved,*
> *And mercy more than life!*
> *America! America! May God thy gold refine,*
> *Till all success be nobleness, And ev'ry gain divine.*
>
> *Oh! Beautiful for patriot dream That sees beyond the years*
> *Thine alabaster cities gleam, Undimmed by human tears!*
> *America! America! God shed his grace on thee,*
> *And crown thy good with brotherhood From sea to shining sea.*

[*Text:* KATHERINE LEE BATES, 1859-1929; *Music:* SAMUEL A. WARD, 1848-1903]

From the Hallmark Art Gallery, we were taken to the area where we could view their actual production personnel, tools, and machinery making and engraving their beautiful greeting cards that bring cheer to the entire world. Here, they would answer our many questions.

As a final farewell, they gave each of us a wrapped gift, which we took with us to the motorcoach that drove us to the airport for our return flight to LAX. I did not open it until I returned home, where I found it to be a *Hallmark Recordable Storybook* of the birth of our Savior Jesus Christ, beautifully illustrated. They also included three post cards: *The Spirit of Kansas City; The Four Seasons,* and *The Hallmark Visitors Center.* How very thoughtful.

The last verse of *America the Beautiful* reminds me of the last book in *The New Testament of our Lord and Saviour Jesus Christ, Revelation 21, 22:*

"And I saw a new heaven and a new earth: for the first heaven and
the first earth were passed away; and there was no more sea.
And I John saw the holy city, new Jerusalem, coming down from
God out of heaven, prepared as a bride adorned for her husband.
And I heard a great voice out of heaven saying,
Behold, the tabernacle of God is with men,
and he will dwell with them, and they shall be his people, and God
himself shall be with them, and be their God.
And God shall wipe away all tears from their eyes;
And there shall be no death, neither sorrow, nor crying,
neither shall there be any more pain:
For the former things are passed away. . . .
He that overcometh shall inherit all things;
and I will be his God, and he shall be my son. . . .
And he shewed me a pure river of water of life, clear as crystal,
proceeding out of the throne of God and of the Lamb.
In the midst of the street of it, and on either side of the river,
Was there the tree of life, which bare twelve manner of fruits,
and yielded her fruit every month: and the leaves of the tree
were for the healing of the nations.
And there shall be no more curse: but the throne of God and
of the Lamb shall be in it; and his servants shall serve him: . . .

*Behold, I come quickly: blessed is he that keepeth
the sayings of the prophecy of this book."*

When I read these verses from the Apostle John's *Revelation,* I am always reminded of an occasion when someone in heaven actually wiped my tears from my eyes:

It started one morning back in 1971 when my husband, GROVER SWALLOW was at Carson City as the Chairman of the Education Committee during the Nevada Assembly Session of that year and I was one of the five member Lincoln County school board. I was the only woman on the board.

As the pharmacist, I needed to open the pharmacy part of our Swallows Drugs at 10:00 A. M. —so with my two-year-old son GROVER in our station wagon, we stopped at our local Panaca postoffice to get our mail, before I drove the 15 miles to Caliente. I was surprised to find that I had to sign for a certified letter. Of course, I immediately read the letter. There was a little fear, for certified letters seem ominous, and the return address showed it was from our Lincoln county school superintendent. I knew he was unhappy with me, for we had some unhappy discussions the previous week, after the school board meeting— but a certified letter? It was not a kind letter.

My original bravado was slowly eaten away as I drove the fifteen miles— alone with my cute little sleeping son and my memories. The school board meeting had been a rather hot one for our communities. The question was about the consolidation of the elementary schools in Panaca and Pioche and the bussing of children the eleven miles between the two towns. I represented the Panaca area on the school board. The people of Pioche were not unhappy—they faced a possible three grades under one teacher, if it didn't pass.

We moved the school board meeting to the largest high school classroom to accommodate the huge group of concerned citizens from Panaca—many of them wanted to speak on the issue, and the temper temperature kept getting hotter and hotter—they felt Pioche had been strongly favored in the arrangement. It was their school that was short on students, not Panaca.

[Note: Pioche is at least 1200 feet higher in the mountains. They always have more snow in the winter. Panaca would be bussing far more students up than were coming down, and their students going up the mountain included all of the kindergarten children plus the third and fouth grades. Only the fifth and sixth grade students were coming from Pioche to Panaca.]

Emotions were charged high enough that the president of the board, coached by the superintendent, called an executive session to decide the vote—which means that only the board and the superintendent would be present. This disturbed me and I questioned this procedure; but the rest of them assured me it was legal, as it involved how many teachers would be needed. The question was quickly called for and seconded without discussion. I voted "No." The Pioche member and one of the Caliente members voted "Yes." The other Caliente elderly member had made promises he would never consolidate any schools, and he simple said, "Not voting." The superintendent quickly declared, "It's two to one and passed." The president of the board (at that time from Alamo), according to our local rules, did not vote unless there was a tie. I protested it was not a majority, but was totally ignored.

The many Panaca people had waited in the hall and were called back in and told that the board had passed the question. They were angry. After the meeting was adjourned, I told these friends that our procedure was wrong and I was going to check my NRS (Nevada Revised Statutes) as soon as I got home. Every assemblyman has his own volumes. At home, I quickly verified the Nevada state school board laws. I was right. An executive session could only be called by the board for individual personnel matters—everything else must be voted publicly, and the vote had to be a majority of the total board—two votes could never be a majority. It was late. I called the superintendent, as the board president was driving the 80 miles to his home—no cell phones at that time. I explained that the vote was illegal and therefore void. He was not a swearing man, but he was a very angry man. There would be another board meeting.

Earlier in our board meeting that night, I had told them I was going to drive the 456 miles to Carson City for a Monday legislative session. I was our board's legislative representative and had been requested by the State School Board Association to be there. They wanted support on a legislative bill that would allow the boards an addional year before tenure became effective.

In determining the date for the special board meeting, the upset superintendent deliberately placed it on the same day as my Carson City meeting and the legislative vote on this school board bill. I had already made arrangements for a pharmacist, someone to care for my children, and was packed to go. I called our school board president and explained that I couldn't attend the meeting that day. They could either change the date, or hold it without me, which I thought would be all right as I would definitely vote "No" if present—which would not help the majority vote they needed. He agreed. He wanted me in Carson City.

When the superintendent found out I was not going to the local board meeting, he called me and talked for nearly two hours—basically accusing me of creating the need in the first place, and then not going. He would not change the date. I had already explained the problem to the Panaca people.

I went to the legislature and sat next to my husband on the floor of the assembly. He was chairman of the Education Committee, whom had given the bill a "Do Pass." He would introduce the school board bill on the assembly floor for the final vote. When he asked me what to do, because the NSEA (union) strongly opposed the bill and had filled the balcony with teachers, I told him:

"Give the school boards a break. We really need that extra year to assess beginning teachers. Pass it."

He spoke briefly on the bill and gave it his personal as well as the committee's "Do Pass" endorsement. It passed the assembly—previously the senate. No one spoke or voted in opposition to its passage, as I remember.

Unions don't like to be beaten, so a phone call from their boss was made to our local chapter president with the message:

"Get rid of Mrs. Swallow on the school board. She's too powerful."

My local friend told me about it. He had simply told them that they liked me on the board, and I had done them a lot of good.

I believe the same man also called the superintendent, although I didn't suspect it at that time. Many school administrators were part of the NSEA and GROVER was an even greater target than I was. The superintendent's vicious participation in events during the following two years is told in *Part II: STANDING FIRM*—which may help to explain why the certified letter, in which he refused to pay my $92 expenses for the journey to the capital, was so personally mean and destructively written.

I was also told by my women friends that the county school board meeting had been held in Alamo—80 miles south of Panaca—too early in the day for the working husbands to attend. Fourteen women drove down early so they could talk personally to the president of the board. He had called them to their faces:

"a bunch of emotional women who were incapable of reason!"

The superintendent had tried to make my absence appear as an affront to those I was supposed to represent, but their anger was against the three that voted "Yes" and the superintendent that obviously manipulated them.

When I reached the drugstore in Caliente after reading his certified letter, my emotions had taken over. I was distressed and felt sorry for myself. The tears were near the surface and I thought my eyes would be red as I placed my sleeping son in the apartment behind the prescription room. I had three customers waiting for prescriptions.

I filled the first prescription and was ringing up the sale on our cash register when the customer saw my face and asked if something was wrong. That did it! I burst into tears. I managed to tell her I would be all right but ran back to the apartment as soon as she left for the front door. I didn't know what else to do.

With the door closed to the apartment and only a small light coming in a tiny back window, I stood by my sleeping son and looking towards the heavens I cried out loud to my earthly father, who had died when I was ten years old:

"All right! You got me into this! Now you get me out of it! I'm tired of it all!"

It was amazing—just like an eraser had passed rapidly through my head. All my pent up emotions were totally gone—along with my tears. My eyes were dry; my self-pity was gone—all in an instant. I immediately went back into the store and filled the waiting prescriptions with total calmness and control of my emotions. I have never forgotten or ceased to thank whoever helped me at that time, but I know that someone is able to "wipe away the tears from their eyes."

That day, with a clear head, I realized that the impassioned letter I had received was a gift—for it was a written document. Copy machines, as we know them today, had not been invented at that time. If we wanted to make copies, we put carbon paper in our typewriters. A very small copy method had been developed and the little machine had been sent us as an introductive gift for our drugstore. My husband was in the stake presidency in our church at that time and had taken it to their stake clerk, who was also a teacher in our high school. When the store closed at 6:00 P. M., I typed an explanatory personal letter and took the two letters to the clerk to make me five copies of each of them. He smiled but suggested he would prefer I not mention that he had helped me. The small machine did a nice job. I then mailed a copy of each letter to each of the four board members and the fifth set to the district attorney.

The next day, after they had received their letters, one of the two Caliente members came in and laughingly told me he would vote to pay my expenses. I got a phone call from the board president in Alamo. He was indignant that the superintendent had refused to pay me. He had told me personally to go to Carson City. That evening the district attorney called me at home. He jokingly told me if the board wouldn't pay me, let him know and he would see that I got my $92.

Early the next morning the superintendent asked me to come to his office, so I went. He was quite pompous and pulled out his tape recorder and started to further explain why he couldn't put my expenses on the agenda. At the first opportunity, I stopped him and explained what I had done. The idea that the copies of his letter had already been sent out to the members of the school board and the district attorney was very disturbing to him. His color was quite ashen, and his hand shook a little when he looked down at his own carbon copy to see what he had said. Needless to say, the travel expense was put on the agenda and the board voted to reimburse me with suppressed laughter in their eyes; but I was also sure that there was not the same good will at the end of the table where the superintendent was sitting with his stotic expression. Unknown to me at that time, but it would become apparent a few years later, I had also gained the respect of the smiling board member from Caliente. After he had lost his election, he was mostly silent but a very effective help in keeping sanity of purpose in the school board through our lame-duck meetings.

The school problem took longer to resolve. The children were bussed as the board had dictated; however, today we have much newer and beautiful elementary K-6 schools in each town with much updated middle and high school complexes. My daughter teaches first grade in Panaca, and her two-youngest-high-school sons are especially delighted with the new auditorium with its much larger stage and lighting for their drama, show choir, community, and band productions. Mostly we now have what we "emotional, incapable of thinking" women of Panaca envisioned for our own children forty years ago.

As I view these new buildings, my thoughts sometimes go back to the 1969 legislative session. My husband GROVER had entered a bill that went to the Ways and Means Committee. With most of our schools deteriorated and condemned and the county trying hard to meet their bills, this bill would give our school district $500,000 (1969 dollars) for a new school complex. During that legislative session, GROVER was struck down with a kidney stone and rushed to the hospital. While he was there, the Committee decided to cheer him up and passed the bill through the Assembly without any opposition. When it was sent to the Senate Finance Committee, I attended the meeting. Our superintendent was there with a few of his supporters. The chairman of the Finance Committee was our old senator from Lincoln County, who had changed his residence to Las Vegas when the reapportionment of the state legislatures had been forced upon all of the states by the U. S. Supreme Court in 1964. Between the superintendent plus his cohorts and the chairman, the bill was quickly killed with very little discussion allowed. When the superintendent was asked by my husband why he had done this, about four years later, the superintendent simple stated:

> "I did it, because you killed my bill to consolidate the Lincoln County School District with the Clark County School District. I thought you needed to know how it felt!"

The bill referred to, for consolidation of the two districts, had been voted down by the people of Lincoln County in a special vote initiated by our county commissioners to give the people of the county a chance to express their wishes. If the superintendent had been willing to work with GROVER, I feel sure that the half million dollar bill would have passed in the Senate to help in any way we needed. Instead, he had deliberately stirred up some of the people of the county against it. It was a simple bill that could have been used toward doing much of what we have today—over forty years later. I still don't understand this type of power play, but our federal government leaders with their cohorts seem to, at times, also ignore, stir-up, deliberately destroy, and try to control (for foolish and selfish reasons) large numbers of our citizens in much the same way. Why does this remind me of Christ overlooking Jerusalem, saying: *St. Luke 13: 34?*

"O Jerusalem, Jerusalem . . . how often would I have gathered thy children together, as a hen doth gather her brood under her wings, and ye would not."

[Note: Part II: STANDING FIRM tells more about the Nevada Legislature, including how GROVER as vice-chairman of the Health and Welfare Committee—with help—spearheaded the *defeat* of the bills that would have made Nevada the first state in our nation to *legalize abortions*. The national pro-choice group had felt Nevada was where they wanted to start the movement, and they threw a large amount of time and money into trying to accomplish it. The pro-choice bills never passed in Nevada. The Roe v Wade Supreme Court decision forced it on us.]

~ IN CONCLUSION ~

BROAD are the BRANCHES
Including all four parts:
DRIVEN,
STANDING FIRM,
REBELLION, and
UNITED STATES ?
Is dedicated to
MANKIND and TRUTH

TRUTH is—the Axioms of Geometry and all Mathematics that never change—upon which all Theories and Reasoning are built. Truth includes the Axioms of the basic Elements of Chemistry (all MATTER), and Physics (all ENERGY—WORK) that act upon each other to create change, but never can destroy themselves, because these basic Axioms are eternal. They cannot be created or destroyed—the building blocks of the Universe, which is endless and which is controlled by a supreme INTELLIGENCE (God), that is Omnipotent (all powerful), Omniscient (all knowing), Omnipresent (always present.) To Him we should be Omni-devoted, because He is the WAY, the TRUTH, and the LIGHT, eternally loving and good, and also because our own eternal intelligence was previously with Him. He in His great wisdom has organized this world from these eternal elements and allowed us to come here to obtain mortal bodies that we may continue to grow in righteousness (good), or choose to stop our growth and degard ourselves (evil) each moment we are here—for there is opposition in all things. Good (happiness) and Evil (misery), are also eternal. We arrive and are nurtured in this world by the goodness and labor of others. We cannot grow individually in righteousness by ourselves, but must include love and service in our lives, not destroy those who are willing to work to do us good by using their many individually earned or inherited talents to make us a family, community, nation, and a world of happier people. To be alone without friends or family (solitary confinement—even in a palace of gold) cannot be happiness, especially if you add to it the absence of God and conscience—also absent—TV, books, all goodness—sans everything. Only memories of what might have been. A "wretch concentered all in self" and where only evil is king.

The HISTORY of MANKIND—started approximately 4000 years before the birth of our SAVIOR, JESUS CHRIST. For that was the time that God had completed his preparations—God took the basic eternal elements and organized them in what he called days [periods of time] and gave us, His Children, mortal bodies of flesh and bones with a *conscience* that we might know the difference between good and evil—[something not previously on this earth.]

Mankind as we know them are CHILDREN OF GOD, made in his image— able to think, learn to read, write, speak and communicate ideas, love and protect others and be loved in return—man with a conscience—with an ability to plan, organize, and do—in an environment fit to help him and his brothers and sisters to rise and grow strong in love together through all seasons of good and adverse conditions while they remain here.

Once more God set his eternal clock—there would be seven more days (in this case, each a thousand earthly years—based on the time for each earthly rotation around the sun. His righteous children were organized and given their opportunities for their individual growth for good, or, if they chose, their own selfish pleasure. We agreed to the plan. If our mortal clocks are right, we are now in the very beginning of this promised Seventh Day that is called in the words of His scriptures—*the Millenium*—a time of peace—but darkness proceeds the dawn. The shadows must be cleared away before the light can come with all its glory. The righteous children, who have joined the angels of heaven, and those who remain on this earth, are preparing for His coming. May we all be among that number of Saints, because of our Faith in his righteousness, our

Hope—by standing firm for righteousness, and above all for our Charity for all of Mankind— past, present, and the future still to come. That is my wish.

Also, remember—It takes a majority! Don't be too hard on the minorities that are trying to do their very best—they need help, not criticism.

BROOKIE CONDIE SWALLOW

*"I heard the bells on Christmas day
 Their old familiar carols play,
 And wild and sweet the words repeat
 Of peace on earth, good will to men.*

*I thought how, as the day had come,
 The belfries of all Christendom
 Had rolled along th' unbroken song
 Of peace on earth, good will to men.*

*And in despair I bowed my head:
 'There is no peace on earth' I said,
 'For hate is strong and mocks the song
 Of peace on earth, good will to men.'*

*Then pealed the bells more loud and deep:
 'God is not dead, nor doth he sleep;
 The wrong shall fail, the right prevail,
 With peace on earth, good will to men.'*

*Till, ringing, singing, on its way,
 The world revolved from night to day,
 A voice, a chime, a chant sublime,
 Of peace on earth, good will to men!"*

[HENRY WADSWORTH LONGFELLOW, 1807-1882
Music by JOHN BAPTISTE CALKIN, 1827-1905]

— ABOUT THE AUTHOR —

Born just before the beginning of the Great Depression of wonderful parents, Brookie Condie spent her early childhood on a large sheep and cattle ranch near Carey, Idaho, by the Craters of the Moon National Monument. Just before Hitler started his invasion of Europe, her beloved father died of cancer, leaving her mother with the ranch and seven young children. Brookie was the third oldest child at ten years old. Shortly after Pearl Harbor, the family moved to Twin Falls, where she graduated from Twin Falls High School with high honors.

Excelling in math and science, she chose pharmacy as a career and attended Idaho State College in Pocatello, Idaho, where she met and married her handsome husband, Grover Swallow, also a pharmacy major, in the LDS Manti Temple in 1948. World War II had ended and there were over two hundred new pharmacists in her 1950 graduation class. They were mostly GI Bill veterans. She was one of only three women pharmacists and graduated summa cum laude. The couple worked many low pay jobs to finance their educations. At college, Brookie played the violin in the Idaho State Symphony orchestra.

To become a registered pharmacist, Brookie worked in Logan and Smithfield, Utah, and Preston, Idaho, where her husband was also working. In 1954, he became a partner in a drug store in Montpelier, Idaho. Always active in church and community activities and playing violin solos, Brookie wrote short plays for local entertainment, and directed one of her ten minute road shows that placed first in the area. Four children were born during these years. As always, Grover was chosen as a leader in church and community organizations. They also became interested in the genealogy of their families. Brookie loved to teach adults and taught in the Gospel Doctrine class—the New Testament, Acts through Revelations. The class more than doubled in size.

Wanting their own drugstore, they purchased the Pioche Pharmacy in Nevada. Brookie sold her first publication to *Sunset Magazine* in 1957 to promote tourism into the area, while writing a fiction novel she chose not to try to publish. She then enrolled in Art Instruction, Inc., later graduating and specializing in illustrations. In the fall of 1958, they purchased a second drugstore in Caliente, which Grover managed, while she was pharmacist in Pioche and did the accounting for both stores.

Living in a three bedroom home, cut into the mountain behind the drugstore in the mining town of Pioche, became more difficult as the children grew and became more numerous. So with the birth of number seven in 1962, they purchased and remodeled a larger home in Panaca with extra acreage, driving north and south to their two businesses. The high school for the three towns was located in Panaca. Ever interested in the education of her children, Brookie was elected as the only woman on their five member Lincoln County school board.

The mandatory U.S. Reapportionment legislation by the Supreme Court in 1964 left the county without a legislator, and the destruction of their local economy began rapidly descending towards zero. They closed the Pioche Pharmacy in 1968. Grover, ever the leader, was unable to find anyone else willing, so he filed for the Nevada Assembly. The odds of his election were one in twenty, but someone at least needed to try. Brookie became his campaign manager. He won, giving the Republicans their first majority in forty years. Keeping all his campaign promises, he won again in 1970. Brookie became the Caliente pharmacist, a strong lobbyist for morals and school boards, and mother of ten during the legislative sessions. In addition, Grover became a member of the LDS Stake Presidency, and drove home every weekend for this assignment—450 miles.

With another reapportionment after the 1970 census, Grover filed for the state senate race in 1972. This area included the south half of Nevada, except Clark County (Las Vegas). He lost this race by a very few votes, in spite of Watergate and the descent of the Republican Party, and was not quite successful in his bid for the one seat in the assembly in 1974, but Lincoln County was no longer ignored in Carson City.

Four children had attended Brigham Young University, a missionary had returned from Guatemala, three children were married, and with a pharmacist/

manager in Caliente, they decided in 1976 to move closer to BYU and purchased a drugstore in the University Mall in Orem from Walgreen's, who with high interest rates and a shrinking economy had decided to sell all their stores in Utah. It was 15,000 square feet and included a restaurant. Brookie worked from 10 a.m. to 3 p.m., with her children in school, mostly doing accounting with some management and pharmacist duties. They later expanded into the Layton Hills Mall in Layton, Utah; but with the national economy still going sour and interest rates zooming near twenty percent, they closed it in 1982.

At home in Provo, Brookie became a typical LDS mother with a missionary in Colombia, Arizona, and Dominican Republic at the same time. She had a gymnast/cheerleader, a girl's basketball star at Provo High, two exciting elementary students, a BYU bishop husband with his office at home, interviewing his single members, while she was Relief Society chorister, Primary teacher and chief cook, laundress, chauffeur, and genealogist. Time brought more marriages, family history consulting, auditing freshman French at BYU, and more intensive research at the best genealogical library in the world, the Family History Library in Salt Lake City. When the lease ended in 1995 for Swallows Drugs in the University Mall, they sold it, and she began to compile and edit her vast collection of genealogical records, which became more and more exciting as new discoveries were made in these and other historical records.

They sold their Caliente store and built a retirement home on their vacant lot, and celebrated their sixtieth wedding anniversary in 2008. In 2009, Grover died. Today Brookie is still in Panaca, Nevada. She has 47 grandchildren, including a Green Beret in the Middle East, and 32 great-grandchildren. After her physical examination, her doctor told her she was eighty years old, going on sixty, so she traded her old Lincoln clunker for a red 2010 Ford Fusion.

⚊ Bibliography for Parts III and IV ⚊
Rebellion and United States ?

A Genealogy of a Cooley family of Hunterdon County, New Jersey and a Tillou famly of French Huguenots, presented by Watchung Chapter N.S.D.A.R., 1937 US/CAN, FILM AREA, 0873024 item 5

Adventurers of Purse & Person, FHL, Salt Lake City, Utah, many volumes.

AF, Ancestor File, FHL, Salt Lake City, Utah, and On Line

Allen, Charles Fletcher, *David Crockett Scout*, J. B. Lippincott Company, Philadelphia, 1911

Americana Encyclopedia, 30 Volumes, First Edison 1945

America's Civil War Magazine, Leesburg, Virginia, March 1994,

Ambrose, Stephen E., *Undaunted Courage*, Simon & Schuster, New York, NY, 1996

Billington, Ray Allen/ Ridge, Martin, *Western Expansion*, Macmillan Publishing Co., Inc. New York, 1982

Bottsford, Byrd; Kirby, Rae, Spencer, *BASIC TRENDS*, THE DELPHIAN SOCIETY, United States, 1939

Brown, Ivan H., *BARTON "All Bartons are Kin"*, privately published, 1976

Brown, Jr., Stuart E., *Rev. Thomas Barton (1728-1780*, FHL, US/CAN 929.273 B285kr

Bullock, Alford and others, *FHL film, 0288405*, includes relationship of William Alexander Ivie to Theodore Roosevelt and Martha Bullock (Roosevelt)

Byrd, William, *A Journey to the Land of Eden*, Macy-Masius, Vanguard reprint, 1928

Bucks County, Pennsylvania Birth Records, for Canby, Morgan, Preston, Wilkinson, Lacey

Calloway, Colin G., *The American Revolution in Indian Country*, Cambridge University Press, USA 1995

Cavaliers and Pioneers, Patent Book No. l---Part I., FHL, Salt Lake City, Utah

Census Records, US, Early Colonial Census, various

Charles City, Virginia, court records from 1655, from official county records

Clay, Lillie I. C., (sister) *They Chose to Serve*, B.Y. U. Printing, 1998

Clint, Florence, *Northumberland County, Pennsylvania, AREA KEY*, FHL, 974.831 D25a, S. L. C., 1977

Colbert, David, *Eye Witness to America*, Pantheon Books, Random House, New York, 1997

Collier, James Lincoln, *The Alexander Hamilton You Never Knew*, Children's Press USA 2003

Commemorative Biographical Record, Dutchess County, New York, J. H. Beers & Co. 1897

Complete book of Emigrants, Vol. 1, 1607-1660 FHL, Salt Lake City, Utah

Condie, Lillie A. I., *journals, books of remembrances, personal genealogical research and records*

Condie, Gibson A, (grandfather), *journals, autobiography, genealogical records.*

Contributions to the History of the Ancient Families of New York, 1879.. FHC microfiche, Panaca, NV

DAR Patriot Index, Centennial Edition, Orem Park Stake FHC, Orem, Utah

Davis, William C., *A Way Through the Wilderness*, HarperCollins Publishers, New York, 1995

Day, Sherman, *Sherman Day's 1843 History, Northumberland County, Pennsylvania*, FHL, Salt Lake City, UT

Dixon, Thomas, *The Southerner*, D. Appleton and Company, New York, 1913

Doctrine and Covenants, The Church of Jesus Christ of Latter-day Saints, Salt Lake City, Utah

Dovell, Ashton, *The Contributions of the French Huguenots in the Cultural Life of America*, Ninth Annual Assembly, Richmond, Virginia, April, 1940

Drake, Samuel G., *The New England Historical & Genealogical Register, Volume V*, A Heritage Classic, Boston, Samuel G. Drake Publisher, 1831

Draper, Theodore, *A Struggle for Power*, Times Books, Random House, New York, 1996

Esposito, Vincent J. Brigadier General, *The West Point Atlas of American Wars*, Volume I 1689-1900, Henry Hotl

Farmer, John; Drake, Samuel G., *The Genealogical Register of the First Settlers of New England*, Genealogical Publishing Co., Inc. 1851

Fawcett, Edward Charles, *The Fawcett family: 1736 (of Fawcett Gap, Virginia & heir descendants.*

Fawcett, Thomas Hayes, *the Fawcett family of Frederick County, Virginia*, FHL US/CAN 929.273 A1 no.. 990

Ferris Robert G; Morris, Richard E., *The Signers of the Declaration of Independence*, Interpretive Publications,

Flagstaff, Arizona, 2001

Fleming, Thomas, *Duel*, Basic Books, New York, NY 1999 *Liberty, The American Revolution*, Penguin Group, New York, 1997

French. Ellen Cochran, *Barton & Hummell Family Histories*,Tribune Printing Company, Fairfield, Iowa 1967;

Part Three, Faucett Genealogy Ireland to Orange Co., North Carolina pg. 398-421

Genealogical and Biographical Annals of Northumberland County Pennsylvania, J. L. Floyd & Co., Chicago, 1911, FHL US/CAN 974.S31 D2go

Goodrich, Thomas, *Gueerrila Warfare on the Western Border, 1861-1865, BLACK FLAG*. Indiana University Press, Indianapolis, 1995

Graham, James, *Life of General Daniel Morgan*, Zebrowski Historical Services, Bloomingburg, NY, 1993

Greenwood, Val D., *The Researcher's Guide to American Genealogy*, Genealogical Publishing Co., Inc., Baltimore,1977

Greenburg, Jan Crawford, *Supreme Conflict*, Penguin Group, USA, 2007

Hamil, Mrs. Lura Coolley, *A Story of Pioneering*, Illinois Printing Company, June 1955

Harwood, Thomas, early journal, *Adventurers of Purse and Person, p. 361-3*, FHL Salt Lake City, Utah

Hamilton, Dr. Alexander, journal, *Colonial American Travel Narratives*, Penguin Classics

Hawke, David Freeman, *Everyday Life in Early America*, Harper & Row, Publishers, New York, 1988

Helligso, Martha Stuart, *George Mason including one line of descent*, US/CAN 929.272 M38/h FHL, Salt Lake City, Utah 1983, also, *The Five George Masons*

Historical records of The Church of Jesus Christ of Latter Day Saints, Church Office Building, Salt Lake City, Utah

Hoes, Roswell Randall, *Baptismal and Marriage Registers of the OLD DUTCH CHURCH OF KINGSTON*, Ulster County, New York, 1660-1809, Baltimore Genealogical Publishing Co., Inc., 1980

Hoover, Herbert, *The Challenge to Liberty*, Charles Scribner's Sons, New York, London, 1934

Huguenot Emigration to Virginia, . . . A partial list of the descendants of Bartholomew Dupuy.ca 1113- 1745

Hymns of the Church of Jesus Christ of Latter-Day Saints, Deseret Book Company, Salt Lake City, Utah, 1985

Ivey, George Franks, *The Ivey Family in he United States*, The Southern Publishing Co., Hickory, N.C.

Ivie, Evan, *Records of wills County of Monroe*, Paris, Missouri, *1833-1845 deed*, also Jasper County, Georgia, *Will of Lot Ivie and other papers.*

Judd, Denis, *Empire,* HarperCollins Publishers, London, 1996

Kantor, MacKinlay, *Valley Forge, A Novel,* J. B. Lippincott Co., Philadelphia, PA, 1975

Kelly, C. Brian, *Best Little Stories from the American Revolution,* Cumberland House, Nashville, TN 1999

Kelso, William M., *Jamestown, the Buried Truth,* University of Virginia Press, Charlottesville and London, 2006

Kennedy, David M., *Freedom from Fear,* Oxford University Press, Madison Ave., New York, New York, 1999

Kennedy, Roger G., *Mr. Jefferson's Lost Cause,* Oxford University Press, 2003 *Burr, Hamilton, and Jefferson* 2000

Ketchum, Richard M., *Saratoga,* Henry Holt and Company, New York, 1997

Klett, Joseph R., *Genealogies of New Jersey Families, From the Genealogical Magazine of New Jersey*

Volume I, Pre-American Notes on Old New Netherland Families, A-Z, Orem Park Stake FHC, 044-119A

Konstam, Angus, *Guilford Courthouse 1781,* Osprey Publishing, Osceola, WI, 2002

Kwasny, Mark V., *Washington's Partisan War, 1775-1783,* The Kent State University Press, Ohio 1996

Langguth, A.J., *Patriots,* A Touchstone Book, Simon & Schuster, New York, 1988

Larned, J. N., *A Study of Greatness in Men,* Houghton Mifflin Company, Boston and New York, 1911

L.D.S. Church records of baptisms and other ordinances: Temple Index Records, Computer, extraction.

Leone, Mark P.; Silberman, Neil Asher, *Invisible America,* Henry Holt and Company, Inc. New York, 1995

Limbaugh Letter Special Supplement, *The Americans Who Risked Everything.* Rush Limbaugh Jr.

Lippincott, Abigail, *Complete Pedigree Chart, four generations, 28 Oct 1753 to 1642*

Louda, Jir'I & Maclagan, Michael, *Lines of Succession,* Barnes & Noble, 2002

Love, Terry Marvin, (1944), *The descendants of Thomas Love of Orange County, North Carolina,,* Lakeville, Minn., 1991
FHL 929.273 L941ev (Faucett)

Lytle, Carolyn , short history of LYMAN PETERS

Mackeys and Allied Families, New York, New Hampshire, Delaware, Pennsylvania, New Jersey, Virginia, South Carolina, North Carolina, British Isles, FHL, Salt Lake City

Maier, Pauline, *AMERICAN SCRIPTURE Making the Declaration of Independence,* Alfred A. Knopf , New York 1997

Martin, Wendy; Imbarrato, Susan; Dietrich, Deborah, *Colonial American Travel Narratives,* Penguin Books, USA, 1994

McCullough, David, *John Adams,* Touchstone, New York, NY, 2001, *1776,* Simon & Schuster, New York, 2005

McCurry, Stephanie, *Masters of Small Worlds,* OXFORD UNIVERSITY PRESS, New York, 1995

McDonald, Forrest, *Alexander Hamilton, A Biography,* W. W. Norton & Company, New York, NY 1979

Mitchell, Broadus, *Alexander Hamilton, A Concise Biography,* Barnes and Nobles, Inc. USA 1999

Morgan, Joy Elmer, Editor, *The American Citizens Handbook,* National Education Association,

Washington 1941

Morris, Christopher, *Becoming Southern,* Oxford University Press, New York, 1995

Moyer, John W., *Famous Frontiersmen,* Rand McNally & Company, Chicago, New York, San Francisco, 1972
National Archives of Canada: Library, Agen: Chez la Veuve Nouabel er Fils, 1791. Broadside.

Nevada "The Silver State", Volume One, Western States Historical Publishers, Inc., Carson City, Nevada, 1970

New Jersey, FHC Park Stake, Orem, Utah, *Lippincott,* pp., 74-77, 46-47, 60-61, 190-195

Norton, Mary Beth, *Founding Mothers & Fathers,* Alford A Knopf, New York, 1996

Oats, Stephen B., *A Woman of Valor, Clara Barton and the Civil War,* The Free Press, New York, 1995

Orton, Chad M.; William W. Slaughter, *Joseph Smith's America,* Deseret Book, Salt Lake City, Utah, 2008

Pruett, Dorothy Sturgis, *Our Thrasher Heritage*, FHL US/CAN 929.273 T412p, Salt Lake City, Utah

Purcell, L. Edward and Sarah J., *Encyclopedia of Battles in North America 1517-1916*, Checkmark Books, 2000

Randall, Willard Sterne, *Thomas Jefferson, A Life*, Henry Holt & Company Inc., New York, 1993, *George Washington*, 1997

Richards, Laura E.; Elliott, Maud Howe, *Julia Ward Howe 1819-1910*, Houghton Mifflin Company, 1915

Ridpath, John Clark, *Ridpath's History of the World, Volumes V & VI*, The Jones Brothers Publishing, Ohio, 1910

Roberts, B. H., *A Comprehensive History of The Church of Jesus Christ of Latter-day Saints, Century I*, Brigham Young University Press, Provo, Utah, 1965

Roberts, Cokie, *Founding Mothers*, HarperCollins Publishers Inc., New York, 2005

Ross, Claude F., *Know Your Presidents*, Grayhul Features, Wichita, Kansas, 1934

Sandburg, Carl, *Abraham Lincoln, The Prairie Years*, Harcourt, Brace and Company, Inc., Cornwall, NY 1926

Scheer,George F.; Rankin, Hugh F., *Rebels & Redcoats*, Da Capo Press, New York, N.Y. 1957

Shannon, David A., *The Great Depression*, A Spectrum Book, Prentice-Hall, Inc. Englewood Cliffs, N.J.

Shipton, Clifford K., *New England Life in the Eighteenth Century*, The Belknap Press of Harvard University Press, 1993

Stone, Conway B., *Ships, Saints, and Mariners, 1830-1890*, Orem Park Stake FHC, BX 8673.4 So59sh, 1987

Stratton, Eugene Aubrey, *Plymouth Colony*, Ancestry Publishing, Salt Lake City, Utah, 1986

Strouse, Jean, *Morgan, American Financier*, Perennial, Harper Collins Publishers, 2000

Sugde, John, *Tecumseh, A Life*, Henry Holt and Company, New York, 1997

Sullivan, Robert (Editor), *In the Land of the Free September 11---And After*, Life, Time Inc., 2001

Swallow, Brookie Condie, *journals, personal knowledge, personal research papers*

The Holy Bible, King James Version

The International Association of Lions Clubs, *SONGS for LIONS*, Chicago 4, Illinois, U. S. A. 1926

The New York Genealogical and Biographical Records, 1879, FHC, microfiche, Panaca, NV

The Spark of Independence, History Book of the Month Club, New York, United States of America, 1997

The State Records of North Carolina, The journal of the convention of North Carolina, 1788

The Story of Samuel Cooley and his descendants, FHL, US/CAN 929.273 C7764

The Virginia Genealogist, Includes land grants, tax lists, and various genealogy of families FHL

Thomas, Evan, *John Paul Jones*, Simon & Schuster, New York, 2003

Toole, Shelby, *The Civil War, A Narrative, volumes 1 and 2*, Time-Life Books, Alexandria, Virginia, 1999

Tyler, Sgt. Daniel, *A Concise History of the Mormon Battalion in the Mexican War*, The Rio Grande Press, Inc., Glorieta, NM 1980

Virginia Company Records, 1622,1624, 1625,1628,1635, 1637,1638,1639, 1640, 1645, 1646, 1649, 1652, 1653, 1654, 1655, 1656,1657, 1659, 1660, Complete Book of Emigrants 1661-1699.

Walter, Alice Granbery, *The Journal of Abigail Langley of Nansemond County, Virginia*, "the Langley, Mason and Thelaball families of Virginia . . . were the progenitors of Abigail Langley. . . 1695, 1723; *General Ped File no. 1122, 1154, 1166-7, 1169*, FHL, Salt Lake City, Utah,

Waugh, John G.. *Reelecting Lincoln*, Crown Publishers, Inc. New York, 1997

Wedgwood, C.V., *The Thirty Years War*, Book of the Month Club, New York

Welch, Douglas, *The Complete Military History of the Civil War*, Brompton Books Corp., Greenwich, CT, 1990

William and Mary Quarterly, collected by James Oscar Ivie, Williamsburg, Virginia, 1891

Wilson, Douglas L., *Honor's Voice*, Alfred A; Knopf, New York, 1998

Wilson, Jr., Vincent, *The Book of the Founding Fathers,* American History Research Associates, Brookeville, Maryland 1974

Winik, Jay, *April 1865,* HarperCollins Publishers, New York, New York, 2002

Young, Robert, *A Personal Tour of Old Ironsides,* Lerner Publications Company, Minneapolis, 1951

Young, Mrs. Jewel Waller, *Lineages and Genealogical Notes, A Compilation of Some of The Lineages And Family Lines In The Genealogy of CLOUD THRASHER BARTON,* B&W Printing & Letter Service, Dallas, Texas, 1973

Your Ancient Canadian Family Ties, FHL, #971D2o, Salt Lake City, Utah

— Index for Part IV —
United States ?